Shining and Other Paths

A *book in the series* LATIN AMERICA OTHERWISE:

LANGUAGES, EMPIRES, NATIONS

Series editors: Walter D. Mignolo, *Duke University*

Irene Silverblatt, *Duke University*

Sonia Saldívar-Hull, *University of Southern California*

Shining and Other Paths

War and Society in Peru, 1980–1995

Edited by Steve J. Stern

Duke University Press   Durham and London   1998

2nd printing, 2005

© 1998 DUKE UNIVERSITY PRESS

Printed in the United States of America on acid-free paper ∞

Typeset in Scala by Tseng Information Systems

Library of Congress Cataloging-in-Publication Data appear

on the last printed page of this book.

for the students

at the Universidad Nacional de San Cristóbal

de Huamanga in Ayacucho, Peru

and for their families

✣ CONTENTS

✤ *Latin America Otherwise: Languages, Empires, Nations* is a critical series. It aims to explore the emergence and consequences of concepts used to define "Latin America" while at the same time exploring the broad interplay of political, economic, and cultural practices that have shaped Latin American worlds. Latin America, at the crossroads of competing imperial designs and local responses, has been construed as a geocultural and geopolitical entity since the nineteenth century. This series provides a starting point to redefine Latin America as a configuration of political, linguistic, cultural, and economic intersections that demand a continuous reappraisal of the role of the Americas in history, and of the ongoing process of globalization and the relocation of people and cultures that have characterized Latin America's experience. *Latin America Otherwise: Languages, Empires, Nations* is a forum that confronts established geocultural constructions, that rethinks area studies and disciplinary boundaries, that assesses convictions of the academy and of public policy, and that, correspondingly, demands that the practices through which we produce knowledge and understanding, about and from Latin America be subject to rigorous and critical scrutiny.

Latin America's postcolonial history has been marked by its neocolonial legacies. Since the middle of the century the continent has erupted in civil war and political violence—including the Cuban revolution, dictatorships in Chile, Argentina, Brazil, and Guatemala, hard fought wars in Nicaragua and El Salvador. While Latin America's new democracies have been much heralded, battles for political power in Peru—between Sendero Luminoso and the Peruvian state—have added a twist to this political complexity.

From the early 1980s to the early 1990s Peru was convulsed by a ferocious civil war. By 1992 predictions of Lima's impending collapse dominated national conversations. Just as quickly, with the arrest of Sendero Luminoso's leader, Abimael Guzmán, this violent, surprisingly successful, and enigmatic movement crumbled. Intellectuals, journalists, and pundits, as well as Peru's political class were at a loss to explain these extraordinary times, compounding Sendero Luminoso's mysterious development, appeal, and failure.

The essays in the collection address the enigmas and exoticisms cloaking Sendero. They attend to the movement's social roots, its ability to compel fierce loyalty and equally fierce rebuke, its varied regional patterns of success and defeat, its gendered contours and consequences, its legacies for political rule and political culture. Placing the seemingly inexplicable in history's thicket of possibilities, this volume, taken as a whole, builds a deep and nuanced historical analysis of Peru's harrowing war. In the process it dissipates the enigmas that contributed to Sendero's terrible cachet.

✣ This book originated when a group of faculty and students at the University of Wisconsin–Madison began discussing the difficulty of understanding the origins, social dynamics, and consequences of the political agony that convulsed Peru in the 1980s and early 1990s. Frustration, urgency, and opportunity all played roles in our discussions. The frustration emerged from a sense that our inherited knowledge and the available intellectual frameworks were inadequate for achieving a deep, multifaceted understanding. Urgency derived from the sense that Peru and Peruvians had been living a great disaster and a decisive watershed period; these conditions seemed to demand, almost as an ethical priority, that we mount an effort to improve understanding and interpretation of Peru's recent history. A sense of opportunity also emerged. A number of intellectuals and activists had "come of age," intellectually, during Peru's war years. Their field knowledge and analytical flexibility, if integrated into a carefully designed and multigenerational collaboration, might help develop the fresh knowledge and analysis that seemed so urgent.

Out of these discussions emerged a planning group for an international conference, entitled "Shining and Other Paths: Anatomy of a Peruvian Tragedy, Prospects for a Peruvian Future." This conference was held at the University of Wisconsin on 27–30 April 1995. We coordinated the conference with student reading and research in experimental courses at the graduate and undergraduate levels. Subsequently, the editor of this volume worked intensively with conference authors to sharpen and integrate their essays. In some instances, the rewriting process led to new or thoroughly revamped essays. Our hope is that we have molded our efforts into an original and coherent book whose whole is larger than the sum of its parts, and that the book captures in some way the intellectual excitement of the conference.

This project drew on the help of many people and agencies. My partners on the symposium planning group included Marisol de la Cadena, Nancy Forster, Florencia E. Mallon, William Ney, Guido Podestá, Frank Salomon, and during his time as Tinker Visiting Professor at Madison, Carlos Iván Degregori. Without their enthusiasm and suggestions, the intellectual design of the conference and our ability to identify and invite knowledgeable participants would have been much weaker. Indispensable logistical support, publicity, and sponsorship of the conference were provided by the staff of the Latin American and Iberian Studies Program, especially William Ney, Kristen Smith, and Carrie Johnson. In addition, Laura Fuentes and Janet Melvin provided translation support for students and community members who attended and participated (the conference was conducted in Spanish to facilitate more fluid discussion and debate among the panelists).

I owe an especially important thank you to the co-authors of this book. Their good will and collaborative spirit at the 1995 conference and during the arduous process of intellectual critique and editorial nagging that followed it reminds me that sometimes, and however imperfectly, the metaphor of intellectual "community" really works. Among the coauthors, I owe special thanks to Carlos Iván Degregori, who was a wonderfully generous intellectual partner during the semester when we team taught and prepared for the conference, and to Florencia E. Mallon, who shared knowledge and provided support and perspective as the conference results evolved into a book.

Several additional intellectual contributions must also be acknowledged. First, the undergraduate and graduate students who worked with Professor Degregori and me during the Spring 1995 semester tolerated experimental team teaching with a great deal of good will and energized the campus community and the conference sessions with their intellectual insights, feedback, and engagement. Second, important contributions were made by scholars who contributed commentaries and related background papers to the panels. These discussants and authors included José Gonzales, Gustavo Gorriti, Christine Hunefeldt, Enrique Mayer, Alfred McCoy, David Scott Palmer, Leigh Payne, Deborah Poole, Gerardo Rénique, Frank Salomon, Thomas Skidmore, and M. Crawford Young. Third, during the postsymposium phase, a series of readers helped sharpen the book manuscript and provided welcome advice. I wish to thank Peter Klarén, John Tutino, and an anonymous reader for their excellent advice, as well as Valerie Millholland,

Rosalie Robertson, the team of editors and production assistants at Duke University Press, and the manuscript's copy editor, Linda Gregonis.

I am enormously grateful to Nancy Appelbaum, without whose assistance this book would not have happened. The bulk of this book was written by Peruvians and Nancy worked heroically in the translation of their essays (chapters 1, 2, 4–6, 9–14). Although we cotranslated the essays and I assume responsibility for any mistakes and infelicities, Nancy did the work of creating quality first-draft translations, tracking exchanges on specific points and problem areas, and incorporating revisions. Nancy also served as the manuscript manager, coordinating communication with the authors and me during a year when I was in residence in Chile and pulling the book together into a unified manuscript and set of diskettes. That Nancy performed these tasks so well while completing her own pioneering dissertation on Colombian history speaks volumes about her intellect, energy, and organization. Thanks, Nancy, for making this book possible.

The maps in this volume were produced by the Cartographic Laboratory of the University of Wisconsin, and I wish to thank Onno Brouwer and Qingling Wang for their superb help. I also wish to thank Danny Holt for providing helpful background research at a crucial juncture. Conference participants supplied the photographs in this volume, and specific credits run as follows: page 48, Eloy Neira and Aroma de la Cadena; page 74, Gustavo Gorriti and *Caretas*; pages 106–7, Rodrigo Sánchez; pages 188, 246 (ronderos at market), 474 (ronderos as patriot-citizens), Ponciano del Pino; pages 246, 361 (Shining Path women), Robin Kirk and Orin Starn; pages 284, 418 (Guzmán on television), Carlos Basombrío; pages 361, 475, Isabel Coral; pages 418–19 (Fujimori photos), Dante Piaggio. Thanks to all, and to Marisol de la Cadena, Florencia E. Mallon, and Patricia Oliart for securing access to various photos.

For economic assistance that made the 1995 conference and this book possible, I gratefully acknowledge the Anonymous Fund, Brittingham Fund, Graduate Research Committee, and Nave Fund at the University of Wisconsin-Madison, the Title VI program of the U.S. Department of Education, and the Visiting Professor Program of the Tinker Foundation.

During and after major collective traumas, the problem of memory and forgetfulness often becomes an important cultural issue. My connection to the Ayacucho region, and to the students, faculty and staff, and families affiliated with the Universidad Nacional de San Cristóbal de Huamanga, runs deep and is a bittersweet blend of affection, hope, and pain. This book's dedication is one way of expressing that I have not forgotten the youth and families who have suffered so much and nonetheless insist on a future of hope, and that I have not forgotten the generosity of those who have welcomed me. This book is for you, gratefully, affectionately, hopefully.

Steve J. Stern
Madison, Wisconsin,
September 1997

❖ INTRODUCTION

Beyond Enigma: An Agenda for Interpreting Shining Path

and Peru, 1980–1995

Steve J. Stern

❖ Enigma, exoticism, surprise: These sensibilities have often marked discussion of Peru during the profound political upheaval and violence that marked the 1980s and early 1990s. An aura of enigma has often swirled around the theme of Sendero Luminoso ("Shining Path"), the Maoist political party that proclaimed an insurrectionary war in May 1980. Sendero launched its war conventionally enough by burning ballot boxes in Chuschi, a pueblo in the Ayacucho region of Peru's center-south highlands. But the symbols used later that year to announce the war in Lima, the capital city and national media center, seemed exotic expressions that invited ridicule. Limeños awoke to the sight of dead dogs tied to lamp posts and traffic lights. The accompanying signs proclaimed "Deng Xiaoping, Son of a Bitch," as if mention of the architect of counterrevolution in China were a sufficient and relevant political explanation.[1]

Given the distant preoccupations and arcane symbolism of Sendero, and the participation of most of the Left in Peru's return to electoral politics and civilian government after an extended period of military rule (1968–1980), the Maoist sect's declaration of war seemed out of step with Peruvian history. Given the snobbery, racism, and indifference that attended Limeño perceptions of the highland Department of Ayacucho—the birthplace of Sendero, noted mainly for the confluence of an extremely impoverished indigenous peasantry in the countryside and a politically effervescent university culture in the region's small capital city—Sendero also seemed an expression of isolation and peculiarity. Odd political trajectories, proclamations, and utopias might mark the political world of educated mestizos and Andean Indians in faraway, backward highland provinces.

The surprises that lay in store added to the enigmatic aura. After all, in

1980 few persons outside the Ayacucho region took Sendero all that seriously. Few, aside from the Shining Path militants themselves, would have
predicted that self-styled revolutionaries from an extremely impoverished
and largely Indian highland region could effectively spread a ruthless war
through much of the national territory, sustain it into the 1990s, then provoke a sense of imminent government and social collapse in Lima by 1992.

By the mid-1980s, Sendero had become harder to dismiss. Its capacity
to function as a tenacious, brutally effective political and war machine had
sparked declarations of emergency military intervention in numerous departments. The war also provided the military with a platform to conduct
an Argentine-style "dirty war" against presumed subversives in Ayacucho,
and yielded massacres of journalists, peasants, and prisoners that seemed
to implicate the military as well as Sendero and sparked media scandals. At
the same time, Sendero's ideological dogmatism and its almost celebratory
embrace of violent bloodletting as purification and heroism became increasingly evident. This was a political force that looked with contempt upon
leftists who approached politics through compromise and coalition. Sendero looked with contempt, as well, upon politics as the process of building
legitimacy through "soft" means—through alliance with semi-autonomous
social movements and grassroots organizations or through campaigns of
discursive persuasion and mobilization. Yet dogmatic sectarianism and a
horrifying will to violence had not implied political ineffectiveness.

Sendero's strangely out-of-step political preoccupations and symbolism;
its birth in a regional world that blended Andean Indian communities, a decomposing rural oligarchy and hacienda system, and radicalized university
intellectuals and students; its amazing capacity to build utopian dogmatism
and contemptuousness into an effective political war machine: these would
have been sufficient to generate an aura of enigma and exoticism. Other
forces worked in a similar direction. For Sendero's supporters and sympathizers, the political party's mystique and intimidation lay precisely in its
self-projection as a force uniquely brutal, effective, and accurate in reading
the march of historical destiny. For Sendero's critics and rivals, the understandable desire to draw moral distance encouraged depiction of Sendero
as a freakish evil force outside the main contours of Peruvian social and
political history—more an invention of evil masterminds and an expression, perhaps, of the peculiarity of a particular regional milieu than a logical
culmination or byproduct of Peruvian history. For supporters, critics, and
agnostics alike, the ethnoracial othering of native Andeans as "Indians,"

governed by a mysteriously different worldview, could also prompt exoticist interpretations. Sendero's spread expressed the cultural marginality and ignorance of Indians, or their disposition toward outbursts of utopian millenarianism to overturn evil.[2]

Small wonder, then, that terms like "idiosyncratic," "magically elusive," "strange dovetailing," and "exotic and enigmatic" attach so readily to otherwise disparate discussions of Sendero. The mixed sensibilities of peculiarity, surprise, and disgust encourage adjectives that draw moral distance and emphasize uniqueness.[3]

But the sense of enigma and surprise was not really limited to Sendero Luminoso alone. In the 1980s and early 1990s Peru as a whole seemed to lurch from surprise to surprise.[4] Consider four such surprises. First, the declaration of armed insurgency in 1980 seemed absurdly out of step with the turn of the polity and the leftist opposition toward competitive electoral politics. Even Patria Roja, the Maoist political group most inclined to reject elections and promote armed insurgency, accepted the turn. The seriousness of the armed conflict—its capacity, along with erratic economic performance and steep declines in real wages, to destroy the effectiveness of President Fernando Belaúnde Terry (1980–1985), and to return the military to a leading political role in national life—defied expectations of regional and political containment. Why did a historically archaic Maoist sect, so at odds with the direction of change among most of the Latin American and Peruvian Lefts, prove so able to wage war, organize a social support base, and read the flow of history?

Second, the victory of the leftist coalition Izquierda Unida in Lima's municipal election of 1983 and the capture of the presidency by APRA's Alan García in 1985 seemed to signify the ascendancy of a Center-Left alternative marked by populist economic assistance and development projects, anti-imperialism, and political rather than military means of defeating insurrection. Within three and a half years, however, the ferocity of a foreign exchange crisis and subsequent economic shock treatment and the failure to win the war against Sendero had destroyed García's credibility and a Center-Left solution. The main contenders of the 1990 presidential elections— Mario Vargas Llosa, as the novelist-turned-candidate of a "new" neoliberal Right, and Alberto Fujimori, as an "unknown" who rejected politics as usual—signified an unraveling of hopes once placed in established Center-Left parties. Fujimori surprised the electorate by winning, then surprised the populace by adopting a harsh neoliberal shock treatment that drove key commodity prices skyward and contracted the economy. Why did Left and Center-Left politics implode so dramatically, and why did a political novice steal the political show even from the neoliberals?

Third, as Peru entered a period of severe neoliberalism and economic hardship (accompanied by cholera outbreaks in 1991) for the impoverished majority, the insurrectionary war intensified in Lima. The insurgents' declaration that they had reached the "strategic equilibrium" stage of the war in May 1991, the urban bombings and the assassinations of alternative political leaders that choked Lima with fear during the next fifteen months, the suspension of the Congress, judiciary, and Constitution in President Alberto Fujimori's self-coup (*autogolpe*) of April 1992 all seemed to signify imminent national collapse. Yet it was Sendero that collapsed when its mythic leader, Abimael Guzmán, was captured in September and the movement's political capacity abruptly declined. Only retrospectively did it seem obvious that Sendero had lost the war between 1989 and 1992, despite appearances to the contrary. In those years, the profound alienation of peasants from Sendero's politics crystallized as organized resistance, facilitated by a certain rapprochement between the military and peasants. The rural resistance to Sendero, along with gains in military-police intelligence, had rendered Sendero vulnerable even as it appeared to approach the threshold of a decisive victory. How could Sendero have approached strategic victory and strategic defeat *simultaneously*?

Fourth, the sense of incomprehensibility was reinforced by the intensity with which Peruvian politics seemed to concentrate distinct historical times and tendencies into a single conjuncture. There were several prominent contenders for political space in the Peru of the 1980s, the armed Maoist revolutionaries preoccupied with the Sino-Soviet split and the course of the Chinese Revolution in the 1960s and 1970s being only one. Leftist and Center-Left populists (Alfonso Barrantes, the Marxist who won the 1983 mayor election in Lima, and Alan García, the president whose election in 1985 revitalized the American Popular Revolutionary Alliance [APRA] party's earlier legacy of social critique) evoked a politics of reform, anti-imperialism, and mass appeal that bubbled to the fore repeatedly in Latin America between the 1930s and 1960s. The avuncular president Fernando Belaúnde, whose election recalled a politics of enlightened centrism and moderation—development projects, frontier colonization, and mild social reformism—that had seemed fresher in the early 1960s resurfaced. More ominous was the guerrilla force Movimiento Revolucionario Túpac Amaru

(MRTA), whose leadership genealogy and eagerness to lead a revolutionary tide sparked by bold armed action and symbolism brought back to life the groups inspired by the Cuban Revolution in the 1960s. Then there was the military, whose anti-insurgency campaign and political control in the provinces evoked the dirty wars and foundational military regimes of South America in the early to mid-1970s. In the neoliberal revolution that redefined political discourse in the Latin America of the 1980s stood a pair of leading prophets—Hernando de Soto, author of the manifesto *El otro sendero* in 1986, and Mario Vargas Llosa, presidential candidate in 1990. Finally there was a political "unknown," Alberto Fujimori, whose election captured the sense of exhaustion with old political schemes and yearning for truly fresh alternatives that launched "new" politicians out of "nowhere" in the Latin America of the late 1980s and early 1990s. How could each of these political players have a bright day in the sun during a relatively compressed historical conjuncture? And why could so many decline so precipitously and unexpectedly from the political heights?

To be sure, Alejo Carpentier noted long ago in his classic novel, *Los pasos perdidos,* that there is a Latin America tendency toward the coexistence of political times that seemed, in other parts of the world, to separate themselves in a more chronologically ordered sequence. As a Carpentier character succinctly put it: "You must remember that we are accustomed with living with Rousseau and the Inquisition, with the Immaculate Conception and *Das Kapital.*"[5] Nonetheless, the Peru of the 1980s and early 1990s presented an extreme case of historical coexistence and compression where populists, developmentalists, revolutionaries, "dirty war" leaders, neoliberals, and unknowns could all build a formidable political presence for a time, yet quickly lose the political magic. The political congestion tested the limits of comprehension, enhanced the probability of sudden surprise twists, and added to a sensibility of crisis and uncertainty.[6]

In short, the surprises and the velocity of Peruvian political life seemed to defy well-worn scripts of classification, chronicling, and explanation. In this sense, the enigma and shocks associated with Sendero were part of a larger sense of enigma and surprise associated with Peru.

The sensibility created by a rush of twists and turns, genuinely surprising and often difficult to explain, is that of day-to-day journalism. Important events seem to fall from the sky, in an unpredictable yet steady stream of happenings that shock and change our social world, for reasons that remain somewhat mysterious. Such events are like acts of God or Nature. An earthquake strikes here, a hurricane there; an assassination strikes here, a massacre there. One rushes to provide a basic chronicling of the event and its immediate consequences. Yet who knows when, where, or why the event happened? Before deep analysis or reflection are forthcoming, another *novedad*—a landslide here, an uprising there—drops out of the sky to command our attention. If the velocity of major surprises and events prevents deep follow-up analysis, the sense of connection and patterning that contextualizes and historicizes events becomes difficult to establish. The sense of a chaotic world buffeted by accident and surprise becomes increasingly difficult to resist.[7]

This sort of sensibility was quite evident in the 1995 symposium that evolved into this book. Particularly in the first days of our intensive meetings, the role of accident or chance in history (*el azar en la historia*) was a recurring refrain. Resort to the phrase did not reflect a lack of empirical knowledge, analytical skill, or theoretical talents by the participants. It reflected an honest expression of the sensations of wonder, unpredictability, and limited deep comprehension forged out of an experience permeated by shock as well as grave seriousness. Life had moved through unsuspected twists and turns that seemed to matter greatly, at least until the next turn of events. Under the circumstances, the futility of prior conceptual frameworks and analytical expectations became all too evident. The refrain expressed, as well, a drawing of moral and intellectual distance from the teleological readings of history promoted by Sendero. After all, it was Sendero that proclaimed a piercing and totalizing ability to read and lead the contradictory march of history toward its inexorable, triumphant outcome. The desire to draw distance from the confident teleologies of Sendero resonated readily with post-modern intellectual skepticism toward grand narrative and totalizing frameworks.

Yet the dichotomy between history as teleology and history as chance event is too rigid and self-defeating. Both poles destroy the blend of curiosity and craft that constitute the art of contextualized historical analysis. If history is a teleological march toward a predestined and irreversible grand conclusion, and all that happens is merely a step on the inevitable road, there is little to analyze, question, or research deeply. The context and the story lines are a given. But if history is a chance sequence of events that happen without cause, or more precisely, for reasons so immediate and so infinitely varied that they constitute the equivalent of a game of chance, then there is also little drive to analyze, question, or research deeply. The context is transparent and immediate, the story line is an episodic string of events.

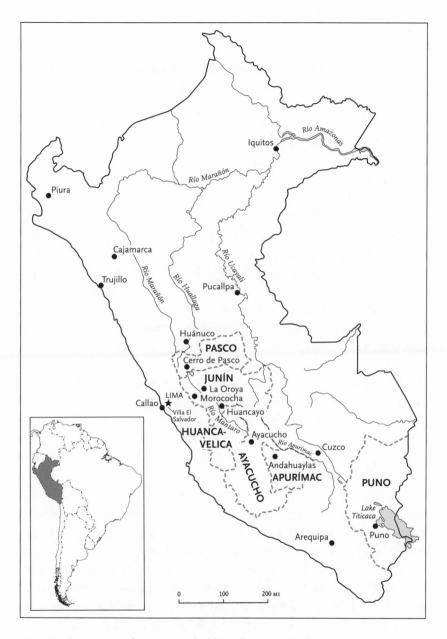

Figure I.1. Peru, circa 1980. Note: Dashed lines demarcate the five departments of the center-south sierra analyzed extensively in part II of this volume, and the Department of Puno, analyzed in part III.

Between the pole of overdetermined teleology and that of near-random chance breathes the art of contextualized historical analysis: the study of human beings in their time dimension as an unfolding pattern of possibilities and probabilities—some realized and others unrealized, some pulling human groups in similar directions, others at cross-purposes, some more structurally entrenched and others more susceptible to change, all constituted in part by human action.

The agenda of this book is to move "beyond enigma" by bringing the art of contextualized historical analysis to the war that engulfed and redefined Peruvian society from 1980 to 1995. I have argued that the sense of enigma that surrounds the Sendero phenomenon and Peru more generally is understandable. But the task faced here is to historicize and contextualize the social origins, dynamics, and consequences of a time that constituted a major watershed, when much was at stake and long-lasting legacies were forged. This task is all the more difficult if we wish to keep our intellectual balance by sidestepping easy, yet shallow apparent solutions. On the one hand, we need to avoid overdetermined explanatory logics that erase altogether the sense of wonder, unusualness, and extreme human condition that constituted part of the experience and its meanings. On the other hand, we must also avoid a reductionism that collapses the wide social experiences and frustrations that generated and fed civil war into its narrowest dimension—the story of a freakish fringe group, led by evil masterminds, who came together in a particular province in the 1960s and 1970s, organized an ideology and a set of cadres, and waged and lost a brutal war in the 1980s and 1990s.

This book, then, is a collective effort to build a historical analysis of war and society in Peru's time of upheaval. We undertake this task through analysis of five themes: the historical roots of political convulsion and revolutionary projects in the highlands, the failed struggle of Shining Path to conquer the peoples of the center-south highlands, the destruction of apparent "third political paths" in Lima and the highlands, the war experience of women and their emergence as new citizen-subjects, and the consequences of the war for political rule and political culture. (See figure I.1 for geographical orientation to the main regions and sites considered in this book.) These themes are considered in parts I to V, respectively, of this book, and in a brief conclusion that sets forth findings that cut across the various book sections. Let us turn to our first major theme: the historical roots of the political sensibilities and projects that plunged Peru into war in the 1980s.

Notes

1. The seven short essays by the editor of this volume (the general introduction, the introductions to each of the book's five major themes or sections, and the general conclusion) are synthetic interpretations that dialogue directly with the information and analyses presented by my collaborators in this book. For this reason, the essays tend to eschew detailed annotations. For readers who wish additional orientation to Shining Path and to the contextual information presented in the essays by the editor, key works are Degregori 1990a; Degregori (ed.) 1996; Gorriti 1990; Manrique 1989; NACLA 1990–1991, 1996; Palmer (ed.) 1992, 1994; Palmer 1995; Poole and G. Rénique 1992; Starn 1991b; and for fuller bibliographical orientation, P. Stern 1995. The story of the dogs slung from posts and lights is well known: see, e.g., Degregori 1994: 51–52; Rosenberg 1991: 146.

2. On the theme of millenarianism and utopias in Andean history and its vexed place in interpretation of Shining Path and violent outbursts as exotic expressions of the Indian Other, the most flagrant example of overheated claims based on little evidence is Strong 1992a, 1992b; compare the critique of Mario Vargas Llosa in Mayer 1991; and the critique of anthropology in Starn 1991a. By far the most subtle exploration of utopias in Peruvian history and culture is Flores Galindo 1988a, a brilliant study that avoids the trap of treating Shining Path as a projection of the exotic Andean Other; see also Brown and Fernández 1991.

3. For the quotes, see Poole and G. Rénique 1992: xiii; Guillermoprieto 1994: 261; Strong 1992a: 61; Rosenberg 1991: 146. It should be underscored that these works are otherwise vastly different in approach. For example, Strong emphasizes the exotic aura of the Andean Other, and Poole and G. Rénique (cf. 1991) seek to strip away exoticism.

4. The "surprises" that follow are based on the discussions at the 1995 conference that evolved into this book, my personal experience and observations of unfolding events, and the sources cited in note 1.

5. Carpentier 1957: 53.

6. The sense of extreme crisis and incomprehensibility contributed, as well, to apocalyptic sensibilities. These emerged not only in the fascination with the millenarian themes described earlier, but in literary works that suggested an end of worlds; see, e.g., Vargas Llosa 1984.

7. Obviously, I refer here to day-to-day journalism in its function as a chronicle of news, rather than investigative journalism by reporters who take a "time out" from the daily grind to write articles and books that probe a social issue more deeply. The best journalists, of course, try to balance the two functions.

✥ PART ONE

Within and Against History:

Conceptualizing Roots

❖ Sendero Luminoso emerged both "within" and "against" history. On one level, the combination reflected Sendero's self-proclaimed place as the agent of a world history destined to conclude in Communist Revolution (an agent "within" history), and as the vanguard whose ownership of Truth and Knowledge set it against the State and revolutionary pretenders (leadership "against" history). On a deeper level, the combination of "within" and "against" reflected the ways Shining Path represented one logical culmination, among several logical culminations, of the forces that bred oppositional politics in twentieth-century Peru. As a probability or culmination "within" history, the Sendero phenomenon belonged to a family of similar phenomena anchored in Peruvian historical processes. As a historical possibility in competition "against" other historically grounded projects and possibilities, Sendero's capacity to dominate the 1980s—to plunge a society and its politics into profound upheaval—fell far short of inevitability, and its unique features would prove important over the course of the war.[1]

In Peru, as in much of Latin America, a certain exhaustion of the Old Regime had set in by the 1960s. To understand the sensibilities that informed this exhaustion, one needs to reach back to earlier moments of twentieth-century critique of the established order.[2] In Peru, as elsewhere in Latin America, a cycle of sharp political dissidence and mobilization defined the late 1910s, 1920s, and 1930s as a time of middle class and worker mobilization against politics as an aristocratic bastion. This was a period when new political parties and leaders emerged and sought to establish a more inclusionary political and social system. In the case of Peru, the social mobilizations of the period involved a remarkable variety of groups—workers and trade union groups in cities, mining camps, and sugar plantations; university youth and intellectuals, including "insurgent intellectuals" from the provinces; indigenous and mestizo peasants in various highland provinces; and urban poor and migrant populations in Lima.

The period also witnessed the birth of oppositional political parties (APRA and the Communist Party) sharply critical of the established order and successful in establishing substantial social followings. The pressures for social inclusion generated an ambience for the emergence of dissident intelligentsias and opportunities for populist political leaders to promote a "new" style of state politics. Several presidencies, those of Augusto Leguía and Luis Sánchez Cerro during the 1920s and early 1930s and of Luis Bustamante y Rivero and especially Manuel Odría during the 1940s and 1950s, would include important populist phases and styles of rule. In short, the new social forces encouraged a certain massification of politics and an environment of critique that placed traditional aristocratic politics on the defensive by the 1920s and 1930s. The new political and intellectual environment undermined national political rule as a series of pacts and intrigues within a club of gentlemen and oligarchs with narrow social bases.

Yet the currents of political critique and social inclusion developed within sharply delimited spaces. Periods of military rule and repression repeatedly "interrupted" or drove underground the social and political organizations, including APRA and the Communist Party, that pressed for a more inclusionary and responsive state.[3] Over time, in part, perhaps, as a survival strategy in a political system inclined toward repressive "interruptions," political leaders and parties retreated from their earlier, more populist and "radical" stances. In addition, they abided by an implicit pact not to press the question of agrarian reform, to leave unchallenged the concentrated land tenure regime and servile social and ethnic relations that structured life in many rural highland provinces. Instead, political demands were confined largely to the needs of the urban groups, workers, and laborers of the coastal provinces who comprised the parties' historical social base. In short, the "new" political currents and parties that had challenged the structure of politics and society and pressed for social inclusion in the 1910s through 1930s had become "old" by the 1940s and 1950s. Their relative ineffectiveness and moderation, relative accession to the continuity of an exclusionary social order made them parts of a reconstructed Old Regime.

By the 1960s, the reconstructed Old Regime seemed increasingly untenable for several reasons. First, it granted more latitude to pressure for social inclusion in the coastal cities, especially Lima, than in the rural highlands, where state support of the hacienda system and ethnic domination continued to reign. In the late 1950s and early 1960s, however, a series of peasant mobilizations in the central and southern highlands (especially in Junín and Cuzco) shook the political order. The land invasions contributed to a sense that land reform and the break-up of servile rural relations in the highlands were issues that could no longer be sidelined or postponed in national politics. Second, the reconstructed Old Regime delivered neither steady economic growth that might satisfy the interest group needs of an expanding middle-sector and urban poor population, nor a political system that effectively incorporated dissident parties and intelligentsias. Import-substitution industrialization failed to yield an economic "take-off" powerful enough to break the effects of international commodity price cycles, a modest internal market, foreign ownership of key economic sectors, and concentrated income distribution. In addition, APRA and the Communist Party, the mass parties that originated as vehicles of sharp political critique and mobilization, had lost much of their luster. As mentioned earlier, periods of military rule and repression had rendered them ineffective as contenders for national political power, and the effort to survive and find spaces in a hostile political system had dulled their once radical edge. Third, the political and cultural impact of the Cuban Revolution made obstacles to social change and inclusion much more difficult to tolerate. The mystique of Cuba undermined the political credibility of slow paths to social transformation and posed the question: Why not a revolution now?

The exhaustion of the reconstructed Old Regime provoked unprecedented political stirrings in the 1960s. The successful presidential campaign of Fernando Belaúnde Terry (president, 1963–1968) included rallies and appeals in the southern Andean highlands, provinces marked by indigenous majorities and mobilizations for land reform. The new campaign style rendered uncertain the implicit pact by which the coastal political system would leave unchallenged the social order of the rural highlands. In 1965, radical youth inspired by the Cuban Revolution split off from APRA and the Communist Party and organized as guerrillas. They proved politically and militarily ineffective, but the campaign to defeat them contributed to currents within the military that questioned the viability of a social order premised on rural degradation. In 1968, the new currents dramatically took over national life. A Left-leaning military government headed by Juan

Velasco Alvarado ousted Belaúnde and launched a "revolution" that included anti-imperialist expropriations, agrarian reform programs in the sierra and coastal provinces, and worker cooperatives in capitalized enterprises.

As we shall see later, especially in the essays by Hinojosa and Mallon, the Velasco regime (1968–1975) had a profound impact on the history of the Peruvian Left of the 1970s. Its rhetoric promoted a Left-leaning "common sense" in popular culture, and complicated the task of differentiation between an oppositional Left and a state that proclaimed similar social objectives. At the same time, its on-the-ground politics—often haphazard and bumbling implementations of proclaimed programs and ideals or disempowering practices that seemed to "betray" general policies and proclamations—opened up breaches between expectation and reality. The breaches fueled radical disillusion.

In short, a new era of radical and reformist politics was born between the late 1910s and 1930s, but by the late 1950s and 1960s the new currents had, by a combination of repression and cooption, become part of a reconstructed Old Regime and its political exhaustion. In the initial period political ferment meant an invention of new languages of political and cultural critique, and new forms of organizing pressure for social and political inclusion. Eventually, political ferment meant the invention of subsequent languages of critique condemning the errors and limitations that doomed earlier efforts at social transformation to failure, and that extended a rather radical oppositional "common sense" to broad reaches of society, including sectors of the military.

Within this broad historical context, the three essays in Part I help specify the sociopolitical dynamics and sensibilities that made Sendero Luminoso a culmination "within" history—within the interplays between the Left, the state, peasants, and dissident intellectuals that shaped the politics of sierra rebelliousness and radicalism in the twentieth century.

Marisol de la Cadena's study traces the emergence and evolution of an insurgent intelligentsia between the 1910s and the 1960s. The insurgent intellectuals promoted a politics of regional emancipation that challenged the aristocratic politics of Lima gentlemen, as well as the cruder politics of *gamonalismo* in the rural highlands. (*Gamonalismo* refers to rule by provincial landowners and their allied merchants, authorities, and intermediaries over Indian peasants and servants. The term evokes "feudal-like" relations of human ownership and physical abuse buttressed by ethnic hierarchies; the non-Indians, or *mistis*, who became petty or grand versions of *gamo-*

nal masters included mestizos and "whites" of tainted social origin.) De la Cadena traces the interplay of race and class, and the role of knowledge and intellectuals, in the emerging politics of critique and emancipation. She shows that during the 1920s, the critical founding period for leftist politics and indigenismo, dissident political figures and intellectuals developed a complex coordination of ethnoracial and class thought. In an era of scientific racism, intellectuals sought to avoid the trap of biologically defined racial destiny, yet their lived experience was thoroughly permeated by racial feeling and sentiment. They responded to this dilemma by promoting ideas that emphasized the cultural and moral bases of racial character and improvement, and by establishing a certain dialogue between positive cultural values inherited from an Indian past and values derived from the politics of class conflict and socialism.

Between the 1930s and 1960s, this creative tension, in many ways the heart of José Carlos Mariátegui's political "agony" and his dialogue with indigenistas such as Luis Valcárcel, gave way to a sharper split. A gulf emerged between a dissident politics driven by a language of class and mass parties on the one hand, and a politics of cultural education and indigenismo, more easily domesticated and subsumed within the politics of a developmentalist state, on the other. Yet as de la Cadena also shows, this divergence did not seal dissident political figures and intellectuals—often mestizos or descendants of highland *provincia* families—from the structures of racial sentiment and hierarchy that permeated Peruvian life.

The legacy of this trajectory, especially in the highland regions, was the rise of a class-driven politics of critique disdainful of ethnoracial languages of analysis and social emancipation, yet nourished implicitly by social statuses, yearnings, and alienations derived from racial hierarchy and degradation. An added legacy was a political culture that tightly joined ideas of social advance and dissidence with ideas of superior knowledge and education. Under these circumstances, radical political projects energized by desires to liberate Indians, or by desires to project persons of "tainted" social backgrounds (persons of racially mixed or provincia descent) into social leadership, might nonetheless resort to class-driven languages and code words. The language of class silenced explicit racial categories and analysis, or referenced them by allusion, even though racial sentiments remained present and important. Under the circumstances, too, dissident intellectuals who laid claim to special knowledge (theory) and higher education (university studies) could establish themselves as forceful players in the politics of regionalism and social emancipation. Indeed, as Florencia Mallon has shown recently, the failure of the national state to build organic bridges to the local intellectuals and political movements of highland rural communities ended up widening spaces for a radicalized political culture *de provincia*.[4]

The nexus of class-driven language, implicit ethnoracial sentiment, and knowledge-based politics analyzed by de la Cadena not only proved central in the formation of Sendero Luminoso (formally, Partido Comunista del Perú—Sendero Luminoso) as a distinctive political party and project under the leadership of university philosopher Abimael Guzmán in the 1960s and 1970s. They were also evident in a wide array of leftist political parties and projects and, to a certain extent, within the Left-leaning "revolution" promoted by the government of General Juan Velasco Alvarado (1968–1975), during the same years.

Ivan Hinojosa's essay analyzes the mix of similarities and differences that place the formation of Sendero Luminoso within a "family" of leftist political parties and projects of the 1960s and 1970s. Hinojosa's analysis helps situate Sendero within the specificities that made the Peruvian version of the Latin American Left unusual, not only for its size, radicalism, and impact on political culture (the creation of a dissident "common sense"), but also for the strong influence of Maoism.[5]

The "radical" military government of Velasco (1968–1975)—which nationalized oil holdings, promoted expropriations of highland haciendas, organized worker coops in more capitalized agrarian and industrial enterprises on the coast, and purchased military equipment from the Soviet Union—played a key role in generating a Peruvian Left whose specific features were unusual within Latin America. Velasco's languages of antiimperialism, land reform, and worker ownership contributed to a more oppositional common sense and political milieu and fostered political spaces and projects that fed popular mobilization and organization. In addition, it complicated differentiation between the state and the Left. The differentiation issue was rendered acute by the Velasco government's discursive claims to have forged a "revolution" between capitalism and Communism; by the disillusion derived from its notorious on-the-ground tendency toward confusion, retreat from social empowerment, and authoritarianism; and by the failure of continuity that culminated, in 1975, with Velasco's replacement by a more conservative, "second phase" military government led by General Francisco Morales Bermúdez.

As Hinojosa demonstrates, the political spaces and differentiations that emerged in the military years help us to understand Sendero Luminoso as one logical culmination, among several logical culminations, within Peruvian and Left political culture. On the one hand, the political spaces, disillusions, and differentiations of the military years contributed to the appeal of Maoism and ideas of armed struggle in radicalized leftist parties and discourses. On the other hand, they also contributed to leftist leadership of a massive wave of political and social mobilizations that contributed to the unravelling of the Morales Bermúdez regime in the late 1970s, and to the re-establishment of electoral constitutionalism and political coalitions whose practical effects undermined armed vanguardism. Within this context of ambivalence and contradiction in leftist political parties and political culture, Sendero distinguished itself neither by its Maoism nor by its idea of armed struggle as a necessity of revolution, but rather by discarding the ambivalence. Sendero rejected the sullying effect of coalition politics with other leftist forces and isolated itself from the wave of mobilizations that marked the late 1970s; it granted top priority to preparing to wage a "popular war" at all costs. Shining Path was a deadly precipitate purified out of a more complex leftist solution.

If Hinojosa offers a history of political parties, factions, and ideas that locates the senderista branch of politics within a tree of related branches, Florencia Mallon probes the experiential processes and frustrations that rendered Sendero-like approaches to politics and utopia—particularly, contemptuous distrust of Andean peasant political culture, and conviction that revolutionary war to conquer state power was urgent and necessary for social liberation—alluring to political activists. Once again, the legacy of the Velasco era proved crucial. Mallon focuses on the politics of land reform and land invasion in Andahuaylas (in Apurímac, the Department that borders Ayacucho on the east) in the early 1970s. The case study matters not only because it came to weigh heavily, as a political allegory, on the consciousness of the Left and the military. It also matters because the experience of key individuals and subregions exposes the *processes* of personal idealism, frustration, and drawing of lessons that rendered activists more receptive to Sendero-like approaches to politics.

Mallon demonstrates the unfolding frustrations that bred Sendero-like omens or conclusions. Individuals whose political beginnings as agrarian activists linked them to the Velasco state (as employees of SINAMOS, the agrarian reform agency and bureaucracy for highland haciendas) came to view SINAMOS and the state as part of the problem rather than the solution.

Activists who varied significantly in their styles of political engagement with peasants—Lino Quintanilla married into a peasant community and leaned toward a deeper and more respectful form of engagement with peasant political culture, Julio Mezzich and Félix Loayza tended toward shallower and more authoritarian links—ended up drawn toward similar self-critiques and conclusions. Radicals who considered the Velasco government's repression of the agrarian movement after negotiating initial accords with mobilized peasants criticized a "treasonous" Left whose compromises with the state betrayed popular needs.

At an experiential level, then, the political commitments and frustrations that emerged in the agrarian turmoil of Andahuaylas, and in the wider consumption of the Andahuaylas affair as political allegory, lent a certain attraction to what Mallon calls "shining omens." For an important fraction of radical activists, the experience of Andahuaylas encouraged sentiments and analysis that defined alleged pseudo-leftists and the state as coprincipal enemies, Andean peasants, including community leaders and elders, as politically suspect, and armed struggle as a paramount priority.

Taken together, the essays by de la Cadena, Hinojosa, and Mallon illuminate the ways Sendero Luminoso emerged as a political phenomenon "within"—not merely "against"—history. The development of a class-driven language of political insurgency led by provincia intellectuals and knowledge claims, yet nourished implicitly by ethnoracial hierarchy, sentiment, and yearnings; the emergence of a radical leftist family of parties differentiated from the failed Velasco project and drawn, ambivalently and paradoxically, toward ideas of armed struggle as well as participation in political and social mobilizations that fed a return to constitutional politics and electoral coalition-building; the specific experiences of political disillusion, "awakening," and drawing of lessons that fed the allure of an authoritarian utopia imposed through revolutionary war: These forces created an environment, within leftist political culture and a popular political culture that incorporated many leftist ideas by the late 1970s, conducive to a Sendero-like phenomenon.

Sendero's launching of a revolutionary war in 1980 was one logical historical culmination, within several plausible and competing culminations, of the interplay between leftist politics and social discontent. Revolutionary war by Maoists was not, of course, the only possible culmination. We will temporarily postpone consideration of "other" political culminations until discussion of the essays in part III. More generally, parts II and III will draw out the many ways Sendero acted as an agent "against" history. For now, however, let us turn to the uncomfortable task of specifying Sendero's place "within" the major currents of twentieth-century Peruvian history.

Notes

1   The other historically grounded projects that represented alternate culminations of leftist history will become apparent as this book proceeds. They included radical and Center-Left versions of populism that pursued transformation largely through nonviolent social mobilization and electoral contests, grassroots activist work that granted less priority to loyalty to particular political parties and lines, and nonsenderista versions of armed struggle.

2   The discussion on the cycle of political discontent and pressure between the 1910s and 1930s, and its eventuation in a reconstructed and exhausted Old Regime by the 1960s, draws on a variety of sources. I am grateful, as well, to Florencia E. Mallon for illuminating discussions. For helpful works, see, in addition to de la Cadena's essay in this volume, Poole and Rénique 1992; Cotler 1991; Bertram 1991; Klarén 1973; Stein 1980; Flores Galindo 1980; G. Smith 1989; Seligmann 1995; and the still useful Handelman 1974 and Bourricaud 1989.

3   A point worth noting is that military governments that repressed and "interrupted" pressures for inclusion organized by political parties and other groups could themselves resort to populist forms of inclusion. A well known example is the government of Manuel Odría, which repressed APRA fiercely but also responded to the aspirations of the urban poor who moved to Lima in search of work and housing. For perspective, see Degregori, Blondet, and Lynch 1986.

4   See Mallon 1995, which may be usefully supplemented by G. Smith 1989 and Seligmann 1995. See also Thurner 1997, an important new study that traces a history of nineteenth-century misencounters between the creole republic and indigenous communities. Thurner's study illuminates the failure of effective organic linkages to local indigenous peoples and intellectuals and provides a helpful backdrop for understanding the racial imagery of "Indians" evident in the indigenismo of the 1920s.

5   On the role of the Left in creation of a dissident common sense, I have benefited from the illuminating study of G. Rénique 1996, which may be supplemented by the fascinating and suggestive treatment of schooling in Portocarrero and Oliart 1989.

ONE

From Race to Class: Insurgent Intellectuals

de provincia in Peru, 1910–1970

Marisol de la Cadena

Have you all noticed what is happening to the *cholo* Tello? They say that now he is a doctor and plans to travel abroad! Don't you remember that he was one of so many *serranitos* who lived poorly and people said he was a "witch" because at night he chatted with "skulls" and "bones of pagans?" Don't you all remember that the police took his skulls to see if he was "crazy" or "possessed" like the newspapers said in Lima? — *Some neighbors of Julio C. Tello in Lima, circa 1917* [1]

Tello is a national institution all by himself, and there is more work going on in his museum with a higher class of personnel than I have seen anywhere else. This old Indian is really as good as the tales that are told about him, and if he falls short by some academic standards I'll still maintain that he is the greatest archaeologist in the New World, and I'll argue the point in detail if someone else wishes me to. Also I'm inclined to think that he is the cornerstone of social science in Peru in spite of the fact that he deals with a distant time. — *Carl O. Sauer, U.S. geographer, 1942* [2]

✣ In the secondary schools of Peru, students learn that Julio C. Tello was one of the first and most important archaeologists in the country. Sometimes teachers will mention that he was born in the province of Huarochirí, in the sierra that overlooks Lima. They never recount, and perhaps do not even know, that the future archaeologist arrived in the capital in the first decades of the century, with his father and a little bundle of clothes. Much less do they suspect that his neighbors in Lima called him a *serranito*, a word that emphasizes his "Indian" physical features, which is how the geographer Carl O. Sauer, without cultural or social inhibitions, referred to him.

This chapter will analyze two periods in the history of Peruvian academic culture that serve to contextualize the preceding quotes. The first, from the 1910s to the 1930s, was an era of "insurgency" by intellectuals from the provinces. The second began in the 1940s when the intellectuals *de provincia* began to capture intellectual spaces. Sauer witnessed this moment and Tello was one of the first provincials incorporated into the intellectual elite of Lima. The second period ended around 1970, when the distinction between provincials and Limeños, although it did not disappear, became more diffuse. The central argument of this essay runs as follows. While in the first period, "race" (*raza*) was a central category of intellectual analysis, description, and diagnosis of "Peruvian society," in the second period the academics decided to replace race with notions of "culture" and social class. Nonetheless, race continued to matter in daily life and in the social hierarchies that governed relationships between intellectuals and other members of the society analyzed by the intellectuals. Thus, the racial taxonomies that the intellectuals used in the first epoch did not lose their importance. On the contrary, although race was no longer used explicitly in academic discourse, the categories of analysis that prevailed after the 1930s referred to race implicitly.

The purpose of this essay is not to analyze intellectual figures or the ideas of the Shining Path elite. I merely seek to describe the academic culture of the provinces and its relationship with Lima before the war unleashed by Abimael Guzmán and the intelligentsia that surrounded him. As we shall see in the epilogue, although Shining Path intellectuals defined themselves as outside of history, in truth they most certainly were not. Not only were they part of Peruvian academic culture, but in this culture they occupied a social space that, like any other, was immersed in historically constructed relations of power. In addition, senderista ideas and sentiments were nourished by the pre-1970 antecedents examined here. In this context it is important to study the relations of subordination vis-à-vis Limeños in which intellectuals de provincia, such as Abimael Guzmán and his immediate circle, found themselves before the 1970s.

The First Decades of the Century

The comments of Julio C. Tello's neighbors enunciated one element of the racial hierarchies that colored life in Lima during the early decades of the twentieth century. Tello lived poorly on money sent by his parents and an aunt, and on incomes from small projects. He rented a small room on Chillón street in a working-class neighborhood. Don Julio shared with his neighbors their economic poverty and their phenotype—brown skin, straight hair, and short height. They were *cholos,* a flexible social label that broadly included all of those who did not have white skin. The difference between Tello and his *vecinos,* however, was that Don Julio was *serrano* (from the sierra). Incrusted in geography, the cultural construction of race in Peru assumed, and continues to assume, that serranos are inferior to *costeños* (people of the coast) because they descend from Indians. Obviously, the Indians occupy an inferior place in the reigning socioracial taxonomy, and because Tello's neighbors had been born in Lima, therefore, they were supposedly superior. But to their surprise, Tello inverted the relation by acquiring a university degree and becoming a "doctor." He was not a folk healer *(curandero),* an occupation with which his neighbors were surely familiar, but rather a medical doctor. He had acquired knowledge that was socially accepted among the "whites" of Lima. Although this title placed him above the masses of *serranitos* ("little serranos") who migrated to Lima in search of a better future, Tello and his cohorts, in their relations with Limeños, had to struggle against the racial stigma of not being socially white.

The racism of "superiors" in regards to the "inferiors" was complicated. The governing elite of the country tempered racism with certain "patriotic exigencies" (in the words of the aristocrat Javier Prado).[3] The elites went from "rehabilitating the indigenous people," to "promoting" education in the provinces, and eventually to accepting the legitimacy of "nonwhite" intellectuals. To patriotism they added, in the first years of the provincial intellectual insurgency, the prestige attributed to science that circulated in political thought in Latin America.[4] One result was that in Peru the idea spread that academic knowledge provided legitimacy to politicians; thus, it was imperative to replace the military-political bosses *(caudillos)* with politician-intellectuals.[5] The equation of academic knowledge with political power, in a context of commercial expansion, opened the space for a large number of middle-class men from the provinces to join university studies with political careers. In addition to renovating the political life of the country, the combination of the academy and politics served as a mechanism of social ascent for individual provincials, first in their places of origin and then in Lima.

An important ingredient in this new conjuncture was the defeat of the political monopoly of *civilismo,* the political group that had governed Peru since 1895 and represented the landowning aristocracy. The downfall of the civilistas began in the early 1910s and culminated when Augusto B. Leguía (1919–1930) became president of the Republic. The name of "New Fatherland" (Patria Nueva) with which he baptized his administration signaled the emergence of a new governing class. At first, the new provincial intellectual-politicians played a preponderant role in the Leguía regime—as part of the Patria Nueva, they personified the opposition to the intellectual aristocracy. By 1923, when the Leguía administration began to withdraw support for the provincials—to the point of exiling and imprisoning them—the intellectual opposition was already incrusted in Peruvian politics. Years later they would become the intellectual elite. From the 1920s and 1930s, the most prolific artists and academics in Peru were either anti-aristocrats, provincials, or both. Nonetheless, neither the avalanche of their production, nor their indisputable preeminence in Peruvian intellectual life, erased the evidence that, like Tello, they were serranos or *provincianos*. Although their academic titles distanced them from the rest of the cholos and silenced public acknowledgment of their skin color, the perception of the provincials as a racially different group was widely accepted.

The Repudiation of Scientific Racism and Racial Sentiments

As in other countries of Latin America, the idea of "scientific politics" (*política científica*) became popular in Peru in the first decades of the twentieth century. Influenced by the ideas of the Uruguayan José Enrique Rodó and the Argentine José Ingenieros, the new Peruvian intellectuals—both conservatives and progressives—sought to replace rule by the military caudillo, and to research the past "scientifically" to find the precolonial and colonial roots of the country. This, they claimed, would help them to formulate policies consistent with the culture of the population and render governance feasible. In general, the new politico-intellectual class sought to invent the Peruvian nation in order to govern it. The generations of Peruvian intellectuals that lived in the first decades of the century believed it their duty to orient their academic knowledge toward the solution of national problems.[6]

As actors in a period in which "race" was considered to be one of the most relevant areas of scientific innovation, the intellectuals perceived the racial composition of Peru as an important national problem. Nancy Leys Stepan, in her study of national projects in Argentina, Mexico, and Brazil, discovered that the efforts of intellectuals in these three countries to reevaluate "the national self were carried out in the name of race, not in

rejection of race as an explanatory variable."[7] The Peruvian case was somewhat different. The most influential among the new Peruvian intellectuals
faced a dilemma. On the one hand, they rejected the scientific notion of
race as a biological inheritance and the racial taxonomies that created definitive racial scales. On the other hand, they continued to believe in racial
hierarchies and therefore constructed taxonomies that included both social
hierarchy and the possibility of "ascending" racially.

Let us begin with one aspect of their dilemma. For José Carlos Mariátegui, the famous radical intellectual, the concept of biological race was
"totally fictitious and assumed" and the notion of inferior races had served
"the white west in its work of expansion and conquest."[8] Hildebrando Castro
Pozo, an intellectual from Piura who was very active in Lima during the first
years of the Leguía government and very influential in Mariátegui's work,
thought that "the racist vocabulary is a convenient cliché without scientific
substance to explain, conceal, and excuse certain socio-economic-political
pretensions."[9] Víctor Andrés Belaúnde, one of the leading intellectual reno-
vators of conservatism, shared this position. He considered "unacceptable
and simplistic the conclusion of the ethnologists who have dogmatized so
much regarding the racial inferiority of the aboriginal race, its defects and
the vices of *mestizaje* [race mixture] and the biological degeneration of the
whites."[10]

Yet, the new intellectuals were also enmeshed in what Mariátegui called
"racial sentiment."[11] The new intellectuals—whites and nonwhites, aristocrats and nonaristocrats, conservatives and radicals—lived lives that were
socially and culturally shaped by racial hierarchies. The experience of the
cholo Tello and his neighbors was not exceptional. Consider, for example,
the case of the medical doctor Nuñez Butrón from Puno:

> In the community of Jasana while the inhabitants called him *misti* . . .
> in the capital of the province of Azángaro they called him Indian . . .
> and after he was educated they considered him misti. In Puno, in the
> School of San Carlos they labeled him a provincial Indian and then
> when he excelled they considered him misti. In Lima, he was consid-
> ered serrano and provinciano . . . in the University of Arequipa they
> called him Indian and *chuño* [desiccated potato] only later to promote
> him to a social category equal to that of his classmates, and when he re-
> turned [to Puno] and to his *pueblo* there was no one who would call him
> Indian. Spain was the only place where they considered him an equal.[12]

Nuñez Butrón did his university studies in Arequipa, Lima, and Barcelona. In the first two cities and in Puno, depending on who would speak with him and where, Nuñez Butrón was classified differently—as nonwhite, but located differently within the complex gamut of numerous, subtle, and culturally constructed racial possibilities that differentiated among nonwhites. His becoming a doctor erased the label "Indian" that had been applied to him as a native of an indigenous community, as the degree of "Dr." elevated him to the level of his provincial classmates. In the eyes of an aristocrat such as Belaúnde, however, he would continue to be seen as a serrano and provincial. Only in Spain, where the cultural construction of race operated differently, did the Puneño doctor find himself free of Peruvian-style racial relationships and etiquettes.

Racial *sentiments*, as meanings and values that are actively lived and felt—in other words as part of what Raymond Williams calls a "structure of feelings"—were a central part of the Peruvian cultural construction of race and they colored alternative racial scientific taxonomies.[13] Peruvian racial sentiments ended up mixing, in complex ways, a rejection of biological determinism with ideas of racial difference and "legitimate" hierarchies derived from them. The new generation of intellectuals shared a sense of shame about the racism of previous generations. Conservatives and progressives relieved their shame by believing that it was possible to improve the "inferior" races. The principle disagreement that divided them (which roughly coincided with the division between Limeños and provincials) was about the most appropriate formula for "improving" the races and changing the racial physiognomy of the country.

Provincials versus Limeños

Provincials and Limeños coincided partially in their diagnostics of the ills that plagued the country. After visiting Cuzco, José de la Riva Agüero, Limeño aristocrat and political ally of Víctor Andrés Belaúnde, complained of the electoral practices of political caudillos: "Election season will arrive with its boisterous retinues and abuses; the vast and solitary plaza will boil with inebriated people, lassoed from the most distant villages; shouts will be heard, ferocious insults, shots, and running; some unfortunates will die without knowing why, nor by whom; the mob will acclaim the candidate imposed, ephemeral feudal *señor*, often incapable of understanding a program or conceiving of an idea, mute instrument of the government or of a friend."[14] During his stay in the "Imperial City," Riva Agüero was a guest of local intellectuals, who probably influenced his opinion of local politics.[15] Note the similarity between the preceding quote and the following affirmation by Luis E. Valcárcel: "The boss (cacique) is omnipotent in his province. His power is unlimited . . . once the electoral base atomizes, no resistance is possible. Then comes the candidacy of an outsider, supported by the central government and through transactions with the gamonal, who cedes to his demands in exchange for a "plate of lentils" represented by a sub-prefectureship."[16]

The agreement between the Lima and Cuzco perspectives ended here. Searching for a way to transform the electoral process they criticized, Riva Agüero's political group blamed the problems on the "provincialism" of the politicians, while Valcárcel's group blamed gamonalismo ("bossism"; for a more extended definition, see introduction to part I). Both concepts interwove racial sentiments and moral judgments. The difference was that provincialism implicated the provincial intellectuals, while gamonalismo excluded them. According to the intellectuals of Cuzco, a group to which Valcárcel belonged, the gamonales were mestizos from the pueblos who lacked the education afforded by the city, the university, or privileged birth. Products of scientific politics, the intellectuals who used both categories believed that education could create morally correct, and therefore superior, individuals.

In addition to identifying the gamonales as the cause of regional vices, the provincials accused the aristocratic intellectuals of centralism (centralismo). The polemic between centralists and regionalists, as the provincials referred to themselves, was not new. The innovation of the period of the Patria Nueva (1919–1930) was the environment of "scientific politics" in which this polemic was immersed and the central role of education in the polemic. In addition to their political debates, the provincial insurgents worked actively in their regions to improve education at all levels. Not only did they consider the contributions of university graduates important for regional progress. The insurgent intellectuals also thought that spreading and raising the level of education in Peru would contribute critically to solving politico-moral problems that plagued the country, from the highest spheres of government to the smallest villages.[17] In the first years of scientific politics, university education served as a catapult for the new political generation. According to Limeños and provincials, the subordination of the latter diminished if they were academics. At the same time, one of the causes of delegitimization of the Lima intellectuals was that they were seen as perpetuating the "monopoly trust of intelligence and culture in the hands of the oligarchy" and thus retarding and opposing the country's progress.[18]

Provincials and Limeños had a complicated relationship: Both groups were very conscious of the social place they occupied in the academy of the capital, where cultural perceptions of race were an important component. Emilio Romero, the geographer from Puno, recounted:

> I cannot forget my life in Lima at that time, the year of the centennial of national independence. The mornings in the patios of [the University of] San Marcos were for us a glorious compensation for our nostalgias, but after mid-day our Limeño friends disappeared along with the grand figures created by our fantasy . . . we admired the great writers and teachers of Lima, but they were unreachable constellations for our humble lives. . . . Some time later, Víctor Andrés Belaúnde, always cordial, democrat to the core, spoke to us of this discriminatory situation of the provincial, telling us that in Lima he who was not proud of being Limeño aspired at least to being *Arequipeño*.[19]

Víctor Raúl Haya de la Torre, who would go on to found the APRA party and become one of the most important leaders of renovation, also belonged to this insurgent generation of provincial intellectuals. Born in Trujillo, the coastal city in which his mother also was born, his father was a serrano from Cajamarca and the son of school teachers. Víctor Raúl attended the University of Trujillo where he and some other future APRA members belonged to a somewhat iconoclastic group self-dubbed as La Bohemia Trujillana.[20] The future party founder himself moved to Lima in 1917, with a small inheritance, to study in the University of San Marcos. Regarding his arrival in the capital, he recalled: "I arrived in Lima thinking about the great honor of being in the same classrooms with personages of whom the newspapers had said so many things. Sr. Smith, the teacher; Dr. Jones, the wise man; the witty Sr. So and So, all produced a certain fascination for me. And the first impression of our men of letters was really admirable. They were solemn, elegant, measured, and courteous men who spoke in high-pitched voices, making theatrical gestures as they conversed, and they seemed to me to be geniuses, absolute geniuses, indisputable geniuses, indeed universal geniuses!"[21]

Later, swept up in the opposition intellectual insurgency and conscious of racial culture in Lima, Haya de la Torre would change his opinion. "Beginning with the Rector . . . the University of San Marcos is . . . a dated institution, conventional, aged. To have a name, money, or to submit to the reigning clique is to be consecrated . . . in Peru it is enough to be the co-owner of the largest and oldest civilista daily for a chair to be conceded to a dandy [*fifí*]."²² Overtly, the political dispute between provincials and Limeños consisted in mutual accusations of academic ignorance, political ineptitude, and immorality. More covertly, the dispute contained racial sentiments. In addition to lacking the economic privileges enjoyed by the centralist intellectuals, as provincials the new intellectuals were marked as non-white. The mark diminished them in daily life, as is clear in the recollections of Romero and Haya de la Torre.

But racial sentiments also transcended daily life and colored the political concepts these intellectuals invented. Regionalism was not only a movement of economic and political revindication through which the insurgents sought to distribute power equitably between the provinces and the capital. It also represented "a redemptive rebellion . . . a movement of racial revindication."²³ According to Luís Alberto Sánchez, the provincial insurgency had to "prove that the 'cholo' is also someone and that he has his valor and his word."²⁴ As in the cases of Julio C. Tello and the Puneño Nuñez Butrón, for many other provincials the insurgency of the new intellectual elite was not simply a space for social ascent. Given the cultural construction that related Peruvian geography and race, regionalism was also a social movement directed by the provincial elite and destined to transform the average phenotype of Peru's governing class. The radical Mariátegui wrote during the 1920s that "Regionalism . . . more than a conflict between the capital and the provinces, reflects a conflict between the coastal and Spanish [read: "white"] Peru and the serrano and indigenous Peru."²⁵ From an officialist perspective, in 1929, in the closing period of the Patria Nueva regime, a pro-Leguía Senator from Cuzco, sensing that regionalism had already emerged victorious, agreed that "electoral regionalism made us face up to struggling victoriously against the voracious appetites of the Limeños who presumed to distribute deputorial and senatorial seats, as one would say, 'in the family,' systematically excluding us, the 'cholos serranos,' even though they had no other titles beyond having been born on the banks of the Rímac [River]."²⁶

Echoing the racial sentiments expressed in José Angel Escalante's speech, and perhaps to distinguish himself from the civilistas he had defeated electorally, Leguía answered the senator from Cuzco by saying: "I do not have *prejudices of caste* or of doctrine. I came to make a country and I am doing so with its own elements. In the coast I irrigate, in the sierra I communicate, in the *selva* I colonize."[27] Leguía's answer used the word "caste" as a synonym for race and juxtaposed the notion with the economic and social geography of the country. His answer also revealed that Leguía embodied a political opening for the provincials. Familiar with the political feuds between Limeños and provincials, during the first years of his administration he played the regionalist card and surrounded himself with socialist and regionalist advisors, among them Hildebrando Castro Pozo and José Antonio Encinas. He ended his government surrounded by conservative provincials, such as the same Escalante quoted earlier, and the hacendado from Huancavelica, Manchego Muñoz. For their part, the aristocratic intellectuals, such as José de la Riva Agüero and Víctor Andrés Belaúnde, chose self-imposed exile or were officially exiled by the government.[28]

A problem Leguía's astuteness did not resolve that also colored the racial aspects of the regionalist revindication was the gendered language used to characterize provincials and Limeños. During the first stage of a competition for "manliness" (*hombría*) among politicians, the provincials constantly associated Limeños, radicals and conservatives alike, with "the feminine." In an era in which being intellectual was a prerequisite for being a politician, such reference implied that the effeminate Limeños were of diminished intellectual capacity and therefore had limited potential to govern. One of the most eloquent in his diatribes against the "effeminate" Limeños was Víctor Raúl Haya de la Torre. Recall, for example, our earlier citation of his denunciation of the mediocrity and corruption of intellectual life. In this denunciation the editor of a civilist daily was a "dandy," or *fifí*, clearly an allusion to the aristocracy and effeminate ignorance that marked an aristocrat.

Toward the end of the Patria Nueva, when the provincials were no longer relegated to the margins of the intellectual-political life of the country, the provincials' claim of hombría associated femininity with conservatism, and manliness with social change and even revolution. Echoing this change, the exiled Haya de la Torre wrote to the editor of the magazine *La Sierra* in 1928: "before the University Reform of 1919, our youth believed that masculinity was Don Juanism and creole talent and spark." Elsewhere he exclaimed: "Peru has seen the end of the deceitful youth consecrated to things of señor de la Riva Agüero, Marquis and boss of a party of *señoritos* [who were] servile to the past, effeminate, and ventral."[29] As for the radicals, Ricardo Martínez de la Torre (a disciple of Mariátegui in the 1920s who later became a Communist Party ideologist) defended the masculinity of the Limeño radicals who had been criticized by their counterparts in Cuzco: "From this 'Limeñismo' of these 'Costeño fags' who 'bathe often,' those champions of a false suicidal provincialism, who are afraid even of their own shadows, have much to learn. Our proletariat of the factories of Lima and Vitarte has conquered a prominent place within the social history of America as the vanguard of the emancipatory movement of the militarized masses who move towards socialism."[30]

Years later, masculinity and revolution—or at least masculinity and "renovation"—would be considered as one. Within this unity, the provincials would continue to claim priority. Once masculinity and revolution were equated, provincials and Limeños still debated who among them would revindicate the men of Peru.[31]

Indian or Mestizo? The Influence of Cuzco in the Intellectual Insurgency

By the mid-1920s, regionalism had a name of its own: *indigenismo*. Indigenismo was a social and cultural movement led by intellectuals of the provincial elite and some Limeños, including peasants and workers. Beyond aspiring to transform the governing class's phenotype, indigenismo also promoted the production of art, music, and literature inspired by the Andean landscape and the supposed customs of its native Andean inhabitants, and destined for local elite consumption. The assumption was that this artistic outpouring would awaken sentiments of appreciation for the country—defined as a symbiosis of landscape and history—that inspired the art. Indigenismo thus represented an effort to create cultural manifestations that might identify Peru as a "nation." This framework was hegemonic among the country's intellectuals. Even conservative intellectuals criticized those who did not subscribe as Europeanized and effeminate.[32] The supposed masculinity of the indigenistas emanated from the sierra, which they exalted as the source of nationalist impulses. Painters, novelists, musicians, and choreographers described serrano scenery, told stories, played melodies, or dramatized legends set in the Andean mountains.[33]

The indigenistas produced cultural manifestations colored by an image of the nation in which the greatness of the Inca Empire was prolonged and offered the possibility of regenerating the "indigenous race," which despite centuries of torment had remained culturally "pure." The new cultural and intellectual Peruvian personality that indigenismo promoted had supposedly freed itself from colonial sentiments of disdain for Peruvian indigenous culture, sentiments that the new intellectuals attributed to the previous generation. Mariátegui wrote: "In the paintings of Sabogal and Camino Blas and the poems of Vallejo and Peralta *the same blood circulates* . . . they fulfill a *complex spiritual phenomenon* that is expressed distinctly but coherently by the painting of Sabogal . . . the historical interpretation of Valcárcel, and the philosophical speculation of Orrego, all of which announce a *spirit purged of intellectual and aesthetic colonialism.*"[34]

Indigenismo was the vehicle of expression of the intellectual personality of the artists and provincial thinkers (including all of those mentioned in the preceding quote) who, regardless of their physical features, saw themselves as members of the same race ("the same blood") because they were capable of creating a culture purged of colonialism. This new race was not merely biological; it was a new spirit that created a culture of sufficient vitality to create a nation and transform the colonialism of the past.

A key indigenista cultural concern of the intellectual insurgents, including Mariátegui, was the premise that culture could transform race. They inverted reigning beliefs whereby race determined culture. Expanding upon its original premise, indigenismo was a political movement that had as its goal "the revindication of the Indian." Despite the renovation implied by the indigenista premise, however, the "revindication of the Indian" accepted the prevailing assumption that the indigenous race needed improvement in order to be included as part of the nation. This idea was shared by nationalist Latin American movements of the period, among them the indigenista movements in both Peru and Mexico. Both movements distinguished themselves from other nationalist movements, such as that of Argentina, for example, because although the Peruvian and Mexican indigenistas were centrally concerned with the "inferior races," their nationalist solutions did not include a continuing process of bleaching through biological mixing with ostensibly "superior" races.[35]

In the Peruvian case, the battle against the ideas of the oligarchy influenced the proposals and revindicatory ideals of the indigenistas. During its period of domination, the Peruvian intellectual oligarchy had advocated eugenics, which the generation of the 1920s found abominable. Such ideas ranged from the physical extermination of the Indians (citing the United States as an example) to matrimonial eugenics. The former proposal did not find many adherents even among conservatives, who with few exceptions condemned it. On the other hand, conservatives of the nineteenth century held hopes about the cross-breeding of indigenous people with "coastal races" to create biological mestizos.[36] It is possible that the nineteenth-century consensus influenced the rejection, also widely agreed upon, of biological notions of race in 1920. As mentioned earlier, the aristocrat Víctor Andrés Belaúnde and the radical José Carlos Mariátegui both considered such notions false. But while Belaúnde proposed the mestizo as the national ideal, the indigenistas of the 1920s, distinguishing themselves from the aristocracy, rejected the idea of the mestizo as the social type to which the Peruvian race should aspire.

Neither of these proposals was free of racial sentiments. Progressives and conservatives shared ideas about the inferiority of "the Indians" and the beneficent role of primary education in regenerating *la raza*. They also believed that "superior" persons were marked by their benevolence toward inferior classes (a benevolence that liberals attributed to education and conservatives to religion). In this context, the politician-intellectuals proposed alternatives to eugenics. Readers of such French theorists as Lamarck, the Peruvian intellectuals incorporated into their proposals the idea that the environment was important in the formation of "social types." In those years this scientific belief freed both groups equally from accusations of racism.[37] Yet, what made some of them progressives and others conservatives, and what differentiated their political projects, was their choice of which natural and cultural environment would provide the ideal scenario for Peru's development as a nation.

For Víctor Andrés Belaúnde and his followers, the environment that would improve the race was that of the Hispanic city, the fountain of social mestizaje, center of the agricultural market and industrial activity, and source of culture and religion.[38] This viewpoint presupposed the absolute superiority of the mestizo in relation to the Indian. Mariátegui did not agree. He believed that "the Indian, in his facility for assimilation of progress and of technology of modern production, is not absolutely inferior to the mestizo. On the contrary, the Indian is generally superior."[39] This quote makes clear that Mariátegui thought about and experienced Peruvian racial hierarchies. Nonetheless, he relativized them. This stance was very important for his political proposals and in his agony—to use the phrase and idea of Alberto Flores Galindo—his effort to merge national (conceived as "indigenous") and international (Marxism and "social class") frameworks to understand Peru and offer solutions.[40] Considering the influence of environment on the races and adding the cultural ingredient enabled Mariátegui to relativize racial hierarchies. He suggested that in the sierra, the Indian was not inferior to the mestizo. "In his native environment, *as long as migration does not deform him,* he has no reason to envy the mestizo." And, although "indigenous society can be more or less primitive or retarded . . . it is an *organic type* of society [and] culture." [41] The inclusion of culture as one component of race permitted Mariátegui to argue in favor of the Indian. Yet, in assuming the superiority of "purity" over "hybridization," he agreed with one of the central paradigms of European theories about biological determinism of race. Ironically he introduced an argument that countered his own efforts to cast racial hierarchies as relative. In the mestizo, Mariátegui found "imprecision and [racial-cultural] hybridism . . . that results from a dark predomination of negative sediments in a sordid and morbid stagnation." [42]

The influence of Cuzco indigenismo and particularly that of its academic leader, the archaeologist and historian Luis E. Valcárcel, was very strong on this point. For the insurgent intellectuals of the 1920s, the Inca capital of Cuzco provided an alternative urban symbol for serrano Peru. In addition, in 1909 Cuzco had been the site of the first university reform movement in Latin America. In 1919, when the new intellectuals were still university students, they chose this city as the headquarters of the National Student Congress (Congreso Nacional de Estudiantes). In the 1920s, the region was the scene of an indigenous political movement that was exceptionally successful in transcending the limits of regional opinion and captivating the attention of the Lima press. According to Víctor Raúl Haya de la Torre, "from Cuzco emerged . . . the new inspiration for Peruvian youth. From it, the popular universities, from it, the interest of educated youth in the social problem, from it, the devotion to the indigenous cause." [43]

Undoubtedly the Cuzco intellectuals were influential in the creation of indigenismo, above all in the political and academic foundations of "indigenous culture" and "the Indian." During its most active years, the indigenismo of Cuzco expressed the same disdain for the "mestizo" that had characterized the racial sentiments of the local elite since colonial times. The concept of gamonalismo was derived precisely from this scorn towards the latifundistas of the rural pueblos. The urban intellectuals characterized these gamonales as ignorant and therefore abusive toward the Indians. One of the most important tasks of the Cuzco defenders of the Indian was the political condemnation of the mestizo gamonal, which implied distinguishing between the gamonal and the just *hacendado.* [44] The difference between Indians and mestizo gamonales was rooted in racial-cultural purity of the former and the hybridism of the latter. When Luis E. Valcárcel founded the Historical Institute of Cuzco (Instituto Histórico del Cuzco) he said, "We still possess the marvelous tongue of the Great Empire's founders . . . but the victor's destructive labor continues to wear it away, to the point of reducing its vocabulary to perhaps only a thousand words, making it more mestizo every day, making it lose its philological individuality. The Instituto plans to cultivate the pure Quechua that is still preserved in certain places and cultivated by many illustrious individuals."[45]

The crusade for the revalorization of indigenous culture was a struggle for purity and implied the condemnation of cultural-racial hybridism. In an apparent paradox, this condemnation was progressive in that it coincided with the conservative repudiation of the eugenicist theses of the nineteenth century. Consider the following comment by José Carlos Mariátegui: "To expect indigenous emancipation through purposely crossing the aboriginal race with white immigrants is an anti-sociological innocence, conceivable only in the rudimentary mind of an importer of merino sheep."[46] Mariátegui would not challenge Valcárcel's condemnation of the mestizo.[47] On the contrary, he shared Valcárcel's opinions regarding the "sordidness" and "morbidity" of the mestizo. Mariátegui, however, criticized eugenics and believed that the social sciences, not the biological sciences, were appropriate for political analysis. His was an uncommon opinion in the first decades of the twentieth century, when biology constituted the epicenter of knowledge about the human species.[48] When Mariátegui, Luis Valcárcel, and their cohort combined environmental theories of race with social sciences, they portrayed the "environment" that "nourished" race as one that included— centrally—"social environment."[49] This stance placed them hastily on the frontiers of knowledge for the period, where they redefined race-biology as race-culture. In addition, in the case of the indigenista followers of Valcárcel and Mariátegui, the choice of the Indian as the race-culture upon which to construct the nation located them in the political vanguard, even though this choice implied a condemnation of the mestizo.

Mariátegui and the Provincials: Race, Indigenismo, and Nationalist Socialism

According to Alberto Flores Galindo, "from his particular elaboration between Marxism and the nation, Mariátegui ended up developing a specifically Peruvian, Indo-American way of conceiving Marx."[50] The many provincials who passed through the home of the founder of Peruvian socialism collaborated in developing this approach. Emilio Romero remembers that when he met Mariátegui in Lima, Mariátegui, already ill and sensing that death was near, told him "that there was no time to lose, that he needed social, economic, and all kinds of information about my native land, Puno . . . proposing to me that I pick a day of the week. He would prepare a brief questionnaire for each week about which we would converse. I asked him for time to converse with some eminent co-provincials of mine . . . to provide a foundation for my conclusions. José Carlos extended both hands to me and I saw two diamonds gleam in his pupils. . . . At times I came to think that Lima would have become intolerable for the provincials had we not had the refuge of his mansion."[51]

At that time, Lima was still a relatively small city, which facilitated contact and exchange among provincial intellectuals. Don Emilio recounts that he visited Mariátegui on the same street—Jirón Sagastegui—where another Puneño, José Antonio Encinas, also resided. Encinas, a lawyer who in Puno had been Romero's primary school teacher, and Valcárcel, an historian, influenced Mariátegui's definition of the Indians as a race-culture of agriculturalists. Mariátegui cited Encinas when he said: to "retire [the Indian] from the land is to alter profoundly and possibly dangerously the race's ancestral tendencies."[52] He was inspired by Valcárcel when he said "the Inkaic people were a race of peasants ordinarily dedicated to agriculture and herding."[53] Combining the historical and legal interpretation of these two intellectuals, Mariátegui concluded that "the indigenous question begins in our economy. It has its roots in the ownership of the land."[54]

Thus, Mariátegui incorporated economic aspects into the notion of race-culture. The leap from this step to an identification of the Indians as peasants would not be long in coming. Let us see how the indigenista interpretation of the "indigenous community" or "*ayllu*" provided elements for the leap. To legitimate his proposals with the "discoveries" of the nascent social sciences, Mariátegui used a book that he considered "in accord with the research methods of modern sociology and economics." The author was Hildebrando Castro Pozo, who had based it on his experience in the Mantaro Valley in Peru's Central Sierra. Castro Pozo balanced out the controversial Valcárcel, "whose propositions regarding the ayllu seem to some to be excessively dominated by the ideal of indigenous resurgence."[55] According to Mariátegui, the Piura-born Castro Pozo concluded "that [the indigenous community] is still a living organism . . . [which] demonstrates the vitality of the indigenous communism that impels the aborigenes to varied forms of cooperation and association."[56] Mariátegui, Valcárcel, Encinas, Castro Pozo, and even Haya de la Torre considered that, historically, the natural social space of the "indigenous peasant" was the ayllu (or community), which they defined as a receptacle for lifeways and culture, in which the Indian could fully develop his faculties. [*Editor's note:* The ayllu has long been considered a key building block of indigenous identity and community groupings, and is now conceptualized by anthropologists and historians as a flexible referent for indigenous groupings that claim descent from a common ancestor. The flexibility of the referent implies that smaller ayllu groups or lineages may be incorporated into larger, "maximal" ayllu groupings that serve as the main branches of an Andean "community" or ethnic group. The larger group identity is held together by a sense of metaphorical kinship within and between ayllus.] Moreover, the community represented a form of land tenure that harmonized with indigenous culture.[57]

Although some of the indigenista intellectuals, including Valcárcel and his Cuzco followers, were not decidedly socialist, the indigenismo of the provincial intellectuals provided Mariátegui with elements to fuse his racial sentiments with his own socialist vocation. Inspired by his readings of the authors mentioned previously, and doubtlessly by other lesser known ones, Mariátegui concluded that "the communist spirit identifies the Indian" and that "the community corresponds to this spirit."[58] As it was defined in the 1920s, the indigenous community gave Mariátegui the intellectual resources to imagine and propose a nationalist socialism, the central component of which was the indígena as a race-culture determined by environment and agricultural labor, and which would be revindicated by receiving land. In addition to the racial and cultural contradiction between the Indian of the ayllu and the mestizo gamonal, he noted a contradiction regarding the forms of property inscribed in each culture. The collectivism of the first opposed the individualism of the second, which resulted in a class contradiction between the hacendado and the campesino.

Not surprisingly, if the agricultural environment molded the indigenous race, then the city also molded the race of its inhabitants. For Mariátegui, while "in the feudal latifundia, the backwards village, the mestizo lacks the means of ascension . . . in the city he is saved by the distances that separate him from the white . . . the mechanization and discipline of [the city] are automatically imposed on his habits." The redemption offered by the city derived from class consciousness and from the labor relations that made such consciousness possible. This was true of blacks as well as mestizos.

"Industry, the factory, the union redeem the black from his domesticity. Erasing among the proletarians the frontiers of race, the consciousness of class morally elevates the black."[59]

Class consciousness—also a result of environment—would redeem certain racial problems. Once acquired, such consciousness would have revindicatory potential greater than that of education, biology, or non-revolutionary socioeconomic progress. On the flip side of the coin, bourgeois social environments, which were racially identified as white, had the effect upon nonwhites of erasing their consciousness of their physical appearance and of producing similar racial sentiments among people of distinct races. For the nonwhites selectively incorporated into such environments, "class solidarity is added to solidarity of race or of prejudice and this sentiment extends to a large part of the middle classes who imitate the aristocracy and the bourgeoisie in their disdain for plebeians of color, even when their own mestizaje may be all too evident."[60]

Socialist indigenismo was very important in the country until the end of the 1920s. Mariátegui's teachings had spread, especially in the sierra, where intellectuals saw in the identification of socialism and nationalism a revindication of and a means of expressing their racial sentiments. From Puno (in a periodical of limited circulation published through the heroic forces of its editorial committee), a provincial intellectual named Emilio Armanza wrote an article eloquently titled "Confessions of the Left." In it he declared: "We will never be able to understand capitalism and our organization will continue to be capitalist as long as we do not examine ourselves. We never believed that the socialist tendencies came from Europe. We are socialists by virtue of our racial spirit and telluric inspiration."[61] During the following years the political debate would drive a wedge between this identification of socialism and national culture. It would displace the notion of raza from the political scenario, which was being transformed by political professionalization.

Political Modernization: From Race to Class and from Indigenismo to the Party of the Masses

The decade of the 1930s marked the beginning of a new political period in Peru. Provincial insurgents (including intellectuals and workers) and rural and urban folk organized opposition political parties. Within these parties, and outside them as well, the provincials reversed their political subordination and became official opposition leaders. The dawn of the period witnessed the dispute between Mariátegui's political group and the Comintern, the death of Mariátegui, and the founding of the Communist Party affiliated with the Soviet Union.[62] Subsequently, Hildebrando Castro Pozo and Luciano Castillo founded the Socialist Party in Piura, and Víctor Raúl Haya de la Torre converted the American Popular Revolutionary Alliance (APRA) into a political party. At the beginning of this period there emerged clearly the idea of the political Left, both electoral and clandestine. In the elections of 1931, Haya de la Torre was his party's presidential candidate; the Communist Party put forward Eduardo Quispe Quispe, a "Puneño indígena."[63]

Distancing themselves from the rhetoric of indigenismo, the radical intellectuals accepted their own identity as mestizo and blamed the "Indiofile current" of having judged "the mestizo with too much injustice and severity."[64] The Piurano writer and Socialist Party co-founder Hildebrando Castro Pozo, proposed that the leader of the Indian was the mestizo—not any mestizo, but rather those mestizos transformed by their class consciousness or their intellectual knowledge. As Don Hildebrando wrote: "The unsuspected mestizos, such as our coastal-serrano workers, and the *yanaconaje* [a reference to sharecropping] from both geographic zones . . . are free from any defect or suspicious interests, and also a group of intellectuals of the same nature who never transgressed their principles of honorable manliness and brotherhood towards the Indian . . . and this because in the present the Indian himself will not know even for various decades how to resolve the problem of his lands, much less that of his acculturation.[65]

The creation of political parties and the new dynamic they imprinted upon popular protest did not mean the disappearance of the patriarchal racial sentiments that also characterized the earlier period. Paternalism toward the Indian as a symbol of hombría was present in Castro Pozo's declaration. Nonetheless, he expressed such sentiments with a renovated vocabulary that interwove race and social class, and the counterpart of class—class consciousness. In using this new rhetoric, the provincials converted themselves into official leaders who spearheaded political and cultural change. For example, the Puno-born lawyer José Antonio Encinas—advisor to the Tawantinsuyo Pro-Indigenous Rights Committee (Comité Pro-derecho Indígena Tawantinsuyo), who had been a primary school teacher of Emilio Romero and one of the inspirations for Mariátegui's indigenista socialism, became the rector of the San Marcos University in 1930. It was the first time that a provincial directed Lima's famous university. Using the new vocabulary to express his racial sentiments and his opinions about the new situation, Encinas remembered: "The feudal castle that was San Marcos came tumbling down in 1930. On its ruins a new type of university began to be built in which we were to venerate all that is our own. The old obsolete University had because of *classist prejudices* neglected our history, our geography, our social and economic problems. The new had the purpose of opening new furrows. This desire that began to crystallize was labeled 'Communism' [by pointing to] student political restlessness . . . in order to impede this liberation that came from the provincial element of the University, they closed San Marcos and placed at its gates a permanent guard of soldiers."[66]

If this had been written in 1920, Encinas would perhaps have called the prejudices of the old San Marcos aristocrats "racial" rather than "classist." Along with this change of political vocabulary, related transformations took place in the 1930s. One of the most important changes, despite the student political restlessness described by Encinas, was the disappearance of personages who fused "political" and "academic" dissent, and intervention in public life, as had the provincial rebels of the indigenista decade. In great measure this disappearance was a consequence of the new forms of activism employed by the opposition organized into political parties. From the Peruvian Communist Party, Martínez de la Torre criticized the intellectuals, calling them "petty bourgeois professionals who seek to contribute their 'intelligence' [sic] to the movement, their labor therein being precisely negative." He called for the "active intelligence" of the political militants to oppose the "inert intelligence" of the academics.[67] In addition, and to no lesser degree, the disappearance of the politician-academic was the consequence of fourteen years of persecution that the country's presidents unleashed against the opposition, beginning in 1931, when General Sánchez Cerro defeated Leguía.[68] The proscription of the opposition political parties ended momentarily in 1945 with the electoral victory of the Democratic National Front, which included APRA, the Communist Party under the name of the Socialist Vanguard (Vanguardia Socialista), the Socialist Party, and two new groups. The leader of the front was José Luis Bustamante y Rivero, who developed a populist policy of confronting dominant sectors, basically the hacendados, some exporters, and financiers.

During the period of political "modernization," which was also in part a period of clandestinity, the politicians became professionalized. The intellectuals, for their part, assumed academic responsibilities. At first, the intellectuals encountered difficulties such as those recalled by Encinas earlier.

In later years, they obtained positions more easily in populist governments. Luis E. Valcárcel, for example, became Bustamante y Rivero's new minister of education.[69]

One of the changes that occurred in this period was that, from the early 1930s through the 1950s, the focus of political activity by opposition leaders shifted from the countryside to the city. [*Editor's Note:* In the late 1910s and the 1920s, by contrast, toward the end of a phase of hacienda expansion in southern Peru, considerable political mobilization and agitation involved and focused on indigenous peoples in rural highland provinces, especially Cuzco and Puno. The volatility of the "Indian South" contributed to the politico-intellectual environment of indigenismo, and was, in turn, stimulated further by indigenista activism]. To the closure of San Marcos (in October 1930) mentioned by Encinas was added a long strike by mineworkers in Morococha, La Oroya, and Cerro de Pasco. In 1931, Lima's autumn darkened even more with a bus drivers' strike; in Talara, workers had gone on strike in July of the same year.[70] The transfer of political attention from the countryside to the city was reflected in the change of political vocabulary. In 1930, in a flyer by the General Confederation of Peruvian Workers (Confederación General de Trabajadores del Perú, CGTP), an organization that grouped together workers and peasants, Peruvian Communists expressed themselves in the following manner: "The class war that has been developing from day to day surges openly in all of its vigor."[71] The similarity with the phrase "race war" (*guerra de razas*), which authorities in some provinces of Cuzco used to refer to the political organization of indigenous peoples promoted by the Tawantinsuyo Pro-Indigenous Rights Committee in 1921, is obvious.[72] Nonetheless, the fact that urban struggles were more important for opposition leaders in this period contributed to the change toward a lexicon of class. It was as if race had been sufficient to explain the rural conflicts but not to explain the urban political struggle. In the city, "social class" resolved these deficiencies.

These years also revealed the strength of APRA. In 1948, the biggest APRA uprising occurred in Trujillo. As a consequence, General Manuel A. Odría overthrew the populist Bustamante and harshly persecuted APRA, forcing its leadership once again into clandestinity.[73] Mobilizations in the north included rural protests, but "the Indian" had disappeared as the protagonist of opposition. (In rural sugar haciendas of the northern coastal provinces, the "Indian" identity of peasants and laborers was in any event less clear and the weight of the "Indian community" less heavy than in the southern highland provinces.) In subversive political discourse the Indian gradually started appearing as the "peasant" (*campesino*), a term that the politicians chose to refer to the agriculturists of indigenous communities. The politico-intellectual construction that identified the serrano peasants with the rural community and collective labor (one of the most permanent achievements of Mariátegui's teachings) provided a vocabulary that implied *indio* without actually saying the word. This vocabulary allowed the opposition leadership to express the paternalist (and obviously hierarchical) racial sentiments they continued to hold. The peasants who worked and possessed their lands collectively were "Indians" even though this word was silenced. The serrano workers of the haciendas who did not receive wages were called *pongos*, a word that also meant Indian, while the opposition rhetoric called the coastal agricultural workers *yanaconas* (a term that became synonymous with sharecroppers) or "rural workers."

The separation of the intellectual from the politician also signified the distancing of indigenismo from the subversive political sphere, which embraced "class analysis" and, until the 1950s, APRA's "Indoamérica." Although the latter concept served as a bridge with the rest of Latin America, it did not play an important role as a cultural symbol in this period. APRA, like the Peruvian Communist Party (Partido Comunista Peruano; PCP), promoted economic improvements and relegated cultural concerns to a second plane. Nationalism consisted of anti-imperialist economic struggles.[74] The new interpretation and rhetoric of nationalism spread to some extent among the governing classes, who also inaugurated a new vocabulary to persecute the subversives. Instead of accusing the opposition of trying to restore the Inca Empire, as had occurred in the indigenista decade, they persecuted "Communists," a category that included not only the members of the PCP, but the opposition in general.

The new rhetoric masked old racial sentiments that continued to weigh down the categories of "peasants" and "workers." To the extent that "class consciousness" and "socioeconomic improvements" did not "improve" the peasants and workers, they would be "led" by those mestizos or whites who had already been transformed by "class consciousness" or by intellectual knowledge (see the citation above of Castro Pozo). In the new hierarchy the "classists" occupied the peak and the "peasants" the base. In the middle were the "workers," liberated by their political militancy.

Leftists of all tendencies preferred "class consciousness" to "race" as a category for analysis of identities and, above all, "social problems." As we shall see, contributing to this emphasis on class was the fact that, from the mid-1940s until the end of the 1960s, the academic indigenista current merged with an "assimilationist" politics of development and strongly occupied the official state sphere. To oppose the state was to oppose indigenismo and its politics of integration based on criteria that the opposition, from the 1940s onward, disqualified as "culturalist" because the indigenistas discussed "culture" rather than "relations of production."

Indigenist Resurgence: State and Anthropology

> He commanded respect, despite his old fashioned and dirty appearance. The principal personages of Cuzco greeted him seriously. It was uncomfortable to walk with him because he kneeled down before all the churches and chapels and ostentatiously took off his hat to every priest he met. My father hated him; he had worked as a scribe in the Old Man's haciendas. "From the hilltop he shouts with the voice of damnation, warning his Indians that he is everywhere. He harvests his vegetables and then lets them rot; he thinks they are too cheap to sell in the cities and too dear to be eaten by his serfs. He will go to Hell, my father said of him." — *José María Arguedas, Los ríos profundos* [75]

Although indigenismo left the political opposition by the early 1930s, it did not disappear. Indigenismo retreated into literature, from where it would reemerge to occupy successfully the official sphere. Andahuaylas-born writer and anthropologist José María Arguedas published *Agua*, his first book of stories, in 1935, and *Yawar Fiesta*, his first novel, in 1941. Between publishing the two works, during 1937 and 1938, Arguedas was imprisoned for political reasons. The novel *Los ríos profundos*, from which the preceding quote was taken, appeared for the first time in 1958, and was followed in 1964 by *Todas las sangres*. Four years later, in 1968, Juan Velasco Alvarado and a group of military officers and civilian men of the moderate Left took over the government. In 1969 they decreed an agrarian reform that attempted to transform radically relations between the "Indians" of the hacienda and their bosses (described in the previous quote without exaggeration), relations that the class-conscious Left also tried to transform. [76]

In the discourse of Velasco and his administration, the Agrarian Reform Law of 1969 was an attempt to put an "end for all time to an unjust social order that has maintained in poverty and iniquity those who have always had to till someone else's land, a social order that has always denied this land to millions of campesinos."[77] But it also represented an effort to detain the radical Marxist opposition and put an end to the rural social movement, which was sweeping across various departments of Peru and had grown very intense in Cuzco since the late 1950s. In this movement the rhetoric of class had replaced completely the revindicatory indigenista lexicon. Nonetheless, this rhetoric indirectly reiterated the racial hierarchies implicit in the dynamic of social subordination, a dynamic also evident in the political parties. One of the most eloquent evidences for this dynamic was the acceptance, without discussion, that the urban workers represented the vanguard of the revolution, and the peasants an important rearguard. In this scheme, "urban worker" replaced "mestizo" much the way "peasant" replaced "Indian."

One of the least-intended consequences of the Agrarian Reform was that it contributed to masking racial sentiments even more, since together with this law, the government of Velasco Alvarado abolished the word "indio" from the official vocabulary and replaced it with the word "campesino." In doing so, Velasco not only appropriated the language that leftist politicians had promoted since the 1930s. He also dealt the final blow to indigenismo and to the racial-cultural rhetoric that had until then served as an official vocabulary for talking about rural problems and development.

The implementation of official indigenismo had been impelled in part by international policies. In 1941 the Panamerican Union promoted the creation of the Interamerican Indigenista Institute (Instituto Indigenista Interamericano), headquartered in Mexico, and Indigenista Congresses in various cities of Latin America. Several years later Luis E. Valcárcel was Minister of Education in the National Democratic Front presided by Bustamante y Rivero. The ministry began unveiling plans to implement educational initiatives inspired by the indigenismo of Valcárcel. In the last months of his government, Bustamante y Rivero attended the foundation of the Peruvian Indigenista Institute (Instituto Indigenista Peruano).[78] The military coup of Manuel A. Odría did not affect this institution; representatives of the military government participated in the Second Interamerican Indigenista Congress that took place in Cuzco in 1949.

One of the important tasks of official indigenismo in this era was the public diffusion of artistic manifestations considered "indigenous." At that time, such artistic manifestations were called "folklore," a concept widely disseminated in Latin America by North American academics that intersected with indigenista ideas already current in countries such as Argentina,

Bolivia, Peru, and Mexico.[79] The "defense" of serrano artistic manifestations promoted by the folklore scholars would be instrumental for the notion of "indigenous purity" evident in the indigenismo of Valcárcel in the 1920s. The folklorists sought out "authentic" interpreters of vernacular art. Evident in this effort, once again, was the intimate relationship between biology, environment, and culture in the racial sentiments of the Peruvian intellectuals. In 1944 José María Arguedas wrote: "The folk songs of the absolutely original peoples, of those who had no other music than folklore, cannot be interpreted by outsiders . . . only the artist born in the community, he who inherits the creative spirit [genio] of folklore, can interpret it and transmit it to the rest." Arguedas made the comment on the occasion of the performance of a Limeña artist, Emperatriz Chavarri, also known as Ima Sumac, whose interpretation seemed to him to be a deformation of Indian music. "A young woman who had grown up in Lima, whose psychology had been molded under the total human influence of the barrios of Lima . . . could not be in worse conditions to seek to become an interpreter of Indian music . . . she has deformed the Andean song to the point of making it accessible to the superficial, frivolous, daily sensibility of the urban public.[80]

The union of race, environment, and culture also influenced the development policies of official indigenismo between 1950 and 1968. Such policies utilized ideas of applied anthropology that came to the Peruvian Indigenista Institute via the North American academy, specifically via the Peru-Cornell agreement. This contract and the Puno-Tambopata project (between the United Nations and the Ministry of Labor and Indigenous Affairs) resulted in a state project of wide scope, initiated in 1959, called the National Integration Plan for the Aboriginal Population.[81] This project was integrationist, based on a diagnostic of Peru as "a nation of two societies and two cultures," one of them the national Euro-American culture, the other the "Andean indigenous culture." The second had to be integrated into the first, in such a way as to respect Andean "norms and cultural values" and to prevent the potentially negative effects of the "cholofication" process. This process was defined as the ongoing urbanization of the countryside, or "a movement of the simpler, folk or indigenous culture and society, toward the more complex urban, or national [one]."[82] This language resonated with the ideas that the North American anthropologist Robert Redfield expounded in the framework of his "folk-urban continuum."[83] In addition, the project reflected efforts to extend the "indigenous problem" from the racial to the cultural and social spheres, as the indigenistas had been trying to do since the early decades of the century. Nonetheless, in the definition of "Indian" utilized by the state, the biological and economic aspects were clearer than the cultural. To the officials responsible for implementing the National Integration Plan, the Indian was "the man who has pre-Columbian blood, not mixed with other races, who lives as a small-holding community-member [*comunero*], or as a tenant [*colono*] in serrano smallholdings, with pre-mercantilist labor relations, and who practices a culture and a way of life of his own." [84]

The ubiquitous Luis E. Valcárcel was perhaps the most important, though not the only, leader of the official indigenismo that marked the 1940s through the 1960s. He relied upon the collaboration of many ethnologists "who [in the Indigenista Institute] have produced more than fifty monographs on indigenous communities of Andean villages." [85] Among his most notable collaborators were the young José María Arguedas, José Matos Mar, Gabriel Escobar, and Oscar Núñez del Prado. The former two were from Andahuaylas and Ayacucho respectively; the latter two from Cuzco. All four were anthropologists. Arguedas and Matos Mar graduated from the Institute of Ethnology of the Faculty of Letters, which was created at San Marcos University in the 1950s. Gabriel Escobar graduated from the San Cristóbal de Huamanga University in Ayacucho, and Núñez del Prado graduated from the University of Cuzco.

In the 1950s, indigenismo once again unified the academic and political components that had characterized the movement in the 1920s. But the new indigenismo was no longer subversive. The new and still incipient insurgent academy was Marxist, acted through political parties rather than intellectual movements, and accused the indigenistas of *culturalismo*. Beyond the question of labels, it is true that in this stage the provincials who embraced indigenismo did so above all as anthropologists. They worked in state bureaucracies or in institutions of the academic elite in Lima, Ayacucho, or Cuzco. [86] The universities in these latter two cities, no longer marginal, became important educational centers in their own right. In official institutions and in the universities, the work of indigenista anthropologists consisted, in the words of Valcárcel, in advising the technicians of development (agronomists) in order "to impede the breaking apart of peasant life, avoiding the abandonment of the countryside and of communal life." [87]

Despite the fact that forty years had gone by since Valcárcel had initiated his indigenista project, his ideas, and perhaps his sentiments, about some fundamental elements of his evaluation of the "Indian" had not changed. In the 1960s he wrote that "the depopulation of the sierra would be truly fatal

INDIGENISTA ICONOGRAPHY. The theme of moral uplift of Indians by intellectuals comes through in the contrast between the visionary gaze of the intellectual on high, and the inert inexpressiveness of the earth-bound "Indian," in this composition from Ocongate, Cuzco, ca. 1956.

for Perú as it cannot be remedied with colonizers from other climes." The implied interdependence of environment and culture in this and the previous quote was even more obvious in Valcárcel's references to migrants from the countryside to the city: "The deserter of his native cultural environment does not manage to be incorporated as a conscious member of the new society: he will remain marginal, with all the consequences of frustration and resentment." Just as Marxist-Leninist "classists" silenced mention of race, official indigenistas also avoided using the term—by referring instead to "culture" and "environment." According to Valcárcel, the "inhabitant of the high zones" (the Indian) was defined by the highland environment and was, in turn, indispensable for dominating "Andean nature." To move him from "his" habitat was to cause a social and economic upheaval.

> The programs of peasant promotion do not contemplate with sufficient depth the need to develop technology in such a way that it does not uproot and distance the man from the countryside. Only a policy that protects the agriculturalist, assuring him good prices for his products, as well as wages that remunerate the worker in a just manner, can be effective in achieving the goal of maintaining and even increasing the peasant population. Such a policy is imperative, especially in relation to the inhabitants of the trans-Andean region, above all if one considers a capital fact: *his ancestral adaptation* [adaptación inmemorial] *to life in the highlands.* He is irreplaceable in the work of the mines and in the fields and each defection brings an impoverishment with disastrous consequences for the human factor in the dominion of the Andean natural environment.[88]

Indigenista racial sentiments still consisted in a complicated and even paradoxical combination of guilt regarding the injustice of social hierarchies, and a necessity for somehow maintaining social hierarchies while erradicating the injustice. With the disappearance of injustice, the Indians would reinitiate the process of development that the colonial Spanish regime had detained. According to indigenismo's decolonization scheme, the potential for evolution should be equal for everyone. In the future all Peruvians would be equal. In the present, there existed cultural-racial hierarchies referenced by allusion in the academic categories used by indigenista intellectuals to formulate development policies. "Andean culture," and later "ethnicity," were silently weighed down by the submerged, but still present, racial sentiments of the indigenistas. For the indigenistas, the ideal of patriarchal benevolence toward subordinates was not only an obvious feature, it was ingrained as a requirement in the personality of the institutional intellectual elite.

Epilogue and Nightmare

"The connections between two such different societies in Peru, the rural and the urban, bring with them the decomposition of many of the autochthonous institutions, makes integration difficult, and the much-heralded communal development will be difficult to achieve under present conditions."[89] This quote is from the book *Ayacucho: Hambre y Esperanza* ("Ayacucho: Hunger and Hope") by Shining Path ideologist Antonio Díaz Martínez. When he wrote it in the late 1960s, he was a professor of agronomy at the Universidad Nacional de San Cristóbal de Huamanga, in Ayacucho. Previously, he had worked in state-sponsored development projects that shared the philosophy of the National Plan of Integration of the Aboriginal Population. From this experience emerged his preoccupation with policies of integration and communal development. Díaz Martínez's language echoes the "redemptive purism" that characterized the racial sentiments of the indigenistas. This is not surprising, given that Díaz Martínez studied in the Universidad Agraria de La Molina, where José María Arguedas taught during the 1960s. Although Díaz Martínez graduated in 1957, he constantly maintained his ties with La Molina. Díaz Martínez's book is of interest because it is the most important text available that expresses at length the ideas and sentiments of an important senderista intellectual at the moment of "origin" of the movement. As we shall see, the book was nourished by ideas and sentiments that emerged in the history presented above.

The incompatibility between the city and the countryside, the first perceived as colonizing and mestizo, the second as colonized and indigenous, was the conceptual framework in which Díaz Martínez inserted his program of defense of the peasant and his "classist" interpretations. The latter were impregnated with connotations regarding the "race" of the peasants, hacendados, and regional authorities of the Ayacucho region. In his description of the hacienda "Azángaro," for example, he noted that the owner was "a white-acting mestizo" [*un mestizo-blancoide*], an "Ayacuchan doctor, who never worked the hacienda." Díaz Martínez defined another hacendado as "belonging to a well-known Ayacuchan family of Hispanic origin, here referred to as decent." As for the Indians, he thought that they "have a great capacity for adaptation and an incredible physiologico-emotional equilibrium," and that they felt "too much love, attachment and gratitude for the Pacha-Mama [Earth goddess or spirit] to break definitively their ties with her." Finally, he believed that among the workers on the haciendas there were so-called "informers" (*soplones*), whom he described as a "traitor group (majordomos, bosses, overseers, or foremen [*mayordomos, caporales, capataces o mandones*]) derived from the peasant class" and whom he considered the "strongest and most dangerous [weapon] of domination." The racial connotations were also present in his description of indigenous communities. He believed that while among the "indigenous" inhabitants there existed "a latent collective and communitarian spirit," the mestizos, or the "mestizo-ized" (*amestizados*) who lived in the communities introduced the individualism that was "strongly rooted in them."[90]

But Díaz Martínez, who had read and conversed with indigenista anthropologists and historians, also thought that the whites/mestizos, on the one hand, and the Indians, on the other, incarnated two different cultures.[91] The first was urban and Westernized. The second was indigenous and rural. In addition, the actors who inhabited these two cultures had class identities: To the first, the "colonizing" culture, corresponded the exploiters; to the second, the "colonized" culture, the exploited. For Díaz Martínez, class and, above all, "class consciousness" were categories superior to race and culture in determining the identities of individuals. Thus, when an Indian lost his status as a peasant comunero or hacienda tenant, he also changed his racial-cultural identity; he "urbanized." The author conceived of this transformation as a deformation, that would produce (as migration had already produced) "grave social crises" in the cities and "traitors" in communities.[92]

The political project that Díaz Martínez proposed in this book can be analyzed at several levels. At one level, he criticized the society he defined as "feudal" and embodied in the opposition of indigenous peasant versus mestizo hacendado. On this level, his vision was not that different from that of other leftist projects of his era. On a second level, he defended the indigenous community. He asked, "will some day the native communities and authentic owners of these sierras, once again have possession of them? Will they once again encounter the *biologic-emotional equilibrium* that they once had?"[93] On this second level, his project was also no different than other leftist projects of the 1960s inspired by Mariátegui's indigenismo of the 1920s. Surprisingly, the leftist indigenismo of the 1960s retained references to the biology of the Indians and its supposed equilibrium with relations of production consistent with "indigenous culture." The racial sentiments of the intellectual elite had not changed much, despite the transformations of their rhetoric and their political work.

On a third level, however, Díaz Martínez introduced ideas that were quite distinct from those of the other "classists" of his era. The others accepted that peasants would "proletarianize" in the process of migration; Díaz Martínez did not. He observed (and described) in his book that peasants, in order to survive, could not merely be agriculturalists. They invented strategies that included migrations to the coast, to the city of Ayacucho, to the tropically forested eastern slopes of the Andes (known as the "eyebrow of the jungle" or *ceja de selva*) along the Apurímac River. He found peasants who, even having enough to survive, found ways to increase their incomes. He also found illiterate peasants who had become merchants and sent their children to universities to obtain degrees. But for Díaz Martínez, these strategies were not valid, because when he interwove his racial-cultural scheme with his ideas regarding class consciousness, he concluded that although such efforts liberated peasants from rural "feudalism," they also trapped the peasants in Western culture and altered their "biologic-emotional equilibrium." Such strategies deformed the indigenous peasants' "natural" consciousness as a class. The juxtaposition of a peasant class "consciousness" and indigenous "race/culture" is evident. Díaz Martínez wondered: "Will [the native communities] be able to escape the mechanistic and utilitarian Western culture that colonizes them today?" [94]

The racial sentiments contained within this scheme left no doubt as to the presumed inferiority of the colonized culture-race. Díaz-Martínez thought that given its primitive level of technological development, the community had not been able to develop according to "the normal rhythm of its own evolution" and that the "cultural shock and unbalanced economic relationships between the two cultures have not permitted the community to modernize technologically, and on the contrary have enclosed it in the magical and conventional principles of its own culture." Communal development should preserve "what is essential in indigenous culture," thereby "conserving the characteristic native features." [95] The project of Díaz Martínez's book postulated that the harmony of the Indian/peasant dyad would permit a "normal" rhythm of evolution. Once this was attained, without deforming the culture, scientific knowledge would replace the inferior forms of knowledge in which the peasants had taken refuge in fear of the advance of Western culture.

Antonio Díaz Martínez, a "classist" intellectual of the 1960s and 1970s

and a *provinciano* member of the new national elite, was inspired by the combination of indigenismo and Marxism created by José Carlos Mariátegui a
half-century earlier. For this reason, Díaz Martínez's political party, the Shining Path, would claim to follow "the path of Mariátegui." But Mariátegui's
vision was characterized by an agonizing doubt derived from his respect
for a reality he perceived as multiple and dynamic, and in which race and
class mixed in complicated ways. Mariátegui did not attribute to himself the
consciousness of the "classist" intellectual that guaranteed infallibility. By
contrast, Díaz Martínez and his group considered themselves infallible. The
sense of doubt that was the source of inspiration for Mariátegui did not exist
in their proposals. Their self-image, as intellectuals who possessed a proletarian class consciousness, gave to Díaz Martínez and his circle the capacity
to decide reality, and gave to the Party the power to implant their decisions.

Saturnino Paredes, a lawyer from the department of Ancash, and Abimael Guzmán, a philosopher from the department of Arequipa, belonged
to the "Red Flag" faction of the Communist Party (Partido Comunista
del Perú-Bandera Roja, or PCP-BR) until 1969, when Abimael Guzmán
founded the faction known today as Shining Path (Partido Comunista del
Perú-Sendero Luminoso, or PCP-SL).[96] In 1970, Saturnino Paredes would
pronounce that "the influence of the race factor as the determining factor
in the class struggle must never be accepted." And, "If we can make some
differentiation between peasants it is not between Indian peasants, mestizo
peasants, and white peasants, but rather between poor peasants, middle
peasants, and rich peasants. The latter is a Marxist-Leninist criterion that
helps the party in its work, since in the end it is the Party that should lead
the peasant movement."[97]

In the 1970s, in the most rigid currents of the Peruvian Left—those
that Paredes and Guzmán led, and to which Díaz Martínez belonged—"the
Party" proscribed taxonomies of racial hierarchy and related sentiments. It
relegated such matters to the realm of "false consciousness." But instead
of eliminating racial sentiment, the Shining Path elite, using ideas of intellectual superiority and party infallibility, justified the racial hierarchies in
which it silently believed. Díaz Martínez's analysis not only ignored the
inhabitants of Ayacucho who were simultaneously peasants, itinerant merchants, temporary workers, and a host of other identities they had to assume
to make a living. Even worse, he considered those peasants who adopted
such an adaptation to try to leave poverty as deformations of race-culture.
Perhaps in this sensibility he imbibed the patriarchal racial sentiments of

Luis E. Valcárcel. But the faction to which Díaz Martínez belonged replaced the benevolence of Valcárcel's indigenismo with the totalitarianism of "the Party."

For anyone who has read Díaz Martínez's book, it comes as little surprise that one of Shining Path's first actions in Ayacucho was to close peasant fairs and market participation, ignoring the mercantile and cultural needs of the inhabitants. The ruthless treatment of those they considered "rich peasants" and "informers" is hardly surprising either. In the intellectual diagnostic offered by the despotic patriarchs of Shining Path, such people were racially "deformed" and thus "dangerous" for the poor peasants, who formed the "natural" social class that was the possessor of autochthonous Andean culture. To annihilate traitors was to contribute to the natural evolution of the productive forces and thereby to defend the Andean culture-race.

The authority that the senderista leaders assumed for themselves derived, perversely, from combined sentiments of racial and intellectual superiority, the former silenced in the rigid "classist" lexicon. The Party, omnipotent mirage that they created, delegated this authority to themselves, the leadership. Even though "the Party" made racial categories clandestine, totalitarian racism was an important component of Shining Path's action. (For an experiential study that illuminates such racial sentiment, see the essay by Mallon in this volume.) An interesting contradiction within Shining Path's project was that the same elite that bellowed for the collectivization of property also utilized its identity as intelligentsia to justify not merely property in "truth," but monopoly of it. But this monopoly was in part related to the racial hierarchies and sentiments that had always marked the insurgent intellectuals of the provinces. Early in the century, the provincial intellectuals were in a sense racial transvestites. They were not socially considered to be white, but they acted and dressed, however awkwardly, as if they were white. By mid-century, these racial cross-dressers had become the intellectual elite and it no longer mattered (as much) if they were not white. By the 1970s and 1980s, to possess the "classist" truth made the intellectual elite of Shining Path perceive itself as utterly "pure," and thus above the social hierarchies, including those of class, that governed the society they sought to change.[98] But the party leaders, people like Abimael Guzmán and Antonio Díaz Martínez, came from the "decent" strata of the provinces— strata more or less "white" by the criteria of their provincial followers, and by the criteria of culture/education that would erase the "serranito" aspects of Julio C. Tello from secondary school teachings in Peru. The perversity of history in the case of the Shining Path leaders was that it was precisely the survival of Peruvian social hierarchies within their party that permitted the grand leaders to situate themselves above hierarchy. When all was said and done, "the Party" was a part of Peruvian society.

Notes

1　Tello 1950: viii.
2　Sauer 1982: 87.
3　See Pareja Paz-Soldán 1954: 282.
4　Hale 1984.
5　Federico More (1929) located the end of "political militarism" in the Piérola administration (1895–1899) during which emerged "technical militarism with purely patriotic goals."
6　On scientific politics, see Hale 1984: 387. Marcos Cueto (1989: 43) notes that until the early decades of this century a military career was sufficient to guarantee a political career. On the influence of Rodó and Ingenieros in the generation of Latin American intellectuals, see Hale 1984 and Sivirichi 1929: 40.
7　Stepan 1991: 137.
8　Mariátegui 1928b: 29, 1968: 34.
9　Castro Pozo 1934: 7.
10　V. Belaúnde 1933: 11.
11　Mariátegui 1929.
12　Tamayo Herrera 1982: 339. Misti is the designation for the "outsider" who supposedly has more power than the inhabitant of the peasant community. The label applies to both "whites" and "mestizos." Chuño is dehydrated potato, made in the highest reaches of the Andean sierra. It is therefore a reference associated with "Indian" as "inhabitants of the heights." Indianness, from within a serrano perspective, is not a function of the coastal-sierra dichotomy, but of relative location *within* the vertical environment of the Andean highlands.
13　Williams 1985: 132.
14　José de la Riva Aguero, *Paisajes Peruanos*, quoted in Basadre 1960: 4694–95.
15　Valcárcel 1981: 158.
16　Valcárcel 1916–1917: 8.
17　On the proliferation of educational centers, publication houses, and university reform movements, see Deustua and Rénique 1984.
18　More 1929.
19　Romero 1979: 13. Arequipeño refers to a native of Arequipa, Peru.
20　Antenor Orrego, one of the Trujillo "Bohemians," wrote about the group: "we had to clash with everything and everybody . . . Trujillo's institutions, public powers, social conventions, university, an insolent and exploiting plutocracy,

its sacred falsehoods, class customs, lack of honesty and honor, a humiliating servileness, its exploitation of the worker, its bureaucracy, professional politics, and general presumptuous ignorance—all had to suffer the ferocity of our attacks." (prologue to Spelucín 1926: 20; quoted and translated in Klarén 1973: 88–89.)

21 Quoted in Klarén 1973: 94. Translation is Klarén's.

22 Letter to Julio R. Barcos, 1925, in Haya de la Torre 1984: Vol. 1: 66–67.

23 Guevara 1929. He would later publish the same article as the prologue to his book with the same title (Guevara 1954: 24).

24 Sánchez 1929.

25 Mariátegui 1968: 164.

26 Escalante 1928.

27 Leguía 1929; emphasis in original.

28 On this point see Flores Galindo 1979: 139–53; Deustua and Rénique 1984.

29 Haya de la Torre 1928, and reproduced in 1984: I,69.

30 Martínez de la Torre 1928: 27.

31 This dyad was agreed upon by provincials, whether Leguistas or non-Leguistas, conservatives or progressives. Thus, for example, Roberto F. Garmendia, a pro-Leguía Cuzqueño, wrote: "Lima and Cuzco need to tighten their connections and march forward in unison to conquer the future. *The first* as the advanced city that lies on the coast and is in contact with all of the countries of the Earth. *The second as virile energy*, as the dynamic force that lives in the renovating protoplasm." (1928, emphasis is mine.) José Antonio Encinas, who Leguía deported, and who in the 1930s became the first provincially born Rector of the University of San Marcos, wrote "Lima has never had *revolutionary* emotion of any sort. . . . The provinces showed the capital duty, honesty, idealism, and *manliness*." (In prologue to Encinas 1954: v. Again, the emphasis is mine.)

32 Even José Gálvez, a conservative from Lima, criticized his conservative friends in the following manner: "They commit a grave error those who in order to universalize, turn their back on their own ambient, those who adopt a distinct environment from their own and waste their vocation in the fatigue of feeling that which generally remains only skin deep." By contrast, he exalted the sierra as the inspiration for national sentiment: "Sabogal as a good serrano is profoundly national . . . it has always occurred to me to point out that in the Sierra there is greater veneration of nationalism than in the Coast" (Gálvez 1921). On the relation between masculinity and indigenismo, see de la Cadena 1991.

33 Praises rained down on artists who presented themes related to the sierra. The magazine *Mundial* was a prime example. For specific examples, see in no. 42 (11 February 1921), the commentaries regarding "two Cuzqueño flautists;" in no. 139 (12 January 1923), the praises of the painter Francisco Gonzales Gamarra, whose paintings bore titles such as "Virgins of the Sun," "The Inca," and "Self-portrait with Chullo"; in no. 463 (3 May 1929), the commentaries re-

garding Inca dances that Carlos Valderrama staged in the ruins of Chan Chan in Trujillo; in no. 476 (2 August 1929), the editorial on the Puneño musician Teodoro Valcárcel.

34   Mariátegui 1928a.
35   In the Mexican case the state assumed the role of forging and universalizing a "mestizo" people through literacy campaigns directed toward Indians and by creating an abundance of cultural manifestations of nationalist iconography for the consumption of the urban elite. See Knight 1990; Brading 1988; and Stepan 1991.
36   Portocarrero 1995: 232.
37   On the particular influence of Lamarck, see Stepan 1991: 136. She writes that "one of the attractions of Lamarckism as a theory was that it was believed to be inherently antiracist." On the influence of the French academics among Peruvians, particularly doctors, see Cueto 1989 and Yépez Miranda 1928.
38   Belaúnde 1964: 96; 1945: 85.
39   Mariátegui 1929.
40   Flores Galindo 1991: 9.
41   Mariátegui, 1929. The emphasis is mine.
42   Mariátegui 1928b.
43   Haya de la Torre 1928. According to Haya de la Torre, who prior to his political career served as the secretary of the prefect of Cuzco, he would not "have felt devotion for the indigenous race nor love for the serrano Peru, nor pain at social injustice, nor rebellion in the face of the barbarically constructed political system had I not lived in person the life of Cuzco."
44   On the colonial Cuzco elite's repudiation of the mestizo, see Lavalle 1988. On the racial culture of the indigenistas of Cuzco of the 1920s, see de la Cadena 1995.
45   *El Sol,* 30 July 1919.
46   Mariátegui 1968: 34.
47   See especially the narrative entitled "Poblacho Mestizo" in Valcárcel 1975.
48   See Stepan 1991 and Cueto 1989.
49   Hildebrando Castro Pozo (1934: 10) wrote in agreement that "the personality of each [people] . . . is more the result of the physical and social environment than of the biological energies transferred through inheritance."
50   Flores Galindo 1991: 24.
51   Romero 1979: 14–15.
52   Mariátegui 1968: 33. He was referring to Encinas 1920: 39.
53   Mariátegui 1968: 45. The work by Válcarcel that Mariátegui used to elaborate his ideas was *Del Ayllu al imperio socialista de los Inkas* (1925): "the land . . . is the common mother, from whose entrails do not emerge nutritious fruits but rather man himself . . . the cult of the Pacha Mama is part of the helio-idolatry . . . of agrarianism." (Valcárcel 1925; Mariátegui 1968: 45).

54 Mariátegui 1968: 30.

55 Ibid.: 66.

56 Mariátegui referred to Castro Pozo 1979. These references are found in Mariátegui 1968: 66–70.

57 The reference to the agreement between Mariátegui and Haya de la Torre is mentioned in Mariátegui 1968: 69.

58 Mariátegui 1968: 69. He also said: "of the influence or alloy of Indigenismo and socialism no one who looks at the content and essence of things can be surprised . . . our socialism would not be Peruvian, nor would it even be socialism, if it did not show solidarity first with indigenous revindications" (Mariátegui 1977: 217).

59 Mariátegui 1928b, 1929.

60 Mariátegui 1929.

61 Armaza 1928, cited in Tamayo Herrera 1982: 262.

62 See Flores Galindo 1991; Flores Galindo and Deustua 1993.

63 Kapsoli 1977: 83.

64 Castro Pozo 1934: 13.

65 Ibid. 1934: 18.

66 Encinas 1954: vi–vii. Emphasis is mine.

67 Martínez de la Torre 1947–1949: 363, cited in Flores Galindo 1991: 143.

68 In addition to APRA and the Communist Party, a political front called the Revolutionary Union led by General Sánchez Cerro also participated in the 1931 elections. With the support of the old civilistas Sánchez Cerro was elected president of Peru, only to be assassinated in 1933. Another general, Oscar R. Benavides, succeeded him and governed until 1939. Benavides proscribed APRA and the Communist Party. Manuel Prado, an aristocrat from one of the richest families in the country, then governed until 1945, the year that the two major opposition parties finally came out of clandestinity. See Kapsoli 1977: 83.

69 See Valcárcel 1981.

70 See Deustua and Flores Galindo 1993: 141.

71 Flores Galindo and Deustua 1993: 150.

72 On the phrase "race war" (guerra de razas) and the way it was used in Cuzco, see de La Cadena 1995; also Kapsoli 1984; chapter 9 in Flores Galindo 1988a; Rénique 1991b; Orlove 1994.

73 See Sulmont 1975: 185–99.

74 In this sense, in Peru the politicians expressed concerns similar to those of their European and African counterparts in the period between the two world wars. See Hobsbawm 1993: 152–53.

75 Quote and translation are from Gall 1971: 281.

76 On relations between hacendados and serfs see, among others, Favre 1967; Gall 1971; and Fioravanti 1974.

77 Speech of Juan Velasco Alvarado, 24 June 1969, quote and translation from Gall 1971: 282.
78 See Válcarcel 1981: 339; Instituto Indigenista Peruano 1948.
79 See Mendoza-Walker 1993.
80 Arguedas 1944, cited in Arguedas 1976: 233–34.
81 Ministerio de Trabajo y Asuntos Indígenas 1983: 57.
82 Ibid.: 6.
83 Redfield 1941; 1956.
84 Ministerio de Trabajo y Asuntos Indígenas 1983: 6.
85 Valcárcel 1964: 9.
86 Arguedas worked first as the chief of the Folklore Section of the Ministry of Education and subsequently directed the House of Culture (Casa de Cultura). José Matos Mar, along with a group of Limeño intellectuals in the 1960s, founded the Institute of Peruvian Studies (Instituto de Estudios Peruanos; IEP), a pioneer institution for studies of Andean communities that became one of the centers of the intellectual elite. Matos Mar directed the IEP until 1985. See IEP 1985.
87 Valcárcel 1964: 15. On the history of Peruvian anthropology during the period see Martínez and Osterling 1983.
88 Valcárcel 1964: 13–14.
89 Díaz Martínez 1969: 135.
90 Díaz Martínez 1969: 196, 75, 248, 246, 275, and 137 respectively.
91 In one of his references to Luis E. Valcárcel, Díaz Martínez says: "as the great historian already said in the decade of the 1920s, Peru is a country of Indians, a fact that is still true in our time" (Ibid.: 165).
92 Ibid.: 138.
93 Ibid.: 167.
94 Ibid.
95 Ibid.: 249, 74–75.
96 Harding 1988: 65–73.
97 Paredes 1970: 31.
98 On "purity" and "purification" see Poole and Rénique 1992: esp. 40–52.

✣ TWO

On Poor Relations and the Nouveau Riche:

Shining Path and the Radical Peruvian Left

Iván Hinojosa

✣ One of the least studied aspects of the Shining Path phenomenon is its place within the larger history of the Peruvian Left. Shining Path seems exotic by Latin American standards, and in the 1980s it advanced at the same time that most leftist movements in the world retreated. As a result, Shining Path remained enclosed in an image so anachronistic and singular that one might think it were the only Peruvian movement that ever advocated Maoism or a popular war as alternatives for the country.

According to this perception, Shining Path was a kind of epidemic disease (armed struggle), which broke out in a remote corner of the country (Ayacucho) and spread rapidly among the poorest and weakest organisms (disenfranchised mestizos) of urban and rural Peru. Subsequently, the terrible consequences of Shining Path's violent actions made it appear disassociated from the well known legal Left. Indeed, the state, in its efforts to eradicate Shining Path, also dealt blows to the Left and to popular organizations that reduced space for radical discourses and practices within legally recognized institutions.

Despite its image as an isolated pathology, however, there are reasons to consider Shining Path as one of the products, if not a particularly gratifying one, of the great mobilization of the Peruvian Left that took place during the 1970s. The Left, in turn, merits a more profound analysis. The Peruvian Left represents a special case in South America given the size and radicalism that it once achieved and the diverse currents and tendencies it embraced. Most notably, Maoism was highly influential in Peru, to an extent unprecedented in the region.[1]

Likewise, it is important to analyze the process whereby Shining Path and the rest of the leftist forces developed out of radical opposition to

General Velasco's reformist military government (1968–1975). Finally, an equally important problem is how Marxist currents with intransigent and authoritarian discourses and practices—to which Shining Path added a sacralized violence—obtained popular support for so many years.[2]

This essay examines the relationship between Shining Path and the radical Left, and analyzes similarities and differences that existed between them since the times before the declaration of armed struggle in 1980. The relationship is defined using the analogy of a "family" of political projects inspired in Marxism that competed among themselves, each seeking to impose its own revolutionary ideology. This competition notwithstanding, the radical groups all recognized each other as belonging to the same "popular camp" or "progressive camp," clearly differentiated from the "reactionary camp" or "bourgeois camp."

Looking at Peru from the perspective of 1995, the analogy may appear somewhat forced. Considered historically, however, we will find that certain proximities and affinities once existed that seem unimaginable today. A moderate and democratic intellectual of the 1990s might have been, fifteen years earlier, a recalcitrant Maoist whose political and personal choices had more in common with Abimael Guzmán than with Javier Pérez de Cuéllar. Moreover, that older radical doubtlessly would have been profoundly offended if someone had grouped him or her with the opposing political camp.

For the Left, or simply for those who at some time considered themselves to belong to the Left, there are reasons to rethink the Shining Path experience along these lines. One can see the *senderista* side of many individuals and organizations during the decade of the 1970s and, with this in mind, weigh the involuntary or unsuspected quota that each contributed to Peru's tragedy. The sharp polemics of the 1980s, trapped in the context of that time, artificially divided reformists against revolutionaries and left these underlying issues unresolved while Shining Path remained active.[3]

Shining Path's Place in the Peruvian Left

At the beginning of the 1990s, to speak of the radical Peruvian Left was to refer to Shining Path. In effect, Shining Path had taken over the political space of Marxist organizations that had, until a short time before, proposed armed struggle as the effective path to power, distrusted representative democracy as an end in itself, and affirmed the necessity of destroying the state and the armed forces in order to construct socialism.[4]

No one could dispute Shining Path's control of this space. Its competitor in the armed struggle, the Túpac Amaru Revolutionary Movement (Movimiento Revolucionario Túpac Amaru or MRTA), decimated by state repression and its own conflicts, was far from superseding Shining Path. Rival revolutionaries within the legal Left, led by the Mariateguista Unified Party (Partido Unificado Mariateguista or PUM) and the Communist Party of Peru-"Patria Roja" (Partido Comunista del Perú-Patria Roja or PCP-PR), appeared trapped by a formalist radicalism circumscribed to the parliamentary arena, and a competition to retain influence among popular sectors. All of this occurred within the grave context of economic crisis and political instability that Peru experienced from 1988 on.[5]

The situation of the PUM and Patria Roja effectively blocked the creation of an alternative to *senderismo* that would have integrated the radicalism of the 1970s with the democratic experience of the 1980s. As is well known, some Marxist groups participated regularly in elections beginning in 1978, when the military government convened a Constituent Assembly in order to initiate a democratic transition. But, only in 1985 did the groups on the Left present a unified coalition in the presidential elections—known as the United Left (Izquierda Unida or IU)—which proposed a profound transformation of the country's socioeconomic structures.[6] These leftist efforts at unity and political practice "within democracy" (*en democracia*) had very little in common with the Left's own discourses of the previous decade, and nothing whatsoever in common with the path outlined by senderista dogma (particularly once Shining Path defined its sectarian and militaristic political line).[7] To arrive at this point, however, the Left had to travel a long distance, characterized by obstacles and retreats, during which not all of its members lowered their revolutionary banners at the same time.

One of the aspects that changed the most after the armed struggle began in 1980 was the image of Shining Path. In the 1970s, for any Peruvian leftist who was more-or-less informed, "Shining Path" was simply the name of one of the fractions that called themselves a version of the Peruvian Communist Party or perhaps constituted one of the university groups known as the Revolutionary Student Front (Frente Revolucionario Estudiantil; FER). In other words, Shining Path was simply one more faction within the above-mentioned popular camp.[8]

In this tangle of Marxist-Leninist groups that together constituted the spinal column of the almost ethereal popular camp, Shining Path occupied the protagonistic role as head of the *infantiles*.[9] Shining Path was considered to be just one of many minuscule organizations, mainly based in universities with little influence among workers or peasants, which tended to use dogmatic and schematic versions of Marxism-Leninism in order "to interpret Peruvian reality."[10]

In addition to its political image, Shining Path also had a pejorative racial image. *Criollo* circles and provincial elites associated ultraleftist dogmatism and rigidity with a stereotype of Andean obstinacy. This prejudice persisted among the Left even after Shining Path initiated its armed struggle. The Left paternalistically underestimated Shining Path and resisted believing that the movement was capable of the actions it undertook.[11]

Nonetheless it would be incorrect to draw a dividing line between the radical organizations of the era based exclusively on ethnic criteria. Other Maoist groups such as the Patria Roja had militants from the same background and even in greater number.[12] What differentiated the cadres of Shining Path from those of its peers were their local character (i.e., their scarce visibility and influence on the national level); their provincialist practice (enclosure within immediate surroundings); and their dogmatism (Marxist-Leninism understood mainly as a repertory of quotes).[13]

These images were strong because the Peru of Velasco was sharply distinct from the Peru of Fujimori, with its celebration of "informality" as a country of *chicha* (Andean beer, usually made from corn) and "ascendant *cholos*." In the earlier period, social classes were more clearly differentiated and stable even though the country was undergoing great transformations and many aspects of present-day Peruvian society were already beginning to take root. Social class and background seemed more obvious (although such identities were not necessarily defined with absolute precision even then). Thus, a party such as the Revolutionary Vanguard (Vanguardia Revolucionaria or VR), which included a minority of "fops" (*pitucos*), "children of the bourgeoisie," and "fake intellectual" (*intelectualoides*) students from private universities, would not have been the first choice of radicalized Andean migrants. Rural students, upon arriving at the universities of the departmental capitals, might prefer to join Patria Roja, Bandera Roja, or Shining Path.[14]

This is precisely one of the factors that explains the surprising growth of some "infantile" groupings in universities such as Lima's San Marcos (Universidad Nacional Mayor San Marcos). Provincial students arriving in departmental capitals, not just Lima, tended to gravitate toward organizations that provided them with group identities, integrated them into a new environment, and permitted them to get through their university studies without major setbacks. This explains the eagerness on the part of all of the parties to do what the American Popular Revolutionary Alliance (Alianza Popular Revolucionaria Americana; APRA) was still doing: to control, or at least to influence, diverse apparatuses of the university system responsible for naming professors, providing services, or determining admission.[15]

Ideological Foundations

Despite the heterogeneity of, and rivalry between, diverse leftist organizations and individuals, they did show certain ideological similarities. A powerful current in the radical Left was Maoism, or more specifically for some, "Mao Zedong thought." In general, such groups developed a vision of Peruvian society as "semifeudal," and of Velasco's military government as "fascist" or "of fascist tendencies" (*fascistizante*). They also developed a great distrust in the "social imperialism" of the Soviet Union, and an expectation that the Chinese path—the "protracted people's war" from the countryside to the city—provided a revolutionary model for Peru.[16]

Indeed, much of the exoticism later attributed to Shining Path (including Maoist quotes and praises, Chinese-sounding expressions, images, and even leaders' ceremonial dress) was not uncommon among Maoist organizations before 1980. Shining Path was neither unique nor original in exalting the Chinese example. But, Shining Path's Chinese leanings became particularly notorious during the 1980s, because they attracted attention at a time when the rest of the Left had abandoned the Chinese model.[17]

Even so, it would be erroneous to assume that only one Maoism existed. In truth, as in the case of Marxism, there were distinct ways of interpreting and practicing Mao's ideas and the lessons of the Chinese experience. There were various "Marxisms" and "Maoisms" that corresponded to Lima or to the countryside, to intellectuals or to peasants, and so on. Thus, the Maoism espoused by the organizations of the New Left, such as VR or the Revolutionary Left Movement (Movimiento Izquierda Revolucionaria; MIR), was more heterodox and cosmopolitan than that of the parties aligned as offshoots of the Communist Party, such as Bandera Roja, Patria Roja, and Shining Path. The latter groups were more orthodox and schematic.[18]

This diversity multiplied when internal struggles, marked by varying degrees of dogmatism and sectarianism, led to splits over differing interpretations of national reality and readings of Marxism-Leninism. Such was the case in the most important divisions in VR, which resulted from debates on the nature of the revolution, on tactics for confronting the military government, and on the problematic of political parties. First the Trotskyists were expelled by Maoists and then the most radical Maoists also left.[19] Vanguardia's tribulations were similar to those experienced by other groups, in part because of changes in global politics and circumstances, and in part because of the singularity of the Peruvian process.

The bitter internal party debates, with their epithets and quotes from party manuals, might now appear, from the detached perspective of the present, simply as elements of Shining Path's protohistory. And to be fair, no one approached Abimael Guzmán's "extremes of suspended common sense" (to borrow a phrase from Josep Fontana). For Guzmán, the answer to any question, even questions about daily life, were to be found in the classic works of Marxism.[20] Yet, this emphasis—at first Leninist and later Maoist— had a wider cultural resonance. It spilled over into the academy, producing a boom in social science scholarship. Such scholarship was motivated by the intellectual agenda of the period. The universities were inundated with monographs and, to a lesser extent, undergraduate theses dedicated to peasant studies, agrarian economy, social movements, social classes, and so forth. In many cases a quick review of these works reveals schematic readings and narrow theoretical frameworks. Even so, outside of the political organizations, a parallel and coinciding effervescence of valuable studies was produced. These studies were inspired by similar problems but framed in nondogmatic approaches to Marxism that, taken together, powerfully increased our knowledge of Peruvian society and history.[21]

For hard-core Maoists who did not succumb to the caprice of departing from orthodoxy, Shining Path resolved ideological tensions with unequaled simplicity. The problem of the national reality was solved by reinventing Mariátegui, after "profound study," as ever vigilant Marxist-Leninist thought. Accordingly, Shining Path labeled its political vision, with Biblical overtones, as "the Road of Mariátegui."[22]

Nonetheless, a great number of social studies, mainly about Ayacucho, were produced by professors and students of that university who would later become prominent Shining Path cadres. For example, the Universidad Nacional de San Cristóbal de Huamanga in Ayacucho published a brief text in 1971 that boasted a singular group of authors: Julio Casanova, Antonio Díaz Martínez, Osmán Morote, and Carlos Tapia.[23] Casanova, Díaz, and Morote would become leaders of Shining Path, while the engineer Carlos Tapia became a militant in a Maoist fraction of the MIR, and thus an adversary. Later he would become a prominent "senderologist." Antonio Díaz Martínez would be killed in the prison uprising in 1986. A comparison of the two editions of Díaz Martínez's important work *Ayacucho, hambre y esperanza*, which appeared in 1969 and 1985, reveals that he was a more flexible thinker in the early years. Díaz Martínez inspired much of the field research undertaken by Huamanga students of the period.[24]

A final ideological characteristic of the Maoist Left of the 1970s was Stalinism. The political and intellectual adulation of Stalin was obvious: His image hung symbolically over the presidium of students' and workers' assemblies, and his texts were used as an "introduction" to Marxism-Leninism or as a "theoretical framework" for analyzing Peruvian reality. The Maoist Left remembered Stalin as the victorious Grand Marshal of the Second World War. His name became a synonym for efficacy and discipline, while his purges and other crimes were considered social sacrifices necessary for the construction of socialism.[25]

The admiration of Stalin predated the development of Maoism. Stalinism was, rather, a distinctive element that emerged from the "trunk" (*tronco*) or core of the Communist Party at the beginning of the phase of exalting the Soviet struggle against fascism, and became a standard element during the Cold War. For this reason, in the 1950s there was a large internal dispute within the party regarding de-Stalinization. Abimael Guzmán, then a young Communist Party militant, was opposed to discarding Stalin, because "to take Stalin away from us . . . is to take away our soul." Obviously, after the Sino-Soviet split, the Communist factions that decided to follow China rather than the Soviet Union continued to emphasize their Stalinism.[26]

Parties and Caudillos

In the 1970s leftist political groups multiplied, each one seeking to become *the* Communist Party of Peru that would direct the revolution. For the Maoist fractions, the old Communist Party "had fallen into the hands of revisionism," for which reason it was critical to undertake its "reconstruction" or "reconstitution" (as Shining Path proposed). No faction was disposed to renounce the name Communist, despite the confusion that resulted.[27]

Those who sought to "organize themselves" into a party had additional motives, not always conscious, beyond their ideological arguments. A party, circle, or cell provided an identity and a collective referent, precious to a social base of university youth who, in many instances, found themselves removed from their communities of origin. They had left behind the formal and disciplined environment of secondary school. Many had left their families behind as well.

Most of the radical organizations were not Limeño, either in terms of the origins of their militants or in terms of their activist priorities. Even though Mariátegui had founded the Socialist Party (which was called the Communist Party after 1930) in Lima, Arequipa and the Andean south would become the traditional bastions of Communism. Decades later, Shining Path would be centered in Huamanga (Ayacucho), while the Communist Party and Patria Roja would prove particularly strong in Arequipa and Cuzco. The southern tendency would be maintained by the organizations of the New Left.[28] On the other hand, the Left as a whole never gained strength in aprista zones such as the "solid North." An exception was Patria Roja, which did obtain some support in Aprista bastions such as Cajamarca and Junín. It would be very interesting (though beyond the scope of this essay) to consider in depth whether Patria Roja's high-flown Maoist rhetoric was perceived in some regions of the country as a form of radical populism akin to the early aprismo.

Beginning with electoral participation in the Constituent Assembly (1978–1979), there emerged a new emphasis on political work in Lima, due to the resonance obtained through parliamentary agitation. Once Patria Roja entered the realm of "bourgeois legality" in 1980, all of the principal parties ended up trapped in a rhythm imposed by Lima. Regional strikes and decentralized struggles continued, but they lost their strategic role. The Left had to think of the country *desde la capital* (from the capital as a point of departure) and gradually declined in relevance elsewhere. To a great extent, the parties had followed the same trajectory as the rural migrants to the capital.[29]

The elections would reveal, moreover, that while the Left had more than enough candidates, it lacked undisputed leaders who might occupy, for example, the space left by Mariátegui. Very few leaders could project themselves outside of their local or partisan ambits, and almost none offered an authority born from unquestionable political and intellectual qualities (such as those that Isaac Deutscher attributed to Lenin) that could have brought other leaders together behind one person.[30]

This lack was important both because of the Leninist demand of a party leadership that would guide the revolution, and because of a certain Peruvian predilection for caudillos. As explained later, electoral victories did not solve any of these problems. In this sense, Abimael Guzmán was unique, even leaving aside his cult following or his pretensions to be one of the "Swords of Marxism" (*espadas del marxismo*). He obtained an indisputable national presence that transcended party lines, and he kept his organization united until his capture. It is worth noting, in addition, that when the youth cadres that would later form Patria Roja first broke off from Bandera Roja, they tried to make Guzmán the leader of their faction.[31]

Left Opposition to Military Reformism

Among the many themes of study related to the Left-leaning social and economic reforms of the "Revolutionary Government of the Armed Forces" of General Juan Velasco Alvarado (1968–1975), one issue that has received little attention is how the regime influenced the development of Peruvian leftist groups. (See, however, the chapter by Florencia E. Mallon in this volume, as well as the discussion that follows.) In reality, there was a tight correlation between the effects of Velasco's policies and the growth of the Left in all of its varied manifestations. Multiple factors affected this process: the general climate of nationalism and anti-imperialism, the massive social mobilization that accompanied the state's recognition of peasant communities and labor unions, and the expansion of public education, among others.

Discussions among leftists in the early 1970s about the "character" of the military government displayed a constant preoccupation with differentiating the Left from the regime. As Guillermo Rochabrún has pointed out, confusion was possible because both projects basically "moved within the same paradigm: development of the country according to a model established by industrial societies and their productive forces."[32] Although it may seem paradoxical, the military undertook reforms directed at demands that had gone unanswered for several decades, including agrarian reform and nationalization of natural resources. And, the military government dealt blows to the Left's great enemies: the oligarchy and APRA. In ideological terms, the military's opening toward "really existing socialism" had unforeseen consequences. The policy of Third World nonalignment implied establishing diplomatic ties with all of the countries then known as socialist—first those of Eastern Europe, then the Soviet Union (from which arms were also purchased), and China. In the case of Cuba, the Peruvian generals were more hesitant because they still had fresh memories of Cuba's support for Peruvian guerrillas during the 1960s.[33] In this manner, Peruvians could be in "contact" with the socialist countries by importing their products, circulating information, and promoting culture through embassies and official exchanges. These policies, when combined with nationalist measures and anti-imperialist rhetoric, left little space for the anti-Communist mystifications common in the Cold War.

This paradoxical situation—a military regime that seemed to preempt the Left—had varied repercussions within the heterogeneous Left. The Communist Party-Unity (Partido Comunista-Unidad or PCP-U), a moderate organization by the popular camp's standards, identified with the military's objectives. The PCP-U collaborated with the regime through its policy of "critical support." Without actually cogoverning, the PCP-U did obtain considerable advantages. First, it benefitted from the campaign against APRA, the secular nemesis of the Peruvian armed forces, which resulted in APRA's political setbacks in the unions and the universities. Second, the government recognized the General Federation of Peruvian Workers (Confederación General de Trabajadores del Perú or CGTP), aligned with the Communist Party, as the official representative of Peruvian labor unions. Such recognition was important in a moment when expanding production was crucial, above all because after the Sino-Soviet split, the majority of the working class base in Peru remained aligned with the pro-Soviet Communist Party. Third, its weekly publication, *Unidad,* gained more weight in national public opinion in a context of repression of the independent press.

But not all was rosy for "official Communism." The PCP-U and the CGTP continued to support the military regime until December 1976, that is, sixteen months after General Francisco Morales Bermúdez rebelled against Velasco and initiated the more conservative "second phase." This situation "tied the hands" of the Communist Party, leaving the field open for more radical organizations that advanced upon the union terrain outside the CGTP framework. The more radical groups channelled popular discontent caused by the deteriorating economy and exacerbated by government efforts to confront the emerging crisis with antipopular policies.[34]

In addition to this unexpected competition within the labor movement, the PCP-U confronted a more serious problem. The party had lost touch with young people and above all with various arenas of the education system. In the schism of 1964, the Maoists—principally Patria Roja—had retained control over party organizing among youth, students, and professors. In addition, the PCP-U's unconditional defense of the Soviet Union, the solemnity of its long-time leaders, and its reluctance to accept armed struggle in place of a slow "accumulation of forces," all caused radical youth to see the party as Peru's creole version of Soviet bureaucracy.

The opposite was true for the more radical organizations, which grew as they opposed the policies of the military government. The radicals cited basic principles. According to a strict class analysis, the armed forces constituted a part and a pillar of the bourgeoisie, and could not be expected to foment a revolution against their own class. What the military proposed, rather, was essentially a corporativist project of class conciliation, which in Peru meant the equivalent of aprismo—in other words, the negation of Marxism.[35] It is hardly surprising, therefore, to find passionate denunciations: "Velasco draped himself ideologically in the word socialism in order to mask his pro-imperialist, monopolist regime, in particular his state capitalism. By reaffirming the old and worm-eaten aprista theses of 'conceptual autonomy,' in addition to the pro-Yankee, Cold War ideology of 'neither capitalist nor communist,' he brought anarchist overtones to his rhetoric of socialism, and spoke of its economic attainment through the 'priority sector of social property.' The flip side of his trumpeted participatory democracy was dictatorship, corporativism, repression, manipulation, promotion of the lumpen, and fascist-like (*fascistoide*) banditry."[36]

Marxist radicals also diverged significantly from the military in the ambit of "political praxis." Even though the military carried out reforms that had been part of the Left's own agenda, the radical Left did not easily forget the military's repressive history. Just a few years before, in 1965, the same army had liquidated the guerrilla *focos*, and as the years went by, the Velasco government exercised an increasingly hard line (*mano dura*) against the "ultra-Left." The military government persecuted Vanguardia Revolucionaria and Patria Roja, in addition to the teachers' union (Sindicato Unico de Trabajadores de la Educación, SUTEP). In August 1975—Velasco's last month in power—he deported twenty-nine dissidents and closed *Marka*, the New Left periodical.[37] Morales Bermúdez's "second phase" signalled a hardening against the Left. The most progressive military men were removed from their posts and the government took a clear turn toward the Right. The growth of social movements and popular discontent resulted in protests and struggles that peaked in the national strike of 19 July 1977. Cornered, the military regime did not hesitate to respond with repression, particularly mass firings of labor leaders and deportations. At the same time, the military courted APRA and the Right by promising to turn the government over to civilians. Given this context, it is not surprising that some leftist organizations came to the conclusion that they were living the beginnings of a revolutionary situation.

In this panorama of sharpening definition and confrontation against the military dictatorship, there was one great absence: Shining Path. Shining Path remained enclosed within its own "philosophical adventure" and turned its back on the protests. Its distance from, and scant influence in, the mass movement was such that Shining Path was not even persecuted. In contrast with the other organizations, not one Shining Path leader was deported. Abimael Guzmán was detained once, by mistake, and quickly liberated.[38]

Nonetheless, some Shining Path militants maintained connections with radical union organizations of the era. A flier by the Callao committee of SUTEP in September 1977, for example, protested the arbitrary transfer from its base of several teachers, including Elena Iparraguirre and Laura Zambrano. (Iparraguirre and Zambrano, it should be remembered, would become important Shining Path leaders detained with Abimael Guzmán in September 1992.)[39] Most likely, Shining Path never abandoned its political work in SUTEP because the education system was the greatest source of cadres for the Left.

The "Popular Camp": Armed Struggle and Democracy

The history of the "popular camp" of the 1970s changed drastically when its most important organizations decided to participate in the electoral process. Most groups were going to apply the Leninist maxim of utilizing elections and parliaments as platforms for agitation and propaganda, only to end up trapped within the very system they had hoped to transform (or even to destroy). By 1978 the period of clandestine structures and leaders began drawing to a close, giving way to the era of public campaign offices and electoral candidates.[40]

Ironically, the election results posed the central problem for leftist groups, even though elections are not supposed to matter too much to those who believe that armed struggle is the only viable path to power. Despite their efforts to limit the legitimacy of the electoral process, the elections introduced a severe disjunction between popular support as measured in votes and as measured in the real size and impact of organizations. Thus, for example, Hugo Blanco, the Trotskyist leader who had become famous during the peasant mobilizations in Cuzco in the early 1960s, surprisingly received the third highest vote total among the candidates for the Constituent Assembly in 1978. His almost 300,000 votes gave the coalition to which he belonged an image of political support that outstripped his actual organizing presence in the popular camp. The Left, characterized by ideological zeal and base activism, had few resources to lead through popular support produced by elections, and was even less able to explain why, out all of the leftist candidates, a Trotskyist received the most votes.[41]

Even so, not all of the groups suffered this problem at the same time. Some of the leftist parties did not participate in the elections and, on the contrary, advocated a boycott. Patria Roja was the largest and most important party to opt for abstention. Shining Path also abstained, but did so according to its own agenda. That is, rather than attempt to coordinate opposition to the elections, Shining Path simply followed its usual policy of holding itself apart from any electoral processes.

It is difficult to calculate the size of Patria Roja in 1978, given that we lack a vote count that might measure popular support and an accessible roster of militants or sympathizers. In any event, Patria Roja was clearly an important party because it controlled the leadership of the teachers' union (SUTEP) and the mining federation (Federación Nacional de Trabajadores Mineros, Metalúrgicos y Siderúrgicos; FNTMMSP). The SUTEP, a key actor in struggles against the military regime, carried out large strikes and street demonstrations that were enormously influential in turning public opinion against the dictatorship. As for the mining federation, forceful action by the mineworkers caused enormous losses. Mining was Peru's principal income-generating export sector, and the mineworkers constituted the faction of the Peruvian proletariat most coveted by the parties of the Left.

In addition to this visibility within the popular movement, Patria Roja also displayed militarist rhetoric, as reflected in the party slogan "power is born from the barrel of a gun." Patria Roja's influence and rhetoric, its reluctance to establish ties with other political forces, its maintenance of clandestine structures, its use of violent shock troops, and its boycott of the Constitutional Assembly of 1978–1979, suggested that Patria Roja was preparing to launch—or at least had made a decision to launch—an armed struggle in the near future.[42]

As a result, the psychosocial campaigns of the military government in its last two years were directed at combating the "blind extremism" of Patria Roja. It was Patria Roja, not Shining Path, that appeared on the verge of mounting armed struggle. There is no evidence, however, that Patria Roja's intentions went beyond political rhetoric. In place of launching an insurrection Patria Roja opted to run in the 1980 elections. Its electoral potential was signalled in advance when Patria Roja made it onto the ballot with the largest number of valid signatures obtained by any of the leftist parties.[43]

What subsequently happened to Patria Roja is symptomatic. It succeeded too well at the polls to maintain such a radical discourse. Over the course of the decade various cadres would be elected as representatives to the congress, and as mayors, council members, and even presidents of regional governments. Unfortunately, it is still too soon to venture an analysis of the destiny of the most radical militants and supporters of UNIR-Patria Roja in the 1980s, when the party leadership remained within the legal framework of democracy. It is revealing, however, that the two most significant fractions that split off from the party ended up either in Shining Path or carrying out actions in the name of Shining Path.[44]

For the elections of 1980 two electoral coalitions were formed. Although these alliances disappeared in the midst of the campaign without ever having been fully solidified, they did divide the popular camp into two clearly defined sectors. The radicals formed the Revolutionary Alliance of the Left (Alianza Revolucionaria de Izquierda; ARI) while the moderates formed the Left Unity (Unidad de Izquierda; UI). ARI included, among other groups, Patria Roja, Vanguardia Revolucionaria, and the MIR, while the principal party in the UI was the PCP-U. It is difficult to say, fifteen years later, how far a radical electoral front might have gone had it been able to overcome its internal differences. The internal conflicts were more prosaic than programmatic, motivated principally by the immaturity of the party leadership, personal appetites, and corruptions divorced from the formal discourses and practices of the organizations. ARI did not last even two months, but it did mark an inflection of the voluntarism of the 1970s, and a sign that many revolutionaries had decided to say farewell to armed struggle.

The radical Left participated in the elections divided into various opposing candidacies, all of which had in common a thorny relationship with democracy that would take time to resolve. Electoral participation was, from then on, both a means of propaganda and accumulation of forces, and a source of responsibilities within the state apparatus as parliamentarians and local authorities. The parties did not formally renounce armed struggle, thus inaugurating a stage of ideological schizophrenia that oscillated between a puritanical defense of the constitution and subversive-like agitation among popular sectors.[45]

THE MAOIST LEFT, ELECTIONS, AND ARMED STRUGGLE, 1980. (left) A candidate of the Maoist Left campaigns for election while brandishing a rifle. (below) Senderista depiction of Abimael Guzmán directing the party's First Military School (Primera Escuela Militar).

In practice, the "progressive camp" had split, since there were still some "organizations and *compañeros*" outside of the legal framework. Of these, Shining Path and the MRTA would in time become the best known. Some radicals, principally Maoists, turned their gaze toward Shining Path. Shining Path, dismissed as somewhat absurd or rustic (*folclórico*) the decade before, took on a profile as a worthy lesser evil. One example is the case of Luis Arce Borja. Before becoming a Senderista representative in Europe and editor of *El Diario Internacional*, Arce Borja was a Maoist militant in one of the organizations of the New Left and an UNIR candidate for provincial deputy in Lima.[46] His trajectory, from "electioneer" (*electorero*) to Guzmán's mouthpiece, including an interlude along the way as Guzmán's exclusive interviewer, epitomizes a path followed by other, less well known radical leftists.

Some Maoist groups remained fragmented, and in university circles that lacked national scope they virtually dissolved. The democratic opening and the new scenario of contention provided by the parliament, local governments, and the communication media (recently liberalized by the Fernando Belaúnde government [1980–1985]) left such groups incidental and marginal. The militants in these groups were for the most part young provincials who lacked family or professional connections necessary to gain niches within the democratic system—in a nongovernmental organization (NGO) for example—so they were left with minimal options. Those who wanted to continue the long march could hope to be accepted into Shining Path. Or, they could abandon their leftist political activities altogether.

Among the groups that had constituted the socialist bloc within the ephemeral ARI, some small New Left organizations shunned the new unified organizations and the electoral arena. Some chose to initiate armed struggle independently of Shining Path, founding the MRTA. The MRTA's heterodoxy and voluntarism was a militarized expression of the New Left of the 1960s and 1970s, with the limitation that it appeared a decade too late. In other cases, these groups became poles of attraction for radical tendencies within the United Left (Izquierda Unida or IU) front, founded in September 1980. Such poles facilitated union activities and demonstrations that did not depend on the rhythm of the IU.

Within this panorama it is possible to detect a certain continuation of the "popular camp" after 1980 despite the armed struggle of Shining Path. Some evidence suggests that processes of conflict and negotiation continued for various years between the militants and the fringes of Shining Path, on the one hand, and other radicalized groups, on the other—official declarations and condemnations of the leaders notwithstanding. The simple reason was that Shining Path and these other groups either competed for the same social space or emerged from similar sections of the political spectrum.[47]

This process constitutes a possible explanation of Shining Path's advance among popular sectors toward the end of the 1980s. This was not so much a case of complicity with subversion as a tragic longing for neutrality on the part of groups not affiliated with Shining Path. They sought to advance a leftist project of their own, however uncertain, that was not represented in either of the two militaristic extremes (Sendero and the military) that fought against each other.[48] By the late 1980s, the differences with Shining Path were more marked. Shining Path never renounced the armed struggle and always repudiated the country's democratization process. No other organization, not even the MRTA, stayed so exclusively aloof from the electoral political scene and concentrated so completely on its "popular war."[49] Nor could anyone compete with Shining Path on the terrain of war—neither in the rhetoric of war, nor in the cult of death as a welcome blood sacrifice, in short in the idea of violence as a permanent and legitimate political resource that transcended any "social cost."

Conclusions

Shining Path was seen by national leftist circles as a sort of poor provincial cousin of the extended family represented by Peruvian Maoist organizations. Shining Path descended from the so-called trunk of the Communist Party and shared with other factions that had split off from the trunk characteristics that would later render Shining Path internationally famous. These included an explicit revindication of Stalinism and a clear determination to replicate the Chinese experience in Peru.

Like the other factions, Shining Path sought to convert itself into the one legitimate Communist Party of Peru and traced its lineage to José Carlos Mariátegui. Likewise, Shining Path counted on militant cadres recruited from the universities and considered armed struggle as the only guaranteed path to power. In contrast to the rest of the Left, however, Sendero never showed any interest in approaching other groups in the popular camp to form any sort of alliance. Indeed, the passing of time underscored Shining Path's emphatic repudiation of all the other groups with which it had once had affinities.

Shining Path's isolation from the rest of the Left permitted it to gain advantage from the many instances when it was underestimated. For example, Shining Path announced publicly, at the end of the 1970s, that it was on the verge of initiating the armed struggle and even provided the script it intended to follow. The announcement was ignored. The state saw danger from elsewhere in the Left. The radical Left was too occupied with themes that seemed at the moment to have greater import, such as debates over participation in the democratic transition.

Once the "people's war" began—apparently at the most inopportune moment, just as a democratic government was being inaugurated after twelve years of dictatorship—Shining Path took advantage of the criticisms it received from those on the Left who saw it as too dogmatic and rustic to embody what should be the revolution in Peru. Shining Path's campaign of hanging dogs against the revisionist Teng, along with its dynamite attacks, seemed a far cry from programmatic advances and mass support enjoyed by the larger organizations at the beginning of the 1980s. It was hard to believe, moreover, that a handful of fanatic followers of Mao, armed with "humble dynamite" (in Guzmán's words), would have any chance against the solid, modernized army Velasco had built.

It is important to explain the paradoxical support that Shining Path gained among popular sectors—support that Shining Path obtained despite dogmatism and its violent terrorist methods—within a perspective that takes into account the regional diversity of the country and the distinct moments of its people's war. Shining Path was able to maintain itself outside of the democratic experience of the legal Left, growing within extra-legal spaces vacated by the Left and taking advantage of the overall deterioration of the country. (For additional discussion of this complex point, within the context of popular resistance also provoked by Sendero, see the essays in Parts II and III of this book.)

In a country such as Peru, in which very few things function systematically and follow a preestablished order, Shining Path followed, in its own manner, the schedule it announced. It is not surprising, then, that Shining Path won over to its cause individuals from radical sectors who were disillusioned with the democratic experience or those who imagined Shining Path as a victorious force in a country that otherwise seemed to be hovering at the edge of a dysfunctional abyss.

In the dark panorama of the five years that spanned 1988 to 1992, Shining Path consistently followed its own dynamic, refused to make electoral deals, and took advantage of the many errors committed in its favor by the participants in the official arena. Among these errors, the Left's scant clarity—in other words, its inability to establish a clear, public difference that offered the country a viable alternative to authoritarianism and savagery—constituted the greatest gift that the Peruvian Left could give to its old compañero from the popular camp. This poor provincial cousin, previously scorned by its Communist relatives, arrived in Lima without asking anyone's permission, burned down the house, and ended up with the family name.

Notes

This essay is part of a larger study on Maoism and the radical Peruvian Left. I thank Steve J. Stern for his detailed and pertinent editorial comments and Elizabeth Haworth for some important changes that she suggested for the final version.

1 The working papers that ex-leftist militants prepared for the National System of Support for the Social Mobilization (Sistema Nacional de Apoyo a la Movilización Social; SINAMOS) are very important sources for studying the Maoist organizations of the era. These documents constitute primary source material and reflect in-depth knowledge of the topic. See ONAMS 1975 and SINAMOS 1975.

2 Even though the Left may have corrected its mistakes by refuting the Shining Path and now may struggle sincerely to defend democratic openings, it is clear that the Shining Path represented a culmination, albeit a perverse and simplistic one, of proposals commonly put forth by the Peruvian Left during the 1970s. The real rupture between the Shining Path and the rest of the Left began in 1982 when the former group initiated its "guerrilla war" of violent actions against everything seen to signify bourgeois democracy. See note 6.

3 In anticipation of potential misunderstandings, it is worth clarifying that my intention is neither to "unmask" former allies of the insurgents nor to provoke a witch hunt against leftists or ex-leftists, whether presently active or retired from politics, for what they said or wrote two decades ago.

4 This radical spectrum was heterogeneous and included not only political parties, but also diverse social movements, and intellectuals and artists, not all of them integrated into organized action. Throughout this essay, however, the principal emphasis will be on the political party ambit of the Left.

5 During the second half of Alan García's Aprista administration (1985–1990), Peru experienced an explosive combination of hyperinflation, social polarization, and senderista advance, that pushed the country to the edge of collapse. In political terms, this crisis provoked the search for new authoritarian solutions, epitomized by Fujimori, and the rejection of the political parties, none of which has won an important election since 1989.

6   The United Left (Izquierda Unida or IU) existed since September 1980, and participated with considerable success in the municipal elections of 1980 and 1983. Despite Shining Path attacks against the groups that composed this coalition, there is no doubt that the IU proposals for governance were very radical compared to most legal alternatives advanced by the Left. This would also become evident, moreover, when IU came in second in 1985 behind Alan García's APRA, which won the presidency with a Center-Left discourse. An IU document produced soon after the elections emphasized that the "IU does not renounce in principle any means of struggle or of organization" (IU 1985: 5).

7   Gorriti 1990 continues to be the fundamental reference for the initial years of the Shining Path's armed struggle. Regarding the point mentioned in the text see chapter 7, "Guerrillas." The Shining Path document that reveals this change is PCP-SL 1982, reproduced in Arce Borja 1989: 181–204.

8   For a description of the popular camp that includes Shining Path, see Letts 1981: 55–67.

9   Lenin (1975) used this term to describe ultra-Leftist deviations.

10 The guidelines for study utilized by the Shining Path are laid out in PCP-SL 1979. The central text from which this pamphlet takes its name, however, was written in 1973.

11 Obviously, this was not the only explanation for the legalized Left's attitude toward the first phase of Shining Path's guerrilla war, but such prejudice did have the impact of distorting the Left's agenda. According to this line of thinking, even if Shining Path were really responsible for all of the attacks, it was "infantile" and would never get very far. And if it was not really responsible, then the Left had to prepare itself for the eventuality of a right-wing coup. See the review of the period in Gorriti 1990: 148–52.

12 On some occasions, pro-Shining Path propagandists outside of Peru, and some misinformed analysts, have emphasized—erroneously—the Indian character of the Shining Path. By the standards of Peru, Guzmán is white, as are many of the other leaders, while most of the militants have been predominantly mestizos of urban extraction. Jorge Castañeda has referred to the Shining Path as "the first Latin American armed organization to massively incorporate the marginalized urban poor into its ranks" (Castañeda 1993: 125).

13 The "provincial" image projected by Mao and the young Communists mobilized during the Chinese Cultural Revolution coincided with that of the social base of the Peruvian Maoist groups. For an analysis, see Hinojosa 1992. On the other hand, for its base of militants, Shining Path made an explicit effort to recruit people who were uprooted, alone in the cities, and without personal or material ties to protect. Interview with César Delgado, ex-militant of the Julio César Mezzich faction, which did not become part of the Shining Path but shared its political line. Lima, August 1992.

14   Ironically, vr worked more with peasants and received more peasant support than did Patria Roja and Shining Path combined. vr's predominance was evident in 1974 when it snatched control of the Peruvian Peasant Federation (Confederación Campesina del Perú; ccp) away from Bandera Roja (one of the other factions that had broken off from the Communist Party).

15   Lynch 1990. Patria Roja would perfect the exploitation of this resource, managing to install itself in various universities of the country. See Tamayo Herrera (1989) for the case of Universidad San Antonio in Cuzco. The Shining Path was not to be outdone. Before converting himself into *Presidente,* Abimael Guzmán was University Director of Personnel in the Universidad Nacional de San Cristóbal de Huamanga (Degregori 1990a: 184). In a little-known document Shining Path leaders protest, albeit anonymously, against abuses by the Huamanga university authorities. See *No basta tener la razón,* 1975. I thank Nelson Manrique for calling this text to my attention.

16   The spectrum of the Maoists—colloquially referred to as the "Chinese" (*chinos*)—embraced diverse offshoots of the Communist Party, each identified by its slogan or newspaper (Bandera Roja, Patria Roja, Sendero Luminoso, etc.). Factions and tendencies of the New Left that had broken off from vr and the Revolutionary Left Movement (Movimiento Izquierda Revolucionaria or mir) also espoused Maoism.

17   A list of all the Peruvian authors and politicians who expressed "Sinophilia," especially during the years of the Chinese Cultural Revolution, would be very long indeed. Anyone interested in looking at some examples, in addition to that of the Shining Path, could begin with the programmatic documents of the pcp-pr (1976) and pcr-co (1979) cited in the reference list, and could continue with articles published in periodicals such as *Crítica Marxista-Leninista* or even *MARKA.*

18   The differences were apparent even in the interior of a given organization, depending on variables such as social extraction, birthplace, income level, and education. These nuances were present, later on, in the Shining Path. Compare, for example, the analyses of the Shining Path in Ayacucho (Degregori 1990a), the Mantaro Valley (Manrique 1989), and Puno (Rénique 1991a).

19   The fundamental text for a balanced, albeit partisan, evaluation of the activism and vanguardism of Leftist organizations up until 1972 is Yawar (actually Edmundo Murrugarra) 1972.

20   Fontana 1992: 10.

21   This affirmation should not be exaggerated, given that quantity superseded quality. The pioneering case of Aníbal Quijano is suggestive. His important works of sociology, which merited discussions within Marxism, were more popular abroad than in Peruvian universities because of the ideological narrowmindedness of Maoist activists and writers. The late Alberto Flores Galindo described the problem with his usual perspicacity: "Fervent readers of [Lenin's]

What is to be Done? did not realize that the real challenge was to write an equivalent book but from the perspective of Peru" (Flores Galindo 1988b: 140).

22 The official Shining Path document is PCP-SL 1975.

23 Casanova et al. 1971. See also the unique bibliographical guide to these works, published by Catalina Adriansén (1978), the widow of Antonio Díaz Martínez, who was herself linked to Shining Path.

24 Díaz Martínez's earlier flexibility is revealed by the fact that in the first edition of his book, issued by the publishing house Waman Puma in 1969, he referred to the Inca Empire as having been a probable example of the Asiatic mode of production (Díaz Martínez 1969: 240). The second edition, published by Mosca Azul in 1985, corrects this heresy, using Maoist terms to label the Inca empire a "slave empire" and a "feudal, theocratic, and authoritarian state" (1985: v–vi). It is important to note that the author prepared the second edition from prison in the midst of the Shining Path's people's war.

25 Stalinism was shared even by more moderate Leftists. In a published interview at the beginning of the 1980s, Alfonso Barrantes, the first socialist mayor of Lima (1984–1986), responded that he liked to call himself Stalinist "because it is a manner of knowing how to act with discipline." *Caretas*, 11 February 1980, reproduced in Hildebrant 1981: 208.

26 The Soviet Union generally enjoyed a rather positive image in Perú. Even many Peruvians who were not Communists admired its degree of development, and ignored its authoritarianism. For radical militants, on their part, the Soviet Union's problems began precisely as a result of abandoning Stalin's example. The Guzmán quote is from Guzmán 1988: 46.

27 Even the organizations of the New Left such as VR and the Revolutionary Communist Party—Working Class (Partido Comunista Revolucionario-Clase Obrera, or PCR-CO) called for reconstructing the Communist Party of Peru. For the Shining Path the question was not simply to "reconstruct," but to do so by "taking up again the general political line of revolution" that Mariátegui had supposedly outlined.

28 The Marxist presence in Cuzco was established contemporaneously with, but independently of, that in Lima. Readers may recall the case of the Communist Cell and the emergence of Cuzco Rojo.

29 It is interesting to note that the Shining Path did not suffer this change as it never participated in electoral processes. The Shining Path could thus undertake actions in Lima during its "people's war" while continuing to see Peru from the perspective of the countryside.

30 Deutscher 1960.

31 Degregori 1991a: 167.

32 Rochabrún 1989: 81.

33 The difficulties were resolved when it became apparent that Cuba had ceased to "export" revolutionary focos. The Peruvian military, for their part, had con-

ceded amnesty to the ex-guerrillas of the failed revolutionary movement of 1965. Many of the former guerrillas, in turn, supported Velasco's reforms and even collaborated with his government.

34 Some Communist Party leaders, such as Gustavo Espinoza, consider the party's support for Morales Bermúdez to have been a "grave error," by which "the CGTP could not keep up" with more radical organizations. See Espinoza 1993: 9.

35 For Patria Roja's position on the military government see PCP-PR 1976: 68.

36 PCR-CO 1979: 92. The text is from a public document of the PCR-CO, which was not by any means a fanatical or "infantile" organization but rather a relatively moderate Maoist party that had branched out of the New Left. A few years later some prominent Peruvian politicians and intellectuals would emerge out of the PCR-CO.

37 Pease 1979: 58.

38 On Guzmán's capture and almost immediate release in 1979 see Gorriti 1990: 19–25.

39 SUTEP 1977.

40 There were some exceptions such as Patria Roja, the general secretary of which continues to use the pseudonym Alberto Moreno, maintains a low profile, and has never run for any public office.

41 To vote for Blanco was to manifest radical protest against the system. But it is difficult to construe such votes as political support for any concrete political program. In his analysis of the electoral triumph of the engineer Fujimori in 1990, Carlos Iván Degregori (Degregori and Grompone 1991) described Hugo Blanco, with reason, as the first tsunami of post-oligarchic Perú.

42 There was broad consensus regarding Patria Roja's reputation. Shining Path itself described Patria Roja in 1973 as a "militaristic" off-shoot of the Communist Party. Reprinted in PCP-SL 1979: 25–26.

43 Patria Roja participated in the elections as part of the Maoist electoral coalition known as the UNIR (Unión de Izquierda Revolucionaria) in which it had an ample majority. In the 1980s UNIR and Patria Roja became synonymous. UNIR got on to the ballot for the general elections as a political party with 59,000 valid signatures (the minimum was 40,000). The figure is high if one takes into consideration that this was Patria Roja's first public appearance after a long period of clandestinity and that it had been the object of a strong negative propaganda campaign during the final years of the dictatorship. In contrast, various other parties did not obtain enough signatures to be included on the ballot. El Comercio (Lima) 2 February 1980: 4.

44 Specifically, Puka Llacta split off in the late 1970s and the so-called "Bolshevik faction" split off a decade later.

45 In 1980, just before the general elections, the Universidad del Pacífico sent a questionnaire to the fifteen different lists of candidates inscribed on the bal-

lot in an effort to publicize their positions regarding key political issues. Five lists on the Left (four Marxist groups and one socialist group) responded that they did not believe in representative democracy as a form of government. A fifth Marxist group headed by Hugo Blanco did not consider it appropriate to respond to the question. Universidad del Pacífico 1980.

46 *El Comercio* (Lima) 1 March 1980: 4.

47 Regarding the "indecision" of the Left see note 11. For an analysis of relationships between the Shining Path and the organizations of the IU, see Woy-Hazleton and Hazleton 1992: 207–24.

48 Many militants and supporters of the Left were assassinated at one or another moment during the 1980s for attempting to maintain this type of position. Obviously, there was very little space to sustain nuanced positions when confronted with inflexible armed extremists. On the other hand, Shining Path cynically utilized the earlier-mentioned proximity in order to infiltrate popular organizations and gain favor or cover. For detailed and nuanced discussions of the difficulties of establishing a "third path," see the essays by Burt and Rénique in this book.

49 As has been noted, some of the future founders of the MRTA were present in the ARI negotiations. Subsequently, the MRTA declared a unilateral cease fire toward the government of Alan García, as a result of the nationalist policies he implemented early in his term in office.

THREE

Chronicle of a Path Foretold? Velasco's Revolution,

Vanguardia Revolucionaria, and "Shining Omens"

in the Indigenous Communities of Andahuaylas

Florencia E. Mallon

¿Hasta cuándo seremos huérfanos en esta nación peruana? (Until when will we be orphans in this Peruvian nation?) — *Song composed in the community of Tankayllo, 1974*[1]

❖ In the province of Andahuaylas, part of the southern sierra department of Apurímac, approximately 30,000 indigenous peasants mobilized between July and September 1974 in an attempt to revindicate their ownership and autonomous control over nearly seventy haciendas partially affected by the military government's agrarian reform law. In the long run, they were defeated: some by the political manipulations of SINAMOS (Sistema Nacional de Apoyo a la Movilización Social, or National System of Support of Social Mobilization), the military government's official organization dedicated to grassroots mobilization; others by the impossibility of maintaining egalitarian agricultural production in a single community or cooperative. The leaders of the Provincial Federation of Peasants in Andahuaylas (Federación Provincial de Campesinos de Andahuaylas; FEPCA), militants and associates of the leftist party Revolutionary Vanguard (Vanguardia Revolucionaria; VR), lived through an intense process of political practice and education that would lead directly to the fracturing of their political party, precisely due to the differences brought about by the Andahuaylas experience. Juan Velasco Alvarado's military government and its populist wings in SINAMOS and the Ministry of Agriculture would lose power in a 1975 internal military coup, in large part because they could not control the intense mobilizations unleashed by the programs they instituted to help the popular classes. Indeed, the case of Andahuaylas, given its great drama, served to highlight the limitations of Velasco's agrarian program.

And finally, in attempting to open up space among the contending forces of the government, the FEPCA, and their own communal organizations, the Andahuaylas peasants reacted in diverse ways across different subregions, depending on previous historical developments within the communities and on the various organizational techniques of VR's leaders.

My focus on Andahuaylas does not bring to bear new empirical data on the existing literature regarding the 1974 movement. Instead, my essay is an initial reflection, a proposal if you will, for a larger project that still needs to be done. In the context of this volume, I think it appropriate to reexamine already existing materials on Andahuaylas in a new light, in order to explain how and why the Andahuaylas experience led a number of the participants toward a relatively positive first encounter with the "softer," comparably more benign Shining Path of the early 1980s.

I begin from several hypotheses. The first is that Shining Path was an organic if exaggerated manifestation of the debates and central tendencies of the Peruvian Left in the 1970s. The second is that Shining Path's political practice in the communities—its shallow engagement with communal institutions, its lack of respect for internal communal processes, its violent manipulation of the indigenous peasantry as a whole—also had its roots in the problematic relationship of the Left to indigenous culture more generally. The third hypothesis is that a part of Shining Path's millenarianism— the impulse to see popular war as an almost religious transformation that would resolve, through the spilling of blood, the contradictions existing within the popular classes—also emerged from the processes and deep frustrations central to leftist popular mobilization during Velasco's "first-phase" military government.

Andahuaylas is a good case for the exploration of these hypotheses. It would be an early and major theater in the Shining Path war, second only to Ayacucho's Río Pampas region. Julio César Mezzich, one of VR's most important leaders active in Andahuaylas, joined Shining Path early on and apparently led the first *senderista* column to enter the area. And finally even Lino Quintanilla, the most visible and heroic leader of the Andahuaylas mobilizations, who died of pneumonia in October 1979, had already left VR in the last years before his premature death and was seeking another affiliation that would provide him a better venue in his tireless quest for agrarian justice. Had Quintanilla not died, there are good reasons to think that he, too, would have joined Shining Path; his widow spent two years in jail accused of being a *senderista* militant.[2]

Lino Quintanilla and the Community of Tankayllo

According to the version presented in his memoirs, in June 1970, Lino Quintanilla appeared at the house of his future in-laws in Tankayllo with the intention of carrying out the Rimaykuku, or traditional wedding ceremony. Accompanied by cousins of his future father-in-law, Quintanilla remembered that "[a]t that moment I acted practically as an orphan, without a father or mother, because my mother lived in Talavera." The Rimaykuku was done according to the customs of the Cocharcas region. The groom-to-be and his companions the Barbaráns, along with the rest of their friends, brought food and drink, "carrying their *ccepires* full of chicha, these are small earthenware receptacles in the shape of [drinking] vessels, . . . the women bringing a little bit of food in earthenware pots and then the godparents" (Quintanilla 1981: 14). When the right moment arrived, Lino's representative explained to the gathering the motive of the visit, while the food was laid out on a tablecloth on the floor.

Quintanilla wrote nearly a decade later that, after an initial resistance, especially by the mother, Maximina's parents seemed to accept the Rimaykuku and thus support Lino's desire to marry their daughter. Maximina herself, on the other hand, "began to cry because she still doubted me, that I wouldn't be faithful to her, that suddenly I might betray her and abandon her after taking advantage of her; perhaps she thought that her parents' attitude was incorrect because they were willing to give her to a strange man, unfamiliar to her, who came from the city; what conduct, what behavior could such a stranger have, she must have thought, and feared for her uncertain future" (Quintanilla 1981: 13–15). In an almost ritual fashion, between the food and the alcohol, parents and godparents began convincing Maximina, who still cried intermittently, to accept the situation. But Lino remembered that "the parents themselves, in the 'tumay' (drinking ritual) also gave out sobs because their daughter would be in the hands of an outsider and who knew where he might take her and what would be their daughter's fate" (15).

When midnight arrived, parents and godparents took Maximina and Lino to the room that had been prepared. They draped crucifixes, first around her neck, then around his; they made them kneel and cross themselves, and explained to them the obligations each would have with the other, in the house and in the fields, with the children. Afterward, Lino remembered, he and Maximina were left in the room already in bed, and the others "closed the door with a padlock and continued drinking." From that moment on, the two of them were considered husband and wife with a mutual commitment to each other, and they began to live together (16).

Since June was a harvest month, the next morning Maximina and Lino went out together to the fields belonging to her family, "in order to finalize the Rimaykuku." As Lino explained, "We built our little hut right in the middle of the field, digging some sticks into the ground and covering them with husks of maize and we stayed there, threshing the wheat. From that moment on I was just another pair of arms working in the fields" (16).

In a book whose subtitle is "Testimony of a Militant," and whose contents are the product of oral interviews subsequently edited by Quintanilla himself,[3] it is important to reflect on why, in a chapter entitled "Fundamental Biography," almost half the pages are dedicated to a description of the Rimaykuku. On one level, this fact serves as an entrypoint into the constructed nature of Quintanilla's narrative. It helps us see how his testimony, in addition to being a valuable though partial window into the community in which he lived and the movement he helped lead, is also an argument about his own participation in the events he narrates. At bottom, Quintanilla's memoir makes a claim about how and why he was a legitimate peasant leader, and one of his purposes is to draw us into that legitimacy. The chapter "Fundamental Biography" is particularly helpful to us in understanding how his claim is constructed.

In the first two pages of the chapter, Quintanilla narrates his origins in the district of Talavera, part of the city of Andahuaylas. He shares with us that his family was always a part of the local elite, and that his father used to be a member of APRA which, even if originally a reformist political party, stopped being so by the late 1940s. He then discusses his experiences at the university in Cuzco, and in Cooperación Popular, the Belaundista grassroots effort of the 1960s, in Puno.[4] These experiences away from home, however, seemed to increase his "interest in integrating myself into my province." And yet, once he returned to Andahuaylas, Lino admits, he realized that "I did not really know the reality of my province." He thus decided to work directly in the countryside, and to dedicate his life to understanding Andahuaylas's agrarian reality (10–11).

Quintanilla began to work in the local office of Cooperación Popular, which with the 1968 military revolution became Promoción Comunal. It did not take long for him to get into trouble with the head of the office, because of his radical sympathies and methods of work. "In this situation," he remembered, "first I decided, well, that I would dedicate myself entirely to working with the rural masses, integrate myself into their lives and, well, give my efforts, my life, to the service of the masses and to the sacred cause of the proletariat. . . . And that is how I decided to marry a peasant woman (12).

From here on, in Quintanilla's narrative, marrying a peasant woman symbolically represents his commitment to the peasantry and to their reality. The marriage will serve, metaphorically, as his entry into communal society. It is his way of creating a direct, concrete commitment to the situation of the peasantry; it is his way of demonstrating that he is serious. And this symbolic connection is further buttressed by two additional decisions he makes at the same time: to quit his job at Promoción Comunal, even though his worth to the office is demonstrated by three refusals to accept his resignation, and not to inform his family in Talavera of what he plans to do (12).

What Quintanilla proposed to do was almost like a baptism, a social rebirth. Beyond deciding to become a part of the peasantry as a class, he also came to realize that he had to make his the peasantry's indigenous and communal traditions, and to do so honestly rather than in a manipulative way. In his own words,

> I made my commitment to my wife taking into account the traditional customs of the region's peasantry. In this sense I moved forward. It wasn't due to my interest in becoming a part of the peasantry, no. Instead, little by little I began to feel that this was correct, that it was normal and that it needed to be accepted as a way to revindicate and respect certain traditions belonging to the peasantry and that this was not shameful but simply a custom, a way of feeling that people had. So when I arrived to ask for my wife's hand in marriage, I did so following the same peasant customs, and looked for godparents among the very same peasants (12).

In Lino Quintanilla's memoirs, therefore, various narrative strands come together to symbolize and define his unity with the community: his desire to marry a peasant woman from Tankayllo; his own individual condition as an outsider and an orphan (this last a condition he himself helps to reproduce by choosing not to inform his birth family of his decision); his political commitment to the peasantry; and his immediate obligation in agricultural labor once he has spent the night with his new wife. Thus for him and for the peasants of Tankayllo, the Rimaykuku is a metaphor unifying all the obligations that Lino accepts, not only to his wife, but also to the entire community, indeed to the entire culture. His obligations of love and work, through his connection to Maximina and her family, tie him to the village as a whole. As has occurred in many cultures and historical periods, marriage serves as a tie that binds men together, through the body and property of a woman.

What makes Lino Quintanilla's case both striking and unique is his honest effort to respect the integrity of peasant culture. Our access to that effort is, of course, circumscribed by Lino's own conscious presentation of himself and his political legitimacy. Only his version of his relationship with the community is available to us. And there are times when his version is too smooth or seamless, even in his discussions of conflict. An example of this is his discussion of the discord that arose with Maximina and her family over his ability to contribute labor to the family economy. According to Lino, the problems arose because of the conflict between his political obligations and his labor commitments to the household. Maxi ended up complaining that he "couldn't even work in the fields and we didn't have enough to last the year." It was not a question of political differences, for Lino's family also supported the peasants' struggle; but simply that Lino was not participating in the family work parties and reciprocal labor exchanges that his position in the community required of him. As Lino remembered it, on the basis of conversation and example Maxi and her parents came to understand the situation. "They understand very well that when the masses decide, and give me a task to carry out, I need to meet my responsibility as a leader, I have to do this above all other responsibilities. Faced with this situation my father-in-law says: 'well, it's all right, you have to do that, you have to live up to their expectations, I'll do the work [here]' and that's generally how it happens" (18).

One is left to wonder how such an agreement was reached, since it goes against customary expectations in kin relations. As both an outsider and a matrilocally established son-in-law (*qatay* or *masay* in Quechua; *yerno* in Spanish), Lino would be expected to offer additional labor to his wife's kin and to occupy a relatively subservient position vis-à-vis his in-laws (Skar 1988: 194; Webster 1977: 39; Isbell 1977: 100). That his father-in-law handled Lino's labor obligations instead suggests an upside-down subservience based on class and political criteria. The absence of such a discussion in Quintanilla's memoirs indicates that there are limits to Lino's openness about his role in his new family and community.

Yet at the same time, Quintanilla was still unusual in the degree to which he took local kinship and communal issues seriously. He recognized the legitimacy of his community and family obligations—"I owe them the *aynis* [equal and reciprocal labor obligations]"—even as he emphasized why, in the conjuncture of the 1970s, he preferentially had to attend to his political obligations (Quintanilla 1981: 18). He also discussed why he and Maxi made a decision to limit their family size to three children, since they could not hope to support more given that, in Lino's words, "my home had to be subservient to the class struggle" (19). Throughout his discussion of his personal life, however, Quintanilla demonstrates an understanding of the painful complexity of the contradiction between family and community and political obligations: "Indispensably, every now and then I must give a day [to family and communal work], even when I have to steal the time from my work with the masses. Thus if we are planting I help my in-laws with the planting, if there is hilling to do I do that, I harvest at harvest time, turn over the earth to let it rest, if necessary I bring firewood for the stove. Finally, depending on when I have time, I occasionally meet my obligation in the communal work parties" (20–21).

Quintanilla's sensitivity to the contradictory nature of communal processes extended beyond the family to the community as a whole. "Always the *compañeros* [comrades or companions] who head the struggles come from either the middle peasantry, more often, or from the rich peasantry," he wrote. This was true both in earlier movements and in the land invasions of the 1970s. "The poor peasants," he explained, "are the most repressed and humiliated." They often did not understand that they had rights, not even in the communal assemblies. Nor were they the first to criticize the oppression of the Catholic Church, nor to understand the class struggle. It was the rich and middle peasants, because of their greater assimilation of political concepts, who "were able to head and to lead the struggle." At the same time, however, there would come a moment when the majority of the rich peasants would tend to separate themselves from the social struggle. Thus, in a contradictory way, even if the leadership of the agrarian movement came initially from the better off peasants, the wealthier individuals "at a certain moment, will oppose the poor peasants, they will oppose the struggle because differences emerge around concrete particular interests" (28–29).

From this discussion of communal politics emerged a need to respect and encourage the participation of local political officials in the agrarian mobilizations. "The lieutenant governors (*tenientes gobernadores*), municipal agents and their respective *varayoc*,"[5] Quintanilla insisted, "including the communal authorities, within the community have participated quite a bit in the land invasions. They have collaborated significantly with the other community members in the recuperation of the land." But this did not occur automatically. These officials had "before been entirely at the service of the exploiters." This occurred because the governor of the district was a local power broker (*gamonal*), and he personally named, "by pointing a finger," the lieutenant governors, who were then pressured to act as representatives of the local power structure within the communities. They recruited people for forced labor, serving the interests of power brokers and landowners, and the *varayoc* carried out the orders of the lieutenant governors (32).

Quintanilla hastened to add, however, that community officials were complicit, not out of conviction, but "because the very structure [of power] encouraged it. Besides, if they did not take this attitude they would be repressed by district and provincial authorities" (32). According to Quintanilla, this changed when the peasants got organized, because with the new organization behind the communal assembly at the beginning of the 1970s, people began to take more responsibility for keeping track of the authorities, and the assembly would remove officials who did not act in the interest of the people. Not only did the communal assembly assert itself in the case of the lieutenant governors, who learned that at any moment they might be removed from their posts by communal vote, but when the annual ceremony for choosing *varayoc* came around, the criteria for election to the position became a great deal more stringent. In Quintanilla's estimation,

> the lieutenant governor and the staff holders (*envarados*) are named at New Year, in a special ceremony connected to the New Year fiesta which is itself connected to the fiesta celebrating the Christ child. They are chosen there, but before the election the *varayoc* who have served the previous year have to search for their own replacements. They have to talk to the possible candidates and they know how to look for people more or less [politically] conscious, no? They treat them to a drink, they talk to them, they convince them to take over the positions. When the election arrives, the old *varayoc* present these new people as candidates. The masses ratify these candidates if they are in agreement with them. And if they are not in agreement, well, the masses change them and suggest other *compañeros* (31).

These were important changes, not only because of the greater political consciousness they made possible, but also because within the communal structure it is the *varayoc* or staff holders who were best positioned to aid in any organizational effort. Explained Quintanilla, "The *varayoc*'s tasks generally include representation and announcements, and in the case of a communal assembly, for example, they call the peasants together, through the *ccayacuy* or nighttime call, a day in advance, or else they ring the [church] bell or go door to door notifying people. In reality they are the ones who are most active" (32).

This consistent yet conflictual commitment to communal political culture was Quintanilla's calling card in Tankayllo and, more generally, in Andahuaylas. Whatever his limitations might have been, Lino took seriously the existing political and cultural traditions of Tankayllo's indigenous peasantry. This bound him to a political style different from that of other political leaders from outside the communities and, ultimately, made for a deeper, more inclusive, and more meaningful process of mobilization in Tankayllo than in other parts of Andahuaylas province. After the peasants of Tankayllo occupied the hacienda of Huancahuacho, they more successfully maintained the unity of their movement, despite the inevitable internal divisions within and between communities. These differences in style, depth, and degree of unity would be reflected not only in the strategies peasants used against military repression, but also in the land invasions themselves, and in the accords signed at the haciendas Toxama and Huancahuacho. But before we begin an analysis of these differences, we must first take a closer look at the political styles and organizational strategies used in Ongoy and Andarapa, the other two centers of rural mobilization in the province.

Leftist Militants in Ongoy and Andarapa

Of the three subregions in Andahuaylas that were most active in the land recuperation movements of the 1970s, we know the least about the district of Ongoy. An important reason for this is that we possess neither a memoir by an important participant, such as Quintanilla's work on Tankayllo, nor an analytical work by a participant observer, such as Rodrigo Sánchez's (1981) work on Andarapa. But in addition, given Julio César Mezzich's subsequent incorporation into Shining Path, the aura of clandestinity surrounding him and his work, and the fact that he apparently led a Shining Path column into Ongoy in the early 1980s (Rojas 1985: 349–51), recovering the specifics of the district's earlier history may need to wait a few years yet. Despite the fogginess of our information, however, it is important to include Ongoy in this analysis, both because of the military and political importance of Mezzich himself—who for some time has been rumored to be the maximum military leader of Shining Path and was in the mid-1990s one of the few top leaders still at large—and because the district had a long and intense history of rural conflict and mobilization dating back half a century.

Indeed, this was probably an important reason for why Mezzich, graduate of Lima's private Jesuit secondary school "La Inmaculada," medical student from Lima's private Cayetano Heredia University, and militant in Vanguardia Revolucionaria, chose to settle in the community of Ongoy when he decided to move from Ayacucho in 1969 (Rojas 1985: 349–51; Sánchez 1981: 86). Most likely it did not hurt that Ongoy was the largest peasant community in Andahuaylas province, both in population and area, and was also the capital of the district of Ongoy (Ministerio de Agricultura 1970: 1; 1971: 23–24). But most relevant for a political organizer was the fact that, for about fifty years, Ongoy had been the center of violent struggles over land, especially in the subtropical zone near the Pampas River and next to the department of Ayacucho. The subregions known as Río Blanco, Chuyama, and Chacchahua, prime locations for the production of *aguardiente*, a locally distilled cane liquor, had been targets for expropriation by outside landowners since the colonial period. After Ongoy was officially recognized as an indigenous community on 28 October 1935, the peasants began a new cycle of protests in an attempt to win back the usurped lands. They were aided in their efforts by members of the community resident in Lima, who also served as Ongoy's representatives vis-à-vis the national government. By 1950, the local landowners apparently had begun to fear a turn against them in the local balance of forces, and they began to divide up and sell the lands they controlled to groups of shareholders, most of whom were either outsiders, mestizos, or rich peasants with no loyalty to the community and its struggle (Ministerio de Agricultura 1970: 19–32).

Between 1952 and 1963, four "sales" of land occurred in four separate localities: Chuyama-Chacchahua in 1952, Cunyacc in 1953, Tururo in 1953, and San Pedro in 1963. In a number of cases, shareholders who had bought lands in one place also bought more in another. In addition, the dynamic of power within the shareholder groups was authoritarian and politically manipulative. According to the 1970 report by the Ministry of Agriculture: "This group of 'misti' shareholders, who as we already said fomented and led the effort to buy the land, included community peasants in the group only to make the buyers look like members of the community, in order to weaken and break the land recuperation movement" (Ministerio de Agricultura 1970: 33).[6]

Tensions intensified with the rest of the members of the community of Ongoy, reaching the boiling point after the "sale" of San Pedro in 1963, when women and men from Ongoy's nearby *anexo* (dependent village) of Callapayocc attempted to prevent the shareholders from planting their new lands. Testimony by the participants in this action, recorded in the same Ministerio de Agricultura report, yields the following:

> At this point the shareholders went to the political and police authorities, and this led to what we already know as the "Massacre of San Pedro," where 17 peasants lost their lives (official figures), although other sources suggest that it was many more. In addition, there were many, many wounded, who have been left permanently damaged, invalid, paralyzed.
>
> This action, in addition to having allowed [the villagers] to recover part of the lands in San Pedro (bordering on Callapayocc) has also allowed them to figure out who are their brothers in the community, and who "are not and never will be members of the community" as one of our informants (a participant in the events) has said, who also tells us what role "these fancy shareholders" played, "who were not content simply to bring the police as if we were murderers or criminals, but also incited them from the hilltops as if they were watching a bullfight and there were some ladies who yelled, pointing, 'get that Indian, get that Indian,' [and that] there was another woman who watched the parade of wounded and dead, and when she saw that they were taking one man half-dead, with his eyes poked out of their sockets, roaring with pain, she took the gun out of the policeman's hand and shot the wounded man in the head, killing him. When questioned, the woman said, 'it was better for him, that way he no longer suffered'" (Ministerio de Agricultura 1970: 33).

And it was only six years later that Mezzich arrived in Ongoy, settling precisely in Callapayocc, where he ended up marrying the daughter of the president of said communal *anexo,* participating in local community meetings, and using his medical training to provide first aid services to the village's inhabitants (Rojas 1985: 349; Sánchez 1981: 86).

The third center of political organization in Andahuaylas province was the district of Andarapa, especially the hacienda Toxama, located within the district, and the hacienda *barrio* of Manchaybamba. In contrast to other communities in the region, by the 1960s Andarapa no longer possessed any communal land. The community of Andarapa was officially recognized as such in 1945, in the middle of a long legal struggle with the hacienda Toxama over grazing rights, work obligations, the use of hacienda lands, and the usurpation of community lands. Despite twenty years of struggle, however, during which Andarapa's migrants resident in Lima had played an important part, during the 1960s the community's hopes were dashed. Such was the level of disorganization and frustration among Andarapa's residents that, when the Velasquista government announced the expropriation of the hacienda Toxama in 1970, it was impossible to avoid the decapitalization of the property. When government functionaries took control of the hacienda in 1973, the previous owner had been able to "sell the animals, machines, tools, grain mill and other equipment, leaving the hacienda in a dismantled state" (Sánchez 1981: 64–81, quotation on p. 81; Ministerio de Agricultura 1970: 36, 57).

Félix Loayza, VR militant from Ayacucho, had settled in Andarapa a few months before the hacienda Toxama passed into the hands of agrarian reform officials. Until 1972, Loayza had worked with Lino Quintanilla in SINAMOS, in Promoción Comunal; but when he also resigned due to political disagreements, he decided to rent a house and agricultural field in Andarapa's district capital and continue his political work there. Loayza found his best allies among the peons resident in Manchaybamba *barrio*, located within the hacienda Toxama (Sánchez 1981: 86–87, 107).

"Félix's activities in Andarapa were not especially successful," wrote Sánchez (1981:116), "due mainly to the peasants' status as independent small proprietors." But if we look carefully at the identity and economic position of Loayza's allies in Andarapa and Manchaybamba, we find that the most important local activists were also "independent small proprietors," people who had begun by working on the hacienda, but who, after some migration experience and having received land through inheritance, had dedicated themselves to small-scale entrepreneurial activities in agriculture. Who supported and did not support Loayza's activities cannot be explained simply through economic factors. Instead, the most convincing explanation lies in Loayza's own political strategy.

In contrast to Quintanilla's practice in Tankayllo, where according to his testimony political changes occurred from within the communal assembly, through the already existing structure of political authorities, Loayza did not integrate himself fully into the community institutions in Andarapa. Although he was accepted as an "assimilated community member" and even elected to the municipal council in June 1973, he used his position to criticize communal structures and denounce them as exploitative of the peasantry. According to Sánchez: "While SINAMOS promoted communal organization in the village and offered support for collective production, Félix's campaign consisted in denouncing the exploitative nature of the communal organization, which favored not only the wealthier sectors in the village, but also the government bureaucrats. As a result, communal work diminished, while at the same time the actions of SINAMOS were blocked" (Sánchez 1981: 116).

In this context, it is hardly surprising that Félix Loayza's most enthusiastic allies in Andarapa were peasants with little stake in community institutions and communal political culture: young men with substantial migration experience and comparatively high levels of education. The fourteen most active peasants identified by Sánchez had an average age of 35.5, had migrated for an average of 5.3 years, and had an average of 4.3 years of primary school. The three peasant leaders, all from Manchaybamba, were between twenty-nine and thirty years old, with a minimum of two years migration experience (and a maximum of twelve years), and had been to primary school for between four and five years. The older peasants—who for generational reasons had the highest access to land, the strongest networks of reciprocal agricultural labor, and the greatest experience in local politics—were not well represented (Sánchez 1981: 107–15, especially p. 110).

Loayza thus attracted a following among individuals who stood out because of their youth, migration experience, education, and bilingual skills. Those members of the community with cultural, political, kin and generational authority were not a part of his group. Rather than engage communal politics on its own terms, attempting to change it from the inside, Loayza denounced communal organizations as tools of the rich. As we shall see, this political style limited the depth of political mobilization and organization in the region because, in contrast to what happened in Tankayllo, it did not make possible a conflictual commitment to, nor a complex engagement with, the internal contradictions of communal political culture.

Agrarian Contradictions in Andahuaylas, 1973–1974

> Antes lo único que podíamos hacer era caminar con un memorial bajo
> el brazo. (Before, the only thing we could do was walk around with
> a petition under our arm.)[7]

Between 1930 and 1960 in Andahuaylas, many communities had engaged
in predominantly legal struggles to recuperate land from neighboring haciendas. With their petitions under their arms, with the help of their
migrant associations in Lima, communal authorities made the rounds of
the state offices created by President Augusto Leguía, hoping to have even
the most minimal attention paid to their demands. Only in the 1960s, in
answer to the rash of land invasions taking place around the country, did the
government of Fernando Belaúnde initiate the first agrarian reform, which
in Andahuaylas abolished unpaid labor services on the haciendas and instituted wage labor. Yet it would only be with the military revolution of 1968,
the 1969 agrarian reform law, and the institutional and populist openings
created by Velasquismo that a new situation in the countryside facilitated a
new cycle of mobilization, during which Andahuaylas's peasants put aside
their petitions in favor of direct action (Berg 1984; Ministerio de Agricultura 1970, 1971; Quintanilla 1981; Sánchez 1981).

A number of tendencies in the late 1960s and early 1970s facilitated
this new strategy. At the national level, agrarian movements, in conjunction with new leftist groups inspired by the Cuban Revolution and guerrilla
movements more generally, had decisively broken the political hegemony
of the Peruvian landed elite. Velasquista populism was a tardy and partial
state response to these trends, but at least it created a new context of structural and social change within which popular mobilization could intensify.
Specifically in Andahuaylas, these changes were reflected in the partial and
contradictory agrarian reform process, the confrontations between peasants
and bureaucrats, and the development of the Federación Provincial de Campesinos de Andahuaylas (FEPCA).

The FEPCA emerged from the organizational work of Quintanilla, Loayza,
and Mezzich, all of whom were, as we have seen, militants of Vanguardia
Revolucionaria (VR). The complexion of the Peruvian Left changed dramatically in the mid-1960s, and one of the many groups that emerged from
these changes was the Maoist VR. After the Sino-Soviet split fractured the
Peruvian Communist Party (PCP) in 1964, a majority of the Peruvian Left

drifted toward a form of Maoism initially unified within the PCP-Bandera Roja. After 1959, the influence of the Cuban Revolution also led directly to a generational confrontation within APRA, the formation of APRA Rebelde, and its evolution into the Movimiento de Izquierda Revolucionaria (Movement of the Revolutionary Left; MIR), which in 1965 formed several ill-fated guerrilla focos in the Peruvian highlands. At about the same time, Vanguardia Revolucionaria was formed out of a coalition of groups that included a faction from the Soviet-allied PCP (Unidad), some Trotskyist militants, a fraction of MIR, and a group from Belaúnde's Acción Popular party.[8] Despite inevitable internal debates and occasional splits, VR survived into the early 1970s as one of the stronger leftist parties, establishing an important presence in the working class organizations around Lima. As of 1974, when the intensification of the peasant movement led to lively debates at the IV Congress of the Confederación Campesina del Perú (Peruvian Peasant Confederation; CCP) and to a massive walkout by peasant delegates protesting the rigid policies of the then-dominant Maoist leadership from Bandera Roja, VR was there to pick up the pieces. When a reorganized CCP emerged in a new congress held months later, the influence of VR was on the rise. And as it turned out, an important part of VR's prestige in the CCP was due to the increasing dynamism of the FEPCA in Andahuaylas (Degregori 1990a: 181, 188, 195; Degregori 1995a; Rojas 1985; Sánchez 1981).

The FEPCA was formally created on 31 January 1973, bringing together four peasant associations created by SINAMOS organizers between 1971 and 1972. In a ceremony held in the conference room of the Andahuaylas teachers' union (SUTEA), the FEPCA declared its program to be "the legitimate defense of the interests" of the peasants "against oppression and exploitation by dominant classes at the regional, national, and international levels" (Sánchez 1981: 95). The organizers also declared at that meeting that they wished to form a political alliance "with the urban and industrial working class and the politically committed intellectual sectors [who] share our goals," and that the joint targets of the struggle should be: the preexisting agrarian system; the bureaucratic agrarian reform that forces the peasants to pay for the land; and state intervention in peasant organizations and in peasant agricultural production. "The authentic agrarian reform," the statement concluded, "will be carried out by the peasants themselves" (Sánchez 1981: 79–80, 94–95, quotation on p. 96; Quintanilla 1981: 39–42).

The FEPCA gained strength in Andahuaylas province between January and April 1973 by supporting an ever more confident and organized peasantry in its rejection of SINAMOS's strategies. In February, for example, the inhabitants of Manchaybamba *barrio*, ex-hacienda Toxama, received notification from the Forestry Service that they had to appear at an already designated location within the hacienda in order to help plant trees. Sánchez (1981: 98) wrote:

> The *manchaybambinos* found the plan to be unacceptable because the area chosen by the experts was entirely within an agriculturally productive zone. This area, apparently abandoned, was in reality laying fallow for three years according to the local system of crop rotation. Another sector that had been included in the reforestation plan belonged to the grazing lands where the peasants kept their animals. Even though the inhabitants had other places where they could graze their animals, they decided at that point that they preferred to have the largest possible area for grazing, rather than to have trees whose productivity would be a great deal further in the future.

Despite protests by the *manchaybambinos*, the bureaucrats from the Forestry Service decided to go ahead with the project using wage labor. In response to this insult, the inhabitants of Manchaybamba sent a commission to talk to the technicians, but they were told that they did not understand the importance of the project, and that, besides, the state owned the land. The peasants answered with direct action. They blocked the road for twenty days and, after a physical confrontation between the peasants and the police, the technicians decided to leave the area. According to Sánchez, the peasants saw this as a "great victory" (Sánchez 1981: 95–99; quote on p. 99).

As this new political climate fed on itself, the peasantry grew ever more assertive about its autonomy from state officials. And every successful confrontation helped intensify peasant militancy and strengthen the FEPCA. "[The FEPCA's] leaders found an ever more propitious climate for their political campaign," wrote Sánchez (1981: 99): "They were always well received in the villages and their links to the peasants became ever closer."

The culmination of this first stage of provincial mobilization occurred in the city of Andahuaylas on 1 May 1973, when the FEPCA organized a demonstration in the city's central plaza and the surrounding streets. A city whose total population numbered approximately 4,000 ended up hosting 15,000 peasants from around the province, who came to protest the form taken by the Agrarian Reform, to share their experiences of resistance against abusive functionaries, and to support the FEPCA's political activities. As state officials duly noted, this was the first time that a peasant demonstration of this size had occurred in the province. And in the following months, SINAMOS's new attempts politically to penetrate the countryside were rejected once again by the peasants of Andarapa and other villages who were full of confidence that they could, by themselves, carry out the necessary reforms in their villages and on their land (Sánchez 1981: 99–107).

After the May 1 demonstration, the FEPCA's top leadership began to plan for a second stage in which they aimed to integrate the provincial movement into a national movement, and to develop a more systematic agrarian program. In August 1973, peasants from Andahuaylas made their first trip as delegates to the National Assembly of the CCP held in Huaura, Lima. Upon their return, these delegates engaged in several long discussions with provincial and national leaders from VR that yielded, by January 1974, an agrarian program that was to dictate the movement's medium-run strategy.

The FEPCA's agrarian program was organized around three main points: peasant control of the land, peasant control over the production process, and peasant control over the marketing and distribution of their products. In order to meet these goals, the FEPCA called for the takeover by peasants of all the land in the province, thus eliminating the hacienda and the local system of power brokerage (*gamonalismo*). At the same time, the FEPCA called for the creation of Democratic Peasant Committees (Comités Democráticos Campesinos) that would consolidate an alliance among the different sectors of the rural popular classes—community peasants, peons, and small proprietors—in order strictly to control the presence and actions of the state, the bureaucracy, and the merchants. The committees would mediate between the communities and the state, and between the communities and the regional and national economies, thus using state investments for effective local development. The committees would also help unify the peasantry and help raise political consciousness (Sánchez 1981: 118–21).

With their agrarian program in hand and a leadership training course organized by FEPCA under their belts, 27 peasant delegates from Andahuaylas travelled to Torre Blanca, Huaral to participate in the alternative IV National Congress of the CCP called by Vanguardia Revolucionaria.[9] Between 5 and 7 May 1974, a total of 336 delegates attended the Congress, representing 144 base organizations—federations, unions, communities, cooperatives, and others—from 13 departments. According to Sánchez (1981: 12) the final resolution of the Congress "established land occupations as the principal strategy for peasant political action" (see also Méndez 1981: 23–25).

Upon their return to the countryside, FEPCA leaders got ready for the land recuperation campaign, calling assemblies in different parts of the province in order to inform the peasants about the decisions reached at the Congress. With the help of militants from the Central Committee of the CCP, FEPCA leaders began to plan clandestinely for the land seizures. "The main decisions were taken in secret meetings, in Lima and Andahuaylas [town], and were communicated discreetly to a few key individuals," Sánchez pointed out. "At least in Andahuaylas [province] the starting date for the actions, as well as the specific plan to be carried out, were not known until a few days before they were to start" (Sánchez 1981: 122).

Lino Quintanilla's arrest, though it was due to unrelated problems arising from a dispute with four livestock merchants in the community of Tankayllo, still delayed the political work of the province's leaders. It was only in the third week of June that Mezzich, Quintanilla, and Loayza began to travel through their districts, attempting to organize the Democratic Peasant Committees that were considered so important to the movement as a whole. According to the FEPCA's agrarian program, the committees were crucial because they were supposed to

a Control the process of land recuperation.
b Decide how the recuperated land should be used, that is decide which fields will be worked individually and who should be given these fields, and which fields will be worked collectively;
c Organize production and work on the recuperated lands that will be worked collectively (Quintanilla 1981: 142).

According to Quintanilla, from the beginning the organization of the Democratic Committees was problematic and contradictory. Perhaps in part it was because the committees were assigned an overly ambitious task; possibly, it was also because they were created and made to function so quickly; but the Democratic Committees never ended up playing the role originally envisioned for them. This should have been, in the words of Quintanilla (1981: 53), "adequately to guide the struggles and then, more than anything else, to prepare the consciousness of the masses." Part of the problem, suggested Quintanilla, was that "it wasn't yet the right moment, because the level of consciousness of the masses was not equal to their level of organization." And for this reason as well, a tension emerged between the need to prepare the invasions clandestinely, and the need to continue public discussion and consciousness raising. "There were disagreements over whether the Committees could have implemented the land invasions or not. In practice we saw that this role was played by the Land Invasion Commands. The Commands were formed clandestinely, while the Committees were formed publicly, even though these were the groups who should be giving political direction. In reality, the Committees should also have been clandestine as far as this was possible, but this was not accomplished" (Quintanilla 1981: 53).

It would be hard to imagine a clandestine political structure that could also engage in consciousness raising among the peasantry. For this reason, effective clandestinity could only have been achieved after a much longer period of political work inside the communities. And here we can clearly see the differences between Tankayllo and Andarapa.

During a lightning trip through Andarapa district between 23 and 28 June, Loayza organized several communal assemblies in order to designate representatives for Andarapa's Democratic Peasant Committee. In the village of Huancas, the individual voted to occupy the position kept insisting that he did not have enough time. On the ex-hacienda Toxama, which everyone considered to be the center of the movement in the district, only 110 out of the 600 ex-peons showed up for the meeting on 28 June. And yet Loayza left Andarapa district shortly thereafter in order to organize more committees in the district of Pacucha. (Sánchez 1981: 132–39).

At a later meeting in Andahuaylas town, Mezzich, Quintanilla, and Loayza recognized that problems had existed in Andarapa district and on the ex-hacienda Toxama, and these were contrasted to the "more animated" assembly held in Tankayllo. "The leaders did not pay sufficient attention to these problems," Sánchez (1981: 141–42) reported, "and concluded that at least the Democratic Peasant Committees had been organized, and that this was the important thing." The way in which the committees had been organized, however, and the political work that underlay them, was dramatically different. And in the long run, as we shall see, these differences resulted in distinct land invasion processes, and in disparities in the peasants' capacity to resist repression.

The Invasions of Haciendas Toxama and Huancahuacho

Yo soy campesino, hombre bien macho. (I'm a peasant, a real man.) [10]

On 15 July 1974, with a time difference of only thirty minutes, the peasants in the district of Cocharcas, where Tankayllo is located, invaded thirteen haciendas. The landowners were caught still on their properties. Some were brought before a popular tribunal, forced to pay their debts to the ex-peons, and expelled from the region. Quintanilla remembered that, in the twenty-four hours between the announcement of the invasion and carrying it out, "the peasants were getting themselves ready the whole night without sleeping, because they were notified around six or seven in the evening. Without sleeping they got their bedding ready, their food, their dishes, their *huaraka*,[11] their tools and their animals in order to enter the hacienda. Not the men, nor the women, nor the children slept that night" (Quintanilla 1981: 55–59, quote on p. 59).

Once the invasions had occurred, the peasants organized themselves to take an inventory of the hacienda, clean the house and the irrigation ditches, and distribute and begin planting the land. According to Quintanilla, all the villagers—men, women, children, and the elderly—participated in the planting. "We had music that accompanied us at every moment during the work, we had chants, we sang." The schools in the district closed for up to two weeks so that everyone could participate in the land recuperation process (Quintanilla 1981: 62–63, quote on p. 62).

After taking the hacienda Huancahuacho, the members of the community of Tankayllo quickly organized the distribution and planting of the land. In addition to administering the orange groves, they planted wheat and corn and, six months into the occupation, they harvested both crops. Planting decisions, cultivating, harvesting, and the distribution of the goods were all done collectively, using principles of labor and communal reciprocity. As Mauricio Rojas, ex-peon of Huancahuacho, recalled,

> As soon as [the wheat] was grown, we harvested and deposited all the grain in a room, we weighed it and returned seed to all those who had given [it]. The rest we divided among all those who had worked and we also gave to the elderly and the widows. With the corn we did the same thing. We sold nothing in the market, it was all for us to eat. It was an agreement we had, to plant first for our stomachs and only afterwards to sell. . . .
>
> With the oranges what happened was that when we entered the hacienda the harvest was about half done. We picked the remaining oranges and gave them out to everyone involved in the occupation. We all tried them, whereas before in the time of the gamonales, . . . no one could try them. Even the workers were guarded and they were even

guarded when they left to urinate. We gave out oranges to everyone, to the men, to the women, to the children, to the elderly (Quintanilla 1981: 78).

In contrast to Cocharcas district, of which Tankayllo formed a part, in Andarapa the land occupations could not occur on the designated date of 15 July. When Loayza and Mezzich arrived in Manchaybamba, they learned that the peasants were participating in a fiesta that would end only on the 17th. The land seizures were therefore reorganized for 18 July, while the leaders tried to convene the various villages in the district through their respective communal authorities, lieutenant governors and staff holders. At every meeting, however, less people turned up than expected; and by the 17th, it was learned that the police already knew the peasants' plans. Meanwhile, the fiesta still seemed to be in full swing, and the peasants were still drinking heavily. Along with the *manchaybambinos* considered the most committed, Mezzich organized a roadblock to prevent the entry of police vehicles, as well as a delegation responsible for waking people at 4 A.M. in preparation for a 5 A.M. takeover of the hacienda Toxama. He chose people to handle security, and a group to spray paint the walls of the village.

Despite these careful preparations, frustrations began to pile up in the early hours of the morning. By 5 A.M. only four leaders were present at the school, designated as the rendezvous spot. "The leaders decided to wait one more hour and to call on people door to door," wrote Sánchez, who was present. "Those who had been drinking the previous day were all sleeping and almost no one answered the calls." By 7 o'clock, the situation had not improved much. Sánchez continued: "Of the 120 peasant adults in the village there were only 5 at the rendezvous spot; in addition, those who had been at the fiesta began drinking again and did not seem interested in the march. Even some members of the leadership group joined the celebration and did not answer the call. . . . Santiago suggested: 'Why don't we go and bring everyone, even by force, otherwise nothing is going to happen'" (Sánchez 1981: 142–47; quotes on p. 147).

With all the preparation and pressure, when people saw a SINAMOS pickup truck come up to the roadblock, there were still only sixteen people at the school. One of the leaders was so frustrated that he shed tears of rage. But another leader cheered up the participants and convinced them to take their flag and drum and begin the march. Luckily, when they arrived at the hacienda two hours later, with the peasants from other villages who had joined along the way, the group had swelled to forty. Hours later, when they managed to open the door to the hacienda's house, there were enough people present to fill the interior patio, and this gave the group a feeling of success and confidence. Only then did three government officials reach the hacienda.

The peasants held a peaceful discussion with the government's representatives, during which the mass of occupiers reached 200, including Mezzich, who listened from the back. An assembly was called after the government officials left, during which Mezzich and Loayza, who had also arrived in the course of the afternoon from the hacienda Bellavista, informed the gathering of the successful takeovers of three haciendas in the district: Toxama, Bellavista, and Santa Elena. The day ended with enthusiasm and confidence for all the peasants assembled there.

Mezzich and Loayza's next organizational strategy in Andarapa district was the occupation of the remaining haciendas on 22 July: Puitoc, Chanta-Umaca, Huancas, and Chuspi. In each place they arranged for a formal occupation ceremony, even though the lands were already subdivided and distributed among the peasants, and named delegates for the Democratic Peasant Committee. In preparation for these events, which occurred during the afternoon of 22 July, that same morning 300 peasants from among the occupiers of the hacienda Toxama arrived in Andarapa, a town from which few had participated in the original land invasion. With a flag, horn, whistle, and drum, they entered the town's central plaza to hold a demonstration. According to Sánchez, they "invited the local authorities, who agreed to participate in the meeting, but reluctantly." Mezzich and nine others went to the school and convinced the teachers and 300 students to come to the plaza. Once nearly the whole village was present, Mezzich addressed them, explaining the FEPCA and its goals in the province. Mezzich "[d]eclared that the peasant struggle did not consist only of occupying the land and throwing out the *gamonales*," Sánchez remembered, "but that the movement was also against those who acted counter to the peasants' interests and exploited them in different ways" (Sánchez 1981: 159–62; quotes on p. 160).

Immediately afterward, Mezzich brought charges against a local merchant and the mayor of Andarapa. Both were accused of working against the FEPCA and informing on the movement; the merchant had also physically abused some of the members of the community.

> [Mezzich] then asked the merchant to present himself at the demonstration. The merchant confirmed the charges and had to apologize for

PEASANTS AND MOBILIZATION IN
ANDAHUAYLAS, 1974.
(above) Vote in a communal assembly.
(right) Lino Quintanilla's experience
suggested that successful mobilization
required interest in and engagement
with entire families, including
children.
(opposite) Peasants occupy the central
patio of Hacienda Toxama, 18 July
1974.

his actions, promising never to repeat them. He offered some goods
from his store as a contribution to the peasant movement. The merchant was thus humiliated in front of the peasants. The mayor had to
face similar charges, given the fact that he almost always opposed the
actions of the municipal agents in the neighborhoods who cooperated
with the FEPCA. The mayor denied the charges and declared that even
if he, personally, were in favor of the Federation, his political position
did not allow him openly to express such support (Sánchez 1981: 160–
61; direct quotation on p. 161).

Between their victories in Andarapa's plaza and on the surrounding haciendas, that night the peasant masses returned enthusiastically to Toxama.
Enthusiasm continued unabated the next day during a long meeting and
confrontation with the departmental representatives who arrived on the hacienda. But by the day after that, the exhilaration caused by the invasion

had begun to decline. Many peasants began to remember their obligations to their neighborhoods, their animals, their fields. The leaders, Loayza and Mezzich in particular, tried to urge the peasants collectively to plant the land, but most of the participants preferred to return to their homes or divide the land up individually. Finally there was no alternative but to allow people to go home, since the food donated for the common pot ran out (Sánchez 1981: 163–78).

At the beginning of August, representatives from VR and the FEPCA met with national state officials. Between 4 and 8 August on the haciendas Toxama and Huancahuacho, they signed accords in which the state accepted the peasants' struggle against the local power structure (gamonalismo) and their occupation of hacienda lands, while the peasants accepted the long-term legitimacy of the agrarian debt. On one level, FEPCA militants considered these accords a great advance, because not only did the state accept the legitimacy of the peasant struggle, but by conceding the validity of the land invasions it also made the violent repression of the movement more difficult. From the standpoint of some of the militants, however, recognizing the agrarian debt, even in the long run, was too large a concession.[12]

Inspired by what they saw as a great victory for the peasant movement, Quintanilla, Mezzich, and Loayza subsequently expanded their organizing into other nearby districts, bringing about mobilizations and land invasions from Ongoy and Chincheros to Argama. In Cocharcas district, previously organized in collaboration with Quintanilla, agricultural work continued uninterrupted on the invaded lands. Not so on the hacienda Toxama, where, according to Sánchez, even though the hacienda

> remained in peasant hands and the bureaucrats had not returned nor showed any immediate plans to regain control of the enterprise, only a small group of 4 to 6 people stayed to watch over the land. Some of the neighborhoods had promised to alternate short returns to the hacienda's house, but they pretty much abandoned their commitment and did not do so. Evaristo, Santiago and Antenor [three of the most committed peasant leaders] visited the hacienda occasionally and continued to remind the rest of the peasants of the need to show up, but without results. The small group on Toxama worked repairing the fences and the house. There was no initiative taken to begin collective agricultural labor nor to carry out acts of effective possession on the land (Sánchez 1981: 185–86, quote on p. 186).

Between mid-September and the beginning of October, therefore, when the military government changed strategies and began systematically to repress the peasant movement, it found little capacity for resistance in the Andarapa region. Loayza and Mezzich, as well as local leaders from Manchaybamba and other neighborhoods, were easily arrested. The peasants arrested from the *anexo* of Chuspi signed documents admitting that the movement had been promoted by "outside agitators" from the FEPCA (Sánchez 1981: 201–8).

In Quintanilla's home territory in the district of Cocharcas, by contrast, serious repression was not felt until November, and even then, it was met with more effective resistance. When the police arrived, people were aware of the need to support those being arrested, to bear witness to the repression. "When they arrested our *compañero* Albino [Mendoza]," *señora* Fausta told Rodrigo Montoya,

> many women followed him at night, with a lantern, until they reached Huancahuacho. When we arrived we found Albino shivering with cold, completely naked. Together with his wife we took him his clothes.
> —Why are you taking him, we asked the police.
> —Because he's a thief, they told us. Hasn't he stolen? We're taking him because he's a highwayman [*asaltador*], they told us.
> —And you, who are you?, one of them asked me. Aren't you Quintanilla's wife?
> —No, I'm not, do you think you know me?, I told him. Why don't you loosen the ropes on him [Mendoza], I said. I knew there were many women on Huancahuacho and I only saw one. I asked where the other women were and one of the policemen told me to be quiet. I asked the lady where the others were. She told me the police had locked them all up. That they had only allowed her out to boil water and prepare breakfast for the policemen.
> —The women aren't guilty, we told the policemen, let them go (Quintanilla 1981: 97).

The general picture one gets in the Huancahuacho area is of women, men, and children presenting a united front against repression, confronting the police, insisting on the legitimacy of the movement and of their actions, suffering beatings and tear gassings. When people were freed, they returned immediately to continue occupying the hacienda and cultivating the land. "They kicked us in our houses, and they entered by breaking down the doors," *señora* Mercedes remembered. " 'You have Quintanilla hidden in these rooms.' And Lino Quintanilla could not be found."[13]

The fact that Quintanilla could not be found, despite heavy repression directed against the whole population on Huancahuacho and environs, bears witness to the different depth of organization in this region versus Toxama. In Huancahuacho the population as a whole suffered repression, and those arrested emerged unbroken to fight again. In most of Andarapa district, by contrast, mobilization had been brought in from the outside, at the last minute. The initial excitement generated in land takeovers and plaza demonstrations soon dissipated and only a few committed militants remained active. Small wonder that Julio Mezzich and Felix Loayza were easily found when the police arrived. Too bad Mezzich apparently chose to question how far the peasantry could be trusted instead of questioning the depth of his organizational strategies.

The Lessons of Andahuaylas

By November 1974, four brief months after the land invasions began, all organized manifestations of the Andahuaylas movement had ended. The last wave of mobilizations occurred in October, when peasants from some Andahuaylas districts blocked roads and held demonstrations in protest against the arrests and repression. On some ex-haciendas, such as Huancahuacho, people were still autonomously cultivating the land. In other areas, SINAMOS had already reorganized cooperatives and, despite widespread absenteeism, was reconsolidating state control over the expropriated land. With the exception of Lino Quintanilla, many FEPCA leaders were still in jail. The movement, when viewed from the provincial, regional or national level, had failed (Sánchez 1981: 191–223).

Entangled within this failure lie a series of important historical lessons. In the first place, the Andahuaylas mobilization taken as a whole forms part of a broader tendency in the Peruvian countryside to confront and defy the terms of the official agrarian reform. In the accords signed at Toxama and Huancahuacho, the Andahuaylas peasant movement forced Velasco's government to negotiate with the peasantry's leaders and to accept the legitimacy of the movement's actions. The generalization of the movement to the whole province and the arrest of the movement's leaders then brought national attention to the failures of rural populism Velasco style, just as the government was attempting to found the official peasant organization, the

Confederación Nacional Agraria. In conjunction with other rural popular mobilizations, therefore, the Andahuaylas movement opened up cracks in the "first-phase" model of military politics. Put most simply, if official attempts at popular organization and social redistribution seemed to generate a radicalization ever more difficult to control, then better to stop Velasco's ill-fated experiments and once again court the confidence of the investing classes. This would be, broadly speaking, the project of General Francisco Morales Bermúdez's "second phase."[14]

The Andahuaylas experience had a heavy impact within the Peruvian Left as well, especially in VR and the CCP. According to Sánchez, at the Asamblea Nacional Sindical Clasista, a national leftist trade union conference called by the CCP for 10 November 1974, "important sectors decided to walk out after denouncing the movement's leaders for having negotiated with the government." And, he continued, "They were referring to the Toxama and Huancahuacho accords, considered a political error that had 'turned the peasantry over to the reactionaries'" (Sánchez 1981: 221). José Fernando Méndez, FEPCA leader arrested in Andahuaylas in October 1974, also remembered in February 1981 that, among the many criticisms he made of the movement's organization, "The overestimation of the value of the Toxama and Huancahuacho accords produced the movement's disarmament, not preparing it for repression and generating in the peasantry an illusion, in the sense that the conduct of the government would be dialogue and not repression [and] this made possible after the repression was over for agrarian reform [officials] and SINAMOS [to enter the area]" (Méndez 1981: 97–103, quote on p. 103).

Méndez further believed that the November 1974 Asamblea Nacional was "the right moment" for the radicalization of the popular movement, but that Ricardo Letts, still convinced that it was possible to dialogue with the government about the repression in Andahuaylas, decided to take the CCP delegation out of the assembly. "What a love affair with the bourgeoisie," Méndez concluded, "VR and Letts achieved their goal: to squash the Andahuaylas movement in alliance with the government" (Méndez 1981: 99–100, 100 respectively).

One of the Left's interpretations of the Andahuaylas movement, therefore, identified the problems only at the national level, in the mistaken interpretation of Velasco's government as open to negotiation. Here the role of Ricardo Letts as leader of VR was crucial, and his past in Acción Popular, the reformist party of Fernando Belaúnde, was enough to mark him as suspicious. In a polemic published with an introduction by Saturnino Paredes—leader of the nonsenderista faction of Bandera Roja—Félix Valencia Quintanilla puts a more radical Maoist spin on this criticism, bringing it closer to the positions espoused by Shining Path. "The deal made by FEDCA [*sic*] leaders with the political authorities of Velasco Alvarado's fascist regime," Valencia argued, demonstrated that the Andahuaylas federation "belonged to the petty bourgeoisie, essentially the traitors of the peasant movement" (Valencia 1983: 87 and 88).

In his self-criticism about Andahuaylas, Lino Quintanilla also emphasized that the defeat of the movement led directly to an engagement with the problem of state power. "We have asked ourselves about the problems surrounding the land invasions. Where do land occupations take us? At first we were not clear about this." If the land invasions in Andahuaylas did not lead to deep and permanent change, Quintanilla reasoned, it must have been because it was impossible to negotiate effectively with the Velasquista state. Ultimately, he concluded,

> the peasantry's agrarian problem and the problems afflicting the Peruvian people will only be resolved through revolutionary war, destroying the power of the semicolonial bourgeois State and constructing another power on the ruins, in other words a State that is truly democratic and popular in which will participate all sectors oppressed by the capitalist system and who, through the leadership of the proletariat in alliance with the peasantry, will be able to guide this State to confront seriously and consciously the problems of the people (Quintanilla 1981: 120).

This impulse, this line of self-criticism, generated the faction of VR known as VR-Proletario Comunista, led by Mezzich and Quintanilla in the years immediately following the Andahuaylas experience. Popular war against the state was seen, in this context, as the solution to the problems that had caused the failure of the peasant movement. "That is why the peasantry begins to formulate more precisely the problem of the State," Quintanilla explained,

> they ask themselves about the need to destroy the State, so that with the strength of the masses behind them, in an organized political way, forming popular armies, they can take power.
>
> At first, we had a preoccupation with armed struggle, but we were not clear as to why. Now we have seen that putting forth the idea of

revolutionary war is not a negative thing. Now we have all realized that it is necessary, indispensable, that there is no other way out but to confront the enemy and his power apparatus in order to destroy it and only then to mete out justice. While the enemy is in power, guaranteed by the State, by the State apparatus, we can do nothing (Quintanilla 1981: 121).

Following this line of argument, we arrive easily at a position that considers popular war and the destruction of the state such high priorities that they become *preconditions* for other transformations. In such a context, any deviation from the highest priority goals is seen as treason, and there can be no place for negotiations because everyone knows what happened with previous attempts at negotiation. In short, with this style of self-criticism we quickly see the "shining omens" appear on the horizon.

"Shining omens" also appeared from early on in the relationship that the Left maintained with the indigenous communities. With the exception of Quintanilla in the Tankayllo-Cocharcas area (where the contradictions appeared much later, and at the larger-than-communal level), in Andahuaylas's other subregions a superficial style of political work in the communities led early on to a high degree of intra-community conflict and to an early disillusionment with the land invasions. Loayza and Mezzich's solutions to these problems—to rely excessively on the militance of a few young peasants with weak connections to the communal power structure and to invade towns and haciendas that had not mobilized independently, "bringing to justice" local authorities in some cases—generated a political unity that was fragile and superficial at best, and that broke apart quickly when faced with repression and state cooptation.

Indeed, it is by demonstrating the fragile yet crucial connection between communal political processes and transformative political and military processes at the regional level that the Andahuaylas movement could potentially have offered the most important lessons to those interested in radical social and political change. Quintanilla's work in Tankayllo, precisely because it took communal traditions and practices seriously, integrating them where possible and challenging them when necessary, helped strengthen community and peasant unity and solidify the invasion of Huancahuacho. The problems in that movement emerged later. In part, they were internal, for the very attempt to reorganize communal production generated differences among the peasants whose solutions, through the medium of the communal assembly, could only have been hammered out over the long run. But at the same time the problems were external: cooptation by SINAMOS of the surrounding communities and petty producers; repression and the destruction of the fields that had been planted after the occupation; and problems of marketing that arose with provincial or regional merchants. Under such conditions, when external pressures prevented the peasants from reaching solutions to their internal problems, it is easy to understand why people began to see state power as the principal problem.

Yet this similar endpoint in the process of self-criticism hid from view the crucial innovations of the Tankayllo experience, creating a false sense of homogeneity that fed easily into an expanding sympathy for Shining Path. Had it been possible to continue highlighting the singularity of Tankayllo politics, especially the conflictual commitment to and serious engagement with communal political processes, the question of the nexus between local and regional political work would have re-emerged. In such a context, the issues arising around the Democratic Peasant Committees would have received more reflection, for in the original conceptualization, it was precisely these committees that should have served as the mediators between the communities and the region. In addition to organizing the land recuperations and supervising the cultivation of the recovered lands, the Democratic Peasant Committees were to communicate between communal institutions and larger political and trade union organizations. Because their effectiveness depended on long-term organizational work, outside of Tankayllo and environs the committees simply became yet another way of bringing together the same militants who had already been contacted through other means. This, too, became a "shining omen."

Lest we blame too much on Andahuaylas and the emergence of Shining Path, however, it might be worthwhile to remember that the Peruvian Left of the 1970s did not invent the problematic relationship between Peru's oppositional political groups and indigenous culture and communal institutions more generally, which has existed throughout the twentieth century. For example, the ill-fated mobilizations of the Comité Pro-Derecho Indígena Tahuantinsuyo in the 1920s made clear, for many of Cuzco's local communal intellectuals, that an autonomous popular movement revindicating indigenous identities as such would not be politically successful at the regional or national levels. Thus, in the 1930s Cuzco's popular organizations began systematically to "de-Indianize" their political identities, not in the sense of negating indigenous traditions and culture, but rather of reinventing them without their negative connotations (de la Cadena 1995).

The Peruvian Left has thus had a long tradition of "de-Indianization" to draw from, and the discourse of the 1960s, which emphasized class struggle, capitalist exploitation, and proletarianization, was only one in a long line of attempts to create a nonethnic popular political identity. Yet as I have suggested throughout this essay, this historically constructed blindness to indigenous political and cultural practices doomed the inclusive and democratic nature of the 1960s and 1970s mobilizations. Leaders who snubbed communal political systems placed indigenous communities once again in a subordinate position, even within a supposedly egalitarian movement. Leaders who gave priority to a class-based political program attracted a small group of young peasants who, for generational and kinship reasons, did not have the political experience or prestige to influence the rest of their communities' inhabitants. This blindness to indigenous political culture, as reconstructed in the 1960s and 1970s, would also link the practice of the Left more generally to the practices adopted by Shining Path.

In the last analysis, the process in Andahuaylas in the 1970s and its critical rethinking by leftist militants and organizations was both an omen and a laboratory for the *senderista* process of the 1980s. The common frustration everyone felt in their attempts to combine political work in the communities with regional political and military work led easily to an overestimation of the value of state power as the principle locus of contradictions in the agrarian struggle. It also led to dismissing the importance and necessity of a long-term engagement with the political and *ethnic* practices and traditions within the peasant communities. In light of all these "shining omens," it is perhaps less surprising that some years later, when Gustavo Gorriti asked some senderista prisoners to explain an assassination attempt against the president of the community of Ongoy because he was affiliated with the leftist electoral coalition Unión Democrática Popular (UDP),[15] the prisoners answered that it had been just "because these people were creating illusions, they were serving the enemy. This is justice, then; justice has meaning in class terms. That is why we bring those people to justice. It is just, it is correct, it is necessary. In addition, this is a revolution; and everyone who opposes this revolution, will simply be squashed like one more insect" (Gorriti 1990: 372). The failure politically to engage indigenous traditions and practices, which emerged in the twentieth century among a variety of oppositional political groups in Peru and was reconstructed within the class-based leftist discourses and practices of the 1960s and 1970s, intensified in the Shining Path vision of 1980s popular war. Indeed, within senderista strategy, a historically created blindness to Indian-ness, linked to the imperative of total war, transformed communal culture and politics into one more insect to be squashed.

Notes

1 Part of the "Carnaval de la toma de Runanmarca," song composed by peasants from the community of Tankayllo during the land invasions in Andahuaylas in 1974. Reproduced in Quintanilla 1981: 133–34.

2 Personal correspondence with Rodrigo Montoya, editor of Quintanilla's memoirs and a friend of the family.

3 Rodrigo Montoya, editor and compiler of the memoir, describes the method of work in the prologue (Quintanilla 1981).

4 Fernando Belaúnde Terry, an architect from the southern city of Arequipa, projected an image of youthful populist change in Peru during the first half of the 1960s. Cooperación Popular, his suggested program for community development, attracted idealistic and reform-minded young people to work in the countryside and in highland villages.

5 A *varayoc* is a local political official, either a mayor or an assistant, whose position of authority is designated by his possession of a staff of office or *vara*.

6 The word *"misti"* is a Quechua term that denotes a combination of lighter skin—i.e., mestizo or white—and abusive political behavior.

7 Testimony of Eulogio Ramírez, in Quintanilla 1981: 50.

8 Though considered a reformist political party, Acción Popular was by no stretch of the imagination a leftist party. The faction that broke from AP to join in the founding of VR was therefore the left fringe; yet as we shall see, the AP origins of this group, and especially of its leader Ricardo Letts, would come back to haunt them later.

9 As mentioned previously, the original IV National Congress of the CCP had resulted in a massive walkout by delegates protesting the political positions of PCP-Bandera Roja. VR called a new IV Congress a couple of months later.

10 Words from the carnival song "Dirigentes FEPCA" ("Leaders of the FEPCA"), collected by Rodrigo Montoya in the Tankayllo region and reproduced in Quintanilla 1981: 128.

11 In Quechua, huaraka (*waraka*) means slingshot.

12 The two proclamations are reproduced in Quintanilla 1981: "Acta de Huancahuacho" and "Acta de Toxama" on pp. 145–50 and 150–55, respectively.

For critiques of these proclamations as "sell-outs," see Valencia 1983: 86–88, Méndez 1981: 30–36, 80–87.

13 Quintanilla 1981: 97–100; the direct quotation appears on p. 100. For more on the repression in Tankayllo, see also Sánchez 1981: 216–17.

14 For a broader view of the legal and organizational implications of Velasco's agrarian reform, see Pásara 1978a, 1978b.

15 The Unión Democrática Popular was founded in 1976–1977. The founding parties in the UDP included the MIR, MIR-Voz Rebelde (IV Epoca), VR, Movimiento de Acción Proletaria (MAP—Movement of Proletarian Action), and the Partido Comunista Revolucionario (PCR—Revolutionary Communist Party). The initial purpose of the coalition was as an electoral front that would field candidates for the 1978 Constituent Assembly and the general elections of 1980. The UDP became a part of Izquierda Unida (IU; United Left) in the 1980s.

PART TWO

The Conquest That Failed:

The War for the Center-South

✧ The center-south provinces of Peru witnessed a "conquest that failed" in the 1980s and early 1990s. It was here that Sendero focused its drive to conquer rural peoples and territories, and to achieve a capacity to strangle Lima from within and without. The impoverished and heavily Indian Department of Ayacucho constituted the regional birthplace and recruitment arena of the party. Ayacucho and the adjoining and socially similar departments of Apurímac and Huancavelica concentrated much of the violent suffering and the accompanying political, social, and cultural processes induced by the war. Strategic areas of expansion lay just north of Ayacucho and Huancavelica in the more mestizo and commercially dynamic central sierra departments of Junín and Pasco, in the montaña slopes that descended toward jungle zones along the eastern fringes of northern Ayacucho and Junín, and toward the jungle and coca leaf zones along the east of Pasco and Huánuco. In Junín and Pasco were concentrated agricultural production and hydroelectric power crucial to Lima's supply of food and energy, mines that supplied a good deal of national export income, and along the western edges of the region, the sierra heights that overlooked Lima and the central coast. The montaña zones along eastern edges of Ayacucho and the central sierra provided refuge territory for guerrillas fleeing from military forces or encounters in the highlands, and access to revenues from the coca-cocaine economy.

The essays in Part II analyze the interior dynamics of this failed conquest. Those by Carlos Iván Degregori and Ponciano del Pino illuminate two remarkable processes at the heart of the war: the consistent capacity of the senderistas both to win and to squander an initial political base—a blend of acceptance and sympathy—in rural Ayacucho; and the subjective experience of living a "double life," as families and individuals willingly or unwillingly drawn into complicity and participatory roles in the insurgency coped with increasing disillusion, alienation, and even rage.

Degregori's account analyzes the transition from a pragmatic partial acceptance of educated youth who were Sendero sympathizers and militants, toward a political alienation and disgust so complete that it sparked organized peasant rebellion against Sendero. The prestige of knowledge and education as roads to social advance lent a certain political space to dissident youth and intellectuals, especially those whose provincial social backgrounds or local kin relations further eased and justified a local presence. In addition, the local injustices and social grievances common in an impoverished countryside of decomposing gamonalismo allowed for political honeymoon periods. Early phases of Senderista action targeted abusers, whether gamonal-like targets such as landlords, hacienda administrators, and merchants, or more subaltern abusers such as animal thieves and wife-beaters. Finally, the military's wave of indiscriminate repression in Ayacucho's "dirty war" phase of counterinsurgency in 1983–1984 deflected wrath and discouraged open rupture with Sendero. Sendero squandered all these political advantages. It came to rely ever more exclusively on violence and coercion to exert a directive political presence, and it would end up facing organized resistance by peasant *rondas* (military patrols) determined to defend communities against incursions and intimidation.

Degregori demonstrates that Sendero sympathizers and militants—however shrewd they may have been in identifying local grievances and ruptures that built an initial legitimacy—fell prey to ideological blind spots and contemptuousness that set them against specific cultural values and social practices of Andean peasants. Among the actions that put Sendero at odds with the local peasantry were its closure of market outlets for agricultural commodities, its contempt for "traditional" systems of community authority vested in elders whose *varas* (staffs) symbolized backgrounds of community service and legitimacy, its neglect of local bonds and social dynamics (age and gender relations, life cycle rituals, social reciprocities) that cut across economic stratification into rich, middling, and poor peasants, and its cult of a killing violence as the preferred form of punishment and heroism. These and other features of senderismo elucidated by Degregori pushed Andeans toward a view that equated senderistas with humanoid monsters (*ñakaq*) destructive of life. In the end, Degregori demonstrates, the hyperideologized vision of Sendero encouraged a contempt that trivialized peasant values as obstacles and signs of backwardness (recall in this context the Andahuaylas experience recounted by Mallon). Teleological certainty allowed one to interpret setbacks as expected steps backward in the march toward triumph.

The growing alienation of peasants—the middling period in their transitions from "resistant adaptation" to open rebellion in relations with Sendero—implied that many peasants lived out experiences of double-life, tensions between conflicting selves, conflicting moral logics, conflicting strategies of survival.[1] The initial adaptive toleration of Sendero ideologues and sympathizers, the emergence of internal community fractions aligned with Sendero, and the survival strategies that, along with intimidation, facilitated the recruitment of youth into ideological training and military service, these dynamics drew the people and kin groups who constituted a local community into a tightening vise of complicity and fear organized by Sendero. Complicity, once initiated, proved difficult to break. It rendered persons and communities suspect by the military, vulnerable to escalating demands by Sendero, and exposed to senderista vengeance if the cycle of complicity were broken.

The tightening vise also generated deeply horrifying and alienating experiences, both because the logic of senderista actions and demands violated local cultural values and social practices and because senderista glorification of violent suffering as a cleansing blood quota allowed for a brutal indifference to the sufferings and deaths of youths drawn into the war effort. During this middling period, especially, peasants could come to experience extreme tension between an external self of complicitous behavior—a self that had lost moral and practical justification—and an inner self that sought to break out of the complicitous mold.

Degregori and del Pino illuminate the experience of double-life and its potential for producing inner rage and spiritual crisis. Del Pino, especially, draws us into a remarkably interior view of the unfolding tension between a rationalist formal ideology that subordinated customary relations of kin and culture to the higher value of revolutionary service and sacrifice, and a rediscovered self whose affective, kin-related, and moral values demanded and justified resistance to Sendero. As the military gained heightened success and confidence in its war against Sendero, and as Sendero's local leaders sensed wavering loyalties and recruited ever-younger children into a near-suicidal war, this tension could reach an explosive intensity.

Within this context of interior tension and double-life experience, mothers and evangelical Protestants proved particularly important catalysts of a culture of resistance to Sendero. Mothers, who were most responsible in practical and cultural terms for the fate of children and family survival, constituted, as del Pino puts it, a "public and discursive vanguard" in the voicing of complaint, rage, and critique. Similarly, evangelical Protestantism could play a lead role in the turn toward resistance, both as a means of resolving the spiritual crisis induced by the tension between interior and exterior selves and as a source of moral values that condemned complicity with senderismo as sinfulness and integrated apocalyptic sensibilities into a sense of order and purpose.[2] By the late 1980s and early 1990s, the extreme cruelty with which Sendero operated in eastern Ayacucho zones it theoretically controlled barely masked the failure of its conquest.

Of course, the dynamics of war, insurgency, and resistance varied by region and microregion. Nelson Manrique draws us into a consideration of commonality and contrast between and within regions. At one level, Manrique provides a regional chronology of the war for the center-south. He demonstrates a shift toward the central sierra, especially Junín, as the decisive sierra battleground of the late 1980s and early 1990s. This shift largely coincided with Sendero's transition to the "strategic equilibrium" phase of war, a prelude to the presumed final crisis and collapse of the national state.

At another level, Manrique's comparison of three microzones within Junín demonstrates the blend of similarity and difference that shaped local experiences of senderista arrival, politics, and struggles for control. In areas whose prior history had yielded rather independent "free communities," such as the high pastoral zones of Alto Cunas, the ability of Sendero to create a reservoir of initial support and an accompanying political honeymoon period proved comparatively shallow. In these areas, communities had a stronger capacity to organize their own independent sense of political will and to place Sendero on the defensive. The independent political capacity and solidarity of communities proved weaker in intermontane valleys whose peasant communities, like Canipaco, had long contended with expansive haciendas and a more "feudal" environment of gamonalista control and abuse. The initial political allure of Sendero also proved stronger: a local political culture organized around hacienda—community struggle and gamonalismo provided targets of peasant ire that converted senderistas into agents of local justice and moral order.

The eastern montaña districts that descended toward the jungle presented a political and cultural environment different from either of the two highland zones. Indigenous groups such as the Asháninka peoples built their sense of ethnic identity—and a degree of cultural receptivity to outside redeemers—out of a history that experienced *serranos* (highlanders) as colonizers, missionaries, and would-be redeemers. And they retained a capacity to organize independent and elusive armies of their own. Like other serrano invaders of the lowlands, Sendero would contend with Asháninka guerrillas and ambushes, notwithstanding a certain capacity to recruit some Asháninka for senderista columns. As guerrilla refuge and coca revenue zones, jungle districts had special importance to Sendero, as well as the competing insurgents of MRTA (the Movimiento Revolucionario Túpac Amaru) and the military. These distinctive features—the serrano-lowlander axis of ethnic identity and politics and the more densely militarized and strategic quality of the area—bred unusually fierce struggles for control. Rapid transits to extremes of violence and war implied, in the locales where Sendero managed to build a strong foothold, the emergence of concentration-camp societies, similar in ruthlessness and loss of life to the eastern Ayacucho scene depicted by del Pino.[3]

Yet, Manrique's discussion also enables us to see the blurred quality of these microzonal contrasts, and the processes in common that partly superseded them. The contrasts between microzones were relative, sometimes more subtle than absolute. Alto Cunas, although an area of free communities more resistant to political penetration and control by Sendero, nonetheless had its share of senderista youths and sympathizers, and pragmatists seeking alignment with a winning political force. Canipaco, although more receptive and vulnerable to senderista control, mixed skepticism and pragmatism as well as political sympathy in its early honeymoon period. Perhaps most important, over time all three microzones ended up experiencing the senderista project as one of extreme subjugation and humiliation that required resistance. Under the circumstances, initial contrasts in local political receptivity, cultural ambience, and leadership style by senderista cadres lost some of their force; experiences in common drove otherwise distinctive peoples and locales in a similar political direction.

One of the most dramatic expressions of the widening movement toward outright opposition to Sendero was the spread of *rondas campesinas* (peasant defense patrols) in peasant communities throughout the center-south highlands. Orin Starn's essay provides an incisive and well rounded interpretation of the rondas. On the one hand, he enables us to see the ronda phenomenon as peasant initiative and achievement, and thereby to set aside the temptation to simplify the rondas as political manipulation or coercion by the military and the state. Starn demonstrates the complex political dynamics that facilitated a certain rapprochement between the state and rural civil society, including the unfolding sense of peasant disgust with Sendero and the transition of the military from indiscriminate dirty war to a politics of rural alliance-building and select repression. The rapprochement, however, did not imply a political praxis that situated peasants as manipulated and uncritical beneficiaries of a benign state. On the contrary, the achievements of the ronderos in establishing a precarious social peace and winding down of political violence, and a rebirth of civil society, fed into a prideful consciousness by Andean peasants that they had won the war *despite* the inadequacies of the military and the state. In this scheme, peasants and *comuneros* were citizen-warriors who led the nation from the abyss, not hapless victims and marginals rescued by military patrons.

On the other hand, Starn's interpretation also makes it difficult to lapse into an idealization of the ronderos as subaltern heroes without blemish or limitation. The masculinized politics of the ronderos, the charges of corruption and political bossism that sometimes attached to this new source of power, the tendency of the military and the state to integrate rondas within a wider structure of exploitation and neglect, the inability of grassroots organizations to invade and transform political structures beyond immediate locales: all point to a certain potential for domination, internal conflict, and disillusion. In short, Starn's complex analysis enables us to see the unfixed and double-edged qualities of the ronda phenomenon. The rondas represent not only a path toward political self-definition and achievement against great odds, they also capture the uncertainties and multiple potentials imbedded within a rebirth of society and politics amidst the ruins, terror, and memories of war.

Sendero launched a "conquest that failed" in the center-south provinces of Peru. Taken together, the essays of Degregori, del Pino, Manrique, and Starn draw out four critical dimensions of the process of failure. First, Degregori and del Pino enable us to see the squandering of initial political advantages that seemed almost inexorable, built into senderista understandings of politics that flowed out of the prior histories analyzed (in Part I) by de la Cadena, Hinojosa, and Mallon. Second, Degregori and del Pino enable us to see the ways that the physical sufferings, clashes of values, and spiritual torments of the war gave rise to conflicted double-lives. Yearnings and angers swelled up and inspired dangerous efforts to break a tightening vise of control. Third, Manrique probes the problem of regional shift and variation. Significantly, his analysis enables us not only to explore contrast — to follow the northward shift of the war within the center-south, to consider the microzonal particulars that pluralized initial experiences of and receptivity to senderista politics — but also to notice processes of extreme humiliation and political alienation that cut across such contrasts. Finally, Starn enables us to explore an ambiguous and unintended legacy of the war: the rise of citizen-warriors among Andean rural peoples, self-conscious that they had won the war and perhaps redefined peasant and ethnocommunity politics, yet aware that walking the edge between uncertain local politics and uncertain national politics is inherently risky.

Notes

1   The concept of "resistant adaptation" used by Degregori and del Pino refers to the ways that real and apparent accommodations to the authorities of an onerous social reality incorporate senses of "right" — of resistant assertion and self-protection — that render such accommodations partial and contingent. "Resistant adaptation" by peasants implies a set of values and ongoing political evaluations that provide a basis for defiance or rebellion if the senses of "right" incorporated into an earlier cycle of accommodation are violated. For fuller discussion, in dialogue with trends in Andean history and anthropology, see Stern 1987: 3–25, esp. 10.
2   For pioneering research on evangelical Protestants and the war in Ayacucho, see del Pino 1996.
3   On the Asháninka experience and the coca zones, see also Brown and Fernández 1991; J. Gonzales 1992.

FOUR

Harvesting Storms: Peasant *Rondas* and the

Defeat of Sendero Luminoso in Ayacucho

Carlos Iván Degregori

Can a spark rebel against a bonfire? . . . How can grains detain the grinding of the mill? They will be ground into dust. —*Abimael Guzmán*[1]

❖ When the war began in May 1980, Shining Path was a party consisting mainly of teachers and university professors and students with little influence among the regional peasantry. Nonetheless, by the end of 1982, when the armed forces assumed military and political control of Ayacucho (figure 4.1), Shining Path had easily displaced the police forces from broad rural zones of the region's northern provinces, and it was preparing to lay siege to the departmental capital.[2]

Rural Youth and the Peasantry

The key to this vertiginous expansion was the significant number of rural youth with secondary-school education, or in some instances no more than a primary-school education, who swelled the party ranks and constituted the most active sector of Shining Path's rural "generated organizations." Subsequently, they were incorporated into the apparatus of the "new state" that Shining Path was constructing. Shining Path clearly *needed* this sector. Where it did not exist, Shining Path encountered difficulties in establishing solid links with the peasantry.[3]

These were the politically and socially "available" youth who, in their secōndary schools, had been exposed either to Shining Path discourse, or at least to what Portocarrero and Oliart (1989) refer to as the "critical idea": thought critical of the social order in a confrontational yet authoritarian manner. The presence of other parties of the Left in some parts of the

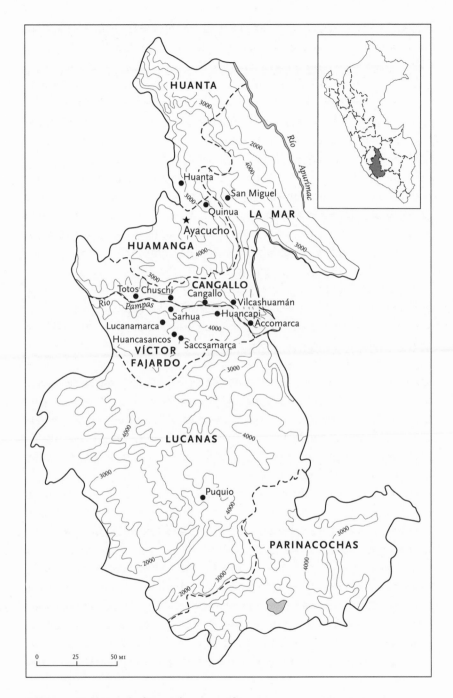

Figure 4.1. Department of Ayacucho, circa 1980.

region, however tenuous, also encouraged youthful radicalism. In addition, these were youth in search of an identity, their parents' "traditional" Andean identity seemed remote after exposure to the "myth of progress" (Degregori 1986). This myth was disseminated in the schools and mass media, and was even promoted by their own parents. These were youth, finally, who had little hope of achieving such progress by way of the market, migration, or more education. Suddenly, they were presented with the concrete possibility of social ascent through the new *senderista* state.[4] Shining Path militancy may thus be seen, in part, as a path for social mobility. Arturo, a youth from the community of Rumi, recalls: "They said that Ayacucho was going to be a liberated zone by 1985. A famous illusion that they created among the *muchachos* was, way back in 1981, that by '85 there would be an independent republic. Wouldn't you like to be minister? Wouldn't you like to be a military chief? Be something, no?"

Power seduced these secondary students, who were also captivated by the examples presented by other youth, the university students-cum-guerrillas, who made up the majority of the Shining Path columns. Nicario, also of Rumi, recalled his encounter with one of them: "I was invited by one who was from the Universidad de San Cristóbal [de Huamanga]. So I, well, agreed easily . . . because at that time, it was '82, Sendero was generating a lot of action . . . a military commander (*mando*) went to the Assembly, who led. He came with his machine gun. I was afraid but I went up to him. He introduced himself and he had a deep voice: yes, *compañero*. So, wearing his boots and all, he greeted me." Power appeared in all of its fearful splendor, and gained the adherence of most youth in Rumi, whom it promised to invest with the same attributes. The young people were intoxicated with this power. Their first actions were to paint walls and set off dynamite in the town, breaking the silence of the rural nights. According to Arturo, "we blew it up just to blow it up, nothing else."

For the university students who constituted the senderista hard core, the party was a "total identity." A sector of rural youth also came to internalize Shining Path militancy to this extent.[5] For many young people, however, what was important was not merely social mobility, but the concrete exercise of power in their own localities, along with a touch of youthful adventure. This was especially the case during the early years, when the violence had not yet spun out of control and everything still seemed relatively easy.

Another important factor was something that we might call the demonstration effect. Youth were inspired to join an organization that was on the rise, prestigious, with a demonstrated effectiveness. Such an organization would empower and transform them. Joining Shining Path had elements of a rite of passage or of initiation into a religious sect: the armed sect.

This beachhead among rural youth enabled Shining Path to spread among the peasantry. It was most successful where there existed a significant generational gap in educational levels. Once converted into an armed generation, in many outlying hamlets (*pagos*) and communities the youth then proceeded to seduce, convince, or pressure their parents, who had sent their children to school so that, rather than grope their way "blindly" through the world, they could encounter paths of mobility in a complex and discriminatory society. Many adults believed that if educated youth said something, it had to have some truth to it. The young people were the "ones with eyes" (*ñawiyoq*), who "saw" things that their "ignorant" parents had perhaps not noticed.[6] Even when, internally, they disagreed with the youth's discourse, the reaction of the adults was ambiguous because of the familial and cultural ties that bound the generations together.

In addition to taking advantage of kinship ties, Shining Path made a show of displaying its coercive capabilities to the peasantry. From the beginning, senderistas included a measure of terror. Shining Path thus occupied the place of the traditional Andean boss or patron (*patrón*). As a "new" patrón, Shining Path was hard and inflexible yet "just," and displaced the generally incompetent and abusive authorities. From this position, Shining Path tried to obtain concrete benefits for the peasantry and located itself at the crux of local conflicts. Berg (1992) has emphasized how Shining Path took advantage of conflicts between communities and cooperatives in some zones of Andahuaylas. Isbell (1992) has noted how in Chuschi Shining Path made some livestock thieves the target of its attacks. Manrique (1989) has referred to how Shining Path worked on the basis of the conflicts between the peasantry and the Cahuide Agricultural Society (one of the SAIS, or Sociedades Agrícolas de Interés Social, large productive enterprises created by Velasco's land reform program) in the high zones of Junín. In addition, the party implanted a very strict moral order.

Ayacucho provided Shining Path with a favorable scenario. In Ayacucho, among the ruins of rural bossism (*gamonalismo*), there still existed small local fiefdoms of abusive *mistis*. The region had relatively few peasant organizations and relatively many students. Education enjoyed a special prestige, to the point that the principal social movement of previous decades had been organized not around demands for land but rather around demands for free education (Degregori 1990a). Under these circumstances, the peasantry was relatively disposed to accept Shining Path as a new patrón, one that appeared more powerful, moreover, than the former local authorities or the State-as-patrón. Shining Path swept out the state's repressive apparatus, the police forces. The peasants' acceptance was basically pragmatic, provided in exchange for concrete gains on a personal, familial, or communal level, as Berg (1992) has demonstrated for Andahuaylas. But, this tactical acceptance opened the door to the possibility, over the long term, of a more strategic identification with the senderista project.

Indeed, Shining Path seemed to be on the verge of gaining deeper peasant support during the second half of 1982, a crucial moment for the region. For Shining Path, this was a moment of euphoria. The party had celebrated its Second National Conference and had begun to develop the last stage of its plan "to unleash the Guerrilla War," which consisted in "hammering away (batir) to advance toward the Bases of Support" (Gorriti 1990: chapter 15). The influence of the party spread like wildfire in the rural zones and also grew in the departmental capital. There, in March, Sendero successfully attacked the jail and liberated dozens of imprisoned cadres; and in September, the funeral of the young senderista leader Edith Lagos drew more than 10,000 people.

But as often occurs, the factors that would contribute to its failure were already emerging, unnoticed, in the midst of all this success. To begin, neither the youth nor the cadres seemed to have a clear medium-range vision. They lived in a present of triumph and they dreamed of a future with marks of a peasantist utopia: The Armed Forces would suffer massive desertions and their helicopters would be shot down with slings (huaracas); Lima would be strangled and the urban poor would return once again to the new rural republic.[7] Toward October, in various places, the party prepared for the first agricultural campaign of the new state-in-construction, where soon there would be no more hunger.

First Points of Rupture

This utopia caught fire in the imagination of the cadres, but it struck fewer sparks among the masses, for whom enthusiasm was ephemeral at best. Shining Path was successful in "hammering the countryside" (Gorritti 1990). Its problems began when, having cleared the terrain, it began to construct its "new power" (nuevo poder). At various levels, fault lines began to appear that would harm the senderista project. Let us consider four points of rupture: the organization of production, the organization of political power, the role of violence in the new order, and the physical security of the peasant population.

THE ORGANIZATION OF PRODUCTION

Shining Path privileged collective forms of organizing production. During the planting season, toward the end of 1982, Shining Path did not seem to encounter great resistance. Resistance became more evident in some places during the harvest, at which point the peasants found out that collectively produced crops were destined for the party.[8]

In other places, finally, problems related to production emerged when Shining Path demanded that the peasants plant only for the party and for self-subsistence, and then proceeded to close off peasant fairs and markets. This strategy of conquering and then closing off territories, in order to block the flow of agricultural produce and thus asphyxiate the cities, clashed with peasant families' own strategies of reproduction. The families' survival strategies transcended the limits of the hamlet or pueblo, and were based on networks of kinship and community origin that established links in different areas of the countryside and in cities (Golte and Adams 1987; Steinhauf 1991). The cities, on the other hand, were not supplied only or even mostly by their immediate rural hinterlands.[9] Elsewhere I have discussed the difficulties that Shining Path encountered toward the end of 1982 upon closing the market at Lirio in the heights of Huanta, where the supposedly isolated Iquichano peasants supplied themselves with a variety of manufactured products (Degregori 1985a, 1985b). Fissures related to production, although present from the early 1980s, would not deepen to the point of irrevocability until the late 1980s.

THE NEW POWER

It was in the construction of a new political power (*nuevo poder*) that Shining Path would encounter greater difficulties from the start. In the second semester of 1982, and as part of its plan to "hammer the countryside," Sendero decided to replace communal authorities with commissaries representing the new power.

According to the Maoist script, in order to wage a more successful people's war, the party had to rely on the impoverished stratum among peasants. These peasants, rather than the middling or rich ones, were "those most disposed to accept the leadership of the Communist Party" (Mao 1971). Shining Path was surprised to encounter, however, its greatest problems in the poorest zones, which were at the same time the most "Indian" and "traditional." Coronel (1994) describes what occurred in the Iquichano communities that were still governed by the *vara* system, a hierarchical and ritualized structure of authority at the pinnacle of which sat the *varayocc* or *alcalde vara* ("keeper of the staff") who personified the community and who assumed that post at an advanced age, having ascended via a community ladder of civic-religious posts or *cargos* (see Vergara et al. 1985). The replacement of these authorities by young senderista cadres was an affront not only to communal organization, but to the community's whole cosmovision. For Shining Path, the peasant world appeared one-dimensional, without historical density or social complexity, divided simply into poor, middling, and rich peasants. Indeed, by proceeding in this manner, Shining Path would end up, often, depending on the youth of the middle and upper strata, neutralizing or winning over the adults of these same strata, and imposing itself upon, repressing, and finally massacring the poorer peasants.

Above all, it was when Shining Path refused to recognize community authorities that the first overt rebellions occurred (Coronel 1996). But even in those communities that no longer elected varayocc officials but organized communal government according to national legislation, the installation of new authorities tended to cause problems. In some, the family connections between "the old and the new power," to employ Shining Path terminology, initially neutralized resistance. In Rumi, *"the old [authorities] did not protest because the president's own son was in the party, definitely. His son had convinced him as well"* (Nicario). But in many other places, the youthfulness of the Shining Path authorities was upsetting. Not only did it break generational hierarchies. In addition, "Gonzalo thought" had not managed to disengage the rural youth from the tightly woven networks of kinship and community relations, with their own dynamic of reciprocities, grudges, hatreds, and preferences, in which they had long been immersed. As a result, the youthful representatives of the new power were frequently dragged into inter- and intra-communal disputes.

An account from the community of Tambo-La Mar explains one of the ways that this dynamic played itself out: "The worst that Sendero had done perhaps was to have trusted very young people in each locality, with very little experience. . . . They completely distorted Sendero's plans for government, they opted to assume attitudes of vengeance, grudges, suddenly a father had a fight with another father over a question of borders between their chacras, or animals, or a robbery, or losses, fights between husband and wife; since Sendero had given responsibility to those of the locality, they began to take reprisals, take revenge, this was what caused the massacres, this caused all the distrust among the people" (José, teacher). The guerrilla column would leave, without realizing it had left behind a hornet's nest of contradictions that could not be resolved.[10] Even if in these cases no overt rebellion took place, the imposition of the new authorities generated initial resentments and the first peasant allies of the armed forces, "informers" (soplones) in the senderista terminology.

VIOLENCE IN THE NEW ORDER

The role of violence in the new order also produced ruptures. By 1980, the grand "semi-feudal" scenario against which Sendero had imagined waging its epic battles, was actually in ruins, already destroyed by the combined forces of the market, the state, peasant pressure, the great rural-to-urban migrations, and the agrarian reform. Inspired by Mao, Shining Path programmed for 1980–1981 "harvest uprisings" and land invasions. The results were meager, as they only took some surviving haciendas (Gorriti 1990; Tapia 1995). The only action that compared with the massive land mobilizations of the 1960s, although carried out under a radically distinct banner, occurred in 1982, when Shining Path demolished Allpachaka, a university-sponsored experimental farm (Degregori 1985b). The senderistas also took some cooperatives that had been created in the agrarian reform (Coronel 1994). But apart from the police, whom Shining Path placed on the run during the early years by dynamiting their rural posts, the most important targets were abusive merchants, cattle thieves, corrupt judges, and drunk husbands.

Without a doubt, all of these people constituted real problems for the peasantry. Nonetheless, to confront them did not require constructing a "war machine," much less the colossal campaign of horror that bloodied the region. The considerable success of the peasant patrols (rondas) in the northern reaches of Piura and Cajamarca had illustrated that peasants could deal with such problems with very little violence (Starn 1992; Starn, ed. 1993; Huber 1995).

But Shining Path had three features that made it different from the northern rondas: an ideology that made violence an absolute value rather than a relative or proportionate instrument, a "molecular" strategy for constructing its "counterpower," and a totalitarian political project. Sendero's ideology took violence beyond the classic Maoist confines of the people's war. For Shining Path violence was, in addition, a purifying force that extirpated the old (the bad) at its roots. The militants' ideological zeal was fed constantly by the leadership, particularly by the supreme leader Abimael Guzmán, who tended to exalt violent purification.[11] Due to the absence of important regional targets, such as large landowners, Shining Path ended up concentrating all of this purifying zeal on the dynamics of micropower, in a kind of "social cleansing" of daily life. In addition, the strategy of Shining Path was to "hammer the countryside" and liberate zones in which Sendero would not only construct a new state, but a new society, controlled by the party even in its most minute details.

Ideological zeal, military strategy, and the totalitarian political project came together in the Fourth Plenary of the Central Committee, celebrated in May 1981. There Guzmán propagated the idea of "the blood quota" (la cuota) that would be necessary for the triumph of the revolution, and warned of the necessity of preparing for an inevitable "blood bath." The militants had to be ready to ford "the river of blood" of the revolution while "carrying their lives in their fingertips." The Fourth Plenary session agreed "to intensify radically the violence," and justified the escalation in the following terms: "they [the reaction] form lakes [of blood], we saturate handkerchiefs" (Gorritti 1990: chapter 10).

It is against this background that we must locate the meaning of the 1982 decision to "hammer the countryside." "In Hammering, the key is to demolish [arrasar], and demolish means not to leave anything." It was necessary to "dislocate the power of the bosses [gamonales], disarrange the power of the authorities and hit the live forces of the enemy . . . clean out the zone, leave an empty plain [dejar pampa]."[12]

The following two testimonies, from the provinces of Huancasancos and Cangallo respectively, refer to Shining Path's "people's tribunals," in which the strategy of "hammering" materialized with heartrending consequences.

> So the woman they punished with fifty lashes because she had talked, complaining of the bad distribution of the harvests. It was a poor family and she had been drinking. And they shaved her hair all off. And as for the other they also gave him fifty lashes and they cut his ear with scissors, so now he is qoro rinri ["mutilated ear"].
>
> And the people, what did they say?

Nothing, well: punish but don't kill. That was what they said, nothing more (Juvenal, adult peasant).

Or, consider a second testimony:

Now the people are unhappy because [those of Shining Path] have done many stupid things. They have killed innocent people saying that they are snitches [*soplones*]. I think—no?—that if they had committed an error they should have been punished, nothing else. They should have given them lashes, they should have cut their hair . . . but not like they have done, like a hog they have slaughtered the mayor.

And the people, what did they do?

Nothing, well. Since they were armed, what could we do, then? That's why I tell you, they have committed many stupidities (Mariano, petty merchant).

The phrase "punish but don't kill" marks the limits of peasant acceptance, at least in the ambit of the so-called people's tribunals. It was a limit that came to exasperate the senderista cadres, as can be seen in the following testimonial from a community in Cangallo, by a young teacher who at that time participated in a Shining Path "generated organization:"

So a person had collected money in the name of Shining Path and they had captured him. Such people were judged in the plaza of the village. Just there they asked the people: "these señores have done this, this, and this," saying "what do you say. Shall we kill them or shall we punish them?" And then the community spoke: "Why kill him, he should submit to punishment," the community said. "Oh, you all still have your archaic ideas about defending yourselves still. From now on we are not going to ask, because we know that you are going to defend. We have to cut off their heads, because the bad weed has to be completely exterminated, because if we are going to be forgiving the bad weed we are never going to triumph, we are never going to exceed ourselves (*superarnos*)." That is what they said (Cesáreo, teacher).

This account illustrates the tragic disjunctures of those years, between the anxiousness of the youthful cadres to "exceed ourselves" and what they considered the "archaic ideas" of the community, that is, between the senderista project and "Andean rationality." The Shining Path cadres, ideologized to the point of fundamentalism, ready to kill and to die for their project, did not know or respect the peasant codes. Their vision was a utopia of cadres, that could not become a code of masses. They were priests for a god that spoke (sometimes literally) Chinese.[13]

Let us explain further. In an environment where rural gamonalismo, although in shambles, still provided codes of domination and subordination, in a region without a strong network of new peasant organizations and with a weakly developed market, in an area that did not have the opportunity to explore the democratic spaces that opened up in other parts of the country after the 1980 municipal elections, the peasants seemed disposed to accept a new patrón and even accept his punishment. Structural and political violence were not new to them. Corporal punishments, including lashings and haircuts, represented continuities from landed society and the old misti power; the peasants knew how to survive such violence and how to ridicule and combat it. But the hyperideological violence of Shining Path was alien to them; this violence did not play itself out according to the traditional codes. In the testimonial just cited, the dialogue with Cesáreo continued as follows:

> But, if they were delinquents, why were the people against killing them?
>
> And their children? Who was going to take responsibility for their families?

In other words, death surpassed the limit of the tolerable, but not simply because the peasants may have a "culture of life." Rather, their reasons were pragmatic. In a society with a precarious economy that establishes intricate networks of kinship and complex strategies of reproduction, one had to take great care to protect the labor force. To kill, to eliminate a link in one of these networks, had repercussions beyond the nuclear family of the condemned. I noted earlier that when Shining Path initiated the war, the landowners had practically disappeared from Ayacucho. Therefore, in many cases the "targets of the revolution" were small local exploiters, arrogant and in many cases abusive, but also linked by connections of kinship, social origin, and daily life to the communities, or at least to sectors of comuneros. A commentary regarding the Allpachaka estate, collected after its destruction, provides evidence of this point: "In Allpachaka, there had been many animal thieves and they have killed them. So their families have become anti-senderistas and have begun to denounce and point out innocent people as senderistas. I think that they shouldn't have killed them but rather punished them so that they would behave" (Alejandro, university student, from a peasant family).

To utilize jargon that presently enjoys a certain prestige, we may say that as far as the economy of violence was concerned, Shining Path's macroeconomic assumptions were not in accord with the microeconomic conduct of the agents. The point of departure for the macroeconomic analysis of Shining Path violence was the idea that everyday structural violence was more lethal. Shining Path argued that its model was more expeditious and, in the medium term, less costly in human lives, because the revolution would eliminate poverty, hunger, and structural violence in general.[14] From the point of view of the peasant agents, however, political violence was added to structural violence. The latter was already more than enough to bear, and the two together would prove unbearable in the short-term. To paraphrase Keynes, in the long term—in this case, the long term envisioned by the Shining Path utopia—we will all be dead.

In juridical terms, the punishments that Shining Path imposed were increasingly out of proportion with the magnitude of the supposed crimes, which, of course, Shining Path categorized according to a totally alien notion of law, distant from everyday common law as well as national jurisprudence. According to Gálvez (1987), in what he called (for descriptive purposes only) "peasant law," punishments often included physical exactions but very rarely included death. Capital punishment was contemplated only when the security of the group as a whole was believed to be threatened, especially in cases of animal thievery, and only after exhausting all other possibilities. The fundamental tenet of the so-called Andean common law is persuasion, aimed at restoring group unity.[15] Therefore, when naming communal authorities and justices of the peace (who are nominated by the community and ratified by the state), the communal assembly takes into consideration mainly who is considered "fair" and "upright" in the eyes of the group. The authorities are individuals who know the people and the customs of the community. This model is obviously an idealization, in practice eroded by conflicts derived from the expansion of the market, peasant differentiation, the increasing prioritization of family over communal interests, and the consolidation of power cliques within the community (Gálvez 1987). But, these problems were not so great as to nullify the general principles outlined above. In addition, Shining Path proved so oblivious to reality that, instead of taking advantage of these contradictions, it stumbled into them and found itself trapped in intracommunal and intercommunal conflicts.

Beyond economic factors, there certainly existed other reasons, of equal or more importance, for peasant rejection of Shining Path. Nicario narrated an episode during the destruction of Allpachaka that reveals the complexity of motivations. "Of the cattle we slaughtered what we could. But when we were slaughtering them the peasant women began to cry: 'the poor animals, why are you killing them like that, how are they to blame?' How the women began to cry, 'poor little thing,' saying this, saying that, we left them. . . . We intended to slaughter all of the cattle but we couldn't kill them because the peasant women started crying." The image of the peasants hugging cows and bulls to avoid their death is not simply romantic and earthy. The women are herders, and the death of their cattle is for them the equivalent of the destruction of a factory for its workers. But if it is true that the herders were *not only* telluric and lovers of life, it is *also* true that they were people who appreciated the lives of their animals.

In Umaro and in Purus (Huanta province), I have seen mature men, elders and former authorities, cry inconsolably when they recalled the mutilating and unbearable *form* in which Shining Path killed. As if slaughtering a hog, the cadres made the victim kneel and proceeded to cut the throat, allow the blood to run, and sometimes crush the victim's head with a stone. In senderista language, the point was "to smash with a stone as if [destroying] a frog." They did this with the deluded economicist pretext of "saving ammunition." And afterwards, they often refused to allow the burial of the victims, the universal rite of mourning. If we take into consideration the violence exercised by the Armed Forces, which in the period 1983 to 1985 and in many zones even until 1988 far outstripped Shining Path violence, we can begin to get an idea of the inferno through which the region lived.[16] One must recall that if all of Peru had suffered the same level of violence as Ayacucho, the national death toll would have been some 450,000, not 25,000.

Ponciano del Pino (1996) describes the most surprising case of peasant repudiation of Shining Path for reasons that transcend mere "rational choice." Evangelical Pentecostals along the Apurímac River resisted Shining Path on the basis of another "total identity." The result was a not-so-holy war that concluded with the triumph of the Evangelicals and, inadvertently, resulted in a victory for drug traffickers as well.

The frequency of death, the social proximity of the victims, and the traumatic context in which the killings took place, also affected the rural youth. They were torn between party ideology on the one hand, and their family ties, communal connections, and common sense on the other. "Of course, the families grieved, but they did not know . . . when these executions were carried out, it could happen in a moment. . . . The people looked and they said, if we happen to know anything or if we see someone who was doing something for the party, it is better to remain silent. If the police come, our line will have to be: 'we don't know; we don't know.' We also had to give this answer. Some did not agree but they endured, they did not say anything, they remained silent and some peasant men, some peasant women, left crying. It always caused fear and grief when killings were done in front of the people" (Nicario). The pain and the grief were two of the various loose threads that, over succeeding years, the extended family and subsequently the rondas, began to pull, until they began to untangle the senderista knot.[17]

THE PHYSICAL SECURITY OF THE POPULATION

The military occupation revealed a fourth fissure, the product of a discrepancy between traditional strategies of Andean domination and the strategy of "people's war." According to Maoist guerrilla precepts, *when the enemy advances, we retreat*. When the Armed Forces entered Ayacucho, Shining Path retreated in order to protect its own cadres. But in doing so Sendero Luminoso clashed with the role of the traditional Andean patrón who *protects* his clients.[18] Thus, Shining Path's retreat left many sectors of the population feeling that they had been greatly deceived. The following account relates what occurred in a hamlet in the valley of Huanta. Similar accounts, with minor variations, were repeated in various other testimonials. "They told us: it is necessary to be ready for the war, to defeat the enemy. We had believed them. But once they attacked Huanta after attacking and killing two guardias they escaped through here and they screwed us; they turned us over; they practically sold us out. Well, this is not manly [*eso no es de hombres, pues*]" (Walter, peasant).

For sectors of the population that Shining Path was not capable of protecting, the Armed Forces became a "lesser evil," or, in any case, an even more powerful patrón than Shining Path, with which it was necessary to retain good relations. This was, moreover, one of the objectives of the genocidal offensive of 1983–1984: to dry up the water in which the senderista fish swam by terrorizing the peasantry and preventing support for Shining Path. What is surprising is that, despite its severity, in many places this strategy did not function perfectly.

Blockage of the First Ruptures

In reality, while it did make already-existing fissures more visible, the overriding consequence of the Armed Forces' strategy in those years was to block the development of contradictions between the peasants and Shining Path. Shining Path was capable of resealing these first points of rupture because, upon unleashing a genocidal violence, the Armed Forces converted the countryside of Ayacucho into an Armageddon. In many instances, this made Shining Path appear as the "lesser evil." Such was the case in the valley of Huanta, according to Coronel (1996). In the words of Shining Path: they burned the prairie and "the reaction fanned the fire."

RESISTANT ADAPTATION

But the "lesser evil" was an external force. The peasants did not internalize Shining Path ideology. Rather, they displayed what Stern (1990) has called "resistant adaptation." The peasants' pragmatic acceptance of the early years did not grow into long-term identification with the Shining Path project. Except in a few pockets, the relationship settled into one of resistant adaptation, located somewhere between acceptance and open rebellion. The following testimonial, from a community of the province of Sucre, clearly illustrates what we mean by resistant adaptation, "The lieutenant governor [of the community] continued [exercising his authority] but clandestinely, that is, when the *compañeros* come we say that we do not have a lieutenant, that we have not had one for some time, that they have taken our stamps away, and so forth . . . and when the reaction comes, fine, they present themselves, in other words, the authorities come out so that there are no problems in the community, that is, they are simply clandestine" (Pedro, young adult peasant). The concept is somewhat similar to that which Scott (1985) calls "the weapons of the weak," which given the extreme situation of that time were the only weapons available for the peasantry. In the following account by a sixty-one-year-old peasant woman from Acos-Vinchos, recorded by Celina Salcedo, the astuteness of resistant adaptation acquires aspects of the picaresque.

> When they had come the *tuta puriq* have told us: "tomorrow in the afternoon you are going to form up and there we will see," they told us, and we were all afraid, thinking: what are they going to do with us? Surely they are going to kill us. When they had gone, everyone got together, men and women, big and small; don Constantino, Jesús, and

don Teodosio have learned and they told us: "we are going to form up like they said and then we'll say we are going to stand watch, and afterwards, when they are all here, we will shout 'the soldiers (*cabitos*)[19] are coming;' and we will come in running. And then they will leave." That's how they told us. [The next day] just as we had agreed, those who had been standing watch started shouting and running and saying "the cabitos are coming! The cabitos are coming!" Then the tuta puriq started to run and escape like crazy. Since then they haven't come back.

EXTERNALIZATION

One shattering episode symbolizes how Shining Path regressed once again into an external actor: the massacre of more than eighty peasants in the community of Lucanamarca (Víctor Fajardo province) in April 1983. Abimael Gúzman himself justified the massacre:

> Confronted with the use of armed bands and reactionary military action, we responded decisively with one action: Lucanamarca. Neither they nor we will forget it, of course, because there they saw a response that had not been imagined. There more than 80 were annihilated, this is the reality, and we say it, here there was excess. . . . [But] our problem was to give a bruising blow to restrain them, to make them understand that the thing was not so easy. In some occasions, such as this, it was the Central Leadership itself that planned the actions and ordered everything, that is how it was. . . . I reiterate, the principal thing was to make them understand that we were a hard bone to chew, and that we were ready to do anything, anything. (Guzmán 1988: 19–20).

Shining Path decided to compete blow-for-blow with the state in the exercise of violence against the population and to beat the state on this terrain as well. Several years later, Guzmán would continue to proclaim that "the triumph of the revolution will cost a million deaths."[20]

Thus, beginning in 1983, most of the region, with a few exceptions, was besieged by two objectively external armies. Each entered the battlefield from opposite extremes. One of the principal slogans of Shining Path was "the party has a thousand eyes and a thousand ears." To put it brutally, in these times Shining Path knew those they killed, even in Lucanamarca; the peasants who submitted to Sendero's dictates would survive. But while the party had a thousand eyes and a thousand ears, the Armed Forces were blind, or, rather, color-blind. They saw only black and white. Recent arrivals in the region, they tried to reproduce in the Andes the same repressive strategies that had proved successful in the Southern Cone. They did not perceive nuances; when they saw dark skin, they fired.

As for the rural youth, their trajectory during the years following the military intervention may serve as a guide to the overall trajectory of Shining Path. These youth, a critical link for Shining Path's expansion in the countryside, remained torn between two logics and two worlds. Torn in Allpachaka between the party orders to kill the cattle and the weeping of the shepherdesses, torn in La Mar between the party's governing logic, on the one hand, and local loyalties, grudges, and family vendettas, on the other. Torn between the party and the market as potential avenues to achieve "progress" and social mobility. The arrival of the military increased such tensions. When Shining Path decided to respond in kind against the state, thus mirroring the latter's violence against the population, a decisive disenchantment emerged among young people.

What happened among the youth of Rumi encapsulates such disenchantment. Nicario's political loyalty to the party broke (see note 17), while others, including a brother, opted to join the party and become the seedbed that nursed, along with other factors, the growth of Shining Path in various regions of the country. But in no other region would the scenario of Ayacucho's rapid growth in the early 1980s be repeated. In the following years, as it expanded into other zones, Shining Path's reliance on terror, and its character as an antisocial movement, would become even more marked (Wieviorka 1988).

In Ayacucho, Shining Path remained in many areas on the social frontier, in limbo, neither inside nor completely outside of the peasant society that adapted or resisted. Converted into one actor among others, armed and thus powerful, but without the kind of hegemony that it enjoyed in the first stage, Shining Path became either a faction within communities; or an implant within some communities caught up in confrontation with neighboring communities, acting out inter-communal conflicts that sometimes dated back even to pre-Hispanic times (Degregori 1985b); or a conqueror of populations that provided "support bases" (bases de apoyo) that would prove increasingly coerced over the medium run.

Second Points of Rupture

With ups and downs for Shining Path, this situation lasted in the region for a half-decade. For large sectors of the population, such a situation was an agonizing quagmire. For Shining Path, this interim represented the normal development of the strategy of protracted war (*guerra prolongada*): "'83 and '84 are the years of struggle around reestablishment versus counter-reestablishment, that is, the counterrevolutionary war to squash the new Power and reestablish the Old and the popular war to defend, develop, and construct the recently emerged Popular Power . . . from '85 until today [we fight for] the continuation of the defense, development, and construction that maintains the support bases [*bases de apoyo*] and [for] the expansion of the people's war to the whole ambit of our mountains from North to South" (PCP-SL 1986: 220). The 1986 pamphlet entitled "To Develop the People's War in Service of the World Revolution," from which this quote is taken, recounts six years of violence in a manner that erases the contradictions and fissures discussed above. For Sendero, such complications seemed less important. Indeed, Shining Path did continue to challenge the armed forces for control over various parts of the Ayacucho region. Even more important, it did indeed manage to "break the siege" and expand into other zones of the country, especially Junín and the Huallaga valley, the principal coca-leaf producing region in the world, and Lima. (See the essays by Manrique, Burt, and Rénique in this book.) Soon after the party's 1988 Congress, the leadership considered that the moment had arrived to attain "strategic equilibrium."

According to Mao (1971c), the "protracted struggle" develops through three strategic phases: defense, equilibrium, and offense. Strengthened by its 1988 Congress and in the midst of the worst crisis of the "old state" (this was the time when Alan García's regime had become a political and economic disaster), Shining Path decided in 1989 to move from the first stage to the second.[21] To achieve such equilibrium at the military level required more combatants, which Sendero could obtain from the youth wing that had always constituted its seedbed, or through forced recruitment in the rural zones where Sendero had established a presence. Shining Path needed more and better arms, which it could acquire based on its stronghold in the Huallaga Valley and its connection with drug traffickers. But if, as Mao said, the guerrilla army had to move among the masses like a "fish in water," then Shining Path needed not simply the peasants' neutrality or passive assent (the "resistant adaptation" discussed earlier) but their more active support. And it was precisely on this point that Sendero's problems increased. Shining Path's demands increased and they battered the fragile equilibrium of "resistant adaptation" that had prevailed in many places. More young recruits, more supplies, more participation of the population as an exposed "mass" (*masa*) in military actions, an intensified senderista discipline prone to the rapid and summary application of the death penalty, all of these pressures undermined adaptation and pushed for resistance. Repudiation became even more blatant in 1989–1990, as a national economic crisis coincided with a prolonged drought.[22]

Shining Path reacted by increasing violence against the peasantry. But, all this achieved was the proliferation of rondas, or "Committees of Civil Autodefense," to the point that, by 1990, Sendero had become trapped in a kind of trench warfare against the peasants (see Starn, in this volume). This constituted the first strategic victory for the Armed Forces and the first real defeat of Shining Path since the war had started. (This defeat was offset, however, by Shining Path's advances in the Amazon Basin, especially in coca-growing zones, and in the cities, especially in Lima. On the latter point, see Burt in this volume.)

Why this defeat of Shining Path? If we look from the perspective of peasant society, Shining Path and the Armed Forces followed opposite trajectories. While the former became more distant, the latter forged closer ties. As Shining Path grew more "external" to peasant society, the Armed Forces became more "internal" to the population. In 1983, the Armed Forces entered an unknown territory in which they exercised indiscriminate repression; anyone was a potential enemy. The marines—from the navy, the most racist branch of the military and the branch whose recruits were heavily drawn from Lima and the rest of the coast—played the key role in the provinces of Huanta and La Mar. Beginning in 1985, however, the army—whose soldiers were more largely drawn from the sierra folk (*serranos*)—replaced the marines. Toward the end of the decade, when the armed forces passed from indiscriminate to selective repression, one might say that they installed themselves at the frontiers of peasant society and began to penetrate it, first through the actions of veteran soldiers who had graduated from their obligatory military service ("*licenciados*") and increasingly in the 1990s, through aid-oriented policies (*políticas asistencialistas*) and infrastructural projects. Thus the military came to represent a state that, despite its extreme crisis, still had more cards up its sleeve than Shining Path, which could only offer more severe hardship. Finally, by recruiting youth who were allowed to do their obligatory military service in their own communities, and by distributing weapons to the rondas—even though these arms were merely shotguns—the Armed Forces, and the state that they represented, demonstrated that they had obtained hegemony in the zone.[23]

It is worth mentioning an important element of this reconquest: The Armed Forces did not seek total control of everyday life, as Shining Path did. To be sure, the obligatory weekly visits of the peasant "commands" to the barracks, the marches, and the attentions paid to the visiting army patrols could be inconvenient. But, the Armed Forces did not otherwise interfere greatly in the daily life of the population, worn down by senderista zeal.

By contrast, Shining Path grew more distant from the peasantry, which had passed from pragmatic acceptance, to resistant adaptation, and finally to overt rebellion against the party. In the initial years, the senderista cadres were natives of the region or had lived there for a long time, and the new recruits were local rural youth who enabled Shining Path to become a force within communities. From this privileged social location Shining Path began to retreat toward the frontiers of community identity, beginning in 1983. Along the frontiers it experienced the peasants' resistant adaptation, and from the frontiers it was eventually expelled by the rondas that closed off, often literally, an ever-expanding territory.

Thus, while the initial years the war made sadly famous the names of various communities demolished by the military—including Secce, Pucayacu, Accomarca, Umaro, Bellavista, Ccayara—by around 1988, it was Shining Path's massacres that populated the map of regional death. In little more than four years, between December 1987 and February 1992, an incomplete count provides us with a total of sixteen Senderista massacres of twelve or more persons (see the report in *Idéele* in no. 34, 1992). While the Armed Forces moved toward a policy of more selective repression,[24] Shining Path moved from "selective annihilations," which it justified as actions "accomplished without any cruelty, as simple and expeditious justice" (PCP-SL 1986), to great massacres. In many places, therefore, decisive sectors of the peasantry would opt for a pragmatic alliance with the Armed Forces (for further analysis, see Coronel 1996 and del Pino 1996).

Two anecdotes illustrate this evolution. In the early years of military intervention a whole mythology emerged around the marines. It was said that they included Argentine mercenaries. Even peasants who had long experienced discrimination could perhaps not imagine that actual Peruvians could treat their national compatriots in such a manner. In April 1994, in a truck that went toward the market of Chaca, in the heights of Huanta, I conversed with a leader of Chaca, who had lived in the Apurímac River zone in the worst years of the violence. He recalled the panic aroused by these supposed mercenaries:

> They lowered the helicopter shooting off their rounds. It could be a leaf that fell off a tree and right away they'd be shooting rounds. They didn't know how to walk, they didn't know the terrain, they were leftovers from the Malvinas War who had been asked to advise. They ended up castaways idling their time listening to strange music.

> They also had the Killers (*Matadores*). In a cage no more they stood, they did not go out. Through a little window they got food. They were male but they had hair down to here [he pointed to his waist]. Once they stuck a terrorist in the cage and they opened his heart and sucked and sucked on the blood that came out, saying "how delicious."[25]

Upon arriving in Chaca, however, we found a lone official of the army passing among hundreds of fair-goers, peasants, and merchants, like a fish in water, with only a pistol and two *piñitas* (a slang word for grenades, literally "little pineapples") hanging from his belt, "just in case." A lot of water had run under the bridges. In San José de Secce, the district seat, the conscripts doing their obligatory military service were Quechua-speaking locals.

By contrast, Shining Path ended up identified with the devil, the Antichrist, or with the terrible Andean *ñakaq* or *pishtaco*.[26] But as much or more than the massacres of comuneros, the event that best exemplifies the externalization of Shining Path in the region was the random death initiated in 1990 against the truck drivers on the Ayacucho-San Francisco route. In one of Shining Path's frequent blockades to demand quota payments (*cupos*) and settle "accounts in blood" (*cuentas de sangre*), one of the drivers escaped and notified a military detachment, which attacked and killed some senderistas. Shining Path retaliated by initiating an indiscriminate massacre of drivers, chosen practically at random.[27] This was the kind of reflex that had been typical of the Armed Forces in 1983 and 1984.

Shining Path's Blind Spots and Defeat

It is strange that Shining Path seemed to miss the significance of the proliferating rondas and the new relationship between the peasantry and the

Armed Forces. Sendero did not consider this development to be an important setback. On the contrary, in 1991 Shining Path proclaimed it was at last gaining "strategic equilibrium."

Until 1991, Shining Path documents did not include an in-depth analysis of the proliferating rondas. That year a Shining Path document, entitled "Let the strategic equilibrium shake the country more!," defined the rondas as mechanisms of counterrevolutionary "low intensity warfare" employed by Fujimori, the military, and Yankee imperialism (PCP-SL 1991a: 52). The document went on to provide a cumbersome *legal* analysis of legislation then under debate to legalize the autodefense committees.[28] Near the end of 1991, *El Diario,* the mouthpiece of Shining Path, went beyond definitions and offered an analysis radically estranged from reality. It affirmed that the rondas, or "armed goons" (*mesnadas*) in senderista slang, had "hit bottom," since "only five percent maintained themselves continuously since they were created by the Marines or the Army. The rest have been recomposed many times and lately dozens have been vacillating without direction, between dissolving and lining up against their mentors" (*El Diario* 1991:3).

Only in 1992 did the senderistas seem to take notice of what was going on. The Third Plenary of the Central Committee affirmed: "The problem is that they express an inflection; this is the problem . . . they have occupied some points and displaced us. So they have subjected the masses . . . with threats even of death, and now they are masses pressured by the enemy. So our problem here, what is it? It is that we are restricted in our infiltration work among the mesnadas and this we must correct in order to penetrate them, unmask them, undermine them, until we make them explode" (PCP-SL 1992). But the new directive, which included a greater emphasis on persuasion, arrived too late.

Shining Path's total disorientation reflected the various blind spots of the party or, if one prefers, of "Gonzalo thought." The party's vision included an "optimistic fatalism," derived from a teleological view of history; a concept of social and political actors as "essences in action," as carriers of structures that inexorably determined their trajectory; a perception of the peasantry as incapable of initiative; a strategy of *prolonged* war through the construction of support bases and liberated zones; and, finally, a disdain for Andean culture. These blind spots meant that Sendero's reading of the Peruvian and global situations did not fit well with real dynamics of Peru and the world.[29]

I have already referred to the themes of violence and the discordance between the logic of the party and social dynamics. It only remains to add
that, in 1982, the decision of the party to increase the violence and the
subsequent initiation of executions (*ajusticiamientos*) contributed to deepen
divisions between Shining Path and the population. And in the late-1980s,
the increase of violence against the rondas reaffirmed those who were
already convinced, convinced the unconvinced, and impelled entire communities into an alliance with the Armed Forces. For Shining Path, violence
was not merely the midwife, but rather the mother and motor of history.
According to their documents, this history did not advance in a straight line
but rather with zigzags and retreats. But such set-backs occur strictly within
the limits of a predetermined general trajectory; more than a script, history
fulfills its destiny.

The Armed Forces, for example, were tagged in the Shining Path documents now and again as "specialists in defeat." Their essential character
could not really change. The military could only go on fatally revealing its
genocidal essence and its dependence on imperialism. In reality, however,
in the 1990s the Armed Forces left Shining Path "off-side" (to use a soccer
metaphor) by not fulfilling their preordained "destiny" of increasing massively their indiscriminate repression.[30]

The peasants, for their part, were for Sendero the "arena of contention between revolution and counterrevolution" (PCP-SL 1991b: 4). Passive
actors, of zero worth, they only obtained value when added to one or another
band. Shining Path, for its part, was the depository of Truth, with a leader
who was a "guarantor of victory"—through his capacity to interpret the laws
of history. The peasants were "condemned to triumph." Sooner or later,
through the development of the protracted popular struggle, the peasants
finally would follow their destiny and gravitate towards Shining Path like
butterflies to a light. Why? "Objectively, [the counterrevolution] does not
represent the interest of the people, we do" (PCP-SL 1991b: 4).

So there was no problem, at least no grave problem. According to Shining Path, the establishment of the "new power" in a zone could be followed
by the reestablishment of the old power for a period and later the counter-
reestablishment of the new power, and so on, until the consolidation of the
liberated zones was achieved and the new republic emerged. The proliferation of the rondas was seen as one more episode of "reestablishment."

The senderistas did not seem to notice that the prolonged character of the war and their strategies of constructing support bases clashed with the peasants' conception of time and space. Such considerations did not matter much, if at all, to Sendero. Yet, despite poverty, the reproduction of the peasantry took place substantially through the market.[31] The peasants, in particular youth, also had aspirations of social mobility that they learned in school and from the mass media. The periods in which families made their plans were measured in the cycles of life (human, agricultural, and animal) and in the time that it took for their children to mature. Such time markers were not those of the protracted people's war that, by the end of the 1980s, seemed to stretch out into unending cycles of establishment, re-establishment, and counter-reestablishment . . . ad infinitum. When Shining Path tried to impose an even tougher rhythm of war, precisely in the years when the peasants were suffering drought and economic crisis, the threads of adaptation finally snapped.

On the other hand, the physical spaces in which the peasantry operated to sustain and reproduce life were vast. Networks of kinship and ethnic origin encompassed both the countryside and the city, and could reach as far as mines in the high tablelands (*punas*) and coca fields in the jungle (*selva*). Such spatially dispersed networks clashed with Shining Path's strategy of taking over bounded territorial spaces and converting them into support bases that tended toward isolation. After the initial years, and especially when the Armed Forces arrived and the peasants found themselves caught between two fires, large numbers of those who could leave joined the flood of refugees to Ayacucho city and to Lima. In many places, Shining Path ended up ruling over half-empty spaces, in which only the weakest remained trapped, that is, poor, monolingual peasants who lacked urban connections, and native Asháninkas of the jungle zones, were those most subject to Shining Path's "total domination."

ANDEAN CULTURE

Shining Path's clash with peasants' notions of time and space was part of a wider collision with Andean culture. I do not refer to notions such as the myth of the hero-redeemer Inkarrí, or the inversion of the world through a *pachacuti* (cataclysm) but rather to the ensemble of institutions important for the Ayacuchan Quechua peasantry. This ensemble included the extended family, the community, principles of reciprocity, generational age hierarchy, and rituals, fiestas, and religion in general.

The religious clash merits particular comment. According to del Pino (1996), the senderistas were exasperated by the militant zeal of the Protestant Evangelicals (who won considerable converts in the countryside) and their refusal "to serve two masters." As for Andean religion and popular Catholicism, Shining Path considered such beliefs archaic and disgusting, and actively tried to suppress community rituals and fiestas.

In addition to the fiestas' economic costs, viewed through a utilitarian lens, the party seemed discomforted by the "inversion of the world" that marked the ambience of fiestas. "Total power" did not permit such openings. Senderista fears were not unfounded. In several places, including Huancasancos and Huaychao, it was during such celebrations that the population rebelled. In a community in Vilcashuamán, the Senderistas suppressed the fiesta "because suddenly when we are in fiesta they might betray us, there could be problems, they say" (testimony of Pedro).

Shining Path's disdain for the cultural manifestations of the Quechua-speaking peasantry was based in a particular theory. "Maoism teaches us that a given culture is a reflection, on the ideological plane, of the politics and the economy of a given society." (*El Diario* 18 September 1989). If this were true, then Andean art and culture were mere remnants of the past, a "reflection of the existence of man under landlord oppression, which reflects the technological and scientific backwardness of the countryside, which reflects the customs, beliefs, superstitions, feudal and anti-scientific ideas of the peasantry, product of centuries of oppression and exploitation that have subsumed it in ignorance. . . . This is the character of what is called 'folklore'" (Márquez 1989).

Parting from this theory and practice, I believe it is valid to characterize the senderistas as the new mistis, influenced by schooling and by Marxism.[32] In a previous work (Degregori 1989b) I likened the senderistas with a third brother of the Aragón de Peralta family, protagonists of José María Arguedas's *Todas las Sangres*. If we take as an example another novel by Arguedas, *Yawar Fiesta*, it is easy to identify Don Bruno with the traditional mistis (Julián Arangüena, for example) who were in favor of the "Indian-style bullfight," and Don Fermín with the national authorities and the "progressive" mistis who opposed the "Indian bullfight" and tried to "civilize" it by bringing a Spanish bullfighter to Puquio. This group would include the university *chalos* (bilingual youth who have been educated and urbanized) who seek "the progress of the town" and help to contract the bull-fighter. But the Indians of the Qayau ayllu manage to capture the ferocious bull Misitu; the university students succumb to the will of the comuneros, and as they are overcome with happiness and pride, they put aside for the moment their "desires for progress." The Spaniard fails in the bullfight and it is the Indians who jump in the ring, to the joy of the progressive mistis. In the last line of the novel, the mayor turns to the subprefect: "See, Señor Subprefect? These are our bullfights. The true *Yawar Fiesta!*"

The ending would have been different if the third brother had been there, who might easily be identified with hypothetical senderista students or professors who would not have succumbed to the strength of the Indians of Qayau. If Shining Path had been present, it might have killed Misitu or prohibited the fiesta. If the fiesta had been permitted, the party would have framed the matter as a strictly tactical concession and perhaps managed to suppress the pride that overcame the Puquiano students.

It is impressive to observe that, in the 1980s, in the Peruvian sierra, the conflict between mistis and Indians portrayed forty years earlier in *Yawar Fiesta* was partially replicated, and that, once again, the mistis, converted into "revolutionaries," ended up defeated by the "Indians," transformed into *ronderos*.

Notes

This chapter focuses on the northern provinces of the department of Aya-cucho. It includes a reworking of materials from Degregori 1991c, which includes testimonies collected in the communities in Cangallo, Huanta, La Mar, Sucre, and Huancasancos. In particular, I refer to an interview with "Nicario," a youth from "Rumi," (a pseudonym for a community in Cangallo) who was a senderista *miliciano* between 1980 and 1983. In the testimonies real names do not appear, only pseudonyms. I do not mention the specific places where the testimonies were recorded, only the provinces. I thank Carlos Loayza, Celina Salcedo, Alex Muñinco, and other friends who remain anony-mous for interviews during the 1980s. I also thank José Coronel and Ponciano del Pino for their invaluable collaboration in discussing these topics and dur-ing my visits to Ayacucho in recent years.

1   Arce Borja, ed. 1989: 142–43.
2   This weakness was, in part, the consequence of a trajectory that Shining Path developed over the course of the 1970s. The resulting project was fundamen-talist in ideology, an "anti-social-movement" (Wieviorka 1988) in its political

stance, and, in its practical organization, a "war machine" that did not prioritize political work in social organizations, communities, or federations, except
in the party's own "generated organizations." These party organizations were
to form the "transmission belt" between the party and the "masses." On the
composition of Shining Path up to 1980 and the evolution of the Shining Path
project, see Degregori 1996.

3   This occurred in the *punas* of Huanta, as José Coronel explains in his essay in
Degregori, ed. 1996.

4   The state as a route to mobility was not an alien notion for them, if we
take into consideration that the bureaucracy of the small towns traditionally
formed part of the old *misti* power structure.

5   Nicario's younger brother, for example, joined the guerrilla column and lived
as a "night walker" (*tuta pureq*) between 1983 and 1986 until, ill, he responded
to the call of his family and went down to Lima. But even some time afterward, when he no longer had an organizational connection to Shining Path, he
did not want to say anything to me about his experience beyond reciting the
official party line.

6   For the peasantry, attending school and receiving an education—understood
as literacy in Spanish—signified passing from blindness to vision, or from
night to day. See Montoya 1980, Degregori 1989b.

7   The complete opposite occurred: massive migration to the cities from those
rural zones where violence had been unleashed and a "dirty war" had begun.
Regarding the utopian ideals of Shining Path youth, see the complete testimonial of Nicario in Degregori 1991c.

8   Nicario participated in the first party-organized planting in Chuschi (Cangallo
province), a community where Shining Path initiated its armed struggle on
17 May 1980. His account is reminiscent of sowing crops, in early times, in the
land designated for the Sun, the Inca, or the landowner. In the eight hectares of
communal land were congregated sixty teams of oxen of Chuschi and of neighboring communities; in the four corners of the plot they planted a red flag. "At
the beginning they set off twelve sticks of dynamite, at twelve six sticks, and in
the afternoon another twelve. The work was successful, but the party did not
get the harvest because the army came in" (Nicario). In Chaca (Huanta province), according to a personal communication of José Coronel, the party did
carry out the harvest in 1983, which resulted in the first rupture with peasants.

9   Lima is an extreme case, but not even the medium-sized cities of the sierra depended principally on their immediate rural hinterlands. See E. Gonzales 1992.

10 In other cases, cadres from outside received negative evaluations, and the local
milicianos appeared to be more understanding. Alejandro, a young university
student, the son of peasants, expressed his opinion about one of these cases,
in which the irresponsible manner in which the cadres faced military confrontation was evident. "It appears that they were not good cadres those who led

the group in Allpachaka; they argued that we were going to win the war, that we were going to take their helicopters, that not to worry because there would be arms for everyone." And he adds, "I think that it depends on the zone, in others there were good elements." This comment is important because it illustrates the wide variety of situations that emerged.

11 Regarding those senderistas who had opposed the position of initiating armed struggle, Guzmán (1989: 155) stated: "We will uproot the poison herbs, this is pure poison, cancer of the bones will take us over; we can not permit it, it is putrification and sinister pus, we cannot permit it . . . we will burn, and uproot this pus, this poison, to burn it is urgent." Regarding Shining Path discourse and purifying violence in the context prior to the beginning of the armed struggle, see Degregori 1996. On the necessity of intensifying the violence for the advance of the revolution around 1982, see Gorriti 1990: chapter 5.

12 PCP-SL December 1982, quoted in Gorriti 1990: 283.

13 A sharp contrast is provided by the example of the Guards of the Iranian Revolution, who died as martyrs on the frontier with Iraq. In an interesting work on the Iranian revolution of 1979, Khosrokhavar (1993) presented a profile of the revolutionaries that showed similarities with the Peruvian case: middle-range provincial intellectuals (in the Iranian case, ayatollahs) and radicalized educated youth who were marginalized by and disillusioned with the Shah's modernization process. But the dynamics and results, as is well known, were very different.

14 A discussion of political violence versus structural violence is beyond the scope of this essay. It is sufficient to note that the latter type of violence substantiated Mao's famous phrase, which Shining Path adopted: "rebellion is justified." The question is: what type of rebellion?

15 Many times the conflicts were resolved in competitions or even ritualized battles, for example, in carnivals. Underlying this vocation for restitution of unity after the conflict is the concept of *tinkuy*. See Ansión 1989.

16 An analysis of the violence of the state and the Armed Forces in Ayacucho also exceeds the limits of this essay. A testimonial regarding the raving, racist violence exercised by members of the Armed Forces in these same years can be found in Degregori and López Ricci 1990.

17 Nicario, for example, was torn between his younger brother, who pressured him to join the guerrilla column, and his other brothers, who called from "the other path" (the informal economic sector) in Lima. In 1983 he opted for this second option and began a mini-business. Over the following years there were other, isolated cases of deserters (*arrepentidos*), which became a significant flow with the expansion of the rondas.

18 Shining Path promised to do so: "Don't worry, we will protect you," said the youth to the women of Rumi who wept as they saw the army trucks descending the highway towards the community. But in the majority of cases, the

senderistas were not in any condition to fulfill their promise and the population became a "terrain of dispute" between the two competing armies.

19 "Cabitos" was the name used for soldiers in the region. It referred to the Los Cabitos military cuartel located in the outskirts of the departmental capital.

20 For a sharp contrast with Shining Path, consider the Zapatista Army of National Liberation (Ejército Zapatista de Liberación Nacional; EZLN) in Mexico: see Collier and Lowery 1994.

21 It is beyond the scope of this essay to discuss the extreme voluntarism that led Guzmán to believe that Shining Path could achieve strategic equilibrium at that time. Tapia (1996) analyzes in detail the differences between Mao's equilibrium in China and the situation that Peru experienced leading up to 1990. See also Manrique 1995a.

22 See Ponciano del Pino's essay in this book for more detailed analysis of these pressures. In Junín and other departments of the central sierra with a greater mercantile development, events progressed at a quicker pace. Until 1987–1988, the peasantry in the high zones had witnessed with astonishment, not without sympathy, Shining Path's destruction of the great SAIS (Sociedades Agrícolas de Interés Social, large agrarian units created by the agrarian reform program of the Velasco regime; see essays by Rénique and Manrique in this volume). But soon the majority of the population passed into opposition, especially in the valleys of the Mantaro, Cunas, and Tullumayo, the breadbaskets of Lima, when Shining Path sought to cut off commerce, directly or indirectly, by blowing up bridges and destroying roads. See also Manrique 1989.

23 The distributions began in 1990, as Alan García's administration breathed its last gasps. The situation was legalized in 1992 by Legislative Decree 747, which recognized the Committees of Civil Autodefense and permitted "the possession and use of arms and munitions for civil use."

24 Military repression continued to produce victims, however. During these same years, Peru also became the world's leading country in persons "disappeared" by the state (*Idéele* 1992).

25 If one believes erroneously that these personages, a mixture of Andean humanoid monsters (*pishtacos*) and the Rambos of video-movie culture, are exclusively the product of the hallucinatory imagination of our informant, consider the ferocious testimony of "Pancho," who served in the marine infantry in Ayacucho (Degregori and López Ricci 1990).

26 In Purus, in October 1994, recalling the ways in which Sendero killed, a former leader insisted that the senderistas were not human but rather devils. On the identification of Shining Path with the Antichrist, see del Pino 1996. On the identification of Shining Path with the *ñakaq* of the Andean tradition, who assassinates his victims in order to rob their body grease, see Isbell 1992.

27 Ponciano del Pino, in a personal communication, called my attention to this episode. TV Cultura filmed a video of a convoy of vehicles that were attacked—

some were burned—in 1991, on the Libertadores highway that runs between Ayacucho and Pisco.

28 It is evident that at least this part of this document is a transcription of an oral intervention by Guzmán. The decree is analyzed article by article, with numerous notations such as "are [the directives] for the emergency zones or not? This is the problem, the previous article does not say anything." (PCP-SL 1991a: 53).

29 For a more specific analysis of senderista strategy, which lies beyond the scope of this essay, see Manrique 1995a; Tapia 1996.

30 We do not overestimate the changes in the Armed Forces, nor do we forget the high degree of demoralization that the military suffered by the end of the 1980s. Nor can we say what would have come to pass had Guzmán not been captured. Toward the end of the decade of the 1980s the counterinsurgency actions seemed to verge toward a "Guatemalan solution." Fortunately, history took a different path and the Armed Forces developed a strategy that can be described as "nongenocidal authoritarianism." (Degregori and Rivera 1993).

31 *Editor's note:* For studies of how such peasant strategies were forged historically in the Andes, see Larson, Harris, and Tandeter 1995.

32 The utilization of Quechua language, Ayacuchan music, and "chicha" music by the senderistas remains to be studied. The use of Quechua by senderistas seems instrumentalist. The *huayno,* music of the sierra, with a simple change of lyrics, becomes "art of a new type." But we still do not know, nor in what measure, if behind the political instrumentalism of the new art is hidden a secret enjoyment of the music—desiring without wanting to desire. In any case, the Montoya brothers (Montoya et al. 1987: 40) have noted perceptively that "strange and terrible is our country; the dominant class that disdains and abuses the Indians also uses their language to express its deepest emotions."

FIVE

Family, Culture, and "Revolution":

Everyday Life with Sendero Luminoso

Ponciano del Pino H.

❖ Until recently it was very difficult to study the internal dynamics of the Communist Party of Peru-Shining Path (Partido Comunista del Perú-Sendero Luminoso; PCP-SL). We did not understand Shining Path's social logics and motivations, and the contradictions woven from within. Similarly, it was difficult to discern Shining Path's social composition and mechanisms of internal control, and the cultural and ethnic values it incorporated. Thus, it was difficult to analyze Shining Path's problems and its possibilities, its triumphs and its limitations, not only as a matter of military strategy, but also as the conservation and conquest of the social bases that facilitated its reproduction.

Work on Shining Path has focused largely on the origins and organization of the armed group, ranging from studies of the political and ideological profile of the party to research on sociological profiles of its militants. These studies have examined the factors that contributed to its growth and its social base of support.[1] To a certain extent, directly or indirectly, the analysis has best helped us understand the inner circle of power, the privileged pinnacle that guided the revolution and forged a political line, that is, the "heroic" discourse of a "Holy Family."[2]

Ideology—the "Guiding Philosophy"—has, to be sure, had tremendous impact among the cadres and the support base by nullifying individual personality and guiding conduct. Nonetheless, ideology has also been modified by the process of incorporation. Internalization of the official belief system becomes more flexible as one descends from the pinnacle toward the social base, and as new contexts emerge in the process of the war. In general terms, one finds among the militants a transition from an initial disposition toward self-sacrifice—"the quota"—to a greater rationalization of violence. On the other hand, in the process of war, the people in the social base express their own intentions, motivated by a conjunction of familial and cultural factors, which in many cases differ from the official partisan discourse. Thus they alter the party's will, the balance of power, and the course of the war.

This essay attempts to approach an understanding of daily life and social relationships within Shining Path. It attempts to understand family and culture as factors that came to weigh against the discourse and to provide an alternative understanding of the party, the war, and the violence. The study thus uncovers internal tensions that accumulated as the years went by. We seek to understand daily life and social relations among the militant cadres, the combatants, and the so-called "masses" (masas) in Shining Path's "People's Committees," and the responsibilities and functions that corresponded to each of these three segments.[3] We argue that the political discourse of Shining Path, whose classist vision is rationally absolutist, constructed the militants and the "masses" as fighters joined together in the service of the revolution, whose only will was to kill or to die for the party. Classist and revolutionary values were to rule over affective ties, traditional family relations, and daily life. That is, Shining Path stopped responding to the population's most basic and felt needs.

When this happened—when Shining Path's discourse did not satisfy the population's deepest needs, not only subsistence but also affective needs and social and cultural values—doubts began to surface. Shining Path was no longer fulfilling the aspirations of its grassroots supporters or *bases*. It was in this context that two distinct logics, often difficult to discern because of terror and silence, began to develop. Over time, they would shape the daily practices of resistance that altered the "revolutionary process." President Gonzalo's scheme of party reproduction, and the life scheme imposed by the party's disciplinary apparatus, would come under question as they collided with the profound and basic felt needs of the supposed bearers of the disciplinary apparatus.

Human needs subverted Shining Path's artificial order. The militants and the "masa" evolved from perpetrators of Shining Path violence to resistant victims, who eventually eroded and battered the political and military structure of the party. Shining Path's problems began when there developed a resistance in its own bases that placed the viability of its whole project in question.

When this happened, Shining Path reinforced its mechanisms of control over the population. Voluntary action or initiative was blocked. The supposed support bases and even the base committees themselves become zones of imprisonment, akin to concentration camps amid the terror and the power of "total domination." This was the reality that the masses, and even the combatants themselves, had to live and confront daily.

Our empirical material consists of testimonies collected in three Shining Path bases in Ayacucho: Sello de Oro, located in the province of La Mar; Viscatán, in the province of Huanta; and the Popular Open Committee (Comité Popular Abierto) of the Ené River Valley, which was connected to Viscatán. (The first two, Sello de Oro and Viscatán, were located on the tropically forested eastern slopes of the Andes mountains, a region known as the *ceja de selva* or "eyebrow of the jungle." See detailed map of the guerrilla zone, later in this chapter.) The sources include testimonies from combatants and members of the "mass" (*"masa"*) who were with Shining Path. In addition, in order to examine the composition of the members of one Popular Open Committee, the research included a survey of thirty people of the Sello de Oro Committee, who turned themselves in under the Repentance Law (Ley de Arrepentimiento) in October, 1993.[4]

Ayacucho: Chronology of War and Fear

In May 1980 Shining Path initiated the armed insurrection that, in one form or another, has lasted until the present [1995].[5] The war did not develop as a linear process, but as a trajectory shaped by the criss-crossing actions of distinct political forces, as well as by the diverse positions and responses among the population. In this complex process the participation of the peasant population acquired importance. Once they overcame fear, the peasants confronted their adversaries and "lifted heads" (*levantó cabeza*), in the words of one peasant.[6]

Huamanga, Cangallo, and Víctor Fajardo were the provinces favored by Shining Path for the political work that intensified in 1977 and 1978. When the war began, ideology defined its course. The "people's war" (*guerra popular*) would progress from the countryside toward the city and the peasantry would provide the principal base of the revolution. The countryside offered the possibility of reproducing the cadres, by supplying food as well as additional young people who would come to form the "iron legions" of the Popular Guerrilla Army. Sendero would establish its first "support bases" (*bases de apoyo*), administered and governed by the party, in the countryside.

In the early years of preparation and war, therefore, Shining Path emphasized political work and building ties to the peasant masses.

The peasants' unmet economic and social needs facilitated Shining Path's ability to approach the rural population. Before the 1970s, the various organizations and institutions present in the region—the church, the political parties, and the state—had not been capable of channeling the demands of the Ayacucho population. Unlike in Puno (Rénique 1991a, and essay in this volume), Ayacucho had experienced a crisis of historical representativity. In the 1970s the Universidad Nacional de San Cristóbal de Huamanga, recently reopened, became known for reformist and leftist politics; the Velasco government attempted to establish a certain state presence in the southern sierra; and political rivalries and social movements proliferated. In short, many new interlocutors and attempts at political mediation emerged in the 1970s, particularly as the transition to the civilian government in the 1980s drew near. In this context, Shining Path gained social spaces by offering— via armed struggle—concrete alternatives in the face of structural problems of backwardness, abandonment, poverty, and marginalization. Rival political forces seemed ineffective and were dismissed by Shining Path as unconvincing and illegitimate. In these conditions, Shining Path appeared, to some, as the only voice capable of opening spaces and gaining certain sympathizers in the countryside. (For further discussion and context, see the essays in part I of this volume.)

Shining Path, moreover, offered a system of order, in contrast to the arbitrary rule of the authorities, police, merchants, and teachers. Sendero seemed to buttress ethical and moral values in crisis by punishing adultery, alcoholism, vagrancy, robbery, and cattle rustling. It seemed to offer not only a just and ordered society, but solutions to concrete problems that the state and capitalism had not addressed (Manrique 1989). In the north of the department of Ayacucho, peasants responded with a certain diffuse sympathy, marked by varying degrees of commitment and acceptance. Within this general context, generational and ethnic factors held significance. Youth more readily identified with the party and seemed disposed to join and to fight, while adults from more traditional and ethnically identified communities were most skeptical of such sacrifices.

In some cases, willingness to collaborate with Shining Path was reinforced by the military interventions that began in 1983. Indiscriminate repression, which did not differentiate between distinct degrees of support for Shining Path, obligated some communities to draw closer to Sendero, now viewed as the lesser (and necessary) evil. Inadvertently, the military occupation reinforced ties between Shining Path and the peasantry in some zones. Nonetheless, in 1983 and 1984 the Armed Forces dealt strong blows to the guerrillas, as even Abimael Guzmán himself (1988) later admitted. These circumstances obliged Shining Path to recruit sympathetic youth in order to replace fallen combatants and to maintain the support bases they had managed to build.

In other cases, however, Shining Path's "hardening" political line and authoritarian attitudes led to problems with the peasantry even before the military occupation. Early in 1982 Shining Path intensified actions oriented to "hammer" (*batir*) the countryside. The idea was to expel the state from the guerrilla zones, and to mount its first People's Committees as a new governing structure (see note 3). The guerrillas tried to "sweep out" (*barrer*) the authorities, the traditional bosses (*gamonales*), and the police. In other words, Shining Path sought to eliminate any presence of the state: "The key is to demolish [*arrasar*]. And to demolish means not to leave anything" (Gorriti 1990: 283). This meant imposing revolutionary authorities and organizational structures to replace expelled and assassinated officials. In places where the population resisted, *batir* meant "to raze, clean out the zone, leave an empty plain [*arrasar, limpiar la zona, dejar pampa*]."

From late 1982, in some high zones such as the *punas* of Huanta, Shining Path sought to impose its rule by demolishing the traditional communal authorities. Sendero was not able to perceive the degree of legitimacy enjoyed by these authorities and by the communities' ritualized social hierarchy and organization. For this reason, on 20 January 1983, less than a month after military intervention had begun, peasants in Huaychao and Macabamba assassinated seven young *senderistas,* in retaliation for the assassination of three communal authorities by Shining Path. The organizational coherence and tradition of these communities, based on hierarchical and ethnically configured structures, allowed them to respond to the authoritarianism and violence of Shining Path. In contrast to the valley populations—marked by small-holders (*minifundistas*) whose experiences included migration and schooling, and among whom Shining Path had managed to establish bases and form local cadres—the high zones resisted from the beginning.[7]

The massacre of eight journalists as "presumed senderistas," in the community of Uchuraccay on 26 January 1983, took place in this context.[8] In retaliation, Shining Path unleashed a wave of overt repression against hostile pueblos. A regional Shining Path leader described the brutal violence in August against the peasants of Uchuraccay in the following words: "We have swept out those *chutos* made of shit."[9]

For Shining Path, or at least for some of its principal cadres, the fight was not only against the "reactionary" government, the bourgeoisie, and the semi-feudal system, but also against the "brutish and ignorant" chutos, who did not understand the revolutionary project. It would not take long for Shining Path's public discourse of equality and justice for the peasants to become contaminated by an ethnic discourse, a hidden script that surfaced to reveal repugnance, intolerance, and racism.[10] (For background on this hidden script, see the essays by de la Cadena and Mallon in this volume.) Later, this secret script would also surface in regards to the ethnic minorities in the Valley of Ené, where sick and invalid Asháninkas would be labeled "parasitic burdens," useless and disposable. Paradoxically, these highland and Amazonian Indians constituted the poorest peasants, those for whom Shining Path claimed to fight.[11]

The response of the peasants of Huaychao in early 1983 marked the beginning of the daily horror that characterized the Ayacucho highlands in the 1980s. The cruelest experience occurred in the punas of Huanta, where sixty-eight communities disappeared as a result of repression by Shining Path and the Armed Forces, and in La Mar, where seventy-five more disappeared.[12] But devastating experiences occurred elsewhere as well. The killing of three Senderistas and the capture of another seven in Saccsamarca (in the province of Huancasancos) on 16 February 1983, would culminate two months afterwards with a massacre of over eighty peasants, in what since has come to be known as the Lucanamarca Massacre.

From then on, peace in the countryside was irrevocably broken. From the beginning of 1984, many communities organized *montoneras* (guerilla bands; the nomenclature reaches back to the independence wars), which is the term they first used to describe the Civil Autodefense Committees (CACS). In many cases the peasants themselves took the initiative in organizing the CACS; in other cases the committees formed under pressure from the army.[13] In any case, even when they were all very weak, the CACS posed the greatest threat to Shining Path. For this reason, the Central Directorate of Shining Path designed a "bruising" (*contundente*) response to these peasants, labeled as government "goons" (*mesnadas gobiernistas*) — simple pawns of the military without capacity for decision making or initiative.[14]

Shining Path had to face two serious challenges: to recover from the harsh blows inflicted by the Armed Forces in 1983–1984, and to confront the organization of some communities into Civil Autodefense Committees. The military presence forced Shining Path to retreat in two directions: eastward toward the *montaña,* the mountain slopes that descended to the jungle and northward toward the central sierra, by expanding its zones of influence toward Junín, Cerro de Pasco, Ancash, and Huánuco, which would become the new zones of operations. (For the retreat and expansion toward the central sierra, see Manrique in this volume.) The guerrillas had to divert the military's attention away from the Principal Regional Committee in Ayacucho.

From around mid-1982 Shining Path had begun to "conquer" bases in the eastern Ayacuchan jungle (*selva*) in order to provide zones of refuge from the Armed Forces. With this in mind, Shining Path established the "San Francisco Guerrilla Zone" (see figure 5.1), with its base of support in the montaña slopes of San Francisco and Santa Rosa, bordering with the sierras of San Miguel, Anco and Chungui in the province of La Mar. They did the same in Viscatán, in the ceja de selva of Huanta, bordering with the departments of Junín and Cuzco. Controlling these frontier zones would facilitate access to highland communities of the sierra as well as settlements in the lowland jungle.

The process of retreat marked a new stage in the development of the war. To maintain bases and control territories, Sendero would recruit additional youth, more by coercive than voluntary means. The guerrillas carried out forced recruitment in both sierra and selva communities. Young supporters were now obligated to join the struggle directly. In contrast to the cadres and militants of the first generation, who had assumed the political line of "total subordination" (*sujeción total*), many of these new militants participated under pressure and out of fear of retaliation. The pressure was particularly evident in the case of families who stayed within the zone controlled by the guerrillas but who resisted renouncing their values and their way of life. Aware of this reality, Shining Path knew that to permit any resistance or internal fractures would risk its forces and the course of the war. To reduce the risk required multiplying its mechanisms of control and subordination.

By 1988, this situation would become quite evident. The resistance of the CACS forced Shining Path into a wider retreat. Communities such as Sachabamba, Vinchos, Acos Vinchos, Huamanguilla—high-altitude communities in the north of the department—had accumulated experience and, above all, overcome fear. Terror and violence had ceased to paralyze a population that,

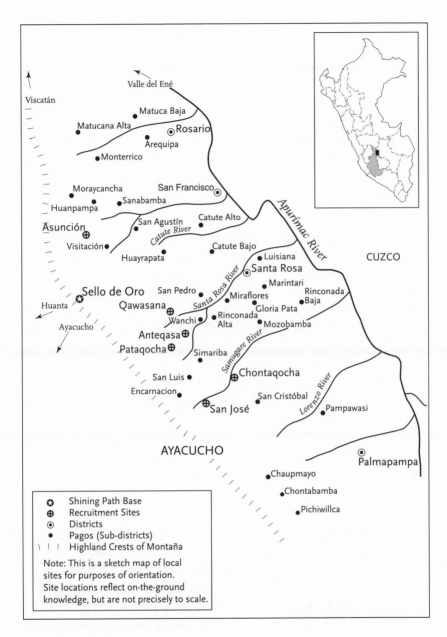

Figure 5.1. San Francisco (Sello de Oro) Guerrilla Zone.

on the contrary, began to resist. Many other such communities chose to move down to the valley towns and the provincial capitals, taking away the bases upon which Shining Path had supported its campaign. Probably the worst defeat for Shining Path in 1988 was its expulsion from the Apurímac valley by the CACS. The military defeat in Pichiwillca marked the guerrillas' definitive retreat from the zone. From then on, the CACS took the initiative and began to organize all of the hamlets of the valley as well as the higher sierra communities of Tambo and Huanta (Del Pino 1994b). In Ayacucho, the countryside was closing up against Shining Path. Sendero had to move on in order to gain control over a new region, open and strategically located: the Ené Valley.

The retreat of Shining Path greatly weakened its power in the Ayacucho region, where it lost territories and social bases. The military's response and the organized action of the civilian population stood in the way of Shining Path's consolidation in its "Principal Region," the historic region that had given birth to the party and initiated armed revolution. This reality cast doubt on Sendero's principal strategy, summarized in the well known and repeated slogan: "enclose the cities from the countryside" (*cercar las ciudades desde el campo*; R. González 1988). Abimael Gúzman, aware of the difficulties that Shining Path faced in the countryside, gave new emphasis to the party's work in the city in the First Congress of the Communist Party of Peru in 1988.

Shining Path's problems in the "Principal Regional Committee" were not only the result of external pressures from the peasantry and the Armed Forces. The problems also resulted from *internal* contradictions that arose within Shining Path's own People's Committees and support bases. The war and the changed composition of the militants had affected the party-military apparatus of Shining Path. Coercive recruitment was beginning to produce the first instances of resistance and repudiation to Shining Path authority.

From 1984 until about 1988, establishing and feeding the People's Committees presented little difficulty. The "masa" cultivated and provided food, while other supplies were obtained through war quotas (tributes) and assaults on merchants and truckers. These circumstances changed notably as the Armed Forces and the CACS passed to the offensive. As of March 1988, the CACS began to organize the Apurímac Valley and to put pressure on Shining Path's support bases in the montaña slopes. Greater territorial control by the organized population made it more difficult for the People's Committees to survive. These difficulties caused the population to question the viability of Shining Path's whole project. Confronted with increasing everyday difficulties, the demands of the "masa" on their commanders would reveal levels of interior resistance that had been silenced during the preceding years. This situation forced Shining Path to improve its system of control and domination. For Shining Path, the bases of support were the very essence of the popular war, without which the war could not continue, much less expand. At this point, Shining Path faced not only the challenge of building new bases of support but also that of conserving those it had once established. The internal problems compounded the external pressure.

Shining Path responded in two ways. First, it strengthened its system of internal control and domination by increasing punishments and exemplary violence within the People's Committees. Shining Path took its accumulated experience of repression against the general population and turned this knowledge inward, to impose "total domination" over the "masa." The second response, even more ruthless, consisted of increased violence against the population at large. The ferocity of senderista actions reached new heights and did not differentiate children from adults, women from men, old people from the able-bodied, or civilians from CAC patrollers (ronderos). All became enemies, from communities organized into CACs to civilians without connection to the war.

Several years earlier, between May 1985 and June 1986, Shining Path intensified its attacks against the population nucleated in the CACs (Granda 1989). The offensive, a kind of eruption of fundamentalist authoritarianism, was facilitated by the retreat of the navy and army from the countryside (Del Pino 1994b). By 1988–1989, Shining Path's actions had become more defensive and indiscriminate, as a result of its own limitations. This new tendency was embodied in the killing *of the family* of the president of the Board of Elections of Ayacucho a few days before the municipal elections of 1989. Shining Path attacks had normally been directed at the civil and political authorities themselves. The episode marked a new stage of indiscriminate attacks, in which the relatives of the authorities also became targets.

Fundamentalist cruelty resounded again with the massacre in December 1989 of forty-seven peasants in Paqcha and Andabamba, and of fifty peasants in Acos Vinchos the following month.[15] In both cases, their throats were slit and their heads smashed with stones. In July 1991, Shining Path attacked the Pentecostal church in Qano, massacring thirty-three churchgoers in the midst of worship by machine gunning them and setting them on fire. The previous month, an incursion by Shining Path into the town of San

Miguel had resulted in the death of fourteen civilian workers. That same year, Shining Path guerrillas went into the small hamlet in Tambo, Huayllao, and assassinated forty-seven peasants, including children and women. In July 1993, the guerrillas went into Matucana Alta in the ceja de selva and assassinated twelve peasants, six of them children. The following month, in Sapito, Shiriari, they killed sixty-two, including both settlers (*colonos*) and native Asháninkas. Shining Path used machetes and *chafles* to carry out these last two massacres.[16]

The victims were not limited to communities organized into CACs, but also included civilians without commitments to either side of the conflict. An attack of great impact occurred on 14 February 1993, when Shining Path murdered sixteen civilians in Qarapa, on their way from San Francisco to Ayacucho, and overturned three vehicles. In August they killed nine more civilians and burned two vehicles. Such rural attacks occurred frequently from 1991 through 1993. The victims were civilians, and included the most vulnerable members of the family: children, women, and the elderly.[17]

Rather than serving to reconstitute senderista forces, these cases of gratuitous cruelty expressed internal difficulties that Shining Path was suffering. The violence was a way to push aside or negate the painful reality of the crisis. Shining Path confronted internal resistance with tactics of terror that silenced all criticism. One tactic was the multiplication of mechanisms of control and submission of the "masas." Another was the display of cruelty, actions designed to create an image of power. The increased ruthlessness of the violence employed against the population was meant to terrorize, block, and paralyze the initial currents of resistance within Shining Path. More than power, this violence reflected fear; more than recovery and strength, it reflected exhaustion and weakness.[18]

Shining Path manipulated an image of power in order to suppress and break apart any resistance. From the beginning, even without an infrastructure of war weaponry, Shining Path sought to terrorize and paralyze opposition, to inspire fear by displaying overwhelming force that demolished the enemy. This logic meant that dozens of people, including youth, women, and children, participated in Shining Path assaults, some acting out of fear of retaliation. According to our tallies, in each Shining Path assault some 30, or 50, in some instances up to 100, people participated, but only about 5 carried firearms. After each attack, stories would be circulated among the population of armed legions of unimagined capacity. This myth was reinforced and massified by the media, which reproduced the fears of the people and—why not?—the fears of the media itself.

The civil defense patrols (rondas) had the advantage of knowing Shining Path's weaknesses. Many of the commanders of the CACS, including Kichca of Santa Rosa, Huayhuaco of Rinconada Alta, and Choque of Pichiwillca, among others, had participated previously in Shining Path ranks, in some cases serving as local officials (mandos). More than with arms, the rondas sustained themselves with their knowledge of Shining Path's weaknesses, and an overcoming of fear.

Sello de Oro: A Case Study of Senderista Social Bases and History

Analysis of Shining Path must consider two factors. First of all, as our analysis descends from the apex to the base of Shining Path's pyramid, we find that the motivations of the participants change and "the science of Marxism-Leninism-Maoism is contaminated by the rural Andean context" (Degregori 1991c: 398). Second, the war included offensives and retreats, processes of expansion and displacement, during which the composition and the intentions of the militants and the "masses" changed.

Studies of Shining Path reflect two tendencies. The predominant approach has been that proposed by Favre (1984) and subsequently developed by Degregori (1989a, 1990a, 1991c), Chávez de Paz (1989), and Manrique (1988a), among others. According to these scholars, the "de-peasantized" and "de-Indianized" population formed the backbone of Shining Path. The second approach, advocated mainly by foreign intellectuals and journalists, describes Shining Path as a movement of indigenous peasant revindication.[19]

A look at one base of support, Sello de Oro, suggests new elements and more complex social dynamics. Members of the base came mainly from the sierra and the upper montaña. Of the adults in Sello de Oro at the moment of its capitulation in October 1993, sixty-five came from the sierras of La Mar, eight from Huanta, three from Huamanga (Ayacucho), and two from Satipo (Junín).

Accusations that the highland population supported Shining Path brought on a wave of repression by the military in 1983. In order to escape, the communities of Paria, Balcón, Pamparaqay, and Challhuamayo, among others in the sierra of Tambo, and Chaca, Llaqllaq, Qisni, Maraycancha, Pulperia, Estera, and Rayama of the San Miguel sierra, retreated together with

Shining Path toward the montaña slopes that descended toward the eastern jungle. They had no better alternative than to flee with Shining Path.

Shining Path began to arrive in the high Andean communities of La Mar in 1980, in the hamlets of the Apurímac Valley in mid-1982. Shining Path's control of the San Miguel heights facilitated its occupation of the hamlets of the upper montaña—Wayrapata, Qawasana, Encarnación, Chontaqocha, Huanchi, and Rinconada Alta—where it established the first bases of support. From these bases, Shining Path began to visit the hamlets of the valley (see figure 5.1).

In the beginning, the population provided food to the guerrillas, took them in, and participated in "people's assemblies." The peasants had lacked such services as health and transportation. They suffered economically from the low prices of produce (such as coffee, *cube*—a plant used to make poison and insecticide—cacao, and *achiote,* which were monopolized by large merchants), and from constant devaluations of currency and rises in the cost of living. All of this meant that the inhabitants looked favorably on those who offered new hope for their lives. The peasants included wage-earning rural workers and small farmers (*minifundistas*) who had migrated to the selva two decades earlier in search of progress, but had never realized their dreams. On the contrary, many of their problems continued without resolution. For Reinaldo, a valley peasant, people accepted Shining Path "because before we had been practically marginalized."

Above all, young people would provide most of the collaboration with Shining Path—"more than the fathers, more than the *señores"*—because of a certain convergence between the discourse of the guerrillas and youthful aspirations. Shining Path promised to end the poverty, inequality, and marginalization from which they suffered. The hamlets (*pagos* or subdistricts) that initially supported Shining Path, among them Cielopunco, Gringoyacu, Anteqasa, Pataqocha, Qawasana, and Chontaqocha, were distant from the valley and lacked city-linked services.

With this support Shining Path formed the San Francisco Guerrilla Zone in 1983, consisting of five People's Committees: Sello de Oro, Vista Alegre (with its native Asháninka population), Santa Ana, Nazareno, and Broche de Oro. They also founded a zone of operations and a Popular Committee of Viscatán in the ceja de selva area of Huanta Province.

The discourse with which Shining Path initially presented itself to the communities did not emphasize the sacrifices that war would entail. Support was forthcoming because Shining Path appeared to provide the communities' needs; it ordered society and put an end to arbitrary acts by authorities and merchants. Shining Path signaled the advent of the new order when, in September 1982, it sacked a store in Santa Rosa that belonged to Edmundo Morales, the richest merchant in the valley. The corruption of the police forces and the authorities added justification to Shining Path's actions. But this initial experience would change substantially as the logic of war took over. Shining Path began to pressure the youth to participate in its attacks and to train for future combat. In 1983, Shining Path began to recruit because, they said, it was no longer time to be producing for the market and making money. The armed struggle demanded sacrifice and total dedication from each and every person; this implied producing the minimum necessary for survival and closing off production for the market and the city.

The first signs of peasant discontent emerged when children were drawn into the war. Mothers recalled that their children "were forced against their will, whether they wanted to or not, they showed them arms, knives, spears; if you don't accept it you'll die." The women might collaborate or accompany their children in actions, but "the fear is only for our children, for what they can take away from us." It was from the mothers, who appeared most sensitive to the suffering of their children, that the idea of resistance began to develop. The children's fate would justify the claim that Shining Path "has deceived us" (*nos han engañado*). These words would be spoken insistently.

Senderista demands obliged many families to flee from the higher reaches of the montaña in 1984. Many young people who in the beginning had been attracted to Shining Path's message no longer wanted to participate. Shining Path responded by sealing off territories and conscripting entire families. Fearful of losing its social bases altogether, Shining Path opted to sacrifice the liberty of the population. All would have to live under its authority, concentrated in the People's Committees. This forced recruitment of entire families initiated a largely unknown stage in the war. As the years went by and as survival became more and more difficult, Shining Path resorted to increasingly ruthless methods to control its own "base."

The composition of the support base of Shining Path in the Principal Regional Committee (i.e., the Ayacucho region) had changed substantially. Sendero was aware of the risks that such changes implied. By the mid-1980s, not all of the militants were seeking immortality and heroism, even less so among those trapped in the ranks by terror. The process of forced recruitment accelerated when hamlets of the Simariva zone organized CACS in May and June 1984. This development obliged Shining Path to attack the civilian population, as in the case of Santa Rosa, which was attacked twice in July 1984. In the second attack seven peasants were killed, six of them Evangelical Christians killed in the church. On September 15, Shining Path went into San Pedro and killed nineteen men and women. Both communities had organized themselves against Sendero in the preceding months—in June and August, respectively—under pressure from the rondas of Anchihuay and Pichiwillca (see Del Pino 1994b). From mid-1984 the population lived under pressure: while Shining Path pressured from the heights, the army and the CACS pressured from the valley. This squeeze accelerated the exodus of the villagers of the higher montaña; some remained to live under the power of Shining Path, but others descended to take refuge in the valley. Families of Qawasana, Qaqasmayo, Antiqasa, and Chontaqocha, among others, came under Shining Path control. Meanwhile fourteen hamlets, among them Wayrapata, San Pedro, Rinconada Alta, and Catute Alto, took refuge in the area around Santa Rosa.

On the afternoon of 24 October 1993—a few days before the voter referendum on the constitution proposed by the new parliament following Fujimori's "self-coup" (autogolpe) of 5 April 1992—the senderista support base of the Sello de Oro Committee capitulated under Decree Law 25499, known as the Law of Repentance (Ley de Arrepentimiento). This group of senderistas totaled 184, including 107 children and youth, 46 women, and 31 men. (See the age pyramid for 167 members in figure 5.2.)

Many of the group had been recruited in the upper montaña and in nearby sierra communities in 1984. The recruits continued as conscripts until just before they turned themselves in (capitularon).[20] Shining Path had used not only fear, but violence, to conscript the peasants. At times, Shining Path killed some family members and conscripted their relatives: such was the case, for example, of María, whose mother they murdered. Claudia (age twenty-seven)[21] was recruited in Anteqasa in 1984, along with her family, including a husband and three sons. Guillermo (age twenty-nine) was taken in Anteqasa as well, after a Shining Path attack on the community in which his wife, two sons, and two brothers were all killed. From the same community, the senderistas also took Marcelino (age twenty-three) after killing his brother. They took Nazario (age fifty-nine) from Qahuasana in 1984, with his wife and one of his sons, after killing the eldest son. They took Rosa (age twenty-five) from Pataqocha in 1984, with her father, son, and one brother. Justina (age thirty-eight) was taken along with her two sons in Asunción in 1984. They took Dina and Elizabet (ages five and four in 1984) as young

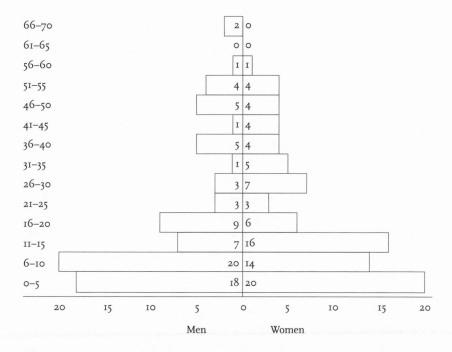

	Men	Women
66–70	2	0
61–65	0	0
56–60	1	1
51–55	4	4
46–50	5	4
41–45	1	4
36–40	5	4
31–35	1	5
26–30	3	7
21–25	3	3
16–20	9	6
11–15	7	16
6–10	20	14
0–5	18	20

Figure 5.2. Population of Sello de Oro Base, 1993 (based on a survey of 167 members of the Sello de Oro People's Committee, by Pichari Counter-Insurgency Base, October 1993).

children, after killing their parents. The mother of Wílmer was conscripted in Chontaqocha in 1984 when she was pregnant, along with her husband and her parents. Wílmer was born while she was in the Santa Ana Committee. Fermina (about twenty-four years old in 1990) was recruited in Pampa Cruz, along with her husband, son, and three brothers in 1990. The last to be conscripted was María (age fourteen at the time, in 1992), of Chaca in the sierra of San Miguel, after her mother was killed and María herself had been shot in one leg. These cases illustrate the new composition of Shining Path's bases from 1984 on.

These families became ramparts, human shields that helped to soften the military blows. But the families also provided food for the combatants. Within this context of prolonged struggle, the children came to serve as the human reserve, destined to replace those who would fall in combat. For this reason, every child was to be taken to the bases—even the children of Shining Path's victims—for preparation and military training.

For Shining Path, it was vital to retain a large base of youth in a pyramid-shaped age structure such as that seen in the Sello de Oro People's Committee (see figure). In 1993 we found seventy-two children under ten years, and minors outnumbered adults (107 versus 77, respectively). More than sixty children who arrived in the military base of Pichari had been born in Shining Path support bases. For Shining Path, children represented hope for the future and had to be raised by whatever means possible: "even if with rags, in order to fight. There have to be babies, we will be finished and the babies will be getting up, standing up," Claudia recalled. What the parents were not doing, the children would do. The parents' lack of identification with prolonged war would be countered by these "iron legions," integrated into what Shining Path called its "war machine." Therefore, from a very young age—eight or nine years—the children were trained militarily, and at the age of twelve they were incorporated into the forces of the base. The children were to be molded to have neither pity, nor family ties, nor affective needs—to be ready to kill or die. For this reason, in almost all of the senderista attacks the children went first, screaming, burning, and looting.

As the children received military instruction (beginning, let us recall, as young as eight years old), they were progressively distanced from their parents, so that once integrated into the "base force" they would live only for the revolution. Affective ties were prohibited, all relations were to be measured as a function of class and the popular war. Persons would no longer be called by their names or addressed according to their familial roles. Terms like *papá* or *mamá* were to give way to the nomenclature of combat, terms such as *compañero* or *camarada*.[22] According to Claudia, "the children were taught, saying we have to call each other compañero, compañera. They didn't talk of uncle, *señora*, only compañero, compañera, that was what they taught us. But we didn't learn easily, we complained."

One of Shining Path's primary objectives was to root out popular and communal organization and, at the same time, to install revolutionary organizational structures. (On the war against "third paths" or alternatives, see the essays in Part III of this book.) Indeed, the "crisis of representativity"—a kind of political vacuum—and the weakness of communal structures in many zones, facilitated Shining Path's presence in the countryside in the early 1980s. Shining Path not only took advantage of political vacuums, but also of weaknesses in family and extended kin structures in their capacity as effective social organization (see del Pino, 1992: 492). Within this line of thinking, tearing up the social fabric, even the family, would ensure domination (for more on Sendero's ideas of identifying fissures and "working the contradiction," see Burt's essay in this volume). At the same time, Shining Path imposed a bundle of values that were to abolish previous ways of life. Thus, for Shining Path, "religion" and "tradition" were merely symptoms of domination and deceit, without redeeming social or cultural value, "remnants of feudalism, that must be demolished by the revolution and disappear in the New Society." Sendero prohibited religion; prayers and beliefs had to die within each person and not be transmitted among the members, particularly not among the children.[23] In the Ené Valley, the Evangelicals were prohibited from speaking of God, under pain of death. In general, members of the Evangelical churches were one of the sectors most battered by violence, because the Evangelicals opposed the Sendero project ideologically and doctrinally (see Del Pino 1994b). According to Gliserio, in the bases people were told: "You all are speaking in the name of God, you don't exist in the sky. Saying 'my God' you are begging. Just because you say 'my God' doesn't mean that things will just come. You have to do something to get things. It's useless to expect anything from God." Shining Path demanded that the peasants "submit" not to God but to President Gonzalo.

Shining Path's arbitrariness and violence provoked Evangelical sectors to respond very early, as in the case of Anchihuay, in the Ayacuchan selva. In the CACS, the Evangelicals also participated notably, and continue to do so, and provided leaders such as "Susi," Zambrano, Jorge Aucasimi, and "Christopher." For Shining Path, religion was merely "the opium of the people," and would therefore disappear once the senderistas took power. People from the base insistently recalled hearing this discourse when the people prayed in some ceremonies, such as burials. In Sello de Oro, Claudia remembered that, even despite all the prohibitions, certain customs reappeared in ceremonies such as burials: "If there are no candles we just light some wood. But if anyone dies we do pray for him. There had been someone who makes us pray. Rosa also knew how to pray the Our Father.[24] Even though they said that now we didn't need to pray we would pray. It's our custom, we would tell them, we're going to pray. Pray then, they said, if it's your custom, you haven't gotten rid of it yet. So we prayed."

The prohibition against religion included traditional religious holidays. Christmas, which had been very widely celebrated in peasant communities, was prohibited. As recalled by Gliserio of the Florida People's Committee in the Ené Valley, the explanation was that "we couldn't celebrate these days that had been imposed by tyrants (gamonales), the exploiters." Instead,

Shining Path imposed its own holiday calendar: the beginning of the armed struggle, commemorated on May 18; the Day of Heroism (a reference to the 1986 massacre of hundreds of rioting senderista inmates in several Lima prisons), on June 18–19; Abimael Guzmán's birthday, on December 3; and so on. Shining Path did not understand the importance of traditional and religious celebrations, not only as socially integrative cultural institutions, but also as social referents in the very identity of the peasant population. These same referents would eventually redefine the peasants' adaptation and condition the process of resistance.[25]

Within a "guerrilla zone" (zona guerrillera) considered a "support base," the senderista leadership organized three combat "forces": the principal force (the guerrilla army), the local force, and the base force (a reserve force). The "masa" that supported the leadership and combatant forces were organized into an Open People's Committee (Comité Popular Abierto) under the leadership of responsables or commissaries: secretary general, secretary of security, secretary of production, secretary of communal affairs, and secretary of organization. This last secretary supervised the "movements" or "generated organisms" of the party: the Poor Peasants Movement, Youth Movement, Feminine Movement, and Pioneer Children Movement. The "masa," dedicated to the production of food for the combatants of the "New State," constituted the base of the People's Committees, whose hierarchy was governed by party militants and whose upper groups included the principal force. The "masa" planted in their own parcels; youth, adults, women, and children participated, producing basically maize, yuca, pitus (a tuber), and beans. To this diet they added preserves and products obtained through assaults and war quotas.

The base force (reserve force), which included children from the age of twelve up to adults who could endure the marches, in addition to producing food, trained militarily and participated in armed actions. They also had to dig trenches and build roads. Those who stood out, young people who were skillful and well trained, were promoted to the principal force. A few managed to ascend to positions of command: Betzon (age twenty-one in 1993), Gregorio (twenty-one), Raúl (twenty), and Rosa (thirty-eight). These mandos mediated between the "masa" and senderista leadership (the General Directorate of the People's Committee) and enforced orders received from the leadership. Many of the mandos had first been recruited as children, between the ages of nine and thirteen. By the ages of fifteen and eighteen, after receiving adequate military training, they assumed their commands.

As the counterinsurgency operations of the Armed Forces and the CACS intensified, conditions for survival deteriorated. From 1988 Sello de Oro became the target of constant attacks, resisting more than twenty, according to various accounts provided by the people who later "settled" under the Law of Repentance. The attacks would oblige them to retreat into the woods, consuming only roots for days or even weeks. This situation got worse as the years went by and the counterinsurgency forces increased their territorial control.

In contrast to the first years of the war, when the base had been able to survive without great sacrifices, by 1988 the families were living in plastic tents, exposed to the weather, and without sufficient clothing. Nutrition was the most serious problem. In the last few years the families virtually stopped consuming salt, sugar, vegetables, and stews. Their diet was limited to what they produced: yuca and pitus, in ever-decreasing quantities. Children were the most vulnerable victims, and those who processed the anxiety most intensely were the mothers, the persons most involved in feeding children and families. Mothers, the most sensitive to the daily drama and pain, showed the greatest resolve to resist and to question the viability of the whole Shining Path project.

Over the course of ten years in Sello de Oro, according to the mothers' accounts, around 100 children and adults died for lack of food. The children who did not have anything to eat often ingested herbs and dirt that caused their deaths. Malnutrition affected everyone, of course, but it destroyed children and left them more vulnerable to disease. According to the survey of 167 base members in 1993, almost every mother had lost at least one child to sickness or malnutrition. They did not have access to medicines or to health workers and treated illnesses with herbs alone. At the moment that Sello de Oro turned itself in (October 1993), 100 percent suffered from anemia, and many were afflicted with tuberculosis, acute bronchitis, and malaria. As a result of malnutrition, many children at two or three years of age still could not walk.

The lack of food and the proliferation of disease affected the "masa" most of all. Since everything was to be destined for the war, the political and military cadres had privileged access to what little could be obtained through attacks and assaults. Yet, as senderista forces became more vulnerable, survival more difficult, and families more decimated, it was not only mothers who felt the pain of the children. Even the mandos of the base force eventually saw reason and lost faith in Shining Path.

The afflictions of extreme poverty made daily life more cruel in nearby bases of Shining Path as well. The Open Popular Committee of the Ené Valley suffered similar effects of the war. Beginning in 1988, Shining Path had retreated to the Ené Valley. In contrast with other zones, Shining Path came to control the whole valley region, and placed forces of "contention" at the entrance and the exit points. The entire population of the valley remained enclosed and immobilized, under the control of the Open Popular Committee. Only in 1991 did the Peruvian Armed Forces and the CACS begin to liberate the valley and "recuperate" the population.[26]

When in July 1993 we accompanied a rescue of 200 people in Selva de Oro, we could document a poorly known reality: the violent construction of a totalitarian order in territories controlled by Shining Path over the years. The population liberated from Shining Path included 160 Asháninkas and 40 colonos. Their state of wretchedness suggested concentration camps. All had lived under Shining Path's power since 1988 or 1989, when the guerrillas had taken over the zone. As the counterinsurgency forces penetrated, survival conditions worsened: the inhabitants were constantly in retreat, forced to abandon their crops. Among the group (80 percent were children and women) all were sick and malnourished, and 95 percent had tuberculosis, anemia, or gastrointestinal disorders. Many also suffered from malaria or typhoid, and ten had leishmaniasis. These alarming figures resulted, they told us, from the hunger they suffered, deprived of salt, sugar, vegetables, and other foods.

Power and Daily Life: Channels of Resistance

Beginning in 1984, as we have seen, Shining Path forcibly recruited young people to replace guerrillas fallen in combat. The bases of the People's Committees consisted of the families that remained under the guerrillas' control. To a certain degree, this would define the new composition of Shining Path's social bases in the countryside. Class consciousness and adhesion to the party line, which presumably empowered the militants and shined their path, had given way to new realities.

At first, while the basic needs of the people in the Committees were being met and no actions required great sacrifice, a process we may call "resistant adaptation" took place. (This concept was developed in Stern 1990; Stern defines "resistant adaptation" by peasants as patterns of real and apparent accommodation to authority within which were enfolded senses of peasant assertion, right, and expectation that made such accommodations partial and contingent, and that might later justify more explicit resistance if "rights" were violated beyond a certain threshold. See also Degregori, in this volume.) This process changed as time passed and as survival became more difficult. Our analysis will attempt to explain how this initial process of resistant adaptation gave way to various forms of resistance that weakened the forces of Shining Path.

From the time that the inhabitants were first organized in People's Committees, they had to assume senderista values and social relations. They were to memorize and repeat constantly the "three golden rules" and the "eight teachings" (advertencias),[27] to submit to the party and to follow devoutly the will of "President Gonzalo." Whoever infringed upon these rules was publicly sanctioned, humiliated, and subjected to criticism and "self-criticism" (autocrítica).

The first currents of resistance appeared when children were forcibly enrolled in the guerrilla army and their mothers fought against losing them. This process would be repeated in many places. Other forms of resistance surfaced when Shining Path imposed its values and organizational structures, ignoring and negating communal traditions. Indeed, some of the earliest responses occurred in communities with the strongest ethnic-indigenous structures, marked by solid social organization and hierarchical patterns of authority, as in the higher reaches of Huanta. The hierarchies and the rituals of traditional communal power were simply ignored by the new commissaries.

In many cases, the communities adapted rather than expose themselves to retaliation from Shining Path. Some communities, however, defended their own ways of life and values. The Evangelical sectors were the clearest example. When Shining Path demanded participation in assaults and executions (ajusticiamientos), the Evangelicals refused, since such acts went against their internalized Christian values: You shall not rob, you shall not kill. This firm ideological opposition to Shining Path would give rise to early forms of organized resistance as Shining Path hardened its line. Resistance also developed around the issue of Catholic religious celebrations. As Degregori also notes, Shining Path tended to suppress traditional community festivals. "They cite the costs involved in these fiestas, but underlying the prohibition is their disdain for customs they consider archaic" (Degregori 1991c: 405).

Such contradictions were apparent from the first, but the peasants adapted to Sendero as long as it solved concrete problems: economic needs, safety concerns, problems of corruption, and immorality. The indiscriminate violence of the Peruvian Armed Forces against the peasants in the early years (ca. 1983–1984) also pushed the communities toward Shining Path. In the cases of the Sello de Oro and Ené Committees, resistance became less sporadic and isolated as living conditions worsened.

According to witnesses, resistance in Sello de Oro came out into the open in 1988. After five years of living under fear of Shining Path violence, the first to resist publicly were the women, impelled by pain and daily anguish as they witnessed their children's precarious lives. Terror no longer paralyzed their wills. The testimony of Claudia is very specific: "We would complain to them: 'we are not used to the cold, our babies are also sick and all the children are dying, we're not well because our children are cold and they are dying, we adults are not well either,' this was how we complained."

Such complaints were not simply personal or private, but became a public questioning. Claudia added: "When they would get us together in the Assembly we would tell them that we need salt, we don't taste meat either, our children have no clothes, no shoes, go barefoot, yet they want us to do guard duty, to work, yes. We did not agree. And so we would argue with them, I also complained to them many times, I wasn't afraid of them."

Up to a certain point, the greater suffering of the mothers was a discursive manipulation of cultural norms regarding gender and family in order to "legitimize" the resistance of both fathers and mothers—to convince husbands, young people and children, and even Shining Path militants and sympathizers, that to resist the destructive demands of Shining Path was legitimate and undeniable. Thus would peasants overcome the patriarchal or *machista* values glorified by the war. The suffering of the children motivated and legitimated resistance on the part of both fathers and mothers, but the mothers became the "public and discursive vanguard" for concrete social and cultural reasons. They were the ones who could most effectively wield the power normally exercised by the men, and who could perhaps mitigate the repressive reaction of Shining Path. In contrast with repression against the mothers, repression of the fathers did not bring pause.

Some couples, facing the pain of seeing their children suffer and die, chose to avoid having more children. In defiance of Shining Path, which placed its hopes in increased natality in order to pursue the protracted people's war, women would resist conceiving more children. Never before had they paid much attention to birth control, but now they did: "Since my little boy did not have clothing or food, they did not know milk, I also did not have any milk to breast feed, so we talked to our husbands, so we no longer had any more children." Claudia would reach this decision after two of her children died of anemia in the Shining Path base.

Hunger was not the only reason women refused to reproduce. They also refused to turn over more children to a cause in which they no longer believed and refused to live for. It was better not to have children than to see them suffer and be taken away at ten or eleven years of age. It was better not to see the children grow up with values completely opposed to those of their parents. Opposition also hardened because girls were forced to go to the base. This provoked the sharpest questioning, a rejection repeated with minor variations in various testimonies. Claudia recalls: "When they took girls who were twelve or thirteen years old to the base that was not alright, they ended up pregnant. For this reason some of us were against it, crying we resisted letting them take my Irma, better to kill us but I will not let her go. Meeting with the masa we told them: 'You are making the girls go to the base so that you can go with them as your lovers.'"

Although the "masa" was subject to the rules and teachings of the party, the mandos could violate them. The mandos simply ignored rules such as "do not take liberties with women," which punished adultery sometimes even by death. Thus the mandos violated the very rules they imposed upon the population. Claudia recalled in regards to rape and adultery: "among them they say it goes on, in the Principal Force and the Base Force, but not in the masa."

Very different from the values of the principal Shining Path nucleus, which had sacrificed families and abandoned children, were those of the peasant families who refused to give up their children, particularly their daughters: "better to kill us but I will not let her go." Cultural values regarding the family split apart. While some were ready to sacrifice all for the revolution, including their own lives, others were disposed to give all, even their lives, to defend their children.

Shining Path demanded what the "Holy Family" had offered and sacrificed: the family and the children. The principal cadres had sacrificed their own children. Osmán Morote and Teresa Durand left their children with the grandparents, the medical doctor Eduardo Mata Mendoza and Yeny María Rodríguez left their daughter with "an acquaintance" only a few months after her birth (Gorriti 1990). The traditional patriarchal family of Ayacucho was transferred to, and utilized by, the party. (On the party's patriarchalism, see the essay by Coral in this volume.) The best known cases of patriarchs delivering entire families to the party include those of the Morote Barrio-nuevo family (Osmán, his wife Teresa Durand, their two children, Elena and Eduardo, his brother Arturo, and Katia Morote); the Durand family (Jorge, Maximiliano, Teresa, and Guillermo, who became a bodyguard for Abimael Guzmán); and the Casanova family (Julio, his wife, Katia Morote, and their children). This appreciation for the family as a sacrifice transferred to the party was meant to be replicated among other militants and in support bases. Military rationality and "scientific absolutism"[28] made it difficult to understand how the militants viewed the institution of the family, or how attitudes may have evolved over time as the composition of the militant ranks changed.

Indeed, it was the family that sensitized many of the youth and made them "see the light" (*entrar en razón*) in the face of totalitarian violence. Mandos of the base force, who had been enrolled as children—as in the cases of Betzon, Gregorio, and Raúl, recruited at the ages of twelve, twelve, and eleven, respectively—had formed families of their own in the base. The training they had received in the bases was topped off with an insensitivity to the pain of others, an absolutist totalitarianism that negated a sense of mercy, even when they themselves had experienced what it means to suffer hunger and misery. Classist and revolutionary values nullified any symp-toms of remorse or sentiments of solidarity. They were the legions of iron, walls of iron, in front of whom the senderista cadres could not show pity or affection. As a result, when the children suffered from scarcity and hunger, the Shining Path cadres were mute. In the words of Claudia, the senderistas "didn't say anything." These were simply the costs of war that the population had to pay.

Upon forming their own families and seeing their own children as vic-tims of the crisis, however, the cadres found their dormant or "repressed" feelings of affection rising to the surface and becoming important in their relationships. They began to doubt the viability of Shining Path's project; they saw Shining Path's forces weakening and living conditions become worse; they started to understand and to note consciously that the triumph of the armed struggle and the taking of power were more an illusion than a reality. Power and ideology were no longer nullifying their own person-alities. On the contrary, spaces began to open for criticism and reason, emotion and solidarity. It was in these circumstances that they decided to rebel against the Shining Path leadership at Sello de Oro by assassinating Elizabet, the leader of the People's Committee, and two of her security people, and by turning themselves over to the counterinsurgency base.[29] The family, as the most important web of social and affective ties, managed to announce the end of the utopia—to break the grip of "total domination."

At the same time that the family and the attendant values of affect and solidarity strengthened, cultural and symbolic structures were being revitalized. Strong resistance emerged in the arena of culture and ideology. Even while religious practice was prohibited and punishable by death, and the party line was supposed to close off all other avenues of thought, cultural and religious values persisted and developed underground. People continued to practice their faith secretly, as in the case of Gliserio. He recounted that more than once he was submitted to "people's justice" and brought to the point of execution for continuing to pray and to speak to God: "in my conscience I would always say Glory to the Lord!" Gliserio realized that to resign himself or to weep would only make the situation worse; he understood how Shining Path operated. Shining Path glorified machismo and exaltation and absolutely prohibited that its members cry. Those who wept were often put to death. According to Shining Path, such resignation was "to become weak," symptomatic of wanting to abandon the party and the revolution. Gliserio, in the midst of the people's tribunal, would recall: "I could not lower my morale, ever. If I was sad, [because] sometimes some [people] are pensive, [well] those accursed ones also had their psychology. So I'd have to be normal, laughing or talking." Gliserio's reaction was the opposite of what Shining Path sought ("you will forget this custom of yours, before you were certainly conformist"). Gliserio became stronger through opposition: "in my inner thoughts I was always refusing, [I was] totally exhausted, oppressed; for this reason I've also left."

The refusal to lose one's customs and faith sometimes set back the ideological power of Shining Path. When someone died, the "masa" would bury him or her with the complete religious ritual; they would cry and pray for the deceased. They broke down the prohibition of rituals, what had been prohibited soon became public and collective practice. As we have seen, the Shining Path cadres would have to content themselves with commenting: "[the peasants] keep going on with their customs, they haven't given them up yet."

These levels of resistance were apparent not only among the "masas," but also among the *milicianos* and combatants. There came a time when many of them feigned sickness or injury to avoid participating in military actions. "I was with my wife and my five children, one who was eighteen years old, but fortunately, certainly God our Father, gave it to us, an *uta* [a tropical disease caused by insect bites that produces open sores and may require amputation of limbs] appeared in the foot of this son of mine, and with this uta they could not take him, not for action or anything, not the principal force, nothing, he was with us. The same [thing happened] to me, uta appeared in both my feet, also I had wounds at the time in my feet, if it wasn't for that they would have taken me away." As in the case of Reinaldo, when Shining Path ordered Sebastián to go out and participate in actions, he claimed to be sick in his kidneys, too incapacitated to walk.

In other cases, people refused to comply with one of the "three golden rules" of the party: "obey all orders in all actions." Píter, a guerrilla in Company 579 of Viscatán base, claiming exhaustion, refused to carry out an order to tear down a tower for a power line. Píter refused even though he was aware that his punishment could be death. Noncompliance was a situation that accelerated the desertion of combatants from the ranks of the Shining Path. Píter deserted, as did Benjamín, leader of the Sello de Oro Committee, who fled with his girlfriend in 1989. Desertion had begun to emerge in 1988, and included both combatants and members of the "masa."

Social Rupture and Totalitarian Violence in Shining Path

Facing internal crisis, Shining Path began to construct new and more terrifying mechanisms of domination, exposing its members to the harshest violence. Shining Path would not openly take note of the internal problems that questioned the viability of its whole project. On the contrary, Shining Path presented an image of itself as invincible and victorious. In this context it entered a new stage of annihilating civilian populations and the organized CAC communities.[30] The difficulties it faced in maintaining control and submission despite growing resistance led Shining Path to increase the irrationality of its violence and the inhumanity of its rule.

More than victories and "unstoppable" advances, the intensification of senderista repression reflected internal problems and the weakening of its forces. Shining Path had to fight on two fronts: demolishing resistance on the internal front and imposing terrifying fear on the national population on the external front.

The internal problems and growing resistance in the bases caused Shining Path to redouble its efforts at submission. At first, sanctions took the form of critique and autocrítica—the public avowal of guilt and submission to the party. When the same fault was repeated, the guilty were submitted to corporal punishment. If that failed, the culprit would be disappeared and assassinated.

Punishment by death became increasingly cruel as the years went on. Sendero killed people who attempted to escape and even those who simply mentioned escape as a possible alternative. Faced with increasing desertion, Shining Path began to retaliate against the families of deserters. Most who fled the base had family ties, so punishment would fall upon those who stayed behind. An extreme case, but not for that reason untypical, was that of Alejandro. When he deserted from the base, Sendero killed his father and two brothers who had stayed behind. Seeing this happen, people who had family ties renounced their plans to flee and chose to remain behind, subordinated and exposed to the most difficult conditions of survival.

When Shining Path captured a deserter, death was immediate and cruel. Sendero would call the people together for a "people's trial" (*juicio popular*) and killed the deserter in front of everyone: "They slit his throat with rope, they choked him, pulled him apart, in front of everyone. The whole 'masa' has to watch, children who were of age, twelve or fourteen years old, would watch. 'Watch this so you don't try to escape,' they'd say." In some cases, Shining Path designated a close relative to carry out the execution.

Shining Path had to paralyze all forms of conspiracy and resistance. It had to carry out sanctions publicly against those who did not comply with the party. At first, Shining Path carried out executions out of sight of the "masa." But by 1988–1989 they forced people to watch the executions and to see the risks of insubordination. But even so, Gliserio recalled, "maybe people were scared, from then on, there were always escapes."

When Sendero captured a rondero or anyone who committed "faults," even an important cadre of Shining Path, the leaders implicated the population in the violence by demanding participation in an "initiation rite" of public execution. By quoting one of the informants at length, we can get a sense of the cruelty of this violence and its searing effect on the "masa."

> They gave me a knife, saying "do it, because the party has chosen you." I did not know what to do, but it was the moment to demonstrate that we were part of them so that they would trust me, and so I would get a chance to escape. I felt like I was in a dream, a nightmare, I became inert while trembling inside, one of them said, "what are you waiting for, compañero, put yourself in the shoes of this wretched guy, in his base they torture you, they make you suffer until you squeal and then

what . . . so that you kill, they deserve it compañero, if not he will be pardoned and you both will be judged . . ." When they gave me the knife I did not know where to start, I went up to him and said forgive me, and I gave him a stab in the chest and I screamed out of fear and I think that the scream helped me to do it . . . then in the stomach, in the heart, while I ended up smeared with blood and not understanding what I had done . . . I wanted to go crazy and escape that very moment.[31]

This was the reality that the indigenous and colono communities ended up living.

Many members of the bases died as a result of hunger and disease, while others were killed by Shining Path. In August 1994, after the army and the CACS invaded four Shining Path bases in the Anapatil region (Nuevo Desarrollar, Nueva Aurora, César Vallejo y Progreso in the district of Rio Tambo, Satipo) they discovered graves filled with the bodies of Asháninka prisoners and Shining Path *arrepentidos*, all murdered by Shining Path within the last few years.

The provincial prosecutor (*fiscal*) of Satipo appeared to verify the statement by General Hermosa that some two thousand people, including colonos and Asháninka prisoners, died over the course of this period, either assassinated by Shining Path or destroyed by malnutrition and disease resulting from the inhumane conditions to which they had been subjected. Hundreds of graves were found in which were buried more than a thousand victims of Shining Path from the years of violence in the central jungle region.[32]

Killings of invalids and sick people by Sendero became common. The clearest denunciation occurred in the Corazón de Quiteni Committee, in the Ené Sub-Region Committee, where Shining Path massacred dozens of sick colonos and Indians considered a "parasitic burden" (*carga parasitaria*). In Sello de Oro, Shining Path began to "liquidate" the infirm who did not collaborate with the war. After killing the husband of Marina Huicho the Senderistas commented that he was "always sick, he never goes out for a confrontation, only being served, sitting there nothing more . . . we have to go out to assault vehicles, to get food, he didn't want to, saying he was sick." In the forced marches, whoever could not continue walking would be killed in fear—the senderistas said that anyone captured by the military would betray them. On a march from Sello de Oro toward Viscatán, just days before surrendering, after having walked three days without food, some of the members were killed—especially those who were already sick—after they fainted and appeared unable to go on. They had become, in the absolutist scheme of Shining Path, a "parasitic burden," an obstacle to be swept away and eliminated without pity. Intolerance in the face of resistance and refutation from the bases fed a disdain for the weakest persons, as well as ethnic minorities.

Another tactic of domination was to maintain the "masa" misinformed and incommunicado. Members of the base did not know what was going on beyond it. Neither the combatants nor the mandos of the base force had access to information, except that provided by the Shining Path leadership. They were told that they were close to triumph and only had to be patient. They should not be pessimistic or complain of problems, because the towns of the valley were suffering hunger and mistreatment at the hands of the Armed Forces. Similarly, keeping base members illiterate was considered an advantage. Of all of the children, only two knew Spanish and none how to read or write. Of the women, only Rosa spoke Spanish. Betzon was the only one of the men who knew how to write, and only with great difficulty.

This state of subordination did not completely paralyze the values and motivations of the people. A certain dissociation took hold inexorably, and implied a critique of the totalitarian order and a desire to put an end to domination and submission. The testimony of Píter, particularly his evaluation of the war, pinpoints the state to which Shining Path arrived.

> Well, as an experience it is a life that in reality goes against the people, against society mainly, mainly striking against the peasants, because they practically all rob the peasants, they kill the peasants, so they're directly striking the peasants, and so they are never going to be able to win like they say, [and] change this society. With the experience I have, that I have been through, they won't be able to change, they don't have a sufficient base on which to rest, a popular base, they don't have the people's support, their forces have diminished, they don't have a big enough group to carry out operations, this is why they are currently in retreat. But before, when they had support from the people, they marched in battalions, a battalion had 1600, 1500 people, there were four or five battalions in every zone.

REBUILDING EVERYDAY LIFE IN
AYACUCHO, 1990S.
(above) Women refugees return to
Purus to build make-shift housing
and re-establish their community.
(left) A displaced woman in the Río
Apurímac Valley.

Conclusion

In 1995, Shining Path was no longer a threat to the country or democratic stability. Sendero was isolated and without social bases, but the isolation was not merely a recent phenomenon. As early as 1984, in some parts of the country, peasants began to refuse to collaborate. And by 1988, not only had the capacity for resistance by peasants organized into CACS increased. In addition, in Ayacucho, Shining Path began to suffer internal problems, as resistance from within its own bases of support reached levels that placed the viability of the Senderista project in question.

Shining Path never would acknowledge its internal weaknesses. On the contrary, beginning in 1989 Shining Path increased its armed attacks, not only against communities organized into CACS, but also against neutral civilian populations that lacked direct connection with the political forces in conflict. Thus Shining Path strengthened its own image of power by heightening the cruelty of its attacks and intensifying the climate of terror. More than the "unstoppable" advance of the armed struggle, these actions reflected Shining Path's fear of internal limitations at a time of growing resistance in the support bases to the life scheme promoted by the disciplinary apparatus of the party.

A dissociation emerged between the party-based scheme of Shining Path and the real and deeply felt needs of the people. Customary family relations, cultural values imbedded in daily life, and human necessities all combined to subvert the artificial order imposed by Shining Path. As problems of survival became more acute, symbolic and cultural structures regained strength. The peasants began to repair their delicate webs of social and family ties, and affective values could once again guide conduct.

Notes

I thank Jürgen Golte, Carlos Iván Degregori, and Steve Stern for their comments and valuable suggestions. This study forms part of an ongoing project entitled "Shining Path: Ethnic and Cultural Dimensions of Violence" (*Sendero Luminoso. Las dimensiones étnicas y culturales de la violencia*) at the Institute of Peruvian Studies (Instituto de Estudios Peruanos), in collaboration with the North-South Center of the University of Miami. For geographical orientation to the Department of Ayacucho, see the map in Degregori's chapter.

1   On the Shining Path, see, among others: Favre 1984; Palmer 1986; Granados

1987; Degregori 1989b, 1990a, 1991c; Chávez de Paz 1989; Manrique 1989; Gorriti 1990.

2   The heroic image of politics is that of privilege, of the actions of an informed circle. Politics is presented as a grandiose public space in contrast to the private sphere in which almost all of us live our daily reality, which is sweaty and unpresentable (Nun 1989). Some important exceptions to my characterization of the literature, and which achieved wider understandings, include Berg 1986; Isbell 1988; Degregori 1991b; Rénique 1991a; and Kirk 1993b.

3   The leadership nucleus of the Shining Path and the combatants have as their goal the "conquest" of new support bases and the "liberation" of the guerrilla zone through "revolutionary violence." In the "liberated" zone they were to construct "Open People's Committees" (Comités Populares Abiertos) through which Shining Path would implement its own governing power structure. The organization of the People's Committees consists of (1) Shining Path nucleus: General Directorate; (2) combatants: Fuerza Principal, Fuerza Local, Fuerza de Base (reserve); and (3) "masa," organized under the following commissaries: General Secretary; Secretary of Security; Secretary of Production; Secretary of Communal Affairs; Secretary of Organizations, responsible for the following "generated organizations": Movement of the Elderly; Youth Movement; Feminine Movement; and Movement of Pioneer Children.

4   We carried out the survey in collaboration with Professor Marilú Criales and four students of the Faculty of Social Sciences of the Universidad Nacional de San Cristóbal de Huamanga.

5   In the last three months of 1995, the Shining Path again appeared in some provinces of the region: in highland pueblos bordering Ayahuanco and Viscatán, Huanta; on the road between Ayacucho and San Francisco, leading to the selva, where they have solicited tributes and provisions; in Ninabamba, San Miguel in La Mar Province; and in Churia, a community bordering on Huancavelica in Huamanga Province, where they killed three ronderos. In addition, some NGOS operating in the provinces of Vilcashuamán and Víctor Fajardo have reported sightings of armed groups moving about the zone. In contrast to the first stage, however, they do not have bases of support and their actions are totally isolated.

6   In collaboration with AYNI-Visión Mundial we have been studying the changes in the community and the rural society during recent years. An unforeseen process was the strengthening of the peasant communities as a result of the war, as communities organized themselves in Committees of Civilian Self-Defense (Comités de Autodefensa Civil; CACs). The crisis in the *gamonal* political system not only left a void in politics, but also produced a retreat by the Catholic church. The latter left fertile ground for the Evangelical churches, which sprang up and grew in the midst of the terror, violence, crisis, and misery.

7   José Coronel has studied the attitudes of high-altitude and valley populations regarding Shining Path. He suggests that the ethnic and organizational aspects of the higher communities were the most important factors in explaining their comparative resistance to Shining Path.

8   For the official report on this incident, see Vargas Llosa 1983.

9   Chuto is a pejorative term used to label the peasants of the high puna zone who are denigrated as "ignorant," "brutish," and "savage" because the majority are monolingual Quechua speakers and weakly articulated with the market and the city. The sources for the quotations and figures cited regarding deaths and attempted assassinations, unless otherwise indicated, are derived from information gathered during fieldwork, especially in interviews with ex-senderistas, arrepentidos, ronderos, authorities, and the like. In many cases the text does not refer to the exact date of events because in the memory of the informants the chronological date is neither the most important point nor the best remembered.

10   The concept of the hidden transcript is taken from Scott 1990.

11   These ideas were discussed and studied with Carlos Iván Degregori and José Coronel in the project "Shining Path: Ethnic and Cultural Dimensions of the Violence."

12   The displaced people who left beginning in 1984 started to return to their communities of origin from June 1993 onward. By late 1995 according to Visión Mundial, an NGO that works with returning communities in Ayacucho, about sixty communities, involving about ten thousand people, returned in the province of Huanta alone. As of October 1993, the author has closely followed this experience by accompanying the returnees.

13   See Coronel 1994, Coronel and Loayza 1992, and Del Pino 1992, 1994b; and the essay by Starn in this volume.

14   This view was also prevalent in some academic circles, which saw the CACS as paramilitary groups "set up" (montadas) by the army. This perspective was held even more openly by some political and human rights groups. For more contextualization and critique, see the essay by Starn in this volume.

15   In 1990 we started working in southern Huamanga, visiting and carrying out interviews in several communities, such as Paccha, for example, seeking to understand the processes of war, violence, and organization of the CACS (see Del Pino 1992).

16   Chafles are instruments used to clear out jungle undergrowth.

17   The author has carried out field research in the selva. On the road one could feel the tension and fear among the people, which would cause the CACS to take control of the route in order to avoid new attacks and assaults. I was also witness to the ruthlessness with which Shining Path killed children in Matucana Alta; their bodies, arms, and heads had been mutilated with machetes.

18   Shining Path's strategy was based on the idea of Mao Zedong (1971) that "We

must appear weak when we are in fact strong and appear strong when we are in fact weak."

19 For a more detailed discussion, see Degregori 1992a.

20 This was how the army referred to people who fled from Shining Path and submitted to the Repentance Law.

21 The ages listed for 1984 recruits subtract nine years from those that were registered at the time of surrender in October 1993. A similar adjustment is made for recruits in other years.

22 Abimael Guzmán (1988: 47) publicly declared that he had no friends, only comrades. When Comrade Meche, Laura Zambrano, was asked about love, she stated "Love is for the class, and in service of the popular war" (Kirk 1993b: 54).

23 Claudia remembered that religion was totally prohibited. Although she continued "secretly" to maintain her faith, her children "no longer knew how to pray, and they didn't want me to teach them."

24 Rosa (age 38 in 1993) was a military commander (*mando*) in Sello de Oro.

25 In an earlier work we analyzed the economic contradictions between the Shining Path and the peasants in the valley of the Apurímac River (Del Pino 1994b). In this essay we limit ourselves to cultural and religious aspects and traditional family relations, emphasizing the analysis of daily life and customary moral values.

26 This "recuperated" population, as the ronderos referred to them, after recovering from malnutrition and regaining their health, began to participate in the rescue of other groups dominated by Shining Path. They knew the bases and the paths that the Shining Path followed. From early on, the defense committees incorporated into their ranks the very communities that had previously been with the Shining Path. Members of the CACS, commenting on the Law of Repentance enacted by the Fujimori government, noted that *they* were the ones who, much earlier, had employed this strategy to beat the Shining Path.

27 See Gorriti 1990: 174–75.

28 The novel by Aldous Huxley, *Brave New World,* is very suggestive. He depicts a world governed by a scientific absolutism that neither leaves room for emotions nor for any manifestation that transgresses the preplanned order.

29 Elizabet, according to the informants, was about forty years old, tall, white-skinned, and was in her fourth year of study in the education faculty of the Universidad del Centro in Huancayo. She had assumed the leadership of the Sello de Oro Committee in 1989, after the previous leader, Benjamín, fled the zone.

30 The increase in ruthlessness and violence of Shining Path actions against the civilian population contributed to fortifying its image in national public opinion as a powerful force. From Lima, the capital city plagued by continual "car bombs," Shining Path's advance appeared unstoppable.

31 Atauje 1995.

32 See Espinosa 1995.

SIX

The War for the Central Sierra

Nelson Manrique

✣ If we consider the fatalities produced by the political violence in the center-south highlands of Peru—specifically the departments of Ayacucho, Huancavelica, Junín, and Pasco—from 1980 to 1991, then we may observe that the overwhelming majority of deaths over the course of the decade occurred in Ayacucho (see Figure 6.1).[1] The numbers are conclusive: out of a total of 11,969 deaths in the center-south, 7,481 (62.5 percent) corresponded to Ayacucho.

Significantly, more than half of the fatalities suffered during those eleven years in Ayacucho happened in just two years, 1983 and 1984 (4,148 deaths or 55.5 percent of the departmental total). The explanation lies in the fact that the administration of Fernando Belaúnde put the Peruvian Armed Forces in charge of suppressing the *senderista* uprising as of 1 January 1983. The military implemented a counterinsurgency strategy based on the indiscriminate use of terror against the peasantry. This merciless campaign of repression, guided by the North American counterinsurgency doctrine absorbed by Peruvian military personnel in the schools of Fort Gulick and Panama, tried to isolate Shining Path by demonstrating that the army could exert even greater terror than the guerrillas (Manrique 1986b). The years 1983 and 1984 marked the peak of the *guerra sucia* ("dirty war") that both sides waged against the peasantry. As we can observe in Figure 6.1, the number of fatalities per year in Ayacucho began to diminish significantly in 1985, and then remained relatively stationary until 1990, when fatalities began to rise again, this time as a consequence of Shining Path's big national offensive. Shining Path leaders proclaimed that they had attained "strategic equilibrium" and that it was time to create the conditions for taking power.

Consider the other departments, particularly the unusual path of Junín.

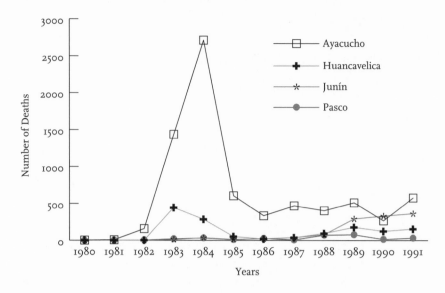

Figure 6.1. Victims of Political Violence, 1980–1991 (SEPAR 1992:29).

The curve that traces deaths produced by the political violence in the department of Huancavelica, which adjoins Ayacucho on the west and historically
has been closely connected economically, culturally, and even administra-
tively to Ayacucho, demonstrates a tendency similar to that of Ayacucho;
the differences are in magnitude rather than direction. The numbers of
fatalities in Pasco were the lowest and remained relatively constant. They
showed a slight increase in 1988 and 1989, when Sendero carried out a
large offensive against the mining centers of the central sierra, and then fell
slightly. The curve that represents the deaths suffered in Junín, on the other
hand, shows a clearly different tendency. The number of fatalities was far
lower than those in Ayacucho, but the progression was constant, without
the sharp increases followed by equally sudden decreases that characterized
Ayacucho and Huancavelica.

These numbers do not allow us to distinguish killings perpetrated by
Shining Path from those perpetrated by the Armed Forces. If in place of
fatalities, however, we turn our attention to terrorist attacks (perpetrated
mainly by Shining Path and, in smaller proportion by the Movimiento Revolucionario Túpac Amaru; MRTA), the tendencies outlined thus far appear
even more clearly (see Figure 6.2). One may observe the following characteristics. First, once again, Shining Path action in Cerro de Pasco proved
relatively stationary. Second, Shining Path attacks in Ayacucho and Huanca-

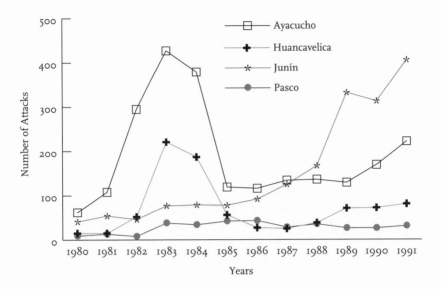

Figure 6.2. Political Violence in the Central Region, 1980–1991 (elaborated on the basis of data provided by SEPAR 1992: 17–18).

velica increased sharply from 1980 to 1983, then fell sharply in 1984–1985, when the repressive offensive unleashed by the Armed Forces obliged the Shining Path leadership to transfer its cadres toward other territories. Sendero attacks increased only slightly after 1985, but more dramatically after 1989, when Shining Path began its great offensive, which would only be interrupted by Abimael Guzmán's capture in September 1992. Third, an uninterrupted rise in Shining Path attacks occurred in Junín from 1980 onward, with a sharply accentuated increase beginning in 1987. After 1987, Junín surpassed Ayacucho in the number of attacks and the breach that had opened between the curves showing the relative intensity of Shining Path action would continue to increase. By 1991–1992, the magnitude of Shining Path actions in Junín in 1991 matched the level in Ayacucho in 1983–1984, when senderista activity in Ayacucho reached its height.

Various are the studies that have analyzed the dynamic of the war in Ayacucho. Their conclusions may be extended without too much risk to the adjoining southern departments of Huancavelica and Apurímac.[2] In contrast, the social dynamic of Junín during this period is clearly distinct and requires a more specific analysis. Violence increased steadily, then explosively after 1987, when Junín became a clear priority to the senderista leadership. I approach the case of Junín by descending from the large numbers, which allow us to outline tentatively the general tendencies, to microsocial analysis—case studies that allow us to look closely at the actors' logic.

The War in Junín: The Mantaro Valley and its Surroundings

Junín played an important role in Shining Path's plans for the center-south sierra since the beginnings of the "people's war." Within Junín, Shining Path concentrated its activities in the Mantaro Valley, considered the heart of the region, and the city of Huancayo, the region's capital and most important city, situated in the Mantaro Valley. The first attacks in the region that caught the notice of the national press occurred in December 1980, only six months after Shining Path began its armed actions.[3] On 12 December, Senderistas dynamited the principal entrance to the office of CONACO (Corporación Nacional de Comerciantes; National Association of Merchants) in the mining center of La Oroya. The following day, the Banco de los Andes building was blown up with high-powered explosives. On 14 December, Tower 211 of Quiulla in the Mantaro utilities network (located twenty-five kilometers to the northeast of Huancayo, in Concepción province) blew up. The same happened to Tower 46 of Huayucachi, ten kilometers south of Huancayo, and to Tower 55, eight kilometers from Huancavelica. The efficiency of these actions led some political leaders to attribute them to navy commandos. On 15 December, four terrorist attacks shook Huancayo. That same day two private autos were blown up in the San Cristóbal mining settlement in Morococha. Groups of saboteurs destroyed the doors and windows of the municipal council building of Sicaya, the district council building of Tambo, and the warehouse of the National Enterprise for the Commercialization of Inputs (Empresa Nacional de Comercialización de Insumos; ENCI), located five kilometers from Huancayo. On the twenty-first, the police managed to frustrate a grave attack when they detected a time bomb in the water plant in Huancayo. In La Oroya, however, the Shining Path activists managed to dynamite a section of the water main and left the town without water. On 1 March, twenty meters of rails and ties were blown up on the railroad line between Huancayo and Huancavelica. Three days later a similar attack destroyed a twelve-meter section between La Oroya and Cerro de Pasco.

These events set the tone for Shining Path's subsequent activities, which included acts of sabotage against public services including transport, drinking water, and especially electricity. The latter had national repercussions, because it compromised the energy supply of Lima (where a third of the

Peruvian population resides), other cities on the coast and towns in the Callejón de Huaylas, the iron and steel works known as SIDERPERU, the mining complex HIERROPERU, and the TRUPAL paper factory in Trujillo. These early acts of sabotage culminated on 17 December 1981, when Shining Path detachments tried to blow up the Campo Armiño facilities of Mantaro Hydroelectric. Other recurring actions included dynamite attacks against public and private entities in the region, and raids on mines to obtain the indispensable dynamite (the raids targeted the minority of mines that refused to pay Sendero a certain quota of explosives). In short, Shining Path generated terror among the population, and demonstrated the inability of the state to guarantee the safety of the citizenry, by carrying out raids to obtain explosives, armed propaganda among the mine workers, and acts of social destabilization aimed at basic services.

The repressive response was ineffective and indiscriminate. A paradigmatic case was the detention of Nicolás Matayoshi, Hans Carlier, and Carlos Taype. Matayoshi, a Huancayo poet and activist in the Izquierda Unida (United Left) Party, was accused of being a senderista leader intellectually responsible for terrorism in the central sierra. Carlier, a Dutch cooperative leader and specialist in rural development, was presented as a terrorist and instructor of senderista guerrillas. Taype was a leader in the Peasant Confederation of Peru (Confederación Campesina del Perú; CCP). The three accused men were publicly well known and declared anti-senderistas. Despite national and international pressure, Matayoshi spent several months in prison, while the Dutch Embassy had to intervene to obtain Carlier's release. Taype had to go underground to escape persecution by the Belaúnde administration's security forces.

Sendero's escalade widened in 1982. In January, Shining Path went a step further when it destroyed a patrol car. Sendero had gone from acts of sabotage to armed confrontation with the police forces responsible for suppressing them. In May, Sendero lit the mountains surrounding the city of Huancayo with giant fires that outlined the hammer and sickle in commemoration of the second anniversary of their armed struggle. In August, Shining Path began attacking the commercial properties of the mayor of Huancayo, Luis Carlessi, a member of President Belaúnde's party, Acción Popular. They repeated the attacks in December. Shining Path had now gone from threatening the indigenous authorities of distant communities to directly attacking the municipal authorities of important provinces.

Even though the Belaúnde administration put the Armed Forces directly in charge of suppressing Shining Path as of 1 January 1983, the senderistas maintained their pressure on the central sierra. That same month, a national guard was gunned down in Huancayo by a Shining Path commando. The guard was left for dead and his weapons were taken. On 9 June, the Nueve de Diciembre army barracks and a military residential compound were attacked with explosives, but tragedy was averted when the most powerful device failed to go off. A renewed attack on 15 January 1984 was more successful: Six bombs exploded. Soon after, more than 100 senderistas opened fire on an army patrol in the village of Parcobamba, Tayacaja province, and engaged the soldiers in a gun battle. Only the intervention of artillery helicopters managed to force the guerrillas to retreat. These attacks constituted only a small slice of rising senderista activity (again, see Figure 6.2).

On 13 December 1983, attacks of singular relevance took place. Around 150 senderistas assaulted the Laive, Río de la Virgen, and Antapongo production units of the Cahuide SAIS. (SAIS, or Sociedades Agrícolas de Interés Social, were associative properties created during the agrarian reform of the government of General Velasco Alvarado out of the great ranching haciendas. On SAIS and other associative enterprises, see the essay by Rénique in this volume.) They burned the main house, seized explosives, and blew up a tractor. The resulting damage was estimated at more than a billion *soles*. The attackers took five thousand head of fine sheep valued at another billion soles. This attack was considered the worst senderista incursion to date in the department of Junín. On 16 December, a battle took place between police forces and fifty senderistas at Tucle, another of the units comprising the Cahuide SAIS. The arrival of reinforcements, urgently solicited by radio, saved this production unit from suffering the fate of Antapongo. These actions formed part of a vast strategic project whose objective was to control the peasantry of the central sierra. During the same period that Shining Path was forced into a general retreat in Ayacucho by the Armed Forces' genocidal tactics (as we have seen, the political violence of 1983 and 1984 alone accounted for more than half of the fatalities of the decade), there was a marked increase in terrorist actions in the central sierra. Beginning in January 1984, Huancayo and its adjoining districts were subjected to recurrent nighttime bombings. As a result, the inhabitants withdrew from the streets after seven P.M. They feared either becoming Shining Path's next victims or suffering detention under accusation of terrorism in the security forces' habitual sweeps. The space for any political expression in the region—apart from armed violence—was constantly contracting. (On the fate of "third paths," see Part III of this book.)

What explains the importance of the city of Huancayo for the Shining Path leadership during this early period, when its material and human resources were scarce? Historically, several factors combined to make the central region, particularly the Mantaro Valley, a strategic territory disputed by those who planned to take power in the Peruvian capital. The area is privileged in its geographic location, as it is an important crossroads for routes that connect Lima with the southern sierra and with the central and northern *selvas* (the jungles that adjoin the eastern mountain slopes). The Mantaro Valley, the key hub of the central sierra, has various cities and a high demographic density. It is an important commercial center: Huancayo is the third most important city in the country and its Sunday market is the most important of the Peruvian sierra. In addition, the Mantaro Valley is close to some of the biggest mining centers in the country, including Cerro de Pasco and Morococha, which together generate an important fraction of the foreign exchange without which the Peruvian economy cannot function (Caballero Martin 1981; Mallon 1983; Manrique 1981, 1986b, 1987b). To these historical factors may be added, during recent decades, the construction of the most important hydroelectric complex in the country, the Central Hidroeléctrica del Mantaro, whose network of high tension cables stretches through the Mantaro Valley toward Lima. Explosion of the project's utility towers proved to be a frightfully efficient tactic on the part of the senderista leadership, not only because of the anxiety and instability provoked by blackouts in the big cities, but also because of their strong impact on the Peruvian economy, especially industry.

The Urban Front and the Universidad del Centro

Another factor of importance was the Universidad Nacional del Centro, in the city of Huancayo. This educational center, founded in the early 1960s, concentrated a significant contingent of students of precarious means from the region and elsewhere. (The university was originally founded as the Universidad Comunal del Centro, which reflects its ties to the region's peasant *comuneros*.) These students made the bitter discovery that their chances of obtaining decently paid jobs upon graduation were rather remote, given the unevenness of academic training in Peru and the ethnic and racial discrimination that places *serrano* students of the interior provinces at an objective disadvantage.[4] (The Universidad Nacional de San Cristóbal de Huamanga in Ayacucho was similar in this regard.) The Universidad del Centro was attractive to the Shining Path command because it was situated in a city of economic, political, and administrative importance, the size of which facilitated clandestine action. As matters turned out, armed propaganda carried out by senderista contingents permitted Shining Path to gain substantial contingents of students who would play an important role in executing urban attacks and incursions into communities of the Mantaro Valley.

By 1986, the university had become a critical battleground for Shining Path and the MRTA (Movimiento Revolucionario Túpac Amaru). For the latter, Junín was a "natural" space for development, given the political work in the area carried out by the Movement of the Revolutionary Left (Movimiento de Izquierda Revolucionaria; or MIR). The MIR, from which MRTA would eventually descend, had been one of the branches of the Peruvian Left that had sprung in the 1960s (see Hinojosa, in this volume, on leftist groups in the 1960s). At that time, the most important MIR guerrilla front was in the central selva (along the eastern fringes of the departments of Junín, Pasco, and Huánuco).

The struggle for control of the Universidad Nacional del Centro was bloody, with political assassinations committed on both sides. According to a denunciation printed in the magazine *Cambio,* the army developed a tactic whereby its military commandos, in the guise of one or the other of the opposing guerrilla groups, carried out political assassinations that would escalate the confrontations and induce among the guerrillas a macabre dynamic of reprisal and counter-reprisal. Incidents in the countryside also suggested such tactics. Dozens of people died from such dynamics, many of them on the university campus. The final phase of the regime of Alan García (1985–1990) was also marked by violence on the part of aprista paramilitary bands (APRA was President García's political party), but the apristas were rapidly crushed by Shining Path's annihilation squads. By the late 1980s, the disappearance of students and teachers from the university and from secondary schools throughout the region had become commonplace. According to many denunciations, they were abducted by agents of the security forces.

Professors who taught during this period in the university recollect a situation of anxiety and instability. In addition to the political violence unleashed by the subversive organizations and the Armed Forces, people took advantage of the climate of generalized violence to settle scores that had little or nothing to do with politics. An example of the extremes to which this multiple and anarchic violence arrived was the proliferation of anonymous letters that threatened professors with death if they did not meet rather banal demands, such as substitute exams in the courses they were teaching.[5]

To Conquer the Countryside

Shining Path's strategy for taking power required consolidation of a solid peasant base from which to launch the assault on the cities that constituted the center of political power.[6] Shining Path's work among students, professors, and teachers of the Universidad del Centro and secondary schools could produce sympathizers of peasant origin who would facilitate its penetration of the countryside (compare the essay by Degregori in this volume). But, it was necessary to have the support of experienced cadres. These came mainly from Huancavelica and Ayacucho, in armed columns that travelled the heights of the western cordillera, a zone populated principally by shepherds and high altitude cultivators in communities and in the various SAIS.

The functioning of the various SAIS units provoked tension between the state bureaucracy that controlled them and the peasantry. The administrative layer instituted by the state had created its own interests and became an unresolvable obstacle to any attempt at change, in a sector that confronted endemic crisis (Montoya et al. 1974). Shining Path took advantage of this situation to advance the project of establishing itself in the countryside. It was no accident that Shining Path carried out its first incursions against the SAIS of the central sierra in December 1983, the same year that the Armed Forces' occupation of Ayacucho had obligated Sendero to remove its most experienced cadres and deploy them elsewhere. The redeployment presumably would preserve these cadres while expanding Sendero's own political presence. In addition to the attacks on the productive units of the Cahuide SAIS already described, Shining Path also attacked SAIS infrastructures for transportation, transformation, and marketing, and SAIS administrators who refused to obey orders to renounce their posts. Indalecio Pino, the administrator of Tucle, was saved miraculously from an ambush that a Shining Path annihilation commando in Huancayo set up, only to die soon after from cardiac arrest.

In addition, Shining Path had to combat the organizations of the legal Left, which had worked substantially with the peasantry of the region, principally through the CCP. The CCP activists were conscious that in their ability to satisfy the demands of the region's peasantry would lie the possibility of blocking Shining Path's ability to gain a following in the region. (For systematic discussion of the hopes placed in "third paths" and the unraveling of such hopes, see Part III in this volume.) In a previous work I described in some depth how this confrontation culminated in the defeat of the CCP activists' proposal for "democratic restructuration" of the Cahuide SAIS. The result was the destruction of the productive units of the SAIS by Shining Path columns; the disappearance of the units' herds, which were distributed among the peasantry with the peremptory order to get rid of the animals immediately (i.e., slaughter them or give them away); and the implantation of Shining Path cadres in the Canipaco Valley in 1988 and early 1989 (Manrique 1989). I now analyze in detail another case at the microsocial level: the construction of senderista power in the neighboring zone of Alto Cunas.

Alto Cunas is a high river valley situated in the southeastern Mantaro Valley, which borders to the south with Canipaco Valley. Alto Cunas is populated principally by communities of herders who also practice high altitude agriculture. It is connected to the Mantaro Valley and the city of Huancayo, more than two hours away by car, by a highway that passes through Chupaca, one of the most commercially dynamic communities of the region. In San Juan de Jarpa, the most important community in Alto Cunas, an NGO created by the Jesuit Order, PROCAD (Centro Promoción, Capitación, y Desarrollo, or Promotion, Training, and Development Center) had been active since the late 1970s. PROCAD developed a dynamic project of peasant promotion in the whole microregion. PROCAD's initiatives in San Juan de Jarpa provide a prime example of its work.[7] This community had only 1,700 head of low-quality sheep (ganado lanar chusco, literally "mixed breed" or "mutt" sheep) when PROCAD began its work. To improve the livestock, PROCAD promoted the purchase of fine breeders from the Túpac Amaru SAIS: 100 head of the Junín breed, including 15 breeders and 85 lambs. Between 1979 and 1988 this select flock grew to 750 animals of high quality. In 1983, the low-quality sheep were sold in order to obtain Andean camelids, twenty alpacas and twenty-five llamas, among them two breeders. This stock grew to 250 camelids by 1988. With a loan from the Banco Agrario the community acquired five heads of Holstein cattle in 1987, and increased this group to nine by the following year. PROCAD also provided support and training for agriculture, with good results. Once trained peasant promoters had graduated, they could make a living by advising agricultural producers. Other PROCAD initiatives including the processing of the peasants' products, particularly the dying of wool with natural herbs, the founding of a communal store, and efforts to resolve land problems among peasants. Uneven distribution of the land left many youth with few alternatives to migration or delinquency. The community of Chaquicocha was convinced to address the issue through a restructuring that redistributed communal lands equally among the members. It was hoped that the experience could be replicated throughout the microregion.

In short, Jarpa had lived through a dynamic and advanced social process. Residents of Jarpa considered petitioning to be elevated to the category of province (a goal since the previous century). But the situation changed rapidly in 1988, with the arrival of Shining Path.

People in Jarpa were aware of what was happening in Ayacucho, but they thought that if Shining Path were to come to their community, the whole community would rise up in resistance. In February 1988 rumors began to circulate that Shining Path had come in the middle of the night to take *comuneros* out of their homes to the edge of the town for interrogations. The authorities investigated with no results, possibly due to fear on the part of those whom the senderistas were presumed to have visited. It was said that Shining Path had threatened them with death. This situation went on until July, and there was a consensus that Shining Path must have had trusted informants in the community. The comuneros no longer dared to walk in the streets at night. Finally, on 17 August at 9:30 P.M., came the armed incursion. Eight masked people captured and savagely mistreated the local *gobernador* (governor), whom they accused of being an aprista (a member of APRA) and of not having renounced his post despite two warnings to do so. They took him to the center of the plaza, ignored his pleas and his promises to renounce immediately, and killed him with two gunshots in the presence of his younger brother, who was also brutally beaten. Meanwhile, other activists wrote slogans on the walls. When the senderistas did not find the mayor, they set his house on fire and moved on to the PROCAD offices—the personnel were fortunately on vacation—and burned the PROCAD as well. They then set the municipal council building on fire, and spread gasoline that prevented people from putting the fire out. As they retreated, they shouted *vivas* to the armed struggle and left a sign next to the cadaver of the assassinated governor: "Just like this miserable dog, all the aprista authorities who are lackeys of the present government will die." Only the next day did the comuneros dare to go out and verify what had happened. "That day the people did not know what to do. Everybody was traumatized and crying and asking one another what we would do when they come back." Only three men and five women attended the funeral, the rest fled to the heights to hide among the caves.

Subsequently, incursions occurred regularly and the senderistas organized community meetings three or four times a week. Not all the comuneros felt victimized by the situation. Sectors of youth looked with favor on the arrival of the Shining Path column and received its teachings enthusiastically. A comunero narrates that "many of the local young people voluntarily joined their ranks, and others were obligated to join the ranks and these same *paisanos* returned with more enthusiasm, believing they were already winning. So they saw anyone who did not obey them as the black sheep whom they later killed with rocks as [they did] to many brothers who today rest in peace, and others they burned alive with gasoline. What a sad and lamentable time we passed, wondering desperately which day we would be killed."

The presence of the senderistas had a profoundly perturbing effect on communal life, quite different from initial events in the Canipaco Valley. There, Shining Path assumed control and organized every aspect of the inhabitants' daily life. Sendero undertook the administration of justice and played the role of a moralizing force. Shining Path settled marital conflicts, supervised the work of teachers, mediated the relationships between the comuneros and those authorities and state functionaries who were not obliged to quit, executed thieves who robbed livestock from the herders and even organized recreation (Manrique 1989). None of this occurred in Jarpa: "There were many people who took advantage of the situation to steal, blaming terrorism, and they took the best animals that one had and we did not have anywhere to go to complain because there were no authorities."

In the coexistence between the community of Jarpa and the Shining Path column that visited regularly, coercion predominated from the beginning. In contrast, Canipaco had initially lived a kind of honeymoon between the comuneros and the guerrilla column, which only ended with the involvement of some senderista cadres in a conflict over lands previously usurped by haciendas within the Cahuide sais, but claimed by two rival communities. The participation of armed Shining Path cadres on the side of one of the communities in a massive confrontation against a confederation of rival communities provoked a rupture with the latter, who decided to turn over two senderista cadres they had captured in the scuffle to the authorities in Huancayo. This action provoked Shining Path reprisals, which culminated in the execution of thirteen peasant leaders. The victims were kidnapped from their communities and assassinated in the central plaza of Chongos Alto (Manrique 1989).

In Jarpa, the peasants noted the ideological inconsistency of the cadres who visited them and proved incapable of explaining the content of the new society for which they struggled. "Really it was clear that they had not been well prepared about the politics they embraced, because when we asked questions they did not respond, they just shut us up with threats to kill us, and they demanded that the community do everything that they said." A source of great tension was the demand that the comuneros get rid of the alpacas, llamas, and cattle that they had sacrificed so much to acquire and raise. When they resisted Shining Path directives, the peasants were warned that the communal ranch would be burned down just like the Cahuide SAIS. This threat obliged the comuneros to divide all of the animals among themselves and divide the remaining equipment among the neighborhoods of the community. It was a painful decision, executed only out of fear of the reprisals that would result from disobedience. The intruders' objective was not only to liquidate all productive projects that might divert the peasants from the path of the people's war, but also, in the words of senderista cadres, "that every type of organization disappear."

At the beginning of 1989, the senderistas obliged the comuneros to block the roads. Shining Path told the peasants that the military would arrive in trucks and attack them. Thus they closed off motor vehicle access to the microregion. From then on, the peasants' only option was to travel on horse and foot paths with their beasts of burden. By October, as municipal elections approached, Shining Path prohibited people from going to the Mantaro Valley. The Sendero leadership had decided on a boycott, and threatened anyone who participated in the elections of 9 November with torture, amputation of fingers in the presence of the community (Peruvian election officials stain the fingers of voters with indelible ink to control the election process), and execution. The threats were effective and people stopped going to the Mantaro Valley, even though they needed to exchange their products to obtain goods they did not produce. During these months, Shining Path recruited many young people from the seventeen communities of Alto Cunas and instructed them to cooperate in enforcing the boycott. Two days before the election, Shining Path evacuated the comuneros toward the heights with their animals. The village was completely deserted.

These actions were carried out in competition with detachments of the

Armed Forces, which at this point only added to the harassment of the Alto Cunas communities. The night of 29 October, military detachments arrived in Jarpa from the counterinsurgency base of Vista Alegre in the Canipaco Valley. The counterinsurgency detachments raided the homes of various authorities, especially those of the municipal agents who represented the barrios of the community. The soldiers tortured two of the authorities to identify members of Shining Path's platoons and commandos. A third municipal agent was in the midst of a family gathering to bid goodbye to a son who was leaving for work in Lima. The soldiers entered firing and shot the owner of the house in the clavicle and lungs, leaving him gravely wounded. The soldiers detained the rest of the guests at the gathering, accused them of holding "terrorism classes," and took them to the house of one of the municipal agents who had already been captured. There, the soldiers tortured the captives through the night.

At dawn, the soldiers kidnapped a municipal official, along with his wife and child, and returned to Vista Alegre. The comuneros found the official dying of gunshot wounds; they tried to take him to Huancayo on a three-wheeled cart but he died on the way. After his burial, which very few people dared to attend, the inhabitants were very tense. They did not know what the future would bring. Unfortunately, they found out almost immediately. In the early morning hours of 2 November, the neighborhoods of Jarpa were occupied by forty or fifty armed *encapuchados* (persons masked with hoods), who entered shooting. The attackers took all of the inhabitants, including women, children, and the elderly, and marched them to the plaza with their hands behind their necks. The intruders said they were militants of the MRTA and obliged the inhabitants to call out *vivas* for this organization. They painted the walls of the plaza with slogans. One of the encapuchados took out a notebook and separated a group of people who were taken to the house of one of the inhabitants. Meanwhile the rest of the comuneros were forced to lie face down on the ground in the plaza for several hours. At noon, the encapuchados retreated. "With a military voice they told us all to stay face down for two hours, 'the first to lift a head will be killed.'" Only after another half hour did the comuneros dare to get up. "One of the youth went up to the house of *señor* Yauli and went in, and before a minute had passed he came out screaming and weeping and said that there were dead bodies. At that moment we went up to the house and it was true, in a pool of blood we found five dead comuneros, including a woman who was the wife of Felimón Aparicio. . . . Then we took them out of the house and carried them to the assembly room and at that time everyone was desperate and did not know what to do nor where to go . . . and at that time many began to flee along the paths to the city of Huancayo."

Apparently, the encapuchados—the comuneros are convinced they were actually government soldiers—had access to reliable information, because four of the five comuneros who had been summarily executed were connected to Shining Path. One may speculate that the intruders proceeded on the basis of information obtained from the family that they had taken three days before to Vista Alegre. The community disbanded, as many escaped toward the Mantaro Valley and left the village virtually abandoned. Meanwhile, those who remained suffered persecution by the senderistas, who assassinated the comuneros they considered informants.

During the first months of 1990, death threat letters circulated against those who might participate in the general elections of April 14. "This is how they totally humiliated the community of the seventeen villages of Alto Cunas. Later on, in the month of March, the soldiers arrived and established themselves in the AB *anexo* ["annex"] and they began investigating the case. Daily they captured suspects as well as innocents from the different villages, especially the annexes, and at the end they found out that the village of Q . . . had been hit in all of its annexes, starting with the annex of S." With military backing, the elections of 14 April were carried out normally.

Apparently, the military show of force was effective in convincing the peasants to make the decision to confront Shining Path directly. On 15 July 1990, the seventeen communities of Alto Cunas made a pact with the military, and committed themselves to organizing peasant defense patrols (*rondas campesinas*). Some time after, they figured among the first communities of the country to receive a donation of arms personally from President Fujimori.

> Day and night we do our patrol duties. When in the end the soldiers retreated to Huancayo, the district petitioned to bring them back. They agreed to our petitions and again the military returns and set themselves up in the principal plaza of Q. Then they begin to do new investigations and capture so many from the annexes and among them once again they determine that the bad elements were from Shining Path; they even rescued our mimeograph machine that the senderistas had robbed from the school. The mimeograph was in the

annex of S and they were the same ones who deactivated the former sais Cahuide Laive.

This was how we were supported by the military and their food was provided by the whole community. The soldiers also committed certain abuses. Considering all of this, it is the peasant community that has to suffer all the consequences, but in spite of it all the village of Q . . . now is becoming normal. Now at least we are passing our Christmas in tranquility, eating our *canchita* [toasted maize] with milk and many with our barley coffee.

The modest dishes with which the peasants celebrated Christmas are most expressive of the privations that they had been made to endure during the preceding years.

At the end of 1990 the soldiers again abandoned the district and billeted in an annex. The community decided to assume its own defense. Subsequently, they elected new authorities and mobilized communal labor to rebuild communal buildings and a bridge that Shining Path had destroyed. "This is all until now," our anonymous informant concludes, "and I hope that they do not come back again to destroy my community, because it has been a progressive pueblo, that works together as one man in its communal tasks, and we do not want to suffer again so much hunger, misery, and injustice."

From the case of San Juan de Jarpa we can extract some important observations. First, Shining Path's use of coercive methods did not prevent them from establishing an initial foothold in the microregion of Alto Cunas. As we saw, at the beginning some young people voluntarily enrolled in their ranks, and even some who were initially recruited by force became more enthusiastic adherents ("believing they were already winning.") What stands out here is an element of the peasant pragmatism that Carlos Iván Degregori encountered previously in the biography of a young Ayacuchan who enrolled in Shining Path (Degregori 1990a; see also his essay in this volume). This period saw the adhesion to Shining Path on the part of a sector of the community's youth and the use of extreme coercive measures, including burning alive or stoning to death those who did not submit.

Second, Shining Path's authoritarianism was much more pronounced in Jarpa than in the Canipaco Valley. In Jarpa, the destruction of procad and the elimination of communal herds against the peasants' will contrasted with the greater openness to dialogue exhibited by the Shining Path column active in Canipaco Valley (Manrique 1989). This difference may be attributed to the Alto Cunas cadres' lesser familiarity with peasants, but it also reflected Shining Path's greater difficulty in occupying zones historically lacking in strong tensions between communities and latifundia. The Canipaco Valley had been characterized historically by conflicts between large haciendas and communities. This social tension was not completely eliminated by the agrarian reform's creation of the Cahuide SAIS, which inherited the lands of the hacienda Sociedad Ganadera del Centro. In effect, while not all the comuneros of the region approved of the destruction of the SAIS, for the majority the measure provided a way out of the impasse provoked by the intransigence of the state bureaucracy that controlled the large SAIS units of the central sierra. Significantly, many of the peasants viewed the distribution of the livestock of the Cahuide SAIS (livestock that had previously been kept from them) as a kind of indemnization for the damages that accompanied the destruction of the ranching complex. For the peasantry of the region, the destruction of the Cahuide SAIS represented a crucial symbolic rupture. Regardless of whether they were for or against the measure, they knew that it broke a stalemate that had resulted from the incapacity of peasant groups influenced by class-driven trade unionism to impose their own alternatives. The intransigence of the SAIS functionaries and the lack of solidarity displayed by the hacienda's former tenant laborers had proved too strong. The former tenants appeared to be the privileged beneficiaries of a vertically imposed government "solution" that only "solved" the problems of a small minority. The creation of the SAIS had not addressed the needs of the large majority of the peasantry, especially in the case of those communities that ended up suing the SAIS over lands that had been usurped over previous decades by the former haciendas.

In Jarpa, events followed a different course. There was no symbolic marker comparable to the destruction of the SAIS Cahuide that could be seen as a solution (or an attempted solution) to a pressing peasant problem. The destruction of the communal animals neither addressed a peasant demand, nor provided a way out of a stalemate. This was purely and simply an antipeasant measure, dictated by the logic of Shining Path's strategic project, which necessitated liquidating "reformist" solutions. Partial solutions to the peasants' problems might lull them to "sleep" and thus cause them to deviate from the only path that, according to Shining Path teachings, could provide an effective solution for their historical demands: the "people's war." The peasants had worked hard to acquire, tend, and expand the very herds that Shining Path divided among them. The peasants could not view the forced distribution as a "gift" or an indemnization; it was simply the destruction of their own hard-won dreams of progress. In Jarpa, the symbolic markers linked to Sendero were negative: the armed occupation of the community, the destruction of the NGO that had effectively helped the peasantry, the execution of communal authorities, the incineration of public offices, the destruction of communal livestock. Sendero framed such acts as the elimination of all forms of peasant organization.

A third point worth highlighting is the different reaction of the peasantry in the zones historically dominated by free communities than in zones marked by a more feudal-like legacy. The difference between Alto Cunas and the Canipaco Valley are in this sense reflective of a wider dynamic. The coercion and violence the peasants of Alto Cunas experienced at the hands of Shining Path and the counterinsurgency forces had certainly not been exceptional. On the contrary, the experience of violence constituted the norm in all of the regions engulfed in the maelstrom of the rural war. But the reaction of the peasantry in Alto Cunas—an area dominated by free peasant communities—was distinct from that of the peasantry in regions such as the Canipaco Valley, where historically the hacienda and the rural tyrant (*gamonal*) had reigned. In the latter case, peasants might accept violence and coercion more pragmatically, as a lesser evil, or as a "natural" occurrence compensated by the tangible benefits brought by Shining Path to an area where the state had ceased to fulfill its functions.[8]

Once Shining Path went beyond a certain limit, its impositions provoked growing resentment among the peasantry. The peasants were filled with the growing sensation that their dignity was being assaulted. "This is how they totally humiliated the community of the seventeen villages of Alto Cunas," says our informant. It was on this substratum of militant indignation, more difficult to achieve in more feudal regions, that the alliance with the military was based. Through this alliance, the communities decided to retake destiny with their own hands. [Ed.'s note: The other essays in part II of this volume make clear that over time, the dynamics of humiliation and resistance described here for the "free" zones also extended to the "feudal" zones, thereby blurring the initial contrasts.]

To be sure, I am referring to a tendency: Not all the peasants in Canipaco sympathized with Shining Path nor did all the peasants of Alto Cunas reject Sendero. Yet, an experience such as that of Canipaco—where during a period of good relations with the communities, a senderista column

convoked a *huaylarsh* contest that went on for several weeks, with the enthusiastic participation of dancers from various communities—would have
been unimaginable in Alto Cunas.

Finally, the community as a structure has played a crucial role in confronting Shining Path and in rebuilding the infrastructure destroyed during
the Shining Path occupation (compare Degregori and Starn, in this volume).
Shining Path never overcame its outsider or alien status among the communities of Alto Cunas, even when numerous young people joined its ranks.
The objective rupture with Shining Path, solidified in the alliance with the
military and the organization of counterinsurgency rondas in 1990, was
symbolically reinforced with the election of new communal authorities, a
violation of Shining Path's interdictions against all forms of autonomous
peasant organization. The hard trial of fire did not liquidate the community
but rather reinforced it. The Jarpa community's legitimacy rested in the
notion that the Jarpinos are "a progressive pueblo, that works together as
one man in its communal tasks." This characteristic had not been erased
(Manrique 1987a).

A study of the war's characteristics among the communities of the eastern side of the Mantaro Valley would require another chapter. I limit the
discussion to pointing out that in this area the situation was complicated by
the rivalry between communities that confronted Shining Path from a position of independence vis-à-vis the military (in some cases, as in Andamarca,
out of sympathy with MRTA columns), and communities that opted for an
overt alliance with the military against both Shining Path and the MRTA
(as in Comas). In addition, the settling of scores within the pro-Shining
Path and pro-MRTA communities gave the confrontation an overwhelming
ferocity. In some communities where the MRTA provided armed responses
to Shining Path abuses, the MRTA went to the extreme of exterminating
not only the senderista cadres, but their entire families and friends as well.
They even killed children, in the words of an atrocious slogan, "so as not to
leave even the seed." Without a doubt, Shining Path paid the MRTA back in
the same coin, wherever it was able to do so. This extreme situation makes
evident the fierceness of the confrontations, as well as the magnitude of
resentments that the impositions and abuses suffered during this period
provoked among the peasantry.[9]

The Central Selva in Flames: Drug Trafficking and the Asháninka Tragedy

The area of the central selva that extends to the east of Comas and Anda-marca was the scene of guerrilla actions initiated by the MIR in June 1965, under the leadership of Guillermo Lobatón and Máximo Velando. The MRTA claimed this experience as part of its own tradition because two of the organizations that came together at the founding of the MRTA had emerged from factions of the historical MIR. In addition, the MRTA included among its own ranks some of the survivors of the 1965 guerrilla movement. The most notable was Antonio Meza, an ex-leader of the Peasant Federation of Satipo condemned to prison during the first Belaúnde administration. Meza was killed, along with sixty-one MRTA guerrillas, in a military ambush in May 1989 in the village of Molinos, near Jauja, when an MRTA column attempted to take Tarma. The military deployed artillery helicopters to pursue the re-treating guerrillas. There were no prisoners or wounded. Within hours, an exultant Alan García arrived rapidly by helicopter and posed for the national and international press. He exhibited the cadavers of the fallen guerrillas as war trophies.[10]

The central selva is occupied by the Asháninka, an Amazonian macro-ethnic group that, with 50,791 members counted in the national census of 1993, constituted about one-fourth of Peru's native Amazonian population. Known colloquially as *campas* (a pejorative term derived from the Quechua word *thampa,* which means ragged, dirty, unkempt), they are a proud people with a long warrior tradition (Varese 1973; see also Brown and Fernández 1991). They occupy the forested zone of the provinces of Satipo and Chan-chamayo in Junín and the Oxapampa area of Pasco, and spread toward the Ucayali Valley region. They are separated in multiple groups, among which there are 21,000 campas Asháninka, who occupy a very broad territory; 6,000 Asháninka Caquinte, who live in the Alto Poyeni and its tributaries; and 4,000 Asháninka Nomatsiguenga of the Alto Pangoa, Sanibeni, Ana-pati, and Kiatari Rivers. Additional groups inhabit the Gran Pajonal, the Alto Perené, the Pichis, and the Ucayali. According to the Ministry of Agri-culture, in 1986 there were 169 native communities, each with its own territory. It is impossible to determine at this moment just how many may have disappeared as a result of the violence. Their language belongs to the Arawak linguistic family and is marked by distinct dialects.

On 8 December 1989, Alejandro Calderón, president of the Apatyawaka Nampistsi Asháninka (ANAP), a federation that grouped fifty-two native communities of the central selva, was kidnapped together with two other native Asháninkas by emerretistas ("MRTAistas"). Taken to an MRTA camp in El Chaparral, they were submitted to a "revolutionary trial," in which they were accused of cooperating with the police in the 1965 capture of the MIR leader Máximo Velando, who was subsequently thrown alive from a helicopter. Sentenced to death by the emerretistas, Calderón and Rodrigo Chauca were killed; the third captive managed to flee and inform his community of the fate suffered by the other two. On 24–25 December, an assembly of native communities of the Pichis River decided to declare war on the MRTA, avenge the death of Calderón, and expel the MRTA—dead or alive—from their territories. The following day saw what has been called the Asháninka Uprising, led by the self-named Asháninka Army, which consisted of natives armed mainly with traditional bows and arrows. The Asháninka offensive expanded almost to Puerto Bermúdez. By the end of January 1990, the leaders of the Federation of Native Yanesha Communities (Federación de Comunidades Nativas Yanesha, or FECONAYA) joined the struggle. They obliged the MRTA to retreat and carry out a public "auto-criticism" (autocrítica) whereby the MRTA recognized that the execution of Calderón had been a political error, and announced a retreat in order to avoid confrontations with the Asháninka. The MRTA wished not to have the Asháninka as enemies but to win them over.[11] The MRTA moved its cadres from the region toward the districts of Perené and Pichanaki, where they set up and maintained a well-equipped and well-trained column that apparently enjoyed a certain amount of support among the local populace.

One year later, during summer 1991, the Second Asháninka Uprising took place. This time, the Asháninka confronted Shining Path guerrillas, who certainly lacked the scruples the MRTA had shown when rejected by the natives of Satipo Province.

Shining Path's occupation of the central selva seems to have followed the footsteps of cocaine traffickers who entered the Ené Valley in the late 1970s and early 1980s. During this period, Colombian drug traffickers were regularly seen in the Cutivireni Airport. The Colombians were trying to convince the natives to cultivate coca. They were impeded by the influence of Mariano Gagnon, a North American Franciscan priest who worked for more than two decades in the mission of San José de Cutiverini and won the respect and support of the Asháninka. Toward the end of 1983, Father Gagnon travelled to Lima to inform the authorities about the difficult situation in Cutivireni. During his absence a Shining Path column attacked and burned down the mission and threatened to kill the missionary if he returned. Gagnon was not deterred; that same year he began reconstructing the mission, which was finished in 1988. In June 1989, a Shining Path column arrived and demanded food, clothing, and medicine. A precarious co-existence was established at the cost, for the mission, of paying a regular tax to the senderistas, principally in the form of ink, stencils, paper, and other printing materials.

In November 1989, in the midst of the senderista offensive against the municipal elections, the mission was assaulted by a Shining Path column of some sixty members. They burned the mission again and kidnapped a Belgian volunteer, Lucas Adins, along with three Asháninka leaders. The following day, the captives' cadavers were discovered. One of the Asháninkas had been crucified. This atrocity provoked the exodus of the seven hundred Asháninkas who had lived in Cutivireni. Lacking weapons with which to confront the senderistas, the Asháninka tried to compensate for their material disadvantage by going deep into the jungle, where they hoped to take advantage of their better knowledge of the terrain. But Shining Path had some Asháninkas among its ranks. After a long march, some frustrated attempts at settling in other places, and the loss of numerous lives, the Asháninka refugees considered an alternative. Gagnon offered a Dominican mission in Urubamba, in territory inhabited by the Machiguenga, and 213 Asháninkas accepted. A very few decided to stay in the region, and the rest sought to establish themselves in the cities of the region. The fate of those who decided to stay is unknown. Similarly dramatic was the fate of the inhabitants of the native community of Matzuriniari. The 1,100 inhabitants of Matzuriniari were harassed by Shining Path: Three guerrilla incursions in 1991 left more than 70 dead. Lacking support from the authorities and facing the threat of forcible enrollment in the senderista forces, the natives decided to leave en masse. Eight hundred people left for San Martín de Pangoa. But they found that they could not stay due to the presence of squatters and the urban character of this settlement, which threatened the cultural survival of the group. So they continued their exodus to Puerto Ocopa, where they were taken in by another Asháninka group. This latter group was more urbanized, had experience in commerce with the city, and considered the recent arrivals to be "uncivilized" (Rodríguez Vargas, 1993).

Shining Path occupied the central selva mainly because of the region's strategic location for the expansion of the "people's war." The area of the Tambo, Ené, and Pichis Rivers constituted a natural corridor to connect senderista work along the Apurímac River, in the Ayacucho selva, with the region of Huallaga. This connection did not rely solely upon the rivers, but was also facilitated by the existence of a highway (*la Carretera Marginal*), extended to Puerto Ocopa in the mid-1980s. In addition, the central selva constituted the natural rear guard for political and military cadres working in the central sierra. Finally, the ties with the drug traffickers in the Huallaga zone (in the northern fringes of the central selva) encouraged Shining Path to continue its work in the central selva. A suspicious plague of fungus that attacked coca plants in the Huallaga led them to an interest in opening new territories in the central selva for coca cultivation. Further south in the Río Apurímac zone, peasant coca cultivators, drug traffickers, and the military had united and established an alliance against Shining Path.

The Apurímac experience repeated what had happened in the Huallaga Valley under the command of General Alberto Arciniegas, who had decided to prioritize the confrontation with Shining Path over and above the political interests of the U.S. government. The United States tried to impose the drug war as the top priority through an antipeasant strategy of coca leaf eradication. Arciniegas managed to break the alliance between the senderistas and the Huallaga peasants by assuring the latter that no one would prevent them from cultivating coca; the only enemy he wished to combat was Shining Path. The clientelist and markedly utilitarian nature of the relationship between Shining Path and the region's peasantry (Manrique 1989) allowed the army to gain the support of the coca leaf cultivators and thereby deal punishing blows to Sendero. Ultimately, Arciniegas was removed from his post due to pressure from the U.S. Drug Enforcement Administration and the U.S. embassy, who accused him of colluding with drug traffickers. Although this accusation was not proved, Arciniegas had to go into exile when he fell out with the military leaders who sustained Fujimori during and after the "self-coup" of 1992 (see Obando, in this volume, for fuller discussion of Fujimori and the military). Evidence that came to light by early 1995, however, demonstrated conclusively that a vast network of alliances existed among drug traffickers and military chiefs of the highest rank and influence in the Peruvian state. These events vindicated those who had opposed entrusting the Armed Forces with repressing drug trafficking because of the corrupting influence of the hugely wealthy drug traffickers.

Social Implications of Sendero's Presence among the Asháninka

Coercion and terror do not suffice to explain the ease with which Shining Path imposed its authority in the region occupied by the Asháninka. There were also numerous Asháninka who joined Shining Path ranks voluntarily. The Asháninka ethnic group are not internally homogeneous. The conflicts among distinct groupings have fed the Asháninkas' fame as excellent warriors. On the other hand, the construction of the Carretera Marginal, a "civilizing project" par excellence, had grave implications for their survival as a people. Along with the roadway came settlers (*colonos*) whose colonization of the land cornered the natives in the most isolated territories. Moreover, the colonos caused irreparable ecological damage, due to the technique (known as *el rozo*) with which they prepared lands for cultivation. They burned large areas of forest vegetation to clear the terrain, where they cultivated coffee, tobacco, cacao, and, recently, coca. Deprived of the forest cover, the soil was exposed to rain and subject to erosion. Within a short period, territories once covered with a dense vegetation were converted into arid deserts.[12] This process intensified in the first half of the decade of the 1980s. The Satipo Cooperative Project, a plan for massive settlement of a million hectares between the Bajo Tambo and Urubamba zones, compounded the problem.

The Asháninka were, therefore, already under siege when the senderistas arrived. It is not surprising that, initially, many Asháninka thought they had found in Shining Path an effective instrument to defend their interests—which they had fruitlessly sought to defend on their own—against external pressures. Marisol Rodríguez suggests that millenarian aspects of the Asháninka cosmovision might have facilitated penetration by the Shining Path. "The encounter with subversion simultaneously produced a new discourse: the idea of a new order, more just and with bases in the countryside, seemed very attractive to them. This discourse coincided with a messianic myth of the Asháninka people, the return of the mythic hero Itomi Pavá (Son of the Sun) who would bring back justice and welfare to the Asháninka" (Rodríguez Vargas 1993: 53; see also Brown and Fernández 1991).

Today it is known that Shining Path's presence did not represent an advance toward the just and prosperous society of which the Asháninka had dreamed. In place of paradise, Shining Path created concentration camps where the natives were forced to work "for the party" in subhuman conditions and endure a thousand privations including corporal punishment and death for disobedience or flight. The majority of the natives rescued by the

Asháninka rondas and by the Armed Forces showed symptoms of critical malnourishment (compare the montaña experience in Ayacucho recounted by del Pino, in this volume).

Shining Path's presence broke down Asháninka ethnic solidarities. Consider the nervous and rather incoherent testimony of an inhabitant of the Tambo River (Rodríguez Vargas 1993: 106). "My community of my problem is now, now, well now, is there, is . . . they want . . . want, how to say it, it is threatened, it wants us to confront Shining Path and no, one cannot dialogue, or rather, converse; in addition our own paisanos they want to kill us and they, there are times that we, in what way can we converse with them, our, our paisano, no, because now it is all dominated by Shining Path, this is why there are times among ourselves, they want, now truly, they want, or rather, they can, attack us in any moment."

This fractured text expresses more than the difficulties of an Amazonian native trying to express himself in an alien language. His discourse is disorganized by the burden of conflicting emotions provoked by the existence of members of his collectivity among the very killers who threaten the group's physical survival. The line that separates the protagonists of the confrontation becomes confused, the difficulty of delineating sharply between friends and enemies produces this painfully fragmented discourse: "In what way can we converse with them?"

The violence has destroyed numerous Asháninka settlements and has forced a vast migration. An estimated one-fifth of the population of the macroethnic group has been displaced as a result of the war. The social structure of the native societies has suffered grave damage; animosities that date to ancestral epochs have been reinvigorated. But the Asháninka have not been victims only of the actions of the insurgent forces; there have also been multiple denunciations of human rights violations committed by the counterinsurgency forces. Such abuses were favored by ethnic and racial prejudices that cast conscripts from the sierra and the coast as superior to the jungle "savages" or *chunchos,* by the relative impunity with which soldiers may act against the local inhabitants, and by the Asháninkas' chronic condition as "suspicious" due to their lack of documents. From the point of view of official Peru, thousands of these inhabitants of the Amazon do not even have legal existence; they are not inscribed in civil registers and therefore are not citizens. The legal limbo in which many Asháninka live excludes them from rights which, at least formally, are enjoyed by legally recognized citizens. Part of the Asháninka tragedy, in their relationship with both Shining Path and the counterinsurgency forces, has its origin in this juridical nonexistence. From a formal point of view, it is difficult to prove the violation of rights of people who, according to law, do not exist.

As in other zones (see Starn, in this volume), the cornering of the Asháninka led finally to the formation of counterinsurgency rondas. During the military parade for the independence celebrations of July 1992, the procession of Asháninka detachments symbolically consecrated the pact established with the state and the Armed Forces to combat Shining Path. The native Asháninka ended up bearing the social cost of the war; on more than one occasion the military has used them as cannon fodder in confrontations with Shining Path. But at least in this way the Asháninka were able to retake the initiative. Confrontations continued [as of 1995] with great ferocity on both sides.

The violence has decreased over the last three years [1992–1995] due to the crisis experienced by the insurgent organizations, the greater presence of the Armed Forces, and the organization of the autodefense rondas. As a result, numerous Asháninka groups that had been abducted by Shining Path and obliged to do forced labor have been rescued. Nonetheless, the tribulations of this suffering people did not end. On 18 August 1993, a Shining Path column, reinforced by numerous Asháninka natives, entered the district of Mazamari, Satipo, with the goal of "teaching a lesson" (*escarmentar*) to those who had organized rondas. Shining Path went on a rampage through the small hamlets along the Sonomoro River and killed men, women, and children. The final tally was 62 Asháninka dead and approximately 2,500 homeless.[13]

Conclusion and Epilogue

In Junín, as in other areas of the Peruvian sierra and selva where Shining Path rooted itself in the 1980s, peasant autodefense rondas proliferated by the 1990s. This outcome was fueled by the disjuncture between a profoundly vertical and authoritarian political project, on the one hand, and a peasantry with a long tradition of independent, solid, and free communities, on the other (Mallon 1983; Manrique 1987b). Sendero tied its destiny not to an effort to win over the majority of the population through persuasion, but to the imposition of a more passive assent. The conscious participation of the peasantry was not necessary; the revolution would be the task of political cadres, the "select minority" that expressed the peasants' historical interests, even against the will of those whom they claimed to represent. While initially Shining Path managed to establish itself as a positive force in some peasant spaces such as the Canipaco Valley, once it had capitalized on the peasants' discontent with the SAIS enterprises, Sendero's acceptance lasted only a few months. In spaces dominated by free peasant communities such as the Alto Cunas, Shining Path was unable to gain consistent sympathy among the communities even during a brief initial period, despite the willing and forced adhesion of a significant contingent of young comuneros.

The peasantry of the central sierra historically has experienced diverse war emergencies, the most significant of which was its resistance to Chilean occupation during the War of the Pacific (1881–1884). The memory of this event is continually renovated in popular festivities known as the Macctada, Cáceres's Army, and the Dance of the Avelinos, performed annually in the villages of the Mantaro Valley region (Mallon 1983, 1995; Manrique 1986a, 1987b, 1988b). The peasants of the central sierra, as Pablo Macera has observed, constitute the only Peruvian social sector that remembers the war with Chile with pride, as a victory rather than a humiliating and shameful defeat.

A question posed by the extension of the political violence into the central region in the 1980s was whether the insurgent organizations would be capable of inserting themselves within the region's bountiful historical traditions of peasant resistance. The definitive answer to this question lies in the failure of MRTA's project to take root and in the complete defeat of Shining Path in the region's communities—Shining Path's forced retreat to the remotest regions,[14] and the generalized hatred that its actions have aroused among the peasantry of the region. The conscious participation of the highland peasantry had been the basis of the region's resistance to the Chilean invasion and its patriotic guerrilla bands during the War of Independence (Manrique 1981). But Shining Path disdained peasant political consciousness. The capture of Abimael Guzmán—the mystified "President Gonzalo"—dealt the final blow to Shining Path's peasant project in the Mantaro Valley. The crisis of the Senderista project, however, had been gestating before, when the peasants decided to organize themselves in rondas and autodefense committees in order to combat Shining Path, in some cases in alliance with the Armed Forces and in other cases on their own. Something similar occurred in the central selva, although in this region the behavior of the Asháninka groups was far more complex, due to the sharp internal conflicts that Shining Path's presence had catalyzed.

Since the early 1990s, it became apparent that Shining Path's presence in the central region—aside from isolated high-altitude zones—was becoming circumscribed to the city of Huancayo and its immediate rural surroundings. A review of the chronology of the political violence ratifies this impression. With the army's military occupation of the Universidad Nacional del Centro and the deactivation of Shining Path's urban network, its presence in the region collapsed. Shining Path's work in the mines, where it had been particularly active during 1987 and 1988, had already undergone a crisis. The mineworkers rejected Shining Path's tactic of assassinating labor leaders who opposed its project (Manrique 1989).

Various bits of evidence suggest that the collapse of Shining Path has not implied a definitive liquidation. Rather, its remaining cadres have tactically retreated, under orders from the national leadership of the self-styled Sendero Rojo ("Red Path"), the Shining Path offshoot that emerged when the captured Guzmán appealed to President Fujimori for peace conversations. (See Part V of this volume for additional context on this development.) The new development split Shining Path's apparently monolithic party apparatus. At least a fraction of the Shining Path cadres who survived the crisis of recent years seem to have retreated to develop a political network and to reorganize their battered forces. Shining Path has not died; press reports of reactivation and attacks in the region surface sporadically, as in the month preceding the April 1995 elections.

In addition, the social problems that prompted the Shining Path to declare that "rebellion is justified" continue unsolved. It is clearly doubtful that Shining Path will once again gain peasant support in the region, after the traumatic experience of these past years. But Shining Path is, above all, one expression of a more profound social crisis. Although its actions sharpened the crisis, Sendero did not generate it in the first place. As long as the causes that are behind the outbreak of this crisis are not faced, a revival of political violence is still possible.

Notes

1   The figures used to quantify the political violence in Peru during the 1980s must be considered relative at best. The reason is simple; the various organizations that have computed the phenomenon statistically have relied for their data on information provided by the national and regional press, which in turn relied on military communiques. After the January 1983 massacre of nine

journalists in the community of Uchuraccay, the press retreated from the war scenario and the military monopolized the production of information. In addition, the 1995 "Amnesty Law" imposed by the government of Alberto Fujimori, canceled judicial investigations in progress and annulled all sentences against members of the counterinsurgency forces accused of human rights violations. As a result, the true magnitude of the internal war in Peru may never be known. For this reason, rather than present exact numbers to measure the significance of this period of Peruvian history, I have chosen instead to sketch curves that permit us to better visualize general tendencies. I have preferred to rely on a regional source because the information that this source provides is richer than that contained in the national dailies, which are analyzed by the institutions that work in Lima.

2   Although I have not considered Apurímac specifically in the preceding discussion, I am confident that this statement holds.

3   Except when otherwise noted, the information used below comes from the data base of the DESCO, Center for Studies and Promotion of Development (*Centro de Estudios y Promoción del Desarrollo*).

4   "An emergent social sector experiencing mobilization and changes in Peruvian society—the provincial university students—will be found exposed to situations of instability and insecurity that derive from the incongruence between expectations and achievements. This condition has probably made them wonder about their personal future within the framework of opportunities offered by society, and they likely become especially prone to thinking about the economic and social problems of the environment from which they come. As a result of their formation, they have some explanatory schemes with which to interpret these problems. The dynamic of mobilization and blockage—on a personal level and on the level of their communities—would make attractive the option of changing structures through the systematic exercise of violence" (Chávez de Paz 1989: 57).

5   A university professor explained to me that the worst part of receiving an anonymous threat was not so much the death threat itself but the impossibility of knowing if the anonymous note was actually sent by the organization that signed it or if it was the work of some personal enemy. In such a case, the uncertainty had a more disturbing psychological effect than the actual death threat. Secondary school teachers confronted a similar situation.

6   As became clear at the conference that led to this book, some scholars criticize the use of the term "peasant" (*campesino*) for obviating the existence of ethnic identities not reducible to class analysis, while others criticize the term for not taking into account the multiple extra-agricultural economic activities of sectors of the rural population. Nonetheless, I consider "peasant" to be a useful and pertinent term. On the one hand, recognition of ethnic diversity in the Peruvian countryside does not nullify the existence of class relations.

On the other hand, while the campesino condition has over several decades incorporated a whole range of nonagricultural activities, and the importance of agriculture in their life strategies is constantly declining, what is decisive, in my opinion, is the logic of the whole. We should not get bogged down in an attempt to define what percentage of the nonagricultural component of peasant incomes signals "depeasantization." Rather, we should consider to what extent family labor is organized around the agricultural calendar and subordinates other needs to agriculture's seasonal demands.

7 The principal sources for this section consist of my own personal knowledge of PROCAD, which I advised in the early 1980s, and the written account by a peasant that obtained the first prize in the *II Concurso de Testimonio Campesino* (Second Contest of Peasant Testimonials), "*Balance y Perspectivas de mi Organización*" ("Results and Perspectives of my Organization"). The contest was sponsored by the magazine *Andenes*, a publication of the Rural Educational Services (Servicios Educacionales Rurales, or SER).

8 Conflicts between communities and haciendas have not been completely absent from the history of Alto Cunas. The most notable confrontation pitted Chupaca and Jarpa against the Aliaga family, which owned the Apahuay estate. But this case is rather exceptional and certainly much less important than the tensions experienced in Canipaco, which in turn were less intense than those conflicts that characterized the zones of greatest gamonal presence in the neighboring department of Huancavelica and other areas to the south (Manrique 1988b).

9 I was struck by a report prepared by the television network Frecuencia Latina on the civil defense patrols of the community of Comas that confronted Shining Path. The report showed the comasinos carrying out a military parade. Great was my surprise to see that the principal weapon they used was the *rejón*, a kind of primitive pike constructed by tying a ploughshare to a large stick— the same weapon that, 100 years before, the peasant guerrillas of the region used to combat the Chilean forces that invaded the region during the war with Chile (Manrique 1981). Comas and the communities of Alto Cunas figured among the first to receive weapons from the hands of Alberto Fujimori, which proved the solidity of their alliance with the Armed Forces.

10 The MRTA officially recognized forty-two of the dead and asserted that the rest were residents who had been assassinated by the military because they were inconvenient witnesses to the execution of prisoners and the wounded.

11 An MRTA leader I interviewed in 1991 in the Castro Castro prison assured me that Fernando Calderón and other Asháninka were tied to APRA through the Universidad Federico Villareal and that they had been organizing a paramilitary force. I have not been able to confirm this.

12 The Asháninka also use this method, but on a carefully limited scale that

does not leave the earth unprotected and vulnerable to erosion caused by the abundant rains that the region receives over many months of the year.

13 An example of a counterinsurgency policy that did not generate credibility was an announcement by high ranking officials that they had found a thousand cadavers of native Asháninkas in a common grave. This report was questioned by those who were acquainted with the way of life of the Amazonian natives. Their skepticism was based on the fact that the region's characteristics do not permit the existence of native communities anywhere near that big. This did not, however, rule out the execution of numerous natives by the senderistas (people who know the region well speak of hundreds of victims), but the victims most likely were buried separately in graves dispersed across a wide territory.

14 As of 1995 there were reports of Shining Path columns moving through zones higher than 3,800 meters above sea level, from which they eventually carry out surprise attacks against vulnerable communities.

SEVEN

Villagers at Arms: War and Counterrevolution

in the Central-South Andes

Orin Starn

> His laughter shatters . . . all the familiar landmarks of my thought—*our* thought, the thought that bears the stamp of our age and our geography— breaking all the ordered surfaces and planes with which we are accustomed to tame the wild profusion of existing things. —*Michel Foucault on the Argentine writer Jorge Luis Borges*[1]

✦ In 1993, I gave a lecture at Ayacucho's Huamanga University. Ayacucho is a city of contrasts, of ponchoed peasants and mini-skirted teenagers and colonial churches and cement-block houses, set against the painful beauty of dry mountains and a turquoise Andean sky. Originally founded under the Spanish Viceroyalty, the university reopened in 1959 as part of the Peruvian government's push to "modernize" the "backward" interiors of the national territory. But the school is best-known as the birthplace of the Communist Party of Peru-Shining Path, the Maoist revolutionaries who have fought a thirteen-year war to topple the Peruvian state.[2] The Shining Path founder, Abimael Guzmán, now imprisoned, taught philosophy there in the 1960s, and the core of his cadre were students. After the occupation of Ayacucho in late 1982, army troops made frequent raids into the university to murder and kidnap suspected rebels. Soon, the Shining Path also began to kill students and staff on charges of collaboration with the military, including seven professors. Fear hung over the entire city of Ayacucho, whose name in Quechua means "Corner of the Dead," as the terror of the dirty war between the army and the guerrillas engulfed the highlands.

Now, however, my friend, a young history professor, assured me that it was calm enough for even a visiting *gringo* to lecture. Before a packed hall (the talk was mandatory for students in the social sciences), I gave a spiel about anthropology in the United States. Still, I was uneasy when question time arrived. A few years before, when I spoke at Lima's San Marcos University, a Shining Path militant stood to denounce "Yankee imperialism" and called for renewed commitment to the "people's war," triggering a chair-throwing melee with his classmates. This time, however, the climate was completely different. One student asked about Clifford Geertz; another about recent debates in Andeanist anthropology. After the class, people had more urgent questions. How hard is it to get a visa to the United States? And had I ever met Yoko Ono or John Lennon?

Leninism displaced by Lennonism? This was how another Peruvian friend described it when I told him the story. To be sure, the recent and violent past has not vanished. Many Ayacuchans, including students, seem to sense the truth of Walter Benjamin's famous injunction that "even the dead will not be safe from the enemy if he wins" and the consequent urgency of "seiz[ing] hold of a memory as it flashes up at a moment of danger."[3] Tales circulate in living rooms and on street corners of loved ones tortured or disappeared by the military, a stubborn refusal to acquiesce to the state's desire to erase the use of terror from collective memory. At the same time, however, few Ayacuchans are attracted any longer by the Shining Path, which has left a grisly trail of massacred villagers, murdered mayors, and burned crops in the name of the fight for a Maoist utopia. With none of the original romance of a popular uprising, and as Marxism and the dream of revolution have unraveled across Latin America, the Shining Path barely survives across the arid mesas and blue-gray peaks of this Andean department of half a million people. Many Ayacuchans from all walks of life speak of a sense that "hemos pasado lo peor—the worst has passed," and even proffer a guarded optimism about the future.

Much of the talk about the war's ebb has centered on the capture in 1992 of Abimael Guzmán. What went far less noticed in the hubbub over the arrest of the man regarded by his followers as "the greatest living Marxist-Leninist" was that the Shining Path's influence had already declined over much of the rural Andes. Their Maoist blueprint projected the encirclement of Peru's cities from the countryside to "put the noose around the neck of imperialism and the reactionaries . . . and garrot[ing] them by the throat," in Guzmán's words.[4] By the start of this decade, however, more than 3,500 villages in the departments of Apurímac, Ayacucho, Huancavelica, and Junín had organized what came to be known as rondas campesinas, or peasant patrols, to fight the Shining Path.[5] Despite the assassinations of hundreds of patrollers, or *ronderos,* the alliance of the peasants and the military pushed the Maoists almost completely out of former strongholds, from the stony canyons of Huanta and snowy peaks of Comas to the rainy valley of the Apurímac River. How to deal with the *rondas* was reportedly a main question at the December 1991 Lima meeting of the Shining Path's Central Committee. The "scientifically guaranteed" logic of Guzmán's plan was upended in a reversal as startling as a *pachakuti,* the inversion of heaven and earth predicted in Andean mythology, as peasants rose in arms against a revolution waged in their name.

This essay examines the history of the rondas campesinas.[6] Easy characterizations of the patrollers as either brutish Hobbesian thugs or noble Tolstoian defenders of pastoral traditions or national sovereignty collapse in the face of this unanticipated turn in Peru's war. "Swings from noble savage to murderous savage, from shattered victim to heroic resister," as anthropologist Irene Silverblatt affirms about representations of Peru's indigenous peoples in the seventeenth century, "have drained the life and lessons" of Andean history under colonialism. To avoid the same mistake with Peru's postcolonial peasants, we need to grapple with the compromised histories—the stiff limits and unintended consequences, split allegiances, missed chances and complicities—that make us "contradictory selves, part of contradictory worlds."[7] The need to push against the confines of dualism and linear thinking is manifest not only in the fragmentation, intertextuality, and massive commodification of the postindustrial megalopolises of Latin America or the United States. In the countryside of the Third World, precisely in those "isolated" and "remote" villages that remain the targets of so much metropolitan discourse of authenticity and Otherness, the wild contours of the social landscape turn out to be just as defiant of our preconceived categories and models, and the world also to be moving in more than one direction.

The Cultural Politics of War and the Rondas Campesinas

"MEDIEVAL VILLAGES" AND ANDEANISM
As I found it in 1993, Cangari-Viru Viru perched on a dry ridge above the Cachi River.[8] The villagers had built eighteen guard towers of adobe brick and red tile into the mud wall that enclosed their fortified settlement of ninety families, five miles to the southwest of the town of Huanta. In the crisp light of the Andean dawn, a stream of women and men headed down

to the riverplain's patchwork quilt of green and brown fields to tend crops and animals. They returned in the evening, herding goats and cows up the winding footpath and inside the walls. By eight p.m., the men on the ronda for the night took their posts with one-shot homemade guns of iron pipe, called *hechizos*, shotguns, and Mauser rifles, ready to defend against raids from across the shallow river. Except for the rifles, the most immediate comparison might have been with a hilltown of Medieval Europe, perhaps San Gimignano or Rocamadour, where the inhabitants of eleventh-century agrarian societies also withdrew at night into walled enclaves to protect against what the Jewish historian Marc Bloch, himself later assassinated by the Gestapo, called the "disorder and havoc" of dangerous times.[9]

Of course, many outsiders have compared the Andes to Medieval Europe. "Feudal," "archaic," and "superstitious" are just some of the adjectives in novelist Mario Vargas Llosa's well-known report on the 1983 massacre of seven journalists in Uchuraccay, just eight hours uphill from Cangari-Viru Viru.[10] Whether as praiseworthy defenders of indigenous ways or, as for Vargas Llosa, backward brutes, villagers figure in the broad tradition of Andeanism as the inhabitants of a primordial "Andean world" isolated from the fast pace and advanced technology of the present-day West. In Peru, this vision maps onto an imagined geography that presents the coast, and especially Spanish-settled Lima, as "modern," "official," and "Western" in contrast with the "premodern," "deep," and "non-Western" Andes. As Vargas Llosa puts it about Uchuraccay's villagers, "they come from a Peru different from the . . . modern European Peru . . . in which I live, an ancient archaic Peru that has survived in these sacred mountains despite centuries of isolation and adversity."[11]

A great deal of recent scholarship emphasizes the need to avoid the trap of the representation of village societies in the Third World as a moribund artifact of a bygone epoch. In fact, the Medieval analogy unravels on a closer look at Cangari-Viru Viru. This village was settled only in 1990. Then-commander of Huanta's Eighth Battalion, Lt. Col. Alfonso Hurtado Robles, known as "El Platanazo—the Big Banana" for his pale skin and unusual height—along with his main lieutenant, Sergeant Jhonny (sic) Zapata, or "Centurión"—spearheaded an aggressive campaign to organize the 56,000 inhabitants of the province's countryside against the Shining Path.[12] In the cactus hills of the lower valley, the army ordered the villagers to leave their scattered farmhouses for nucleated settlements, or *agrupaciones*, and to organize into a patrol system. "Centurión arrived and told us to agruparnos and start rondas, or we'd see what happened," remembers Antonio Quispe, who owns an acre of land and works in construction in the town of Huanta.[13] The families of two scattered settlements along the Cachi River—Cangari and Viru Viru—built and moved into the hyphenated village. Everyone became a rondero under the command of the two villagers entrusted by the army with the titles of "comando" and "civil defense committee president." Another reminder of the flimsiness of the fiction of the timeless Other, and the untenability of the distinction between societies "with" and "without" history (see Wolf 1982), Cangari-Viru Viru proves a product of these last years of the twentieth century, and in particular of a military plan to block the Shining Path's bid for revolution.

So does Cangari-Viru Viru boil down to coercion? Critics have charged that the military organizes by force, placing unarmed peasants on the front line of a vicious war. "Peasants become cannon fodder for Shining Path reprisals," as one leftist senator told me in 1989.[14] Many journalists and scholars have pointed to the danger of the resettlements and patrols devolving into "paramilitary groups" that "extort," "blackmail," "rob," and "pillage," pitting the poor against the poor to quicken the disintegration of the delicate fabric of Andean life.[15] To these observers, the history of the rondas campesinas appears the same as the Guatemalan army's Vietnam-inspired "strategic hamlets" and civil patrols, an extension of the brutalization of the poor majorities by repressive Latin American regimes.[16]

It might be asserted that the Peruvian military's recruitment of peasants echoes the Spanish Conquest, when Pizarro's band of 150 adventurers used a mass of native auxiliaries to topple the Inca Empire.[17] Imposed resettlement also has a colonial genealogy. As part of a design to "civilize" Andeans, and to establish a steady labor supply for the giant mines of Potosí and Huancavelica, Viceroy Francisco Toledo forced the dispersed native population in the 1570s into Spanish-supervised villages, or *reducciones*.[18] Historian Alberto Flores Galindo invokes these historical antecedents in his 1987 description of the counterinsurgency forces as a "colonial army," the evil protagonists of a vicious war of disappearance and massacre of Quechua-speaking villagers in Ayacucho's impoverished countryside.[19] Then-commander Clemente Noel, who studied at the U.S.-run School of the Americas in Panama, relied mostly on outright intimidation, including the assassination of patrol opponents, to start the first rondas, then more commonly known as "Comités de Defensa Civil" (Civil Defense Committees).[20] Navy infantrymen controlled the first resettlements, or *"bases civiles"* (civil bases) like Ccarhuapampa outside the town of Tambo. Meanwhile, Shining Path columns assassinated suspected military collaborators with the troops, dubbing them "*yanaumas*," or black heads, for the ski masks that some of the first patrollers wore to conceal their identities. The rebels also raided villages where rondas had started. In July 1986, for instance, they descended upon Ayacucho's Cochas, slitting the throats of eighteen villagers, including a four-year-old girl and an eighty-two-year-old woman, amid shouts of "Death to Wretches [collaborators with the rondas]" and "Long Live the Revolution and Gonzalo" (Guzmán's *nom de guerre*).[21] Much of the counterinsurgency's history backs a view of the rondas campesinas as furthering the suffering of Andean peasants, deepening what another of Peru's leading historians, Nelson Manrique, has called "*manchay tiempo*" (the time of fear).[22]

But Cangari-Viru Viru also undercuts this reduction of the rondas campesinas to simple coercion. Initially, the Shining Path won the sympathy of many Huantinos, including on the Cachi River, for its punishment of adultery and thievery, and appeal to the desires in an impoverished countryside for a more just order. Many of the high school and university students who formed the bulk of the cadre came from rural families, and sometimes used local ties of kin and friendship to promote the revolutionary cause.[23] Mistakenly, if perhaps understandably, some U.S. scholars proclaimed the Shining Path a "peasant rebellion" or "agrarian revolt."[24] A view of the Maoists as an indigenous insurrection dovetailed with the Andeanist vision of the mountains as a primitive locale of perennial turmoil and rebellion as well as the concept of the insurrectionary villager that was a mainstay of U.S. scholarship on rural upheaval in the wake of the Vietnam War. But this portrayal overlooked that the Shining Path was begun by privileged intellectuals in the city of Ayacucho, and that the revolutionaries were, by 1983, as active in metropolitan Lima as in Andean villages. More broadly, it ignored that the party operated through a rigid hierarchy by race and class that replicated the social order it sought to overthrow. Dark-skinned kids born in poverty filled the bottom ranks under a leadership composed mostly of light-skinned elites.[25] Although it had the approval of some poor farmers in particular places over specific periods of time, the Shining Path was never an organic uprising of the downtrodden, much less one of what anthropologist Eric Wolf calls "the peasant wars of the 20th century."[26]

These tenuous roots help to explain the Shining Path's decline along the Cachi River. By 1990, most villagers realized that the military was not about to "collapse before the glorious advances of the people's war," as the first cadre in Cangari had promised in 1982. For example, Lidia Vásquez, who owns the "Emerald of the Andes" juice stand in Huanta's market, remembers how the rebels "fled like sheep" across the Cachi River when the army arrived in 1989, leaving villagers to face a house-by-house search by angry troops. Although it would be a mistake to present the rural poor as the makers of "rational choices" as if they were outside culture and ideology, historian Steve J. Stern rightly underscores that "peasant societies, to survive, are notoriously sensitive to changes in power balances." Mounting evidence of the Shining Path's weakness clearly lessened the luster of the revolution.[27] Vásquez and many others also tired of the Maoists' missionary zeal: for example, "Commander Percy's" order that the standard expression of "Ay, Jesus!" be replaced by "Ay, Gonzalo!"[28] The rebels angered more peasants still with forced recruitment, demands for food, and executions of suspected *soplones,* or stool pigeons.[29] A decade of revolutionary war only intensified the insecurity and impoverishment of an already harsh world, where no one knew whose mutilated body might appear on the dirt highway or at the bottom of a rocky canyon. No longer was the Shining Path a vessel of dreams for a more egalitarian future. To the contrary, many Huantinos blamed the revolutionaries for the nightmare of a war without apparent end. "All of us supported them at first, but all they have brought us is misery," says José Huamani, a stooped man of forty-five, who lived for many years in a jungle colonization in the Apurímac Valley before moving back to his native Cangari.[30]

Moreover, the military was positioned to exploit growing discontent with the revolution. Although the indiscriminate brutality of the counterinsurgency in 1983 and 1984 forced many peasants to reconsider the wisdom of backing the Shining Path, it also foreclosed the possibility of alliance with the troops. By 1990, however, the military had launched an uneven bid to improve relations with the peasantry. Thus the Big Banana went to birthday parties and holiday festivals in Huanta's countryside; and he delivered speeches about "peasant pride" and "the suffering of the poor" that harked back to Peru's so-called "military socialist" regime of the late 1960s and early 1970s, popular with many Andean villagers for breaking the grip of big landlords in the sweeping agrarian reform of 1969. To be sure, this was an authoritarian, and even fascist, populism. The Big Banana did not hesitate to blow apart with hand grenades captured rebel leaders. "Commander Raúl" and "Commander Percy's" remains were found in Huanta's Cáceres Square at dawn in July 1991, a reminder to the entire province of the grim price of support for the revolution. Still, the decline of indiscriminate violence by the army contributed to new cooperation of peasants in resisting the Shining Path. As the Huanta-born anthropologist José Coronel concludes, "many villagers were weary of war, ready to take any measure to end a revolution that had brought them only suffering and death."[31]

Thus many villagers in Cangari and Viru Viru were willing to move into a nucleated settlement in 1990, even though they knew it was a declaration of war against the Shining Path. It took less than a month for most families to build adobe houses on the hill. Over the next year, the Shining Path launched three nighttime raids. Once they catapulted hand grenades into the village from a stony outcrop. But villagers, dug in behind their earthen walls and an outer fence of brambles, suffered no casualties. Rather than spread fear, the attacks strengthened a feeling of common cause. Peasant society was reconstructed, as villagers built a chapel, school, health post, and a dusty plaza named "Lucas" after a Cangari patroller killed in 1989. The army donated five shotguns in 1992, and villagers held a barbecue to raise funds for a Mauser rifle with a longer range. "When Centurión arrived, we thought he was going to kill us all . . . but now we're very grateful to both him and the Big Banana, because we're living in more tranquility," affirms Juan Sinchitullo, who has returned to Cangari-Viru Viru to plant beans and corn on his riverside plot after six months as a watchman in a Lima paper factory.[32] In the improbable turn of this Andean history, a pair of army officers occupy a privileged place in the collective memory of hundreds of peasants in Huanta's countryside.

ANDEAN DIFFERENCE(S)

Cangari-Viru Viru should not be taken as a "typical" case. Even before the Incas, the mosaic of diverse ethnic polities already belied the concept of a single Andean culture or worldview. The rondas have proved to be no exception to this history of regional variety in the Peruvian Andes. The implementation of patrols coincided with resettlement in Cangari-Viru Viru and other villages on the Cachi River. In other areas, peasants built walls and mounted patrols in preexisting settlements, whether refugee camps or established hamlets or towns. The strength of the rondas also differs from the fledgling patrols in Ayacucho's Víctor Fajardo and Lucanas provinces to the paraprofessional armies of the Apurímac Valley. As we will see in a moment, however, disenchantment with the Shining Path, along with the new alliance with the military, mark the central themes in the explosive growth of the organizations throughout the south-central Andes. By 1993, almost every village had a ronda steering committee across hundreds of rugged miles from Andahuaylas to Junín. Every night, thousands of peasants head out into the uncertain darkness for their weekly or monthly turn on patrol. Sentry towers of wood or mud loom over hundreds of villages and towns, and ronderos staff hundreds of checkpoints along the pot-holed highways that criss-cross the interiors. Out of the harrowing matrix of blood and death, peasant resistance to the Shining Path had mushroomed into a powerful, and perhaps decisive, force in the conflict that ravaged Peru's rugged mountains for more than a decade.

Perhaps the most striking sign of the changing terms of the counterinsurgency came in 1991. The army began the massive distribution to Andean peasants of more than 10,000 Winchester Model 1300 shotguns. At ceremonies presided by a general or even Peru's President Alberto Fujimori, and with the Winchesters blessed by a priest as if for a Holy War, the arms were handed over to peasants in little plazas of hamlets and towns across the war zone. During the Conquest, the Spaniards rigorously banned Indians, even trusted auxiliaries, from possessing either horses or swords, the instruments of Iberian supremacy in the deadly arts of war. Giving out guns would have been just as unthinkable for the Peruvian officers in the first years of the fight against the Shining Path, as the military was no more trustful than the original band of European conquerors of the real allegiance of the Andean villagers.[33] Many peasants, including those in Cangari-Viru Viru, complain about the inadequacy of the allotment of four or five guns per village. They also want automatic weapons, to match the Shining Path, with its Kalashnikovs and FALs stolen from the police, and radios to call the army. Nonetheless, the Winchesters were welcomed in hundreds of villages, the culmination of months and sometimes years of petitions to the authorities for the means to defend themselves, besides machetes, spears, hand-grenades of "Gloria"-brand evaporated milk tins, gunpowder, and nails, and the one-shot *tirachas*. A national law in 1992 recognized the right of the ronderos to arms, codifying the reversal of the colonial withholding the technology of war from Andean peasants, and signaling the confidence of Fujimori and his generals in the strength of their unlikely alliance with the peasantry in the war against the Shining Path.[34]

Andean villagers have always made their lives within extensive structures of economic interchange and imperial rule. Already in the ethnic kingdoms of pre-Columbian Peru, and even more so after the Spanish Conquest, traffic was heavy across the permeable lines of local politics and state-making, provincial custom and official religion, village barter and regional commerce. These busy intersections have always belied the proclivity to imagine the separateness, in the parlance of American anthropology of the mid-twentieth-century, of the "folk" and "urban," or "Little Tradition" and "Great Tradition." Undeniably, however, the incorporation of Peru's interiors into national and transnational life has intensified. Today, Andean villagers, the protagonists of the rondas, buy tennis shoes and Nescafé, tune in twenty-four-hour news from Lima on battered radios, and head to the national capital and even the United States or Europe to work for months, sometimes years, as maids, gardeners, construction workers, students, and streetsellers dreaming of the comforts of a middle class life.[35] In the process, as the Peruvian anthropologist Carlos Iván Degregori underscores, the myth of the return of the Incas has given way to the myth of progress through roads, bridges, schools, and other markers of Western-style development.[36] To be sure, the advent of modernity has not meant the loss of a distinctive, sometimes fierce, sense of independent identity. Yet what it means to be Andean can no longer be understood, if it ever could, as the petrified inheritance of an "archaic" or "feudal" past. In the Andes, as elsewhere around the planet, identity and difference unfold in the charged context of the interlinked field of communities, classes, and nations in the contemporary global system.

Nevertheless, for many prosperous Peruvians in Lima, often more likely to have spent time in Miami or New York than Andahuaylas or Apurímac, the eruption of the Shining Path seemed only to confirm the eternal alterity of the provincial, the dispossessed, and the Andean. Most conversations in the wealthy enclaves of San Isidro and Casuarinas, as well as some of the first writing by U.S. pundits and policy makers in the nascent field of "Senderology," ignored that the Shining Path was a Marxist party, notable for its lack of appeal to "indigenous" or "Andean" roots, and that the leader was a white intellectual who cited Kant, Shakespeare, and Washington Irving in his most famous speeches. To the contrary, the Maoists were cast as primitive rebels from a "non-Western" world, as, in the sensationalizing exoticism of one British journalist, a child of the "magical world of the Indians" and the "cruelty" and "ferociousness" of "the Indian Mind."[37] Many in the privileged classes in Lima, largely of European descent, came to think of *"ayacuchano"* (Ayacuchan) or even *"serrano"* (mountain-born) as a synonym for "terrorist," as old anxieties about the irrationality of "the Andean" interlaced with new fears of "international terrorism" of the Reagan-Thatcher years in the stigmatization of the rebels as "crazed subversives" or "demented criminals."

By contrast, the Fujimori government uses the rondas to suggest it has rechanneled the dangerous energy of Peru's poorest inhabitants to the defense of democracy and nationhood. Each year, beginning in 1993, the army has trucked thousands of ronderos into Lima to march on July 28, Peru's Independence Day. Newspaper photos and television news footage overflow with the "exotic" imagery of ponchoed peasants, along with a sprinkling of Amazonian militiamen in jaguar-tooth necklaces and war paint. This coverage exhibits, and even reinforces, the old conviction of the perennial Otherness of Indians and peasants. In this context, however, the difference of the Other electrifies what Fujimori calls "our crusade to eradicate the scourge of terrorism," as legions of villagers, Winchesters over their shoulders, march through Lima's streets with columns of nurses, engineers, schoolchildren, doctors, and squadrons of policemen and soldiers. Despite, as we shall see, their marginalization from ronda leadership, women wearing the "traditional" garb of bowler hats and wool skirts also parade with spears and guns, an invocation of the popular image of the Andean woman warrior, which traces as far back as the pre-Columbian deity Mama Huaco, and an extension of the guarantee of the government's ability to harness the peculiar powers of multivocality and diversity, in this case the "female" as well as the "Andean." The extremes of violence and reason, male and female, "the Andean" and "the Western," "the primitive" and "the modern" converge in a public spectacle of national unity, staged by the government as part of the cultural politics of state-building in the wake of harsh years of political violence and economic crisis that have torn so deeply at the fiction of the imagined community of a united nation.

Marks of oppression and division hardly disappear, however. The triumphalism of the pageantry effaces the war's human costs, including the massive human rights violations under Fujimori and his two predecessors, Fernando Belaúnde and Alan García. Meanwhile, the Winchesters of the peasants look like pop-guns next to the rocket-launchers and bazookas of the regular troops, an obvious reminder of the military's ultimate supremacy. Sleek generals and ministers occupy the position of privilege on the reviewing stand, magisterially elevated above the marching columns of

Andean peasants, in a straightforward reflection of the power of white over brown, rich over poor, and city over country. Indeed, the very existence of the rondas speaks of the second-class citizenship of peasants. Wealthy creoles pay for Dobermans, armed *guachimanes*, or watchmen, electric fences and cement walls to protect themselves from crime and political violence. By contrast, Andean peasants possess only the option of collective organization, still another example of how the desperate inequalities of race and class govern the logic of survival in Peru. Even as it plays on the politics of inclusion and diversity, the spectacle underlines the subordinate terms of the incorporation of Andean and peasant identity into the fabric of nationhood.

After the march in 1993, most of Cangari-Viru Viru's fifteen marchers stayed in Lima to visit with relatives in the gray shantytowns of Huaycán and Villa El Salvador. Eventually, Antonio Quispe and his fellow villagers trickled back to the mountains, to the animals and plots that offer a fragile livelihood. In Cangari-Viru Viru, life is hard: the rivalries of local politics, the worry about drought or floods, the danger of a Shining Path raid from the desert hills across the Cachi River. Still, and in a precarious security guaranteed in large measure by their own initiative in the rondas, villagers also carve moments of reprieve, whether the quiet excitement at a new baby's birth or the raucous energy of the San Juan's Day fiesta. Against the landscape of want and terror, the intertwining of desperation and hope, pain and delight, and loss and enjoyment stand as tenacious, if bittersweet, witness to the last line of a poem by Peru's greatest Quechua-speaking writer, José María Arguedas, "*kachiniraqmi*, I still exist."

COUNTERREVOLUTION AS SOCIAL MOVEMENT

Until recently, anyone who spoke about Peruvian "peasant mobilization" referred to left-allied federations, or the village patrols in the northern departments of Cajamarca and Piura, also known as rondas campesinas, which grew rapidly in the 1970s and 1980s to stop thievery and then to resolve disputes and supervise small public works projects.[38] Leftist journalists and scholars, myself included, framed the phenomenon of Andean self-defense committees in a contrast between the "grassroots" and "independent" patrols of the north and their "imposed" and "manipulated" namesakes in the south and center. Rondas campesinas has a grassroots sound because of its association with the antithievery movement in the north, mostly untouched by the war. When the military borrowed the name in the early 1980s for the anti-Shining Path patrols, this appeared as a blatant bid to gloss over the compulsory character, and very different mission, of the new organizations. No one imagined that these patrols, too, would turn into a massive movement with an important degree of popular participation and autonomy from the state. The entire existence of the rondas suggests the instability of the line between "grassroots" and "imposed," "autochthonous" and "forced," "autonomous" and "manipulated." This instability reiterates the imperative of openness to how activism from below can defy our expectations about and for the disenfranchised.

At the same time, flexibility ought not mean abandoning a rigorous effort to unpack the origins and consequences of any movement for change. A good place to start may be with the question of causality, already an axis of debate in the extensive literature on rural mobilization in the 1960s and 1970s. In retrospect, much of this scholarship was mired in an illusory quest to establish a single "model" to explain the outbreak of peasant revolt, as if the particular circumstances behind the multiplicity of uprisings could be summed up in a unitary formula. At the opposite extreme, the aura of indifference, and sometimes even contempt, towards "metanarratives" and "teleologies" in poststructuralist theory can lead into slipshod analysis that does more to mystify than illuminate the politics of protest. Instead of an abrupt dismissal of all concern for origins as "authoritarian" or "totalitarian," scholars might recognize the need for specificity and precision, and to avoid the reduction of the study of social movements to a simple quest for "causes," yet without a wholesale abandonment of careful inquiry into the forces behind the fraught decision of people at a specific time and place to organize to alter's history course.

Disenchantment with the Shining Path represents a basic cause for the explosive expansion of the rondas. The insightful work of a number of journalists and scholars, mostly Peruvian, suggests a pattern of initial acceptance among the peasantry, or at least tolerance, followed by mounting disaffection.[39] Although this loss of support has much to do with the arrival of the military, and the realization of the price of opposition to the government, it also represents a reaction against the Shining Path's myopic inflexibility and planned use of mass violence. In the upper mountains of Huanta in 1983, and again to the north in 1988 and 1989 in the Mantaro Valley, the Maoists' order to stop the sale of surplus crops to towns and cities, part of the plan to "strangle" the cities, provoked angry discontent, as the marketing ban shut off a source of social interchange and economic income so long a fulcrum of Andean life.

Inflexibility also proved a problem in the guerrillas' refusal to stop forcibly recruiting children, some as young as eight or ten. The same was true of the fierce and unsuccessful campaign to wipe out Pentecostal churches in the Apurímac Valley in the mid-1980s. Rebel leaders saw the mushrooming of these congregations in Peru's interiors as a direct challenge, unlike the generally less organized and fervent Catholics, and burned churches and murdered pastors. In reaction, Protestants developed an apocalyptic view of Guzmán's followers as the armies of the Anti-Christ, and ultimately mobilized against them. In many areas, finally, villagers resented the Shining Path's "popular justice." The execution of a cattle rustler or corrupt mayor might be applauded at the start. Eventually, however, the increased number of killings, especially of suspected "collaborators" and "servants of the reaction," and the macabre means—often by stoning or slitting throats to heighten fear and save bullets—backfired against the Maoists in many areas. The murders often embittered the friends and relatives of the dead, and extended the erosion of the initial aura of the Maoists as beneficent champions of the peasantry. An absolute, even arrogant, certainty about the dictums of "Marxist-Leninist-Gonzalo Thought" and the infallibility of the revolution turned out to be a serious liability for the Shining Path, as the guerrillas were incapable of compromise with the peasantry. Instead of a progressive consolidation of rural backing after the fashion of the Chinese Red Army or Viet Cong, the Shining Path laid the foundation for the explosion of armed revolt against its revolutionary design.

The other key force was the improved relation between the military and the peasantry. Unlike its counterparts in, for instance, Argentina or Chile, the Peruvian military has a tradition of populism as well as authoritarianism. In particular, the army has served as a rare avenue of social mobility in Peru in the twentieth century, always with a sprinkling of dark-skinned generals of humble origins. This largest of the three branches spearheaded the agrarian reform and nationalization of foreign companies under General Velasco's presidency. Noel's counteroffensive of 1983 and 1984 displayed the most brutal and imperial side of the military. Torture, rape, and murder of suspected rebels remained a mainstay of the counterinsurgency in subsequent years, leaving Peru the world's highest number of "disappeared" from 1988 to 1991. Already by 1985, however, and especially with the evident ability of the rebels to survive the storm of violence, many officers recognized the need to combine intimidation and persuasion in a so-called "integral" strategy, including "sociopolitical development" and "civic action" to build support among the peasantry. Selective killing began to predominate over wholesale slaughter, as civilian deaths at the hands of the military declined by more than two-thirds after 1983–1984. More soldiers were recruited from local villages and provincial towns. Showy generals like Alberto Arciniega and Adriano Huamán played up their own peasant origins, posing for pictures with babies and dancing and drinking at parties and festivals.

Although some troops maintained a colonial posture of distance and superiority, the new ties were reflected in a rapid rise of requests from peasants in the late 1980s and early 1990s for garrisons to be stationed in their villages and towns, a graphic illustration of the partial shift of the military's image from occupiers to protectors. As historian Jaime Urrutia, himself kidnapped and tortured by the army at the start of the war, emphasized in a recent retrospective, the army "has changed . . . [officers] like the sadly celebrated Commander 'Butcher,' who headed the Cangallo garrison . . . are no more than a bitter memory, and peasants no longer live in terror of disappearances and arbitrary arrests."[40] The Shining Path still claimed, in 1988, to rest "on the poor peasants."[41] Ironically, however, the military, stern and forbidding, yet also able to compromise, outmaneuvered the Maoists in the battle for the countryside.

The rondas grew at the intersection of the new ties between peasants and the military. By 1990, Quechua-speaking officers travelled to the high moors of Ayacucho and Huancavelica, dressed in *chullos* and ponchos, to urge their "brother peasants" to take up arms against "the enemies of Peru."[42] "Ronderos and Armed Forces—Together We Will Make a Peru of Peace," proclaimed an army-manufactured pennant on the wall of the municipality in the Ayacucho village of Quinua, a ceramics center I visited in 1993. To cement the image of profitable partnership, the military also promised, and sometimes provided, donations of tools, medicine, and food as well as guns. In 1991, I attended a meeting of fifty leaders of the rondas in the walled army headquarters in the Mantaro Valley, where a general mixed in promises of tools and tractors with the exhortation to "continue in your rondas." The military later donated 200 Japanese trucks, as a reward, in the general's words, for their "collaboration" against the Shining Path. The threat of force hardly disappeared, and, in fact, some inhabitants of Quinua remember how a mustachioed lieutenant threatened in 1989 to take "drastic measures" against villagers who refused to participate in patrols. Still, the inclusive rhetoric and material incentives, along with hate for the Shining Path, encouraged the interest and sometimes even enthusiasm about the resettlements and patrols on display in Cangari, Viru Viru, and dozens of other villages.

Finally, the rondas took on a self-reinforcing logic. At first, the Shining Path often succeeded in putting down the patrols by force, as in the 1983 massacre of 80 peasants in the Ayacucho village of Lucanamarca, justified by Guzmán as "annihilation in order to defend . . . the people's war . . . demolish the imperialist dominion . . . and wipe them from the face of the Earth."[43] By the 1990s, however, the rebels were increasingly on the defensive in many areas, in some cases almost entirely expelled, as in the Apurímac Valley. Success emboldened villagers to maintain *rondas,* and adjoining hamlets and towns to organize, all the more so with the news from Lima of Guzmán's capture. Resistance to the Shining Path snowballed with startling speed in 1991 and 1992, most notably in Huanta and the Mantaro Valley, where thousands of peasants across hundreds of mountainous miles organized into a strong network of patrols and resettlements in little more than a year. In many places, like Cangari-Viru Viru, attacks to put down resistance only deepened contempt for the rebels and strengthened the *rondas.* Shining Path propaganda promised the "miserable mercenaries . . . will be disinflated like a circus balloon."[44] To the contrary, the rondas expanded in 1993 into Vilcashuamán, Víctor Fajardo, Cangallo, and Huancasancos, the last Ayacucho provinces where the Shining Path had significant influence. The feeling of impotence in the countryside diminished as the rondas evolved into a movement that burst beyond the ability of Guzmán and his followers to contain or repress.

THE CONSEQUENCE(S) OF MOBILIZATION

Many scholars of rural mobilization have emphasized the urgency of careful evaluation of the limits as well as achievements of any initiative for change. By the end of the 1980s, caution tempered the initial, and sometimes utopian, ebullience of progressive researchers about the emancipatory potential of social movements in Latin America. On close inspection, the ghosts of clientelism, factionalism, and bossism haunted even the most seemingly "democratic" and "grassroots" of popular initiatives, like Ecuadoran indigenous federations and Brazilian gay and lesbian coalitions, belying the proclivity of scholars to assume a clean break between the "old" and "new" politics of struggle. More broadly, it was difficult to ignore, in the short term at least, and with the possible exception of the Workers' Party in Brazil, the failure of movements from below to translate into national politics of structural transformation while the Left withered in the face of the avalanche of neoliberal victories in congressional and presidential elections. As political scientist Sonia Alvarez concludes, "a certain pessimism set in [by the late 1980s]" about the "seemingly limited gains of social movements in the face of political violence and economic crisis in Latin America."[45]

In the rondas, one of the most obvious problems centers on gender. Many women speak enthusiastically of a greater peace and security with the rondas. They do the cooking and childcare that allows their sons and husbands to patrol. Women, armed with clubs and kitchen knife-tipped spears, also act as sentries, and as a last line of defense. Yet the confluence of ideologies of public leadership and war as male domains have led the rondas to perpetuate and even fortify an old history of female subordination in village affairs and, more broadly, the national politics. Except in the public theater of Lima marches, only men carry guns, the supreme symbol of ronda power. No women are elected as comando or civil defense committee president. "The people got macho," villagers of both sexes will say in a masculinization of the patrols that writes out women's vital role. The Peruvian anthropologist Marisol de la Cadena asserts that peasant women tend to be viewed negatively as "more Indian" than men by virtue of the greater likelihood that they will not speak Spanish and remain more "traditional" in dress and duties, like herding and weaving.[46] The rondas reinforce the ideology of second-class status of women and "the female" in Andean societies.

A second and related problem involves corruption and bossism. Andean villages have always been far less egalitarian or harmonious than might be suggested by the organic-sounding label of "peasant community."[47] Rumors of misappropriation of funds or misuse of authority by local leaders, whether of irrigation committees or village councils, represent a familiar feature of the social landscape. "Small village, big hell," as a Spanish aphorism has it. The rondas have been no exception. Many comandos and civil defense committee presidents have faced accusations, in some cases justified, of everything from stealing money donated by the government to excusing relatives from patrol duty. The close ties of ronda leaders in some places to the military can give them an undue leverage in local politics, as in Junín's Comas, where some village presidents complain of a decline in their authority. In the extreme case of the 1980s in the Apurímac Valley, where the rapid growth in the 1980s of coca cultivation into a source of dollars exacerbated the climate of uncertainty and volatility, the first leaders turned the rondas into personal fiefs. This was the case of schoolteacher-turned-denture-maker Pompeyo

Rivera Torres, "Commander Huayhuaco," who operated as a jungle warlord before his 1989 arrest for drug trafficking.[48] All of these histories undercut the effort to reduce the rondas to a tidy tale of innocent peasants against evil guerrillas, or to imagine a uniform backing for the organizations.

Corruption and bossism extend to the relation of the rondas with civil and military authorities. Some politicians have used the organizations to, in effect, buy votes. For example, the current mayor of Huanta campaigned by handing out bullets in the countryside, and persuaded (reportedly promising future favors) some comandos and civil defense committee presidents to speak in his favor at village assemblies. More centrally, the military maintains a strong influence, an accountability codified into Legislative Decree No. 741, which stresses that every *ronda* committee "must be authorized by the Joint Command of the Armed Forces . . . and operate under the control of the respective Military Commands [in their region]."[49] In practice, the military's authority assumes a variety of forms in the day-to-day operation of the rondas, from mandatory barracks meetings to demands for overnight lodging in villages for soldiers. In all of these relations, examples exist of military corruption, like the sale of bullets supposedly donated by the government, by officers to peasants. More broadly, as many ronderos do not hesitate to complain, the entire rise of the rondas exploits the unpaid labor of villagers, who must guarantee the public safety that was previously the duty of the state. "We sit out here in the dark waiting for the next attack, keeping the peace," the Comando in Cangari-Viru Viru explains, "while the colonel and the brewery owner dance and drink in town." Far from an unambiguous tale of rural "initiative" or "agency," the *rondas* mark the partial reinscription of Peru's colonial hierarchy of town over country and state over peasantry.

Finally, the rondas do not tie into a broad program for change. If anything, their achievements have reinforced convictions about the worthlessness of "politics" and "the politicians." Some of the lowest turnout for recent regional and national elections have come in places where the rondas are strongest. Alberto Fujimori presents himself as a champion of the rondas, helicoptering into the backlands to preside over the distribution of food and medicine as well as guns to ronderos and praising them on television "as some of Peru's greatest patriots." But even this master of populism wins only a tepid backing from most peasants, signaling a widespread cynicism about the political system. The lack of enthusiasm about representative democracy is understandable given a history of flagrant government corruption and broken promises. Obviously, too, the intensity of the battle for survival can assume an overwhelming precedence over events in Lima. Yet indifference also points to the preeminently local thrust of the rondas that leaves the terrain of national politics to the populist authoritarianism of Fujimori and his military allies. Broadly congruent with the exhaustion with utopias in the post-Cold War world, the disinterest of the ronderos in electoral politics and national change may not last.[50] Perhaps the organizations will turn into a vehicle for a more articulated platform in the remaking of economic structures and state policies. Currently, however, the movement meshes with the end of the days of strikes, marches, and mass protests and the virtual absence of a collective response to the devastating policies of deregulation and austerity, which have disproportionately slashed into the already meager incomes of Peru's majorities. No challenge grows to what the Uruguayan novelist Eduardo Galeano labels the "structures of impotence" of Latin America in the teeth of economic neoliberalism.[51]

One of the obvious lessons of this survey of the limits of the rondas is to reiterate the heterogeneity of the make-up of any kind of social mobilization. Thus, as we have seen, women play a different, and mostly subordinate, role than men, while leaders are better situated than followers to gain from favors of politicians or army officers. The unified sound of the label of "movement," no more than the familiar stand-bys of "culture" or "society," should not conceal the inevitable differences in interest and standpoint of the differently positioned participants in popular initiatives. Instead of a unilateral focus on consensus of liberal and functionalist models, or, conversely, on fragmentation and partiality in some brands of poststructuralist theory, the rondas suggest the urgency of a sensitivity to the delicate and sometimes explosive dialectic of difference and commonality, polyphony and solidarity, and conflict and consensus in every bid for change around the world.[52]

"NO LONGER TAME LAMBS TO THE SLAUGHTERHOUSE"
Stubborn contradictions and limits pervade rural mobilization against the Shining Path. Yet it would be just as wrong to ignore as to overplay the inroads of any social movement in Latin America or anywhere else, perhaps even more so in light of the tremendous, sometimes almost preposterous, courage demanded to make even modest gains against the grain of the savage dangers of the contemporary order. In dozens of cases, from shantytown soup kitchens in Honduras to indigenous federations in Ecuador to the rondas in northern as well as southern Peru, activism from below

means the margin of survival in daily life as well as a challenge to the very terms of cultural domination and political exclusion between the elite and the dispossessed, the white and the brown, the rulers and the ruled. These challenges occur in subtle as well as open ways. More than just the glory of slaves, these dynamic initiatives remain a welcome sliver of hope in the struggle for justice and dignity in today's world.

A greater peace represents the most obvious achievement of the rondas. The Shining Path still attacks patrollers and resettlements, as in a September 1993 raid on the Ayacucho village of Matucana Alta, where twelve Quechua-speaking farmers were murdered, including five children. In general, however, the rondas have vastly reduced the Shining Path's ability to operate in the Andean countryside. In their former stronghold of Huanta, a ragged and hungry band only descends from the freezing moors of Razuhuillca to steal food and cattle in sporadic raids. Checkpoints and patrols have pushed the rebels out of the Upper and Lower Tulumayo Valleys in Junín, where peasants, in the words of one leader, began to fight in 1990 with "clubs, machetes, rocks and slings." With almost no help from the military, the rondas have also expelled Shining Path from another of the war's bloodiest battlegrounds, the Apurímac Valley. In these and many other war zones, many peasants confirm a greater, if by no means total, sense of security and calm with the rondas. "There are no more massacres, not even attacks, nothing," concludes Juan Pardo, the comando in the village of Vinchos, which lies on the windy grasslands above the city of Ayacucho.[53]

To be sure, many rondas have not shied away from recourse to deadly violence. In 1991, I cut a deal with a taxi driver to take me to the district of Comas, six hours above the city of Huancayo. Halfway up the winding track into the icy mountains, the muffler fell off the rusted Nissan, forcing us to turn around. On the way back down, we met a pick-up filled with ronderos returning from a meeting at the Huancayo army headquarters. It stopped, blocking our path on a rocky curve. In the gray light of the mountain morning, I watched with a sinking feeling as twenty ronderos jumped off the bed, grabbed stones, crowbars, and shotguns, and moved, silently, to surround us. Fortunately, and at the last moment, one of the weather-beaten farmers recognized the taxi driver as his cousin. Tension dissolved. "The terrorists ambush, and we have to be ready to defend ourselves," one of the gun-toting villagers explained, apologetically. My apprehension, however, had not been altogether a product of negative stereotypes about peasant ferocity. Just a year before, Comas peasants stoned thirteen suspected guerrillas, sliced off their heads, and took them in a blood-soaked burlap sack to army headquarters.[54]

Any discussion of violence by villagers risks a fall into the essentialist view of the intrinsic brutality of the Andean peasantry, displayed in one Peruvian historian's incautious claim about "the frequency of unrestrained cruelty in peasant wars." Yet it would also be irresponsible to ignore the ronda killings of "suspected subversives" from Huaychao in 1983 to Paccha in 1992. Understandable, if not justifiable, against the explosive background of fear, personal and village vendettas, and mass violence by the Shining Path and the military, these examples of ronda terror undermine the inverse, and ultimately just as condescending, essentialism of the view of Andean peasants as the universal bearers of a noble ethic of "punish, but do not kill."[55] Once again, the rondas defy easy judgment or sweeping generalization, in this case even of "life-giving" or "life-taking" or "violent" and "peaceful." Instead, they exemplify the mobile and multiple contours that shape any social movement.

I do not wish to minimize the problem of violence, but it should be emphasized that killings by ronderos have fallen substantially, and are now a relative rarity. The rondas resemble their northern Andean namesakes in this respect. There, the lynching of suspected rustlers, although never as frequent as that of suspected rebels in the center and south, also declined after a measure of order was reestablished and the threat to survival and livelihood diminished. In a surprising number of cases, former guerrilla supporters have even been reincorporated into village society, if willing to abandon the doctrine of revolution at any cost. "We lived in misery, and it was understandable that some would make the mistake of joining the Shining Path," as Hugo Huillca, the Apurímac leader, explains this strong, if not universal, ideology of forgiveness.[56] Several current comandos and civil defense committee presidents in the Apurímac and Huanta were former Shining Path collaborators, in striking testimony to the surprising elasticity of the rondas in the evolution into mass organizations.

In the broad view, an intricate array of factors lie behind declining violence in the war zones, including the capture of top guerrilla leaders and the drop in disappearances and massacres by the military. But a superficial look at the statistics of the last few years bears out the claims of Pardo, Huillca, and others about the patrols' significant role in restoring peace. The massive expansion of the organizations in 1990 and 1991 corresponded to a 30 percent decline in recorded casualties and deaths in the departments of Andahuaylas, Apurímac, Ayacucho, and Junín. As late as 1991, human rights organizations still asserted that "the patrols have contributed to the escalation of violence."[57] This position can no longer be sustained. By contrast to, say, the cases of Angola's Eastern Provinces or Colombia's Middle Magdalena, the militarization of the civilian population has become the precarious path out of one of the fiercest and bloodiest wars in late twentieth-century Latin America.

Today, many critics admit the rondas have contributed to a surprising resurrection of civil society, a second benefit of the organizations. There are regular meetings of the entire village to discuss ronda business, whether fund-raisers for guns or scheduling patrols. As in the northern patrols, all men in the village must patrol and attend assemblies. Skulkers may be fined or even whipped. Nonetheless, in most places this participation no longer rests as much on military intimidation as on the collective conviction among villagers that rondas are desirable. Comandos and civil defense committee presidents are no longer named by army officials in most villages. Instead, open assemblies elect them like other village leaders, part of what historian Ponciano del Pino calls the *interiorización* (interiorization) of the rondas into the everyday fabric of Andean villages.[58]

A panoply of other civil organizations, such as parent-teacher associations, women's clubs, and irrigation committees, have also been reactivated with the new security provided by the patrols, expanding the room for local participation in village organizations shattered by war. Increasingly, too, the rondas themselves have expanded beyond a purely military mission. When cholera broke out in the Apurímac Valley's Palmapampa, for instance, a ronda delegation traveled to Ayacucho to request rehydration salts from development organizations and the government. Many rondas even incorporate old modes of village cooperation, holding *faenas*—or collective work parties—to build guard towers and walls, or, in the case of Chaca, a potable water project. A system of *chasquis,* or messengers, after the Incan communication system, links the villages in the upper reaches of Huanta so that word of guerrilla sightings and attacks is shared. In part, then, the rondas have been "Andeanized," "peasantized," and "villagized," reconfigured to local logics of necessity and tradition. Rather than hastening the demise of mountain traditions or institutions, they have become a vehicle for the

RONDEROS AND COMMUNITY SELF-
DEFENSE IN AYACUCHO.
(left) A rondero at his post.
(below) Ronderos relaxing.
(bottom) Ronderos protecting a peasant
market.

defense of village interests and life, another chapter in the painful history of recomposition and transformation that has characterized Andean societies for so many centuries.

A final and interrelated achievement has been to restore a sense of agency among villagers in the war zones. The harshness of rural life in Apurímac, Ayacucho, and Huancavelica—three of the poorest departments in an impoverished country—partially explains the initial receptivity to the Shining Path's call for radical change. But the war spun the world into what peasants call *chaqwa*, Quechua for chaos and disorder. Massacres were routine by both sides. More than 600,000 were forced to flee for their lives.[59] By contrast, for many peasants the rondas have become a sign of their ability to be more than eternal war victims. "We're no longer tame lambs to be led to the slaughterhouse," says the Quechua-speaking civil defense committee president in Ayacucho's Vinchos.[60] In the Apurímac Valley, villagers even celebrate the anniversary of the founding of the local ronda with ballads, poems, and speeches. They speak of themselves with pride as "ronderos" as well as campesinos (peasants), comuneros (villagers), and peruanos (Peruvians). Common throughout the south-central Andes is talk of superiority even to the military. "We're able to do what they never could," says one man in Chaca, "that is, restore tranquility in these communities." Much of Peru's national culture still affixes the qualities of backwardness to "the peasant" and "the Andean." Despite its claim to represent villagers, the Shining Path's urban vanguard also presumes a superior understanding of "science" and historical destiny, arrogating to itself the obligation to "beat ideas into the heads of the masses through dramatic deeds," as one party document proclaims.[61] Against the stigma of ignorance and inferiority from the Maoists as well as national ideology, peasants have made the rondas into an affirmation of partial control over their hard world.

WAKEFUL THEORY

It should be apparent that the "limits" and "achievements" of the rondas cannot be neatly disentangled. "Systems of power are multiple," as anthropologist Lila Abu-Lughod underlines, "overlapping and intersecting fields."[62] A social movement may reinforce the operation of oppression at one level, yet cut against the grain of domination and misery at another. The rondas remain caught within the disturbing logics of sexism, corruption, and bossism, and within a neoliberal offensive, even as they carve a promising stability out of the relentless fear and chaos of war. To be sure, the weave of the "negative" and the "positive" is especially dense in this unanticipated case of rural mobilization, even if my own feelings tilt toward admiration, even astonishment, at the achievements of the ronderos against the grain of a difficult history. Nevertheless, the multilayered and sometimes compromised trajectory of the rondas also stands as much as the norm as the exception in these unruly times at century's end, epistemologically and politically uncertain, emblematic of the world's willful reluctance to rest inside the categories we in the academy invent to contain and explain. It will not do to jettison the hope of understanding the interplay of culture, action, and political economy that defines human experience, much less to lose respect or empathy for the ingenuity and boldness of so many of the political initiatives of the disenfranchised. Surely, however, good analysis depends on the ability to press beyond the imperial legacy of stationary polarities and preconceived narratives. On this terrain, admittedly insecure and unstable, scholars will struggle to define the terms for remaking of social thought.

In *Beyond Good and Evil*, Friedrich Nietzsche warns against a "solemn air of finality" in social theory, "no more than a noble childishness or tyrranism." This most trenchant of nineteenth-century critics of emptiness and pretension launches a savage attack on "audacious generalization" and "dogmatic philosophy." He imagines no pure place for the social analyst outside of history or politics, always insistent that we too are, as in the title of another of his most famous treatises, "Human, All Too Human." And yet, even Nietzsche refuses to relinquish the possibility of limited yet serious understanding. As the unexpected eruption of the revolt against the Shining Path reminds us with desperate poignancy, the "task is wakefulness itself" for a "philosophy of the future" to understand the beauty and agony of the workings of the world.[63]

The Politics of Postmodernism

CULTURE ON THE FRONTIERS

Some observers continue to paint the rondas in the old frame of the Peruvian Andes as a place of primordial and millenarian customs. "Time stands still in the Andean countryside," writes one Lima journalist, as another compares the ronderos to "Atahualpa's Inca warriors."[64] More productively, however, the rondas' particular history might be viewed as an indicator of Latin America's broader predicament at century's close. After all, many critics emphasize that themes of fragmentation, displacement, and transculturation have always been fundamental to millions of Latin Americans from East Los Angeles to Caracas and São Paulo. Already in the early eighteenth century, before anyone spoke of "intertextuality" or "pastiche," the young Topa Inca posed for portrait in a Spanish waistcoat with an Inca royal tassel, or *llautu*, draped across his forehead. Two hundred years later, José María Arguedas linked his admiration for Western machinery with a celebration of the Andean *apus*, or mountain spirits, in his famous Quechua poem "An Ode to a Jet Plane." As literary theorist Alberto Moreiras concludes, "the marginality and deferment of all colonial societies with respect to what happens in the metropolises led Latin American culture, from its beginning, to be a culture of translation and transculturation."[65] Moreiras and a number of other scholars assert that postmodernity arrived in Latin America before it came to the First World. In this view, Latin America's past stands as continuous with its present and its future of flux and transculturation—the advent of instantaneous communications, rapid technological change, "flexible" capital accumulation, and the other hallmarks of what David Harvey calls "time-space compression" around the world.[66]

Even many Latin American critics leave out the countryside in their talk about the "postmodern" and the "postcolonial." In his otherwise fine *Culturas Híbridas*, for instance, Argentine Nestor García Canclini describes the subcontinent's condition in terms of "a multitemporal heterogeneity" of the "traditional" and the "modern." His link of "the traditional" to the "pastoral," the "rural," and "the folk" marks a partial return to the evolutionary chronology that denies the coevalness of Latin America's fifty million small farmers, presenting their customs and visions as the artifacts of a premodern past. As we saw in the case of Cangari-Viru Viru, an adobe village built only a few years ago amid war's heat, this thinking overlooks the fact that even the most ostensibly "traditional" Latin Americans do not live, as some of us anthropologists still put it not so long ago, "submerged by the tides of history."[67] To the contrary, as this essay has emphasized, Latin American peasants also build their lives at the volatile intersection of the local, regional, and global. Values and traditions in the countryside can only be understood within the same temporal and spatial networks that bind us all in the startling reality of interdependence on a global scale, no matter whether one chooses to calls it "postmodernity," "postcolonialism," "post-Fordism," "late capitalism," or even, as one critic suggests, none of these labels that can become "so empty and sliding as signifiers . . . [as] to be taken to mean anything you like."[68]

If the countryside must be a part of our thinking about cultural mixture and political flux in Latin America, the rondas also underscore the dangers of presenting this condition as a blithe Rabelaisian carnival of polyphony. Perhaps because of their focus on the art, music, and literature of Latin America's cities, and scantier attention to rural areas and shantytowns where histories of poverty and terror are more likely to be the norm than the exception, many theorists slide towards a depiction of the heteronomous logic of kitsch and pastiche as a neatly positive development.[69] On display in the rondas is the spliced spectacle of "comandos" who speak Quechua and worship mountain spirits, even as they go by war names like "Jehovah" and "Rambo." Yet the stark predicament of these farmers warns against a "luddic postmodernism" where the politics of difference reduces to "play" and "pleasure," and highlights the need to avoid the neoregionalism of the "more-postmodern-than-thou-by-virtue-of-our-hybridity" syndrome of some Latin American scholars, as if plurality or hybridity were somehow by their very nature a sign of the good, the "subversive," the "transgressive," or the politically progressive.[70] The interactive, improvisational dimensions of contemporary life reflect joy and possibility, but also pain and destruction, especially for those at the precarious margins of global society.[71]

Still, García Canclini's axiom that "culture everywhere is on the frontiers" offers one way to reckon with the hard struggle of the ronderos.[72] On one of my last days in Ayacucho in June, I traveled a mountain highway with a journalist friend to the village of Chaca, at 11,000 feet in Ayacucho's Iquicha moors. Nineteenth-century priests and present-day observers have described the Iquichanos as part of an "ancient archaic Peru" of "strange customs" and "incomprehensible enigmas."[73] In the little plaza, a fierce sense of a distinctive past was on display in the "Indian" dress of men in chullos and ponchos and women in embroidered blouses and wool skirts. As usual, one did not have to look far for signs of invention and recombination. The bright aluminum linings of National-brand cigarette packages gleamed elegantly between the carnations and roses that single women have long pinned on their black bowler hats. Contrary to the view of the rootedness of Andean peasants to the land, three ponchoed men had just returned from Lima, eighteen hours away by truck and bus. Most of Chaca's peasants are refugees from higher up in the moors. Now, they want to repopulate their Andean hamlets, recreate the village life that has taken on a nostalgic glow after forced flight, poverty, and racism in the shantytowns of Ayacucho and Lima. Out of the space of terror, and through the rondas, the "traditional," the "peasant," the "Iquichan," and even the "Andean" may be recreated, as they have been so many times in this rugged region with its long history of periodic upheaval and displacement.[74] Culture and tradition, as the Peruvian critic José Carlos Mariátegui already insisted in 1927, are "alive and mobile . . . always remold[ing] themselves before our eyes . . . [they are] suffocated by those who want them dead and inert, who want to stretch the past into an exhausted present."[75] Rather than a return to essential or primordial origins, the rebuilding of Iquichan society will unfold at the crossroads of old legacies and new influences, the weight of the past and the unpredictability of the future.

That night, the Chaca schoolteachers warned me to keep my tennis shoes close when I went to bed in their thatch-roofed adobe compound, and to run for the canyon if the Shining Path attacked. But the only sounds to break the night's still were Quechua hymns from a nearby Pentecostal church. In the frozen dawn, a group of ronderos from Puros arrived to take us up the winding trail to their now abandoned village. The burned, stony ruins perch on a windy saddle that feels like the top of the world. There men and women spoke of their plans to return, to build a school and health clinic (along with guard towers to protect against the still-present danger of rebel raids), and to remake village society. Their journey embodies the fragile struggles of millions everywhere to gain a measure of control over their lives in the tumultuous violence of a world where so much that seemed solid has melted into air. "We are faced with a transitory landscape, where new ruins pile up on each other," concludes writer Celeste Olalquiaga, and "it is in these ruins that we look for ourselves."[76]

"JEREMIAH" AND "THE SAVAGE"

As I flew out of Ayacucho after my university lecture, the plane cruised between the clouds above the Mantaro Valley before its plunge down the Andes to Lima's grimy airport. The Mantaro's history offers a possible scenario for the rondas. Here the future Peruvian President Andrés Avelino Cáceres rallied peasants to fight the Chileans in the War of the Pacific (1879–1883), as most of the Mantaro's aristocracy collaborated with the invaders. When the war ended, Cáceres promptly sided with the elite to repress his former followers' demands for property rights. Four peasant leaders were hanged in the main square of the department capital.[77]

A century later, Peru's leaders looked again to highland villagers to save the nation. If the rondas end in the same way, without any real gain for peasants, they will be another parable of the persistence of savage inequalities in Peruvian and global society. The difficulty, perhaps impossibility, of any escape from hardship's grip was a favorite theme of Peru's greatest poet, César Vallejo, nicknamed *El Indio* (The Indian), and a child of the Andes, who wrote "The Nine Monsters" while in Paris in the shadow of the Spanish Civil War: "Pain grasps us, brother men/from behind, in profile/and it crazes us in cinemas/nails us up on record players. . . . I can no more with so many pine boxes/so many minutes/so many lizards/and so many reversals, so much thirst for thirst."[78]

Yet much has also changed in Peru. Since the betrayal of the montoneros a century ago, this restless country has witnessed what anthropologist José Matos Mar calls *desborde popular* (popular overflow): the eruption of the "informal economy" and popular culture, the explosion of Lima into a labyrinthine megalopolis of over six million, the pervasive discontent with traditional political parties, and the break-up of the oligarchical state.[79] If Peru remains riven by exclusion and hierarchy, neither is it any longer what the nineteenth-century critic Manuel González Prada labeled a nation of "gentlemen and serfs." Although they may hold no grand promise of forward progress, the rondas fit with the stubborn refusal of Peru's majorities to accept a perennial role as history's passive spectators, or as second-class citizens in a nation that promises equality for all.

The future of the rondas will be written in the struggle within and against the desires for recognition and the forces of exclusion and marginalization. In the process, the "Andean" may be reborn, as it is in Puros. Or it may take less familiar paths. On one of my last days in Huanta, I visited a ronda-organized fish fry and soccer tournament in the cactus hills of the lower valley. People from Cangari-Viru Viru and many other resettlements and villages, including comandos like "Jeremiah" and "The Savage," raced and yelled as they played next to the rubble of an experimental farm burned by the Shining Path five years before. One of the gun-slinging ronderos explained in Quechua-accented Spanish that the fish came from a new artificial pond, and that a nearby resettlement wanted to turn the soccer field into a tourist complex with a hotel, volleyball courts, and canoeing. It is hard to imagine the success of a resort in mountains where guerrillas and soldiers still roam. But no one ever imagined that the rondas might forge peace from war in the first place, said the rondero with a sly laugh. Against the bustle of jokes and food and ballads of this day's Andean fiesta, and on the brink of an uncertain future, one can only hope for the sounds of more of the Borgesian "laughter [that] shatters the familiar landmarks of our thought . . . [and] ordered surfaces" to leave these women and men with something better.

Notes

Grateful thanks for comments on earlier drafts of this essay to Carlos Iván Degregori, Paul Gelles, Gustavo Gorriti, Alma Guillermoprieto, Charles Hale, Robin Kirk, Donald Moore, Charles Piot, Linda Seligmann, Frances Starn, Randolph Starn, Steve J. Stern, Ajantha Subramanian, and Clare Talwalker. This is a revised and abridged version of an essay that appeared in *Cultural Anthropology* in November, 1995.

1 Foucault (1971: xiv).

2 Two of the best studies of the Shining Path are Degregori (1990a) and Gorriti (1990). For a fascinating look at the important role of women in the Shining Path, see Kirk (1993b). Palmer ed. (1992) collects some of the best work on the Maoists in English.

3 Benjamin (1968: 257).

4 Abimael Guzmán, "We are the Initiators" in Starn, Degregori, Kirk eds. (1995: 461). This is a translation of the speech delivered by Guzmán on April 19, 1980 to call for the beginning of the armed struggle.

5 The figures for the numbers of village participants come from an unpublished survey from 1993 by the Instituto de Investigación y Defensa Nacional (INIDEN) in Lima. The name of the militias is a matter of confusion. Initially, they were mostly known as "Civil Auto Defense Committees," and this remains their name in the legal statutes that recognize them. Probably in an effort to improve the image of the then mostly forced organizations, however, army officers started to use the name of rondas campesinas, after the patrols begun by peasants in northern Peru to stop thievery and then resolve disputes and supervise small public works. For the purposes of simplicity, I use the words rondas campesinas and ronderos in this essay to refer to the patrols against the Shining Path. As part of its counterinsurgency strategy, the Peruvian government also attempted to form *rondas urbanas,* or urban patrols, in Lima, although these organizations have not grown in anywhere near the strength or proportions of their rural counterparts. Adding a further layer of complexity, there are also urban rondas independently organized only to fight crime, in both Lima and poor neighborhoods in the northern cities of Chiclayo, Trujillo, Sullana, and Piura. Despite their very different histories and missions, the rise of these different brands of self-defense organization grow out of the broad context of the failure of the besieged Peruvian state to guarantee order in the 1980s and early 1990s.

6 José Coronel (1992, n.d.; Coronel and Loayza 1992) and Ponciano del Pino (1992, 1994b), have done the best work on the *rondas,* and I am indebted to both of these Ayacucho-based scholars for their insights in our many conversations. Other sources on the *rondas* include Starn (1991c, 1993b), Starn ed. (1993), and IDL (n.d.)

7 Silverblatt (1994: 290–91).

8 On a second visit in July 1994, villagers maintained the same watch system, but spoke of a feeling that threat of Shining Path attacks had lessened, if not disappeared.

9 "The walls and palisades with which Europe began to bristle were the symbol of a great anguish," wrote Bloch (1961: 39).

10 See Vargas Llosa (1983: 65–90). For useful discussions of Vargas Llosa and Uchuraccay, see Salcedo (1987) and Mayer (1991).

11 Vargas Llosa (1983: 69, 82).

12 Many soldiers and officers take war names to protect themselves from future Shining Path reprisals and prosecution for human rights violations.

13 Here and elsewhere I have changed names and places for security reasons. This and all subsequent translations from the Spanish are mine, unless otherwise indicated.

14 Andres Luna Vargas, interview, Lima, July 1989.

15 The quotes come from Burneo and Eyde (1986).

16 See Americas Watch (1986) on the Guatemalan patrols, as well as several of the articles in Carmack (1988).

17 Many Andean ethnic groups were ready to rebel against the Incas, and the empire was itself divided in the wake of civil war of succession between Atahualpa and Huáscar. One of the best, and most accessible, histories of the conquest is Hemming (1970).

18 Stern (1982) offers a good introduction to the reducciones, and their role in Toledo's social engineering.

19 Flores Galindo (1987: 395).

20 Noel (1989) has written an interesting, and self-serving, memoir of his bloody years in Ayacucho.

21 See Balaguer (1993: 15).

22 See Manrique (1989).

23 See González (1982).

24 For an early view of the Shining Path as a peasant rebellion, see the otherwise insightful essay by McClintock (1984).

25 Chávez de Paz (1989) offers statistics on the social make-up of the Shining Path, based on judicial records.

26 The title of Wolf's (1969) fine book of peasant revolt.

27 Stern (1982: 30).

28 Most leaders of the Shining Path were known to villagers only by pseudonyms.

29 This information comes from my own interviews in the area in June 1993 and from Coronel (n.d.).

30 Interview in Cangari-Viru Viru, June 29, 1993.

31 Coronel (n.d.: 92, 45).

32 Interview in Cangari-Viru Viru, June 27, 1993.

33 The preceding president, Alan García had handed over 200 rifles in 1988 to patrollers in the Apurímac, but Fujimori was the first to approve the large-scale arming of the peasantry.

34 The right to arms appeared in Decreto Legislativo No. 757, reprinted in *El Peruano*, the Peruvian government's official newspaper, October 15, 1992, p. 134791.

35 The diaspora of migrants from some Andean villages, like Cabanaconde in Arequipa department, stretches from Lima to Europe and the United States, as wonderfully illustrated in a new film by anthropologists Paul Gelles and Wilton Martínez, *Transnational Fiesta*.

36 See Degregori (1985b).

37 Simon Strong (1992a: 47, 72).

38 For more on the northern *rondas*, see Gitlitz and Rojas (1983) and Starn (1992).

39 See, for instance, Coronel (n.d.), del Pino (1994b), and Isbell (1992).

40 Urrutia (1993: 88).

41 Central Committee of the Communist Party of Peru (1989: 35).

42 A *chullo* is the wool cap often worn by peasants in high villages in the Andes.

43 Central Committee of the Communist Party of Peru (1989: 68, 80).

44 This quote comes from a Shining Path declaration of October 1989, which a news announcer in Huanta was forced to read over the radio under the threat of death.

45 Alvarez (n.d.: 23); cf. Fox and Hernández 1989.

46 See de la Cadena (1991).

47 Mossbrucker (1990) offers a useful analysis of the utopian strain of much of the scholarship on Andean communities.

48 See del Pino (1994b) for more on the history of the rondas in the Apurímac Valley. IDL (1990) offers more on "Commander Huayhuaco," including his implication in major violations of human rights.

49 Decreto Legislativo No. 741, November 8, 1991, reprinted in *El Peruano*, the Peruvian government's official newspaper, November 12, 1991, p. 101687.

50 I borrow some of this phrasing from Ajani (1993: 5).

51 Galeano (1992: 282). Seligmann (1993) discusses the responses of Cuzco market women to Fujimori's austerity program.

52 My emphasis on heterogeneity should not be taken to imply that all earlier scholars of Latin American social movements ignored the problem of hetero-

geneity; see, e.g., Nash (1978) for an Andean case; and more generally, Wolf (1969).

53   Quoted in Starn, ed. (1993: 47, 43).

54   This story made *The New York Times:* "Peasant Farmers Said to Kill Rebels," March 14, 1990, section 1, p. 13.

55   For an account of the events in Paccha, see Amnesty International (1992: 25). Historian Nelson Manrique (1989: 167) makes the point about the brutality of peasant wars. Carlos Iván Degregori (1989a and essay in this volume) takes issue with Manrique, and advances the case for the existence of a "punish but do not kill" ethic, in a response to Manrique. Although in disagreement with the essentializing thrust of both sides in this debate, I want to emphasize my broad admiration for the work of both of these scholars, who are among the most perceptive observers of contemporary Peru.

56   Interview on December 12, 1991.

57   This quote comes from Americas Watch (1991: 15), although I wish to stress my general admiration for their usually sharp-sighted work on behalf of human rights in Latin America.

58   Quoted in Starn, ed. (1993: 53).

59   Kirk (1991, 1993a) has done the best work on Peru's internal refugees.

60   Quoted in Starn, ed. (1993: 43).

61   Quoted in Degregori (1989b: 24).

62   Abu-Lughod (1990: 53).

63   Nietzsche (1990: 31, 32).

64   Quoted in Balaguer (1993: 15).

65   Moreiras (1990: 15).

66   Harvey (1989: 289).

67   Valcárcel (1950: 1).

68   Hall (1992: 22).

69   See, for instance, the overly enthusiastic claim of the normally perspicacious Celeste Olalquiaga (1992: 91) about Latin American cultural hybridity as "a directorial and spectorial delight."

70   I borrow this phrasing from the title of an article by Teresa Ebert (1992) and from George Yudicé (1992: 546).

71   See Shohat (1992) for a critique of postcolonial theory along these lines.

72   García Canclini (1990: 7).

73   Vargas Llosa (1983: 70).

74   Husson (1992) has published a fascinating history of Iquichan revolts of the nineteenth century.

75   José Carlos Mariátegui, *Mundial,* November 25, 1927, p. 21.

76   Olalquiaga (1992: 94). On a return visit in 1994, I found that sixty Puros families had indeed returned, part of a broad, and often painful, process of re-

building of dozens of villages in Iquicha, including Marcaraccay, Uchuraccay, Cunya, and Paccre.

77   Mallon (1983) details this history.

78   César Vallejo, "The Nine Monsters," translated by Robin Kirk in Starn, Degregori, and Kirk, eds. (1995).

79   "*Desborde popular*" is the title of an influential book by Matos Mar (1984).

PART THREE

Obliterating Third Paths:

The Battles of Lima and Puno

✛ The rebirth of willful local communities, endowed with capacities of self-organization and political direction that rendered them something other than mere extensions of the will of Sendero or the military, was not supposed to happen. Much of Sendero's efforts and the military's efforts, in contested regions in the 1980s and 1990s, aimed precisely to *destroy* independent organization and political will. The prosecution of the war implied reductionism: an erasure of alternate political and social pathways that would leave only two stark choices, the path of Sendero and that of the military or state. In this scheme, semiautonomous expressions of local authority —for example, those found in the elder or *vara* system of rural Andean communities in the center-south—became a potential threat and target of intimidation, even if such authorities adopted a stance of "apolitical" avoidance of supralocal politics. The mere potential for independent organization or nonaligned will was grounds enough for suspicion and hostility.

In this scheme as well, "third" paths that represented a more explicit political alternative to Sendero and the military, whether organized as grassroots expressions of will unaffiliated with particular political parties and tendencies, or as local instances or branches of a wider political project, constituted an impermissible threat. Particularly in its dirty war phase, the military tended to react to third pathways by equating leftists and nonaligned activists critical of the state (for example, human rights and Church activists) with Sendero. For Sendero, leftist and nonaligned activist alternatives to senderismo (including the staffs of NGO-based development projects) constituted dangerous enemies. They fed illusions, they competed for support around social justice issues, they encouraged treasonous negotiation, coexistence, or alliance with a reactionary state. As Mallon demonstrated (in Part I), this view was rooted in earlier leftist retrospectives on the Velasco government and the land invasions of Andahuaylas in the 1970s. Yet as we have also seen, Sendero constituted one among *several* logical culminations of leftist politics by the early 1980s. In this sense Sendero stood as a force "against" history, including the history of the Left. The nonsenderista Left, heavily involved in the mobilizations that unraveled military rule in the late 1970s and in the politics of electoral coalitions and mobilized social bases in the 1980s, constituted an alternative culmination within oppositional politics. In some regions of the country, in the 1980s, this alternative culmination seemed strong and effective.

How, then, did Sendero manage to prosecute war in regions whose political spaces and cultures were "densely" populated, compared to rural Ayacucho, with competing Left projects and grassroots organizations? In these more congested political spaces, did the array of competing players and forces constitute an effective barrier to senderista expansion? Once such regions were drawn into active struggles for political control and reductionism, did apparent third paths prove fragile or resilient?

These critical issues are taken up in the case studies of Lima and Puno by Jo-Marie Burt and José Luis Rénique. Burt focuses on Villa El Salvador, a municipality within metropolitan Lima whose shantytown origins and strong tradition of effective grassroots mobilization and leftist political organizing captured the imagination of those seeking an alternative to Sendero and the state. As Burt explains, the prevailing wisdom held that if *any* of Lima's barriada communities were to enjoy a certain immunization to the advance of senderista sympathy and political control, surely it would be Villa El Salvador. Given the drastic social misery and impoverishment that accompanied the disintegration of Alan García's populism and the turn toward neoliberal shock policies in the late 1980s and 1990s, and given the simultaneous intensification of Sendero's political organizing and violent intimidation in Lima as the insurgency moved toward its "strategic equilibrium" phase, the relative capacity of Villa El Salvador to chart a third political path held enormous symbolic power.[1]

Yet as Burt demonstrates, this stronghold of the Left and organized grassroots associations proved surprisingly vulnerable to senderista political expansion and intimidation. Part of the explanation lies in the sheer severity and desperation of subaltern life. The severity of economic survival crises brought physical suffering (hunger) and fear (anxieties about predatory violence as well as economic survival). The severity of senderista violence and intimidation also provoked fear and desperation. The extremes of physical suffering and fear yielded a powerful mix of willing and unwilling complicity with Shining Path. Yet as Burt also shows, these pressures do not suffice to explain Sendero's advance.

Two additional factors also proved crucial. First, senderista political strategy emphasized the acquisition of knowledge about specific fissures, tension points that yielded potential for local polarization, disillusion, and definition of enemies. By discovering and "working" (drawing out and intensifying) such contradictions—for example, corruption rumors and abusiveness charges about specific leaders, or resentments between established old-timers and newly arrived residents of shantytown communities—senderistas could discredit leaders who represented a third pathway, destroy or reshape grassroots civic organizations from within, and build a political base.

Second, the Left's own ambiguities and splits on crucial political questions created a certain zone of tolerance for Sendero, a degree of acceptance and co-existence that enabled senderista sympathizers to develop a presence, accumulate knowledge, wait for fissures and opportunities to develop. Hinojosa's and Mallon's essays (in Part I) are particularly relevant for understanding the zone of tolerance uncovered by Burt. Even though Sendero viewed leftist rivals as coprincipal enemies with the state, its leftist rivals had forged many of their political understandings out of the same formative era, and did not necessarily reject the legitimacy and pertinence of armed revolutionary struggle by a vanguard force. This baggage, along with the urgency of critiquing a state implicated in dirty war repression and in economic policies that intensified and spread indigence, encouraged ambiguity on a decisive point. Should Sendero be treated implicitly as a "wrong but misguided" political relative whose defeat was desirable but should not be pursued at all costs? Or should it be interpreted as a sui generis force, so evil and dangerous that its defeat might justify political collaboration with the state?

The ambiguities implied a learning process. Over time, the leaders and other participants in leftist parties and grassroots civic associations might shift their initial answers and move toward a hard-line stance against Sendero. The ambiguities also encouraged uneven movement in stances toward the state, Sendero, and armed struggle; such unevenness compounded the divisiveness and competing political personalities and ambitions that often afflicted leftist politics. The consequences of the learning process and the divisiveness that flowed from it included a zone of tolerance and freedom of political action that enabled Sendero to pursue its strategy of building a local knowledge and presence, and working local contradictions that undermined third pathways. As Burt shows, the consequences also meant that dynamic grassroots leaders such as María Elena Moyano could find themselves exposed and vulnerable as they moved toward a sharpening antagonism to Sendero. Moyano's assassination by Sendero in 1992 was fraught with devastating symbolism. The dynamite that blew apart Moyano also blasted the hope that communities like Villa El Salvador pointed the way to a viable third path, built by and for the poor and the dispossessed.[2]

As we have seen, political ideas and contenders rooted in distinctive historical eras seemed somehow to coexist and congest the political spaces of Peru during the 1980s and 1990s. As the nation's political and media capital, economic center, and mega-city, metropolitan Lima constituted the prime site that concentrated an amazing number of contending political players. But political crowding and contentiousness, although especially salient in Lima and its surrounding shantytown communities, also developed elsewhere. José Luis Rénique shows vividly that in Puno, in the far south of the Peruvian highlands, there also developed a fierce struggle to build and to obliterate an apparent third path. Indeed, the Puno of the mid-to-late 1980s witnessed land invasions backed by militant peasant federations. Key political projects included not only those of Sendero and the military, but also the populism promoted by Alan García and the revitalized APRA party, the nonsenderista revolution promoted by the PUM (United Mariateguista Party), and the grass-roots democratization promoted by a progressive Church, NGOs (nongovernmental organizations), and peasant communities and federations.

One of the striking aspects of Rénique's political analysis of Puno is a certain consistency with Burt's study of Villa El Salvador. To be sure, vast differences of social and political environment separated the two cases. Puno was an agrarian and majority-Indian social world, not an urban metropolis.[3] Its regional history and political culture configured the Left and grassroots self-organizing as important, but less hegemonic forces than in Villa El Salvador. Nonetheless, certain political dynamics cut across these contrasts. In Puno, as in Villa El Salvador, an apparent third path crumbled under pressure. In Puno, as in Villa El Salvador, ambiguities within the Left on decisive points—politics through armed struggle, alliance with non-leftist forces and the state against Sendero—widened spaces for senderista advance. In Puno, as in Villa El Salvador, Sendero proved astute at identifying real or potential fault lines and "working" the contradictions.

Of course, the resonance of major political dynamics in the two regions does not imply absence of specificity in the more detailed narratives of obliteration. In Puno, unlike Villa El Salvador, a politically adept military rather than Sendero proved the immediate beneficiary of a crumbling third path. In Puno, unlike Villa El Salvador, the timing of Sendero's war advance meant that the PUM's project represented not so much a "bulwark" against senderista advance as an effort to push APRA and Sendero out of their established turfs of control and intimidation. In Puno, Sendero worked fault lines specific to the locale, for example, the varied political visions and inclinations that might sunder working relationships between the PUM and the Church. And in Puno, unlike Villa El Salvador, peasants played important roles within a regional history of peasant politics and social alliances before and during the crisis of the 1980s, and they achieved a rapprochement with the military more reminiscent of the rural center-south than Villa El Salvador.

The analyses of Burt and Rénique yield three important conclusions about the expansion of insurgency war and politics into zones beyond the center-south. First, wars of territorial expansion were also wars of political reductionism: a struggle to destroy third political paths, often Left-oriented culminations of prior regional histories of social effervescence and struggle. Wars to reduce political options to a bipolar scheme meant that for Sendero and the state, the nonsenderista Left often constituted a coprincipal enemy. Second, third paths often proved more fragile than resilient under pressure. A certain poignancy attaches to this conclusion. The very congestion of political spaces in Peru points to deep yearnings for a more just social order, and its corollary, a creative experimentalism that sought to build new citizen-subjects and new forms of politics. But third paths, however expressive of yearning and creativity, gave way to a two-path scheme that destroyed alternate political contenders or rendered them superfluous. Third, the vulnerability of third paths was partly self-inflicted. To be sure, external pressures and forces rendered third paths difficult at best. War between two armed parties that did not hesitate to use violence against rivals wore down activists and the populace. Economic crisis and political disillusion poisoned good faith in grassroots or democratic alternatives and encouraged receptivity to order by authoritarian fiat. Nonetheless, Burt and Rénique also demonstrate that the architects of third paths fell prey to ambiguities, divisions, and blindnesses that, while understandable within the context of the times and prior political experiences, compounded the fragility of their efforts. Under pressure, these fragilities came to the fore. Even the most promising third paths crumbled.

Notes

1   For additional backgrond on Villa El Salvador, the outstanding scholarship is that of Blondet (see 1991, and the works cited therein).
2   On the isolation of grassroots leaders and the assassination of Moyano, see also the essay of Coral in Part IV. Coral argues that Moyano and women leaders of grassroots organization came to understand the priority of opposition to Sendero more quickly than leftist party leaderships.
3   For fine works that illuminate the region's history and particulars during the nineteenth and twentieth centuries, see Jacobsen 1993; J. Rénique 1991b; and for the southern provinces more generally, Poole 1994.

❖ EIGHT

Shining Path and the "Decisive Battle" in Lima's

Barriadas: The Case of Villa El Salvador

Jo-Marie Burt

❖ In a 1988 interview, Shining Path mastermind Abimael Guzmán signaled that the time had come for the Maoist organization to increase
its presence in Lima, the capital of Peru and home to a third of the country's
inhabitants. The development of the "prolonged popular war" in the countryside, he reasoned, had progressed to the point that it was time to prepare the
ground for the urban insurrection that would lead to Shining Path's seizure
of state power. Key to establishing a foothold in Lima was gaining control over the enormous *barriadas,* or shantytowns, that ringed the city and
housed nearly half of the capital's population, forming what Guzmán (1988)
called the "iron belts of misery" from which the poor would rise up against
their "bureaucratic-capitalist oppressors."[1] As Shining Path's newspaper, *El
Diario,* would note in July, 1992: "Lima and the surrounding shantytowns
are the scenario in which the final battle of the popular war will be defined."[2]

Few observers took Guzmán's remark seriously. The organization had
done best in extremely poor and historically marginal areas of the country characterized by a weak state presence and little organizational life; it
seemed unlikely to be able to compete on the more complex terrain of
urban politics. Shining Path developed in remote regions of the country like
Ayacucho, where the state's reach was tenuous, where political parties were
largely absent, and civil society was weak (Degregori 1985b). The weak development of democratic social organizations among the peasantry in these
regions permitted Shining Path's authoritarian leadership style to flourish.
In contrast, it was argued, Shining Path would encounter serious obstacles
in other parts of the country where democratic social organizations had developed and would serve as a kind of social bulwark against Shining Path's
organizing efforts.[3] As events unfolded in the mid-1980s, examples such as

Puno, where the organized peasant movement and its political allies did in fact challenge Shining Path's attempts to radicalize their struggle for land, seemed to confirm this argument. It became conventional wisdom, and was increasingly adopted by left-wing scholars and activists alike.

The "social bulwark" theory seemed particularly valid for Lima. Not only was Lima the center of government; its political space was also populated by a broad spectrum of political and social groups. Political parties ranged from the center-right Popular Action (AP) and Popular Christian Party (PPC) to the American Popular Revolutionary Alliance (APRA) party and the left-wing coalition United Left (IU). In shantytowns, grassroots organizations had been mobilizing since the late 1970s to demand government services, challenge antipopular economic and social policies, and resolve local problems on a self-help basis. The result was the emergence of a vast network of neighborhood associations, communal soup kitchens, women's clubs, and youth groups, many of which received technical training and financial assistance from progressive sectors of the Catholic Church and nongovernmental development organizations (NGDOs). Progressive scholars and left-wing activists pointed to the link between these social organizations and the United Left, forged during the struggle against military rule in the late 1970s, and consolidated during the 1980s, when the left won municipal elections in numerous popular districts in Lima.[4] The IU represented a viable alternative for democratic and nonviolent social change that provided poor people with an alternative to the desperation and frustration that underlay Shining Path's political violence.

Villa El Salvador, a popular district of 260,000 inhabitants 18 miles south of Lima, was perhaps the most important symbol of left-wing organization and community development in Peru. A settlement originally designed as the urban showcase of General Juan Velasco's reformist military government (1968–1975), Villa El Salvador became a center of left-wing organizing and grassroots mobilization against the more conservative Morales Bermúdez regime (1975–1980). The vast network of grassroots organizations in the district was not only an opposition force; it was also the basis of widescale community efforts to resolve local problems on a self-help basis. Left-wing parties played an important role in supporting these grassroots efforts. After Peru's return to democratic rule in 1980, the IU won successive municipal elections in Villa throughout the 1980s. Considered to be the Left's most advanced model of popular participation and self-management (*autogestión*), Villa El Salvador was touted as a model of local organizing and a viable alternative to a neglectful state. Its model of urban planning and community participation was replicated in other barriadas in Lima, most notably Huaycán, and its achievements were celebrated nationally and even internationally. As Shining Path sought to extend its presence beyond its initial base in the south-central Andes, Villa El Salvador was held up as an important example of a well-organized community based on solidarity and democratic participation that was virtually impenetrable to an authoritarian organization like Shining Path.

Analysts initially doubted Shining Path's ability to develop in Lima, but by 1990 growing evidence that Shining Path was making important inroads in the capital forced a reappraisal of the group's capacity to expand into new areas. In late 1991 and the first half of 1992, Lima was a city under siege. Successive Shining Path offensives rocked the capital during this period, and the scope and intensity of Shining Path's military operations increased dramatically. By-then familiar acts of sabotage against banks, government buildings, and basic infrastructure had escalated into potent car-bomb attacks, "armed strikes," and political assassinations. But these armed actions were only the most obvious evidence of the Maoists' urban presence. There was also growing evidence of Shining Path's presence in Lima's immense barriadas.[5] What surprised many observers, however, was Shining Path's growing influence in barriadas like Villa El Salvador, where the IU-popular organization matrix was most developed. The Maoists advanced relentlessly in popular districts like Villa, demonstrating important levels of influence in specific geographic areas as well as in the very popular organizations that were supposed to comprise the "social bulwark" against Shining Path.

Villa El Salvador was an important objective for Shining Path for strategic and geopolitical reasons. As the largest popular district in Lima's southern cone, Villa El Salvador was a strategic area to control for Shining Path's larger plan of encircling Lima. In geopolitical terms, on one side Villa borders the Pan-American Highway, Lima's main link to southern Peru; on the other, across the foothills of the Andes, it links up to other shantytowns that surround Lima, forming part of the "iron belt of misery" that Guzmán said would encircle and strangle the capital city. Aside from these strategic considerations, Villa El Salvador was also an important political objective for Shining Path. Its status as "model district" for important sectors of the Left made it a dangerous symbol for Shining Path. Peaceful organizing was not part of Shining Path's agenda; only violent revolution could produce "real" changes in Peru. In fact, an important part of Shining Path's ideological battles were fought not only against the state or the Right, but against Peru's legal Left and the organizations that had become associated with it. The legal Left participated in elections, had members in Congress, and ran local municipal governments. For Shining Path, this "revisionism" meant that the Left had been "contaminated" by the "putrid old order" that they sought to destroy by force. The real battle, Guzmán is reported as saying, was against this "revisionist Left"—its principal competitor for popular support. Villa El Salvador—the Left's showpiece of grassroots organizing and local participatory government—was a key symbol of the "revisionist Left" that Shining Path was bent on obliterating. By gaining influence in precisely those areas that, like Villa El Salvador, were such crucial symbols of the mainstream Left, Shining Path could "unmask" the "revisionism" of the IU and prove that it offered the only truly "revolutionary" alternative for social change.[6] As one of my interviewees stated when asked why Shining Path wanted to control Villa El Salvador: "Shining Path knows that if they can control Villa, they can control anything."

Politics in the Barriadas

Changes in Peruvian economy and society led to widespread rural-to-urban migration in the 1940s, converting Peru into an urban society and Lima into an immense metropolis. A city of 500,000 in 1940, today Lima has 6 to 7 million inhabitants, nearly a third of Peru's total population. Rising unmet demands for low-cost housing led many rural migrants and urban slum dwellers to organize land invasions on the outskirts of Lima, where they built precarious dwellings on their own and struggled to obtain basic services.[7] Although some invasions were met with repression, the state often let the squatters stay, thereby defusing popular anger while exonerating the state from developing a housing policy (Driant 1991). These areas—known traditionally as barriadas and more recently as "*pueblos jóvenes*" or "young towns"—generally lack basic infrastructure (water, electricity, sewage, public transport, health and educational facilities, etc.), and community residents have alternatively mobilized to demand basic services from the government, and pooled local resources to provide some services themselves on a self-help basis. The growth of Lima's barriadas has been dramatic over the past 25 years. In 1961, some 316,000 people lived in the barriadas, about 17 percent of the overall population. By 1981, nearly a third of Lima's population lived in barriadas (1.5 million), and estimates a decade later maintain that 3 to 3.5 million Limeños live in barriadas today—about half of the capital's total population.[8]

Underlying this process of rapid urbanization was a development model based on import-substitution industrialization, which centralized economic growth in urban centers, especially Lima. In the 1970s that model entered into crisis in Peru, as in other parts of Latin America. The 1980s witnessed various attempts to implement structural adjustment programs and alternative heterodox programs whose eventual failure led to the collapse of the Peruvian economy by 1988.[9] Negative growth rates and dramatic levels of hyperinflation reduced living standards to 1960s levels, and the resulting fiscal crisis led to a dramatic collapse of the government's capacity to provide elemental public services,[10] including basic levels of social order and security. In Lima, crime and common delinquency rose sharply, particularly in the *pueblos jóvenes*. The police force was rapidly losing its credibility for its inability to detain growing crime rates. Numerous cases of police involvement in violent crimes, including extortion, armed assaults and kidnappings, led to a further deterioration of the public's image of the police. Open confrontations between members of the police and army forces in the street reflected the deep institutional crisis of the Peruvian state.[11]

Neoliberal restructuring in 1990 and 1991 exacerbated these conditions.[12] The stabilization program implemented in August, 1990, just weeks after Alberto Fujimori was inaugurated president, pulverized living standards. Price increases and cuts in social expenditures nearly doubled the number of Peruvians living in conditions of critical poverty—from 6 to 11 million overnight, fully half of the country's population.[13] In Metropolitan Lima, consumption expenditures, which had already dropped by 46 percent between 1986 and 1990, fell 31 percent *more* between June 1990 and October 1991, just before and after Fujimori's economic package was implemented (FONCODES 1994). Government cut-backs further decreased the state's ability to respond to growing popular demands and the crisis of internal order.

For Shining Path, this large—and growing—population of urban poor, mostly concentrated in Lima's barriadas, was fertile terrain to build a support base for its revolution. Moreover, Lima's barriadas were central to Shining Path's overall plans in geopolitical terms: controlling Lima's barriadas meant controlling travel routes to the north and south of Lima along the Panamerican Highway, and to the east along the Central Highway, the principal route to Lima's breadbasket and center of crucial supplies and export earnings, principally mining. The barriadas were the chokepoints—the "iron belts of misery"—from which the enemy forces, centered in historic downtown Lima and surrounding commercial and residential districts, could be encircled (McCormick 1990, 1992). In order to construct "strategic equilibrium"—the crucial stage before the final strategic offensive, which would lead to the urban offensive and the final seizure of state power—Shining Path would have to obtain political, if not territorial, control over key populations.[14] Well over half of the capital city's population lived in Lima's barriadas, and their situation of economic deprivation made them—as far as Shining Path was concerned—a captive audience to their call for revolutionary change.

It did not seem coincidental that Shining Path began to focus on organizing in Lima at this precise moment. After 1988, Peru's overall political, social, and economic situation began to deteriorate dramatically. The initial success of García's heterodox experiment, spearheaded by a demand-led recovery of the economy between 1986 and 1987, collapsed under the weight of foreign exchange constraints and looming government deficits by 1988. Spiraling hyperinflation—1,722 percent in 1988 and 2,775 percent in 1989—forced a sharp decline in real wages and a 25 percent contraction of the economy between 1988 and 1990 (Pastor and Wise 1992). This provoked massive labor unrest and seriously weakened the government's fledgling legitimacy. The process of state decomposition that followed the economic fiasco, and the consequent decline of public services and the drying up of social programs caused major discontent. Political violence was growing and expanding into new areas, adding to the sensation of a situation gone out of control.

Popular support for APRA eroded quickly. For a short time, it seemed possible that the IU—APRA's principal competitor for support among the lower classes—would pick up votes from disaffected apristas in the 1989 municipal elections and presidential elections the following year. But in early 1989, long-standing tensions between moderates and radicals within the coalition culminated in the division of the IU, deflating the Left's electoral chances.[15] The division of the Left fed the growing perception that representative institutions were incapable of resolving the political and economic crisis. People increasingly saw political parties across the ideological spectrum as vehicles of personalistic power and patronage and parliament as an ineffective body that spent hours debating irrelevant points while the country veered toward instability and chaos. The political expression of this growing disaffection was the election of independent candidates who played up their status as "outsiders": Ricardo Belmont won the 1989 municipal elections, while Alberto Fujimori defeated novelist Mario Vargas Llosa for president in 1990.[16]

This combination of a devastating economic crisis and the collapse of traditional mediating mechanisms between state and society were the background against which Shining Path stepped up its organizing activities in Lima after 1988. The exacerbation of the economic crisis fed feelings of frustration and desperation among important segments of the urban poor. Hyperinflation was especially devastating to the poor, who often had few available cushions in times of crisis. The growing incapacity of the state to mediate popular demands, and to provide even basic public services, including public order, left the poor with few resources to negotiate the crisis. This was particularly true for newer migrants. Whereas governments from the time of Odría (1948–1956) sought to obtain the support of the urban poor via specific social programs and clientelistic handouts (Collier 1976), the fiscal crisis after 1988 eroded the government's capacity to respond to growing demands for housing and infrastructure.[17] The closing, or collapse, of traditional mechanisms of interest representation, such as political parties and trade unions, meant that poor people had fewer options in seeking redress for their grievances. These combined factors are important contextual variables that help explain why Shining Path's push into the cities was more successful than originally predicted. The growing frustration and discontent among important sectors of Lima's urban population gave Shining Path a crucial window of opportunity to organize in Lima.

These structural conditions undoubtedly favored Shining Path's push into Lima and its bid for "strategic equilibrium" but structural conditions alone cannot be considered the necessary *and* sufficient causes of Shining Path organizing in the city. Numerous studies in recent years have addressed the inadequacy of structural analyses in explaining political outcomes and their failure to address key issues of human agency. Although they vary in approach—some address subaltern behavior using rational choice-inspired models such as that elaborated by Samuel Popkin (1979), while others seek to develop more historically sensitive models to understand subaltern patterns of accommodation and resistance to authority (Scott 1985, 1990; Stern 1987)—they share a concern with understanding the varied dimensions of human agency, subaltern consciousness, and political decision-making.[18] The complex dynamics between the structural variables that shaped Shining Path's organizing opportunities in Lima and the day-to-day political mediations between Shining Path and local groups can be explored in one barriada district, Villa El Salvador.

Many left-wing grassroots activists and local organizations tried to contest Shining Path and its attempts to establish influence in Villa El Salvador and its organizations. The Maoists did not hesitate to use coercion, threats, and assassination when it suited their cause, but these terrorist activities were only one element of Shining Path's repertoire of actions. Sendero acted on a political level in many arenas, and in many ways Shining Path's capacity to negotiate the complex terrain of urban politics was underestimated. A detailed examination of Shining Path's activities in Villa El Salvador, the responses to their presence by local actors, and the nature of popular attitudes and responses toward Shining Path will highlight some of the key aspects that permitted Shining Path to gain a significant foothold in this popular district as well as in other *barriadas* in Lima.[19] It will also provide a more contextualized understanding of grassroots attempts to resist Shining Path's overtures, as well as instances in which there was greater receptivity toward Shining Path's activities.

In order to understand the dynamics of Shining Path's expansion into Lima, and particularly into Lima's barriadas, this essay sets out to examine the nature of the political relationships that the Maoist organization sought to establish with potential constituency groups.[20] Few studies have set out to examine to the dynamics of Shining Path's expansion into Lima, the nature of their interactions with local populations and other actors, and local attitudes toward Shining Path actions and presence.[21] Exploring how the relationships between Shining Path and its potential constituents were constructed, mediated, and negotiated will help explain not only the expansion of the Shining Path insurgency; it will also provide insight into the relatively quick isolation of the group in the wake of the capture of its maximum leader, Abimael Guzmán, in September 1992. After describing Shining Path's initial attempts to organize in Villa El Salvador, I analyze the peak period of Shining Path activity in the district between 1991 and 1992, when Shining Path exercised important levels of influence over key social organizations in Villa El Salvador as well as in certain geographic areas of this popular district.

Villa El Salvador: Creating a Model District

Villa El Salvador was founded in 1971 in response to a land invasion organized by poor migrants and slum dwellers. The original invasion on state-owned land was organized by 200 families, but within a few days over 9,000 families had joined the invasion, which spilled over onto privately owned land. The military regime of General Juan Velasco Alvarado—under pressure to prove its commitment to the poor Peruvians that its "revolutionary" experiment promised to benefit—decided to relocate the invaders to an extensive piece of barren desert land eighteen miles south of Lima. Thousands of poor families were given land by the Velasco government in this new settlement, which residents called Villa El Salvador, and which would become the urban showcase of Velasco's "revolution." State planners were charged with turning this spontaneous invasion into Peru's first planned urban community, simultaneously resolving the pent-up housing crisis and obtaining popular support for the military regime.

The community's structure was laid out block by block, in grid fashion. Every block was composed of twenty-four family lots, and sixteen blocks constituted a residential group. Each residential group had an area demarcated as communal land for the future development of community projects such as preschools, meeting houses, soup kitchens and soccer fields. Today, 126 residential groups are assembled into seven large sectors.[22] This territorial division was designed not only to rationalize the urbanization process, but to facilitate local organizing as well. Each block elected three representatives, and of the forty-eight chosen from each residential group, eight were selected as the main group leaders. State planners created a centralized governing body called the Self-Managing Urban Community of Villa El Salvador (CUAVES), which would oversee the development of the community and represent it before the government and other outside agencies. The rank and file of the CUAVES was made up of the leaders of the residential groups, from which a ten-member executive council was elected. Areas were also slated for the future development of an Industrial Park and an agricultural zone as part of Velasco's design to make Villa El Salvador a self-sustaining and self-managing community (comunidad autogestionaria). Although state planners oversaw community initiatives, the "self-help" model promoted by the Velasco government helped nourish a vibrant network of social organizations that sought to mobilize collective efforts to improve the local community.

The palace coup led by Francisco Morales Bermúdez in 1975 marked the hardening of the military regime's posture towards Peru's popular sectors. Not only did the central government abandon its assistance program to Villa El Salvador; it also stepped up its repression against popular protests, which picked up in the aftermath of the regime's implementation of harsh austerity measures. Villa El Salvador reflected the changing balance of forces in Peruvian politics. Once a pet project of the military government and a bastion of pro-Velasco sentiment, it swiftly became a center of left-wing organizing and community development independent, and often in confrontation with, the central government. Villa and its organizations became the vanguard of the barriada protest movement against the military regime, and the emerging parties of the "New Left" jockeyed to gain influence in the settlement.

The increasingly antipopular stance of the military regime opened up important political spaces in places like Villa El Salvador. The parties of the "New Left," which were more critical of the Velasco government than the traditional Moscow-line Communist Party, saw in the spontaneous popular mobilizations of the poor and working classes the seed for a true revolutionary change in Peruvian society (Nieto 1983). Organized labor, shantytown organizations, and the New Left groups joined forces to challenge the military regime and its policies on the streets. Three successful national strikes between 1977 and 1979 against the regime's economic policies, and against military rule in general, helped push the military toward a return to civilian rule. Although the New Left parties initially hoped to see this mobilization turn to more radical directions, most of them agreed to participate in the Constituent Assembly called by the military to lead the transition process to democratic rule.[23] In the 1978 Constituent Assembly elections, the New Left parties emerged as a significant force in Peruvian politics, winning a combined 30 percent of the vote.[24]

Moving to the forefront of the opposition against the military carried its costs. As state resources dried up, Villa El Salvador was left on its own to meet the challenges of providing basic infrastructure to its growing population, which increased from 105,000 residents in 1973 to 168,000 in 1984. Villa El Salvador turned to the municipal government of neighboring Villa Maria del Triunfo, of which it formed a part, but little assistance was forthcoming. The new democratic government of Fernando Belaúnde Terry (1980–1985) continued to implement austerity measures, feeding the economic crisis. In Villa El Salvador, members of the community worked hard to fill in the gaps. Women, for example, began organizing after 1979 to meet their families' basic nutrition needs by forming communal soup kitchens, often with the assistance of the Catholic Church and other development agencies. The CUAVES, however, had lost its resource base and many of its projects faltered, generating mistrust among the population.[25] Municipal neglect fed a growing movement to establish Villa El Salvador as an independent municipality, which was granted by Congress in 1983.

In that same year, the majority of New Left parties joined forces in an electoral coalition, Izquierda Unida (IU-United Left), in anticipation of the municipal elections to be held in the fall of 1983. The Left's poor showing in the 1980 presidential elections—attempts at presenting a unified candidate collapsed at the last minute and the Left won only 14 percent of the vote—suggested that only by presenting a unified front could they do well electorally. The bet paid off: Alfonso Barrantes, architect of the IU coalition, was elected mayor of Lima, and the IU won twenty-two of forty-one districts in Lima. The Left did especially well in poorer districts like Villa El Salvador. Barrantes came in second to Alan García in the 1985 presidential elections, establishing the IU as the second most important electoral force in the country.

Michel Azcueta, a Spanish-born teacher at Fe y Alegría, a well-known experimental high school in Villa El Salvador, and leader of the movement to make Villa an independent municipal district, was elected mayor of Villa El Salvador for two consecutive terms in 1983 and 1986 on the IU ticket. He proposed an ambitious project of promoting grassroots participation and community development through local government. Azcueta hoped to reactivate the CUAVES and the block-level organizations, and new elections were held for the executive council of the CUAVES. His first act as mayor was to formally recognize the CUAVES as the central representative organization of the community, and he promised to respect its organizational autonomy. Azcueta conceived of a partnership between the municipal government and the CUAVES, and he hoped that together they could develop a coherent plan of development for the district. In Azcueta's retooling of the model of self-management, the municipal government would provide institutional support to the community organizations and use its resources to decentralize government and devolve power to the community organizations. The Left helped promote the formation of new organizations in Villa El Salvador, including the Women's Federation (FEPOMUVES) and the association of small business owners (APEMIVES). The latter would become a key protagonist of the Industrial Park, which Azcueta helped get off the ground with assistance from the central government and international donations. The Industrial Park was crucial to the self-management model, because by supporting local industry it would help promote local business initiatives and dynamize the district's economy.

Through its status as local government, the Left promoted grassroots organizing and participation in local decision-making, in some cases devolving control of municipal-run programs to the community organizations. This was the case, for example, with the Glass of Milk program, initiated under the Barrantes administration, in which the municipal government provided a glass of milk each day to children and pregnant women in Lima's shantytowns, and women organized local committees to distribute the milk. Azcueta signed an agreement devolving control of the milk program to the Women's Federation (FEPOMUVES), which continues to run the program. This was part of the left-wing project of building "popular power."

After Alan García was elected president in 1985, there were numerous attempts on the part of the APRA party to broaden its appeal among Villa's inhabitants. The government established clientelistic programs such as the PAIT temporary work program, which strong-armed workers to become card-carrying members of APRA. The government also created parallel social organizations in Villa El Salvador and other barriadas throughout Lima, such as the mothers' clubs, which competed with other established organizations for scarce resources. Nonetheless, the IU dominated local politics in Villa during the 1980s.

The way the IU was structured, however, would prove to have dire consequences for left-wing organizing in Villa El Salvador and elsewhere in Peru. The coalition was based on a loose structure of affiliation with no strong central leadership. This flexibility permitted each party to retain its own sense of identity while being able to participate in the IU coalition. What worked in terms of national-level politics, however, often had negative consequences at the grassroots. In effect, rivalries emerged among the different parties in the search to control social organizations and establish hegemony vis-à-vis other left-wing parties. As one left-wing activist and former member of the IU said, "relations between the different parties in Villa were cordial and fraternal, but they were also very complicated. It was difficult to figure out who was working for the [united] front [the IU] and who was working for his or her political party." These rivalries would grow and fester, with important repercussions both for the future of the IU and for the district as a whole, as we shall see.

Villa El Salvador won international recognition for its accomplishments, including Spain's Prince of Asturias Award in 1987 and the title "City Messenger of Peace" by the United Nations in 1985. Social scientists and radical political activists alike considered Villa El Salvador to be a paradigmatic case of the "barriada movement," noted for its strong grassroots organizations and the construction of a new local identity based on membership in the community ("vecino," or neighbor) (Tovar 1986). The daily practice of these organizations was highlighted for its democratic and participatory nature, in contradistinction to the national political order, marked by hierarchy and authoritarianism (Ballón et al. 1986). As Shining Path sought to develop its presence in Lima, these positive elements of Villa El Salvador's development were highlighted as factors that would block Shining Path's incursions. A city constructed by poor people through organization and sacrifice would not succumb to the authoritarian dictates of the Maoist insurgents.

Events during 1991 and 1992 suggested, however, that things were much more complex. In fact, Shining Path came to exercise significant levels of influence in organizations like the CUAVES, the Women's Federation, and the small industrialists' association that constituted the key pillars of the district's unique and much-heralded model of self-management. Shining Path used terrorist tactics, including intimidation, threats, and outright assassination, to discredit local leaders and eliminate those who resisted their advances — as in the case of María Elena Moyano, vice-mayor of the district and former president of the Women's Federation, who was brutally murdered by the Maoists in early 1992. At the same time, however, the Maoists also operated at the level of politics in the district, seeking to build sympathy among local populations by championing popular causes, and by establishing tactical alliances with different fringe groups in the district to further their cause. It was precisely at this political level that Shining Path was underestimated. Especially in newer and poorer parts of the barriadas, Shining Path was able to mobilize sympathy among the local population by exploiting the institutional voids in these areas to its advantage.[26] Shining Path played upon the state's incapacity to provide basic security to its citizens, and its actions of intimidating and sometimes physically eliminating thieves, delinquents, and drug addicts won it a great deal of sympathy. At the local level, Shining Path attempted to construct an image of itself as a harsh but fair imparter of justice in a country in which justice was routinely bought and sold, and where conflict resolution mechanisms at the grassroots were sorely lacking.[27] It "punished" local authorities, vendors, and community leaders who it claimed were corrupt, and in many instances successfully manipulated popular outrage at petty acts of corruption in its favor. This broadly paralleled Shining Path's attempts to build sympathy and support in rural areas, where it focused on conflicts revolving around land ownership in the aftermath of the agrarian reform, and played on popular resentment against merchants, state-run cooperatives and local state authorities (Berg 1992; Isbell 1992). At a more political level in Villa El Salvador, Shining Path tried to demonstrate the futility of peaceful strategies for social change, an attempt both to discredit the left-wing parties that continued to organize and were its chief rival on the ground, and to radicalize popular struggles in its logic of confrontation with the state. Focusing on Shining Path's political strategies is not intended to downplay the organization's use of terrorist tactics, but to examine an aspect of their overall strategy in Lima that has not been adequately explored. Examining the case of Villa El Salvador will permit a closer look at Shining Path's lethal mix of politics and terror.

Laying the Groundwork: Subterranean Organizing in Villa El Salvador

In order to understand how Shining Path gained a foothold in Villa El Salvador and challenged its most important institutions and organizations in 1991 and 1992, it is important to look back to Shining Path's previous clandestine and subterranean organizing activities in Villa since the early 1980s.[28] During these initial years of the war, Shining Path's public presence in Lima was minimal. It mainly engaged in armed attacks against the state security apparatus, government agencies, economic infrastructure, and centers of economic activity as a way of disrupting normal activity and demonstrating its presence. Since armed attacks in Lima were more likely to be covered by the press both nationally and internationally, these acts of sabotage had significant symbolic and propaganda value (McCormick 1992). In Villa El Salvador, a relatively small number of armed attacks were carried out between 1981 and 1986 against government agencies, the district's only police station, and economic infrastructure such as banks and electricity pylons (the latter's dramatic effect of submerging the city in darkness was the Shining Path signature for years). Occasional agit-prop activities were also carried out in Villa El Salvador, including huge bonfires outlining a hammer and sickle on the hills surrounding the district. But for most of the residents of Villa El Salvador, Shining Path was a movement in far-off Ayacucho that rarely impinged on their daily lives.

Several reports indicate that there was low-level organizing activity going on in many Lima shantytowns as well as public universities and trade unions (especially the teachers' union, SUTEP) in this early period. Clandestine organizing in the city was paid little attention as analysts focused on the war raging in the countryside where Shining Path armed activity was strongest and military counterinsurgency harshest. Meanwhile, in Lima, radical student groups in San Marcos University, La Cantuta University, and the National University of Engineering organized small cells that later galvanized student support for Shining Path's insurgency. A small nucleus of students from San Marcos organized study groups in Villa El Salvador (and other shantytowns) to recruit new members.[29] One high-ranking member of Shining Path, Nelly Evans, was a professor during the late 1970s and early 1980s at Fe y Alegría, one of Villa's most important high schools, where she reportedly promoted study groups of the literary works of Peruvian novelist José María Arguedas to recruit young students to the "revolutionary cause."

By 1987, there was some evidence of Shining Path's intention to establish a more organic presence in Villa. While sabotage activities continued, there were signs of more grassroots political activism. Reports indicate that new discussion groups and cultural associations were created to recruit followers, as were technical academies, where many high-school graduates with scant chance of entering the university sought training for—or at least a delay of their entrance into—an otherwise unpromising job market. After 1988–1989, Shining Path's agit-prop activities became more visible. For example, small Shining Path contingents participated in activities and protest marches organized by legal left-wing groups, often directed against government economic measures or human rights violations committed by the military, but raising the banner of violent revolution as the only solution.

Many local left-wing activists considered Shining Path to be misguided in its use of violence. There was, however, an important element of ambiguity in the Left's perception of Shining Path, rooted in a common ideological legacy that saw armed struggle as both legitimate and necessary to bring about structural change.[30] This was not only the case in Lima's barriadas, but in the trade union movement as well, which had a long trajectory of combatting the military regime and was struggling to cope with economic austerity and new anti-labor legislation (Sulmont et al. 1989; Balbi 1992). The government's poor human rights record—including the arbitrary detention of hundreds of left-wing activists not affiliated with Shining Path, and massacres and forced disappearances—made it difficult for mainstream Left activists to challenge Shining Path's characterization of the regime as repressive.

This ambiguity at the grassroots level reflected split opinions within the IU coalition toward Shining Path and its struggle. While moderate elements distanced themselves from Shining Path in the early 1980s, more radical groups within the IU maintained a more permissive attitude. Although critical of Shining Path's terrorist methods, they noted the "popular extraction" of Shining Path's militants, their moral commitment of realizing the march toward socialism, and the confluence of positions between the Left and Shining Path against a common enemy—the capitalist state[31] (Pásara 1990). As one national leader of the IU stated: "These more radical elements in the IU did not see Shining Path as an enemy that had to be defeated." Within the sector that defined Shining Path as an enemy, there was a great deal of controversy over *how* to defeat Shining Path: "Supporting or collaborating with the Armed Forces was a hard pill to swallow," said the same IU leader. "For some, it amounted to treason."[32]

An important segment of Peru's mainstream Left came to value the political and civic liberties guaranteed by a democratic system, and tried to defend Peru's democracy while challenging the violence unleashed by both Shining Path and the Peruvian government. For others, however, the massive human rights violations committed by the Armed Forces throughout the 1980s reinforced their vision of the state as an essentially repressive and antipopular entity (Abugattás 1990). By the end of the 1980s, some, increasingly frustrated with the meager results of a decade of left-wing participation in democratic government, flirted with Shining Path, and some joined its ranks.

Over the course of the 1980s, the barriada population grew dramatically, from 1.5 million to an estimated 3 to 3.5 million in the early 1990s. Continued rural migration to Lima was one factor in fueling this rapid growth, but it was also largely due to the doubling of family units within Lima's existing barriadas, as young families set out to build their own homes by organizing small invasions on the outskirts of existing barriadas (Driant 1991). Villa El Salvador was no exception. Between 1984 and 1993, the population had grown from 168,000 to 260,000, a 5 percent annual growth rate. According to the 1984 census carried out by the CUAVES, new invasions made up 27 percent of Villa's overall population, consisting mainly of young couples with smaller families and lower incomes who lived in precarious houses of cane matting (CUAVES/CIDIAG 1984). More recent figures are not available, but new invasions have continued to grow since the late

1980s in the sixth and seventh sectors, as well as the fourth sector, known as Pachacamac.[33] Most of these families lacked land titles, although the municipal government usually adopted a permissive attitude toward squatters. These new invasions lacked the basic infrastructure (piped water, sewerage, electricity) that older, more established parts of the district had obtained in the 1970s and early 1980s, and that the government, increasingly constrained by the fiscal crisis, was unable to provide them as in the past. This internal diversification of Villa El Salvador meant that while some parts of the district had progressed in terms of meeting their most basic needs, including housing and basic infrastructure, a significant and growing part of the district had fewer personal resources as well as less access to outside assistance to improve their local living conditions.

Shining Path's organizing efforts focused especially in these parts of Villa El Salvador. Local observers say that after 1989 they began to note the presence of Shining Path cadre in newly formed settlements such as Pachacamac, which had grown dramatically. It was relatively easy for Shining Path members to join a land invasion and become part of the local community. Many became active in the local neighborhood councils that formed the rank and file of the CUAVES, the centralized community organization in the district. Squatters organized these councils to improve conditions in the community and petition the government for infrastructure. Shining Path sought to win local sympathy by taking up the demands of the local population. For example, Shining Path took up the banner of land tenure for squatters in Pachacamac. Some local leaders in these areas became sympathetic to Shining Path's cause, especially as the economic crisis deepened and peaceful means of social change seemed increasingly unviable after 1989. Shining Path actively sought to encourage this perception, often challenging IU leaders at the local level over their proposals to organize protest marches and petition the authorities. By radicalizing popular struggles, Shining Path hoped to reveal the state's unwillingness to respond to the local population's demands and the need for more drastic alternatives.

Little attention was paid to Shining Path's subterranean organizing efforts in shantytowns like Villa El Salvador. Some of the group's activities were so unobtrusive that they were difficult to perceive except to the most informed local observers, and by the early 1990s, Shining Path activists and new recruits worked side-by-side with their unwitting neighbors at the local level, forming water and electricity committees and seeking to gain positions of influence in local community councils linked to the CUAVES.

Wall slogans announce the presence of Sendero Luminoso in an urban neighborhood.

Other more open organizing efforts were tolerated, in part out of fear—
"snitches" were sure targets for Shining Path reprisals—but also because of
the continuing assumptions among segments of the legal Left that despite
Shining Path's misguided methods, they were ultimately fighting the same
enemy: a corrupt and increasingly delegitimized state. Coupled with long-
standing mistrust of the police and the military, this prompted many local
activists with knowledge of Shining Path activity simply to stay quiet. As
Shining Path's intentions of destroying the self-managing project of Villa
El Salvador became more apparent, many activists who strongly identified
themselves with Villa El Salvador and the larger project of self-management
and popular participation that it represented began to challenge directly the
Maoists in the district. But this initial permissiveness allowed Shining Path
a crucial space to organize, collect information, and establish a local network of sympathizers and activists that was central to its campaign of direct
confrontation in the early 1990s.

Destroying the Myth: The Politics of Confrontation

After 1991, Shining Path began to engage in more direct confrontational
politics in Villa El Salvador as part of its larger plan of upping the ante of

the war in Lima. Guzmán's announcement in May 1991 that the organization had reached "strategic equilibrium," meant launching more aggressive
campaigns on all fronts, especially in the strategically important barriadas,
where the "decisive battle" would be fought.[34] Gaining influence in a left-
wing stronghold like Villa El Salvador would not only promote Shining
Path's strategic objectives of strengthening its hold on Lima's barriada districts; it would also have significant political impact by demonstrating that
the organization was in fact capable of manuevering in the more complex
terrain of urban politics.

Shining Path's subterranean organizing and recruitment activity laid the
groundwork for its more direct confrontational politics by permitting the
organization to elaborate an exhaustive diagnostic of the political and social
situation in Villa El Salvador. Operating on the Maoist maxim of the "principal contradiction," the organization sought to identify the central sources
of strife or conflict in a given area, which it then deliberately tried to exacerbate in its logic of confrontation politics and "deepening the contradictions."
Shining Path identified local popular demands and struggles that were not
being addressed and sought to radicalize them to win popular sympathy and
discredit local and national authorities. At the same time, it played on existing conflicts within and among local organizations as a way of discrediting
the Left leadership, enhancing its status, and polarizing local society.

Based on this logic of the "principal contradiction," Shining Path engaged
in a head-on confrontation against the United Left leadership in Villa El
Salvador. The Left was targeted not only because Shining Path considered
it "revisionist" and the principal "enemy" of its "revolution." In addition,
after nearly a decade in formal, institutional power in Villa El Salvador,
the mainstream Left had become part of the local power structure around
which a series of local conflicts—some recent, some more long-standing—
had emerged. Shining Path identified conflicts such as that between the
IU municipal leadership and the CUAVES as foci around which it could
agitate disgruntled groups, discredit the IU leadership, create the social
space for its own organizing and propaganda activities, and demonstrate
the futility of peaceful organizing and the necessity of revolutionary armed
action. Pinpointing local conflicts and seeking to exacerbate them would
help undermine the "revisionist left" and its project of self-management
while permitting the Maoists to build up their local presence by exploiting
local grievances. By radicalizing popular struggles and exacerbating conflict
between different actors in the district, Shining Path sought to provoke the

military repression which it believed would ultimately favor its cause. This not only had importance for Shining Path's designs in Villa itself; it had repercussions at the national level given the symbolic significance of Villa El Salvador and its central organizations such as the CUAVES.

The IU was the dominant actor in Villa El Salvador's formal politics since the coalition first formed in 1983. Michel Azcueta led the campaign to establish Villa as an independent municipality in 1983, and he was elected mayor on the IU ticket two consecutive terms between 1983 and 1989. His administration obtained many impressive results. Starting from scratch, he got the municipal government working by mobilizing volunteer support. Committed to the Left's model of popular participation, Azcueta not only promoted the formation of new organizations like the small industrialists' association, APEMIVES, and an association of street vendors, FUCOMIVES, but he also devolved control of municipal programs to community organizations, as was the case with the FEPOMUVES, which assumed administrative control of the milk program. Azcueta was also able to muster international support for various local development projects, and progress could be counted in the number of paved roads, street lights, and municipal garbage trucks that kept the district clean. In conjunction with local NGDOs that were active in Villa El Salvador—many of which promoted small workshops and lent assistance to popular organizations like the soup kitchens and the milk committees—the municipal government devised an Integral Development Plan, which laid out a series of proposals for the district in different policy arenas such as housing.[35] The mayor also obtained government and international assistance to implement the Industrial Park, where nearly 200 small business owners had set up workshops or factories by 1990. Villa El Salvador became a model of popular participation and grassroots decision-making, which was held up by the Left as an example of its capacity to govern and offer concrete solutions to Peru's structural problems of poverty and unemployment. This was a crucial experiment for the Left, which was a serious contender for the presidential elections in 1990.

The IU easily won the 1989 municipal elections in Villa El Salvador. Johny Rodríguez was elected mayor, and María Elena Moyano, former president of the Popular Women's Federation (FEPOMUVES), was elected vice-mayor.[36] The Rodríguez-Moyano administration was faced with more difficult times. In Peru's highly centralized political system, municipal governments in Peru have always operated under serious budget constraints, especially in poorer districts. But the ravaging effects of hyperinflation decimated the municipal government's budget. And as Villa El Salvador grew and became more internally diverse and heterogeneous, the problems that community organizations helped resolve in an earlier epoch became more complex. In the district's more established areas, in fact, there was a general demobilization of the neighborhood councils as their communities obtained basic infrastructure. New squatters turned to the municipal government to resolve their problems of infrastructure and land tenure, but it had few resources available. And political violence in the district began to intensify.

Azcueta, Rodríguez, and Moyano all belonged to the United Mariateguista Party (PUM), one of the best organized parties in the IU coalition, until PUM's split in 1988. The party's division was due in part to growing discrepancies over conceptions of armed struggle and the role of the Left in supporting Peru's fledgling democracy. The radicals within the PUM, known as *libios*, maintained that armed struggle was still valid and necessary, thus compromising their commitment to democratic rule and making a clear split with Shining Path difficult. The moderates, known as *zorros*, reiterated their commitment to strengthening Peru's democracy and condemned Shining Path, although there was still controversy over the degree to which they should collaborate with the state in the struggle against Shining Path. Along with an important block of followers in Villa El Salvador, Azcueta and Rodríguez joined the newly formed Revolutionary Mariateguista Party (PMR), while Moyano later joined the Christian Left party, Movement of Socialist Affirmation (MAS). Both groups remained in the United Left coalition, but tensions with the more radical sectors remained. With the approaching 1990 presidential elections, these tensions, coupled with conflicts within the IU over leadership and the apportionment of electoral seats, led to a split in the coalition. Alfonso Barrantes, the ex-mayor of Lima, was selected as presidential candidate for the more moderate Socialist Left (IS), while the IU chose sociologist Henry Pease as its candidate. On the ground, however, the IU coalition was a dead letter. Each political party focused on defining its own political profile and popular support base. This would have grave ramifications in barriada districts like Villa El Salvador, particularly as Shining Path sought to up the ante in Lima's "iron belts of misery."

The division of the IU led to the surfacing of the underlying tensions that had existed within the left-wing coalition on the ground well before the formal split in 1989. While Azcueta was able to mobilize important levels of support for his project in Villa El Salvador, there were nonetheless important levels of jockeying for grassroots support among the different IU parties, and partisan rivalries were often intense. The fact that Azcueta's project was dominant did not mean that it was uncontested. While PUM had gained prominence in many of Villa's key organizations, other IU parties were also seeking to establish their own influence, reflecting the gravest weakness of the IU coalition. The fact that the electoral coalition permitted each organization to maintain its particular party structure and goals often translated into intense struggles to establish "hegemony" within local contexts. As one PUM activist noted in 1994 during a workshop to discuss the impact of political violence on the district, "this struggle for hegemony dominated the Left's actions in Villa, and led to divisions within the organizations, which all the different parties tried to control." This partisan jockeying intensified after the 1988 split of PUM, making united action among the Left in Villa El Salvador far more difficult. The divisions between small radical left-wing groups within the CUAVES that remained marginalized from the IU coalition throughout the 1980s was also a significant source of conflict within the district, as we shall see later.

By 1991, Shining Path's presence in Villa El Salvador had become decidedly more aggressive and high-profile. An open campaign to intimidate and eliminate local authorities—in similar fashion to their tactics of "sweeping up" the countryside—had begun. In June, Shining Path killed the governor of Villa, Alejandro Magno Gómez, who was affiliated with the governing party, Cambio 90.[37] Between 1989 and 1992, Shining Path's newspaper, El Diario, frequently and vociferously criticized Villa El Salvador and its principal leaders. Azcueta and Moyano were singled out as "opportunists" and "revisionists," and the Left's experiment of self-management in Villa El Salvador was sharply attacked as a sham designed "to castrate the combativeness and the revolutionary potential of the masses."[38] Moyano, along with other left-wing mayors and vice-mayors of barriada districts in Lima, was accused of corruption and "working against the Maoist revolution" in El Diario in 1991.[39] Rodríguez and Azcueta began receiving repeated death threats from the Maoist organization, and between 1991 and 1993 both survived unsuccessful assassination attempts.

As the Maoist organization began directing more focused attacks against the local leadership and its intention of expanding its influence in key community organizations within Villa El Salvador became clear, local authorities began to denounce actively Guzmán and his followers. Azcueta, Rodríguez, and Moyano were at the forefront of these efforts. They helped mobilize a core group of local left-wing activists linked to the PMR and the MAS, who began to react to what they increasingly perceived not only as attacks against the project they had dedicated their lives to building, but to their very lives as well. As one grassroots activist who was a member of PMR stated: "Before we weren't so clear as to what Shining Path wanted in Villa. We thought we could coexist in a way. But soon we started to realize that they didn't want to coexist with us; they wanted to get rid of us, they wanted to get rid of Villa." As some leftists sharpened their critique of Shining Path, however, others retained a more ambiguous stance.

In September 1991, a bomb exploded and destroyed one of the central warehouses where the FEPOMUVES stored donated foodstuffs that were used by the soup kitchens in their daily cooking. Moyano accused Shining Path of the attack, and she became an open and unrelenting critic of the Maoist organization.[40] Moyano admitted in an interview shortly after the bombing that her criticism of Shining Path had been muted until they began attacking the Women's Federation: "Until some time ago I thought that Shining Path was a group that committed errors, but that, in some way, they were trying to fight to obtain justice. But when they killed labor leader Enrique Castillo [in October 1989], I repudiated them. However, I didn't dare condemn Shining Path's terrorist attitude. But now they have attacked the grassroots organizations, where the poorest organize . . . They are trying to undermine these organizations. . . . I no longer consider Shining Path a revolutionary group."[41] Moyano was especially critical of the leaders of the IU for permitting the coalition to split. This division, she said, caused many people to feel disenchanted with the Left, leaving them few alternatives. As a result, she said, "some people from the popular barriadas look at Shining Path from afar, they see them as almost mystical, and they say that they fight for justice. . . . And the most radical sectors of the Left did not distance themselves from Shining Path when it was opportune to do so. And now, what left-wing party has made a statement about what is happening in Villa El Salvador? Not one, no political leader has come to see what is happening here."[42]

In the same interview, Moyano said that the women's organizations in Villa would resist Shining Path, and that she would promote the creation of autonomous neighborhood defense groups (*rondas vecinales*) to combat Shining Path.[43] Subsequent attempts to organize urban rondas were quickly disbanded after Shining Path visited the homes of the ronda organizers, one by one, warning them of their fate should they attempt such an endeavor. Nevertheless, Moyano became something of a local celebrity for her outspoken criticism of Shining Path, and she was featured on the news and in

Lima's newspapers and weekly magazines as an example of how to combat Shining Path. The division of the IU and the subsequent weakening of the Left as a political force meant that grassroots leaders like Moyano were increasingly, and dangerously, on their own.[44]

As mayor, Rodríguez tried to use the institutional backing of the municipal government to create a broad-based front against Shining Path in the district. In late 1991, he announced the formation of the Peace and Development Forum,[45] a broad-based coalition uniting the Catholic Church, local human rights groups, popular organizations, and the municipal government. The objective of the Peace Forum was to develop alternative strategies to respond to Villa's social problems and to check Shining Path's growing influence in the community. One of the Peace Forum's member groups, the Youth Coordinating Committee, was one of the most active and daring. For example, the Youth Committee, loosely affiliated to the PMR, mobilized groups of young people to paint over Shining Path graffiti in the district.

While these attempts at building unity continued, a decisive blow for Villa's democratic forces came on 9 February 1992, when a small business owner, Máximo Huarcaya, was elected president of Villa's microenterprise association, APEMIVES, with the open support of Shining Path. Activists of the Peace Forum attempted to preempt Huarcaya's victory by convincing the different left-wing parties operating in Villa to back a single candidate in the elections. The recent history of divisions had sharply marked the Left in Villa, however, and there was no agreement on a consensus candidate. With the Left ticket split, Huarcaya won the election.

APEMIVES was one of the members of the Autonomous Authority (AA), the governing body of the Industrial Park in Villa El Salvador. The mayor of the district was also a member of the AA, along with a representative from the government, private industry, and the president of the CUAVES. Conflict had been brewing within the Industrial Park over several aspects of the Park's administration. Most conflictual was the situation regarding usage of the land plots that were loaned to the small industrialists, who had the obligation of constructing locales on the plots and transferring their workshops to them. Many industrialists, hard hit by the economic crisis, lacked sufficient resources to build on their plots, and reacted negatively to the AA's assertion that they would have to give them up if they did not develop the plots as agreed. Shining Path activists took up their cause, with Huarcaya at the head, demanding that no industrialist be evicted from the Park. They accused the AA of using its power to assign plots in favor of small industrialists linked to Azcueta and the PMR. Another controversial issue was the AA's administration of international donations and a loan program for industrialists set up with international funding. The AA maintained that the books were in order and open for all to see, but other informed observers suggested that there was a problem of corruption within the AA. In any case, Shining Path and Huarcaya played on this issue and demanded that control of the resources be transferred to the APEMIVES alone. After all, they reasoned, the donations were a "gift" for the "poor"; therefore they alone should administer them, and they should not be forced to pay back the loans. This discourse became increasingly common after the onset of the economic recession, and was often exacerbated by the failure of the NGDOS to be more transparent about their sources and administration of funding (SASE-Instituto APOYO 1993). In Lima's shantytowns and in rural areas where NGDOS have been active for over two decades, Shining Path played on long-standing resentments and promised to return control of the money to "the people."[46]

Four days after Huarcaya's victory, a meeting was held in the Industrial Park to discuss the gravity of the situation. Moyano urged Huarcaya and Filadelfo Roa, president of the CUAVES, who also appeared to be forging alliances with Shining Path, to sign a document stating their opposition to Shining Path, but both refused. Moyano decided that a test of wills was in order. The following day, Shining Path declared an armed strike in Lima, and Moyano argued that Villa and its organizations should protest the strike in a public demonstration against Shining Path. Many activists declined to participate out of fear—Shining Path's penchant for killing those who openly opposed it was well-known. Other left-wing groups who were active in Villa also refused to participate, citing the need to maintain their own "profiles," reflecting the context of division within former IU coalition partners that mitigated against the formation of a united front against Shining Path.[47] Only about fifty people participated in the march, carrying white banners to symbolize peace.

Shining Path decided immediately to punish Moyano's defiance. The next day, she was killed at a community barbeque by a Shining Path hit squad and her body was destroyed with a stick of dynamite. In El Diario and in flyers that circulated throughout the district in the following days, Shining Path accused her of corruption and favoritism, and said that she was a soplón—a "stool pigeon"—who deserved punishment. A massive funeral procession was held for Moyano, but numerous observers noted that local participation was minimal, and that Shining Path's intended objective—to inculcate fear and inhibit any further efforts at resistance in Villa El Salvador—had largely succeeded.

For example, some of the FEPOMUVES leaders initially noted their indignation against the brutal murder of their former leader and their determination to resist Shining Path. But Shining Path continued to pressure and intimidate the Women's Federation's top leaders. Just months after Moyano's assassination, the president of the FEPOMUVES, Ester Flores, suffered a nervous breakdown and left the country. Many other leaders quit their positions, while others continued to work but avoided a political discourse. The vice-president of FEPOMUVES, Pilar Anchita, assumed control of the organization. Anchita was from Ayacucho, and her brother was allegedly a member of Shining Path. Her own inclinations in favor of Shining Path became increasingly evident.

A notable shift in Shining Path's discourse appeared around this time. In the late 1980s, *El Diario* had severely criticized the soup kitchens and the milk program as the "shock absorbers" of the dominant system that inhibited the poor's "revolutionary consciousness." Guzmán (1988) said these organizations "sold out the revolution for a plate of beans." Now, the Maoists claimed that they were not against these organizations, but against the "corrupt leaders" who had "sold out" the poor.[48] Thus, Shining Path's concern was not only with controlling the Federation at the level of the leadership, but with winning sympathy among the rank and file by playing on existing conflicts within the organization. As in the Industrial Park, Shining Path played on controversial issues like authoritarian leadership within the organization, the control and mishandling of the organization's resources and donations, and political favoritism. In particular, it played on the issue of corruption, a particularly sensitive issue for organizations like the FEPOMUVES that often had weak mechanisms for administering and accounting for donated resources and dealing with conflicts over resource administration, giving rise to suspicion among the rank and file that the organization's leaders were seeking personal benefits from their positions of leadership.[49] This was undoubtedly exacerbated by the context of economic deprivation, which heightened suspicions of those with access to resources and power at all levels of society (Burt and Espejo 1995).

In the aftermath of Moyano's murder, the Peace and Development Forum disbanded. Rodríguez and his allies continued to denounce Shining Path and groups within Villa El Salvador who had allied themselves with the Maoists, particularly the CUAVES leadership. Roa, the CUAVES president, refused to sign a document condemning Shining Path for the murder of Moyano, and later emitted a document that said that Michel Azcueta was ultimately responsible for her death because he had "manipulated" her.[50]

This presaged the CUAVES' assumption of a more open role in criticizing the Left leadership of the municipal government in terms very similar to those used by Shining Path. In fact, radical groups within CUAVES had established a tactical alliance with Shining Path against what they perceived to be their "common enemy," giving new meaning to the Machiavellian axiom, "the enemy of my enemy is my friend." This was another critical blow to the Left in Villa, because CUAVES was Villa's centralized neighborhood association and the community's main symbol of the self-management model. Shining Path was adept at manipulating the resentment of disgruntled groups like those in the CUAVES, and its pragmatism permitted it to establish tactical alliances with diverse groups as long as it furthered their longer-term goals. Roa was likely not a Shining Path activist, as some accused him of being, but he did willingly forge an alliance with the Maoists in order to undermine and discredit the left-wing leadership in the municipal government.

This alliance manifested itself soon after Moyano's death. In March, the Executive Committee of the CUAVES and the "District Committee of Struggle"—a Shining Path front group—mobilized hundreds of protestors against the municipal government to demand the impeachment of Rodríguez "for promoting the militarization of Villa El Salvador" and to declare Michel Azcueta persona non grata. The largest contingent on both occasions was from Pachacamac, where hundreds of squatters had invaded an abandoned urban housing project in 1989. The residents had requested the municipal government's assistance in obtaining land titles from the central government, but the government's inaction created a situation of hostility and tension between the squatters and the municipal government in Villa. Shining Path had been active in Pachacamac since these land invasions began, playing on the institutional voids in this new and poor barriada to win sympathy and maintain an important beachhead in the district.[51] As the situation over the land titles deteriorated, Shining Path ably manipulated the moment to use this local grievance and turn it into a larger issue of confrontation against the left-wing municipal leadership. When a military base was established in this area just after Moyano's death, Shining Path activists convinced the Pachacamac residents that the mayor had brought the army in to force them off the land, mobilizing hundreds against the mayor and the "militarization" of Villa El Salvador.[52] The sensation of Shining Path spreading its tentacles throughout Villa El Salvador had an impact not only within the district; it was also noted with alarm by the national press.[53]

As a result, many grassroots activists began staying home and avoiding participation in any activities that might compromise them. A core group of activists strongly identified with the left-wing project of Villa El Salvador remained willing to mobilize to defend the project that they had helped to build. In the aftermath of Moyano's murder and growing evidence of extensive Shining Path influence in Villa El Salvador, a handful of these activists, leaving aside their historic mistrust of the police forces, sought to build closer ties with the local police force to rout out Shining Path. Activists who at one point did not consider Shining Path an enemy to be confronted now believed not only that it was important for the Left to fight Shining Path head-on, but that the old fears about collaborating with the state had to be put aside given Shining Path's intention of completely wiping them off the map. Initial discussions about how best to combat the Maoists on the ground were disrupted, however, in the aftermath of the April 5 *autogolpe* (self-coup) of President Alberto Fujimori. Local efforts to bridge the state-society gap to confront the Maoists crumbled, as old fears about the repressive nature of the state and the security forces resurfaced. Days after the coup, Shining Path launched an all-out offensive in Lima. A potent bus-bomb was launched against the municipality of Villa El Salvador, destroying part of the municipal building, the police station, the Center of Popular Communication (an NGO started by Azcueta to promote popular education), and several dozen near-by homes. One police official was killed in the attack and several others wounded.

Despite these military attacks, Shining Path's most important activities in Villa El Salvador continued to be focused at the political level. Shining Path won an important symbolic victory in August 1992 when its proposals were adopted by majority vote in the VI Convention of the CUAVES. Shining Path's influence in the CUAVES was evident to informed observers by 1991, when radical left-wing groups forged a tactical alliance with Shining Path sympathizers within the CUAVES in order to oust the standing president of the organization, Roque Quispe. Quispe was a militant of UNIR (National Union of the Revolutionary Left) who had won the presidency of the CUAVES with the support of the PMR. During a meeting in which the CUAVES was to help the municipal government establish priorities for investing the municipal property taxes that were to be collected that year, these radical groups put forth a motion that, given the economic situation, the municipal government should not impose the property tax. Although the tax was progressively scaled according to the type of housing construction, the proposal to eliminate the property tax became widely popular among the CUAVES rank and file. Roque refused to recognize the motion, and he was voted out of office. Filadelfo Roa, then vice-president, took over the CUAVES with the tacit support of Shining Path.

Roa's alliance with Shining Path came to light the following year, after he refused to denounce Shining Path for Moyano's murder. Radical elements within the CUAVES—part of the Marxist left but not linked to the IU and known as the "Cuavista current"—had long held a grudge against Azcueta and his political allies dating back to the mid-1980s when the municipal government was first formed.[54] The Cuavistas always feared that the municipal government would impinge on the CUAVES' autonomy and its role as the principal community organization in Villa El Salvador. Azcueta signed a compromise deal with the CUAVES upon assuming the mayorship, promising to respect the CUAVES' autonomy. As the municipal government expanded its influence, helped develop new organizations like the APEMIVES, and obtained international resources to develop projects in the district, the CUAVES felt its institutional feet were being stepped on. Conflicts began to emerge between the CUAVES leadership and the IU municipal leadership over issues of power, political rivalries, social legitimacy, and control over resources. Shining Path astutely manipulated these rivalries, establishing alliances with disgruntled sectors within the CUAVES against their common enemy—the "revisionists" in the municipality—in order to deepen the contradictions within the district, delegitimize the IU, and destroy the self-management model that Villa El Salvador represented.

The final document of the VI Convention openly attacked the municipality as part of the "old, rotten and extinct state" and called for its deactivation; it also called for the removal of the Armed Forces, the urban "rondas," nongovernmental organizations, and some private enterprises, called for an end to the municipal property tax, and demanded that all international technical and financial support be channeled through the CUAVES. The original proposal included several names of leaders to be "liquidated," though this list was not included in the final document.[55] Less than half the usual 500 delegates participated in the convention; delegates linked to the PMR, MAS, and PUM abstained from participating so as not to legitimize the convention, while others stayed home out of fear. Nevertheless, it was an important symbolic victory for Shining Path, not only within Villa El Salvador but at the national level as well, as it demonstrated their ability to penetrate into the very heart of "left revisionism."

Immediately after the convention, the municipal government publicly denounced the CUAVES leadership for their conciliation with Shining Path and stated its refusal to recognize the legitimacy of the VI Convention and the CUAVES leadership.[56] Some forty grassroots CUAVES members issued a joint statement stating their refusal to recognize the incumbent leadership, and their intention to renovate the CUAVES from the grassroots. But the damage was done. By building alliances with disgruntled groups within the CUAVES against the municipality Shining Path not only infiltrated the CUAVES and manipulated the VI Convention, it effectively delegitimized the entire organization. Popular sentiment in Villa still recognizes the CUAVES as a "historical" organization of Villa El Salvador, but its leaders are not widely recognized or considered legitimate. Shining Path had achieved an important goal: it had driven out the "revisionists" and dealt a stinging blow to a key element of the self-management model. This paralleled the outcome of Shining Path's ascendancy in the Industrial Park as well. Shortly after Huarcaya became president of APEMIVES, international donors cut off assistance to the Industrial Park. The government also withdrew from the Park, leaving the entire project to flounder. In both cases, Shining Path's goal was not to take over the CUAVES or the APEMIVES in order to lead these organizations, but rather to destroy them and the experience of self-management they embodied, to extend Sendero's own influence in the district, and to provoke military repression. In the logic of "deepening the contradictions," fomenting conflict and greater polarization would hasten the "revolutionary victory."

Conclusion

This strategy of undermining alternative projects for change, promoting the radicalization of popular demands, and provoking military repression might have panned out had Shining Path been able to culminate its series of offensives in Lima through 1992 and into 1993.[57] In March 1992, the organization had advanced to the point that the U.S. State Department began to urge more decisive U.S. action to prevent Shining Path from seizing state control.[58] Since the early 1980s, Shining Path's logic of confrontation had been pushing the country toward greater levels of polarization and political violence, as Fujimori's autogolpe of 5 April 1992 revealed. Many observers feared that increasing military control would play into Shining Path's hands and strengthen its possibilities of victory.

Terror was a crucial element of Shining Path's ability to extend its influence in Lima's barriadas. At the same time, however, Shining Path's capacity to operate on a political level was also significant. Ultimately, Shining Path's political organizing was intimately linked to what it perceived as the imminent collapse of the capitalist state. Its overall strategy of confrontation and provocation sought to hasten that moment and presumably, ultimate victory. All that was cut short on 11 September 1992, when Abimael Guzmán was arrested by DINCOTE, a special police intelligence unit.

The surprise capture of Guzmán led to a radical altering of the balance of forces, which shifted—probably for the first time in twelve years of political violence—in favor of the state and the Armed Forces. While Shining Path continued to carry out significant military campaigns in the months after Guzmán's capture, the scope and intensity of its military operations has waned significantly since 1993. The future of Shining Path as an effective guerrilla force was further called into question at the end of 1993, when Guzmán's call for "peace talks" with the government provoked a sharp confrontation within the Shining Path between the imprisoned leadership, who rallied behind Guzmán's peace proposal, and the leadership that remained at large, led by Oscar Ramírez Durand (alias "Comrade Feliciano"), who argued for the continuation of the "popular war."[59]

In this new context, the tentative nature of Shining Path's political alliances at the local level became increasingly evident. By focusing their political mediations with the local population on radicalizing popular grievances and promoting confrontation and polarization, Shining Path was able to advance at the local level by locating the weak points in specific local contexts and exploiting them to their advantage. Shining Path was able to obtain sympathy by acting as a local vigilante, punishing thieves and corrupt leaders, but it rarely sought to consolidate its popular appeal by offering people viable alternatives to other local problems. In fact, the Maoists were not concerned with building a mass popular movement, or leading local organizations. They were operating on their own politico-military logic, which calculated that the crisis of the capitalist state—and ergo their victory—was at hand, and that provoking confrontation and polarization would hasten that moment. This failure to build more enduring bases of support meant that as its power and authority declined within Villa El Salvador after

Guzmán's capture and the withdrawal of many of its activists from the district, local groups became emboldened to challenge Shining Path. This was especially the case with the Youth Coordinating Committee and the women in FEPOMUVES. In October 1993 the FEPOMUVES held a convention in the midst of great tension and fear, while young people from the Youth Committee provided security and support. They criticized Pilar Anchita for her conciliation with Shining Path and her dealings with Villa's new mayor, who was seeking to withdraw the Federation's control of the milk program.[60] The assembly voted to oust Anchita and chose a new leader. This was a tentative, but hopeful, sign of new times in Villa El Salvador.

Yet, Shining Path's ability to expand in Villa El Salvador—a prominent symbol of community organizing and leftist politics—remains a disturbing paradox. A district celebrated for its democratic and participatory politics and community organizations, Villa El Salvador also became a terrain of effective Shining Path political organizing. Changing structural conditions certainly favored Shining Path's organizing attempts in Villa El Salvador: the deepening of the economic crisis after 1988 and the disengagement of the state from its most critical public functions as a result of the fiscal crisis led to popular frustration and anger that provided Shining Path with plenty of raw material to exploit to its advantage in barriadas like Villa. Shining Path ably played on the growing situation of insecurity and public order in barriadas like Villa El Salvador by offering harsh but effective measures against thieves, drug addicts, and delinquents. Understanding Shining Path's capacity to operate in more politically and socially complex environments is also crucial to explaining their expansion in districts like Villa El Salvador. Shining Path was adept at locating the fissures and cracks within local contexts and exploiting them to its advantage. Pinpointing local points of tension and conflict permitted Shining Path to insert itself into the local body politic, undermine rivals, and gain local sympathy by taking up popular struggles at a time when traditional mediating mechanisms were in crisis—most notably the mainstream Left.

The problems of local institutional development in barriadas like Villa El Salvador and the degree to which Shining Path could manipulate these problems to its advantage were not sufficiently appreciated. Shining Path was adept at playing on problems internal to local community organizations—rivalries among leadership, partisan infighting, corruption, and weak mechanisms of conflict resolution—to undermine left-wing leaders and gain sympathy among the rank and file, as it did in the Industrial Park and the Women's Federation. Moreover, partisan divisions among organizations and institutions in Villa El Salvador seriously debilitated the ability of these organizations to form a common front against Shining Path. It was, in fact, these very conflicts and divisions that Shining Path exploited to establish its influence in key peak organizations in the district and mobilize public opinion against the local leadership. Left-wing discourse, which focused on promoting the experience of self-management and popular participation, tended to downplay the problems of local institutional development and the partisan rivalries among left-wing groups. The silences and ambiguities of the sectors within the Left vis-à-vis Shining Path also played in Sendero's favor. With the decline in Shining Path activity, perhaps local activists will learn from this dramatic and tragic episode in Villa El Salvador's young history to address the problems of local institutional development that will help solidify local organizations by building more effective mechanisms to administer resources, resolve internal conflicts, and develop local capacities.

Notes

I am grateful for the generous support of the Inter-American Foundation, the Institute for the Study of World Politics, the United States Institute of Peace, the Aspen Institute, and the North-South Center at the University of Miami, which allowed me to carry out extended fieldwork in Lima between 1992 and 1994, and make a follow-up visit in 1995. My thanks to my advisor, Douglas Chalmers, and Margaret Crahan, Steve Stern, Deborah Levenson, Kay Warren, Nena Delpino, Luis Pásara, Nelson Manrique, Carlos Iván Degregori, José López Ricci, Carlos Reyna, Rosario Romero, and Carmen Rosa Balbi.

1   The term barriada, commonly translated as shantytown, refers not only to a physical space of underdeveloped housing and basic services, but denotes a mode of access to housing via organized land invasions and the eventual, often piecemeal, development of housing and other basic services, usually through the self-help efforts of the barriada residents (Driant 1991).

2   Shining Path had slowly infiltrated the left-wing newspaper, *El Diario de Marka*, establishing full control by 1988. Renamed *El Diario*, the newspaper began to appear on the streets of Lima, covering labor disputes and events in the shantytowns, and professing an openly pro-Shining Path line.

3   See Degregori (1985b) for an initial discussion of this nature. IDS (1989) published a study outlining this argument in more detail. See also Woy-Hazelton and Hazelton (1992). Much more significant than these studies, however, was the growing acceptance of this argument among left-wing activists.

4   The United Left was influential in municipal-level government in Lima

throughout the 1980s, particularly in the poorest districts of popular extraction. In 1980, IU won 9 out of 39 municipal districts; in 1983, when Alfonso Barrantes of IU won the mayorship of Lima, IU won 22 out of 41 districts. In 1986, IU lost ground to APRA, which was riding on the tailcoat of Alan García's presidential victory in 1985, losing control of 11 districts. Reflecting a larger crisis of the political party system, as well as its own shortcomings, the IU won only 7 out of 40 districts in 1989, and in the wake of the coalition's division, became a marginal political force. In 1993 no left-wing group won a single municipality in Lima, which were dominated by so-called "independents."

5 In 1992, the Institute of Legal Defense, a leading human rights organization in Peru, noted ominously: "Shining Path has grown in the popular barriadas of Lima not only in relation to the number of attacks and armed actions; they have also managed to construct a vast social base. The [neoliberal] economic policies that have pushed a high percentage of the families that live in the shantytowns into a situation of extreme misery has helped Shining Path's plans" (IDL 1992:211).

6 In this respect, Shining Path's attempt to gain influence and control over Villa El Salvador had important parallels in Puno, where similar symbolic issues were at stake in infiltrating the local campesino movement.

7 Since the wave of rural migration began in the late 1940s, successive governments adopted a laissez-faire attitude toward the barriadas, permitting land invasions to prevent pent-up demands for housing from becoming a political problem, but not engaging in comprehensive social policies to improve the living conditions of these settlements. The one, brief exception was Velasco's attempt to more actively promote self-help efforts as a way of obtaining local support for his reformist experiment. See Driant (1991).

8 Census information provided by Driant (1991).

9 For an excellent discussion of these policies, see Gonzales de Olarte and Samamé (1991).

10 "The problems of Lima today are linked to the exhaustion of its capacity to reproduce itself as a city and as a market. The exaggerated dimensions of the city make it nearly impossible to provide basic infrastructure, and borders on collapse. This is reflected in the rationing of water and electricity, for example, which at the most critical point reached 66 percent in 1992" (Olivera and Ballón 1993).

11 "Sicósis en Lima: Delincuencia," *Caretas,* 25 March 1991 (Lima): 39–45; and "El vacío interior," *Caretas,* February 3, 1991 (Lima): 6–14.

12 Otárola (1994); *Caretas,* April 21, 1994 (Lima): 33–36; *Expreso,* January 9, 1994, (Lima): 20–21.

13 An official document of the Ministerio de la Presidencia (1993) recognizes a continual decline in social spending after 1986 in real terms. Social spending dropped from 4.61 percent of GDP in 1980 to 1.78 in 1991 (Fernández Baca

and Seinfeld 1993). The education sector lost three-fourths of its value between 1986 and 1990, and the situation was similar in the health sector. The widely accepted estimate of people living in critical poverty was corroborated by official government figures from 1994: 54 percent of the population, or 13 million people, lived in *critical poverty*, defined as insufficient income to cover a basic food basket for a family of five, while 23 percent of the critically poor suffer *extreme poverty*, defined as insufficient income to cover minimum nutritional requirements for a family of five. Figures are taken from a recent study commissioned by the Fondo de Compensación y Desarrollo Social (FONCODES), the government-sponsored social emergency fund which was founded in August, 1991, a full year after the initial adjustment measures were applied. See FONCODES (1994).

14 In this crucial stage in the development of the prolonged popular war, Shining Path claimed it had obtained the capacity to fight on equal terms with state security forces despite the superior man- and fighting-power of the latter.

15 Disagreements over the presidential candidacy of Alfonso Barrantes, an independent and former mayor of Lima, sparked the division. For moderates, a Barrantes candidacy would attract support among centrist and independent voters and carry the IU to the presidential palace. Radical parties within the IU had long-standing qualms about Barrantes' centrism, and they opposed his proposal of a broad-based front to save Peru's fledgling democratic institutions from the onslaught of the economic crisis and Shining Path's violence. Other more long-standing conflicts underlie the split, however, including personal rivalries, different visions about political democracy, strategies for achieving social change, and attitudes vis-à-vis Shining Path (Pásara 1990).

16 This disaffection was also reflected in April 1992, when Fujimori closed Congress and suspended the Constitution, winning wide popular support.

17 Driant (1991) offers an excellent description of the process of consolidation of older land invasions, as squatters slowly build up their homes from cane matting to brick and concrete, basic services such as water and electricity are obtained, and other local infrastructure develops. This progression is contrasted with new land invasions, largely after 1984, that often encountered greater difficulty in obtaining government assistance to develop their local communities.

18 For other works that point to subaltern political decision-making and agency as irreducible to structural analysis, see Mallon (1995) and Moore (1978).

19 This discussion is based on fieldwork carried out in Lima between 1992 and 1994, preliminary research carried out in 1990, and my own personal experiences living in two barriada districts (Villa El Salvador in 1986–1987 and San Juan de Miraflores in 1989). During the formal research period, I carried out semistructured interviews with over fifty community activists and residents in four barriada districts, and with more than two dozen informed observers who lived or worked in these communities. I also carried out several focus groups

of community residents and grassroots leaders in three of the barriadas, and was able to participate in numerous community meetings as well as informal discussions within these communities.

20 Migdal (1974) discusses what he calls "exchange relationships," i.e., the goods and services a political organization offers to its constituency, and how these relationships shape popular responses to the political organization seeking support.

21 McCormick (1990, 1992) offers a good analysis of the role of Lima in Sendero's macro-level strategy. Smith (1992b) examines Shining Path activity in the strategically important popular district of Ate-Vitarte. Good journalistic accounts of Shining Path's urban activity can be found in *QueHacer*, a bimonthly publication of DESCO, and *Ideéle*, a monthly publication of the Instituto de Defensa Legal. Sectoral studies of the trade union movement have been carried out by Sulmont et al. (1989) and Balbi (1992).

22 The fourth sector did not follow this grid design. The Belaunde government constructed a housing project in this area, which came to be known as Pachacamac.

23 A handful of groups decided not to participate, most notably Patria Roja and Shining Path. While Patria Roja later participated in elections, in 1978 it joined Shining Path in criticizing the "electoral farce." Most left-wing groups, however, sensing the popular mood in favor of elections, decided to participate, but most saw this as a tactical resource to improve their position vis-à-vis other groups (Nieto 1983). The Left parties made a distinction between "formal" democracy (i.e., elections) and social democracy or "real" democracy, a distinction that would shape the Left's ambivalent relationship to political democracy in the course of the 1980s.

24 The APRA party won 35 percent of the vote, while the Popular Christian Party won 24 percent. Among the Left parties, the Trotsky-inspired Worker Campesino Student and Popular Front (FOCEP) won 12.3 percent, the Revolutionary Socialist Party (PSR) won 6.6%, the Moscow-line Peruvian Communist Party (PCP) 5.9 percent, and the Popular Democratic Unity 4.5 percent. See Tuesta (1994).

25 Most community projects collapsed with the retreat of government support. This was the case, for example, of the credit union, and many families lost their savings. Charges of corruption in the management of these enterprises further undermined confidence in the CUAVES and its leaders. Partisan infighting among the left-wing parties in the CUAVES also undermined the organization's image. See Burt and Espejo (1995).

26 Elsewhere I explore this dimension of Shining Path's urban activities. See Burt (1997).

27 The two principal institutions charged with providing justice and order—the judicial system and the police—have received consistently low approval ratings

in national surveys carried out by Apoyo, a Lima-based polling firm. Based on a review of annual polls between 1987 and 1994 published in Apoyo's monthly magazine, *Debate*.

28 This discussion is based on newspaper and magazine accounts, flyers and pamphlets published in Villa El Salvador, and interviews carried out in Villa El Salvador in 1993 and 1994. I would like to thank Liliana Miranda for her capable research assistance in compiling the data base of Shining Path activities in Lima from DESCO archives. Some material is also gleaned from my previous work and research in Villa in 1986–1987, 1989 and 1990. For obvious reasons, my interviewees must go unnamed.

29 *Sí*, 24 February 1992.

30 The literature that discusses the Left's relationship with Shining Path often misses this ambiguity, focusing instead on the different practices of the legal Left within democracy and Shining Path's armed violence. See for example Haworth (1993) and Hoy-Wazelton and Wazelton (1992). There were of course many differences, but it is also important to examine the commonalities and ambiguities in order to fully understand the dynamics of the relationship between the Left and Shining Path.

31 In 1987, Jorge del Prado, general secretary of the Moscow-line Peruvian Communist Party, said that Shining Path was a "revolutionary force" and that they should not be "excommunicated" from the rest of the Left. See Pásara (1990).

32 Author's interview with Santiago Pedraglio, Lima, May 1994. An interview by Hernando Burgos of Carlos Tapia, of the IS, and Santiago Pedraglio, of IU, reveals these discrepancies. Tapia advocated that the Left should collaborate with the state in order to defeat Shining Path, which he argued had become the enemy of all Peruvian society. See *QueHacer* 70, March/April 1991.

33 The official census carried out in 1993 did not distinguish between new invasions within specific districts. However, one indication of these newer and less developed areas is the census data on basic infrastructure. In Villa El Salvador, 35 percent of the population lacks access to piped water (though even those that have piped water are subjected to rationing), and 24 percent lack electricity.

34 See *El Diario*, January 1992.

35 See *El Plan Integral de Desarrollo de Villa El Salvador*, Lima: DESCO and the Municipality of Villa El Salvador, 1986.

36 See *El Diario* 545, 26 April 1989; 547, 10 May 1989; 551, 7 June 1989; 554, 28 June 1989; 568, 11 October 1989; and 571, 1 November 1989.

37 *La República*, 23 June 1991.

38 *El Diario* 551, 7 June 1989.

39 What ever happened to the "projects" and "programs" of the revisionists and reactionaries? They were only a crass trafficking of the poor that permitted the illicit enrichment of a few at the expense of the poverty of thousands. This is the case of the traffickers Azcueta, Paredes, Moyano, Zazzali, Cáceres, Mo-

reno, and Quintanilla [all ɪᴜ leaders who worked in municipal governments], among others who worked against the Maoist revolution in our country. *El Diario* 613, 1991.

40 In leaflets it distributed in Villa El Salvador, Shining Path disclaimed responsibility for attacking the warehouse, and accused Moyano of orchestrating the attack to cover up her alleged misuse of the organization's resources.

41 *La República*, 22 September 1991. The first registered assassination of a female leader of the milk program or the soup kitchens was that of Juana López, leader of a soup kitchen in Callao, who was killed on 31 August 1991. Over 100 community activists, including trade unionists, neighborhood council leaders, and women active in the soup kitchens and milk program were killed by Shining Path.

42 *La República*, 22 September 1991. In a workshop of over forty grassroots leaders linked to the Left from several popular districts in Lima which I observed, a leader of the milk program made a more biting critique of the Left: "The Left is the only party that is concerned with the people, but they are selfish. They are concerned with their partisan interests and not those of all the people. Too often they talk from above but they don't live among us. They do not experience the lack of water, electricity, or mothers who go to the market and cannot afford to buy food for their children."

43 Moyano explicitly stated that the rondas would be independent of the police or Armed Forces, since the people lacked confidence in these institutions.

44 For a brief but sensitive treatment of this issue, see Montoya and Reyna (1992).

45 *La República*, 5 July 1991.

46 My interviews with ɴɢᴅᴏ workers revealed a similar pattern of popular responses to development projects, especially after 1989 with the worsening of the economic crisis. The "assistentialist mentality" that Delpino (1991) describes was ably picked up by Shining Path, who used it to attack ɴɢᴅᴏs— many of whom were linked or sympathetic to the ɪᴜ. In another research project about ɴɢᴅᴏs undertaken by sᴀsᴇ and Instituto ᴀᴘᴏʏᴏ, two nongovernmental research and development centers in Lima, in which Nena Delpino and I served as the primary researchers, we uncovered a similar logic in the countryside, where a number of ɴɢᴅᴏ leaders described how Shining Path used this discourse to their favor in the countryside.

47 In a public letter to the leaders of the other left-wing parties, Michel Azcueta of the ᴘᴍʀ wrote: "For more than a week, María Elena, Johny Rodríguez, José Polo, and I have been clearly denouncing Shining Path's intentions in Villa El Salvador and about the continuous threats—now confirmed—against our lives. No one said a word. On the contrary. . . . María Elena asked ᴘᴜᴍ to support an act of unity in the Industrial Park. . . . What was ᴘᴜᴍ's response? 'No, we have to strengthen our own profile.' That was their literal answer to María Elena. . . . We now see the results. Neither ᴘᴜᴍ, nor the Communist

Party, the Democratic Popular Union (UDP) or the Popular Front supported the peace march." Published in *Ultima Hora,* 17 February 1992.

48 It is instructive to compare the following cites from *El Diario,* the first from 1989 and the second from 1992. First, "The objective of the so-called 'self-management' model is to ensure that the masses do not combat this bureaucratic, oligarchic state, and that they content themselves with palliatives within the system so that they can ostensibly resolve their problems. . . . The same thing happens with the soup kitchens and the milk committees, that is, making the masses, with their unpaid labor, conform themselves with receiving charity from the NGOs, so they won't fight for their rights" (*El Diario* 551, 1989). Second, "The PCP is not against the soup kitchens, the milk program, or the mothers' clubs. . . . But we are against those counter-revolutionaries who defend the old state and its rule of exploitation and oppression. . . . We are against those who traffic with the popular sectors' demands. . . . We are against those who want to make us eternally poor, to eternally receive 'charity,' 'pity,' 'assistance,' or 'philanthropy' from the rich of our country and abroad via NGOs." (*El Diario* 620, 1992).

49 This is developed further in Burt (1997). See Delpino (1991) for an excellent discussion of the problem of the fragile institutionality in women's organizations.

50 In an interview, Roa reiterated this position: "[Roa]- 'Michel Azcueta, with his economic power acquired from [international] donations, uses people and keeps them as his puppets, to use as he pleases.' [Sí]- 'Are you saying that Maria Elena Moyano was a puppet?' [Roa]- 'We are perfectly aware that that's the way it was.'" *Sí,* 6 April 1992.

51 Local residents reported an active Shining Path presence in Pachacamac, which they used partially as a zone of refuge. They reportedly carried out marches and exercise drills in this part of Villa El Salvador in the early morning or late at night.

52 Carlos Reyna, "Villa El Salvador: La Batalla por la CUAVES," *QueHacer* 76, March/April 1992 (Lima): 48–55. *La República* (March 3, 1992) covered the first march, but mistakenly took the banners against the "militarization" of Villa El Salvador to be a spontaneous protest of Villa's residents against the army.

53 See the editorials in the conservative newspaper *Expreso* on 22 March 1992 and 5 April 1992. Later, in a 5 July 1992 editorial, *Expreso* lauds Fujimori's crackdown on terrorism after the autogolpe, but notes the failure to address the continuing presence of Shining Path in Lima's shantytowns.

54 For a detailed description of the rivalry between the CUAVES and the municipal government, see Tuesta (1989).

55 "Acuerdos de la VI Convención de la CUAVES," Mimeograph, August 30, 1992.

56 *Expreso,* 31 August 1992.

57 The military was nonetheless relatively restrained in responding to Shining

Path's growing influence in Lima's barriadas. While Shining Path expected a more arbitrary and repressive response—similar to its behavior in the countryside—the military in fact was testing new tactics to deal with Shining Path both in Lima and the countryside. In the barriadas, the military began carrying out late-night sweeps in which suspected Shining Path leaders were arrested. These were followed by the distribution of medicine and foodstuffs to the local population.

58 See the statement of Bernard Aronson, Assistant Secretary of State for Inter-American Affairs before the Subcommittee on Western Hemisphere Affairs, House Committee on Foreign Affairs, 12 March 1992.

59 For a discussion of Shining Path after Guzmán's capture and his peace overtures, see Burt and López Ricci (1994).

60 The mayor, Jorge Vásquez, was elected on the independent "Obras" ticket of former Lima mayor, Ricardo Belmont. From the beginning of his tenure in early 1993, Vásquez criticized and denounced local organizations like the FEPOMUVES and the former municipal administrations linked to the mainstream Left in terms similar to those used by Shining Path. For a period of several months Vásquez allied himself with Roa and Anchita to discredit the Left and its associates in Villa El Salvador. Vásquez's administrative incompetence and blatant corruption led local organizations to demand his ouster. He was arrested on illicit enrichment and other charges in early 1994.

NINE

Apogee and Crisis of a "Third Path": *Mariateguismo,*

"People's War," and Counterinsurgency in Puno,

1987–1994

José Luis Rénique

❖ "The People's War," boasted Abimael Guzmán Reynoso in 1988, "is making them see that the sierra exists."[1] A year later he reiterated: "it has become very clear that we are expanding in the sierra." For its part, the center-south was the "axis of the historical vertebration," which in the War of the Pacific "had been the region that defended itself most" against the Chileans, constituting a zone of retreat and refuge "in the face of foreign attack."[2] Based on the stronghold that it claimed to have established in the Andean highlands, by the beginning of 1992 the Peruvian Communist Party–Shining Path appeared to have advanced to the "enclosure of Lima," the siege that was supposed to culminate a war waged from the countryside to the city.

Early in 1992, it was difficult to perceive the actual destiny that awaited the armed insurgency: the detention of its leader and of a substantial part of its central committee later in the year; the effective containment of Shining Path across entire regions and the beginning of its dismantling. With the support of the state, numerous "civil defense committees" (Comités de Autodefensa Civil or CACs, also known as patrols or *rondas*) had risen up against their supposed liberators. With its leadership crippled by mid-year, the senderista "war machine" fell apart as vertiginously as it had been erected. Contrary to what Guzmán had predicted, the southern sierra would not become a zone of retreat and refuge for his forces; 1992 was not 1882, nor was the Peruvian Army an occupation force of the kind that the Chilean Army had been a century before. Those who were "caught in the crossfire" had opted to throw in their lot with that of the military and thereby impose the beginning of the end of the "people's war."

Was this outcome inevitable? Did there exist any possibility of a different result—more democratic and less "militarized"—of the conflict initiated in

1980? To what extent, in the face of violence by insurgent and counter-insurgent forces, would it have been possible to construct an alternative resolution to the crisis, based on the social movements and popular organizations that had arisen in Peru in the late 1970s?

Shining Path's expansion throughout the sierra was not uncontested. The resistance of diverse segments of the rural population would limit the extent of Shining Path penetration. There was no political organization, however, capable of coordinating the resistance provoked by Shining Path's methods. The Left had a tenuous and sporadic rural presence toward the end of the 1970s and went on to privilege municipal and parliamentary work during the 1980s. Thus it left organizing spaces open, and Shining Path opportunely and efficiently took advantage of this situation.

Puno, in the extreme south of Peru (figure 9.1), would seem to be the exception. There, with the support of the Church and the Unified Mariateguista Party (Partido Unificado Mariateguista, or PUM), and even as Shining Path stalked the peasantry, a coalition of peasant organizations carried out in 1987 the biggest wave of land invasions in the Peruvian sierra since the 1960s. In part activated by rural struggle, moreover, a dynamic regional movement had since the early 1980s shown a defiant attitude toward the central government. The Puno movement actively opposed the declaration of a state of emergency, which would have meant placing the department under military administration. Thus, the movement constituted an exceptional instance of opposition to the government's counterinsurgency strategy. By the mid-1980s, even as the rest of Peru became increasingly polarized, Puno seemed to prove the viability of a "third path" for resolving the armed conflict. This option rested on the social movement's capacity to interject itself between the two polarizing agents while developing, at the same time, its own democratizing potential.

By the early 1990s, however, all that remained of these aspirations were memories. The peasant federations had lost their influence and the regional movement had vanished without a trace. The PUM had practically disappeared while the militant Church of the 1980s had opted for a "low profile." The army appeared to be the axis of a new stability. The new Regional Government, which had raised certain expectations when it was installed in 1991, turned out to be a decorative entity, generally subordinate to the directives of the military departmental command. What had happened? How do we explain the frustration of the "third path?" What was the itinerary that led to this outcome? This essay seeks to respond to these questions.

Figure 9.1. The Department of Puno.

Land and Peasant Organization

In Puno, Velasco's agrarian reform signaled the marginalization of the peasant communities (see table 9.1). Because of the necessity of retaining the experience and the accumulated technology of the large altiplano cattle haciendas, the peasant community was not considered a valid option. The authors of the reform believed that to turn over land to the communities would encourage minifundia. "Associative" entrepreneurial models, such as the Agricultural Societies of Social Interest (Sociedades Agrícolas de Interés Social; SAIS), Agrarian Production Cooperatives (Cooperativas Agrarias de Producción; CAPS), and the Rural Social Property Enterprises (Empresas Rurales de Propiedad Social; ERPS), on the other hand, would guarantee productive continuity while incorporating former peasant workers from the old estates (*feudatarios*) and community members (*comuneros*) into the reform process. The CAPS and ERPS followed a classic co-op model: a collective administration of indivisible units of production. The SAIS, by contrast, were born from the fusion of various haciendas under a centralized administration, supervised by a hired manager and overseen by the Ministry of Agriculture. Associated with the SAIS, the surrounding communities would have access to services and technical assistance as well as to new employment opportunities.[3]

Part of a wider plan of national socioeconomic restructuring, with the fall of General Velasco, the chief of the military revolution, in 1975 the agrarian reform was cast practically adrift. The associative enterprises of Puno were left on their own and became disputed terrain between their beneficiaries and the comunero population that saw in them the continuation of the old haciendas.[4] The dismantling of Velasco's apparatus of agricultural assistance, the economic crisis into which the country was sinking, and the effects of one of the worst droughts suffered by the Puno altiplano in several decades combined to sharpen the tension.[5] Three factors combined, in these circumstances, to strengthen peasant organization: (1) the support of the Church, (2) the progressive radicalization of the agrarian leagues formed by the Velasco regime, and (3) the presence of activists of the Peasant Federation of Peru (Confederación Campesina del Perú, or CCP). In 1979, these organizers founded the Peasant Federation of Puno (Federación de Campesinos del Puno, or FDCP), which would serve as the umbrella organization for the land struggles of the 1980s.[6]

Perhaps more than in any other region of the country, in Puno the

Table 9.1   Adjudication process in Puno, 1981.

Type	Number of Enterprises	Properties Adjudicated	Hectares
SAIS[1]	23	447	1,025,125
CAP[2]	15	119	499,269
ERPS[3]	5	174	216,846
Peasant Groups	41	101	84,658
Peasant Communities	67	89	49,192
Individuals	135	135	28,161
Pre-Cooperatives	2	2	24,805
GAST[4]	26	24	22,032
Use right ceded	11	11	15,893
Agrarian Unions	2	1	239
CAS	16	—	—
Communal Coops	3	—	—
Totals		1,103	1,966,218

Source: Caballero Martin 1991.

1. Agricultural Societies of Social Interest (Sociedades Agrarias de Interés Social).

2. Agrarian Production Cooperatives (Cooperativeas Agrarias de Producción).

3. Rural Social Property Enterprises (Empresas Rurales de Propiedad Social).

4. Groups of Agriculturalists without Land (Grupos de Agricultores sin Tierra).

arrival of a series of North American and European religious orders beginning in the late 1950s signified a true renewal of ecclesiastic labor. Not only did they reactivate numerous rural parishes. They also promoted an "Andean pastoral" that assimilated local culture and adjusted to communal life while promoting rural development through peasant organizing.[7] The pastoral agents cleared the path that the CCP consolidated. The drought of 1983–1984 opened new horizons for the peasant movement. The communal drama became a departmental problem and parliamentary debate on a new Regionalization Law gave the movement's leaders an opportunity to connect the land problem with that of regional poverty. A regional development strategy, distinct from that imposed by centralism, was needed to put an end to the "historical suction of the altiplano resources" and to create a solid agricultural and animal raising sector constituted by communal enterprises. The latter would be based on a restructuration of the ERPS, SAIS, and CAPS, with technical assistance and credit provided by the state.[8]

This proposal reflected notions shared by the religious and lay activists who promoted the movement: an idealized vision of the community and of its political, social, and economic potential; a belief in the democratizing role of the regional movement, as a strengthening civil society displaced local traditional powers; and a conviction that a development alternative based on Andean productive, social, and political practices (in a predominantly peasant and indigenous region) would be feasible.

Events appeared to confirm their aspirations. Puno had been in conflict with the central government since the first days of the "transition to democracy." The drought accentuated the conflictive atmosphere. Faced with inaction by the central government, the mobilizations, strikes, and proliferating local and regional Defense Fronts (Frentes de Defensa; FEDIP)— encouraged by the growing presence of the Left in Puno's municipal governments—gave rise to what many saw as the strongest regional movement in the country.[9] In November 1985, a Regional Departmental Assembly declared Puno a region and urged the new APRA administration of Alan García to accelerate the implementation of the legal framework mandated by the 1979 Constitution.[10] The following month, various communities invaded the lands of the Kunurana ERPS in the province of Melgar with the active support of the Ayaviri Prelacy. Over the following weeks, torrential downpours and floods once again critically threatened agriculture in the department. Important roads were affected, and the migration of flood victims toward the towns put added pressure on the municipal governments.[11] Once again, the central government's slow reaction to the disaster reactivated demands for land as well as calls for the implementation of regionalization. People generally believed that the creation of the administrative region would permit the autonomous and expeditious use of "enormous departmental resources" in order to attend to local necessities.

Puno was a volcano on the point of erupting. The government's delay in resolving communal demands, according to general opinion, favored the subversion of Sendero, whose armed columns were making their presence increasingly known in northern Puno. In February 1986, finally, the government promulgated the long-awaited legal measures to begin to restructure the rural associative enterprises of Puno. These measures brought APRA (the Alianza Popular Revolucionaria Americana, or American Popular Revolutionary Alliance, the party of President Alan García [1985–1990]) and the PUM into direct conflict.

Mariateguismo versus Aprismo

After four years of working within the "state of law," the so-called legal Left still had not defined a coherent strategic course. Founded in 1984, the PUM constituted an intent to respond to this problem. The PUM offered possibility of taking the United Left (Izquierda Unida, or IU) out of its paralysis by countering the "electoral path" with an option that—following the Central American example—would cast aside old "vanguardist" attitudes without losing the revolutionary mystique that was so rapidly being eroded by "parliamentary democracy, capitalist modernization of the country and the biological cycle of the leadership itself." [12] The project was embodied in the formula: "revolutionary party of the masses" (*partido revolucionario de masas*). The PUM's "principal mass base," the sierra peasantry, would have a central role in the new party's construction. The *pumistas* maintained that a powerful rural-urban movement could be generated from the combination of district and provincial FEDIPS ("defense fronts") that had sprung up in the sierra, and rural organizations that struggled around local demands (for land, against the remains of gamonal power, for services and small public works) and regional demands (for resources, decentralization, and large-scale infrastructure). The party should empower and lead this movement toward a rupture with the prevailing legality. This would create a situation that the revolutionaries, with legitimacy on their side, could resolve through "unleashing a war." This war would be a "democratic insurgency" rather than a "mechanical continuation of politics." [13]

The plan would require a territorial distribution of party forces that would permit them to dispute both Shining Path and APRA for control of the sierra. The PUmistas aspired to create a "democratic corridor of masses" that would articulate a series of geopolitical spaces (Ancash, the Cajamarca and Piura sierra, Amazonas, the central selva, and the southern Andean altiplano) in which, simultaneously, the party would initiate pilot projects of "constructing mass PUM organizations." Puno was the most important of these regions. What happened there would determine "the possibility of widening the struggle for regional governments." [14]

In a similar manner, for President Alan García Pérez, Puno was to be the starting point of the government's campaign to recuperate the sierra from the hands of subversion. [15] Throughout 1986, the APRA leader undertook a campaign aimed at displacing those, such as the PUM and armed subversives, who sought to manipulate "the legitimate demands of the comunero population." Without solid partisan bases in the region, the success of this campaign depended on the capacity of the president of the Republic to generate popular support for his policies. It was during the events known as Rimanakuy—publicized as regional dialogues between the government and the presidents of peasant communities—that the Peruvian president's procommunity rhetoric reached its peak.

"You are the most genuine expression of Peru," President García intoned at the inauguration of a communal leader, "and I speak with you as President to President because each of you is as much a president as I am." He promised land as well as a new national organization without "intermediaries" and based in the transformation of the peasant communities into "local organisms of the state." As such, they would have the right to receive their own budgetary appropriations, whose use would be decided by their own communal assembly.[16] As proof of his commitment to the peasantry he would promulgate a series of measures in favor of the countryside—investments in public works, implementation in rural zones of emergency employment programs, loans without interest, price supports for peasant products, and a generous policy of legal recognition of communities.[17] In return, he asked the peasants to have a little patience and not to be seduced by the siren song of the "traffickers in hate."

The triumph of the government party in seven of the ten altiplano provinces in the municipal elections of November 1986 seemed to confirm the success of the *alanista* campaign.[18] In a relatively brief lapse, the new chief had demonstrated his capacity to convert an old party dream into reality: to create a constituency in the southern sierra and thereby make APRA a truly national party.

The PUM responded by seeking to "unmask" the demagogy of APRA's promises. The gap between the presidential promises and the frustrating reality of an ill-conceived restructuration program, constantly stymied by conservative local representatives of the government party who resisted turning over the land, offered the perfect target. Thus, when the president promised to transfer more than one million hectares to Puno communities, the FDCP demanded the total liquidation of the agrarian associative enterprises (SAIS, CAP, ERPS, and the like), and the adoption of the communal enterprise as the one and only production unit model.[19] More than a "technical formula," a PUM leader explained, this demand represented a "political formula" or tactic that would block Alan García from "stealing our great banner of struggle."[20] With respect to the communal enterprise, our informant recalled: "We knew beforehand that we were offering an alternative that was not going to work. We knew that in the context of Puno poverty it was going to be impossible to move it forward. The transaction that we arrived at was a formula that we could use but it was not a real alternative."

To the extent that the process of restructuration did not satisfy communal demands, this tactic enabled the FDCP to establish itself as the recognized voice of communal dissatisfaction. But at least two factors complicated the future of the movement headed by the PUM: (1) its demand for "liquidating the enterprises" converted the *feudatarios* (peasants of the ex-haciendas) into acrimonious adversaries of the FDCP, and (2) APRA's triumph in the municipal elections of November 1986 left the "regional movement" practically disinflated. (The leftist municipal governments had played a decisive role in the regional movement through the formation of the FEDIPS, or "defense fronts.") These factors contributed to a certain political isolation of the struggle for land that was further accentuated by internal conflicts within Izquierda Unida after its electoral defeat. The IU practically ceased to function on the departmental level.

Nonetheless, in a kind of "forward retreat," the PUM advisors of the FDCP prepared to carry out a militant action: to invade the lands that the president of the Republic had promised and that his local representatives were still refusing to turn over. The case of the community of Chapioco, in Lampa Province, illustrated the type of conflicts in which Aprista restructuration was bogging down.

Months after having received its property titles from the hands of President García, the community's members still had not managed to obtain possession of their lands:

> in the RIMANACUY '86 the land title was given . . . by the Señor Presidente of the Republic, according to the directoral resolution . . . dated 12 September 1986, in which the Community of Chapioco was adjudicated a part of the Agrarian Cooperative of Parina. . . . To date we have not received the land; all we have is paper and not the land, because the señores of the Cooperative refuse to turn the estate over to us and say that they don't want to hear anything about the laws or the restructuration . . . the chief of the restructuration for the Agrarian Region of Puno says that he cannot turn over Parina because they are the owners, this makes us think that there is an agreement or bribe on the part of the Cooperative.[21]

According to the comuneros of Chapioco, the Parina CAP was seeking recognition as an "entrepreneurial community," and one of its promoters was a director of the cooperative who had been "an employee since the time of the Asociación Ganadera del Sur [the hacienda that has preceded the CAP]." For this reason, "since the Ministry does not listen to us nor do those of Parina, the community has decided to take the adjudicated land at any moment, because we have the property title and an act of delivery of the same cooperative of Parina dated 14 October 1986 by the gentlemen of the restructuration commission."[22]

The opportunity to launch land invasions came in early May 1987. A strike wave was sweeping the country. Even the national police had suspended its labors and was protesting aggressively in the principal streets of the capital. The General Workers Confederation of Peru (Confederación General de Trabajadores del Peru; or CGTP) was pressed into convoking a national strike for May 19. According to the FDCP's tallies, on that date 156 communities, among them the comuneros of Chapioco, occupied some 280,000 hectares belonging to some twenty enterprises. Around 60,000 more hectares would be taken over during the following months. The FDCP's audacious call to action had resonated with the prevailing mood in northern Puno.

Authorities received petitions in the days following the land invasions. The communities explained the reasons that had led them to use force: (1) noncompliance by authorities with legal deadlines for turning over lands; (2) the refusal by the same authorities to recognize historical titles presented by the communities to justify claims in given properties (authorities proceeded, on the contrary, to turn over lands which often were located at considerable distances from the principal territorial nucleii of the beneficiary communities); (3) the certainty that the "power groups" of the enterprises, in complicity with the relevant functionaries, created "ghost communities" and other ruses to manipulate the restructuration process and maintain control over the land; and (4) fear that the land legally assigned to a given community would be invaded by another. In light of these and other problems, the peasants hoped that their actions would spur President García himself to intervene and rectify the fraudulent conduct of local functionaries, and thus implement, finally, the presidential promise.[23]

The Left, on the other hand, saw the mobilization as a challenge to the regime, which revived their hopes for a "third path." Not only had the government opted against repression, but Sendero also had remained silent throughout the land invasions. The FDCP, securely established as the representative of the Puno peasantry, was disposed to negotiate with peasant participation the concluding stage of restructuration. The question was whether PUM would be able to transform this social energy into some form of political action. Against this goal there loomed a series of weaknesses that the Mariateguistas proved unable to overcome during the following months. First, the PUM did not have party structures in the countryside; its militancy was concentrated in urban zones and worked through the Church and NGO networks. Second, the FDCP lacked a leadership team capable of coordinating the district peasant federations that had sprung up during the restructuration struggle. Third, the struggle over land was geographically concentrated in the provinces of the north of the department (mainly Melgar, Azángaro, and Carabaya), where the most important animal-raising enterprises of Puno were also concentrated. And fourth, the possibility of converting this conflict into a truly department-wide struggle was constrained by other local divisions, including conflicts between Aymaras and Quechuas for the leadership of the departmental federation.

The government, perhaps perceiving these vulnerabilities, ignored accords it had achieved with the FDCP in July and October 1987, and pronounced the restructuration of the associative agrarian enterprises of the altiplano to be concluded. According to the Puno federation, less than half of the promised 1.1 million hectares had been distributed, while another 364,000 hectares taken by the peasants since 19 May remained in legal limbo. Seeking to expose the hypocrisy of presidential promises, the PUM leadership proposed that the FDCP itself take over the process of giving out titles.[24] According to a top leader of the party, as "an act of popular power without precedents," this "usurpation of functions" would lead to "surpassing the reigning legality" and convert the peasant organizations, in practice, into agents of power, "expressions of command and authority."[25] Another witness close to these events recalls, however, that "handing out titles was a desperate act to affirm, however symbolically, the triumph of the FDCP in the land question."[26]

"People's War" versus Mariateguismo

If for the PUM the Puno movement provided the opportunity to construct practically the "revolutionary party of the masses," for Shining Path it permitted a demonstration of the superiority of armed struggle. The experience would provide a "slap in the face to the demagogue who calls himself president [a reference to Alan García]" and a blow to the "followers of the opportunistic chameleon who leads the Left [Alfonso Barrantes Lingán, Mayor of Lima (1983–1987), and leader of Izquierda Unida]."[27]

More than a product of shifting circumstances, Shining Path's stance against leftist "revisionism" was a central element of its ideology. Thus Shining Path rejected the "vanguardist" tactic of land invasions in favor of a policy of "demolition" (arrasamiento), the complete destruction of feudal relationships with the intent of "disarticulating the productive process."[28] "Our policy is to demolish, not to leave anything; the livestock must be made into dried meat [charqui], what does it matter if the whiners [babosos] protested because the animals are burned and the dogs are hung? . . . It is necessary to break the fences and remove the cattle, it is what the peasants of '56 did and, where we cannot take them, we burn them and do not leave anything. In war what cannot be used or taken is burned and destroyed."[29]

"The land," Guzmán stated in early 1986, "is defended by the peasants, not by us." The peasants "have to learn that land is conquered with arms and defended with arms." "We have to put thousands of peasants" in this political line, he continued, "and let the rest see what we do so that they too will do it."[30]

By the middle of 1988, "Gonzalo" went further and claimed for himself the leadership of the altiplano land movement. He affirmed that "we are the ones who initiated the land invasions in Puno while the PUM argued with APRA over how to do it." Thus the PUM contributed "to lowering the water pressure," and repeated "what they did in 1974 when they were VR": to negotiate, compromise, and liquidate the movement. (See Mallon and Hinojosa in this volume for details on Guzmán's allusions to the 1974 land invasions in Andahuaylas, and to Vanguardia Revolucionaria.) Guzmán demanded that the pumistas "perform an act of contrition and reveal if they have even informed on us in order to batter our forces."[31] At the beginning of 1988, "revisionism" had become the "principal danger" to the evolution of the "people's war."[32]

As Guzmán recognized, what the PUM did in Puno demonstrated the "explosivity of the masses" in the region and the importance of not overlooking the concrete demands of the population.[33] In contrast to the revisionists who sought to assert themselves as a "scab leadership [costra dirigencial] in the service of reaction," however, Shining Path was going to the "base and the depth of the masses."[34] Shining Path would polarize local conflicts in order to undermine the organizational edifice that revisionism had erected to "shackle" the masses and to deflect them off their rebellious path. Thus, Sendero's "armed strikes" served not only to confront the state but also the Left "defense fronts" (FEDIPS), those "outmoded guild forms" that revisionism needed "to mount the backs of the masses." [35]

Active in Puno since the late 1970s, it was only in the mid-1980s that Shining Path passed from "armed propaganda" actions to true guerrilla attacks. These intensified in the context of competition with the PUM. Shining Path realized more guerrilla actions in 1986 than in the preceding half-decade. Various of the associative agrarian enterprises were attacked in actions that involved, in some cases, hundreds of people. As the state retreated, the insurgent advance seemed to gain greater proportions. Shining Path's operations, however, depended upon the extraordinary mobility of an armed column formed largely by cadres from outside of the region. It would take a year for Shining Path to reinitiate actions after the armed column was decimated by the police. Once recomposed, Sendero's armed forces seemed to become the lords of northern Puno within weeks; they expanded their geography of operations, formed new platoons of "local force" militias; and initiated "People's Committees." These committees, which in some cases assumed an open form, were local embryos of Shining Path's "new power." (See del Pino, in this volume, for more information on Shining Path's local structures.) The debacle of the APRA regime, the spiraling hyperinflation, the abuses committed by the police in presumed hunts of terrorists in communities, and the poor results of the negotiations between the FDCP and the authorities, all combined to give to Shining Path propaganda an appearance of verisimilitude previously lacking. [36]

Once it was securely established, the new column directed its efforts to battering the bases of PUM revisionism. Thus, in May 1989, after killing the provincial mayor of Azángaro, Shining Path went on to demolish the Instituto de Educación Rural "Waqrani" de Ayaviri, which was a project of the Prelacy of Ayaviri dedicated to rural development. The director was an official of the PUM in Melgar province. [37] Such attacks would permit Shining Path to obtain a triple objective. First, they deprived peasant federations of northern Puno a fundamental space to meet and exchange experiences. Second, they despoiled PUM's essential infrastructure, including vehicles, offices, and institutional cover for communicating with peasant leaders in the zone of the most important PUM bases. Third, the attacks deepened the division between PUM and the Church, which would face increasing risk in allying with those who were becoming the principal target of Shining Path attacks. Later in 1989, Shining Path concentrated its military operations around the boycott of municipal elections. Executions (*ajusticiamientos*) rose from twenty-three in 1988 to eighty-two in 1989. In December, a few days after the elections, Shining Path's attack on Orurillo in Melgar Province had perhaps the greatest political impact for the PUM. Eight people were eliminated in this nocturnal incursion. They included Tomás Quispesayhua, the recently elected leftist mayor and secretary general of the district peasant federation; his brother Víctor, governor of the locality; Godofredo Marrón, general secretary of the SUTEP (teacher's union); Pedro Pablo Tito Limache, a primary school teacher; Julio Céspedes, director of the agrarian high school (Colegio Agropecuario); Nicolás Cahuata, Justice of the Peace; Mario Lizandro, a peasant; and Benito Isidro Mamani Condori, a driver. The report by the Solidarity Vicariate of Puno noted that "after the massacre, the senderistas dynamited the municipal offices and the medical post and lit the homes of the victims on fire." [38]

Tomás Quispesayhua Aguilar, at thirty-two years of age, was the youngest of the victims, whose average age was forty-five. He was considered one of the most outstanding "peasant militants" of the PUM. He had led the Orurillo federation in the land struggle and its effort to centralize the sale of alpaca and sheep wool produced in about forty surrounding affiliated communities. They had sought to obtain better prices than those paid by the monopolies that controlled the purchase of the product. [39]

Eight widows, thirty-one orphans, and a people without leaders were left behind by the Shining Path action. The attack formed part of the process of constructing Open People's Committees. In this process, according to party directives, it was necessary "to pay ever increasing attention to attacking the authorities. It is good. Almost fifty mayors have been liquidated. In South Vietnam 13,000 authorities were liquidated to create a power vacuum." [40] To be effective, however, selective annihilation required careful preparation. It was necessary to choose the "most recalcitrant and hated" personages at the highest possible level: "the more responsibility and the higher the level the better." It was fundamental, at the same time, to explain to the population that individuals such as these were nothing more than traitors who "although having the complexion and appearance of humble peasants, served and serve the exploiters and betray their class; they did it in the times of the Conquest and they do it now in the Republic." [41] With the majority of its cadres based in the city, and dependent upon the infrastructure of the Church and NGOs (nongovernmental organizations) to operate in the countryside, the PUM could do little to compete with Shining Path in those local arenas where the battle for control of Puno would be decided.

From Mariátegui to Clausewitz

Three years after its founding, the young party still found unity difficult to achieve. Toward the end of 1987, the confrontation between factions known as the *libios* ("Libyans") and *zorros* ("foxes") within the PUM was public knowledge.[42] The internal debate would climax in the Second National Congress of the party in July 1988. The libios sought to complete the building of the "revolutionary party of the masses" by bringing the party to a turning point (*viraje partidista*) that would include preparation for armed self-defense. In the context of a "structural and protracted" crisis, they argued, the country was moving toward an "open and generalized confrontation."[43] The party would therefore have to prepare itself for a "war of the whole people" and not a "political insurgency," as their adversaries advocated. The zorros, for their part, maintained that the project of the libios would push the popular vanguard into an "isolated confrontation" that "risked years of party building."[44]

Tensions were also evident in attitudes toward Shining Path. The libios saw the senderista insurgency, despite its "great deviations," as contributing to the wearing down of the regime.[45] The zorros perceived Shining Path as a "regressive force" that fostered a profoundly disintegrating kind of polarization that paved the way for "dirty war" repression and popular defeat.[46] In this view, "eclectic mixtures around program and strategy" with Shining Path were impossible.[47] For the libios, then, differences with "Gonzalo" were not sufficient to make them support "the antiterrorist front, nor to equate Shining Path with the reactionary armed forces."[48] The zorros, on the other hand, were open to a broad coalition agreement against the insurgency. Defeated at the end of a stormy congress marked by mutual accusations of disloyalty, the zorros would leave the party.[49]

In the hands of their rivals remained the responsibility of proving the feasibility of the party turning point. With its broad "organizational labor-economic-religious network," favorable geopolitical conditions, and a certain "strategic vulnerability," Puno presented, in the judgment of PUM strategists, "objective conditions to attempt to fracture the system of anti-democratic and militarized domination of a centralist state, by empowering the countryside and the regional movement and by constructing power 'from below.'" For this reason, in June 1989, the party approved the "Red Ande Pilot Plan," (Plan Piloto Ande Rojo; PPAR), the object of which was "to organize an insurrection and popular uprising in the region." The key question asked by the PPAR was how to jump from "economistic-movementism" to building a "popular army involving communal leaders." The plan's redactors argued that natural disasters, a new agricultural political economy, militarization, and the end of restructuration, created a conjuncture favorable for launching "strike waves" that would lead to a "general attempt at popular uprising." Shining Path's confrontation with the communal movement, on the other hand, had opened "an impassable abyss with the masses," and created "objective conditions for autodefense to generalize and legitimately take up arms." After two attempts in March and September 1989, however, the PPAR would be abandoned, because it failed to push "the forging of concrete people's power." The PPAR threatened to become "successive and costly 'eruptions' that culminated in signing statements that afterwards we would lack sufficient strength to carry out."[50]

In March 1990, the party prepared to carry out a new effort, this time more clearly military in nature. Cadres with experience in the Salvadoran war were sent to the zone of Asillo in order to create the first armed column of the PUM, the development of which would gain force in the context of renewed land invasions that signalled a reopening of the restructuration process. Through popular assemblies and a regional strike they would seek "to expand the mass base and cover of the movement."

Puno was not Morazán, however, and the PUM was not the FMLN. The details of this new failure are lost amid the coded language of the documents and the silence of the protagonists. A testimony reveals the awakening to reality that the PUM cadres had to confront: "Our calls to form popular assemblies and FEDIPS ['defense fronts'] fell into a void. The train had already passed us by. Shining Path was more deeply rooted than we had imagined. Its work of constructing people's committees had advanced considerably. They had the advantage of illegality. To construct our own bases we would have had to abandon Azángaro, go to San Juan del Oro, to the Sandia selva, with a very long-range vision, almost of resistance. If we had done so, however, wouldn't we have become even more marginal?"[51]

In May, finally, the failures in the military terrain reverberated in the party's own directorate, which "now convoked the struggle against 'militaristic apparatism' just as the construction of military forces had begun in the Party." Surprisingly, they used for this purpose some of the same arguments that the zorros had first tried out two years before. The change was part of a larger retreat. "The leadership nucleus of the party"—the former libios of 1988—"has proceeded to reposition itself," reviewing for this purpose "central issues of strategy integral to People's Power and the GTP ['war of all people,' or *la guerra de todo el pueblo*], going back to the debate of issues supposedly resolved in the Second Congress."[52]

Almost without shooting a single shot, the PPAR initiative passed into obscurity. The policy heaves of the leadership and the bewilderment of the demoralized membership—which observed the "null response of the party to the aggressions suffered from Shining Path"—bore witness to a new and effervescent rural reality.[53] The implacable facts of this new reality ended up convincing PUM strategists that the era of Red Ande had come to an end.

Crisis of the "Third Path"

Product of the disputes within the Izquierda Unida and the PUM about the real potential of the Puno movement, the radicalization induced by the PPAR had contributed to accelerate Left fragmentation. Grass-roots party activists perceived the definitive "turning-point" of the PUM's Second Congress as a kind of "schizophrenia" in which "the discourse of the party went in one direction and the practice and morale of the people went in another." "If memory can be trusted," a militant commented in April 1991, "never have our analyses been so muddled and counter to reality."[54] Another questioned the "peasant guildism" of the party that led it to reproduce, in new contexts, an ideological line unchanged over "the last twenty years," a road to "self-isolation."[55] A third affirmed "what was at first a virtue, that is to say the comunero content of our proposal, little by little was converted into a weakness and an obstacle for resolving the agrarian problem of the region."[56] He later explained: "we suffered an ideological block that stopped us from having an exact appreciation for the meaning of the comunero movement." This meant that "We enclosed ourselves in the defense of supposed 'communal interests' and in 'collectivist' style alternatives, without appreciating that the process of peasant differentiation, and the recomposition of local powers were redefining relationships among comuneros, between comuneros and the feudatarios, and between the diverse sectors of rural society [who were] affected in addition, by a protracted economic crisis, by populist politicians [Alan García] and extension workers [i.e., NGOs, the Church], by a decade of natural disasters, and by the growing violence that acted as a de-structuring factor."[57]

Another PUM leader recalled: "we had dreamed of a sierra populated by communal enterprises, forgetting that we were dealing with a poor peasantry." They would have needed enormous subsidies to put into operation the dozens of communal enterprises the PUM envisioned. "How to protect them without misconstruing the market?"[58] The great error had been "not to appreciate economic processes that have many years behind them. To believe that we could defeat the market on the basis of transferring resources from development programs. Maintaining the comunero-feudatario tension had been absurd. To try to establish whatever collectivist or statist form was contrary to history. In all the places where we had this experience it turned out like this."[59]

In effect, throughout the areas affected by the land invasions, a complex panorama that resisted any type of ordering "from above" began to unfold. Alongside intimidation and the efforts at eviction there also developed accords between communities and cooperatives of recent formation, while community units of ancient origin were once again excluded. Víctor Caballero Martín observed the emergence of "new contradictions that escaped the control of the FDCP," confrontations between comuneros and feudatarios, between comuneros and comuneros, between feudatarios and non-peasant families that received land, and so on. A real blossoming of "negotiations, struggles, accords, acts, compromises" was forged "by the comuneros and feudatarios themselves." Such processes culminated in "informal accords" that the state functionaries were limited to rubberstamping.[60] Confronted with the failure of the party to organize the peasant "selfdefense," the latter followed a similar trajectory of grassroots accord and initiative.

In some cases, the communities seemed to accept the conditions that Shining Path imposed, while establishing, at the same time, "mechanisms to protect local authority."[61] To assume leadership posts rotationally was another option. In some cases customary communal organization camouflaged itself within senderista "People's Committees" from which—despite the opposition of the commanders—connections were maintained with the few development assistance entities that still worked in the "red zone" of the department. Nuclei of feudatarios closed ranks with leaders of the associative agrarian enterprises in defense of what remained of their properties. They armed themselves, or sought the installation of military garrisons on their lands, or they negotiated some sort of pact with the Shining Path column. It mattered little what the documents said; in the real world everything was negotiated, case by case, without a common reference.

Confronted with war and new economic realities, the peasantry responded with a "realistic calculation of its own capacities." The peasants obtained land and sought the way to protect it, in some cases opting to divide it in parcels. If the risks increased, peasants left the land in someone else's charge and migrated, to return when conditions would permit. "It is on this concrete political and military situation that the comunero peasantry acts, organizes its life, production, and festivities; it calculates, resists, and learns without committing itself; it shuts up, hides, supports, denounces until it decides to punish with its own hands and organize to protect itself."[62]

The PUM's frustrated armed experiment had a highly negative effect on the relationship between the PUM and the Church. The latter moved toward a more moderate tone of commitment to the land movement, converting itself into "a site of appeal in the conflict, a voice of counsel, information, and support."[63] The Prelacy of Ayaviri opted not to reopen the Waqrani Institute after its destruction in 1989 and distanced itself from the ex-director and some members of his staff who persisted in confronting Shining Path on their own. The radicalization of the movement, a PUMista leader recognized, had a "dissolving effect" on the pro-comunero bloc.[64] Thus, the declaration of a state of emergency in various altiplano provinces in 1990 did not produce a mobilization like that of the mid-1980s. The measure appeared to be the death sentence for the already weakened "third path." At the same time the state of emergency declaration awakened fears that Puno would become "another Ayacucho."

The Paths of Counterinsurgency

Between the military's arrival in Ayacucho in 1982 and its arrival in Puno in 1990, however, significant changes had taken place in the counterinsurgency vision of the Peruvian Armed Forces. The "Argentine solution" lost its attraction and the military showed a certain inclination—to use the terms of Gustavo Gorriti, in remarks at the symposium prior to this volume—for "the British model." The military questioned the validity of the "emergency zone" model, which affords great prerogatives to the military but in the long run is supremely costly in political terms. Instead, the Armed Forces focused on gaining the support of the population.[65]

After a decade of experimentation, moreover, the army had developed its own strategy, which had a "notorious authoritarian character" but lacked the "genocidal" sheen of the counterinsurgency practices, for example, of the Guatemalan military.[66] The application of this strategy placed the civilian regime in the dilemma of having to choose whether to take direct control of the war by subordinating the Armed Forces, at whatever cost, or to promulgate the legal framework demanded by the military as a necessary condition for terminating subversion. Fujimori's "self-coup" (*autogolpe*) of 5 April 1992 would provide the response to this dilemma. (For more on Fujimori, the military, and the autogolpe, see the essays by Obando and Oliart in this volume.)

In Puno, as in other departments of the sierra, the traditional police forces had been the first line of defense against Shining Path. Poorly trained and armed, they had to retreat. In a second stage, specialized forces were introduced, along with new schemes of combined military-political action — Tactical Antisubversive Units (Unidades Tácticas Antisubversivas) and Special Operations Detachments (Destacamentos de Operaciones Especiales). Installed in the associative enterprises and the mining centers, their presence signified a partial recuperation of initiative in the rural zones. But their operations provoked controversy. According to the Church and the human rights organizations, these operations were really directed against those who fought for land. "We do not want Puno to live the dramatic moments that the people of Ayacucho are living" — proclaimed the Vicariates of Solidarity a few weeks after the state of emergency was declared — as a product of a "dirty war in which the principal victim has been and continues to be the poor people."

These fears, however, would diminish as the months passed. A year later, in 1991, a representative of the Vicariate of Juli declared: "Our relationship with the Armed Forces was initially strained. But when as Vicariates of Solidarity we presented them with denunciations of human rights violations against the civilian population, they reacted differently. They investigated and punished rapidly. The relationship has changed. There are no disappearances, and except for the case of Chillutira, there are no extrajudicial executions. They came intending to arm the peasant rondas and because of the strong resistance channeled by the regional government they desisted in this. So they are responsive."[67]

The army, in sum, showed a surprising self-control which many saw as a suspicious reluctance to act against Shining Path. To some it seemed that the military strategy consisted of hoping that Shining Path and the peasant movement "confront and wear each other down alone."[68] The military officers themselves provided another explanation for their cautious mode of action. One observed that "it would be easy to order a massive attack on a presumably terrorist community, but this would be to lose all that has been gained until now in support for the population and in addition there is the human rights problem." Behind the apparent passivity, however, lay a new strategy. One of the officials in charge of the altiplano counterinsurgency plan would explain: "we knew that after their defeat in Ayacucho, Puno became their most important theater of operations. Here, the problem was that the subversion had penetrated all of the social spheres. It required, therefore, a comprehensive strategy."[69]

In this context, the crucial step was to win over the world of the NGOs, the development projects, and the Church. The military pursued this step by adopting a policy that combined pressure, dialogue, and relative openness. With a certain subtlety, the military went about engaging the neutrality of sectors whose support would be crucial to sustain the possibility of a "third path."

The creation, in early 1990, of the José Carlos Mariátegui Region (RJCM), which combined the departments of Puno, Tacna, and Moquegua, would permit the Left to reactivate its proposal for pacification under civilian leadership with participation of the population.[70] The PUM recognized that "frustration with the persistence of violence and death" prevailed in broad sectors of the region's inhabitants. Nonetheless, the party, whose militants occupied the highest positions of the new regional government, reaffirmed the necessity of blocking "the government, the Armed Forces, and the reaction," from capitalizing on this "elemental and instinctive pacifism" to gain "support for the antisubversive war."[71] The PUM reaffirmed, therefore, its position of "denouncing the government as a factor contrary to a true, lasting, and just peace," and agreed to a "minimum platform" to create conditions for "a political and democratic exit to the war" that included "dialogue with the armed rebel groups."[72]

By 1991, however, many in the "legal Left" believed in the necessity of building bridges to the Armed Forces in order to defeat Shining Path.[73] Disagreements around this issue would lead Romeo Paca Pantigoso, president of the RJCM (the new regional entity that combined Puno, Tacna, and Moquegua) and a member of the PUM, to break with his party. His efforts at including the army in debates over regional pacification strategy were seen by the PUMistas as attempts to form a "regional military-civilian government."

His was not an isolated case. The failed PPAR initiative and the effort to bring the RJCM government to a confrontation with the central government—similar to that which had occurred with the peasant movement—were seen as policies imposed by a clique impervious to the points of view of the regional "bases." Thus, following a course assumed by Paca Pantigoso, the party leadership in the province of Melgar declared itself in rebellion against the national leadership. In the following months, the division reached into the heart of the FDCP. The division in the peasant federation meant, in practice, the pulverization of the regional bloc. In mid-1991, the Bishop of Puno declared "Here in Puno the Federation itself is divided as a result of the split in the PUM, this is scandalous. How then can we make common cause against the violence? The region must embrace pluralism, I do not agree that it be hegemonized by only one party. This is what is making it fail."[74]

In fact, for many within the Church, the struggle for peace did not imply the same levels of confrontation with the government as during the late 1980s. At the beginning of 1992, the Church had organized the semi-official Council for Peace and Life (Consejo por la Paz y la Vida). In the days that followed the "self-coup" of 5 April 1992 (the suspending of the constitution, accompanied by closing of the congress and disbanding of the judiciary, by decree of President Fujimori), some of the Council members proposed making a public pronouncement regarding the events. It was impossible, however, to reach an accord regarding their significance. One of the members argued that the Council should come out against the "coup," in coordination "with all the political parties and leaders of the different organizations." Another proposed that they write the President of the Republic to "express to him their broad approval and support of the measures taken by the Supreme Government to moralize Parliament and the Judicial Power," and to ask Fujimori "to take measures necessary to ensure that the National Pacification is not enmeshed in situations of violence." Finally, a third member opposed making any pronouncement because it would be seen as a "political question," whereas "the organization that we installed on the twenty-fourth of last March . . . only seeks to obtain the pacification of Peru by taking Christian principles as its essence." With the self-coup, the Peace Council's existence no longer had any meaning.[75] The fact was that without the restrictions that the legislature had imposed, the regime could fully implement the institutional framework demanded by the military.[76] The fall of Guzmán, six months later, appeared to prove that the military had been right.

Puno, July 1993

Whoever traveled around the provinces of Azángaro or Huancané in mid-1993 could not help but notice a new element in the local scenery: buildings festooned with greens and browns, in camouflage style, surrounded by turrets, machine-gun nests, and palisades. Originally municipal government buildings or medical posts, they broke the harmony of village architecture, which remained little altered otherwise—save perhaps for parabolic antennae that symbolize the arrival of impetuous modernity to remote corners of Peru. These counterinsurgency bases (Bases Contrasubversivas; BCS) had come to dominate a territory that, some years before, had been disputed between peasant organizations and Shining Path columns.

The visitor also could not escape noticing the control posts on the roads, the lines of passengers who waited for soldiers to compare their documents against mysterious and feared lists of "wanted elements," and the mobile patrols that reconnoitered areas that for many years had not seen the presence of government forces. In Putina, the soldiers prepared an allegorical float for the celebration of the local patron saint, cleaned the municipal pool, or prepared for Sunday visits to the communities, where they provided medical attention and provisions to be distributed after raising the national flag.

Perhaps one breathed an air of normality. The insurgency, however, was not a fact of the past. The BCS of San Antón and Putina and the headquarters of the National Police of Mañazo were attacked in the mid-1990s. The slogans that covered the walls of the towns of the area were silent testimonies of the Shining Path presence: "People repudiate the control and vigilance of the army," "People do not permit that your children serve the genocidal army," "Long live the open popular committees," "Against the robbery of the lands," and "Down with the Council for Peace."

In 1992, according to a military report, "as a consequence of the permanent and continuous production of intelligence," the military now had material that revealed "the organization of Shining Path and the names of the most important cadres and zones of action." The existence of the BCS also allowed the military to act with greater alacrity on the basis of information gathered. With these new elements, the army carried out its repressive action toward the middle-level and base sectors through which Shining Path had sustained its activity. For the first time, there was a real possibility of systematically dismantling Shining Path platoons, local forces, support bases, and popular committees.

A list of those detained from the peasant community of San Miguel illustrates this new turn in the counterinsurgency operations. Of ten arrested, only one was accused of direct participation in armed action, while the others were labeled with terms such as "commissary of livestock," "commissary of agriculture," "commissary of justice," "in charge of transportation," or simply "element of support." Interrogated in the counterinsurgency base of Asillo, they would have to respond to detailed questions regarding their community, the conduct of authorities or teachers, and the persons who "receive visits of unknown persons" or give lodging or provisions to "foreign elements." Two weeks later the detained would be sent to the city of Puno. One of them remained in the base of Asillo "to be used in counterinsurgency operations." The new information, meanwhile, would form the basis of new detentions.

But efficiency has its costs. Abuses abounded. Accusations were made out of fear or vengeance. "Is it true that the mayor of your village gives food to unknown persons?" asked an officer in a routine interrogation. "I have no knowledge, but from rumors in the community I know that the indicated person wants to join the terrorists." Such a comment could lead to an arrest. The testimonies and the lists of names emitted by military intelligence, in this context, acquired a monstrous weight. No one investigated the accusations. The judges felt the military pressure, while doubting, in silence, the constitutionality of the proceedings. "This attitude of the Armed Forces has been simply and plainly the result of a calumny on the part of a cattle thief," declared a community in Asillo in a petition to the Superior Court of Puno. The petition continued: "We, Mr. Judge, know our community and its members, we have full knowledge of the activity of every comunero, we know the newcomers and the outsiders . . . it is unjust that because one single person or gratuitous enemy labels someone a terrorist, it is enough for the person to be imprisoned . . . we can all manifest his innocence before your office."

After three weeks of detention in the BC of Asillo and in the antiterrorism headquarters in Puno, the subsecretary of the FDCP issued the following opinion: "Today to be a leader is to place yourself in a hell. Shining Path looks for you. Since you throw yourself at the State, the military also looks for you. You have to think about it a hundred times before agreeing to be a leader. There is no CODEH or Vicariate that will defend you. Before, who was going to be able to do this to us? We have been diminished. Military intelligence is today more than the people. I am amazed by the military intelligence."[77]

Conclusions

Toward the mid-1980s, Puno was an area of effervescence. Through a series of diverse organizations, the Puno population attempted to remedy the devastating consequences of the natural, economic, and political disasters that had wracked the region. In diverse ways, Shining Path, APRA, and the forces of the Left grouped in the PUM managed to reflect the demands of certain sectors of the population. In the Puno ferment, these political forces saw an opportunity to promote their respective national agendas. For PUM and APRA, Puno was a chance to reverse the expansion of the insurgency, while for Shining Path, Puno provided the opportunity to open the "altiplano front" and to expand from Ayacucho to the rest of the Peruvian sierra.

With the decisive rhetorical contribution of Alan García, the self-styled "comunero president," the government party generated enormous expectations of land distribution. At least temporarily, APRA blunted the effect of Shining Path propaganda and captured the attention of the most combative rural sectors in the restructuration process. The abrupt collapse of the APRA regime and the internal contradictions of the party, however, blocked the conversion of such expectations into solid ties between the government and the communities. The gaps in the restructuration process, moreover, permitted the alliance of pastoral agents, leftist activists, and certain leaders of the comunero peasantry to breed organizational ties of broad reach and appreciable dynamism. Local peasant federations and the urban movement—with support of the Church, NGOs, and professional and intellectual sectors—conformed the regional bloc that held out a "third path" as a possible outcome of regional conflict.

In the context of increasing deterioration of the peasant economy, Shining Path managed to transform an intense but highly localized work of implanting itself in rural support bases into a guerrilla war column. The column depended, however, on periodic reinforcements brought in from the outside. Restructuration and land invasions displaced the Shining Path column, and military blows obliged it to retreat. Shining Path's brief reign in northern Puno, toward the end of the 1980s and the beginning of the 1990s, rested on displacing the PUM, intimidating the Church, and attacking their communal allies. The political costs of this method were not light and ended up producing a deepening breach between the guerrillas and the rural population. In their attempts to respond to Shining Path via the radicalization of the peasant movement, on the other hand, the PUM in-

Table 9.2   Structure of land tenure in Puno, 1985 and 1992. (The 1985 figures are before restructuration. The 1992 figures are from December.)

Type	Number of Enterprises 1985	1992	Hectares 1985	1992	Percent 1985	1992
Associative Enterprises[1]	45	9	1,766,045	224,395	48.1%	6.1%
Peasant Communities	985	985	920,592	1,848,314	25.1%	50.4%
Individuals			726,561	1,192,144	19.8%	32.5%
Other			255,802	404,147	7%	11.0%
Totals			3,669,000	3,669,000	100%	100%

Source: Author's compilation based on diverse sources.
1. "Associative Enterprises" refer to the units known as SAIS, CAPS, and ERPS in 1985, and to the units known as SAIS, CAT, and ERPS in 1992.

advertently contributed to undermining the cohesion of the regional bloc upon which the possibility of the "third path" was sustained.

At the margin of this corroding dynamic, the army distributed its forces with discretion and caution, without committing the repressive "excesses" of the Ayacucho campaign and with an astute utilization of intelligence and civic action. When, in April 1992, the military obtained a favorable political balance, based on its previous work, it set its counterinsurgency machinery into motion in Puno. For a rural population tired of violence and whose appetite for land had been partially satisfied (see table 9.2), collaboration with the Armed Forces seemed an attractive possibility. Not only had the puneños avoided the traumatic "dirty war" situations that peoples of other sierra regions experienced. In addition, the Puno population had come to realize that the army provided the most effective defense against senderista impositions. The government forces' increasing ability to capture the countryside, in any event, left few options.

Beyond the party activists' interpretations of regional events or their use of political capital accumulated within the formal political system, were the actions of the peasants themselves. The peasants, in accord with their own vision of regional and national events, made key decisions that determined the evolution of the "battle for Puno." They tolerated, supported, or punished the guerrillas. They allied with pastoral agents and militant leftists in an effort to realize their own agenda. Or, they took the words of President García, demanded that he fulfill them, and brought his pro-comunero rhetoric to its logical conclusion. Likewise, their conditional acceptance of the military program ended up becoming the essential factor in the outcome of the struggle.[78] In the end, it was the peasants whose actions made the "third path" a real possibility and later confirmed its subsequent irrelevance.

It was in the communal context, with all of its internal contradictions and differentiation, that the decisions were reached that determined peasant stances. Facing the various revolutionary, reformist, and modernizing proposals put forth by party, Church, and state intellectuals, local "peasant intellectuals" articulated political visions sustained in long-standing local traditions. The sense of continuity of these visions, however, did not delete the currency and pragmatism of their contemporary decisions. Thus, even when their discursive forms were inherited from the past, as Steven Feierman notes in his study of "peasant intellectuals" of Tanzania, "the peasant must make an active decision to say that they are meaningful at this moment, to select a particular form of discourse as opposed to other possible forms, and to shape the inherited language anew to explain current problems."[79]

On the basis of her research on peasant Mexican and Peruvian communities, Florencia Mallon postulates that much of agrarian history can be summarized in the search for these moments of consensus and unity, occasionally achieved and rapidly lost.[80] Thus, to achieve an adequate comprehension of the peasant as a political actor it is important to locate peasant actions in a long-term temporal frame. As Stern suggests, "it should at least include the period considered relevant in the rebels' own historical memory, and the period during which the last enduring strategy of resistant adaptation was developed."[81]

In the case of the northern Puno peasantry, such an approach requires a reference to the first decades of the century, when the communal project was defeated by the haciendas as wool production for export expanded. The triumph of the Puno haciendas did not signal the massive proletarianization of peasants nor, much less, the disappearance of the community. It was the beginning, rather, of a silent struggle that, over the course of various decades, implied the incorporation of new actors, as well as new schemes of domination that might assure the continuity of the hacienda scheme defined by 1920.[82] It was through their prolonged dealings with development projects, international organizations, Adventist missions and Catholic congregations, state agencies, and NGOs, that the altiplano peasantry forged a political culture of multiple alliances and coalitions. The alliances, both ephemeral and more-or-less lasting, both genuine and deceptive, were perhaps crucial for guaranteeing survival, but they proved insufficient to put an end to the peasants' marginalization.

Notes

1 Guzmán 1988: 27.
2 PCP-SL 1991 [1989]: 4.
3 Martínez 1991: 77 ff.
4 Caballero Martín 1984, 1990; Scurrah 1987.
5 See the following articles in *Sur:* "Reforma Agraria o Gamonales?" No. 29 (July 1980), 19–20; "Denuncia de la Liga Agraria Ciro Alegría de Lampa y San Román," (February/March 1982), 27–28; "Poder local y retorno de Gamonales en Puno" No. 43 (October 1981), 30–34; "Acora: La organización campesina cultural después de la toma de tierras," No. 37 (April 1981), 8–11; "Puno: Poder local divide y enfrenta a campesinos," No. 45 (December 1981), 33–41. On the drought and its social and economic impact, see, also in *Sur:* "Sequía en Puno y problemas regionales en el sur," and "Puno, la sed del Perú: sequía agudiza la crisis pero no es la causa," both in No. 61 (April 1983), pp. 11–18 and 36–42, respectively. See also CORPUNO 1984.
6 In 1974, Revolutionary Vanguard (Vanguardia Revolucionaria; VR) had displaced the Maoist "Red Flag" faction of the Communist Party (Partido Comunista del Peru-Bandera Roja; PCP-BR) for control of the CCP. During the following years, this federation became one of the most important peasant organizations in Peru. See García Sayán 1982; Quintanilla 1981; and the articles by Hinojosa and Mallon in this volume.
7 Klaiber 1988: 358 ff.; Judd 1987; Campredón 1992; Llanque 1985; Pásara 1986.
8 Vega 1989; Robles 1987.
9 "Puno 2,000: ¿Proyectos y desarrollo en una región?" *Sur* 69/70 (December 1983), 10–15; Barrenechea 1983: 189–98. In the municipal elections of 1983, Izquierda Unida candidates gained 35 percent of all votes in the department, as opposed to 23 percent by the government party, Acción Popular, and 9 percent by APRA.
10 The Constitution of 1979 delineated the principles of a new regionalization of the country and of the establishment of regional governments in place of departments. The specific terms of these measures were to be defined by a new Regionalization Law. Debates over this law advanced very little under the administration of Fernando Belaúnde Terry (1980–1985). From the beginning

of his administration, however, Alan García promised to carry out regionalization. See Pásara 1989.

11 "Puno: la tragedia y el coraje de un pueblo," *Sur* 95 (May 1986), 33–36.

12 PUM 1985: 8; and "Diagnóstico del Partido" in PUM 1986: 18. The PUM included most of the groups that broke off from VR over the course of the 1970s as well as groups that came out of the Movement of the Revolutionary Left (Movimiento de Izquierda Revolucionaria; MIR) and the Christian Left.

13 PUM 1985: 8.

14 Quotes from PUM n.d.: 13, and "Diseño básico del Plan de Asentamiento y Construcción Estratégica," in PUM 1986.

15 Alluding to its cartographic profile, García Pérez called the provinces of the southern Andean region the "Andean trapezoid" (*trapecio andino*). In these provinces were concentrated the greatest pockets of poverty and marginality in the entire country. See "Proyecto de Plan Trapecio Andino" *Sur* 94 (April 1986), 3–21.

16 Centro Bartolomé de las Casas 1987: 70, 9.

17 The 562 communities recognized by the APRA administration exceeded the 531 that had been legally recognized throughout all of 1926–1985, according to Trivelli 1992: 23–37.

18 President García traveled to Puno on numerous occasions during the weeks before the municipal elections in order to lend his personal support to the candidates of his party in the Trapecio Andino. His visits would be accompanied by the distribution of goods and articles of consumption as well as diverse donations to the local population. These expenditures were not monitored as there were no laws that regulated the use of state resources in electoral campaigns.

19 "Tercer Congreso de la FDCP," *Sur* 99 (September 1986), 3–21.

20 Interview with Raúl Wiener, Lima, 7 August 1992.

21 Comunidad Campesina de Chapioco, Ocuviri District, Lampa Province, Oficio No. 012-87, 2 March 1987.

22 Ibid.

23 This paragraph is based on analysis of some fifty petitions (*memoriales*) in the archive of the FDCP.

24 FDCP 1987.

25 Harnecker 1990.

26 Interview with Víctor Caballero.

27 Notebook, Archive of the National Directorate of Counter-Terrorism (Dirección Nacional de Lucha Contra el Terrorismo), Puno.

28 PCP-SL 1984.

29 PCP-SL 1986.

30 "Intervención de la dirección," ibid.

31 Guzmán 1988: 37.

32 PCP-SL 1988a, "Informe de la dirección en la Sesión Prepatoria del Primer Congreso del Partido Comunista del Perú" (6 January 1988) in Gonzales 1990: 10.

33 PCP-SL 1988a.

34 "Bases de Discusión," in Arce Borja 1989: 305–88.

35 PCP-SL 1988a: 16.

36 On the debacle of the APRA administration, see Crabtree 1992; Graham 1992.

37 On the attack against the IER, see Smith 1992a: 93, 94, 95.

38 Chronology of violence provided by the Vicariate of Solidarity of Puno, corresponding to the month of December 1989. See also IDL 1990: 41–42.

39 Ibid.

40 PCP-SL 1988a: 16.

41 *Causa Proletaria* 5, n.d., Gorriti Archive.

42 See Wiener 1987. The zorros (literally "foxes") were a group of PUM members who formed part of the editorial board of the magazine *El Zorro de Abajo* ("the foxes of below"). The nickname libios referred to the ephemeral anti-imperialist fame that the Libyan leader Muammar Khadafi gained at that time as a result of his confrontations with the president of the United States, Ronald Reagan. The zorros had intellectual affinities and social-democratic inclinations, while the libios were the ultimate militants who, in contact with the party bases, led the most combative fronts. According to the zorro Alberto Adrianzén "we would call them libios because of their vocation for isolation."

43 PUM 1988a.

44 PUM 1988b: 54, 87.

45 PUM 1988a: 76.

46 PUM 1988b: 84.

47 PUM 1987: 82–83.

48 PUM 1988a: 76.

49 Immediately after the congress, some leaders of the losing faction denounced in the press the "militaristic" course that the new leadership sought to impose upon the party. See, for example, "El PUM echa humo," *La República* 10 July 1988: 24.

50 PUM 1991b: 2, 1, 9–10, 5, 14.

51 Ibid.: 17.

52 Ibid.: 17, 18.

53 PUM 1990: 4.

54 PUM 1991a: 3.

55 Interview with Víctor Torres, Lima, 19 August 1993.

56 PUM 1991c: 7. Some time later, the secretary general of PUM would recognize "the volunteerism, inmediatism, and absence of priorities," and the lack of a serious analysis of the changes that had been produced in the mass movement

through which the party aimed to cover its underlying intent to "produce jumps of accumulation (embrionic organs of new power, new forces, etc.) and prop up a government of rupture" (PUM 1993: 16–93).

57 PUM 1991b: 7.
58 Víctor Torres, Lima 19 August 1993.
59 Interview with Dante Vera, Lima 19 August 1993.
60 Caballero Martín 1991: 133–57.
61 Y. Rodríguez 1992: 131–54.
62 Consejo de Desarrollo Alternativo de Puno 1992: 3.
63 Calderón [Bishop of Puno] 1991: 11–12.
64 Interview with Víctor Torres, Lima, 19 August 1993.
65 In addition to the essay by Obando in this volume, for the evolution of the counterinsurgency strategy of the Peruvian Armed Forces, see: Mauceri 1989; Degregori and Rivera 1993.
66 Ibid., 14. On Guatemala see Carmack 1988 and Falla 1992.
67 Gallegos 1991: 31. The changes in the perception of the Puno situation can be followed through the following articles published by *Ideéle* throughout 1991: "Estado de emergencia en el sur, persistiendo en el error" (no. 24), "Qué pasa en las nuevas zonas de 'emergencia,'?" (No. 25), "Puno: Entre la emergencia y la pacificación" (No. 28), "Puno y San Martín: La paz busca un cambio" (Nos. 32–33), "La batalla por Puno" (No. 39).
68 Paca 1991: 81–91; Smith 1992a: 109.
69 Interview with Peruvian Army Colonel Alberto Pinto Cárdenas, Puno, 24 February 1995.
70 See Paca 1991; Smith 1992a.
71 PUM 1991d.
72 PUM 1991e.
73 See for example Pedraglio 1990 and the debate between Javier Diez Canseco and Carlos Iván Degregori in the magazine *Sí* in March of 1992. Pedraglio and Degregori left the PUM after the Second Party Congress in July 1988.
74 *Ideéle* 28 (August 1991): 12.
75 The cited documents are all from the archive of the Vicariate of Solidarity in Puno.
76 See Vidal 1993; Tincopa and Mollo 1992.
77 Interview with Percy Añazgo, Puno, 24 August 1993.
78 Results from recent elections in Puno reveal that the significant amount of support for the government party in the elections for the Democratic Constituent Congress (Congreso Democrático Constituyente) in November 1992 subsequently gave way to massive opposition to the approval of the constitutional text in the referendum of October 1993. In fact, Puno was the department with the highest percentage of "no" votes (79.69 percent). President

Fujimori had to make numerous trips and to increase radically government action in the area in order to convert this repudiation into the mass support that his candidature received in the May 1995 elections. See Rénique 1995.

79   Feierman 1990: 3.
80   Mallon 1995: 324.
81   Stern 1987: 13.
82   See in regards to this history, Burga and Reátegui 1981; Hazen 1974; Jacobsen 1993; and Tamayo Herrera 1982.

PART FOUR

Women as Citizen-Subjects:

Exploring the Gendered War

❖ The war for Peru had generative as well as destructive consequences. In Part II we discerned one of the major generative consequences
of the war: the formation of peasant *rondas* and a reborn civil society in
the rural center-south. As we have seen, this painful birth and renovation
was a product of growing alienation from Sendero, limited rapprochement
with the military, and at times, double lives that provoked moral crisis
and renewal. In Part IV, Isabel Coral assesses a second generative aspect
of the war: the emergence of women as new citizen-subjects, major and
visible protagonists in struggles over politics, survival, and reconstruction.
To some extent, this argument has been anticipated in del Pino's discussion
of women as a leading force in the transition toward open resistance to Sendero in eastern Ayacucho, and in Burt's analysis of grassroots organizations
and leadership in Villa El Salvador. The gendered dimension of the war has
also been anticipated, in part, by Starn's reflections on the intersections of
ronda organization and masculinized peasant politics.

Coral's study extends and complements such insights by exploring more
systematically the gendered dimensions of the war, especially women's experiences and responses. Her ambitious essay crosses conventional genres.
In part historical analysis, in part testimonial, in part advocacy, the essay
draws on Coral's experience as President of CEPRODEP (Centro de Promoción y Desarrollo Poblacional), a leading NGO whose support activity has
concentrated on women and displaced migrants in Lima and Ayacucho.
This experience has enabled Coral to achieve an exceptionally well informed
and multifaceted overview of women's experience in the war.[1]

Coral's wide angle view offers an important corrective to the temptation
to focus more narrowly on woman-as-warrior within the Sendero Luminoso

insurgency. Women and female youth were actively recruited and drafted into senderista soldiering and militancy. Their visibility as fierce warriors of revolution, whose political and military roles were at once "nontraditional" yet resonant with the image of female self-sacrifice (life in the service of a higher cause defined by authoritative men), captured the cultural imagination. Thousands of onlookers, mourners, and celebrants—not all of them Sendero sympathizers—flocked to the funeral mass and burial of Edith Lagos, a fallen guerrilla leader, in Ayacucho in 1982.

Yet as Coral demonstrates, narrow focus on the mystique of the senderista female warrior in many ways deflects attention from the more complex and contradictory pattern of female participation in the senderista insurgency. On the one hand, the insurgency *did* create new and visible spaces for women and female youth to assume roles and responsibilities at odds with conventional social restrictions. These new spaces, along with Sendero's attacks on male drunkenness and domestic violence in rural communities, generated a certain responsiveness by women to Sendero. On the other hand, notwithstanding their new roles and responsibilities, female participants in Sendero found themselves inserted into insurgent versions of patriarchal subordination. The party and its leaders became the new patriarchs who controlled the private and affective lives of female subordinates; techniques of gendered humiliation that stigmatized the feminine remained a standard part of political warfare; women who achieved special esteem were celebrated for their capacities to act as men, as brave *macha* warriors whose readiness to inflict and to suffer violence would enforce the will of the revolution. In short, Sendero's politics of gender opened new spaces for women but tended to integrate them within an insurgent brand of patriarchalism.

Perhaps most important, Coral demonstrates that women's "awakening" as more visible and empowered citizen-subjects developed largely outside of, and often in opposition to, Sendero Luminoso. Women played lead roles in grassroots civic organizations that addressed the major practical life issues—economic survival, war-induced displacement, human rights violations, political stances toward Sendero and the state—that shaped a war-torn and impoverished society. As leaders and participants in mothers' clubs and federations, in relatives-of-the-disappeared organizations, in migrant associations, popular soup kitchens, and glass-of-milk committees, and in community crafts and employment workshops, women built roles as visible protagonists of society. They became the organized claimants who channeled resources and political pressure beyond those mobilized by masculinized political parties and grassroots organizations.

Although they pointed to new models of community self-development and state-society relations, these activities ought not be romanticized as an unproblematic "third path" of self-mobilization by women. The achievements of women were tied to revenue streams from NGOs, the state, and community economic projects that were vulnerable to political change and to neoliberal economic shocks. In addition, and as Coral observes, as women gained prominence and leadership they came to contend with increased pressures by political parties to build controlling, manipulative relationships with grassroots organizations. They also contended with increased pressure by Sendero to infiltrate women-run organizations and to undermine independent or antagonistic leaders. In comparing the women's movements in Lima and Ayacucho, Coral notes that Lima's women leaders, despite greater political experience, were rendered especially vulnerable by the pressures of political parties and Sendero. All in all, Coral's discussion of external pressures and internal tensions provides a corrective to romanticization reminiscent of the correctives offered in Starn's analysis of peasant rondas.

Nonetheless, women's new prominence as citizen-subjects, with their own political organizations and agendas, has left an important and probably irreversible legacy. Since the capture of Abimael Guzmán in September 1992 and the transition toward a reconstructed society and politics, political parties and the state have had strong incentive to establish working relationships with women's organizations. In addition, women have insisted on a version of "normalization" that will not return them to invisible political status. In Ayacucho—the highland region with the greatest political symbolism for a reconstructing society and state—women have figured prominently in debates on the framework for return by displaced migrants to rebuilding rural communities, and on the cultural, economic, and political shape of the rebuilt communities. Given the prestige and masculinized quality of peasant rondas outlined by Starn, the political proposals and self-awareness of women-led organizations traced by Coral, the general uncertainties that mark the reconstruction of society and politics out of the ruins of war, and the likelihood of variation among specific subregions and communities within Ayacucho, directions of change in the political culture of the highlands are not entirely clear. In this sense, all the citizen-subjects of a rebuilding polity stand at an uncertain crossroads in the mid-to-late 1990s.

What is clear, however, is that the crises of war have impelled and enabled women to establish themselves as insistent citizen-subjects in the shaping of a post-war polity. It is important to bear in mind, of course, that oral interviews and field work can lead to an overstated—flat and misleading—sense of discontinuity. Analysis and testimonials of a self-conscious female "awakening" can encourage misplaced assumptions of the near-complete dormancy and political invisibility of women in the prewar years.[2] Notwithstanding this caveat, a certain threshold was indeed crossed during the war years and will be difficult to reverse. A return to relative female invisibility is unlikely to take place without considerable conflict and struggle.

Notes

1   For additional work on women's experience within Shining Path, the outstanding study is Kirk 1993b; a more problematic work, but useful as a vision sympathetic with Sendero, is Andreas 1985. For a splendid study of urban women's experience that includes the prewar and war years, for the case of Villa El Salvador, see Blondet 1991. I wish to acknowledge here that my understandings of women's experiences have benefitted greatly from Weiss 1996, a pioneering discussion of war, gender, and subjectivity in Peru, and from extensive discussions with Narda Henríquez and Jean Weiss.

2   This point comes through strongly in Weiss 1996, who notes that the literature on urban migrants in Peru also tends to put forth a vision of "awakening" that may overstate women's invisibility and dormancy in rural society before migration. For insights on women, migration, and shantytown communities, see Degregori, Blondet, and Lynch 1986; Blondet 1991. For discussion of conceptual issues and difficulties, when considering women's assertions of gender rights and family and community needs in "preawakening" historical periods, see Stern 1995: chapter 13.

TEN

Women in War: Impact and Responses

Isabel Coral Cordero

❖ Little has been said and written about the impact of the war in Peru on women and gender relations, yet such an analysis could be useful for understanding—and empowering—Peruvian efforts to construct a lasting peace. To reflect on women and gender relations is to pose the following questions. How were women's lives situated before the war? What interests and hopes for gender relations were proposed during the war, and to what degree and through what mechanisms were such desires incorporated? How should we understand the transformation experienced by women directly involved in the war, from relative invisibility to visible protagonism? How were women's lives situated after the war? What changes have been envisioned for gender relations, and how might they be consolidated and sustained?

This chapter outlines some responses to these questions based on an analysis of women's experiences in two important scenarios: Ayacucho, the center of war action in the sierra, and Lima, the national capital and the terrain where Shining Path would suffer its decisive defeat. I focus my analysis on the experience of women of humble social circumstances, that is, peasant women and poor urban women. Empirically, the chapter is based on interviews with women, especially leaders of social movements, oriented toward capturing their life histories and their memories of events. (For obvious reasons, the identities of the interviewed women remain anonymous.) The direct observation and personal experience accumulated through my own accompaniment of women's processes also serve in the analysis that follows.[1]

Before the war, especially before the 1970s, women suffered from being made invisible—a product of patriarchal relations that excluded and devalued women's experiences, hopes, and interests, and that fomented, as well, women's own low self-esteem. Nonetheless, toward the 1970s, the economic crisis and the growing politicization of civil society led women to search for new spaces of expression and participation.

The principal recognized activities of women were those dedicated to domestic activities or those seen as extensions of domestic activities. In the man, as family head, was supposed to concentrate decision making. He was the public representative of the family, the producer par excellence, the guarantor of the income and resources necessary to sustain the family. In the familial space, women were assigned responsibility for domestic activities. Mothers counted on their daughters' assistance while fathers progressively incorporated sons into productive economic activities. Sporadically, fathers might fulfill some domestic duties, such as providing water and caring for babies.

On the other hand, although women formally did not have authority to make decisions about the allocation of household resources, family housing and location, family planning, and the buying and selling of goods, they developed informal strategies of negotiation through persuasion, pressure exerted by their older children, and intervention by the extended family. In addition, women assumed total responsibility for providing food, caring for the health of family members, and educating their children. Such activities were not fully acknowledged or valued even by the women themselves. Nonetheless, they provided spaces within which women could make relatively autonomous decisions. Food was a concern that, before the war, was still resolved individually and privately, while health and education required collective action from women. They had to interact with institutions of the external world such as schools and health centers. The fulfillment of these tasks led to the emergence of the first mostly female organizations, including health committees and parents' associations, which sprang up mainly in the cities. In the cities as well, women's participation in the building of new neighborhoods on unused lands invaded by migrants and squatters also pushed them into public spheres of contact and revindication.

In productive economic activities, the invisibility of women's contributions was blatant; the many activities carried out by women were simply attributed to men. The women themselves conceived their principal occupation as "the home," or perhaps, "helping their husbands," and national occupational registries reflected these assumptions. Yet, women's participation in agricultural labor was continuous. Women participated in important activities such as soil preparation, weeding, and harvesting produce in the field; selecting and distributing products (especially selecting seeds); packing products for transport; and providing food for work parties. In addition, the care of animals, both large and small, was almost completely the responsibility of women, girls, and the elderly.

In addition, women in both the countryside and the city participated in generating family resources through small-scale commerce. In the city, women organized small, generally informal trades that sold or resold products such as fruit, vegetables, meats, prepared meals, and clothes. In the countryside, women sold small production surpluses in local market stands (generally informal), or by participating in fairs and intercommunal exchanges of products.

Another source of income was the sale of domestic services, generally to the middle and upper sectors of society. Among urban women this activity took the form of working full time as servants, or of providing specific services such as washing clothes, cleaning homes, or looking after children. In the case of rural women, young girls and adolescents more often worked as domestics, while adult women offered more sporadic services such as processing grains or assisting on special occasions such as family fiestas.

In all of these cases, women's economic contribution was rendered invisible because they received payment in kind, bartered for products, or immediately spent their earnings on articles of family consumption, usually food.

Public space and political activity were in varying degrees off limits to poor women, even in the rural communal ambit. Local political representation and decision making were reserved for men except in particular cases in which female household heads were recognized and admitted as such. In marginal (i.e., newly expanding) urban areas, some such women were even able to obtain leadership roles. Just as important, depending on what was on the agenda, women occasionally sought admittance to communal assemblies. Even when they had no formal vote or voice in the debate, the pressure they exerted on their husbands and on other influential persons conditioned the decisions that were made. Without a doubt, an important achievement of women was tolerance of their presence and influence in these spaces. This achievement was all the more important because women's contact with political parties was low. The parties focused their activities on organized associations (*organizaciones gremiales*) of workers, students, professionals, marginal urban residents, and peasants that were dominated by men. Although women's participation in political parties expanded before the 1970s, their increased presence derived almost exclusively from middle-class, student, and professional sectors.

During the 1970s, especially the late 1970s, the combined effects of economic crisis and an increasingly politicized civil society drew poor urban women into a search for broader spaces of participation. On the one hand, the economic crisis, especially in the cities, and its resulting unemployment and inflation called into question the role of men as household producers and earners. Whole families had to confront the situation by diversifying their economic activities and by participating in collective strategies of survival such as communal kitchens, small workshops to generate complementary income, and health programs. These programs were supported principally by non-governmental organizations. On the other hand, the politicization of poor women, while tentative, took place mainly through two channels. First, nongovernmental organizations (NGOs), mainly feminist and many of whose members were linked to political parties, mobilized masses of women. Through different organizational forms linked to survival strategies, the NGOs encouraged reflections on politics and gender. Second, the ideological work of the political parties mobilized youth and adults with leadership capacities and would include women as well, although in smaller proportions than men. In contrast to the NGOs, the political parties organized around general demands without incorporating even the most immediate gender interests.

Thus women, inspired to seek solutions to problems through new spaces of participation as social actors, became more visible and assertive than in previous generations. In the 1980s, this tendency would grow and become consolidated in a context of severe crisis. [*Editor's note:* It is important to note that the mobilization and "awakening" of women in the 1970s and especially the 1980s do not imply an absence of dynamics of conflict, negotiation, and affirmation by popular women to defend their needs in earlier times. The subjectivity produced in a process of social "awakening," and the fact that female dynamics of assertion were less organized as such and less visible in public spaces in earlier times, can create an exaggerated vision of the earlier past as an era of overwhelming domination—without reply, negotiation, struggle, or affirmation. The experiences of popular women in the 1970s and especially the 1980s did, however, represent a turning point toward a stronger, more organized and visible, affirmation by women as social actors and protagonists in public spaces.]

Women in Shining Path

The interaction between war and economic crisis in the 1980s redefined socioeconomic relations in public as well as private spaces. Women of the popular sectors, including those of poverty-stricken marginal urban zones and peasants, emerged onto the public stage and asserted themselves as social actors who confronted the problems of economic crisis and war.

Let us begin with women in Shining Path. The presence of women in Shining Path was undeniable, even though their presence derived more from their own expectations and desires to enter new spaces of participation than to a senderista sensibility that incorporated gender interests in the Shining Path project. On the contrary, Shining Path established an instrumentalist relationship with women, whereby patriarchal relations were reproduced to benefit the party.

Shining Path's ideology and actions on gender were contradictory. On the one hand they conceived of politics and particularly war as the work of *machos* and attacked their opponents as "fags" (*maricones*), "cowards," and "little women" (*mujercitas*). On the other hand they made significant efforts to recruit women and constituted women's committees within the party structure and at the level of the "mass front" (*frente de masa*) in Ayacucho.

Since the 1970s, in the university ambit Shining Path gave priority to organizing in faculties such as the social sciences, education, agronomy, nursing, and obstetrics. The criteria were the size of the mass (*masa*) that could be mobilized and the role that it could fulfill within the project. With the exception of agronomy, the composition of these departments were in the majority female. Women's acceptance into the Shining Path seemed to have two basic requirements: capacity for leadership and readiness to give oneself over to party activities, to the point of renouncing responsibilities such as work and study and renouncing familial and affective ties. Thus arose the first nuclei of Shining Path women, who mostly came from middle-class university and professional sectors and, in a lesser proportion, from popular neighborhoods in the cities. These women were more characterized by their total identification with the project and their great will to work and to struggle than by theoretical and political qualifications compa-rable to those of the male leaders. These nuclei were those that supported institutionalizing the women's committees.

But the acceptance of these women did not imply changes in gender relations. On the contrary, in this initial stage, traditional gender relations were reproduced and even reinforced. Arguing that they had to guarantee the security of the party, the Shining Path leader-patriarchs sought to con-trol the private lives of their members—the places they lived, their life style, and even their choice of mates. Many were the couples who broke up on party orders or formed in the interests of the party. Even worse, Shining Path used romance as a strategy for recruiting women, and to this end orga-nized "youth fiestas" formally inaugurated by prominent party leaders. The internal division of labor within the party was disadvantageous for women, who tended to fulfill "logistical" tasks rather than those of organization and leadership.

These relationships of dependency were reinforced through a kind of cult around the most important party leaders, such as Abimael Guzmán and Antonio Díaz Martínez, who assumed lordly attitudes and intellectual airs and distanced themselves prudently from the common concerns of mere mortals. In the bases, there was a strong tendency to idealize and deify the leadership, a situation that enabled leaders to exploit women for diverse ends, some of them unrelated to party matters. The experience of one woman's committee provides an example. This committee received, apparently in recognition of its merits, the delicate assignment of providing security for the top leader of the "mass front," who at the same time was a well-known party leader. But in reality they were no more than ladies-in-waiting who, in disciplined shifts, were responsible, not only for minor political tasks but for attending to his domestic and personal needs.

But what most surprises about Shining Path is the manner in which senderista men and women confronted their adversaries by denigrat-ing women. Public campaigns frequently discredited antisenderista male leaders through flyers that recounted their wives' infidelities. To present the men as cuckolds was the best way to humiliate them and undermine their authority. The hostility was even greater toward female leaders considered adversaries, who were called prostitutes, women of ill repute, and lovers of male leaders. Sexual accusations and incidents of physical aggression ex-pressed a profound contempt for women. I obtained the testimony of one woman who for ideological differences left Shining Path and attempted to combat these positions from the outside. Her bravery resulted in a campaign to discredit her, in which she was accused of having contracted venereal diseases through prostitution. Even more unsettling is the fact that intelligent and strong Shining Path women participated in tactics of self-denigration. In one student confrontation in which Shining Path was defeated and lost control of a university residential dormitory, a group of Shining Path women, some of them married, sought to recast what had happened by waving their underwear in public and accusing their adversaries of raping them.

After armed actions began in 1980, the number of women in Shining Path steadily increased. There has been much speculation about the sex-ratio of senderista participants and even assertions that a majority of militants were female. Those of us who followed the process closely can affirm that while women's presence remained a minority one even at the high points of Shining Path expansion, it was still significant. Women achieved a visibility never before seen in any political party in Peruvian history. The women militants continued to come mainly from the cities, from upper, middling, and lower middling (*medios empobrecidos*) sectors. Some were daughters of migrant families establishing an urban life. An important wing of young urban women came from impoverished marginal neighborhoods and from the peasantry; these women were recruited through "popular schools" or were drafted by force. Shining Path's influence and links with poor women (*mujeres populares*) tended to pass through two channels: through affective engagement of female relatives of senderistas already involved in the armed insurgency, or through forcible recruitment to attend to the militants' survival needs.

There has also been speculation about the spaces gained by the women in Shining Path and the suggestion that from the perspective of gender Sendero was a relatively democratic and committed party. But this female presence did not produce substantial changes in gender relations. On the contrary, instrumental relations continued to reign between the party and its women. The party sought to benefit from women's capacities within a framework established by a patriarchal patron-leader. Initially, in the official documents of the early 1980s that we could obtain, and even as late as the so-called "interview of the century" (Guzmán 1988) that supposedly summed up Shining Path's project and strategies, we could not find a single reference to the problem of gender. By 1988, Shining Path leaders were certainly aware of the strength of feminine organizations and numbers in society, but there was still no place to discuss gender interests as such. In a private Shining Path event, Abimael Guzmán commented: "we must see that we sidestepped the popular feminine movement, women being the half that holds up the sky; to fight the enemy that is transitorily strong with one arm tied behind one's back is foolish. The struggle for the emancipation of the woman is part of the liberation of the proletariat—this is the Communist way of understanding the problem—from which derives equality before the law and equality in life."

Over the years, women did indeed broaden their spaces of participation in Shining Path. "Logistical" activities increased and remained fundamentally their responsibility, and women were also given the tasks of propaganda and popular aid. In addition, they participated in intelligence and military activities, commanded columns and operatives, and came to attain leadership positions in all areas of the organization. On the one hand, Sendero came upon hard times as the war progressed (see the essays in Part II of this book). Activities multiplied; opposition grew; and paths closed despite the images of senderista power and expansion. The combatant ranks, at first mainly male, suffered casualities; dismay and frustration spread. Sendero needed to fortify its resources and in this context came to value certain qualities of women—discipline, persistence, capacity for persuasion, efficiency, and, above all, loyalty and reliability. Shining Path leaders sought to make use of these qualities by encouraging ferocious competition and the most destructive feelings among the women to reach the condition of brave macha warriors.

On the other hand, rising to high positions did not necessarily imply gaining policy responsibilities or escaping party-based patriarchalism. Shining Path always had an authoritarian structure and steadily concentrated power and decisions in the person of Abimael Guzmán, the "fourth sword" of Marxism and "guiding thought" until his capture in 1992. To assure his own hegemony it was necessary to establish unconditional loyalty and operative efficiency as the fundamental criteria for accumulating merit. In such conditions, access to leadership positions did not imply influence over fundamental decisions of the party, but rather some limited prerogatives in making operative decisions. In the process leaders exposed themselves to high risks because of internal and external tensions. After the capture of Abimael Guzmán and the subsequent blows dealt to Shining Path, we learned the names of the new members of its central committee and the intermediary leadership and women proved important. Even at the moment of his capture, the "guiding thought" himself was practically surrounded by women, most of whom had high party posts. But these women were there as a result of their loyalty, reliability, dedication, and operational efficiency— the gap between their intellectual, ideological, and political qualifications, and those of the few women who had belonged to the previous central committee was all too evident. Without underestimating the capacities, political will, and mystique of these women, it is clear that they were also responsible for the care and attention of the personal and survival needs of the patriarch.

In sum, although Shining Path received a flood of women in search of new spaces of participation, and while these women achieved an important presence at all levels within Shining Path, Sendero was not capable of programmatically incorporating their gender interests. Shining Path established an instrumental relationship with its female members that reproduced patriarchal relations to benefit the party.

Women in Ayacucho

Shining Path began its phase of organizing and preparing for armed warfare in the late 1970s. Sendero prioritized its relationship with peasant communities in the four provinces of northern Ayacucho (Vilcashuamán, Huamanga, Huanta, La Mar) and with the poor in the larger towns, especially the departmental capital. In the interior of these communities, Shining Path initially privileged relationships with teachers who had already been recruited and indoctrinated in university classrooms and in the senderista-controlled teachers' union. Teachers' prestige in popular and rural communities made them ideal bridges for reaching the population. (On the prestige of knowledge and intellectuals, see the essays by de la Cadena and Degregori in this volume.) In these spaces, the teachers, along with youth and Shining Path leaders, organized "popular schools." In this period, Shining Path related to the population through a discourse of change, of a new society without poor or rich people, and with a new state. They argued that a people's war was the only way to obtain these changes, and they sought to internalize this discourse in the consciousness of the population through the popular schools.

For a population that had already had organizational experiences with political parties of the Left, this discourse was familiar (see the essays by Hinojosa and Mallon in this volume). In addition, the years of reforms under Velasco had increased the people's hopes for change—modernity and progress with social justice. As the schools developed, Shining Path remained a more or less marginal presence in the communities—an affair of youths and party leaders that the population observed with a certain tolerance. On their own initiative and attracted by the novelty of senderista activities, which consisted basically of indoctrination and military "practice," some female adolescents attended the schools. They first had to pass a special process of selection to overcome the cadres' distrust. Testimonies collected from women who are now adults mention posts and responsibilities (secondary ones, of course) that they were assigned, and pseudonyms that they now recall with astonishment.

Beginning with these contacts, in some communities Shining Path moved on to build a structure of popular committees that could become a vehicle of control. Through this new structure the party could vertically assign new community posts to new representatives, and thereby reproduce *patrón*-serf relationships between the party and the community. (For more information on popular committees and the senderista structure of community power, see the essay by del Pino in this volume.) In the communities in which Sendero developed an important presence and influence, adult women were also indirectly involved, induced by their children to provide food and housing for senderistas and to carry messages. Subsequently, they would be involved in providing foodstuffs as a community contribution on a more periodic basis, by orders of senderista commandants. Already in this stage women experienced a certain discontent because of the burdens this relationship placed on their precarious household economies. The women recall, as well, that they were not well informed. They observed the activities of youth and party leaders and were kept at a distance from all decision making. They were simply informed of decisions already made and of the tasks that they were to complete.

Shining Path initiated its armed offensive in Ayacucho and its transition from talk to action involved the population in acts of sabotage, confrontations with special police forces, and a thorough unhinging of communal life and expectation. This situation generated confusion in the communities involved. The arrival of the Armed Forces in 1983, which unleashed a "dirty war" marked by indiscriminate repression, revealed the limits of Sendero's project and opened a breach between the senderista project and the population's aspirations. Shining Path tried to resolve this situation by accentuating its authoritarianism and recurring to pressure, threat, and extortion.

The population found itself virtually trapped between two fires: the military's offensive, principally against youth and leaders labeled terrorists, and Shining Path's efforts at forced recruitment, which targeted the same groups. In the face of the pressure from both sides, resistance developed along two lines: migration to cities or other pueblos, and armed confrontation through organizing autodefense patrols (rondas). Bit by bit, these actions produced three new social actors: the refugees (*desplazados*), a kind of "emissary" group from regions under siege who made denunciations and raised awareness; the ronderos, who carried out specific functions of community defense; and women, responsible for ensuring individual and collective survival. The defense of life reordered the roles of women. The war called into question masculine protagonism, because men were the principal target of both sides in the war and women would be the ones who had to confront the new situation.

One of the first actions undertaken by a woman was to organize her family's dispersal. A woman would stash her husband and the adolescent children at greatest risk from both sides in zones of refuge as far away as possible—Lima or Huancayo, if possible, or the city of Ayacucho. She would try to relocate her middle children in homes of relatives, co-godparents (*compadres*), or other friends in more secure communities in the countryside or in the city. She would leave family elders at home in order not to lose her family's stake in the community. (The elders presumably faced lesser risk and in any event were more reluctant to abandon the community.) Such women, carrying their smallest children with them, would then become itinerant wanderers—moving back and forth between these different spaces to look after the well-being of their relatives and to coordinate economic and family activities. This process of dispersal and subsequent coordination was repeated as safety conditions changed in the zones of refuge. The life histories collected suggest that many families experienced four successive displacements during the war.

During the "dirty war" of 1983–1984, massive violence—principally by the military in this period—targeted mainly men, because women were devalued as "useless" or "harmless." Nonetheless, women, because they were the most stable element in the communities, and because they confronted the situation, ended up becoming targets as well. They were victims of physical abuse and psychological torture, they were obligated to witness alongside their children the executions of loved ones, and they were raped. These repressive activities had the purpose of intimidating the population and, presumably, gathering information. Profoundly affected and sensitized, the women became the principal protagonists in the defense of human rights. They were spurred not only by the painful process of burying the dead, seeking the disappeared, and trying to free prisoners, but also by the desire to preserve the physical integrity and lives of those who remained with the women.

Women from these battered and violated sectors, with no more resources than their will and creativity, burst onto the public stage to assume the giant task of defending human rights. Their work was not easy, because they did not know what rights they had or what mechanisms existed for exercising such rights. They had to discover all of this through the life experience of confronting a previously unknown world. The first seeds of women's organizations were semiclandestine groups of relatives of victims, which formed spontaneously to provide moral support and share information about mechanisms and procedures in pressing their demands. Through these networks of solidarity, these Ayacuchan women began to define and assume their responsibilities. They organized searches for the disappeared, dividing up their forces geographically and exchanging information that might identify family members. They coordinated information on the dead, the disappeared, and the detained; on using legal mechanisms; and on access to national and international organisms of pressure and assistance on human rights. They organized pressure on military and police posts for the release of the detained, and they learned how to project themselves in the media. They developed individual and collective tactics to protect themselves from danger.

At the same time, the ferocity of the war and the profundity of the economic crisis fomented a veritable crisis of the family space. Absences of men from families were massive and growing, whether permanent absences as a result of death, disappearance, or abandonment, or prolonged absences as a result of migration for security or economic reasons, or temporary absences as a result of participation in self-defense rondas. Women had to fill the void by assuming the role of formal or real household head. While this situation implied burdens of work and responsibility, it also implied greater protagonism. Three large consequences resulted from the expansion of women's protagonism and responsibilities. First, the necessity for family planning began to surface. In the countryside as well as in the city, demand for information and practices of abortion, contraception, and sexual abstinence increased. Second, as women assumed greater responsibility for leading and preserving their families in a highly destructive context, they socialized the responsibility. They simplified domestic activities and distributed them to other members of the family and to neighbors, with whom women shared responsibility for tasks such as preparation of meals and provision of childcare. Third, since these individual adaptations were insufficient to sustain families, women, on their own initiative and as a result of external influences and resources (for example, advising and resources provided by NGOs), developed collective projects to generate alternative sources of income. They implemented food services, workshops to produce commodities, and communal gardens.

The profound imbalance between income and consumption needs, far more severe than the gap that preceded the 1980s, brought about the massive incorporation of women into productive activities that generated family income. In the countryside, whether as a result of the absence of the male head or of family dispersal and migration, women took over much or all of family productive activity. In poor urban sectors, three-fourths (77 percent) of those surveyed carried out paid economic activities, and two-fifths (42 percent) of the families lived either exclusively or principally from incomes generated by women. (The percentages are based on our survey of 300 women in 1992).

Over time, confronting the enormous tasks of defending human rights and organizing family survival impelled women to form more stable organizations, especially mothers' clubs. These organizations facilitated negotiating for resources and jobs before offices of the state and developing links of collaboration and support with organizations such as NGOs and human rights groups. Acquiring knowledge about state assistance programs proved very important. Many women had offered their labor or that of their children for domestic tasks in urban middle-class families in exchange for food and housing and had thus reproduced a world of servile relationships. Frequently, when women recalled this stage of their lives, they broke out in sobs; they remembered being objects of humiliation and even physical mistreatment as a result of their inexperience, illiteracy, and condition as *indias*. In the rural communities as well, organizing as social actors in public spaces proved important. An important step in the conquest of this space was legitimation as full members in communal organization and assembly. At an individual level, many women took on the role of representing their families and thereby acquiring the right to voice opinions and take part in decision making. On a collective level, this legitimation took place as a result of dynamism and representativeness of the women's local organizations (the mothers' clubs).

Within this context, women increased their engagement with communal endeavors and leadership. They participated with great dedication in communal services and work parties, and in some zones at moments of great danger they also participated in autodefense tasks and assumed responsibility for controlling and protecting the community while the men left for areas of confrontation. The sharing of communal labor and responsibility facilitated women's access to debate and decision making. Their opinions came to matter in communal decisions. These advances were manifest in the increasing frequency with which female leaders were assigned communal posts of representation and even governance.

From about 1986 on, the efforts of the rural population, organized in autodefense *rondas* supported by the military, began to isolate Shining Path in the countryside. Sendero reacted to these adverse conditions by opening new fronts and expanding toward the central sierra, especially Junín, without abandoning the Ayacucho region (see Manrique's essay in this volume). Shining Path also responded to difficulty by exemplary punishments— surprise attacks on communities that showed the greatest capacity for resistance. As a result, some 300 communities in the region were razed or abandoned, mostly at the hands of Sendero. In this period, Sendero's reprisals constituted acts of genocide, incursions that usually resulted in a massacre of dozens of people, principally women, children, and the elderly. Such attacks could occur repeatedly, up to seven times in some cases, and condemned the whole population to a situation of permanent anxiety, with extremely grave ramifications for the mental health of the inhabitants.

In this context of terrifying reprisal, expanding and strengthening the mother's clubs was especially important to preserve and encourage the capacity for action. Women's organizations had first appeared in Ayacucho in the 1960s, as a result of initiatives by the state and especially the university, but their expansion was limited mainly to the small urban poor population. By the end of the 1970s there were only sixty mothers' clubs in the whole department. Nonetheless, during the war years women accumulated tremendous organizational experience and a tremendous necessity for taking initiative. Mothers' clubs multiplied throughout the Department of Ayacucho. The expansion made evident, however, the need to transcend disconnected actions at the local level of clubs and their communities. Thus there developed a process of linking and coordinating the women's organizations and in 1988 women founded the Federation of Mothers' Clubs of the Province of Huamanga (Federación Provincial de Clubes de Madres de Huamanga). The inaugural event included 270 mothers' clubs as well as delegates invited from other provinces. (Huamanga province includes the city of Ayacucho, known in colonial times as Huamanga, which is the capital of the Department of Ayacucho). One important aspect of this event was the presence of male communal leaders who served as advisors to their respective mothers' clubs, on the grounds that the women would not know how to organize and press their demands. The women themselves had asked for the men to be present.

This experience of expansion and coordination was reproduced almost spontaneously in eight other war-torn provinces in Ayacucho, each of which constituted its own federation. The expansion provided a foundation for organizing the First Departmental Congress of Mothers' Clubs, attended by representatives of 1200 mothers' clubs in November 1991. At the beginning of the Congress, the organizing committee consulted the delegates about the necessity of having male advisors present and the Congress agreed that the men should withdraw in order to permit the women delegates to participate autonomously.

In this manner, even as other social and political organizations came apart or were reduced to minimum expression, the women's movement advanced against the current of the war and created the most representative and largest organization in the department. By 1995, the Departmental Federation of Mothers' Clubs of Ayacucho (Federación Departmental de Clubes de Madres de Ayacucho; FEDECMA) had come to include eleven provincial federations, 1400 mothers' clubs, and approximately 80,000 affiliated women, both urban and rural. FEDECMA organized around two key concerns: the defense of human rights and the struggle for economic survival. It carried out these tasks with relative success, given the difficult circumstances confronting the region. FEDECMA organized an extensive network of female leaders that covered the whole department, provided information, and transmitted alternatives and responses back to its bases. It forged access to programs and resources of the state and other institutions (NGOs) in the areas of food, health, and education. It promoted food services, such as community kitchens and daily glass-of-milk programs, and workshops for generating income. FEDECMA served, as well, as a space for accumulating experiences and sharing strategies and mechanisms for defending human rights.

Shining Path initially tolerated the women's organizations, especially when the mothers' clubs were relatively isolated and dispersed. At bottom, Sendero devalued the significance of the clubs. But once the women organized the provincial federation for Huamanga in 1988, Shining Path sought to block the process by intimidating the recently elected directorate, espe-cially the president, who suffered a physical assault and death threat. The incident sparked the resignation of five leaders, who were replaced the fol-lowing week. Subsequently, Shining Path tried to infiltrate the organization on at least two occasions, but the efforts were rapidly detected and the sen-deristas expelled from the organization. Sendero then changed its strategy. Senderistas kept a close watch on the federation's activities and on several occasions insisted on dialogues that turned out to be efforts to give orders to the federation. The women managed these situations skillfully. The reality was that once the women consolidated their organization, Shining Path could not find a way to control it.

One of the first actions undertaken by the mothers' clubs federations was to collaborate in organizing a nation-wide march for peace in August 1988. The mobilization of many institutions and social and political organizations, with the support of local government, marked a milestone in the history of the war. It provided a forum for public demands that Shining Path answer for the consequences of the war, a forum from which Shining Path isolated itself. At least half the persons in attendance in Ayacucho were women, and they carried various placards with slogans in Quechua: "those who kill should die," "because we give life we defend it," and "the fear is gone." Shin-ing Path attempted to break up the mobilization by exploding petards of dynamite in the area but failed to disperse the concentration. Then senderis-tas tried to take over the gathering by seizing control of the microphones. I have never seen such strength, decision, and fury as when those women leaders went up to the dais and screamed and hit the intruders until they had to recede. The women managed to throw the senderistas out.

With their organizations as a foundation, women also designed alterna-tive strategies for two central problems that emerged from the war. First, the community self-defense rondas in many instances involved several males from the same family and removed them from productive and income-generating activities. The women proposed that each family contribute one person to the autodefense committees and that any family member, accord-ing to the family's necessities, be allowed to assume this burden. In this way, many men would be able to return to agro-pastoral activities. They also proposed that the functions of autodefense should be limited to inter-nal community space and that the military assume other tasks. With these proposals, the women initiated a process of redefinition of roles and respon-sibilities between the rondas and the army. Second, once the displaced com-

WOMEN IN THE POLITICS OF
WAR AND PEACE.
(right) Shining Path women
project strength in Canto
Grande prison, 1991.
(below) A Mothers' Club delegation joins an International
Women's Day march in
Ayacucho.
(bottom) Provincial delegates
at a training workshop of the
Departmental Mothers' Club
Federation of Ayacucho.

munities began to return to their sites in the early 1990s, women impelled an important debate about how to organize best the process of return. Male leaders wanted the families to return all at once so that, once located in their communities of origin, they could pressure the state for the help that they needed with greater force. The women opposed this strategy as too dangerous for their families and particularly for their children since the community zones were still not entirely pacified. They envisioned the return as a process. A series of campaigns in the refuge zones would be launched to rebuild houses, to reinitiate agricultural activities, and to organize the community and its autodefense. The transferral of the family would come last, once these minimal conditions for survival had been created. Various communities attempted to implement the strategy proposed by the male leadership but many of these attempts proved short-lived and communities switched to the process proposed by the women. The women had been more realistic.

On the basis of these experiences and their organizational force, women in Ayacucho obtained legitimacy, a recognition from the authorities and regional public opinion as social actors. They had built up the most solid and representative organization of the region during the war years. As of 1995, there was no official act—political, social, or academic—in which the Mothers' Federation did not participate or attend as a special guest.

Women in Lima

During most of the 1980s, life in the popular sectors of metropolitan Lima was marked by the coexistence of two conflicting projects: the armed project of Sendero, and a project of mobilization based on the historical trajectories of urban popular movements and the electoral Left. Shining Path organized secretly over much of the period in the midst of the tremendous disorder generated by the economic crisis. Whether out of sympathy, affinity, or underestimation, people tolerated Shining Path's presence during these long hard years. In general, the effects of the war were indirect—a sharpening of an economic crisis that reached alarming dimensions—or at least less extreme than the drama in the sierra—electric blackouts rather than mass assassinations. In addition, the information and imagery of senderista effectiveness transmitted by the mass media encouraged a certain senderista mystique—expectations and even sympathy among significant sectors of the politicized population.

From the beginning Shining Path meant to insert itself in Lima. Its strategic scheme envisioned Lima as the site of the final insurrection of the people's war (Guzmán 1988: 35). Nonetheless, a series of setbacks in the sierra provinces of the country pushed Sendero to intensify its urban actions and accelerate its schedule. Shining Path gave priority to Lima's urban poor (*sectores urbanos marginales*). "Since 1986 we have the directrix for the work in the cities. To take neighborhoods and shantytowns as bases and the proletariat as leaders is our mandate" (Guzmán 1988: 35). Shining Path chose the so-called "eastern cone" of Lima as its center of operations because of the area's strategic importance as a popular-industrial zone. The "southern cone," particularly Villa El Salvador, became a key objective as well, since Sendero wanted to destroy an experience of autonomous communal governance and development (*autogestión*), linked to the non-Senderista Left, that had become a symbolic example (see the essay by Burt in this volume).

Shining Path also prioritized certain sectors of the population. Organized workers and poor urban neighborhoods constituted a first priority, followed by university students and state employees' associations, principally the teachers' union, which Sendero intended to use for indoctrination and propaganda.

The preparatory phase for Sendero had two differentiated moments: physical insertion, and organization to launch an offensive. The years 1984 to 1986 marked the period of insertion, when Shining Path sought to situate its cadres in the priority zones to accumulate information through its mere presence as well as a tracking of human activities. Only occasionally did Shining Path appear explicitly on the local scene, spreading flyers on dates commemorated by Shining Path. Although it might seem incredible for Shining Path not to have perceived the dynamism of poor women's organizing in this period, one must recall that in the shantytown communities there had developed two significant spaces of popular mobilization. One was the neighborhood movement, now in crisis and protagonized predominantly by men, and the other was the movement of "functional organizations," led by women. For Shining Path, the functional organizations, oriented to daily survival struggles, was a less important space. [*Editor's note:* The "neighborhood movement" refers to community organizing to gain land title, urban social services such as electricity, potable water, and sewage, and legal recognition of identity and governing structures for "young" shantytown and working class communities that had sprung up in metropolitan Lima through direct actions including land squatting and invasion since the 1940s and 1950s. The "functional organizations" refer to grassroots groups that attended to specific survival functions, such as distribution of milk, preparation of food in communal soup kitchens, or implementation of primary health campaigns.]

Not until 1987–1989 (years that would coincide with the political disintegration of Alan García's presidency, and with the emergence of a devastating hyperinflation in Lima) did Shining Path initiate preparation for its Lima offensive. Shining Path started organizing more openly; its presence could now be detected with more clarity, at least on the local scene. Sendero worked to coopt prominent leaders, and through them to infiltrate and control the neighborhood movement. Shining Path also sought to agitate and mobilize the population by appropriating inhabitants' just demands and to make a psychological impact through periodic parades of Shining Path columns. It is important to note that the effort to coopt leaders was directed at the male leaders of the neighborhood movement. Shining Path was at this stage concerned with female leaders insofar as they represented the "neighborhood" rather than the "functional" organizations.

Parallel to these developments, poor women forged their role as new social actors and constructed an alternative project to respond to the economic crisis. (They also tended to underestimate the presence and work of Sendero.) In the 1980s, the economic crisis had the effect of deepening and generalizing already existing social problems. In those circumstances, not only the problems of physical space (land sites, housing, etc.) and infrastructural development (access to water, electricity, transport) had to be addressed collectively. In addition, the problems of unemployment and personal survival also transcended the family sphere and demanded prompt and effective solutions. Extensive sectors of the population became involved in the search for solutions. This was especially true for women, who demonstrated a great capacity to resist adversity, to forge ties of solidarity, and to raise up organizations that could establish strategies of collective survival. Without a doubt, the fundamental demand was for jobs. Faced with a shrinking formal labor market, massive layoffs, and deteriorating working conditions, people tended to develop informal economic activities to attend to their basic needs. In the face of this problem, women gained valuable experience in self-employment and income-generation. They set up workshops and microenterprises, mainly with their own labor and resources, and in some cases with the support from the state or NGOs.

The other great problem was the deterioration in health and nutrition that resulted from the widening gap between income and consumption. It was the women of the popular sectors who took on the titanic task of constructing survival alternatives in the areas of nutrition and health. Through at least 5,000 communal kitchens (*comedores populares*) they came to produce 570,000 rations of daily meals and through the glass-of-milk program they came to attend 1,200,000 people daily, most of them children. By the mid-1990s, these organizations benefitted approximately 17 percent of all Lima families (Blondet and Montero 1995). Basically, the women coordinated and improved the scope and quality of the assistance available from the state and from NGOs. In addition, the rise of women's associations to run the comedores, and women's health committees and glass-of-milk committees served to constitute extensive networks on local, district, and metropolitan levels. The strength of these networks and organizations converted women into the protagonists of the most important social movement in Lima in the 1980s and early 1990s.

This experience introduced into urban social and economic processes a new proposal for integral and autonomously generated development. Until the 1970s the predominant focus of development strategies in the urban marginal sectors was infrastructural improvement. The neighborhood organizations were organized around demands for access to space (through gaining titles to land), and access to basic services such as electricity, water, sewage, and transportation, among others. Toward the 1980s, as the social problems deepened and became more complex, this development model came into crisis. The women's movement introduced a new concept of sustained integral development that transcended the earlier focus on infrastructure. This new vision incorporated the notion of *autogestión* (self-development), which assigned a more active role to organizations in development planning at a local, zonal, or district level. Autogestión also implied negotiation and formalization of accords with the state and with some private sector agents based on proposals derived from discussions by all the diverse actors involved in the problem. Access to various levels of decision making was thus an important aspect of this perspective. This renovation movement bred the idea of a new relationship between state and society, a relationship that would commit the state to a development project conceived, planned, and directed from within civil society. This relationship was to be mediated by local and regional agents of government branches and over time would yield the modernization and transformation of the state, which would become more responsive to the needs of society.

This valuable contribution and experience of women was supported by NGOS, mainly feminist in orientation, and political parties, mainly on the Left. But although these alliances were important in consolidating the movement, they also caused problems. On the one hand, the inward-looking tendencies of the women's movement, along with tendencies by traditional leaders to underestimate women, created tensions and misunderstandings with the neighborhood movement that retarded the consolidation of the project. On the other hand, given the quantitative and qualitative importance of the women's movement, political parties sought to establish an instrumentalist relationship and initiated a process of cooption and party-oriented politicization of important leaders. The cooption campaign diverted some from the immediate interests and strategies of their own movement and damaged unity, as sectarian divisions emerged from the leaders' party affiliations. The worst tension emerged between the autonomously organized comedores, ostensibly aligned with the Left, and the mothers' clubs, ostensibly affiliated with APRA.

Fujimori's presidential administration began in 1990 with an economic readjustment measure that became known as *Fujishok*. Gasoline prices multiplied by thirty and the cost of living rose by some 400 percent in August. Survival strategies that women in poor urban neighborhoods had developed during the 1980s quickly fell apart. This situation coincided with Sendero's Lima offensive from 1989 to 1992, when Sendero appeared openly to dispute spaces with rival political forces. The chaos and confusion generated by Fujimori's economic measures favored Shining Path's efforts to channel popular discontent and mobilization for its own ends.

The Fujimori administration, in the face of evidence of the severe consequences of the austerity measure, proposed creating the Social Emergency Program (Programa de Emergencia Social; PES) and convoked civil society (including the functional organizations, the Church, and the NGOS) to participate in implementing the program through the creation of a central coordinating committee and local emergency committees. This proposal sparked an important debate at the grassroots level. The traditional sectors of the neighborhood movement, encouraged by Shining Path, opposed participation in the PES and proposed instead to create district "struggle committees" (*comités de lucha*) that would begin a process of mobilization and confrontation with the state. The women, on the other hand, proposed to participate in implementing the program, but to do so in a way that transcended its limitations. They proposed creating emergency and development managing committees with greater prerogatives and functions than those assigned formally by the state. They sustained that confrontation would be fruitless; it would require large amounts of time, would pose security risks, and above all would fail to deliver solutions to their demands.

The results of the debate favored the women's proposal. In the zone of greatest senderista influence four committees for the emergency and development were established, and only one struggle committee. A similar tendency marked the organizing process in most of Lima's districts. From then on, the women participated intensively in implementing the PES, which served to fortify their organizational strength and to reactivate their survival strategies—communal kitchens, glass-of-milk programs, "communal pots" (ollas comunes), and income-generating workshops, all of which had been paralyzed by "Fujishok." Toward the end of 1990, in a meeting of grassroots leaders in Lima's "Eastern Cone" (the center of senderista activity in Lima), the leaders discussed and overcame the tensions that had developed between "neighborhood" and "functional" organizations, and committed themselves to designing a project inspired by the vision of the women's functional organizations.

Sendero Luminoso, faced with this situation at a time of preparation for a final offensive in Lima, realized that underestimating the women was a repetition of the same error committed in Ayacucho. Sendero adjusted its strategy accordingly and began to dispute the space claimed by the women's organizations. In the beginning, Shining Path attributed the women's attitude to external agents. The NGOs and the churches were "filtration channels" for an imperialist ideology that had "gnawed away" the minds and wills of the leaders, who in turn induced the "masses" to follow "mistaken paths" (quotes synthesize various senderista discourses). It did not take long to mount a campaign to discredit the leaders of the women's movement as "sell-outs" and "thieves" who trafficked with the interests of women and their families. Shining Path assumed a posture as savior and "moralizer," situated itself between the leaders and the bases, and carefully distinguished among women leaders, dividing them into enemies, salvageables, and allies. For the "enemies," Sendero launched a campaign of death threats and executions. For the "salvageables" Sendero applied a mix of blackmail, pressure, and persuasion that would involve the leaders in tasks for the Shining Path project. Finally, Shining Path manipulated the "allies," most of them popular base leaders whose inexperience and fear left them very vulnerable.

As a result of this offensive, Shining Path achieved certain advances. It took over some of the popular dining rooms located in its priority zones and took advantage of these services to supply itself with foodstuffs. It co-opted some leaders, infiltrated some organizations, and sharpened tensions between "leaders" and "base." (For a more detailed analysis of this process, for the crucial case of Villa El Salvador, see Burt's essay in this volume.)

Nonetheless, these advances also provoked resistance. The most important case was the response of women in Villa El Salvador who, led by María Elena Moyano, convoked popular mobilizations for peace on at least three occasions at the local level. In 1991, the women transcended the local space by calling for a metropolitan-wide march of women's organizations in a central plaza of the capital. Even more important, they convened diverse institutions and social organizations for a march in San Juan de Lurigancho, a zone practically controlled by Shining Path. In organizing these events, tension surfaced in relation to the "struggle" oriented program. While for the political parties and some of the institutions that accompanied the process, the central problem was one of political economy and economic crisis, for the popular sectors and the women's movement, *the war itself* had become the principal problem.

Unfortunately, the formulations of the women did not find the opportune echo or support they needed and the women leaders ended up politically isolated. Despite the ferocity of the Shining Path offensive, and perhaps precisely for this reason, the disjuncture between the political struggle program and the antiwar program was not resolved. Although a consensus had been reached in condemning violence, the problem that remained was whether to define the government or Shining Path as the principal enemy.

In early 1992, the women's heroic resistance began to decline and Sendero's political offensive reached its highest point. Shining Path's assassination of María Elena Moyano in February marked the breaking point of the women's resistance, not only because she was the most outstanding leader of the movement but also because of the nature of the killing itself. Undoubtedly, shooting María Elena down and blowing up her body in the presence of her children and *compañeras* in struggle, in the midst of a public event, was an application of the "exemplary punishment" strategy. Aside from eliminating the most important leader of the women's movement, Sendero sought a psychological impact, especially on the female population. Institutions withdrew from the scene as a result of Shining Path threats, and the political parties pressured women leaders to retreat.

The women leaders, in a confusion of feelings marked by fear and indignation, wanted to continue in their work. But under pressure from their husbands and relatives, they began to retreat. The organizations were reduced to a minimum profile and expression even as they continued to provide services. Even under these low profile conditions, however, the return to the "shell" allowed for an evaluation of what had happened and for adoption of some security measures, basically making sure they knew "who was who" among their own ranks. After the burial of María Elena Moyano, some efforts were made to mount responses such as peace marches and similar actions in the various sections of Lima, but the reality was harsh. Operational capacity was lacking. Shining Path intensified the terror and the threats forced popular leaders, mainly women, to take cover. Toward the end of March 1992, Sendero seemed to have taken control of the urban marginal sectors of greater Lima.

The Post-War: Women in the Work of Reconstruction and Development

The capture of Abimael Guzmán in September 1992 inaugurated a new period characterized by a decline in the intensity of political violence, a transition from tasks of emergency to tasks of reconstruction and development, and efforts to recover spaces that had been lost. Shining Path's new situation was irreversible. (For greater detail on the disintegration of Sendero's strength and cohesion, see the introduction to Part V of this book.) At certain moments Sendero achieved a relative recomposition but it would no longer be the country's principal problem. Nonetheless, Shining Path's local presence in regions such as Ayacucho and the Amazon continued to pose dangerous situations for sectors of the population.

After the defeat of Sendero, the principal problem would be the task of overcoming the cumulative effect of emergency situations experienced for more than a decade—the task of reconstruction—and the task of establishing a foundation for future economic development. The population initiated a process of reactivating organizations, an effort to normalize economic, social, and cultural activities and to recover lost spaces. With a winning spirit, initiative, and creativity, the affected population set about forging proposals of reconstruction and local and regional development. The broad popular support given to Fujimori in the elections of April 1995 expressed the population's recognition of the political will Fujimori had demonstrated to end the war, but it also included an expectation that economic problems would be resolved and that support would be provided for reconstruction and development in the zones devastated by the war.

In this context, women proposed to legitimate their presence and the spaces they had won by participating as a "social subject" in local and regional tasks of reconstruction and development. This effort occurred amid the tensions produced by a process of "normalization" that also implied the reconstitution of more traditional actors and protagonists. While risks of women's return to invisibility were present, as we shall see, women's achievements proved fundamentally irreversible. Nonetheless, a regional contrast is worth noting. The women's movement of Lima, which had had the most experience and the highest degree of politicization, suffered the greatest difficulties in sustaining its protagonistic role. On the other hand, the women of the Ayacucho movement, not without difficulties, showed greater capacity for initiative and organizing in an ascendant process.

To explain this contrast is difficult, but the difference undoubtedly had to do in part with the war's impact in each area. Activist women in Lima, as a result of their own experience and qualifications, proposed solutions that had a more political character, and needed to do so precisely in the conjuncture in which Shining Path was playing its last card. Sendero would be disposed to achieve its objectives at any cost. In addition, the women in Lima confronted difficulties of party-oriented sectarianism, and subsequently a certain abstentionism that ended up isolating the women even in their own urban barriadas. In the case of Ayacucho, women without prior political experience had had to work in a space already under siege by senderismo and adopted a strategy of working with the human dimension of the problem, thereby avoiding direct confrontation with Shining Path. Only when Shining Path was more isolated and the women had acquired more experience and force did they respond in more explicitly political ways. This response was possible in part because, although abstentionism by national-level institutions afflicted Ayacucho, the women managed to achieve joint action with actors on the local scene.

By the mid-1990s, the general tendency among women's organizations was reactivation. While in Lima the movement was rebuilding from the bottom up, in an effort to recuperate its earlier strength, in Ayacucho the women's organizations survived and grew, in a climate of greater optimism. In both cases, these processes were not free of difficulties, including problems of bureaucratization and internal conflicts, principally at the leadership level. In Ayacucho there was a certain exhaustion of the leaders and an exacerbated sensitivity by women in situations of conflict; these were symptoms of the war's impact on energy and mental health. In Lima, bureaucratization, linked to personal interests and to the weight of state and private institutions, generated tensions among leaders. Notwithstanding these problems and a consciousness that the tasks of reconstruction would demand consensual interaction with other actors, the women's movement continued to be an important space for affective support, politicosocial expression, and learning for women.

In Ayacucho, by 1994–1995, the three collective actors that had shown the greatest capacity for resistance and response during the war years — the displaced refugees, the ronderos, and the women's organizations — developed their own proposal for reconstruction and development on the local and regional levels. Let us consider the central features of this proposal.

1 The proposal involved the entire population of the devastated areas, on the grounds that the war victims included not only those who fled but also those who remained in their communities and resisted.

2 The proposal integrated demands related to the emergency and to development over both the short and medium term, in order to address structural problems as well as the effects of war.

3 The conception of development transcended communal frameworks on the assumption that the objectives could not be achieved separately as communities. Intercommunal relationships, in spaces linked by historical, economic, or cultural ties, would be needed.

4 The experience of war demanded thinking of a new country-city relationship capable of transcending a dividing line between city and country that had implied backwardness and impoverishment. The idea was to have urban benefits nourish the countryside via fluid economic, social, political, and cultural relations between the country and the city. The new context would foster a maintenance of connections to the urban zones of refuge.

5 As a result of the war experience, the proposal looked for the emergence of new models of community that, while drawing on "traditional" content might also incorporate advances in science, technology, and other knowledge learned during the period of exile. There would thereby arise "intermediate communities" between city and countryside, whose level of development would put a brake on migration and encourage displaced refugees and economic migrants to return.

6 The proposal required a new social subject, with the necessary qualifications for planning, leading, and carrying out the process. It

advocated constituting Committees of Reconstruction and Local Development (CORDEL), which with the support of local governments would convoke the participation of all of the relevant actors, including representatives of the communities, autodefense committees, producers, the women's movement, and local branches of the state.

The women of Ayacucho, conscious of the breadth of the project, perceived a need to specify their own role within the process. So they defined a program of work that established some priorities.

1 The first priority was to reaffirm their participation in production and in generating employment and income for women and their young children. Their arguments expressed fear that with "normalcy" men would re-establish an advantage in access to the labor market.

2 They also proposed to defend and develop the population's nutrition and health. The women were conscious of the deterioration suffered during the war, and feared the consequences for their children. They sustained that the state's assistance programs would not solve the problem and that the theme would have to be included in an integrated development planning process that would include everyone in the building of an effective and sustainable response.

3 A priority concern would be to attend to women migrants displaced by the political violence, whether they were returning to their communities or remaining in zones of refuge. The women's organizations faulted themselves not having addressed this problem sooner, given that 40 percent of their members had been displaced. The words of one leader are very expressive: "so long have we lived taking care of others that we have not been able to see each other."

4 The rehabilitation of the mental health of children victimized by political violence, and the subsequent development of the children constituted a profound concern. The women worried that their children could not grow into normal adults and pressed the urgency of dealing with this situation to rescue the future of their families and communities.

The women also discussed the practical conditions required to implement the proposal. They noted various needs: the need to coordinate the women's organizations on local, regional, and national levels; the need to learn Spanish (the majority of the women were Quechua speakers whose experience taught them that they would be more effective if bilingual); and the need for family planning, partly because the women had become profoundly sensitized to the suffering of their children during the difficult years, but also to relieve their domestic burdens.

The implementation of proposals such as these was still in a very initial stage in 1995 and 1996. In the case of Lima, women participated in very localized experiences, on the initiative of local networks, and with the difficulty posed by an almost total absence of support from the state. In Ayacucho the rhythm of work and achievement was faster, perhaps in part because Ayacucho was a symbolic priority region for NGOs and the state. Even so advances have been tentative.

What has been evident in the post-war stage is the determination of women to participate actively as relevant social actors in the process of reconstruction and development, in dialogue with other actors. In this process of participation the women demonstrated a new consciousness of the importance of gaining access to the decision-making levels of state and society. This stance was evident in their important efforts to reach agreements with representatives of the state—ranging from local offices to the government ministries—around concrete proposals dealing with poverty and with women. Although there emerged an important opening and initiatives by the state and the administration on the themes of gender and women, it did not prove easy to institutionalize the participation of women's organizations.

Prospects and Conclusion

Unfortunately, the conditions confronting the country in the mid-1990s were not very encouraging. The war had had highly destructive effects on varied spheres of national life. The hopes for a resolution of grave economic problems after the reelection of Fujimori in April 1995 proved illusory for the poverty-stricken majority, and surveys in 1996 demonstrated increasing discontent. [*Editor's Note:* It was in this context of great politicosocial discontent, expressed in high disapproval ratings of Fujimori in public opinion surveys, that a crisis erupted when an MRTA group seized hostages in the Japanese Embassy in Lima in December 1996. The spectacular resolution of the crisis, in a military operation that freed with life all but one of the remaining hostages late in April 1997, returned Fujimori to high approval ratings in the following weeks. But discontent proved stubborn. By June, controversies about political abuse and authoritarianism, along with continuing massive indigence, had once more yielded high disapproval ratings.]

Although popular mobilization and participation in formulating and carrying out creative proposals for regional reconstruction and development were evident in the mid-1990s, substantive economic changes in economic policy were not likely to occur in the near future. Even though compensatory social programs may expand, they will not be sufficient to meet the demands placed upon them. Without the political will to designate resources sufficient to attend to emergency and development needs, especially in the zones devastated by the war, the proposals that have been made will probably be blocked. Such an outcome would risk losing a historical opportunity to revitalize Ayacucho, the most backward and devastated region of the country, and to prevent future situations of political violence.

Even in such a harsh scenario, however, one could observe positive dynamics and legacies. In spite of difficulties and the destructive effects of war, women in Peru managed to reshape their roles and their social visibility. They achieved a transition from "traditional" roles that situated them as "invisible," toward explicit and visible affirmation as protagonistic social actors. In this valuable experience shaped by women there emerged important changes in gender relations. Women drew themselves toward spaces of political power and decision making to press their needs and perspectives, they relocated themselves in spaces of productive economic activity and work, they partially restructured familial relationships of authority and self-esteem. In this sense, the processes of "awakening" and actuation have proved fundamentally irreversible. Something was achieved in the area of gender equity and affirmation in the 1980s and 1990s. "Normalcy" will not bring a return to the point of beginnings.

Notes

1   Although most of the information in this essay derives from interviews and direct participant-observation, I have also relied on various written documents: Archivo CEPRODEP 1988, 1991a, 1991b, 1994, 1995; Centro Manuela Ramos 1996; Fujimori 1995; Guzmán 1988. I have drawn, as well, from knowledge presented by various writers: see Blondet 1991; Blondet and Montero 1995; Byrne 1996; Coral 1990, 1994, 1995; de la Cadena 1991; Degregori 1983, 1994; Degregori and Grompone 1991; Kirk 1993b; Oliart 1994, and chapter in this book. See also: Vargas 1992.

✢ PART FIVE

Political Rule, Political Culture:

The Ironic Legacies of War

❖ By 1995, the war had wound down. An insurgency that had profoundly affected national politics and everyday life had diminished to more sporadic and offstage struggles. Five or ten years earlier, Sendero's insurgency dramatized political reach: a capacity, backed by internal cohesion, to destroy alternate paths, to engulf new locales and regions in struggles for control, to create an aura of invincibility. Now, the insurgents wrestled to regain the sense of direction and the recruitment capacity without which a war campaign seemed futile. The April re-election of Alberto Fujimori as a can-do president backed by a large majority symbolized the changed state of affairs.

The turning point was the capture of Abimael Guzmán in a raid on a Lima safe house on 12 September 1992, but there was more to the capture than met the eye. First, the taking of Guzmán offered Fujimori and the state a tremendous opportunity to puncture the mystique of effectiveness that had accrued to an insurgency "scientifically" led by Guzmán, the larger than life intellectual whose ideas and direction required absolute loyalty. Over time, the state capitalized on the opportunity with media events that reduced Guzmán to a fallible and soft human being, a supplicant who petitioned the conquering president for peace. (See the photo in the chapter by Oliart below.) Second, and equally important, the capture was a dramatic episode within a larger process of intensified intelligence work, since 1990, to identify, seize, and dismantle systematically the leadership of Sendero. As Nelson Manrique has observed, the intelligence work succeeded. Nine-tenths of the high leadership was captured, along with Guzmán, in 1992, in part because Sendero had overextended its politico-military capacities by "fleeing forward."[1] The Sendero leadership had responded to the spread of peasant political resistance and ronda organizations in the center-south provinces not with self-critique of its political vision or practice, but with a declaration of "strategic equilibrium" that prioritized the conquest of Lima.

The gamble almost worked—as we have seen, collapse seemed imminent in Lima in the early months of 1992—but it proved fatal. Already on the defensive in the center-south highland provinces, Sendero lost its stranglehold on Lima. Within little more than a year of Guzmán's capture, Sendero's mystique crumbled, Guzmán recognized President Fujimori as the war victor and petitioned him for peace on television, the remnants of the uncaptured insurgent leadership suffered internal division on central points. By 1995, the hold-outs who rejected the veracity or wisdom of Guzmán's call for peace and his genuflection toward Fujimori could no longer mount an effective insurgency campaign. The hard-line insurrectionists who had reorganized as "Sendero Rojo" ("Red Sendero") under "Comrade Feliciano" would have to settle for cumulative political work and infighting behind the scenes, punctuated by occasional acts of bombing, assassination, and intimidation.[2]

Yet even as the war wound down to a lower grade of intensity, its legacies ran deep. In particular, it had generated profound and often ironic consequences for political rule and political culture. Some of these consequences we have already visited (in Parts II–IV) at the level of specific regions, social sectors, and political tendencies that fell short of nationwide scope or hegemony. At these grassroots levels, we have observed the emergence of peasant rondas, reborn civil societies, and peasant-military rapprochement in the center-south; the destruction of "third paths" and nonsenderista culminations of Left history; and the emergence of women as visible and forceful citizen-subjects—as "warriors" within Sendero's culture of insurgent patriarchy, as leading voices in base-level turns toward open opposition to Sendero, as organizers of community response to severe economic crisis—within a polity shaken by war crisis and neoliberal austerity.

The essays in Part V complement these findings by exploring two key transformations in political rule and political culture at the national level: on the one hand, the emergence of President Alberto Fujimori as a decisive political force, on the other, the significance of violence and human rights as markers and catalysts of changing political values and sensibilities.

The essays of Enrique Obando and Patricia Oliart offer complementary understandings of Fujimori's rise to power. Obando traces the fascinating inside story of civil-military politics through the presidencies of Belaúnde (1980–1985), García (1985–1990), and Fujimori (1990–). Tense relations between presidents and the military, facilitated by the suspiciousness inherent in the return of the previously ousted Belaúnde to power, by a long history of APRA-military conflicts, and by an initial underestimation of Sendero Luminoso, were more the norm than the exception. Such tensions impeded and damaged the ability of the military to formulate and execute a coherent, national-level counterinsurgency strategy. Moreover, the turn toward presidential interventionism in the politics of high command promotion, retirement, and loyalty generated deep internal tensions within the military. As Obando also demonstrates, however, Fujimori—assisted by Vladimiro Montesinos, a former army captain and the chief of the SIN (Servicio de Inteligencia Nacional), and by his eventual chief of command, General Nicolás Hermoza—nonetheless achieved a presidential-led symbiosis. The new presidentialism that governed civil-military relations was anchored in the fusion of patronage and efficacy: on the one hand, the promotion of select officers as allied caudillos within a chain of patrimony, and, on the other hand, the organizing of a successful campaign against the military's war enemy, Sendero Luminoso. (As this book entered its final copy editing phase in mid-1997, Montesinos and Hermoza remained firmly ensconced as key advisors.)

One aspect of *fujimorismo*, then, was the astute consolidation of institutional power at the top. Fujimori not only undermined the independent standing of parliamentary and judicial institutions in the *autogolpe* ("self-coup") that suspended constitutional procedure in April 1992. He also undercut the integrity and political weight of the military as a national institution. At regional levels, of course, the capacity of the military to intervene directly and cohesively in the political life of specific provinces might run high. At the national level of civil-military politics centered in Lima, however, the new regime of civil-military relations marginalized the *institucionalista* officer currents that critiqued the loss of the military's political independence and its institutional culture of command and promotion. In this perspective, Fujimori's presidentialism succeeded because it undercut potentially countervailing institutions, especially the military, within the state.

If one side of fujimorismo was the art of consolidating institutional power at the top, the other side was more diffuse: a play of images and actions that elicited receptive responses and thereby refashioned political culture. Patricia Oliart's essay explores this politico-cultural style and its appeal. As Oliart points out, despite his promotion of neoliberal economic policies in vogue with economic elites and which he had opposed in his first presidential election campaign in 1990, Fujimori's political style ran in a contrary direction. His style emphasized an almost intuitive, affective connection with the racially mixed and humble subaltern layers of Peruvian society. Fujimori was, in the words of an early campaign slogan, "a president like you"—dark in phenotype, alien to the Europeanized aristocrat circles that once embodied politics in creole Lima and that seemed reborn in the 1990 presidential campaign of Mario Vargas Llosa, and inclined to hard work and accomplishment rather than the discursive flights of fancy that characterized APRA's García, the Left, and "old" politicians and parties more generally.

The "ethnographic present" in Oliart's essay is 1995, a precaution worth noting since Fujimori remains in power as this manuscript goes to press, and because his style and effectiveness may evolve significantly. In his second term, post-war reconstruction and austerity issues are likely to assume a more central and perhaps intractable place in Peruvian politico-cultural life. As they do so, the patience and approval offered to an authoritarian hero deemed uniquely effective may wear thin, and high-handed abuse of power may itself become a focus of polemics and popular discontent. "Unexpected" incidents by guerrillas, such as the MRTA's capture of hostages in the Japanese Embassy in Lima in December 1996, may also erode Fujimori's mystique as the conqueror of terrorism. In short, the euphoric atmosphere of 1993–1994 may become a more distant, less politically relevant memory. The intractability of reconstruction and austerity issues seemed evident in the aftermath of the spectacular military raid that put an end to the MRTA hostage crisis in April 1997. Fujimori's political rebound as a conqueror of terrorism proved short-lived, and by late May he was once again mired by low approval ratings, a sense of economic disappointment or desperation in vast sectors of society, and hostile reactions to his efforts to circumvent legal obstacles to a re-election campaign in the year 2000. The hostility to the latter effort to ignore legal institutions—Fujimori had lost in the tribunal that ruled on the legality of a re-election campaign in 2000—contrasts sharply with the popularity of his shutdown of the Congress and his revamping of the judiciary in the "self-coup" of 1992.

Oliart shows that even in his first term, Fujimori's social identification with the humble and the hard-working implied not a politics of democratic dialogue with the dispossessed or with organized grassroots associations, but rather a politics of trustworthy paternalism displayed in organized media events. At the micro level, the symbolism of trustworthy paternalism often took the form of local visits, announcements of public wellbeing or economic projects, and gift exchanges that consolidated Fujimori's standing as a warm doer (*hacedor*) and benefactor who identified intuitively with the needs and values of the local folk. At the macro level, within his first presidential term, Fujimori's conquests of Guzmán, hyperinflation, and ineffectual parliamentary and judicial institutions consolidated a mystique as a uniquely efficacious ruler. In a real sense, the mystique and yearnings for order and effectiveness that once accrued to Sendero and Guzmán had transferred to Fujimori.

Fujimori's success at the level of political culture had profoundly authoritarian implications. As Oliart shows, Fujimori's popular style as a "new" politician disdainful of the old ways—the political parties and leaders, and countervailing state institutions, defined as almost inherently duplicitous and corrupt—not only sealed a vertical model of personal political leadership. It was also accompanied by a discrediting of the languages of right and the oppositional sensibilities that had worked their way into Peruvian political culture by the 1970s and early 1980s. Discourses about social rights and injustices had become inherently suspect—associated with the vices and ineffectiveness that had thrown Peru into a time of profound violence and fear.

The rise of fujimorismo, then, raises important questions about the legacy of the war period for political values and sensibilities. In two poignant essays, at once analysis and testimonial, Carlos Basombrío and Hortensia Muñoz, explore the problems of violence and human rights during the war and consider their significance for future directions in political culture as the war winds down.

Because struggles in defense of human rights invoke a concept of universal right and mobilize international support networks, it is easy to lose sight of their historicity and specific politico-cultural contexts. The essays of Basombrío and Muñoz illuminate the distinctive contours that marked the violence and human rights problems in Peru. Basombrío explores the unusual political context of human rights work in the Peru of the 1980s and 1990s. Unlike other leftist guerrillas and insurgent movements, Sendero handled human rights themes not as an allied cause, but as a contemptuous disguise for bourgeois rights that violated the true rights of the people. Indeed, instead of recoiling from the idea of violence against unarmed civilians, Sendero glorified the shedding of blood as a necessary and purifying force.

As Basombrío shows, these circumstances brought distinctive challenges—and dangers—to human rights struggles in Peru. Normally conceptualized as opposition to violations by the state, human rights struggles in Peru had to develop a two-front framework that denounced and resisted pervasive political violence against civilians by Sendero as well as the military. Normally conceptualized as a humanizing defense of rights that required political neutrality, human rights struggles in Peru seemed to require that activists take a political stand and consider conditional alliances with the state, even as they continued to denounce and organize against human rights violations by the state. Normally conceptualized as a defense of the inherent rights of all human beings, human-rights struggles in Peru pushed activists toward two-tiered defense practices that distinguished between suspected senderistas and nonsenderistas. As Basombrío shows, these transitions from normative points of departure were extremely difficult and painful to achieve, and they did not spare human-rights workers from dangerous accusations of collaboration with subversion and terror.

Muñoz's subtle essay illuminates the changing sensibilities and languages that accompanied such transitions. She shows that although the concept of human rights implies universality, the language of rights is organized around specific, war-defined categories of humanity, referents that provide a defining (and humanizing) guide to right, victim, and aggressor. In the Peruvian context, the key referents and sensibilities changed under the pressure of events. As Muñoz shows, initial normative referents, similar to those developed elsewhere in Latin America, defined the disappeared (persons arbitrarily kidnapped by state agents yet institutionally unrecognized as detainees of the state, and eventually presumed dead) as the victim and symbol of human violation; the state as the aggressor in a "dirty war" of its own making; and the insurgents as a political opposition to a violating state.

Over time, however, the standard referents grew increasingly tenuous. Sendero's acts of political violence and repression assumed greater objective and subjective weight in the war, and political alienation from Sendero grew increasingly stark and urgent. Perhaps most revealing, fear of Sendero's notorious capacity to invade and undermine grassroots organizations dissuaded relatives of the newly kidnapped from joining the organizations that promoted the cause of the disappeared. By the late 1980s, a new set of referents and sensibilities—compatible with the transitions discussed by Basombrío—had taken hold. In the new scheme, the symbol of human victimization was not the disappeared person (who now bore the complicating taint of "possible senderista"), nor the *desaparecido*'s family members, but the displaced refugee. The aggressor was not the state, but the generalized violence created by two key aggressors, both the state and armed insurgents. The label of (legitimate) political opposition to a violating state no longer applied to those who failed to distance themselves from armed struggle concepts. Muñoz hypothesizes perceptively that the winding down of the war may yield a new key referent. The new symbol of violated victim may become the innocent person wrongly detained or abused by an ascendant authoritarian state.

The juxtaposition of Basombrío's and Muñoz's essays defines the crossroads reached in a shifting political culture. On the one hand, Basombrío's conclusions corroborate and extend Oliart's depiction of the transition to profoundly authoritarian political values. Despite the efforts of human-rights activists to mount a two-front campaign attentive to Peru's specific conditions of war and political violence, they could not block the ascendance of values that associated human-rights work with subversion, that accepted the primacy of ends over means, that buried memories—lives lost, ideals held—that might question the road to order. On the other hand, Muñoz identifies more hopeful notes in the legacy of human-rights struggles for political culture. The legacy includes the building of new citizen-subjects who assert the right to have rights (something more than asking a paternalistic authority for favor), and the emergence of a new "common sense" that formulates violence in its many forms as something that violates a right. This new sensibility was evident, in the mid-1990s, in a heightened receptivity to issues that evoke physical abuse, such as children's rights and women's rights. As is clear in their essays, both authors are fully aware of the countervailing currents to each of their conclusions. In the tension between Basombrío's depiction of a political culture that has come to value results and to disdain its human cost, and Muñoz's depiction of a political culture that has suffered a great sensitization to themes of violence and violation, lies the ambivalent and contradictory crossroads bequeathed by an experience of fear and upheaval.

The legacies of the war for political rule and political culture are filled with irony. The mystique of authoritarian effectiveness passed from Abimael Guzmán to Alberto Fujimori. The ascendance of Fujimori weakened the integrity of the military as a national-level institution even as it gained a heightened political significance at regional levels and a diffuse esteem that flowed from Sendero's defeat. At the level of political values, a war waged from the Left ended up destroying the influence of leftist critiques and idealism as oppositional "common sense" within subaltern political culture, and laid a certain groundwork of legitimacy for an authoritarian regime embarked on a neoliberal path. Yet no one knows how lasting or precarious this groundwork will prove. Perhaps the ultimate irony of the war comes through in its ambivalent legacy for the political value placed on violence and human suffering. On this crucial issue, a war fought to reduce the maze of political combat to a clear choice between two paths, and that claimed perhaps 30,000 lives in the process, left matters deeply unresolved.

Notes

1   Manrique 1995a: esp. 22 (quote), 24.
2   In April to June 1996, as I composed the first draft of this introduction, these divisions also captured attention on the internet. The cybernet wars featured a "Luis Quispe" as a leading hard-line voice, an "Adolfo Olaechea" as an advocate of the peace negotiation line, and charges of counterrevolution against non-senderista cybernet voices (including a "Simon Strong"). Some of the various missives were imported and circulated on the electronic "Temas Andinos" list, and I am grateful to participants on the list, especially Florencia Mallon, who forwarded me the relevant postings.

    As Senderista hard-liners settle in for long-term political work, especially in urban barriadas, occasional acts of violence and political intimidation still burst into the news. In May 1997, as I revised this introduction, two such incidents, including a major bombing in Ate Vitarte (Metropolitan Lima), drew attention and provided a gruesome "commemoration" of the anniversary of the war's initiation in May 1980.

ELEVEN

Civil-Military Relations in Peru, 1980–1996:

How to Control and Coopt the Military

(and the consequences of doing so)

Enrique Obando

✤ This chapter provides an analysis of civilian-military relations in Peru after the return to civilian rule in 1980. In general terms we may say that the Fernando Belaúnde administration (1980–1985) tried to appease the Armed Forces by not intervening in their internal organization and by providing them with a large quantity of conventional arms. At the same time, Belaúnde tried to weaken the military politically by cutting the budget of the intelligence service and by not supporting the military's planning system. Alan García, in contrast, sought to control the military forces through direct intervention in their internal organization. The García administration (1985–1990) created a new National Defense System at the same time García coopted the high command. The new system sought to control the military rather than make it more efficient. Administrative chaos resulted. Alberto Fujimori, finally, went further than García. Fujimori intended not only to control the Armed Forces, but also to rely on their support to implement his neoliberal political program. For this purpose he perfected García's system of military cooptation and control by designating the top officers himself.

Nonetheless, over time the man whom Fujimori named as president of the Joint Command—General Nicolás Hermoza—began to become more independent, to the point that Fujimori could not replace him. This meant not the political capture of Fujimori by the command he himself had created, but rather a symbiosis that had a political price Fujimori would have preferred not to pay. Some military officers resisted civilian cooptation of the Armed Forces. Such opposition first appeared during the García administration and became more active under Fujimori. Nonetheless, Fujimori did not limit himself to controlling and utilizing the Armed Forces, but won the active support of an important sector of the military by providing the full political backing they needed to combat subversion.

Civilian-military relationships from 1980 to the mid-1990s evolved in an extremely complex context. In the first place, two subversive groups were active. Shining Path and the Revolutionary Túpac Amaru Movement (Movimiento Revolucionario Túpac Amaru; MRTA) had taken up arms in 1980 and 1984, respectively, and terrorist action drove the Peruvian state to the edge of collapse by 1992. Second, narcotrafficking began in the late 1970s and eventually produced an alliance between drug traffickers and subversives. In the third place, Peru suffered perhaps its worst economic crisis of the twentieth century. Only recently, under Fujimori, has the economy begun to recover. Finally, and related to the economic crisis and the drug trade, there was corruption. Corruption spread to almost all sectors of the nation, including the Armed Forces and political parties.

The Fernando Belaúnde Administration (1980–1985)

Civilian-military relations during Fernando Belaúnde's second administration were poisoned from the outset because twelve years earlier Belaúnde's first administration had been deposed by a military coup. The Comandante General of the Army in 1980, General Rafael Hoyos Rubio, had been the very colonel who had expelled Belaúnde from the Government Palace. On the military side, there still existed an important group of pro-Velasco officers who espoused a statist and leftist ideology and were not happy about the presence of neoliberal ministers interested in dismantling the protectionist and interventionist state they had created.

The civilian officials not only distrusted the military, they actively resented the Armed Forces. The civilians returned to office ready to take revenge for twelve years of military government and they did so by refusing to cooperate in implementing the National Defense System, which, in accord with new ideas promoted by the Inter-American Defense College, required civilian participation. The new theory was that war, whether external or internal, took place not only on a military terrain, but also on economic, political, and psychosocial fronts. The politicians' refusal to implement the Defense System, at the very same time that the worst subversive uprising in Peruvian history was beginning, allowed Shining Path to expand. The politicians clearly were more afraid of the military than of the subversives. Yet, military spending, curiously, did not suffer. The Belaúnde government approved the majority of arms acquisitions proposed by the military.[1] The government thus sought to avoid provoking greater discontent in the barracks, even though these expenses were not income-generating investments and increased significantly the external debt.[2]

Meanwhile, as the years passed, the national economy deteriorated. In 1983 gross domestic product fell by 11.7 percent, and in 1984, inflation reached 127 percent. Government corruption was notorious and a constant topic in the news media. In 1968, in a less chaotic situation, the military had overthrown the government. Now, however, the military did not have its own project. Moreover, the post-Velasco military administration (1975–1980) and the subsequent fight against Shining Path led the military ideologically to the Right and weakened the *velasquista* group. By the end of the Belaúnde administration, the surviving velasquistas clearly constituted a minority within the increasingly conservative Armed Forces. In addition, the military officers were conscious that twelve years in power had been debilitating. So they stayed in their barracks.

The struggle against subversion was another source of tension between the military men and civilians. The Armed Forces wanted to intervene to suppress the insurrection, but the administration initially refused. Belaúnde did not want to project the image that a recently elected democracy needed military force to maintain order. From 1980 to 1982, the police were in charge of suppressing the guerrilla movement, which continued to grow. Finally, in December 1982 the administration decided to put the Armed Forces in charge of suppressing the subversive movement in Ayacucho. But the Armed Forces could not control the subversion either. In military circles, officers tended to blame this failure on civilians. They argued that Belaúnde's refusal to call on the military from the beginning had facilitated the guerrillas' expansion and made them much more difficult to defeat. The real circumstances were not so simple. The outgoing military government of General Francisco Morales Bermúdez had known of the Shining Path's intention to initiate an armed struggle.[3] Yet the military decided not to act upon that knowledge for political reasons. Military leaders thought that to attack a political party just at that moment, when they had called for elections and a return to civilian government, would prejudice their image. They left the problem for the civilian government to resolve, under the assumption that the government would call upon the Armed Forces to confront the subversives.[4]

The military had another reason to blame the civilian government for the failure of its counterinsurgency efforts. Belaúnde's administration weakened the Intelligence Service because the military government had used the service to control the political parties and deport activists. This measure deprived the military of an indispensable tool for the counterinsurgency struggle.

Thus the military was brought into the counterinsurgency war late and suffered from inadequate intelligence. Its failure also derived, however, from internal problems. The Armed Forces lacked experts in counterinsurgency warfare. The commanders and officers in the emergency zones were replaced every year, which impeded them from gaining experience. The Armed Forces had not studied successful counterinsurgency wars such as the British experience in Malaysia or the Philippine experience in suppressing the Huks. The Peruvians' knowledge of counterinsurgency theory was limited to two manuals, dating from the 1950s, which they had copied from the French Army.[5] The counterinsurgency campaign lacked a centralized command structure. Military leaders in each emergency zone fought independently. In the end, the Armed Forces not only failed to suppress the subversive movement, they failed to block its expansion. By 1984, the departments of Ayacucho, Apurímac, Huancavelica, Huánuco, and a province of San Martín—in addition to the capital of Lima—were all militarized. In September 1984, another subversive group appeared, the MRTA.

During 1983, the Political-Military Chief of the Ayacucho war zone, General Clemente Noel Moral, resorted to "dirty war" practices: disappearances and assassinations. This elicited no reaction from the Belaúnde administration, despite denunciations issued from various political sectors. As the administration lacked a counterinsurgency strategy of its own to replace that of the Armed Forces, Belaúnde gave them a free hand. Although human rights violations did not provoke friction between the military and the civilian government, such abuses did cause internal problems within the Armed Forces. The Peruvian Armed Forces (especially the army) were made up largely of officers from lower middle class origins, often from provinces outside of Lima. This modest social profile was one of the reasons that, when military officers took over the government in 1968, they sought not to defend the oligarchy but rather to destroy it and modernize the country.[6] The experiment ultimately failed but in 1983 some military sectors still favored social change and did not want to resort to a purely repressive counterinsurgency policy. Some officers thought that the best solution would be to win the support of the population through economic and social assistance from the government. In January 1984, a representative of this current, General Adrián Huamán Centeno, was named to the Ayacucho leadership post. But the Belaúnde government, which had not opposed General Noel's repressive policies, clashed with Huamán's civilian assistance policy, principally for economic reasons. The economy of the country was in crisis and Huamán's strategy was costly. Huamán publicly criticized the government and was for this reason removed from the post.[7] His successor, Colonel Wilfredo Mori Orzo, returned to the practices of Noel. The civilian government, ignorant of counterinsurgency strategy, ended up allied with the military hardliners simply for economic reasons.

The counterinsurgency war went poorly. In July 1984, collective graves of victims of military extrajudicial executions were uncovered and provoked an international scandal. Amnesty International had been exposing and denouncing such practices, and by December 1984, hundreds, if not thousands, of Peruvians had been disappeared.[8] By the end of the Belaúnde period, the prospects for success in the counterinsurgency war seemed dim. The civilian government had rejected proposals for a military policy oriented toward social assistance, yet still lacked an alternative to the strategy of the military hardliners, whom the civilians ended up defending.

The Alan García Administration (1985–1990)

Upon taking office in 1985, one of the principal concerns of Alan García and his political party, APRA, was to obtain the support of a sector of the military high command as insurance against a coup. The Armed Forces and APRA had a long history of confrontations that dated back to 1932, when APRA mounted an insurrection in which army officers were assassinated. A year later, an APRA militant assassinated the president, General Luis M. Sánchez Cerro.[9] As the years passed and APRA drifted toward the right, however, the rancor softened somewhat, particularly during the military's Morales Bermúdez period (1975–1980).[10] Nonetheless, the apristas continued to distrust the Armed Forces and wanted to coopt a sector of the high command. The method was to offer certain generals and admirals high posts within their institutions, or as attachés and ambassadors abroad. This system functioned throughout the regime and damaged the Armed Forces by exacerbating internal feuds for promotion to the highest levels. The high institutional posts allowed military men to manage very flexible budgets in circumstances where few questions were asked about expenditures. In addition, since the income of officers depends on rank, the economic attractions of ascent in rank or service as a military attaché abroad were obvious. García took advantage of the economic crisis, in which military salaries had deteriorated notably, to control the Armed Forces.

Within five years, the identification of younger officers with their leaders had plunged into crisis. Junior officers perceived the high command as having sold out to the administration. Among young officers, the rumor began to spread that coopted generals and admirals had obtained incomes through illicit means that damaged military capacity, and that the system of cooptation functioned to facilitate the continuation of corruption and to guarantee the fidelity of the officer in question. This rumor gave rise to the appearance of a group of clandestine military opposition, known as COMACA (a Spanish acronym that referred to "Comandantes, Majors, and Captains"), made up of officers of inferior rank who accused the generals of supporting an immoral aprista administration. COMACA began to accuse the administration and the high command of misappropriating funds, appropriating narco-dollars, damaging military operational capacity, neglecting military subordinates and the poor, and thereby "propitiating the development of terrorism, abuse, and injustice."[11] García's cooptation policy worked, but it poisoned his relationship with the young officers and revived almost-forgotten military hatred of APRA.

Government policy on human rights in the counterinsurgency campaign changed radically when García took power. García declared that he would not permit the dirty war, which placed him in conflict with the Armed Forces. On 16 September 1985, García demanded the renunciation of the President of the Joint Command of the Armed Forces, Lieutenant General César Enrico Praeli, following an investigation that implicated the army in the assassination of civilians. This was the first time that a chief of state had fired a president of the joint command, the highest military officer. The following day, General Sinecio Jarama, Chief of the Second Military Region, and General Wilfredo Mori, Political-Military Chief of Ayacucho, were also removed from their posts. In July 1986, for the first time, eleven police officers were tried for the assassination of thirty-four peasants near the community of Soccos in Ayacucho.

Tensions related to human rights policy exploded in 1986. On 18–20 June 1986, Shining Path prisoners took over three prisons in Lima. The president ordered the police and military forces to suppress the uprisings. A massacre resulted: All the inmates in the Lurigancho prison and almost all those in the Frontón prison were killed. The president himself confirmed that a high number of senderistas had been executed after having surrendered. As a result, twenty-four police officers, including a general and a colonel, were detained and tried, as was the army General Jorge Rabanal, who had commanded the operation.[12] The Chief of the National Guard (Guardia Republicana), General Máximo Martínez Lira, was removed from his post. The military responded by leaking to the press that the order to execute the prisoners had come from the president. Because the president's orders were verbal, the truth was never known. The controversy definitively broke the relationship between the military and APRA. The first consequence of these events was the military's refusal to take certain initiatives in the counterinsurgency war. Officers in the field consulted directly with Lima and in cases considered politically delicate, demanded written orders from the administration before they would act. The most pathetic case of refusal to act without written orders occurred in 1988, when Shining Path attacked the police post at Tocache, located in the Department of San Martín. The country listened by radio and television to messages sent by the chief of the post. Surrounded, he begged Armando Villanueva, the leader of the Interministerial Coordinating Commission for the Counterinsurgency Struggle (Comisión Interministerial Coordinadora de la Lucha Antisubversiva, or CICLAS), for reinforcements. The pleas went on for eight hours, until the commander and his detachment were annihilated. Lacking written orders requiring them to do so, military forces located within fifty kilometers refused to assist the besieged detachment and gave the excuse that they feared an ambush and could not send helicopters due to "bad weather."[13]

While the military were refusing to fight, APRA turned to the police. The administration began to give weapons for warfare to the police, which provoked military resentment. The army discovered that armored vehicles had been purchased for the police and successfully demanded that the vehicles be given to the army instead. The problem for the military was that the police formed part of the Interior Ministry, which APRA controlled. In July 1988 another subversive group appeared, this time on the Right. The Rodrigo Franco Commando,[14] named for an aprista leader supposedly assassinated by Shining Path, attacked presumed senderistas and APRA's political adversaries. In a rare agreement, the legal parties of the Left and the Armed Forces considered the commando to be supervised by the Interior Ministry and controlled by APRA. Rumors circulated in military circles that the Rodrigo Franco Commando was preparing to take power through a coup.[15]

Beyond the officer groups directly coopted by the García administration, tensions between apristas and the military had arrived at an extreme.

The policy of the Belaúnde administration had been nonintervention in military institutions to avoid rejection, but the García government's policy was maximum intervention in an effort to control these institutions. In March 1987, the administration created the Defense Ministry by fusing the former War, Navy, and Aeronautics Ministries, plus the Joint Command of the Armed Forces, and the National Defense Secretariat.[16] The military sustained that the new ministry was designed to drain political power from the Armed Forces by diminishing their representation on the Council of Ministers from three ministers to one. In addition, the decree theoretically subordinated the military to civilian authority by allowing a civilian to be named as defense minister. Ultimately, the administration did not dare to name a civilian to this post, although it had no need to do so, given the cooption of the high command.[17] The measure also deprived the military institutions of control over acquisitions, now placed under the Minister's control.

The reform of the defense system sparked a new confrontation between the military and the government. Although army leaders had for forty years lobbied for a Defense Ministry, the military viewed the new ministry with distrust because it was APRA that had finally brought it about. The air force and the navy, by contrast, had always opposed the project, because it implied their subordination to the army. The General Comandante of the Peruvian Air Force (FAP), Lieutenant General Luis Abram Cavallerino, manifested his opposition to the president by ordering Mirage aircraft to carry out maneuvers over the Government Palace. Like the previous general comandante, he was forced into retirement. In addition, the FAP watched as the president ordered a cut of its planned purchase of twenty-six Mirage 2000 aircraft down to only twelve. García appointed a loyalist, Lieutenant General Germán Vucetich, as the next comandante general of the air force. This action provoked a split within the air force between Vucetich's followers and his enemies, who considered him an APRA man and rallied around the Chief of the Military Staff, Lieutenant General César Gonzalo Luza. This internal struggle also poisoned relations between the three branches of the Armed Forces and largely marginalized the air force from the military's political maneuvers during the rest of the García administration.[18]

The creation of the Ministry of Defense had grave collateral repercussions. It caused administrative difficulties in defense planning, since incorporation of the Joint Command and the Defense Secretariat denied them direct access to the president. In addition, the military was occupied during 1987 and part of 1988 in implementing the changes, which demanded a new organizational structure and chain of command. This process got in the way of planning the struggle against subversion, which by the final years of the García administration had spread through the greater part of the country.

The collapse of the García administration began in 1988. As we shall see, one consequence was coup-oriented rumors and plotting. The previous year García had tried to nationalize Peruvian banks but encountered tremendous resistance among the opposition, Parliament, and his own party. The measure could not be implemented. In addition, the economy had entered into crisis. [*Editor's note:* The reasons for the severe economic crisis are complex, but may be glossed as the combined effect of poorly financed populist economics, war attrition, and corruption. Toward the end of the García administration, hyperinflation in Metropolitan Lima had soared to an annual rate of more than 7000 percent, and per capita gross domestic product was falling at an annual rate of more than 10 percent.] The year closed with a negative economic growth of 8 percent. That year something strange happened in the army. The Chief of the First Military Region, General Víctor Raúl Silva Tuesta, was obliged to renounce by the high command for allegedly plotting a coup. Silva Tuesta belonged to the group of generals coopted by García. The military leaked to the press that Silva Tuesta had been involved in planning a "self-coup" (*autogolpe*) whereby García sought to preserve his image and escape from responsibility for the approaching chaos by urging military friends to organize the self-afflicted takeover.[19]

Meanwhile, another coup plot was brewing from below. The grave economic crisis was affecting the supplies of the army units that were fighting against the subversives. They were short on gasoline, food, and even munitions. (The value of the soldiers' salaries also declined noticeably.) In 1989, a unit of the army (BAS 28) stationed in Pucallpa rebelled because it had not received its rations for three months.[20] The fact that the coopted high command exerted only very slight pressure on the administration to solve these problems contributed, finally, to breaking the chain of command. Young officers began to view their superior officers as traitors to their own institutions and planned a coup against their own commanders as well as García. At the center of these plans was the COMACA group just mentioned.[21] The theory of the plotters was that the shortages were intended to weaken the military, allow Shining Path to expand, and create a chaos that would render the elections of 1990 unfeasible. According to this theory, a sector of APRA would prolong the mandate of García with the support of the Rodrigo Franco Commando and the police.

Finally, some officers in the high command found out about the intentions of the dissident junior officers and planned their own coup in order not to be overthrown by their subordinates.[22] They planned a new government under the code name *Libro Verde* (Green Book).[23] In the end, the assumption upon which the coup plans were based never occurred. Shining Path was not able to block the 1990 elections, which proceeded relatively normally, and the coup plots subsided.

The Fujimori Administration (1990–1995)

The Armed Forces participated actively in the 1990 elections. The principal contenders were APRA and FREDEMO, the latter an alliance of conservative parties with Mario Vargas Llosa's neoliberal Liberty Movement (Movimiento Libertad). The navy bet on Vargas Llosa and put its intelligence service at his disposition.[24] The army perceived Vargas Llosa as the lesser evil but did not identify closely with his program. After ten years of failures by the traditional parties, the Peruvian people castigated the professional politicians by voting for an obscure candidate of Japanese ancestry, Alberto Fujimori, who took second place in the first electoral round. The navy unleashed the rumor that if Fujimori were to win the run-off election, the Armed Forces would revolt. Fujimori did win but the coup did not occur. The rumor, intended simply to deprive Fujimori of votes, cost Comandante General of the Navy Vice-Admiral Alfonso Panizo and his chief intelligence officer their jobs. Fujimori put an end to air force disputes between the followers of Vucetich and those of Gonzalo by forcing them both to retire. These first moves set the tone for Fujimori's administration; the president would consistently maintain control over promotions and retirements.

Before the run-off round of the elections, President García, who opposed Vargas Llosa on ideological grounds, secretly ordered the chief of the National Intelligence Service (Servicio de Inteligencia Nacional, or SIN), General Edwin Díaz, to support Fujimori's campaign.[25] General Díaz had played an important part in García's cooption system and had tapped the telephone lines of the top military officers.[26] Through General Díaz, Fujimori learned about the system of cooption and found it useful. Over the following years, Fujimori would expand cooption more than García had ever dared. Once in power, Fujimori tried to maintain General Díaz as the head of SIN, but protest from opposition and military circles for designating the very man who had spied on their activities led Fujimori to replace him with General Julio Salazar Monroe. The person who would exercise the real power of the SIN, however, would be a civilian, Vladimiro Montesinos.

Montesinos was brought into Fujimori's circle during the campaign in order to resolve a judicial investigation that FREDEMO wanted to bring against Fujimori for evading taxes in a real estate sale. Electoral laws prohibited the candidacy of individuals with pending trials, but Montesinos, a lawyer with the right contacts, managed to put a "friendly" judge in charge of the case. The investigation went nowhere and Montesinos steadily gained Fujimori's trust. Fujimori had neither an organized political party nor his own unions or seasoned political allies upon which to base his government. He sought to gain the support of a sector of the military, in the hopes that the Armed Forces would not see him as a dangerously weak president and try to replace him. In Fujimori's efforts to coopt a sector of the military, Montesinos proved extremely useful. He was a former army captain who knew who was who in the army and knew how to confront the subversive threat, the most important problem that Fujimori had to face.[27]

Montesinos made himself irremovable. He became a key advisor who suggested which generals Fujimori should retire, which ones to promote, and which to place in key posts. He began to construct his own power base among the generals who owed him their promotions or their posts. Montesinos, however, also had some serious disadvantages. Years before, when he was a captain, he had been accused of treason for allegedly providing classified information to the U.S. government. The accusation was never proved but he was expelled from the army for deceit and insubordination when he was found in Washington, D.C., while he was supposedly on sick leave in Lima.[28] As a civilian lawyer, he had worked for drug traffickers, which sparked distaste among the opposition and the Armed Forces. Montesinos's exercise of power over the Armed Forces, whereby he hired and fired generals but also organized the counterinsurgency struggle rather efficiently, caused a split within the military between those who insisted that he was a person of great importance for national defense whose past should not impede his present services, and those who saw him as an unscrupulous person who could bring disaster to the institution.

Fujimori's own efforts to place unconditional supporters in the high command only served to worsen the conflict. A military opposition group, the *institucionalistas*, was composed of independent-minded officers who thought that a semiautonomous status for the Armed Forces was necessary to defend the interests of the institution. This group was very reluctant to give unconditional support to civilian authority. Fearful of a possible coup, Fujimori decided to replace the institucionalistas with less independent men, who could be found among officers with less successful careers, disposed to do whatever necessary to get promoted to the high command. Fujimori and Montesinos cashiered the institucionalista leadership and installed loyalists (leales).

In December 1991, the administration retired three institucionalista generals (Luis Palomino, José Pastor, and Jaime Salinas) slated to serve as comandantes generales of the army in 1992 and 1993 and as chief of the military staff in 1992. Fujimori replaced them, upon Montesinos's recommendation, with General Nicolás Hermoza Ríos as comandante general of the army. This appointment was preceded in November by the new Law of Military Standing,[29] which mandated that the comandantes generales would be designated by the president from among the generals of highest rank. The comandante general no longer had to be the most senior general, as earlier, nor would he pass into retirement until and unless the president decided to relieve him. Fujimori, unlike García, would not need to coopt a series of new comandantes generales. It was enough to find a loyal man and maintain him in his post throughout the administration, which was exactly what Fujimori did with General Hermoza. These measures angered the institucionalistas, especially when they found out that Montesinos had been behind them.

Nonetheless, Fujimori managed to contain the discontent. In contrast to García and Belaúnde, Fujimori concerned himself with the operational capacity and efficiency of the Armed Forces in the counterinsurgency war. In this endeavor, Montesinos also proved very useful. For the first time in eleven years a Peruvian presidential administration adopted an actual strategy for counterinsurgency operations. In November 1991, the administration proposed a series of legislative decrees for pacification.[30] The Peruvian Congress, however, vetoed some decrees and modified others that they considered violations of individual liberties guaranteed in the Constitution. One of the decrees so modified was the National Defense System Law, which was central to the counterinsurgency strategy.[31] This law would have given the Political-Military Command in each Emergency Zone control over the civilian sectors of the state. The congress replaced the system of political-military chiefs with a tripartite structure consisting of a regional prefect who would represent the president of the Republic, a regional president elected by the people, and a military authority. The Armed Forces warned that a command divided in three would not function.[32]

By December 1991 a serious confrontation was taking place between Congress on the one hand, and the President and the Armed Forces on the other. But this conflict was not the only problem. In counterinsurgency warfare, the judicial system must be a key tool for imprisoning subversives, but in Peru the judicial system was both inefficient and corrupt. Rebels threatened judges and went free. After Fujimori's election, two hundred terrorists were liberated. During the García administration, the congress approved a law to protect judges from these threats by guaranteeing them anonymity, but the judges did not accept such protection because it violated the "majesty of judicial power."[33]

Given the legislative and judicial impasse, on 5 April 1992 Fujimori, supported by the military, closed down the congress in order to implement the blocked counterinsurgency decrees and to reorganize the judicial system. Fujimori had not expected the international reaction that his "self-coup" (*autogolpe*) provoked, and agreed to convene new congressional elections. Shining Path, meanwhile, assumed that the coup signaled a government offensive against the subversives, and set off car bombs in Lima in April and May. Many people, including in military circles, believed that the deepening national crisis might lead either to a Shining Path victory or to a foreign invasion to prevent it.[34]

The sensation that Sendero's subversion was becoming uncontrollable angered the institucionalista officers who had been forced to retire from the Armed Forces. Their discontent extended to active-duty officers of inferior and middle rank for various reasons—the incredibly low and compressed pay scale (US$283.42 a month for a division general, US$212.78 for a second lieutenant), the lack of victories in the counterinsurgency war, and the low operational capacity of the Armed Forces.[35] Clandestine opposition groups within the Armed Forces included COMACA and "León Dormido," formed by institucionalistas who had also opposed the García administration. COMACA explored the possibility of a counter-coup against Fujimori and sought the support of retired institucionalista army generals. On 12 September 1992, however, Guzmán was captured by the DINCOTE (the antiterrorist police, known by its Spanish acronym). The mortal blow to Sendero eliminated the risk of a possible triumph by Shining Path, and the institucionalistas, led by General Jaime Salinas, ended up abandoning the idea of a coup. Nonetheless, they had been infiltrated by SIN. More than forty officers, including five generals, would be arrested and placed on trial.

This was the moment of Fujimori's greatest triumph. He had captured Shining Path's leader Abimael Guzmán, and two months earlier had captured Víctor Polay, MRTA's leader. He had convinced the international community that he was returning to democracy by holding elections for a new congress that provided him an ample majority of supporters. And he had dismantled the institucionalista military opposition. This was the perfect moment to pardon the institucionalistas and gain the Armed Forces' total support, but Fujimori decided instead to destroy the institucionalistas. The Armed Forces was composed of three groups: the pro-Fujimori *leales* (loyalists), the anti-Fujimori institucionalistas, and a group of institucionalistas who were loyal to Fujimori but not coopted. The latter group believed that the military had to support the president because he was carrying out important work, and functioned as a cushion that blocked greater opposition. This group included Division General José Valdivia, who served as Chief of the Staff of the Joint Command and who had formulated the military aspect of the counterinsurgency strategy; Brigadier General Alberto Arciniega, who had been an effective political-military chief in Huallaga; and Division General Rodolfo Robles, Comandante of the Third Military Region (the most important in the country). General Valdivia was subject to house arrest and subsequently sent to Washington in "golden exile" and finally to the Ukraine. General Arciniega was passed over for promotion and pushed into retirement. General Robles received a post without troops to command—Director of Instruction. Similar fates befell other loyalist institucionalista officers, and left the coopted leales and the hard-line institucionalistas with no cushion to soften the confrontation. The stage was set for a clash. The retired General Arciniega and General Luis Cisneros, a retired former Minister of War under Belaúnde, publicly criticized the action of the Army Comandante General, Nicolás Hermoza, and would be tried in military court. Arciniega was deprived of his military protection—a measure equivalent to an invitation to Shining Path to assassinate him—and had to leave the country. The confrontation continued in the form of two letters from nineteen former comandantes generales of the army. The letters criticized General Hermoza for the treatment of the institucionalista officers who had taken part in the counter-coup attempt. Fujimori publicly defended Hermoza and accused the entire high command prior to Hermoza of inefficiency and corruption.

After Fujimori's and Hermoza's clash with the institucionalistas, the latter sought to discredit Hermoza and thereby to oblige the president to replace him. They accused Hermoza of human-rights violations, at a time when Peru's human-rights situation was receiving tremendous international attention, especially in the United States. During 1993, the discontented groups within the army leaked information to the press and the opposition that revealed violations of human rights by an army command known as the Colina Group. The gravest accusation implicated various coopted generals, including Comandante General Hermoza, in the capture and murder of nine students and a professor from the Universidad Enrique Guzmán y Valle "La Cantuta." When the Congress tried to investigate Hermoza he put tanks on the streets of Lima. Subsequently, he sent the case to a military court, to block parliamentary access by arguing that, according to Peruvian law, one case could not be judged by two different state organisms. Fujimori and his supporters in Congress suggested that the denunciation sent by the military opposition was anonymous and therefore could not be taken seriously. But General Rodolfo Robles—one of the loyalist institucionalistas persecuted after the counter-coup plot—solicited political asylum in the U.S. Embassy and revealed the names of the commando members who had assassinated the students.[36] He directly implicated the presidential advisor Vladimiro Montesinos and General Hermoza in this and other massacres, such as the massacre in the Lima district of Barrios Altos. The official response was that Robles was lying and could not prove that the disappeared students had been assassinated in the absence of cadavers. The institucionalistas then leaked information to the press on the location of the bodies. Journalists went with a judge to the site and they found the bodies. The judge opened the case in a civilian court, and the government disputed the court's jurisdiction because the case was already in a military court. The administration got its majority in the Congress to pass Law 26291, on 8 February 1994, which simplified the procedure on the Supreme Court and made a simple majority sufficient to decide jurisdiction. Since the Supreme Court had voted three to two in favor of military jurisdiction, the issue was now legally resolved.[37]

The institucionalistas, however, continued their campaign to force the replacement of Hermoza. Having failed to achieve their objective through human-rights accusations, they turned toward accusations of collaboration in the narcotics trade. It was assumed that the United States would not remain aloof, given that the drug war was the centerpiece of U.S. foreign policy. The relationship between the Armed Forces and drug traffickers during the Fujimori administration was no different than that which had prevailed during previous administrations. Rumors were always circulating among the military that a considerable number of officers colluded with drug traffickers.[38] Simply comparing the exterior signs of wealth displayed by certain officers with their salaries gave reason to suspect that there was something wrong. What changed was that now there existed a military opposition disposed to reveal publicly what before had only been known internally.

The involvement of officers in drug trafficking became a political weapon that COMACA and "León Dormido" used in their efforts to topple Hermoza. These groups leaked information to the press that a large number of officers posted to coca-producing zones were involved in narcotics trafficking. Normally, such officers were paid "not to see" what the drug traffickers were doing a few kilometers from their bases. The accusations included the political-military chiefs of Huallaga, the chief of army aviation, and Hermoza himself. Hermoza denied all participation of officers in these kinds of activities. Nonetheless, in 1995 he ended up accepting that at least one hundred officers were presumed to have ties to drug traffickers, on the condition that they be investigated by military courts.[39] The high chiefs supposedly implicated included Generals Jaime Ríos Araico, Eduardo Bellido Mora, David Jaime Sobrevilla, and MacDonald Pérez Silva. The former two were political-military chiefs of the Huallaga Front and the latter two were in charge of the Mantaro Front. All were tried except General Bellido, who was Hermoza's brother-in-law and a key member of Fujimori's military group. Every attempt to investigate him proved useless and Bellido was sent to Israel as a military attaché. Major Evaristo Castillo, who had accused Bellido, fled into exile in Spain. Nor was Hermoza's complicity in drug trafficking ever proved. COMACA claimed that the members of Hermoza's leadership clique were exempt from the investigations.[40]

The military conflict with Ecuador in 1995 offered another opportunity to discredit Hermoza. That year was a presidential election year. Fujimori seemed to have victory assured over his closest competitor, Javier Pérez de Cuéllar of the Union for Peru (Unión por el Perú; UPP), an alliance of anti-Fujimori politicians of all camps. The only possibility for a UPP triumph was a grave error on Fujimori's part. In January, the opportunity seemed to arise. Ecuadorean troops were discovered in Peruvian territory in the frontier zone of Alto Cenepa that Ecuador considered its own. Once efforts to secure a peaceful withdrawal of the troops failed, the Peruvian Armed Forces proceeded to expel the Ecuadoreans under the assumption that it would be a simple operation. A similar situation had occurred in 1981 and the expulsion had been accomplished easily. This time, however, the operation took a month and a half and yielded substantial Peruvian fatalities, especially in the air force, and failed to expel the Ecuadoreans from their last bastion at Tiwinza, although Tiwinza was surrounded and its communication lines cut. The Ecuadoreans finally withdrew as a result of an international accord.

The political opposition led by Pérez de Cuéllar and the military opposition both made use of the military difficulties encountered in this conflict. Both criticized Fujimori and Hermoza for not having prevented the conflict with Ecuador and for having neglected the military's supply of armaments. The institucionalistas pointed out that Fujimori's practice of placing generals in key posts in reward for their loyalty, rather than for professionalism, had led to errors in the confrontation with Ecuador. They criticized the Comandante General of the Air Force, Air General Enrique Astete Baca; the Chief of the Aerial Wing of Chiclayo, Lieutenant General Barrantes; and Hermoza himself.[41] As in the past, this attempt to discredit Hermoza went nowhere. Hermoza remained in his post. His response was to retire the active-duty generals who had criticized him within the institution (General Walter Ledesma), and to try to imprison those retired generals who criticized him in the press (General Carlos Muricio, Ledesma himself for making additional criticisms once he had retired, and Navy Comandante Mellet).

In the 1995 elections the retired institucionalistas supported the opposition candidates and lost badly. Of the fifteen retired military officers who ran for parliamentary office, thirteen were endorsed by opposition parties. Equally telling, none of them were elected. The preferences of Hermoza and the military leadership for Fujimori were also clear although they were careful not to influence the vote count. Interference did not prove necessary in any event. Fujimori won the election with a majority of over 64 percent of the votes cast. His overwhelming victory placed the institucionalistas in a difficult position. Before the elections the SIN had already damaged the "León Dormido" group. Now, the election results revealed that the public impact of the accusations of human rights abuses, drug trafficking, and incompetence during the Ecuador conflict had been slight. The majority saw in Fujimori the man who pacified the country after fifteen years of internal warfare and who stabilized the economy after years of crisis. (On Fujimori's political style and image, see the essay by Oliart in this volume.) They wanted to believe that he would bring progress during the next five years. The rest did not matter.

The Second Fujimori Administration (1995–)

As of 1996, the Fujimori government maintained an alliance with the command of the Armed Forces, led by General Nicolás Hermoza, based on four elements. First, the state would continue to implement its counterinsurgency policy. The Armed Forces completely approved the strategy, even though they had not originally designed it (the strategy was designed by a group of SIN analysts). Second, the top leadership circle of the Armed Forces would continue, although this coopted group of loyalists has shown, since 1993, increasing independence from the president and from his advisor Vladimiro Montesinos. Third, Fujimori would not permit investigation of human rights violations committed by the Armed Forces in the counterinsurgency war. To this end, an amnesty law was passed in June 1995 that interrupted trials and liberated those detained for such abuses, including the commando that committed the crimes of La Cantuta and Barrios Altos. This law also conferred amnesty on those officers who were courtmarshaled for "insulting a superior" because they had criticized General Hermoza during the Ecuadorean conflict, as well as those officers involved in the counter-coup plot of 1992. Fourth, no investigation would scrutinize misappropriations that the military leadership had effected or permitted within the Armed Forces. To all of this was added the fact that most of the military leaders supported the government's economic program, which managed to stabilize the economy and generate economic growth. In addition, most had approved the "self-coup" of 5 April 1992, and human rights have not been their principal concern.

Who has coopted whom? The question emerges because Fujimori, who has demonstrated a great facility for disposing of ministers when they become inconvenient, showed an odd loyalty to Hermoza despite internal political and military pressure for his resignation. According to internal army sources,[42] Fujimori tried unsuccessfully in December 1993 to name Hermoza Minister of Defense and put another comandante general in his place. Hermoza refused to leave. The same effort and outcome were repeated in 1994. The moment to replace Hermoza would have been at the beginning of the new administration in 1995, when the re-elected Fujimori enjoyed overwhelming popular support. The military leadership, including the comandantes generales of the navy and the air force and the Minister of Defense, was relieved of its duties, but Hermoza was retained.

Does this mean that Hermoza and a sector of the military governed, rather than Fujimori? Definitely not. In the first place, it was not the military as an institution that was in control, but rather Hermoza himself. Hermoza maintained his command, moreover, at the behest of Fujimori rather than the Armed Forces. Within the army, Hermoza had become a *caudillo* (personalist leader or strongman) who managed the institution on the basis of a series of alliances with other officers as well as internal espionage and personal protection provided by the Special Protection Operations Battalion (Batallón de Operaciones de Protección Especial; BOPE). Hermoza reproduced Fujimori's cooption system within the army, but this time at the service of his own interests, not those of the president. But, this situation did not mean that Hermoza ruled the country. Neither Hermoza nor the Armed Forces were interested in intervening in nonmilitary spheres of the state. They did not intervene in economic policy, privatization projects, foreign policy, agrarian policy, and the like. Their main interests were the defeat of subversion and the maintenance of impunity in the face of political investigations of human rights violations, corruption, and links to drug trafficking.

Hermoza's power did not signify power for the Armed Forces as a whole. As an institution, the Armed Forces were weaker now than ever. Hermoza is basically a powerful caudillo who manipulates the military institution, and once he retires the military will remain in its position of political weakness. [*Editor's note:* As this book went to press in 1997, Hermoza remained in power.] If we compare the prerogatives that the military used to enjoy with what they had by 1996, it is clear that the military's power diminished in a process that began with Belaúnde, continued under García, and concludes with Fujimori. This was a military that no longer elected its comandantes generales, and in which the president and his advisor, Montesinos, made key decisions about retirements, promotions, and postings of generals. The Armed Forces no longer decided unilaterally, as they once did, who were the country's enemies. Their capacity to exert pressure to obtain approval for their budgetary requests has declined almost to nothing, as was evident during the conflict with Ecuador. Their officer pay scale had become astonishingly low (in March 1994 a division general received US$280.00, a second lieutenant $230.00), and like civilians, they suffered the surveillance of the SIN. SIN's power reflected not military power so much as Montesinos's own power; he was the real chief of the SIN.[43]

The relationship between Fujimori and the Armed Forces proved more complicated than appearances. Fujimori used the Armed Forces first to maintain himself in power while implementing an intelligence war against Sendero and a neoliberal economic shock program. Hermoza, and the military clique that revolves around him, used Fujimori to obtain power within the army and arrive at the point where it would be difficult to remove them. In short, a strong symbiotic relationship had developed between Fujimori and Hermoza. At the same time, among the majority of "neutral" officers who were neither institucionalista nor Fujimori loyalists, a symbiotic relationship with the president, based on pragmatism rather than ideology, also seemed evident by 1995–1996. The old dream of the Armed Forces was to achieve a country that compared favorably, in terms of power, with its neighbors. In another era, some officers believed that this goal was best achieved through the kind of socialism *a la peruana* promoted by Velasco, while others opted for the corporatism of Morales Benítez and others favored fascism. In the 1990s, many came to believe that the best route was through economic neoliberalism. Fujimori, with his counterinsurgency victories and economic successes, seemed to provide this path. But the price was heavy. The military had become politically strong as a tool of the president or of the caudillo Hermoza, but politically weak as an institution. The military had lost the capacity to elect its own commanders, develop its own program, and defend its own interests.

This process of weakening as a political institution at the national level did not imply a lack of popular support or of political importance at regional and local levels of power. After all, the power of the military in regional and local governments increased drastically with the installation of political-military chiefs in the emergency zones. In the sierra regions where the peasant defense patrols (*rondas*) proliferated, the Armed Forces sought to handle them as an extension of the military's organization. At the least, the military sought and received the rondas' support. The political parties, submerged in a profound crisis, were not capable of participating in forming rural rondas and as a result had no influence over them. Thus, the Armed Forces were closer to the rondas than were the parties. The process of rapprochement was facilitated in part by the fact that the Peruvian Armed Forces evolved from a "dirty war" approach to counterinsurgency toward an emphasis on gaining the support of the population. Military operations in the countryside and in the marginal zones of the cities gradually shifted toward civic action and intelligence and became official policy in 1993. The theme of human rights, moreover, did not block popular support of the military much, once human-rights violations became very selective, in part because the political culture gave preference to effective authoritarian "solutions" over democratic governments incapable of solving "problems."[44]

Conclusions

Three principal conclusions follow from the preceding analysis. First, civilian control of the military did not always guarantee democracy. During the three governments of Belaúnde, García, and Fujimori, there had always arisen tensions between civilian authorities and the military, and by one means or another the civilian presidents sought to control the Armed Forces. Nonetheless, the president who went the farthest in creating a system of control and cooption that enabled him to control the Peruvian Armed Forces was Fujimori. But he used this power to close the congress. Civilian control was not necessarily synonymous with democratic governance.

Second, cooption of the military leadership could provide an apparent stability in the short run, but exacted a high cost in the medium run. It provoked grave conflicts within the military as well as between the military and civilians, and it weakened the military's professionalism as well as its institutional integrity and strength. To the extent that the military is organized vertically, coopting the high command may seem like the best way to control the whole institution. Nonetheless, in the medium term, cooption led a sector of high and middling officers to perceive that their superiors defended neither the subordinate officers' interests nor those of the institution. As we have seen, time and time again such perceptions produced grave conflicts that threatened subordination—both the chain of command within the military, and the subordination of the military to civilian authority. As was evident in the crisis of military supplies and in the poor performance in the 1995 conflict with Ecuador, the selection of high leaders by criteria of loyalty and cooption also weakened professionalism and institutional strength. The most "loyal" officers who aspired to promotion were not necessarily the most capable ones in military terms, and loyalists who benefited from a symbiotic personal relationship with the president did not necessarily press hard for institutional needs.

A certain irony attached to the use of cooption to control the Armed Forces. In 1990 the newly elected Fujimori feared a coup, because the lack of a party machinery and governing team made his administration seem, at first, like a quick route to chaos, and because pro-coup efforts were already evident toward the end of the García administration. This was the perception that enabled the advisor Vladimiro Montesinos to consolidate his power; he presented himself as a person knowledgeable about the Armed Forces who (aside from organizing a strategy to defeat Sendero Luminoso) could prevent a coup by placing loyal officers in key posts. Fujimori demonstrated his own effectiveness from the first moment and was not ideologically objectionable to the military. Therefore, he might have been able to dispense with cooption. The president's own insecurity, however, fed first by Montesinos and then by Hermoza, led Fujimori to attack the institucionalista sector and thereby provoke the very "countercoup" plot that he had sought to avoid. The sequence was a self-fulfilling prophecy.

Our third principal conclusion is that notwithstanding the institutional weakening of the military, the Armed Forces have achieved a presence of "high compatibility" with society and power in Peru. This high compatibility has three important elements. First, as we have seen, the military leadership has developed strong symbiotic relations with the Fujimori administration. Second, military thought shifted from statism to neoliberalism. The military junta of 1962–1963 created the National Planning Institute and issued an agrarian reform law. Velasco's military government (1968–1975) carried out a profound agrarian reform; it nationalized petroleum, railroads, large-scale mining, the fishing industry, and part of the banking system; and it made the state into the key planner and intervenor in the economy. The Morales Bermúdez military regime (1975–1980) did not expand the state sector of the economy but did not dismantle it either. The military scheme of rule and economics failed, however, and the discredited military turned power over to civilians. During the course of the 1980s, military thought evolved toward a rejection of the interventionist state, and by the time a military sector planned a coup against García in late 1989, their Libro Verde plan for governance called for a neo-liberal program. Precisely for this reason, the military did not put up much resistance to Fujimori's neoliberal scheme, which reverted the reforms of the 1968 military government by privatizing mining, petroleum, and communications, and by passing a new Land Law that eliminated the effects of the Agrarian Reform.[45] The third component of the military's "high compatibility" is linked to social perceptions. Given their evolution from a "dirty war" policy of massive and indiscriminate repression toward a policy of select repression and civic action, and given that Shining Path's brutality provoked a great rejection by the Peruvian population, the Armed Forces managed to achieve a certain popular support as fighters against senderista terrorism.

Notes

1 See SIPRI 1982–1987.
2 Tulberg 1987.
3 Gorriti 1990.
4 Interview with General Francisco Morales Bermúdez, 5 July 1989.
5 Escuela Superior de Guerra 1980a, 1980b.
6 Lowenthal 1976; Stepan 1978; Urriza 1978; Fitzgerald 1979; Pease 1980; Palmer 1982; Rodríguez Beruff 1983; Kruijt 1989, 1991.
7 Interview with journalist Alejandro Guerrero, 27 August 1992.
8 One must be careful with the numbers of disappeared as there are notable discrepancies between sources. For example, by 1984, according to DESCO (1989, vol. 1: 51), 466 people had been disappeared, while Perupaz (1994 bulletin in possession of author) reported 1,288 disappearance victims, and *Idéele* (1992, No. 34: 2) counted 2,108.
9 Thorndike 1969.
10 The sons of President (and General) Francisco Morales Bermúdez and General Javier Tantaleón (one of Morales's most important ministers) were apristas. During this period the Armed Forces suspended its annual pilgrimage to the tombs of officers assassinated by APRA in 1932.
11 The quotation and the accusations are from a typical clandestine COMACA flyer, left on the desk of a colonel (whose name remains confidential) in the Secretariat of National Defense in 1989. The flyer directly implicated President Alan García as a beneficiary of embezzled funds deposited in a foreign bank account.
12 DESCO 1989, vol. 1: 147–48.
13 The CICLAS was the aprista administration's attempt to create a coordinating entity for the counterinsurgency struggle, but it was discredited after the Tocache episode and disappeared. CICLAS's work was never very important; it had only met once during a period of eight months.
14 DESCO 1989, vol. 1: 177. Tensions between the army and the police also arose in connection to the fight against drug trafficking, to U.S. congressional accusations of army collusion with traffickers, and to support of the police by the U.S. Drug Enforcement Administration. For overviews of the drug trafficking problem, see Obando 1993; J. Gonzales 1992.
15 The Rodrigo Franco Commando's first attack came on 28 July 1988, when it assassinated Manuel Febres, the defense attorney for imprisoned Shining Path leader Osmán Morote. The suspicion that APRA controlled this organization from within the Interior Ministry seems consistent with the fact that its paramilitary operations ceased when Alan García left office.
16 "Decreto Legislativo 435, "Modifican, sustituyen y adicionan varios artículos al Decreto Ley 22654—Ley del Sistema de Defensa Nacional," *El Peruano*, 27 September 1987, 57862–57863.

17 At that time, the possibility was debated of naming Raúl Chávez Murga, Technical Director of the National Defense Department, as the first civilian Minister of Defense. Chávez was a career functionary—velasquista with Velasco, an anti-velasquista under Morales Bermúdez, a Popular Action supporter of Belaúnde, and, finally, an aprista with Alan García. The Armed Forces would have accepted his past, but not his recent aprista militancy. Moreover, Chávez had been the one to propose that the Defense Ministry include the Secretariat of National Defense and the Joint Command of the Armed Forces, which caused grave administrative and planning problems. For these reasons, the Armed Forces finally vetoed his nomination.

18 Internal opposition within the air force to Vucetich's command grew to such a point that the air force's Intelligence Service tape recorded Vucetich's telephone conversations, in which misappropriations were revealed, and turned the tapes over to the journalist César Hildebrandt, who played them twice on Peruvian television.

19 Interview with General Alejandro Antúnez de Mayolo, who had been Chief of the General Military Staff of the Army at the end of the García administration, 7 September 1995.

20 Interview with Captain Hugo de la Rocha Marie, 3 February 1996.

21 I became aware of these plans in 1989 when I worked as advisor to the High Directorate of the Secretariat of National Defense.

22 Interview with "Colonel A," who participated in the High Command's coup plot. He remains in active duty, for which reason he has requested anonymity.

23 Some parts of the Libro Verde were subsequently leaked to the press and published by *Oiga*, 12 July 1993 and 19 July 1993. The U.S. Embassy obtained knowledge of the coup preparations and an Embassy functionary met with one of the generals organizing the coup in order to state that the United States would oppose it.

24 This assertion is based on conversations with retired naval officers who worked for Vargas Llosa's campaign.

25 Interview with Juan Velit, advisor to the SIN during the period in question, 16 January 1990.

26 I obtained evidence of wire tapping in 1989 during my tenure in the National Defense Secretariat. Employees normally assumed that their telephones were tapped by the SIN.

27 The strategy for confronting the subversion was not entirely a creation of Montesinos. During the last years of García's administration, a group of civilian and military advisors of the SIN had taken the initiative to design a counterinsurgency plan that included legislation necessary to confront the problem. The head of this group was Rafael Merino Bartet. This information is based on an interview with "Colonel B," a member of the group of SIN consul-

tants who elaborated the counterinsurgency strategy. He is presently on active duty, for which reason he has requested anonymity.

28 Interview with General Edgardo Mercado Jarrín, 17 February 1994.

29 "Decreto Legislativo 752, Ley de Situación Militar," *El Peruano* (12 November 1991), No. 4130, 101700-101708.

30 Vidal 1993.

31 For an example of the Left's criticism of these decrees, see Comisión Andina de Juristas 1991.

32 The military position was evident in the conference organized by CEPEI (Centro Peruano de Estudios Internacionales) in January 1992.

33 Lecture given by Carlos Blancas, Alan García's former Minister of Justice, Instituto de Estudios Peruanos, 1992.

34 This was the impression left by two speeches to the Peruvian military establishment, in August 1992, by Dr. Manuel Migone, advisor to the High Command of the Navy, in the Escuela Superior de Guerra Naval, and by Retired Colonel José Bailetti, Director of the Instituto Nacional de Investigaciones de la Defensa Nacional (INEDEN). Active-duty army generals were present in the second lecture and the impression that their commentaries left was one of defeatism.

35 In July and August 1991, Ecuadorean troops incurred into Peruvian territory and it proved necessary to resort to a diplomatic accord, disliked by sectors of the Armed Forces, because the military was not sufficiently operational to repel the foreign troops from national territory. For low morale provoked by low operational capacity, see also the letter from then-Minister of Defense General Jorge Torres Aciego to then-Minister of the Economy Carlos Boloña, in Torres y Torres 1995.

36 As the United States is not a signatory to the accord signed in Caracas in 1954 on diplomatic asylum, its embassies do not provide asylum and Robles ended up taking asylum in Argentina.

37 Rubio 1994: 4–7.

38 Interview with "Lieutenant Colonel C," 5 February 1987, member of the organizational staff of the Army's Intelligence School, and currently a brigadier general. He maintained that during the García period more than a third of the students (majors and comandantes) of the Advanced Course in Intelligence had been involved in one manner or another in drug trafficking.

39 *La República*, 9 January 1995.

40 It is of interest to notice that in 1992, when friction developed between the army and air force officials assigned to intercept drug planes in the Huallaga Valley, the air force officials claimed that a sector of the army colluded with drug traffickers. This was precisely the period of Bellido's command in the region. Interview with "Journalist D," 6 June 1993, who, for reasons of safety, has requested anonymity. This same information was confirmed through conversations with different air force officers.

41 Interviews with "Air Force Colonel E," "Air Force Colonel F," and "Air Force Comandante G," 6 April 1995.

42 For obvious reasons, these sources must remain anonymous.

43 For further discussion of the atrophied power of the military, see Obando 1994.

44 On this point, the national survey of attitudes on issues associated with the strengthening of democracy carried out by the Apoyo Institute in July–August 1994 is very revealing. See APOYO 1994.

45 For further discussion of military thought on economic policy, see Obando 1995.

TWELVE

Alberto Fujimori: "The Man Peru Needed?"

Patricia Oliart

❖ This essay explores sociocultural aspects of the "Fujimori phenomenon," particularly his significance as symbol or force that expressed
popular aspirations that institutional political formulas could not fulfill in
1990–1992. From the electoral triumph that first swept him into the presidency in 1990, to his reelection in 1995, the government of Alberto Fujimori received the constant support of broad sectors of the population. From
1990 to 1994, the polling agency IMASEN reported that Fujimori received
the support of 65 percent of Peruvians surveyed among various regions,
age groups, and economic sectors. Their surveys found that support for the
president ran particularly high in the departments of the Andean sierra.[1]

The reasons for this support have been the object of much debate and
commentary. I believe, however, that a particularly important subject for exploring and understanding the acceptance and support received by Fujimori
is his interaction with different groups within the population. Through his
short public speeches, his plain style of speaking (and perhaps, for this
reason, a style of great impact), his gestures, and even his clothing, he
demonstrates his particular understanding of Peruvian society, his distance
from traditional formulas, and his knowledge of the political culture of distinct social, cultural, and regional groups of the country. Beyond the impact
of his concrete political measures, the emotive response generated by these
manifestations appears crucial to Fujimori's popularity among diverse social
sectors. We Peruvians have access to Fujimori's style through his frequent
presidential visits to different places in the country, fragments of which
are transmitted constantly in the media. In visiting small communities,
the president makes use of diverse backgrounds to project himself to all
Peruvians.

Concretely, I suggest that Fujimori, from 1990 to at least 1995, symbolically satisfied, through his presence in power, the need for inclusion and recognition by groups previously excluded. In addition, he demonstrated to the middle classes that he could take care of their needs without committing them to an ideological affiliation or call to action. Finally, I propose that the president established a relationship of complicity with the majority in not reinforcing institutions or seeking organized popular participation, and in leaving untouched the traditionally distant relation between citizens and political power. This approach also implied leaving perennial corruption untouched, as well as providing new extra-legal routes for obtaining benefits without complying with norms.

On the following pages I develop these ideas, first by reviewing briefly how Peruvian intellectuals explained Fujimori's triumph. Then I discuss some features of the social and political context within which emerged the political figure of Fujimori. I subsequently refer to the characteristics of his particular style and its engagement with aspects of national culture. Finally, I discuss the implications of this relationship for the future of Peru.

The "Fujimori Phenomenon"

The election of El Chino ("the Chinaman," which in Peru is a common way to refer to persons of Asian appearance or origin) in 1990 elicited many comments and explanations on the part of Peruvian intellectuals. All agreed that the crisis of the traditional parties had left them unable to sell presidential candidates successfully (one communications specialist referred to a crisis of "electoral marketing"). The dominant political cultures were exhausted, unable to take responsibility for emergent social groups. The form of democracy that the traditional parties had embodied was in question.[2]

Fujimori's triumph was therefore interpreted as an emergency exit, a popular gamble on the unknown in the absence of a national leader capable of representing the "new Peru." The election results expressed the autonomous suffrage of those who did not want to elect a "snob" (*pituco*) as president. That is, they did not want Mario Vargas Llosa. During the 1990 campaign, Fujimori clearly demonstrated that he was not subordinated to the *criollos*, or white coastal elite. He represented for the *cholo* bourgeoisie the possibility for emancipation from criollo power. (In Peru, "cholo" is a common term for persons of quite dark phenotype who are neither "Indian" nor necessarily "mestizo" in culture or racial descent, and is often synonymous with the idea of "popular" or humble social background. In many contexts, it is also synonymous with the idea of "not far removed from 'Indian' and rural ancestry.") Jürgen Golte has said that in voting for Fujimori, the *serranos* (people from the sierra) expressed their desire for change and their capacity to adapt to what was new, and to project their own development on the basis of it. The criollos, on the other hand, were incapable of absorbing such desires or innovation.[3] Isidro Valentín, on the basis of interviews, concluded that Fujimori won because of a Peruvian propensity to believe in unexpected solutions. Thus, an obscure man could plausibly be the person Peruvians were waiting for, the leader who would solve the country's grave problems.[4] Many also identified with Fujimori as a man who was not white. But, he was not quite cholo either, susceptible to denigration by others. Fujimori was the son of Japanese immigrants; he also appeared to be unassuming and hardworking; he did not talk too much; "he is like us." Fujimori has demonstrated a profound understanding, although perhaps only an intuitive one, of some elements of Peruvian political culture, elements little used by other politicians.

Some Antecedents

I begin these reflections on the "Fujimori phenomenon" by mentioning a process and an institution not generally included when we talk about social actors in the new Peru. I refer to the emergence of a new middle class and to the role that state universities played in this process. In the 1960s, some social scientists and intellectuals perceived that new social groups were emerging in Lima, consisting of people who arrived principally from the small cities of the interior and from rural Andean areas. Aníbal Quijano would define these cholos as constituting a social stratum in formation, which emerged by differentiating itself culturally from the indigenous masses in order to assume new economic and social roles.[5] Francois Bourricaud announced the arrival of a new mestizo middle class, leaving aside the question of its potential political orientation as an unknown factor, difficult to predict at that time.[6]

The following decades witnessed the vigor of new groups that, although diverse in ideological markers and in economic activities, nonetheless shared some common cultural characteristics. Two of the more important commonalities in the development of a new, mostly mestizo, middle class have been their nonwhite (or at least non*limeño*) ethnocultural identity, and their need to legitimate their social situation and their recently acquired economic standing through access to higher education and, for some, to professional careers.

I think that these characteristics basically describe the environment out of which emerged two central political figures in the Peru of recent times: Alberto Fujimori and Abimael Guzmán. Both leaders were formed intellectually in public universities and began to forge the bases of their future political power while they were authorities in those universities. The role of the Peruvian university in this process of social emergence was not foreseen by either Bourricaud or Quijano in the 1960s. Nonetheless, the state university has served as a fundamental cultural institution for the development and circulation of ideas that have given political and cultural force to the new middle class. Diverse agents and circumstances converged to facilitate the growth of the university system in recent decades. In Lima, and especially in the provinces, the universities made themselves into alternative centers of political opinion and ideological influence, counter to the perceived dominant culture controlled by the mass media.[7]

The ideas expressed in the universities circulated fluidly at diverse social levels, among other reasons because one of the distinguishing characteristics of the new Peruvian middle class was the diversity of social spaces in which it moved and reproduced. This fluid circulation and dissemination of ideas was possible due to various phenomena. In addition to the expansion of the educational sector, the growth of the state, and the development of the popular organizations, there was the fact that money had changed hands, giving rise to a very dynamic social sector. This sector's origin in the popular classes and movement in different social ambits created unprecedented bridges of communication between different economic groups, and strong social-cultural affinities difficult to understand without experiencing these processes. The political behavior of this new middle class and its spheres of influence represent a complex phenomenon of political culture, in need of study if we are to identify clearly some of the obstacles to institutional modernization and democratic development in Peru.

As they emerged, the new middle classes made use of ideological currents such as Marxism, *indigenismo,* and various versions of populism to open a political and social space in the country through discourses of opposition to oligarchical rule and imperialism.[8] They were relatively successful in this project. But the capacity for mobilization and achievement through such discourses entered total crisis in the decade of the 1980s; such ideological currents could no longer serve to legitimate more recently emerged sectors of society. The exhaustion of these ideologies—to mention only domestic factors that converged in the late 1980s—was a result of great disillusionment with President Alan García, the disintegration of the Left as a serious political force, and the fear and repudiation provoked by Shining Path intransigence. Together these factors provoked the tumultuous fall of an ideological current until then relatively successful for a new middle class and those popular sectors allied with it. (Compare the discussion of the fate of "third paths" in Part III of this book.)

The terrain was thus prepared for the emergence of some kind of alternative, a new use of political space as self-recognition and for construction of a political and social identity distinct from that of the criollos.[9] Vargas Llosa, and the groups he led, definitely did not offer such an alternative. Vargas Llosa and his allies reproduced with utter clarity the exclusionary style and language to which the country has been so susceptible.

One last cultural element in the climate that gave rise to Fujimori was the relationship that the masses have always had with national political authority. This has been a relationship of distance and pragmatic rapprochements, but without the participation of the civilian population in decision making and without a clear sense of representation of collective popular interests in the corridors of power. Carlos Franco illustrates this relationship by tracing the constant fluctuations between political loyalties and populism in Peru. The politician who wins popular support is the one who in the exercise of this remote power shows concern for the people and provides certain significant benefits.[10] It is not difficult, therefore, to understand that people often related personally to the president and assumed that the president himself made all the important decisions. Indeed, given widespread mistrust of authorities and the bureaucracy, the relationship with the president himself may have seemed more secure.

The Fujimori Style

Fujimori's first electoral campaign was marked by various gestures that gained the sympathy of the poorest sectors. The candidate would arrive in various pueblos in his "Fujimobile," a cart pulled by a tractor. Fujimori himself designed his publicity to be deliberately rustic in appearance; he used regional clothes and danced to the music of the communities he visited. Thus he transformed the scenes through which candidates traditionally presented themselves to the nation.[11] His motto was "Honor, Technology, and Work." And he promised to be "A President Like You."

Once in the presidency, Fujimori developed a style of communication directed principally at the popular sectors. He has demonstrated from the beginning that he is very conscious of the media; he never forgets what will be seen by the public. Thus, in the middle of a nationally televised official meeting he might throw out a highly colloquial phrase such as "the meat of the matter is . . ." (*la verdad de la milanesa es . . .*). Regarding this consciousness of the media and the production of political events through the television screen, the media critic Javier Protzel sustains that there has been a change in Peruvian culture and in the relationship between the president and the media, a change that Alan García initiated when he lost his own party's support.[12] Fujimori has developed his own technique for politically manipulating his image, thereby reinforcing the "media driven leadership" (*liderazgo mediático*) that, according to Protzel, replaces obsolete and discredited party structures through elaborate discursive engineering. During the first two or three years of the regime Fujimori seems to have consulted with experts in the production of "media events." Some were intended to create a specific psychological impact in moments of difficulty for Fujimori. Such was the case when Fujimori prayed for the future of the country before weeping images of the Virgin in Lima. Thus, free from any references to ideological doctrine, the leader establishes contact with the masses through emotions, through a knowledge that tunes in to aspects of emergent political cultures.

The image that Fujimori seems to have of poor Peruvians is actually quite traditional and for this reason, perhaps, arouses little opposition from the poor or the middle classes. Fujimori appears to direct himself toward a people that needs someone to care for them with wisdom and firmness. In simple language the president basically informs the country of what he does and what he will do. In the same simple language, he responds to the critiques of adversaries. His style contrasts with that of any other national leader since he does not assume the role of politician-educator. In his discourse, Fujimori neither insists, demands, nor suggests that people change their behavior. This approach contrasts markedly with Alan García who, in his daily speeches from the balcony of the presidential palace, told Peruvians that we had to plant trees, eat *kiwicha* (an Andean cereal), and include more fiber in our diets, among the many other topics he considered relevant for the country. Conveying this advice, he used a language obviously influenced by readings of recent academic literature. Fujimori distanced himself completely from this image. He sustained that in Peru it is necessary to do things, that "philosophizing and speaking pretty does not get anyone anywhere." To the popular masses he presents himself as a doer (*hacedor*), he offers public works such as schools in his own name, and he takes credit for the successful projects carried out under his administration. "I work like this, silently. You all want a new school for your children, and here it is now, so that your children may enjoy it. I do not make false promises. Watch out for those who will come to offer you things and then will not follow through. You know them by now and you know me and you know that I come through with what I offer."[13]

When the president goes to a community he often establishes an accord for a local development project to benefit the very same locality. In an improvised meeting he learns about the community's most urgent priority and then commits to financing the materials, in exchange for which the community commits to providing the labor.[14] The flip side of Fujimori's stance as a "doer, not educator"—and something that perhaps generates feelings of comfort and affinity on the part of most Peruvians—is his attitude towards legal procedures. Fujimori appears ready to disregard legal norms when they get in the way of what he wants to do. Examples of this relaxed and even disdainful attitude toward institutional norms came through on the occasion of the "self-coup" of 5 April 1992 in his evasive and even blatantly false answers to international human rights organizations, and in declarations to the press after the Bahamas meeting.[15] With these and other actions Fujimori seemed to suggest that if the law was not in accord with his plans, he would find a way to obviate it or, in the best of cases, change it to do what he considered right. Such a president becomes appealing in a society in which legality is in any event subverted by corruption—in which public officials commonly accept bribes, judges charge for a favorable verdict, and police cancel a traffic citation in exchange for a U.S. dollar.

As a president who is a "doer" rather than a "talker," Fujimori declared that his administration "has put an end to the cocktail-party style of governing" (*gobernar en coctelitos*). Rather, he has always been "right there where events were happening" (*el lugar de los hechos*) in order to ensure that everything would be done right. He personally knows the needs of all Peruvians, since his presidential helicopter can take him anywhere. Fujimori's declarations have commonly referred to that which other politicians have promised and abandoned, and how little they have actually seen of the country. Fuji-

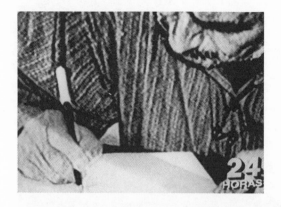

MEDIA EVENTS: FUJIMORI AS
CONQUEROR.
(left) Abimael Guzmán, now
a prisoner, signs letter petitioning Fujimori for peace on
national television.
(below) Fujimori as a ruler
and partner of the victorious
military.

mori has referred to the traditional political class as a group alienated from
the interests of the country. He has established a discourse in which they
are "the other" while he and the people are "us."[16]

In the western political tradition the political parties provide vehicles for
the representation of different sectors of society. For Fujimori this role is
not valid because he himself represents the interests of the majority. He has
taken it upon himself to travel the entire country constantly in order to see
personally to satisfying the needs and demands of the "forgotten pueblos,"
as he likes to call them.

In his effort to distance himself from traditional political behaviors, Fuji-

MEDIA EVENTS: FUJIMORI AS POPULIST.
(above) Fujimori begins conventionally,
but ends with a spontaneous affective
connection.
(left) Fujimori dons Andean garb to
speak at a rally in the highlands.

mori has broken with convention at unexpected moments. He may throw
water at people, mount a bicycle, donkey, motorcycle, or tractor, or simply
decide to wet his feet in a creek as he hikes to some outlying village. He has
made informality part of his style and his audience expects to be surprised
by some of his gestures.

When Fujimori arrives somewhere, whether at some tiny hamlet or a
provincial capital, he generally is showered with gifts, including typical regional clothing. Fujimori always puts on one or more of these items, so that
he is pictured in the media in local dress, a gesture that may mean a lot
to the people he is visiting. He wraps himself in whatever might be given

him; he chooses hats, ponchos, *cusmas* (Andean tunics), feathered crowns, and even flags. He knows how to tell the people that he is one of them. All that Fujimori seems to ask of the people is that they let him do his work. In exchange he expects only their approval and trust. His "new form of doing politics" consists, in synthesis, of adjusting himself to the type of relationship that large sectors of the population have traditionally had with the state, but cleansing his discourse of doctrinal elements while developing a personal and affective relationship that is much more intense and direct as a result of his constant travels.

With the middle classes the relationship is different. The criollo middle classes support Fujimori without necessarily feeling committed to him. In 1992, one such middle-class woman from Lima described the attitude of Peruvians toward Fujimori as something similar to the gestures of circus seals: they shake their heads as if in disapproval while clapping their flippers in applause. Perhaps because of this ambiguous relationship—an ambiguity that Fujimori doubtlessly perceives—the president does not demand from the criollo middle- and upper-class groups any kind of personal identification. At the same time, however, he does not offer them anything that might sound demagogic. In 1991, after the antidrug "summit" with President George Bush in San Antonio, Texas, Fujimori visited the University of Texas in Austin. A representative of Peruvian undergraduates asked him what he wanted from youth who had left the country to study. Fujimori responded that they must feel very happy to be studying abroad, a privilege enjoyed by few Peruvians, and that all he could offer them was employment at $300 (U.S.) a month. In short, Fujimori did not recur to the easy rhetoric of demagoguery. He does not try especially to please an urban, criollo, middle- or upper-class audience. He distances himself ostensibly from the privileged, but he does not ask them to sacrifice anything either. Thus he establishes his independence from the traditional criollo style of politics, while avoiding populist references to notions of justice and injustice.

It is interesting to note that even references to the importance of pre-Hispanic culture for national identity, so frequent in recent administrations, have been quite scarce in Fujimori's speeches. His project expresses an intent to construct a collective identity based not on past history but, rather, on what is to be done in the future. After his first electoral campaign, in which he pitted *cholitos* against whites (*blanquitos*), Fujimori has not gone back to interpellating Peruvians according to ethnic labels. Possibly, this was also part of his success, since to obviate all references to what has been and is a permanent source of conflict is one of the possible options for registering changes in the country's ethnic relations.

The New Politician

From the beginning of Fujimori's administration, the struggle against Shining Path and the MRTA (Movimiento Revolucionario Túpac Amaru) occupied an important place in the president's discourse. In his words and attitude, he demonstrated himself as firmer and more emotionally committed than either of his two recent predecessors, and conceded nothing to the armed insurgents on an ideological or political terrain. To some extent he had the advantage of dealing with known enemies. Unlike Belaúnde, for example, who believed the guerrillas to be agents imported by an anachronistic international Communist movement, Fujimori's experience as a university authority and his particular relationship with the intelligence services allowed him to perceive terrorists with a more visible local face and with weaknesses that could be attacked.

In 1990 the police obtained a video tape in which Abimael Guzmán and high senderista leaders appeared dancing. Fujimori played the tape for the nation and seemed to direct it particularly at Sendero sympathizers. Fujimori used a very basic argument to puncture the Guzmán mystique. The mythic leader was a drunk who partied while thousands of Peruvians, including Guzmán's own combatants, died in a war launched by Sendero. On this and other occasions Fujimori has used the mass media to confront Shining Path by counterposing his image with that of Guzmán. He has lashed out against Shining Path constantly and has challenged it in territories where Shining Path had previously appeared to be the sole actor. Peruvian television has shown a very active head of state traveling throughout the country, supervising public works projects and addressing the public in unconventional scenarios, always associated with the task of constructing and generating resources, at a time when Shining Path's message was perceived as one of total destruction.

Another clearly identifiable feature of Fujimori's political style has been his disrespectful and hard-line treatment of the opposition. Any criticism of his government is taken (by him or by firm political allies, such as Marta Chávez) as an offense and an expression of overt opposition, almost a manifestation of ingratitude. Fujimori generally refers to his adversaries in two ways, either as traditional politicians who are only motivated by personal wellbeing and have no real concern for Peru, or as pawns of terrorism with whom it is not worth debating because the whole world has already turned its back on them. He has not demonstrated much capacity for listening or for modifying his policies through dialogue.

The anthropologist Xavier Albó has described how leaderships are formed among the Aymaras and how, once the leader is chosen, there is no social place for those who do not accept his leadership, for opposition, or for processing of conflicts through negotiation or conversation. Rupture becomes the only way to resolve conflict.[17] For this reason any kind of divergent opposition or opinion is seen as a threat to the community and is not accepted. I think that this difficulty with dialogue, in addition to the belief that it is neither necessary nor desirable to oppose the leader, are also characteristics of a political culture shared by many Peruvians. Such characteristics perhaps become more obvious in times of crisis.

In the Peru of recent years, one could perceive attitudes of extreme aversion toward opposition and toward anyone who used terms associated with leftist language. After the experience of daily fear, with violence and spilling of blood becoming common, the government's struggle against Shining Path—particularly the capture of Guzmán—represented the promise of peace, a tranquility which many Peruvians wanted preserved at all costs.

As a result, those who had been away from Peru from 1990 to 1995 could perceive a change in lexicon notable at every level, among the mass media, one's friends, and even in the language of social sciences. Terms that allude to oppressive social relations were now almost never mentioned, and the criticism of power was now focused, in the best of cases, on the abuse of authority or on authority badly used. Some people could not tolerate listening to any language that smacks of Marxism, social complaint, or radical criticism of either the government or the exercise of power and domination in Peru.

The Calandria research group carried out some surveys and interviews during the 1995 electoral campaign and found that informants frequently associated ideas of hatred and social resentment with leftist affiliation. This fear and repudiation of candidates identified with leftist positions led many people not to vote for the list headed by Javier Pérez de Cuellar.[18] Fear of returning to the years of war, combined with the failure of the most radical currents in politics and in the ability to represent popular aspirations, made the Left appear as a potential threat to the peace that had been achieved.

This association of leftist candidates with terrorism was promoted by official spokespersons of the government and found an echo among many people. Two taxi drivers with whom I conversed a few days before the elections serve as examples. One told me that he would not vote for Pérez de Cuellar because there were known leftists in his list, and that they were resentful people. In Peru, he observed, we no longer supported such resentment. The other taxi driver told me that the true terrorists were those who hid in the legal system in order to become parliamentarians and then use their official posts to assist the senderistas. Another example of repudiation of anything remotely smacking of criticism of the government came from a middle-class woman who became indignant when her son mentioned how the government continued to abuse human rights. "Don't tell me, I don't want to know, I only know that now I'm not afraid to go out, I don't suffer when my children get home late thinking that they died from a car bomb." Significantly, in earlier elections this same woman had sometimes voted for candidates of the Left.

Thus we can discern a climate in which Peruvians' aspirations for their country have been reduced to something very basic and almost primitive: a guarantee of survival in tranquility. Given the disdain for political discourses, the fear of dialogue and debate, and the overestimation of concrete gains, the future does not appear to shine brightly. Rather it is somber, although perhaps stable. Certainly, progress with peace is a general aspiration that Fujimori seems to offer. But the connection of material progress and the modernization of society, in political terms, is not guaranteed. The president seems to fear the popular organizations, which in his eyes are neither convenient nor valid interlocutors. Few are those who discuss desirable ways of life that go beyond increasing people's capacity for consumption. In this climate, mention of the ideals of justice or equality seems risky, an invitation for violence to return. The fear of politics has created a propitious space for the renewal of forces such as Opus Dei (an international Catholic organization that represents very conservative sectors of the Catholic Church and also allies with Rightest regimes), some of whose members collaborate with the government.

Nonetheless, several decades of constant exposure of the population to radical political discourses have not been in vain. A continuing legacy of this exposure has been a clear sense of distance and liberation from the influence, or ideological power, of the traditional criollo political class. But this popular autonomy merely provides a point of departure from which Peru may now go in almost any direction.

Notes

1 Compiled from figures published in various issues of *IMASEN Confidencial* (Lima), 1990–1994.
2 Protzel 1994. Interpretations by Peruvian intellectuals include Valentín 1993a, 1993b; Grompone 1990, 1991.
3 Golte 1994.
4 Valentín 1993a.
5 Quijano 1980. This slender volume consists of two long essays, "Dominación y Cultura" and "Lo Cholo y el Conflicto Cultural en el Perú," originally written in 1969 and 1964 respectively. The essays and the ideas they contain have been circulating in Latin America for the past three decades.
6 Bourricaud 1989, originally published as *Pouvoir et société dans le Perou contemporain* (Paris: Librarie Armand Colin, 1967) and published in English as *Power and Contemporary Society in Peru* (London: Faber and Faber, 1973).
7 Degregori 1990a, 1990b; Bernales 1972; Lynch 1990; Gorriti 1990, 1992.
8 Nonetheless, I think it is important to identify the ideological and cultural elements that this new middle class shared or shares with the oligarchy and the landowning culture, and with the present dominant groups, independently of whether these groups emerged with an identity distinct from that of the traditional criollos.
9 Boggio, Romero, and Ansión, 1991.
10 See Franco 1991.
11 Jochamowitz 1993.
12 Protzel 1994.
13 Excerpt from inauguration speech in a secondary school in Huaycán, October 1994.
14 Personal communication from Liliana Choy, broadcast journalist for ATV *Noticias*.
15 In a press conference following the Bahama meeting, to which he had been summoned to explain the parliamentary situation in Peru, Fujimori told journalists he had agreed to sign a document that would satisfy those who had summoned him but that in reality would not change any of what he had already begun to implement.
16 Notes by the author from Peruvian television programming and printed media, 1994–1995.
17 Albó 1992.
18 Personal communication from Arturo Granados, researcher for Calandria. The results of this survey have not been published.

THIRTEEN

Sendero Luminoso and Human Rights:

A Perverse Logic that Captured the Country

Carlos Basombrío Iglesias

❖ The doctrine of human rights as we know it today has a short history. It emerged as a reaction against the horrors faced by humanity as a consequence of fascism and World War II. The United Nations formulated the doctrine on 10 December 1948 in the Universal Declaration of Human Rights. Since then, there has been considerable progress in developing concepts, designing mechanisms of protection, and taking concrete action to protect human rights. It is well known that this process has been essentially and almost exclusively directed toward controlling and sanctioning abuses that states have carried out against individuals and groups. This is the raison d'être and the principal feature of global and regional intergovernmental organizations that focus on human rights, and of the thousands of NGOs (nongovernmental organizations) that operate from civil society, in every country in the world, to pressure governments to comply.

The explanation for this consistent focus on the abuse of governments is obvious: States are responsible for protecting the rights of citizens. To achieve this, people concede authority to the state (or the state appropriates such authority). In addition, the state monopolizes the exercise of force. Therefore, when a state, rather than fulfill its protective role, opts to violate the rights of its citizens, whether incidentally or systematically, we find ourselves confronted with a special type of abuse against which individuals find themselves practically defenseless. This situation requires that the abuse be denounced before the rest of humanity, regardless of national frontiers, as a violation of human rights. Within the predominant conception of human rights, crimes committed by individuals and irregular groups should be prosecuted by the state, and in such cases, the human-rights question only involves ensuring that the state follows the law and procedures of due process.[1]

In periods of violence the behavior of states and irregular groups received monitoring through what is known as International Humanitarian Law, which mandates minimum standards of conduct for forces engaged in armed conflict. Initially, International Humanitarian Law was intended to apply principally to international conflicts. Subsequently, the Additional Protocols to the Geneva Convention (which Peru signed) extended the jurisdiction of humanitarian law. These protocols elaborated on points already included in Article 3 of the original convention and established rules of conduct for actors in internal conflicts. The logic of action by the International Committee of the Red Cross, the institution charged with looking after the application of these accords throughout the world, is different, however, from that of human rights organizations. Among other differences, the Red Cross's action is exclusively humanitarian and guards absolute secrecy: It addresses its reports and recommendations only to the parties involved.

Within this general context, let us turn more specifically to Latin America. Latin American human rights movements have emerged almost exclusively as responses to abuses by the state. For this reason, they have held the sympathy of armed rebel groups that, for reasons of principle or political convenience, found the conduct of such organizations to be positive. Demands for respect for International Humanitarian Law have, more often than not, emanated from irregular armies seeking to humanize conflicts. Governments, in contrast, have often resisted such demands out of fear that they would impede the effectiveness of repression.

The eruption of Shining Path in 1980 and its conduct over the succeeding years broke the schemes that had previously shaped the human rights theme in Latin America. For the first time in the region, an insurgent force on the Left developed a systematic practice of violence against the civilian population that matched, and perhaps surpassed, state-sponsored violence. Shining Path's profound disregard for human life, its contempt—in both theory and practice—for the discourse of human rights, and its refusal to ascribe to the norms and principles of International Humanitarian Law rendered it unique on the continent.

Nothing could be further from the intent of this essay than to justify the costly errors and atrocities that the Peruvian state has committed against human rights in recent years. We are diametrically opposed to the argument that human rights are relative and that one must grant a sympathetic latitude in the face of extreme circumstances. Nor do we in any way sympathize with those who attempt, nationally or internationally, to use denunciations of Shining Path's actions to mask the state's own crimes and responsibilities. I believe that my personal trajectory,[2] including more than a decade of human rights work in Peru during which I have clearly condemned and denounced all kinds of atrocities by the Peruvian state, should in any case block a misunderstanding of intent. We reaffirm here that the logic of conduct by the Peruvian state in matters of human rights has been, and in many ways continues to be, unacceptable and counterproductive. It is unacceptable because, in the name of suppressing armed subversion, the state has incurred massive (some would say systematic) violations of human rights. Peru became a country of disappeared persons and torture victims, of people displaced and unjustly detained, of common graves and extrajudicial assassinations, all with absolute impunity. The state's conduct is counterproductive as well because such repression has not only violated the rights of persons, who in the most cases were innocent and poor, but because it also has served as the "gasoline" that helped "to light a prairie fire."

Yet because this book aims to understand Shining Path and its effects on the life of the country, permit us on this occasion to invert the usual practice. Let us begin not with the logic of state conduct, but with that of Shining Path. That is to say, let us try to see how this movement influenced the form that the human rights debate took in Peru. Let us examine how Shining Path defined human rights conceptually and in actual practice, consider how these resonated with the state's own vision and practice of human rights, review what repercussions Shining Path had for the struggle for human rights in Peru and for the consciousness of the population. Finally, with the insurgency defeated, let us consider the new challenges that this heavy inheritance leaves for the future of the human rights question in Peru.

Different from the Beginning

Unlike other Latin American countries, such as Guatemala and El Salvador, that underwent intense processes of political violence during the 1980s, Peru neither lived under a seemingly unending dictatorship nor experienced grave human rights violations before the start of the insurrection. (Both circumstances, one should note, were important factors for understanding the upsurge in violence in the other countries). In Peru, as we know, the incubation of Shining Path's politico-military project culminated toward the end of the 1970s, just as the military government was in retreat and a complex but real political transition toward representative democracy was emerging. (For context, see Hinojosa's essay in this volume.) In 1978 elections took place for a Constituent Assembly, in the midst of great social turbulence and with significant levels of political repression. But none of these limitations blocked the political presence of any sector that chose to participate.[3] The most obvious example is that of Hugo Blanco, the Trotsky-ist ex-guerrilla of the 1960s who had been a prisoner for many years and who obtained 12 percent of the vote without ceding any of his radicalism. Altogether the Left received a third of all votes cast.

But Shining Path remained totally aloof from the decision of the rest of the political forces of the country to participate in the political process that would bring the military government to an end. Shining Path abstained even though the political movements that opted to participate included those of the most radical Left. None of the parties that participated in the presidential elections encountered any significant obstacles. Even the Communist Party of Peru-Red Flag (Partido Comunista del Peru-Patria Roja; PCP-PR)—the most influential Maoist party in the country, whose slogan, "power is born from a gun," clearly revealed its worldview, and which chose to boycott the Constituent Assembly in 1978—ran its own presidential candidate in 1980.[4] In short, it was by choice that Shining Path excluded itself from participation in the open political process. Sendero demonstrated its opinion of the process by initiating armed action on 18 May 1980, the day of the general elections that brought President Fernando Belaúnde to power.

Shining Path also remained aloof from another equally important and real process of democratization. We refer to the emerging participation of popular social sectors in social and political life, a new phenomenon for the country that resulted from mass migration to the cities, increased access to education, and, above all, a generalized and multifaceted process of popular organization that provided new, once unimaginable mechanisms of participation. Of course, in the 1970s the process was still in its initial stages and had not wiped away the terrible imbalances and exclusions of the past. Yet it was rapidly becoming a complex yet interesting challenge to the formal institutionality of the country, traditionally so distant from the common people.

Thus, the surge in political violence in Peru, in clear contrast to the other countries we mentioned, cannot be explained by the impossibility of legal political participation by the future insurgents. Nor, we might add, did the start of the insurgency gain legitimacy from a situation of massive human rights violations. In Peru, despite the prolonged military dictatorship and despite a social storm of great proportions in the late 1970s, human rights violations paled in frequency and in form to those that convulsed countries such as El Salvador and Guatemala. Certainly, we did not live in anything even approaching the best of worlds. Restrictions of press freedom and political party activities were common practice, along with detentions, deportations, mistreatment of street demonstrators, and torture in prisons. But extrajudicial executions and forced disappearances were not yet part of our vocabulary, as they tragically would become just a few years later. Political crime was virtually unknown.[5]

An explanation for the emergence of this particular case of violence must therefore come from another angle. Perhaps relevant is something I heard Hubert Lanssiers say some time ago, in a debate with those who cited the terrible structural conditions of the country as the principal cause of the violence we were experiencing.[6] In his view, what such terrible conditions generated, usually and spontaneously, in the people that suffered them was not rebelliousness, but rather fatalism, passivity, or religious resignation. Lanssiers maintained that the explosions of violence could only be understood if given social conditions came together with an ideology that deliberately and consciously proposed exercising violence as a response.

According to Lanssiers, all ideology serves as an "arm of combat," an "instrument of power," a "mechanism of defense against objectivity," and a "pretext to escape moral criticism." He adds that "the value [of ideologies] is not found in the rigor of their construction or in the quality of their argument, which are rather poor and schematic. . . . What is important is that they tell us essentially what we need to think; they express what is needed to make a thought collectively operative. Their mobilizing energy is more useful than the content of their concepts, the orchestration of the themes is more important than their richness."[7]

Shining Path provided an ideological reading of reality, totally independent of the political process under way, and converted this interpretation into the guide and fundamental motivation to initiate armed action. As we have already suggested, the political changes of that time, which any analysis might consider as pointing away from justifying armed rupture, were absolutely dispensable facts for Shining Path, given the ideological edifice it had constructed. "The problem, *Señores* revisionists," Shining Path said disdainfully to the legal Left, "is not whether those in government are wearing collars and ties instead of uniforms and boots, or that they still sport beards and tie their pants with rope [a reference to Hugo Blanco], because this does not negate their reactionary position nor does it make them revolutionaries. We are not talking about civilian dictatorships versus military dictatorships. We are talking about class dictatorships. . . . *Do we not know that power is conquered with violence and maintained through dictatorship,* that 'revolution is an act in which one part of the population imposes its will upon the other with guns, bayonets, and canons . . . *and where the winning party is necessarily obliged to maintain its dominion by the fear that its arms inspire in the reactionaries?*' as Engels teaches?"[8]

Abimael Guzmán, only days before the ILA (the initials which signify the Inicio de la Lucha Armada, or initiation of the armed struggle, in Shining Path literature), pronounced the closing speech at Sendero's "First Military School." Without a trace of modesty he entitled his speech: "We are the Initiators." Among other things, he provided a preview of the practices Peru would have to endure during the following years:

> Comrades: our labor with our hands unarmed has concluded. . . . A period has ended. Here we seal what has been done; we open the future, the key is action, the objective power. This we will do, history demands it, the class needs it, the people has foreseen it and wants it, we must comply and we will comply. We are the initiators. . . .
>
> The people's war will grow more every day until it overturns the old order, the world is entering into a new situation: the strategic offensive of the global revolution. This is of transcendental importance. . . .
>
> [A]nd the people gets up on its hind legs, arms itself, rises in rebellion, and places a noose around the neck of imperialism and the reactionaries, grabs them by the throat, tears off their flesh, and will strangle them. [The people] will tear the reactionary flesh, leave it in shreds, and drown these black wretches in slime; what is left will burn and the ashes will scatter to the ends of the Earth, so that all that is left is sinister memory of what will never return, because it cannot and should not return. . . . Marxism-Leninism-Mao Zedong thought, the international proletariat and the peoples of the world, the working class and the people of the country, the party with its bases, cadres and leaders, all the grand combined action of centuries has culminated here. The promise opens, the future unfurls. ILA 80[9]

At that time, only a few faithful followers knew of this important warning. Understandably, the rest, even those who might have known of it, still did not have any reason to take it seriously.

Human Rights and People's Rights

A comparative vision of other countries that confronted internal insurgency continues to be useful, as we enter into an analysis of how Shining Path dealt with the issue of human rights once it embarked upon the project of a "protracted people's war." Upon surveying the continent, we find that guerrilla movements in Latin America generally sought to have the cause of human rights on their side. Some doubtlessly held this position with great conviction and honesty; others embraced human rights with varying degrees of political instrumentalism, as a means to isolate the state nationally and internationally, and to justify the guerrillas' own course of action.

Therefore, denunciations of the state as the principal violator of human rights usually have formed an important part of the political discourse of guerrilla movements. At the same time, guerrillas either described their own abuses as inevitable costs of the confrontation or simply denied that they occurred. In reality, and without in any way justifying the crimes committed by insurgent movements, their violations generally seem to have been significantly less in number, importance, and frequency than abuses attributed to agents of the state.

In Peru, however, we lived a very different reality. Shining Path openly repudiated human rights in both doctrine and practice. To achieve its goals, Shining Path would not hesitate to attack the civilian population and to use varied methods of terror against persons uninvolved in the conflict. In the point of departure for this approach, we find, once again, an "ideological justification": Shining Path insisted that human rights originated in a bourgeois conception of the world and were opposed to "the rights of the people [*derechos del pueblo*]."[10]

According to Abimael Guzmán,

> For us, human rights contradict the rights of the people because we base ourselves in man as a social product, not in an abstract man with innate rights. "Human rights" are nothing more than the rights of the bourgeois man, a position that was revolutionary in the face of feudalism; thus *liberty, equality and fraternity were advanced bourgeois criteria in the past.* . . .
>
> In so far as the people's rights are the rights that the proletariat and the immense popular masses conquer with their own struggle and blood, and that they establish as the guiding principles of the New State, in service of the interests of the classes that conform the people,

the rights of the people are the rights and obligations of class, superior to so-called human rights in the service of the masses, the poor especially, of the New State, of socialism and of future communism; the people's rights [are ones] that only the People's Republic of Peru, in our case, will be able to guarantee.

Guzmán went on to explain that by people's rights he referred "principally to the supreme right to conquer Power and to exercise it in order to transform the old existing order, oppressive and exploitative, and to construct a New State and a New Society for the people and the proletariat" (Guzmán 1991).

With his usual conviction that what he was said constituted incontrovertible truth, Guzmán maintained that "the Marxist-Leninist-Maoist, Gonzalo-thought conception makes us understand the bourgeois, reactionary, and counterrevolutionary character of the so-called Human Rights that are so manipulated in the world today, and [shows us] how to understand the rights of the people." In Guzmán's rendition of the history of human rights, the Universal Declaration of Human Rights was an instrument to establish "the expansion, domination, and influence of imperialism," and the United Nations as "a pro-imperialist organism, guarantor of the superpowers and imperial powers." He concluded with a vision of human rights as anachronism:

And today as imperialism falls into general collapse, it recurs to the old bourgeois reactionary banners, to its old resurrected principles, because it can no longer create anything new or progressive, and it covers them with a "humanitarian" varnish to hide its counterrevolutionary class nature whereby it seeks to contain the principal historical and political tendency in the world, which is revolution; cunningly hiding that human rights are one instrument more for imposing its reactionary ideology (the core of which is idealism, and the most vulgar pragmatism, totally contrary to dialectical materialism) and its fallacious bourgeois democratic politics of bloody reactionary dictatorship. . . . And all for the defense of the expired imperialist system, bloody parisitic barbarism that scorches the Earth, contrary and totally opposed to the socialist system, the great innovation of the twentieth century, the only system that will lead humanity to the reign of liberty: Communism. (Guzmán 1991)

Before moving on to examine the practical repercussions of such belligerent opposition to the human rights perspective, one might add that this belligerence did not impede Shining Path from developing, when convenient, an absolutely pragmatic attitude regarding human rights. Thus, when human rights appeared useful for its political and military objectives, Shining Path demanded compliance with these principles and the laws that embodied them. Sendero's absolute attachment to legal technicalities to defend well known leaders, who without any scruples denied their obvious leadership positions, became rather notorious. (Osmán Morote, for example, claimed to be only a "social researcher.") Sendero leaders attempted to exploit the deficiencies of the Peruvian legal system to their own advantage, and only later, in the event of a conviction, would they reassume their original positions.[11] Also well known, to name another example, was their denunciation of violations of liberty of the press, whenever necessary to ensure that their mouthpiece *El Diario* could continue to circulate.[12]

From Word to Deed

This disdain for human rights, whereby Sendero reduced respect for the rights of others to the interest and necessities of "class" and "revolution" (read: the Party) provided a basis for Shining Path's cruel and relentless military conduct against others. In addition, it informed the scant value placed on the lives of their own militants.[13]

Shining Path's cruelty in war actions is widely known. Never, for example, have Shining Path guerrillas been known to carry out military operations in which they ended up taking prisoners or treating the wounded. Certainly, the same may be said about the operations of the Peruvian Armed Forces. Even worse, the military battles, per se, can account for perhaps 10 percent of the war's victims over the course of fifteen years. The immense majority of deaths resulted from unilateral actions against an enemy without any capacity for response, that was annihilated without contemplation. Shining Path assassinated hundreds of police for no other reason than to take their arms. The Armed Forces were responsible for numerous extrajudicial executions and forced disappearances.

I am interested here, in particular, in the role of Shining Path. Continuing the methodology of drawing comparisons with other realities in Latin America, note that in other countries, the guerrillas took great care not to produce victims in sectors that they considered potential allies for their cause: political parties on the Left, popular organizations, NGOs, and so forth. And, perhaps for this very reason, these groups suffered repression by the state. In Peru, however, this was not the case. Shining Path, because of its vision of human rights and its general conception of politics and war, perceived all such groups as direct enemies of its armed struggle and did not hesitate to use the most violent methods against them. One might argue that Shining Path, even more than the state, affected directly and systematically these sectors of civil society, or what was long known as the popular movement.

Thus, Shining Path guerrillas massacred peasants who dared oppose them. The most notorious case was that of Lucanamarca, where Shining Path assassinated more than eighty villagers, including women and children, with the purpose of sending a message to a third party, the Armed Forces. In Guzmán's words, this massacre was intended to give "a decisive blow to restrain them, to make them understand that the thing was not so easy." Always with intricate justifications, Shining Path killed many other people as well: humble local authorities ("representatives of the bourgeois state in the countryside"); candidates in any electoral process ("we warn all the electioneers that seek to run for office that if they persist in the farce we will annihilate them sooner or later"); politicians on the Left ("revisionism is the advance of the bourgeoisie in the bosom of the people"); labor and popular organizers of all kinds ("reactionary agents infiltrating in the ranks of the people"); members of different churches ("death to the worshipers of imperialism, death to the preaching dogs"); members of local and international NGOs ("they corrupt the popular leaders with foreign money and promote aid policies [políticas asistencialistas] to enrich themselves at the cost of the hunger of the people"); and so forth.

The flip side of this logic was evident in the attitude that Shining Path leaders assumed toward the suffering and terrible deaths faced by thousands of their own militants and supporters (see the essay by del Pino in this volume). Shining Path justified this attitude with the same notions of purity and ideological reinforcement. In his "Interview of the Century," Guzmán (1988) is very clear on this point:

> The reaction attempts to use its armed forces and repressive forces in general to wipe us out (barrernos) and disappear us. And for what reason? *Because we want to do the same to them*, to wipe them out and

to disappear them as a class; Mariátegui had said that only by destroying, demolishing the old order can a new social order be created. In the last instance, we judge these problems through the lens of the basic principle of war established by President Mao: the principle of annihilating the forces of the enemy and preserving our own; and *we know well that the reaction has applied, applies, and will apply, genocide, on this we are absolutely clear. And, in consequence we face the problem of the quota, the problem that to annihilate the enemy and to preserve our own forces, and even more to develop our forces, it is necessary to pay a cost of war, a cost in blood, the necessity of sacrificing a part to ensure the triumph of the people's war.*

For Abimael Guzmán the crowning moment of this "vital and principal" sacrifice was the barbarous repression produced by the intervention of the Armed Forces in Ayacucho in 1983 and 1984. *"There took place the greatest show of massive revolutionary heroism and our greatest forging ahead as well."*[14] The connection between the sacrifice of militants and the strengthening of the organization and political project is confirmed in senderista reference to the massacre of more than 200 senderistas in the prisons of Lima in 1986 as the "Day of Heroism." "The 19th of June," said Guzmán, "is a date that demonstrates to our people and to the world *what firm Communists and committed revolutionaries are capable of doing."*

When analyzed from a perspective informed by respect for human life and the dignity of persons, Shining Path's conduct could not have resulted in a worse outcome. We cannot for this reason avoid mentioning how, when subjected to rigors much less harsh than those he himself imposed upon his enemies or demanded of his own followers, Abimael Guzmán broke weakly. In exchange for minimally decent prison conditions, he acceded to negotiate the same peace he had always described as the worst of betrayals.

When Combatants Converge

Let us complete this complex panorama by noting that in Peru a perverse convergence emerged. We refer to the practical and conceptual appraisals of human rights by the Shining Path insurgents and the agents of the state who planned and conducted the counterinsurgency campaign.

For example, both sides would blame the preoccupation with human rights on unacceptable intervention by the United States for purposes of domination. In 1994, at no less an important occasion than the Fourth Summit of Heads of State in Latin America, Fujimori affirmed his "rejection of underhanded interventions with the pretext of defending continental democracy or human rights." He went on to sustain that "each people must resolve as best it can its own internal affairs," including in "the cases of Haiti and Cuba."[15] Guzmán was not outdone. He sustained that "today, imperialism, principally Yankee, uses human rights to impose international norms that justify its intervention in whatever part of the world and to submit everyone to its hegemony" (Guzmán 1991).

Another area of impressive convergence was the evaluation of the role played by NGOs in human rights. One very interesting poll asked more than 100 commanders and majors of the Armed Forces to provide their opinions anonymously regarding human rights (de la Jara 1994). In response to a question about human rights groups, nearly three-fifths (57.26%) of these military men replied that human rights organizations were only concerned with terrorists and only promoted the organizations' own interests or those of other countries. Nearly a third (31.62%) responded that although such groups have had laudable goals, in practice they favored subversive actions. Indeed, the respondents would have found it difficult to think differently since this is what they have heard from their superiors and successive presidents over the years. Fujimori, in particular, has made the denigration of human rights groups into a personal crusade.

Here I repeat only two of the many allegations made against us: "We know that the terrorists and their front organisms, or useful fools, are not going to give up and will use every resource to damage the image of the country arguing that the Armed Forces systematically violate human rights." In addition, "these professional organizations are not coherent in the defense of life and human liberty because, in some cases, *they are legal arms of subversion, but we will unmask them.*"[16]

The state's accusations that the human rights groups were biased, and did not understand the underlying reasons for what they did, mirrored accusations by Shining Path. "When in the context of developing the people's war, the PCP applies military actions of selective liquidation against informers, functionaries of the state, and others, as in the execution of María Elena Moyano ("Mother Courage"), the 'human rights defense organizations' exclaim: 'horror!' *But when the armed forces and police assassinate defenseless people, including children, the organizations do not say anything. They maintain a nauseating complicit silence.*"[17] Abimael Guzmán would maintain, in an epoch in which his utterances constituted virtual death threats: "we have not encountered until today among the NGOs [referring to human rights organizations], an organization that openly and valiantly defends the rights of the poorest people, much less advanced revolutionary positions; at most we find bourgeois humanitarian positions, *but the great majority are lackeys, conscious or unconscious, of imperialism*" (Guzmán 1991).

I still experience a certain chill upon considering Guzmán's references to the institution to which I belong. In the text just cited, he used this organization as an example to illustrate his point: "Among the NGOs: the Institute of Legal Defense (IDL), a nongovernmental organization that defends human rights in the service of mainly Yankee imperialism . . . always serving the demands of its imperialist masters and acting as their soft hand, against Marxism and the people's war, and marking off and even criticizing reactionary governments when imperialism necessitates."

Let us consider one last theme where both sides converge. At times, both recognize certain "excesses" against the civilian population and consider them acceptable in exchange for advancing the principal objective, finishing off the enemy. Martha Chávez, the most prominent pro-Fujimori parliamentarian, would sustain: "I weigh the balance between the war against terrorism and subversion on one side and, on the other, *the question of the human rights of some . . . it is painful, but I end up choosing the war against subversion.*"[18] Guzmán complements this idea from his perspective, when he analyzes the "excesses" that he admits his men committed in the Lucanamarca massacre: "excesses might be committed, *the problem is to arrive at a point and not to pass it,* because if you pass it you go off track, it is like an angle that opens only to a certain degree and no more" (Guzmán 1988).

Enormous Challenges

By this point, it should be easy to imagine the difficulty of the work of human rights organizations over the course of fifteen years (1980–1995). It is worth adding, of course, that similar difficulties also faced those who expressed a consistent commitment to human rights in the communications media, in the Christian churches, in the academic world, and (in this instance the numbers can be counted on one's hands) in the political parties.[19]

The accusations and threats under which the human rights activists worked are well known and originated in the elements described previously: we are only concerned with the rights of terrorists and remain quiet when the victims are caused by the subversives; we tie the hands of the forces of order, impeding them from acting efficiently; we are "useful fools" (or *candelejones*, "silly ones," as Luis Bedoya Reyes once called us), or in more extreme versions, occult allies of terrorists. The other side called us embellishers of the system, accomplices of imperialism, and so forth.

To face up to this political problem constituted the fundamental challenge of the Peruvian human rights movement. The first difficulty to overcome was to break with the inertia of following the usual quasi-universal schemes of defense of human rights, according to which our work should focus exclusively on denouncing the abuses of the state.[20] In spite of the fact that no human rights group or individual activist had any inclination whatsoever, at any moment, in favor of Shining Path—and on this I can give personal testimony—there was, particularly in the first years, an intense debate regarding our role. We debated whether it was our responsibility to denounce Shining Path in the same manner that we denounced the state. The doctrinal referent in these arguments was an international juridical tradition that viewed the state as the sole violator of human rights.

The process was intense and complex, but had clear results. In our favor was the fact that all of us united early in a common coalition, the National Coordinating Committee of Human Rights (La Coordinadora Nacional de Derechos Humanos, hereinafter "La Coordinadora"),[21] which all of us decided to use as our political voice at a national and international level. Little by little, La Coordinadora opted to leave aside any theoretical disquisition that could be interpreted as weakness in the condemnation of Shining Path. We decided to denounce each and every crime committed by Shining Path with the same energy and conviction with which we denounced violations by the state.[22]

In addition, differentiating ourselves from most Latin American human rights groups, we broke with the idea of neutrality, or intent merely to humanize conflicts. We announced with absolute clarity that we opposed Shining Path, that our struggle for human rights was intrinsically associated with obtaining peace, and that for this purpose, we felt solidarity with civil society's desire to defeat Shining Path and we supported legitimate efforts by the state to accomplish this goal.[23] In addition, we decided to convert our political choice into a matter of principle. We demanded that all groups and individuals who wanted to join our organizations adhere to four principles: repudiation of all forms of violence, revindication of democracy as the best political system, independence in regards to the state, and opposition to the death penalty.

This manner of addressing the issue of human rights had practical repercussions in our daily activities. The human rights groups consciously decided that our primary commitment was to the innocent victims of the confrontation, to whom we had to dedicate our best efforts. In cases in which senderistas were subject to human rights violations, we decided to act only if their lives were at risk. This of course did not mean in any case endorsing the crimes committed by the state simply because some or all of its victims might be senderistas. Many of the best known cases of disappearances and extrajudicial killings to which we dedicated so much effort included known Shining Path members among the victims.

The distinction was clearer in cases of detained persons. The human rights organizations decided expressly not to provide legal defense through our lawyers to people whom we considered with reasonable certainty to be members of Shining Path or the MRTA.[24] This decision certainly caused many conflicts of conscience, above all in the final stage, since in some cases we ended up turning ourselves, in a sense, into anticipatory judges. That is, we did not give the accused the benefit of the doubt, even though we knew that judges, in deciding the innocence or guilt of an accused person, considered it important to know who was behind the defense.

It is necessary to state clearly that this choice, which in my opinion was not only made out of conviction but also because it was the only choice that was politically viable, in effect silenced a response to certain abuses. Thus, while no one among us doubted the justice of convicting Abimael Guzmán and other Shining Path leaders, we never publicly stated with sufficient firmness the evident truth that they did not benefit from minimum guarantees of due process and that the legal validity of the trials was quite relative.[25]

Nonetheless, our declarations of principle and our daily conduct did not suffice to end accusations of partiality and complicity with subversion, accusations which persist today and have become, in great measure, popular common wisdom. Without underplaying our own errors and limitations it is important to consider the extraordinary difficulty of defending human rights, given the pressure from Shining Path and its effects on public opinion. One must add, however, that although this perception in the general public may have been, and may now be, honestly held, the political and military leaders with whom we argued all these years, and even sectors of the communications media, knew better. They understood perfectly well that the accusations were mistaken, yet purposely encouraged the confusion. What they sought was not that we take an impartial and balanced position, but rather to neutralize our capacity to denounce the state's violations of human rights.

Inevitable Consequences

For human rights in Peru and for the struggle to ensure their enforcement, Shining Path brought many negative consequences and, ironically, a positive consequence as well. The many negative effects are overwhelming, so let us begin with the effect that might be considered positive.

If one asks who were the victims of human rights violations in Latin America in those countries that recently or currently suffer armed internal conflicts (such as Colombia, El Salvador, Guatemala, and Nicaragua) one will find that the victims have been mostly peasants not directly involved in the confrontations, as in Peru. But in those countries, in contrast with Peru, the state's victims also frequently included activists in popular organizations, political leaders of the legal Left, student leaders, and members of human rights organizations. This generally did not happen in Peru. Over the years, the Peruvian cases in which these sectors suffered state repression have been quite isolated and never constituted a systematic pattern.[26]

In my view, this difference has to do principally with the type of movement that Shining Path was, and the clear division between the distinct camps in Peru. That is, Shining Path, according to its own ideas, did not have, did not want, could not have alliances with legalized sectors that would have served to broaden its political project or its social base. Sendero's fanaticism, expressed in an absolute and exclusive conception of its own role, facilitated this separation between the world of Peruvian politics and that of war. Thus, in contrast to the other countries cited, and despite the voices that (with more malice than ignorance) proclaimed the contrary, in Peru one could argue, even in the worst moments, that there were no ties between the legal Left (however radical its language) or between activists in all kinds of social organizations (however confrontational their practices or incisive their criticisms) and armed senderistas. This situation rendered it more difficult to justify systematic repression of the legal Left and activist social organizations. In the particular case of the human rights organizations, and in contrast to countries such as Guatemala or Colombia, this situation allowed us to continue and to develop further our labor over the course of this whole period, despite having to confront difficult situations and instances of violence, and despite having to work in a climate of repeated verbal aggression.[27]

The negative effects to which we alluded earlier were without a doubt very great. Shining Path's conception of human rights was a decisive factor that contributed to increasing contempt for human life in Peru. Such contempt applied to Shining Path's own victims in all social sectors as well as to those who had to suffer in retaliation. In my judgment, the type and magnitude of the violence that we had in Peru, and particularly the way in which Shining Path exercised violence with absolute disdain for its consequences upon the civilian population, generated in the great majority of Peruvians a cynical and pragmatic attitude toward democracy and human rights. Sendero, in short, induced a weakening of the consciousness of the population on the importance of respecting human rights and the dignity of persons.

By the end of the 1980s, when the sense of frustration and desperation had spread to the majority of the population, it became common sense that sacrificing democracy and human rights, and damaging the lives of innocent people, were costs well worth paying in order to get rid of Shining Path. According to this perspective, which today is lamentably predominant, any price was worth paying to overcome the threat of Shining Path. This view coincides with the beliefs of the senderistas that the ends justify the means.[28] The psychological climate was certainly encouraged and embodied by Alberto Fujimori and constituted one of the reasons for his popularity—for the support that he received in the "self-coup" of 1992 and for his overwhelming electoral victory in 1995.

With this sentiment so widespread among the population, the struggle for human rights became, and remains, much more difficult and complicated. The struggle for human rights, by its nature, only has an impact if national and international public opinion takes it up and makes it their own.[29] But we are still far from achieving the possibility of juridical, political, and moral sanctions against those who have committed human rights violations as part of the state. For example, Peru is far from obtaining a Truth Commission. Different versions of such a commission were established in Argentina, Chile, El Salvador, and in Colombia for one specific case, and will soon be established in Guatemala.

The experience of human rights groups when we denounced a massacre in the Alto Huallaga River in 1994 was very revealing. This was probably one of the gravest denunciations, and one of the best-documented with eye-witness accounts, that we have been able to make in recent years. In the early days of April 1994, on the left bank of the Huallaga River, in the localities of Moyuna and Moena, counterinsurgency troops of the army, after a show of rapes and other terrible acts of cruelty, assassinated dozens of peasants. The troops allegedly used artillery helicopters. Despite restrictions of access to the zone even for the International Red Cross, and despite not being permitted to go to the specific place where the peasants indicated that the majority of the victims were to be found, twelve cadavers were recovered.

La Coordinadora spearheaded the denunciation of the facts and produced a voluminous, detailed, and documented report that presented the testimony of more than thirty witnesses from the zone, including priests and nuns. Nonetheless, the government ably exploited the public's fears that such accusations might have a negative impact on the continued successes—already visible—of the counterinsurgency campaign. The government maliciously described our denunciation as a desperate attempt to stop the most important and final offensive against the guerrillas. My point is not simply to affirm my profound conviction that we acted correctly in making this denunciation. The point is that, for the reasons already given, the government managed to ensure that our action was negatively received, even by sectors that had traditionally identified with our cause. The government thus managed to bury, perhaps forever, one of the worst crimes committed in recent years in impunity and forgetfulness.

Return to Normalcy?

Even though all that we lived through with Shining Path and the war that it unleashed happened very recently, for many Peruvians those experiences already belong to the past. In our particular style of confronting national problems, the collective consciousness has preferred to forget what occurred among us.

It is not the intention here to inventory all the war has signified for the country. I note only that, in great measure because of the war, we have fallen decades behind in terms of democratic institutional development. The hope that Peruvians would construct a solid democracy, based on the initiative of sectors that emerged from below, is only a memory from the past. Today, we Peruvians have become more cynical and pragmatic about public affairs and politics, and about our own participation in them.

As one might easily imagine, there is tremendous unfinished work from a human rights perspective. In addition, new problems confront us and will demand our attention. Perhaps the most important task, however, will be to contribute to an understanding—and reversal—of the fact that even though Shining Path lost utterly on the military terrain, it achieved some unforeseen victories at the level of consciousness and values. Ironically for its authors, the amnesty law approved by the Peruvian government in June 1995 represented the triumph of this mentality.[30] Its first article is so revealing, that in place of an explanation, it merits an extensive excerpt: "General amnesty is conceded to military, police, and civilian personnel, whatever their police or military or functional role, who have been denounced, investigated, prosecuted, tried, or condemned for common or military crimes, under the common or military codes [of justice], respectively, for all of the events derived or originated upon the occasion of or as a consequence of the struggle against terrorism and that could have been committed in individual or group form since May of 1980 until the promulgation of the present law."

If this law is not an important indication of the emergence in Peru, as a consequence of this unwanted war, of a profound degradation of our appreciation for the essential dignity of human life, then what would be? One might find hope, however, that this is not an irreversible tendency in the unforeseen and massive repudiation that the amnesty law provoked among the Peruvian citizenry.

Notes

1 The ideas in this introductory section have been amply discussed in other works. See for example O'Donnell 1988.

2 The author is a member of the Legal Defense Institute (Instituto de Defensa Legal; or IDL), a nongovernmental organization dedicated since 1983 to the defense and promotion of human rights, the strengthening of democracy, and the construction of peace. The IDL, like similar organizations in Peru, has had to work in very adverse conditions, openly confronting the practices of both the Peruvian state and insurgent groups.

3 In the elections for the Constituent Assembly the noticeable absence of Acción Popular was considered to be a highly risky political ploy on the part of Belaúnde, but one that was successful, as his party emerged triumphant two years later.

4 In fact, since then, the Peruvian political system attracted the participation of all of the political forces. The Left, including even the most radical sectors that

continued to affirm armed struggle as their ultimate objective, participated in the electoral process, at times successfully, as in the Lima mayor's race in 1983.

5 As in other Latin American countries, leftist sectors were the most likely targets of these violations. Nonetheless, Peru, in contrast to many other places, did not witness significant and systematic state repression against the Left. We have to reach as far back as 1962 to find a massive round-up and imprisonment of leftist leaders.

6 Lanssiers is a priest of Belgian origin who has resided for many years in Peru, and is perhaps one of the most lucid minds in Peru today.

7 Cited in IDL 1992.

8 Document cited in Gorriti 1990. Emphasis in this and subsequent quotes are mine.

9 Cited by Gorriti 1990.

10 *Editor's note:* The word "pueblo" as people carried a connotation of "common people" or "people of modest means" in common Spanish usage.

11 This contrasts, again, with attitudes displayed by other guerrilla movements in Latin America, exemplified in the case of Peru by the MRTA. These groups refuted the political and moral authority of such tribunals, publicly revindicated their actions, and as "prisoners of war" refused to exercise their rights to defense.

12 In their favor we might add that they did not hide it: "As far as our violating human rights is concerned, our point of departure is that *we do not subscribe to the Universal Declaration for Human Rights,* nor to that of Costa Rica. *But we do use their legal mechanisms to unmask and denounce the Peruvian Old State,* its institutions and organisms, its authorities, beginning with those who lead it, functionaries and subordinates who violate human rights in defiance of their own international promises" (Guzmán 1991).

13 We should add that in contrast to other armed movements in Latin America, Shining Path has never demanded respect for International Humanitarian Law on the part of the Peruvian state. Nor has it practiced such principles in its own acts of war.

14 The Armed Forces' entrance into Ayacucho marked the beginning of what in Peru also has been known as the "dirty war," which escalated the conflicts to unforeseen levels. Thus, during 1983 and 1984 in just five provinces of Ayacucho (Huamanga, Huanta, Cangallo, La Mar, and Víctor Fajardo) there were 5,645 deaths, that is, 46 percent of all that were produced in Ayacucho during fourteen years of violence and, perhaps even more revealing, 20.5 percent of all that were produced in Peru during the same period. Equally illustrative of the level of violence in this zone, "for Lima to have had the same proportion of casualties that Huanta suffered, for example, rather than 2,014 that really

occurred, there would have to have been 213,453! And on a national level, rather than 24,117, there would have been 816,540!" (Basombrío 1994).

15 *El Comercio,* 15 June 1994 and *Expreso,* 14 June 1994.

16 Cited in IDL 1991.

17 *El Diario Internacional,* no. 18 (March 1993).

18 Declarations in *Panorama,* reproduced in *La República,* 12 July 1993.

19 It is hard to think of anyone in Acción Popular or the Popular Christian Party (Partido Popular Cristiano, or PPC) who worked for the human rights cause. In APRA, there is only one person, Javier Valle Riestra. The political discourse of various sectors of the Left referred to human rights, but only Javier Diez Canseco, Enrique Bernales, Rolando Ames, and Henry Pease carried out concrete and consistent action as protagonists of human rights. In Cambio 90, Fujimori's group, the only person who was sensitive to the issue was the second Vice-President Carlos García, who distanced himself from the regime almost as soon as it started.

20 Years later the journalist Guido Lombardi, who was not known for any pro-Shining Path inclination, publicly criticized us for not having persevered in this perspective: "I want to express my frustration over the fact that the human rights groups have ceded to the pressure from those who demanded similar condemnations for the violations committed by the state and those committed by terrorism . . . it is not a hindrance to keep thinking that those that proceed from the state are more grave and intolerable, because it is the state that should be the first guarantor of their protection" (Lombardi 1994).

21 La Coordinadora presently includes some fifty civic and religious organizations that work in the area of human rights in Peru.

22 We did this, according to our abilities and resources, through communiqués and notes for the press, through visits and private letters of solidarity with the victims, through international denunciations, and, increasingly, through humanitarian aid to victims of Shining Path. In fact, La Coordinadora has given concrete and effective humanitarian aid to many more of Shining Path's victims than has the state.

23 One could cite dozens of public communiqués that expressed this sentiment. The most revealing was, however, that which the human rights groups issued after Guzmán was captured, manifesting our satisfaction with, and approval of, the methods by which the capture had been achieved.

24 We should point out that as a rule they also preferred not to associate with us, and sought out legal assistance from the Association of Democratic Lawyers (Asociación de Abogados Democráticos).

25 In addition, Fujimori's authoritarianism impeded the trial against Abimael Guzmán from becoming a moment of political and moral sanction of his crimes, one that would have demonstrated the superiority of those who fought

against him and judged and condemned him through strict adherence to the norms and principles of legality that Guzmán so disdained.

26 The most notorious exceptions to this rule were the assassinations of the peasant leader Jesús Oropeza and the mining leader Saul Cantoral.

27 The worst attacks against human rights organizations were the detention and subsequent disappearance of the president of the Comité de Derechos Humanos (Human Rights Committee) of Huancavelica, Angel Escobar Jurado; the package-bomb that cost an arm, and almost the life, of the lawyer Augusto Zúñiga of COMISEDH; and the bombs that went off in the offices of the Andean Commission of Jurists and Amnesty International.

28 There is no element of sublime sacrifice for the nation in this reasoning given that, of course, the assumption was always that someone else would pay this price.

29 There were notable exceptions, however, when a particular set of events led many sectors of the Peruvian citizenry to join in a common cause and to corner politically the perpetrators of human rights violations. These events revealed the true nature of the regime and contributed to making sure that these types of violations could not be repeated. Such was the case, for example, of the massacre of nine students and a professor of La Cantuta University by a military death squad in July 1992.

30 For the amnesty law and human rights in 1995, see CNDDHH 1996.

✤ FOURTEEN

Human Rights and Social Referents:

The Construction of New Sensibilities

Hortensia Muñoz

✤ To speak of human rights is to refer to an ensemble of subjects and mechanisms that have been assembled by the international community as well as to procedures of promotion and response in situations of systematic abuse.[1] When the defense of human rights becomes an urgent and painful issue, the particular forms by which potentially affected persons and groups exercise these rights vary in each society. The path that victims must travel to assert tangible rights, recognized by the state and supported by society, is a difficult path indeed. On this journey they work out and transform their condition as victims when they encounter and identify their respective rights as citizens.

This journey has to be, in the first place, a journey of sensibilities, since ongoing pain, anger, and fear must become a foundation for constructing a concept of injustice that justifies a demand. For this demand to be effective requires formulating a discourse and learning to open spaces for this discourse to be heard. On a related level, those involved must learn norms and procedures that create a movement of institutional pressure, and that generate mechanisms of dialogue with institutions, such as human rights organizations, that have already established specific frameworks and modes of intervention. These organizations, in turn, continually must strive to gain social space in a process of ongoing negotiation with the state, with international institutions, and with diverse sectors of society.

In Peru, the defense of human rights developed in a context of violence unleashed by armed rebel groups as well as the state. In addition, the victims of the war had not previously perceived fully their own condition as citizens in a political community with corresponding civil rights.

These basic conditions are not sufficient, however, to explain the obstacles to human rights work or the gains that have been made.

Between 1980 and 1993 it was necessary to construct distinct "social referents" that could embody the victims who needed attention. At the same time, the subject denounced as the aggressor shifted as human rights demands moved away from an exclusive focus on the state—as normally recognized on an international level—and came to focus, as well, on violations by armed rebels. I will examine this process of constructing "social referents" in the present essay.

In my view we can distinguish three social referents. The first constructed the victim as a "disappeared person" (*desaparecido*) or, by extension, as a relative (*familiar*) of a desaparecido. At that moment, the state appeared clearly as the aggressor. The second referent equated the victim with the "displaced refugees" (*desplazados*), in other words, as civilians caught in the cross fire. The aggressor in this context was identified as violence in general, whether provoked by the armed insurgents or by the state's overreactions. The third referent has been constructed as innocent people unjustly accused, with the state once again cast as the aggressor. This time the state has been "personified" by those who administer justice for crimes of terrorism, a function identified with the military. To analyze the entire process in detail would exceed the scope of this paper; for this reason I will discuss in some detail only the construction of the first social referent: the disappeared.

The year 1980 marked not only the beginning of the internal war unleashed by the Communist Party of Peru-Shining Path. At the same time, it also set off efforts to build a space for human rights work in Peru.[2] At some moments this labor has resonated with the sensibilities provoked by war, at other moments the opposite has occurred.

The first reading of the war understood Shining Path as a social movement—as a peasant uprising or as a guerrilla uprising—against the state.[3] The war began and Shining Path, a political offspring of the Maoist Left, conjured up images of the Latin American guerrilla among intellectuals, activists, political figures and activists, and sectors of the Church. Many considered Shining Path mistaken in the violent methods that it used, but even the president equated Shining Path with established ideas of a guerrilla movement.[4] The military thought the same.

But in January 1983 an event occurred in the *punas* (high tablelands) of Huanta (in northern Ayacucho) that cast doubt upon the image of Shining

Path as a guerrilla force supported by "the people" or "the peasantry." Peasants in the community of Uchuraccay, apparently incited by military forces stationed in the area, killed a group of eight journalists and their guide. Days before, a neighboring community, Huaychao, had confronted and killed Shining Path militants. The communities of the area feared retaliation.[5]

From that moment the war invaded television sets, radio stations, and the press. Various explanations were spun out to confirm, excuse, or negate the facts. Some commentaries cited culture to "explain" what happened and assumed that the collective violent reaction had ancestral origins. Others cited the peasants' agreeable and hospitable customs to deny that they could be capable of such an atrocity, and pointed to the Armed Forces as directly or indirectly responsible—they either killed the journalists or incited the massacre.

Beyond the truthfulness of such commentaries, the doubts provoked by Uchuraccay—were the peasants victims of Sendero? did they fear Sendero?—expanded the space for discussion and concern about human rights and violence. The strategy that the Armed Forces adopted after arriving in Ayacucho in late 1982 produced, during the next two years, more than 5000 deaths, including some 1000 desaparecidos, and a still-undetermined number of extrajudicial executions, for which the discovery of graves provides evidence.[6] The massiveness of this response left no doubts about who was the aggressor.

Functionaries of the state initially denounced violations of the right to life by the Armed Forces in Ayacucho. Around mid-1983, successive government prosecutors (*fiscales*) in Ayacucho denounced disappearances in the press and also accused the regional politico-military command of impeding their investigations. As a result of these accusations, some prosecutors lost their jobs.[7] Possible doubts about their charges disintegrated upon the discovery of the first mass graves that contained the corpses of disappeared persons previously detained by the army. The response to the prosecutors' accusations made clear that to change the military's mode of operating would require strong political and social pressure.

In this context, the disappeared began to emerge as the social referent around which the methodology of human rights work would develop. In 1983 the National Association of Family Members of the Detained-Disappeared (Asociación Nacional de Familiares de Detenidos-Desaparecidos; ANFASEP) was created. The following year, in Lima, relatives of the disappeared residing in the capital founded the Committee of Family

Members of the Detained-Disappeared (Comité de Familiares de Detenidos-Desaparecidos; COFADER). There were two reasons for founding a second organization. First, Lima provided the opportunity for negotiation and political pressure supported by leftist parliamentarians. Second, the ecclesiastical authorities in Ayacucho opposed the progressive line that animated the Episcopal Commission of Social Action (Comisión Episcopal de Acción Social, hereinafter CEAS) and refused to allow this commission to enter the region and directly support the victims.[8]

The organizations of relatives adopted the model of the Latin American Federation of Associations of Family Members of the Detained-Disappeared (Federación Latinoamericana de Asociaciones de Familiares de Detenidos-Desaparecidos, hereinafter FEDEFAM). This model emerged from experiences of repression in Argentina, Chile, and Uruguay. Thus, forced disappearance was defined by this organization as the "kidnapping, hiding, and negation of the whereabouts of members of the political opposition to the states."[9] The aggressor against human rights was clearly the state while groups who had risen up in arms were understood as political opposition. Even before we had news of forced disappearances in Peru, we were familiar with the methodology and procedures developed by FEDEFAM. For example, in mid-1982, even before the military intervention of Ayacucho, Lima hosted a FEDEFAM congress inaugurated by the Bishop who served as president of the CEAS.

In this initial stage the organizations of family members of the disappeared developed in relation to the Catholic Church, the human rights organizations, leftist congressional representatives, and Left-oriented lawyers and peasant unions in Ayacucho. By mid-1984 the groups involved in human rights work came predominantly from two currents: a current that consisted of progressive Catholics grouped around CEAS, and a current linked to leftist congressional representatives who belonged to the Human Rights Commission of the Chamber of Deputies. These currents were united by their will to transform Peruvian society, but they were separated by different perspectives on political violence.

With the war advancing, urged by the need for increased pressure against the state and by the limits of such pressure because of the disproportionate presence of the Left in the defense of human rights, progressive sectors of the Catholic Church sought to expand the space for denouncing human rights violations by incorporating other social and political sectors. In this manner they could influence the delicate equilibrium implied in the relation between the discourse of human rights and that of the Left, which had not achieved a clear differentiation from Shining Path. The tragic combination of the doubts raised by Uchuraccay, and the crushing character of military aggression against civilians in 1983 and 1984, permitted expanding the frontier of "fighters for human rights" to include new sectors. The new participants included liberals of the Right, who repudiated the military strategy and the lack of political will to regulate the military, in addition to repudiating Shining Path violence. Thus, beginning in mid-1984 a group began to form that later would become the Commission for Rights of the Person and the Construction of Peace (Comisión de Derechos de la Persona y Construcción de la Paz; CODEPP). Participants in CODEPP included not only personages of varying political orientations, and bishops and priests, but even retired generals who disagreed with the military strategy employed in Ayacucho.[10] CODEPP held the state responsible for human rights violations and affirmed that "terror cannot be an answer to terror."[11]

At the same time, intellectuals associated with the Church perceived the need for a language—a kind of lingua franca—that might comprehend the wider context of violence, including themes of economic and social rights and Shining Path's emergence, without recurring to Marxist terminology. In July 1985 the Peruvian Association of Studies and Research for Peace (Asociación Peruana de Estudios e Investigación para la Paz; APEP) organized a seminar to present research findings. The papers presented for discussion show how a series of "latent conflicts" together "conform a violent structure in society." This concept of "structural violence"[12] allowed for ambiguous positions that subsumed various types of violence within one concept. By then, a key referent for dialogue and pressure was available: "the disappeared." The disappeared personified state terror and provided a certain degree of flexibility because they were not linked to a specific political line.

The inauguration of Alan García in July 1985 generated hopes for human rights.[13] In his inaugural speech García stated that "to struggle against barbarism it is not necessary to fall into barbarism." He also announced the creation of a Peace Commission to review the cases of those who were detained and accused of terrorism and to convoke a dialogue with Shining Path. Two months later, President García retired the military chiefs responsible for peasant massacres in Ayacucho and installed the Peace Commission. But only four months later, the commissioners resigned due to difficulties with the García administration and the obstacles that impeded their work.[14]

In this context, La Coordinadora, the recently-constituted committee that coordinated dozens of human rights organizations,[15] convoked a "March for Peace" in Lima. The objective was to pressure the government, which was beginning to show political weakness on pacification strategies.[16] At the same time, as its first massive public act, the march also served as a test of La Coordinadora's capacity to mobilize support. Leading the march were university rectors, Catholic bishops, Left-wing and Christian Democrat parliamentarians, members of the "Commission of Personalities" of CODEPP, organizations of family members of the disappeared, and leaders of popular organizations. They were accompanied by congregations from parishes of the poor, institutions of research and outreach, artists' groups, and some professional associations and worker organizations. At the end, a bishop and member of the Peace Commission read a statement that outlined various elements of a peace proposal.[17]

Taking part in the march, as if in a ritual, were all the sectors that had laboriously constituted themselves to demand that the state take responsibility for enforcing human rights. Among the participants were family members of the disappeared who had travelled from Ayacucho to represent the victims of state aggression. The march took place in Lima because the organizers believed that the capital was the site in which they had to build the capacity for denunciation.

From Tears to Words

As mentioned earlier, around the end of 1985 the human rights organizations realized that President García was disposed to tolerate the form that military strategy was taking. The turning point, however, was the violent suppression of the June 1986 prison insurrection in Lima. Prisoners accused or sentenced for terrorism rioted simultaneously in Lima's three penal institutions; the date coincided with the Congress of the Socialist International in Peru.[18] President García met with his cabinet, declared the prisons a "restricted military zone," and ordered the intervention of the Armed Forces to put down the uprising. The military incursion resulted in about 240 deaths.[19] The outcry came quickly. Diverse institutions, churches, popular organizations, and civil associations all issued public statements repudiating the government's strategy.[20]

In this context, the human rights institutions shifted the focus of denunciation from Ayacucho to Lima; they converted juridical accusations about a group of concrete cases before regional prosecutors, into political denunciation before the press, the congress, and the government. In this trajectory one learned how to be a "family member of a disappeared person" (*familiar de un desaparecido*). People with little or no daily experience of possessing rights as citizens learned how to demand justice from the state through becoming conscious of the right of life.

Invoking the right to life and physical integrity, institutions of human rights promoted the organization of the relatives of the disappeared as *protagonists* of the denunciation process, above and beyond any ambiguity that arose from the possibility that a desaparecido was linked to Sendero. For their part, by grouping together the relatives imbued the invoked right with "social reality." They configured themselves as a social organization, with the powers and conflicts that such an organization implies.

Every family member (*familiar*) has a story to tell. Working with the lawyers who ordered the facts to build legal cases, the family members learned to select from their experiences the elements necessary to elaborate their testimony, which they would repeat and go on adapting according to the context. The family member gave form to her or his narration—leaving aside what might harm the image of the desaparecido, ordering precisely the circumstances of the forced detention, electing those aspects that highlighted the poverty and goodness of their missing relative, and learning to harmonize their experiences with the discourse of "structural violence."

Beginning in 1985, in Lima and in Ayacucho, groups of *familiares* participated in workshops with representatives from FEDEFAM (the Latin American federation of counterpart organizations of familiares).[21] They exchanged testimonies and organizational experiences and learned mechanisms of negotiation with local and international entities. They also learned about the struggles shared among Latin American associations of family members of the disappeared: "always with FEDEFAM they converse with us; they talk to us; they tell us. I learn a lot when I go to these meetings: that I have to denounce and that I cannot be silent. Before I had those thoughts that one shouldn't, I thought: if the disappeared could be subversives, I should be quiet, but this cannot be."[22] Thus the Peruvian organizations learned a methodology for protest. They constructed a common and homogeneous discourse marked by the style of FEDEFAM, even when this discourse did not fit with all of the Peruvian reality. For example, the discourse understood groups in arms as "political opposition." Nonetheless, this discourse permitted an international projection when FEDEFAM lobbied in the United Nations for ratification of the Convention on Forced Disappearances.

Until the end of 1986, the organization and identification of the familiares as a social referent in Lima took place in the streets. In demonstrations they drew attention to their demands and collectively overcame their fear and armed themselves with angry courage (coraje). They convoked marches in the principal plaza of the city to demand an audience with the President. To participate in the march and preside over it jointly with the Lima familiares, was a delegation of Ayacucho familiares, sometimes accompanied by representatives from FEDEFAM. In the plaza they learned new forms of protest. Like their counterparts in Argentina's Plaza de Mayo and in Chile, they carried immense photos of their relatives along with their names; they resisted police efforts to eject them violently from the plaza; and they gave their testimonies to journalists.[23] The family members learned what communications media were sympathetic and on whom they could count.

The familiar groupings were fundamentally women's organizations (as in Santiago and Buenos Aires), for various reasons. Approximately 89 percent of the disappeared were men.[24] In addition, the public image the familiares constructed of themselves was that of mothers of the disappeared (recreating images of the Madres de la Plaza del Mayo). Possibly they assumed that mothers were carriers of a greater sensitivity than fathers, even though from the beginning there were men among the leaders and members of the Lima and Ayacucho organizations. When familiares took to the streets, the press would call them madres, mamachas, or "peasant mothers" (madres campesinas).[25] In the same newspapers, the photos of an Andean funeral ritual known as velaciones de ropa[26] of the disappeared reflected a mix of elements drawn from the international image of the disappeared and from local cultural sensibilities and traditions regarding death.

To put more pressure on the government, the family members visited congressional representatives and gave press conferences in which they offered public testimony. They made presentations in parishes and universities in order to generate consciousness and a solidarity that began to be directed toward themselves. They received visits of foreign commissions and petitioned embassies. They participated in teach-ins on human rights and learned the basic elements that a denunciation should contain. They configured themselves as protagonists and as living symbols of their disappeared relatives.

I did not know what this thing called a "forum" is, what this thing called an "encounter" is, what this thing called "rights" is, what "human rights" are. I knew what an organization was . . . like a mothers' club, but I did not know what my rights were.[27]

I have learned how to organize, how to participate, what to do when others bring denunciations, what are the parts of a denunciation, what else has to be brought. To keep the organization from disappearing it is necessary to create encounters, denunciations, picket lines, marches, protests, letters to the president asking "where to find [my family member]."[28]

Throughout this first stage, the human rights institutions sought to enlarge the spectrum of those committed to the denunciation, by accompanying them, arranging the appointments, and organizing.

Protagonists of Denunciation

The presidents of the two Peruvian organizations of familiares learned to elaborate a discourse that offered an image of themselves as leaders, and that legitimated their representation within the space they sought to occupy. They oscillated from fear and pain in the face of lived experience, to the urgency of denunciation and the demand for justice and the search for a public space. They configured themselves as embodiments of a tragedy . . . they were victims and heroines at the same time.

Both leaders were women from Ayacucho who had lived in urban environments since before the war. María, of peasant origins, was bilingual (in Quechua and Spanish) and illiterate.[29] She lived in the city of Ayacucho and had migrant children in Lima. María presided over ANFASEP in the emergency zone of Ayacucho. (ANFASEP, let us recall, was the Ayacucho-based national federation of familiares, while COFADER was the counterpart committee of familiares based in Lima.) Teresa, president of COFADER, on the other hand, was rather *mestiza* and had been to school. Originally from Huanta, she lived in Lima, where she owned a business.[30] Both had children who had been disappeared, and Teresa also had other family members who had been executed extrajudicially.

The women of FEDEFAM (the Latin American counterpart federation) provided role models for the Peruvians to construct themselves as *presidentas*. Working with FEDEFAM, the Peruvian leaders discovered the commonalities that united them. They shared a tragedy and had to struggle together at both the national and international levels in order to obtain justice (investigation and punishment of the perpetrators, international pressure, and ratification of the Convention on Forced Disappearance in the UN). But they also encountered differences that separated them. The Peruvians perceived the FEDEFAM leaders as professionals, "trained and educated" (*capacitadas*) women who managed their own local organizations autonomously.[31] As Asunción, a leader in one of these organizations, noted: "the ones from other countries are from middle-class families, here in Peru the most affected are the poor humble people of the sierra. Those of the other countries are better trained, they are not just anybody, they are doctors, teachers, mainly lawyers those who come in these commissions as delegates."[32]

In this relationship, the Peruvian women came to discover, as well, the limitations and the possibilities offered by differences among themselves. With FEDEFAM's support, the two Peruvian leaders traveled on various occasions to Europe to denounce the actions of the state and to gain support for their cause. María, the president of ANFASEP, would dress in Andean *pollera* and *lliclla*, would speak first in Quechua and then in Spanish to denounce the Armed Forces' violations of human rights in Ayacucho, and would emphasize this region as the epicenter of human rights abuses.[33] Teresa, the president of COFADER, would speak in Spanish to accuse the state of violations and would embrace the whole national territory in her denunciation.

The tensions generated among leaders over who would represent the "Peruvian case" were negotiated in Peru with the human rights organizations, as well as with FEDEFAM, which served as their bridge to international forums. The president of COFADER, headquartered in Lima, was in a better position to create a space for representing Peru. Because she lived in Lima she was the immediate contact point for the international commissions that visited the country, and she was able to establish a direct relationship with politicians and to accompany the parliamentary Human Rights Commission in investigation of specific denunciations. She established a direct relationship with the leadership of FEDEFAM, through which she had access to information necessary to approach the international networks of support for Peru. All these connections allowed for a certain degree of autonomy vis-à-vis the Peruvian human rights organizations.

The president of ANFASEP, on the other hand, had to rely on the Lima-based human rights organizations in order to develop relationships beyond the Ayacucho region. She had her own distinct set of resources. Her knowledge of Quechua allowed her to negotiate a terrain of local leadership that enabled her to overcome a certain competition by more urban and literate leaders. Another specific resource was her ability to work in Ayacucho to support the children of the disappeared, to organize a communal kitchen (*comedor*) for the orphans, to confront the barbarism of the dirty war in Ayacucho, and in doing so, to represent a certain kind of collectivity. In sum, her role was to speak in the name of voiceless peasants.

María managed to situate herself above her own circumstances (her peasant origins, illiteracy, and difficulty when speaking Spanish) in her desire to constitute Ayacucho as the symbol of the dirty war. Yet her abilities encountered their limit when she had to compete for leadership space with Teresa, who was mestiza, urban, and literate, in the link to FEDEFAM. In 1987 the president of COFADER was elected member of the Latin American directorate of FEDEFAM. As a result, the tension between the two Peruvian organizations increased, canceling any possibilities for mutual coordination.

Displacing the Disappeared

Between 1987 and 1992 the number of disappeared persons once again increased.[34] During this period, Shining Path established its violent presence in other regions besides Ayacucho and intensified its selective assassination of authorities and local leaders.[35] Thus, the victims of violence increased.[36] The media provided daily news coverage of these events, accompanied with photographs and dramatic images.

In this context of increasing violence and human rights violations, the Second National Conference of La Coordinadora (II Encuentro Nacional de la Coordinadora Nacional de Derechos Humanos, held in 1987) took place and the executive committee of this coalition was enlarged to incorporate institutions that represented quite diverse political sectors.[37] The conference created the Executive Secretariat of La Coordinadora and charged it with reinforcing and coordinating the work of the national network in order to promote joint strategies. Above all, the secretariat had the difficult task of creating a space for social dialogue that would facilitate a more effective labor in defense of human rights.[38]

Publically denouncing the state for violating Peruvians' right to life, while at the same time condemning Shining Path violence, La Coordinadora inaugurated a new stage. In 1988 it convoked a national campaign with the slogan: "Sign for Life" (*A firmar por la vida*, a play on the words *firmar*, which mean "to affix one's signature," and *afirmar,* which means "to affirm"). The goal was to sensitize public opinion against forced disappearance of persons. The campaign managed to collect more than fifty thousand signatures in protest before the state. This action situated the human rights groups as the protagonists of denunciation.

This petition drive occurred at a moment when the organizations of family members mentioned above were hobbled by their mutual conflicts and had lost the capacity to mobilize their bases. La Coordinadora tried to encourage the organization of family members of the disappeared in the emergency zones.[39] Nonetheless, the family members of the newly disappeared turned to the institutions and commissions of human rights in Lima and the Peruvian interior to present their denunciations, but avoided the organizations of family members. When they did approach the latter, their attendance was sporadic.

Ironically, the organizations of familiares declined in the context of increasing numbers of disappeared persons. Should this decline be attributed exclusively to the tensions and conflicts among the leaderships of these organizations? In my view, other elements in play better explain the declining capacity of these organizations to convoke support. In the first place, the image of Shining Path as attacking the peasants and their leaders, and in general violating their human rights, became increasingly clear. Second, the repeated appearance in the mass media of Shining Path as an organized bloc that strictly regulated and controlled the internal dynamic of the prisons in which its militants were detained, and the suspicion that from prison they issued war directives, generated distrust toward the family members.[40] The organizations of familiares not only suffered from suspicion that they were relatives of Shining Path militants. In addition, they could no longer embody the huge number of war victims (on the contrary, they might embody one of the aggressors). Disappearances continued, but public sensibilities regarding the war, its victims, and its aggressors, had been shifting as the years went by.

In effect, as noted earlier, the repression of the Shining Path prison riots in Lima in June 1986 marked a turning point in sensibilities about the war's victims and aggressors. Although there had been strong reactions against the method used to suppress the riot, the first sentiments expressed by Peruvians were anxiety and fear aroused by Shining Path's ability to organize and coordinate actions from within prison walls. "I have and continue to have a profound anxiety, because of what is going on in Peru, where society is becoming more and more violent; where every day, violence is more natural, a tendency against which nothing, or almost nothing, is done." Other persons expressed "fear of losing my way of living" and that the "system, as it is, is indefensible." [41]

The expectant population felt that Shining Path was closing in, and people commented in the street and even in the daily press about a supposed Shining Path plan to invade the city of Lima. Speaking before television cameras, people interviewed in the streets expressed their fear and demanded that order be imposed upon the prison rioters. This was the case even though six months after the fact, 64 percent of the same population of Lima disagreed with the methods used to quell the uprising. [42]

But the experience of the prison uprisings also made people feel that institutions were not working. On television one could see how some judges and prosecutors, in accord with their responsibilities, attempted to enter the prisons and were pushed aside when they tried to cross the military barricade around the buildings. "Perhaps the circumstance that we have come to expect . . . has been a dramatic intersection in which the extreme crisis of each and every one of the civil institutions—including the Executive Power, the Legislative Power, the Judicial Power, the Public Ministry—has been unmasked. It has been a Dantesque circle in which all the pieces that compose it and the steps that were taken all led to this result. [43]

Another element that began to work itself out was the idea that not only the state violated human rights, but also Sendero. When in its actions Shining Path violated the physical integrity of human beings, this too became an aggression against human rights. [44]

A second event that also reflected this turning point in sensibilities regarding human rights violations was the 1988 massacre of comuneros in Cayara, Ayacucho. In retaliation for a Shining Path ambush of military troops, the military extrajudicially executed peasants in a neighboring community. The testimonies of survivors revealed a perverse situation: Shining Path had ruled the community through terror, and after the ambush had abandoned it to the army's retaliation. The peasants had no options as both sides said, in effect, "with me or against me." The civilian population was caught in the cross fire. [45]

A change in sensibilities toward war configures new social referents. The victims of the armed confrontation became known as the victims of violence in general, that is, a violence attributed to two aggressors. Already in 1987, in the annual meeting of the Permanent Seminar on Agrarian Research

(Seminario Permanente de Investigación Agraria), held in Ayacucho, young researchers from the zone proposed a new twist on the apparently neutral topic of peasant economy. They suggested study of the displacement of the population as a product of violence in the peasant economy. At the same time, they were studying peasant strategies in a "war economy."[46] Thus, a second referent for human rights was beginning to emerge: the victims were *los desplazados,* "the displaced" refugees who perceived themselves as trapped in a crossfire.

An analysis of the desplazados—their trajectory and decadence as a referent in the discourse of human rights—would exceed the limits of this essay. It is enough to suggest, as a hypothesis, that new "sensibilities" and new actors in the war would change the social referents used in the discourse of human rights. The violent transfer of the war to Lima by 1989 (manifested in car bombs and the assassinations of popular leaders), the growing involvement of peasants in the Autodefense Committees alongside the Armed Forces and against Shining Path, the detention of Abimael Guzmán; the reforms of the justice system to deal with terrorism (including use of Faceless Judges, the Military Code, and the Repentance Law), and the process of pacification that was underway: All these developments combined to produce new social referents by the mid-1990s. The victims of human rights abuses increasingly were identified with the innocently detained; the aggressor was no longer the army itself, nor even Shining Path (whether in retreat or defeated), but rather the justice system.

Between Oblivion and Memory

"Before people here paid attention to us, [now] no one pays attention to us, we are like lepers."[47] Today both ANFASEP and COFADER oscillate between survival, oblivion (*olvido*), and memory. Both focus on self-financing through small income-generating projects. ANFASEP is isolated; in 1993 it was not admitted as an organization by the Ayacucho coalition that works with the region's violently displaced refugee population. In 1994 it was not included in the agenda of an international commission that traveled to Ayacucho to observe the consequences of violence in the region. Today its former president is dedicated to producing a testimonial or memoir that narrates all the events of past years so that someday "justice will be done."

The situation in Lima is similar. The current president of COFADER, who lives in Lima, has returned for the first time to the community where her father was assassinated by a military patrol, carrying a commemorative plaque that she has placed in the cemetery in memory of all of the local victims. She sustains that it is necessary to keep the organization going so that the victims are not forgotten, and so that in the future "justice will be done."

But memory keeps alive not only pain, in the face of forgetfulness or oblivion, but also courage and anger (*coraje*) and acquired knowledge. In February 1994 a woman whose relative had disappeared in 1984 after a military operation in an Ayacucho community forcefully noted the reasons that she had stayed in the struggle: "[T]hey are people with names! they have been poor, someone has to look for them, one's little animal disappears you want to find it and why, just because we are poor, aren't we going to denounce this injustice? It is our right! . . . [T]hey look at us badly, as if this organization shouldn't exist, but it exists because they have forced us, they forced us because they killed us they disappeared us."[48]

Some Final Considerations

During the war years the human rights organizations built an organized social base capable of protest, as a method for defending human rights and denouncing abuses. This experience gives one the impression that the process of elaborating social referents served to enclose the victims within certain categories that identified them as "the disappeared," "the displaced," or "the innocents." Such labels have lifted them out of their social and economic context, and placed them in what Sinesio López called "the scenario of war."[49]

For this reason, my first reflection refers to the possible effects of the journey taken by the familiares on their consciousness as citizens. What relevant points should we emphasize out of the narrative I have just presented? One would be that the forced disappearance of a relative from the "private" ambit of affection, caused the family members of the disappeared to transform their "private" need into a "public" demand for justice from the state. In other words, for the familiares the life of the relative was no longer a personal favor that one solicited or demanded individually from some military officer or judge. It became a political right to be demanded from the state. The apprenticeship that the relatives underwent has led them, at the very least, to the conviction that they have "the right to have rights."[50] Clearly, the journey was a painful and difficult one in a country antagonized by war and marked by multiple social exclusions. For this reason they had to arm themselves with courage, and the learning needed to take the necessary steps.

Moreover, this conviction was attained through a process of demanding equality before the law. This was a demand to be included in the privilege of law: "why, just because we are poor, aren't we going to denounce this injustice? It is our right!" Thus, while the organizations of family members of the disappeared were formed with the specific purpose of recovering their relatives, the dynamics they developed located them in the ambit of the institutional pressure movements of the period that constructed a notion of citizenship.[51]

The efforts of the leaders of these organizations to situate themselves above their own circumstances may be understood in a similar vein. The tensions and conflicts present in the relationships between the leaders of the two organizations, and between these women and the national and international human rights organizations, unmask the dimensions of exclusion present in the dynamic of society. At the same time they show how these leaders tried to reverse the negative meanings of their own limitations in order to construct a space for themselves in society.

Nonetheless, it is necessary to consider that even as the familiares traveled a route from consciousness about the human right to existence to consciousness of rights as citizens, this same path revealed to the participant-actors the weakness, or absence of a juridical apparatus that protected the rights guaranteed by the constitution.[52] At the same time, their experiences revealed the fiction implicit in the affirmation that we are all equal before the law and the state. On the other hand, one should not give into the temptation to convert the term "family members of the disappeared" into a homogeneous model or to assume that every familiar travelled the exact same path. More likely, their diverse circumstances produced heterogeneous elaborations and may, as a result, lead to diverse paths in the future. Even so, the argument enunciated earlier still seems plausible to me: during the war, at the same time that they felt pain and anger before the injustice and the blatant discrimination that they experienced, these individuals became convinced that they had the "right to have rights." Accordingly, they became oriented toward constructing a notion of citizenship that was associated in part with knowledge of procedures and participation.

This appreciation brings us to a second reflection: the whole process of war and extreme violence to which the Peruvian population has been subjected appears to have made the idea that violence itself is wrong into an almost common sense assumption, despite the fact that daily life is pervaded by overwhelming violence. One thinks automatically in terms of a corresponding right that has been violated. In Peru today it is almost impossible to live a violent situation without it raising instantly the ominous idea of a violated right. This is the flip side of the violence. The association between violence and a sense of violated right has resulted from the unbearable excesses and from broad national debates about human rights, which have sensitized public opinion. This sensibility is evident in the great receptivity of the communications media today to such themes as the rights of children, linked to denunciations of violent abuses to which they are submitted, or to themes such as violence against women.[53] The media now embraces discussion of diverse violations of rights that were previously considered marginal or irrelevant issues. Regardless of the agreement or disagreement among the actors, the discussion of a broad spectrum of rights will modify some norms or ensure that others are applied more effectively. The discussion is encouraging a series of initiatives on the part of society and even on the part of the state.[54]

It is the process of reflection and open discussion on human rights, accompanied by efforts to elaborate a "neutral" discourse independent of political party frameworks, that has yielded a near-automatic linkage of the representation of violence with that of transgression of human rights.

Does all of the above signify the emergence of new cultural routines? The narrative presented above permits us only to affirm that we have "new lexicons." To propose the configuration of "new grammars" it is still necessary to analyze, from the perspective of ideas of rights, the processes that were elaborated over the course of the war. (And it is necessary to include those of us who worked in human rights as part of the dynamic of being studied.)

But there is still another final reflection: Today's agenda includes a closing of the period of the war. In this agenda, themes such as the administration of the social decomposition in the zones of narcoterrorism, the existence of hundreds of innocent persons unjustly detained and even condemned, the ambiguous character of a state that is efficient in the control of terrorism but does not respect democratic institutionality: these are all still unresolved issues. The institutions of human rights have to find new ways to tune in to the sensibility of the population and to elaborate a new political strategy.

Paths, there are many. The journey taken by sectors of the population toward notions of rights, toward demands of inclusion and participation, permit hope that it will be possible to confront this new challenge. In addition, we can count on the political will and the journey of apprenticeship by the human rights organizations, on the one hand, and on the knowledge acquired by the population, on the other.

Notes

1   I formed part of the Commission for Rights of the Person and Construction of Peace (Comisión de Derechos de la Persona y Construcción de la Paz; CODEPP) since its foundation in 1985, and I was Executive Secretary of the same organization during 1987–1991. In this capacity I served on the Executive Committee of the National Human Rights Coordinating Committee (Coordinadora Nacional de Derechos Humanos, hereinafter "La Coordinadora"), also from 1987 to 1991. I was also one of the initiators of the civic movement "Peru, Life and Peace" (PERU, VIDA Y PAZ) in 1989 and since 1993 I have coordinated its national network. For these reasons I have witnessed directly or indirectly (through testimonies and investigations) many of the experiences that I discuss in this essay.

2   La Coordinadora (see note 1) brings together forty-two organizations oriented toward the protection of human rights and the denunciation of violations. It was formed in January 1985. Before that date there were already diverse human rights commissions in Peru, in both Lima and the interior. Some had emerged in the late 1970s to support victims of the social repression (of those who pressed for economic rights) by the government of General Morales Bermúdez, while others were formed from 1982 on. Promoters of the human rights movement in the country who have not oriented their work toward denunciation of specific violations also include the Peruvian Network of Human Rights Education (Red Peruana de Educación en Derechos Humanos), founded in 1987, and the civic movement PERU, VIDA Y PAZ, founded in 1989.

3   Degregori 1993b: 69.

4   Belaúnde 1993: 27–29.

5   In a press conference President Belaúnde recognized and congratulated the peasants of Huaychao for their action. Uncertainty about the reports in the national dailies on the actions of the peasants in that confrontation led eight journalists to travel to verify on site the facts that had appeared in the press. Upon arriving in Uchuraccay they were killed. Various hypotheses were put forth at that time because people found it difficult to believe that the peasants were the assassins. One hypothesis was that the president had provoked the deaths in Uchuraccay by lauding the Huaychao peasants' actions. Others pointed to the military as having incited or carried out the killing. Since the victims were journalists, the events of Uchuraccay invaded all of the media

during the months of January and February 1983, for which reason it is diffi-cult to cite one report in particular. Moreover, the importance of the events led President Belaúnde to name a special investigating commission headed by Mario Vargas Llosa. The results of this commission were debated profusely and publically. Extensive documentation regarding the case of Uchuraccay can be seen in the Centro de Documentación of the Asociación Pro Derechos Humanos in Lima. Doubts about the initial image of Sendero came after Uchuraccay. As a leader of the Left put it a few months after the massacre, "it is a fact that there are communities that confront Shining Path and suffer the consequences of its reprisals" (Pease 1983: 49).

6   In 1982 there were 170 victims. This number increased to 2,807 in 1983 and 4,319 in 1984. See Chipoco 1992: 213. The number of denunciations of disap-peared persons according to statistics compiled by La Coordinadora in 1990, in its accusation against the state before the Permanent Peoples' Tribunal (Tri-bunal Permanente de los Pueblos), reached to 696 and 574 for the years 1983 and 1984 respectively, in CNDDHH 1990: 30. See also: Blondet and Montero 1994: 227, 327. In order to understand the urgency with which it was nec-essary to form organizations and institutions dedicated to human rights it is important to note that in those years according to Amnesty International the disappeared amounted to 1,000 persons (Chipoco 1992: 213).

7   See CNDDHH 1990: 28, 42.

8   Despite the prohibition, Catholic pastoral workers did accompany the victims of the violence of Ayacucho. The religious institution that worked in Ayacucho was the National Evangelical Council (Concilio Nacional Evangélico), an orga-nization that unites approximately 80 percent of the Protestant Evangelicals in the country and that created the human rights service "Peace and Hope" (Paz y Esperanza).

9   FEDEFAM: 1989.

10   Among the participants was the former attorney-general of Peru, Alvaro Rey de Castro. He had been the first jurist of this rank who, during the govern-ment of President Belaunde, acknowledged the existence of unmarked mass graves in Ayacucho.

11   The declaration of principles of this commission as well the list of its members appeared in El Comercio, 20 May 1985.

12   MacGregor and Rouillón 1985. Father MacGregor, who had been Rector of the Catholic University of Lima, founded APEP.

13   In June 1985 the Working Group on Enforced Disappearances of the United Nations visited Peru, establishing a direct relationship with human rights in-stitutions and with organizations of family members of the disappeared.

14   Faced with the extrajudicial execution of sixty-nine peasants in Accomarca, Ayacucho, "President García ordered an investigation and, as a result of it, forced the exit of the Chief of the Joint Command of the Armed Forces and

two generals who had commanded this emergency zone" (Chipoco 1992: 214). President García never adequately defined the mandate of the Peace Commission, five members of which also belonged to CODEPP. The majority of the members resigned in January 1986 because the government attempted to use this commission as an instrument in the government's own defense.

15 See note 2.

16 The extrajudicial executions did not stop. Nor was attention paid to the denunciations presented. The relevant documentation is on file in the Centro de Documentación of APRODEH in Lima.

17 The march took place on 21 November. The text of the declaration referred to may be verified in the archives of the human rights institutions.

18 The APRA party, to which García belonged, is a member of the Socialist International. García needed this forum to legitimize his political mandate, thus it was important to him that this event proceed without problems.

19 Ames et al. 1987: 85, 127, 169.

20 Over the two weeks that followed the suppression of the prison riots, the communiqués to which I refer were published in the press, especially in *La República*. Because of the importance of these events, all of the media editorialized about them.

21 The signifier *familiares* ("family members") comes from terminology provided by FEDEFAM and is used to designate the relatives of the disappeared and, by extension, their organizations.

22 Ayacuchan woman from the zone of Parcco, who migrated to the city of Huamanga in 1986, member of ANFASEP, interviewed in Lima in 1988.

23 For information on such developments, see especially *La República*, 12 May, 25 May, and 20 September 1986; *El Nuevo Diario*, 12–16 May 1986; *La Voz* and *El Nacional*, 20 September 1986.

24 Blondet and Montero 1994: 238.

25 See *La République*, 12 May, 25 May, and 20 September 1986; *El Nuevo Diario*, 12–16 May 1986; *La Voz* and *El Nacional*, 20 September 1986.

26 Especially in the rural zones of the Andean sierra, after burying a dead person, it is customary to return home and set out the clothes of the dead on a table or directly on the floor and *velarla* ("accompany," as in a wake) for five to eight days, depending on the region. The ritual ends with washing (or, in some places, burning) the clothes.

27 Migrant woman from Ayacucho, whose parents were disappeared in the zone of Huanta in 1985. From then on she participated in COFADER, interview 1989.

28 Ayacuchan woman, currently residing in Lima. Participated in the leadership of COFADER, interview 1993.

29 The names I provide here of the leaders are pseudonyms. In 1979 illiterate people obtained the right to vote. María exercised this right for the first time in the presidential elections of 1980.

30 While I have noted that both leaders had urban experience, it is important to differentiate between living in a city like Huamanga, which is still close to the rural experience, and living in a metropolis like Lima, which implies a rupture with the countryside. On the difference between provincial city and metropolis in Peru see G. Rochabrún 1994: 17–31.

31 In their testimonies, the Peruvian familiares tend to use the term *capacitadas* to refer to the leaders from FEDEFAM.

32 Interview 1993.

33 *Pollera* is the long skirt that peasant women of the Andes use; *lliclla* is a small manta wrapped over the shoulders and closed with a clasp over the chest.

34 In these years the number of disappeared persons increased from 125 in 1987 to 410 in 1989, and then declined to 230 in 1992 and to 69 in 1993 (see Blondet and Montero 1994: 237). In August 1992, the Human Rights Sub-Commission of the United Nations noted Peru as the country with the most disappearances that year.

35 From 19 authorities assassinated in 1984–1985, the number rose to 136 in 1988–1989 and 138 in 1992–1993.

36 The victims increased from 1,376 in 1986, to 2,878 in 1989, to arrive in 1990 and 1992 to 3,708 and 2,633, respectively (Blondet and Montero 1994: 227).

37 In the executive committee participated human rights commissions from four provinces (Puno, Cuzco, Ica, and Chimbote); two institutions from Lima with national coverage, APRODEH and the National Commission for Human Rights (Comisión Nacional de Derechos Humanos; or COMISEDH); the Episcopal Commission of Social Action (Comisión Episcopal de Acción Social; CEAS) of the Catholic Church; and CODEPP and ANFASEP also joined. In addition it includes as permanent guests of the executive committee, the Institute for Legal Defense (Instituto de Defensa Legal; IDL), the Andean Commission of Jurists, and the Peruvian section of Amnesty International.

38 Despite having incorporated very diverse political sectors in the denunciation of human rights violations, the human rights institutions had been labeled leftists and accused of not sufficiently condemning Shining Path. At the same time, changes in the interior of the Catholic ecclesiastic hierarchy had resulted in a greater presence of conservative bishops who are not disposed to take a leading role on these issues. It was necessary to construct a civic space to legitimate the work of La Coordinadora. In this sense the new composition of the executive committee offered possibilities, because it allowed for the organization to reach a larger audience.

39 In 1988 they organized the first National Day of Family Members of Disappeared Persons (Jornada Nacional de Familiares de Desaparecidos); in 1989 they supported the organization of the Ninth Congress of FEDEFAM in Lima; in 1992 national institutions still sought to join the familiares and organized an Encounter of Departmental Coordinators.

40   Salcedo 1986: 60–67. In the months leading up to the riot and massacre of
      1986, reports on Shining Path's control on the prisons appeared repeatedly
      in magazines such as *Caretas* and *Oiga,* and in newspapers and on television
      and radio.

41   See Moreya 1987: 90, 92 (in Cotler 1987, a compilation that was the result
      of a series of roundtables organized by the *Instituto de Estudios Peruanos* on
      July 14–16, 1986, more than a month after the riot was quelled).

42   Survey of public opinion realized in Lima in January 1987 by APOYO S.A. upon
      the request of CODEPP.

43   García Sayán 1987b: 171.

44   Chipoco 1988: 43–45. La Coordinadora petitioned the Permanent Peoples'
      Tribunal, asking that in its fact-finding session in Peru (which took place in
      1990), the tribunal pronounce not only on the state's violations of human
      rights, but that it also "contemplate the judgment of crimes against humanity
      committed by armed rebel organizations that, without a doubt, constitute an
      essential factor in the increasing spiral of violence" (CNDDHH 1990: 9). For
      a similar opinion, this time alluding explicitly to Shining Path as violating
      human rights, see DESCO/Andean Commission of Jurists 1989: 363.

45   The massacre of Cayara was profusely covered by the different press media.
      A Senate Investigating Committee was named, headed by the aprista Carlos
      Enrique Melgar, who concluded the investigation by pronouncing that the
      victims never existed. The prosecutor Carlos Escobar, who was in charge of
      the case, presented evidence that contradicted Melgar's conclusions and as a
      result was relieved of his post.

46   Loayza Camargo 1988; Pérez Liu 1988.

47   Asunción, interviewed in 1993.

48   Marina is 48 years old, resides presently in Lima and participates in literacy
      courses.

49   López 1989: 15–19, 1991: 65–109.

50   Arendt 1973.

51   This was the case in the women's movement as well. The difference is rooted
      in the velocity with which the processes unfolded; the organizations of family
      members of the disappeared were born, grew, and declined in only six years,
      thus giving rise to tensions and conflicts. The women's movement, on the
      other hand, went through a longer maturation process.

52   Rubio 1995: 201–214.

53   While it is true that during the war some communications media criticized
      the labor of the human rights institutions, it is also true that there were
      others who strongly supported them. Moreover, in some cases of violations
      committed by the state—they would be too many to enumerate—most of the
      media highlighted the news and repudiated the violation committed.

54   We will only cite two examples: the enthusiasm with which the proposal for

creating a Defender of the Child (Defensor del niño) was accepted in different parts of the country; and the conduct of the Lima judge Antonia Saquicuray as regards the Amnesty Law promulgated by the government on 16 June 1995. This law in its first article "concedes general amnesty to military, police, and civilian personnel who have been denounced, investigated, prosecuted, tried, or condemned . . . for all of the events derived or originated upon the occasion of or as a consequence of the struggle against terrorism . . . since May of 1980." The judge Saquicuray declared the law inapplicable in the case of the massacre of Barrios Altos, a decision that was approved by a large majority of the citizenry (70%) and was confirmed in other places in the country (see CNDDHH 1996: 15–29).

✤ CONCLUSION

Shining and Other Paths: The Origins, Dynamics, and Legacies of War, 1980–1995

Steve J. Stern

✤ In the introductions to each of the five major parts of this collaborative book I sought to contextualize and draw out the implications of the studies specific to each of the book's five major themes: the historical roots of the political convulsion that overwhelmed Peru, the failed conquest struggle by Sendero in the center-south highlands, the destruction of apparent "third paths" in Lima and the highlands, women's war experience and affirmation as citizen-subjects, and the legacies of the war for politics and culture. Our hope, however, is that the whole of the collaborative work is larger than the sum of its parts. As one steps back to consider this book's cumulative interpretation of the origins, dynamics, and legacies of the nightmare that convulsed Peru, several major conclusions stand out and cut across specific book sections and essays.

First, we have argued that the Sendero Luminoso phenomenon must be viewed as a force both "within" and "against" history. The essays in Part I (de la Cadena, Hinojosa, and Mallon) help us to conceptualize the roots of the Sendero phenomenon as one logical culmination among several of the history of highland and Left politics before the 1980s. These essays anchor the key elements that would mark Shining Path within wider historical processes: the turn toward a class-driven language of radicalism implicitly nourished by racial and *de provincia* sensibilities, the appeal of Maoism within a Left that differentiated itself from the Velasco revolution and took up mobilization against the post-Velasco military regime, the activist experience of rural political mobilization and disappointment that fed disgust with political compromisers and "ignorant" Indians, and that fed belief in the necessity of violent insurrection led by a vanguard.

The essays by Burt and Rénique in Part III deepen our awareness of Sendero's place both "within" and "against" history. On the one hand, Sendero's campaign to destroy "third paths" underscores its stance as a unique and uncompromising force—"against" the history that had yielded rival Lefts and popular illusions. On the other hand, the zone of tolerance that enabled Shining Path to invade specific locales and organizations, and to "work" local fissures and contradictions, demonstrated a rootedness "within" history that tragically affected the course of war and society. Burt and Rénique's studies illuminate ambiguities within nonsenderista Left politics—anchored in the historical experiences that also yielded Sendero Luminoso's project—that widened Sendero's freedom of action and that contemplated the necessity of nonsenderista versions of armed struggle.

Second, Sendero Luminoso demonstrated an astonishing capacity, in its political practices, to blend extreme astuteness and extreme ignorance. The juxtaposition of Parts II and III helps clarify how Sendero could know so much and so little *at the same time.* On the one hand, the essays in Part II (Degregori, del Pino, Manrique, and Starn) demonstrate an almost inexorable drive toward ideologically inspired blindness. Again and again, Sendero squandered its initial political advantages and legitimacies, and seemed unable to process the politically fatal implications of deeply alienating practices that would spark open peasant resistance. All setbacks and problems could be inserted within a hyperideologized vision of the dialectical and scientifically revealed path to revolutionary triumph. On the other hand, the essays in Part II also make clear the impressive local knowledge and presence of many senderista activists. The essays in Part III (especially Burt's study of Lima) illuminate the astuteness with which senderistas processed this local information, identified fissures in the social and political fabric, and "worked the contradiction" to undermine competing authorities, leaders, and institutions. Coral's discussion of Lima, in Part IV, corroborates this astuteness. Taken together, the essays somewhat dissolve the paradox of an intimidating awareness and practical ability to use information ("the Party has a thousand eyes and a thousand ears"), and a self-defeating obtuseness that blocked vital information or ignored its implications ("the Party is amazingly blind and deaf"). Senderista political practice tended to channel information narrowly, to achieve goals of political presence, intimidation, and domination. The narrow channeling allowed the larger field of ideologically driven vision and blindness to remain relatively intact.[1]

Third, the essays in this book suggest that for many Peruvians the war years brought experiences of double-lives and inner conflicts. At one level, the drama of doubled lives derived from the tensions and ambiguities of coerced complicity. The depictions of community life by Degregori, del Pino, and to some extent Manrique (in Part II) demonstrate that in many locales, a mix of complicity and tolerance initially facilitated relations of coexistence, adaptation, and in some instances sympathy with the senderistas. Yet even as peasants traveled the inner transition from tolerance and complicity toward rejection and resistance, they could not necessarily act in accord with their inner sensibilities. After all, it was precisely in the communities of greatest tolerance or sympathy that Sendero could most easily construct vises of coerced complicity that rendered resistance difficult, if not suicidal. The effects of draconian coercion and the ambivalences posed by kinship— whether reluctance to consider senderista kin as enemies, or reluctance to place nonsenderista kin at risk of vengeance—could introduce a widening breach between "inner" and "outer" selves.

The breach did not only afflict peasants and comuneros. At another level, the drama of doubled lives derived from the ambivalences and learning processes experienced by the Left and by human rights activists. The essays in Part I (by de la Cadena, Hinojosa, and Mallon) on the roots of senderista-like political visions, and the zones of leftist tolerance drawn out in the studies by Burt, Rénique, and Coral, make clear that leftist opposition to Sendero was often tempered by a sense that the state and its devastatingly regressive or ineffective economic policies constituted more urgent targets of critique and resistance. Like the human rights activists whose doctrinal background had focused on the state as the key violator of rights (see the essays by Basombrío and Muñoz), many leftist activists underwent a complex "learning process" before they could "arrive" at a focus on Sendero as a priority target of resistance. Such learning processes also implied ambivalent, doubled lives—periods when an "outer" self did not yet act in accord with "inner" knowledge or sensibilities. For many activists and intellectuals, therefore, the terrors of war were not only physical. The war also yielded a drama of moral crisis and renewal.

Fourth, beyond its destructions of life, economic resources, and the geography of human settlement, the war had an extremely destructive impact on political culture and institutions. Earlier, in the general introduction to this volume, we noted the extraordinary coexistence, in the Peru of the 1980s and 1990s, of political visions and players who seemed to represent distinct historical eras. In the Peru of the 1980s and 1990s, prominent political players included guerrilla revolutionaries of the 1960s–1970s (both in their "Cuba-inspired" and "China-inspired" varieties), Left-leaning populists of the 1930s–1960s, moderate developmentalists of the 1950s–1960s, "dirty war" military rulers of the 1970s, and neoliberals and unknown "new" politicians of the 1980s–1990s. The war generated a profound clearing effect on these richly congested political spaces. The essays in Part III (Burt, Rénique) brought the clearing effect into sharp focus by demonstrating the political richness that generated apparent third paths, often rooted in nonsenderista culminations of leftist history, and the reductionist pressures that destroyed them. Yet as the essays in Part V make clear, the disintegrative effect of the war on political institutions and values went beyond the fate of Left and Center-Left parties, or the influence of leftist ideas in political culture. Obando traces the ways the war struggle impelled a presidentialism that weakened countervailing institutions, including the military, within the state. Basombrío illuminates the ways the war struggle impelled an interest in results and a cynicism about politics that weakened respect for life and rights to fair process, and that could taint critics as knowing or unknowing agents of terrorism. As the war wound down, the congested quality of Peruvian political life had cleared. By 1994–1995, few tenable alternatives to fujimorismo and neoliberalism were apparent.

Fifth, the war crisis had important generative impacts on politics and society, and not all these generative impacts were negative. Oliart and Basombrío illuminate the bleaker side of such impacts in their examination of the consolidation of a political culture of popular authoritarianism, identified with subaltern needs and identities, and rather dismissive and cynical about discourses of human rights and social justice. But as we have also seen, not all the generative impacts of war proved bleak. The essays in Part II (Degregori, del Pino, Manrique, and especially Starn) depict transitions to antisenderista resistance through which peasants and ronderos have refashioned themselves as patriotic citizen-subjects who won the war and claim the right to have a future. Although military intelligence work that dismantled Sendero's leadership was also critical in "winning the war," the ronderos' self-image is warranted. The analysis by Obando of deep splits between presidential administrations and the military, and within the military forces as well, underscores the importance of the ronderos in winning regional wars in the countryside. Similarly, Coral's analysis of women's experience, supplemented by del Pino's and Muñoz's portraits of mothers and Burt's

NEW CITIZEN-SUBJECTS.
(left) Teodora Ayme, as president
of the Departmental Mothers' Club
Federation of Ayacucho, addresses
a propeace rally.
(opposite) In the heights of Huanta,
Ayacucho, poorly armed ronderos
see themselves as the patriot-
citizens who defend Peru and their
community.

study of grassroots organizations in Villa El Salvador, depict the unforeseen emergence of women as citizen-subjects. The women depicted in these essays intervened forcefully in the crises of rural and urban politics, and claimed a voice in the politics of post-war reconstruction. Finally, Muñoz identifies expanded sensibilities of right—repudiations of violence that open new spaces for a language of children's rights and women's rights— that provide a certain counterweight to more dismissive and cynical values.

The generative impacts of the war crisis have opened as well as closed doors. Through these doors walk the new citizen-subjects of Peru, insisting on the right to build paths of life over death, sustenance over hunger, agency over intimidation.

Note

1   As close observers of Sendero are aware, this point does not imply absolute uni-
      formity of vision at all levels of the party hierarchy or an absence of debate that
      includes dissent based on realistic field information. What it *does* imply is the

ability, through hyperideological analysis, to win internal senderista debates and impose a "correct line" that blocks out the unraveling implications of inconvenient information. Early in the transition to war, Guzmán was already a master at internal debate to establish a correct line: for vivid and reliable analysis, see Gorriti 1990.

❖ ABBREVIATIONS AND ORGANIZATIONS

AA Autonomous Authority

ANAP Apatyawaka Nampistsi Asháninka

ANFASEP Asociación Nacional de Familiares de Detenidos-Desaparecidos, Association of Family Members of the Detained-Disappeared

AP Acción Popular, Popular Action

APEMIVES Small business owners' federation

APEP Asociación Peruana de Estudios e Investigación para la Paz, Peruvian Association of Studies and Research for Peace

APRA Alianza Popular Revolucionaria Americana, American Popular Revolutionary Alliance

ARI Alianza Revolucionaria de Izquierda, Revolutionary Alliance of the Left

Associación de Abogados Democráticos

BCS bases contrasubversivas, counterinsurgency bases

BOPE Batallón de Operaciones de Protección Especial, Special Protection Operations Battalion

CACS Comités de Autodefensa Civil, Committees of Civilian Self-Defense

Cahuide Agricultural Society

CAP Cooperativas Agrarias de Producción, Agrarian Production Cooperatives

CCP Confederación Campesina del Perú, Peruvian Peasant Federation; Peasant Federation of Peru

CEAS Comisión Episcopal de Acción Social, Episcopal Commission of Social Action

CEPEI Centro Peruano de Estudios Internacionales

CEPRODEP Centro de Promoción y Desarrollo Poblacional

CGTP Confederación General de Trabajadores, General Confederation of Peruvian Workers

CICLAS Comisión Interministerial Coordinadora de la Lucha Antisubversiva, Interministerial Coordinating Commission for the Counterinsurgency Struggle

CODEPP Comisión de Derechos de la Persona y Construcción de la Paz, Commission for Rights of the Person and Construction of Peace

COFADER Comité de Familiares de Detenidos-Desaparecidos, Committee of Family Members of the Detained-Disappeared

Colina Group Dissident military group

COMACA Dissident military group

COMISEDH Comisión Nacional de Derechos Humanos, National Commission on Human Rights

Comités de Defensa Civil, Civil Defense Committees

Comités Democráticos Campesinos, Democratic Peasant Committees

Comités Populares Abiertos, Open People's Committees

Comité Pro-Derecho Indígena Tawantinsuyo, Tawantinsuyo Committee for Indigenous Rights

CONACO Corporación Nacional de Comerciantes, National Association of Merchants

Concilio Nacional Evangélico, National Evangelical Council

Confederación Nacional Agraria

Consejo por la Paz y la Vida, Council for Peace and Life

Cooperación Popular

La Coordinadora La Coordinadora Nacional de Derechos Humanos, National Coordinating Committee of Human Rights

CORDEL Committees of Reconstruction and Local Development

CUAVES Self-managing Urban Community of Villa El Salvador

DESCO Centro de Estudios y Promoción del Desarrollo, Center for Studies and Promotion of Development

Destacamentos de Operaciones Especiales, Special Operations Detachments

DINCOTE Dirección Nacional contra el Terrorismo

ENCI Empresa Nacional de Comercialización de Insumos, National Enterprise for the Commercialization of Inputs

II Encuentro Nacional de la Coordinadora Nacional de Derechos Humanos, Second National Conference of La Coordinadora

ERPS Empresas Rurales de Propiedad Social, Rural Social Property Enterprises

FECONAYA Federación de Comunidades Nativas Yanesha, Federation of Native Yanesha Communities

FEDECMA Federación Departamental de Clubes de Madres de Ayacucho, Departmental Federation of Mothers' Clubs of Ayacucho

FEDEFAM Federación Latinoamericana de Asociaciones de Familiares de Detenidos-Desaparecidos, Latin American Federation of Associations of Family Members of the Detained-Disappeared

Federación Provincial de Clubes de Madres de Huamanga, Federation of Mothers' Clubs of the Province of Huamanga

FEDIP Frentes de Defensa, Defense Fronts

FEPCA Federación Provincial de Campesinos de Andahuaylas, Provincial Federation of Peasants of Andahuaylas

FEPOMUVES Popular Women's Federation

FER Frente Estudiantil Revolucionario, Revolutionary Student Front

FNTMMSP Federación Nacional de Trabajadores Mineros Metalúrgicos y Siderúgicos

HIERROPERU State mining corporation

IDL Instituto de Defensa Legal, Legal Defense Institute

IEP Instituto de Estudios Peruanos, Institute of Peruvian Studies

ILA Inicio de la Lucha Armada

IMASEN Polling agency

INIDEN Instituto Nacional de Investigaciones de la Defensa Nacional

Instituto de Educación Rural "Waqrani" de Ayaviri

Instituto Indigenista Interamericano, Interamerican Indigenista Institute

Instituto Indigenista Peruano, Peruvian Indigenista Institute

IS Izquierda Socialista, Socialist Left

IU Izquierda Unida, United Left

Ley de Arrepentimiento, Repentance Law

MAS Movement of Socialist Affirmation

MIR Movimiento Izquierda Revolucionaria, Revolutionary Left Movement

MRTA Movimiento Revolucionario Túpac Amaru, Túpac Amaru Revolutionary Movement

NGDO nongovernmental development organization

PAIT temporary work program

Patria Roja Communist Party of Peru-Red Fatherland

PCP Partido Comunista del Peru, Peruvian Communist Party

PCP-BR Partido Comunista del Perú-Bandera Roja, Communist Party of Peru-Red Flag

PCP-SL Partido Comunista del Perú-Sendero Luminoso; Sendero Luminoso; Sendero, Communist Party of Peru-Shining Path

PCP-U Partido Comunista del Perú-Unidad, Communist Party of Peru-Unity

PCR-CO Partido Comunista Revolucionario-Clase Obrera, Revolutionary Communist Party-Working Class

PES Programa de Emergencia Social, Social Emergency Program

PMR Revolutionary Mariateguista Party

PPAR Plan Piloto Ande Rojo, Red Ande Pilot Plan

PPC Partido Popular Cristiano, Popular Christian Party

Red Peruana de Educación en Derechos Humanos, Peruvian Network of Human Rights Education

PROCAD Centro Promoción, Capacitación y Desarrollo, Promotion, Training, and Development Center

Promoción Comunal

PUM Partido Unificado Mariáteguista, Mariáteguista Unified Party; United Mariáteguista Party

SAIS Sociedades Agrícolas de Interés Social, Agricultural Societies of Social Interest

Sendero Rojo Red Sendero faction

SER Servicios Educacionales Rurales, Rural Educational Services

SIDERPERU State iron and steel works company

SIN Servicio de Inteligencia Nacional

SINAMOS Sistema Nacional de Apoyo a la Movilización Social, National System of Support for the Social Mobilization

SUTEA SUTEP affiliate in Andahuaylas

SUTEP Sindicato Unico de Trabajadores de la Educación

Tribunal Permanente de los Pueblos, Permanent Peoples' Tribunals

TRUPAL Paper factory

UI Unidad de Izquierda, Left Unity

Unidades Tácticas Antisubversivas, Tactical Antisubversive Units

UNIR Unión de Izquierda Revolucionaria, National Union of the Revolutionary Left

UPP Unión por el Perú, Union for Peru

VR Vanguardia Revolucionaria, Revolutionary Vanguard

Vanguardia Socialista, Socialist Vanguard

Abugattás, Juan. 1990. "El Leviatán apedreado: La polémica sobre el estado en el Perú." In Juan Abugattás et al., eds., *Estado y sociedad: Relaciones peligrosas*, 81–107. Lima: DESCO.

Abugattás, Juan, et al. eds. 1990. *Estado y sociedad: Relaciones peligrosas*. Lima: DESCO.

Abu-Lughod, Lila. 1990. "The Romance of Resistance: Tracing Transformations of Power through Bedouin Women," *American Ethnologist* 17 (1): 41–55.

Ajani, Fouad. 1993. "The Summoning," *Foreign Affairs* (September–October): 2–9.

Adriansén, Catalina. 1978. *Bibliografía seleccionada de publicaciones acerca del campesinado de la región de Ayacucho*. Lima: Proyecto SINEA.

Albó, Xavier. 1992. *La paradoja Aymara*. La Paz: CIPCA.

Álvarez, Sonia. n.d. "Theoretical Problems and Methodological Impasses in the Study of Contemporary Social Movements in Brazil and the Southern Cone: An Agenda for Future Research." Ms., Department of Politics, University of California, Santa Cruz.

Americas Watch. 1986. *Civil Patrols in Guatemala*. New York: Americas Watch.

———. 1991. *Into the Quagmire: Human Rights and U.S. Policy in Peru*. New York: Human Rights Watch.

Ames, Rolando, et al. 1987. *Informe al Congreso sobre los sucesos de los penales*. Lima: OCISA.

Amnesty International. 1992. *Human Rights During the Government of Alberto Fujimori*. New York: Amnesty International.

Andreas, Carol. 1985. *When Women Rebel: The Rise of Popular Feminism in Peru*. Westport, CT: Lawrence Hill.

Ansión, Juan, ed. 1985. "Violencia y Cultura en el Perú." In Felipe MacGregor and José Luis Rouillon, eds., *Siete ensayos sobre la violencia política en el Perú*. Lima: Fundación Friedrich Ebert and Asociación Peruana de Estudios e Investigaciones para la Paz-APEP.

———. 1989. *Pishtacos. De verdugos a sacaojos*. Lima: Tarea.

Apoyo, S.A. 1987. *Encuesta sobre los Derechos Humanos*. Lima: CODEPP.

————. 1994. *Actitudes hacia temas vinculados al fortelacimiento de la democracia en el Péru. Encuesta nacional de opinión pública.* Lima: APOYO.

Arce Borja, Luis, ed. 1989. *Guerra popular en el Perú: El pensamiento Gonzalo.* Brussels: no publisher.

Archivo CEPRODEP (Centro de Desarrollo y Promoción Poblacional). 1988. "Sendero Luminoso. Informe, bases, y aparatos." Ms., CEPRODEP, Lima.

————. 1991a. "Memorias del taller de trabajo. Cambios en el rol de las mujeres y la federación departmental de clubes de madres de Ayacucho." Ms., CEPRODEP, Lima.

————. 1991b. "Memorias de reuniones—las jornadas con las familias desplazadas en Lima y Ayacucho con ocasión de la Misión ICVA. Ms., CEPRODEP, Lima.

————. 1994. "Memorias del taller de trabajo: Mujeres displazadas, con participación de las líderes de la Federación Departmental de Clubes de Madres de Ayacucho." Ms., CEPRODEP, Lima.

————. 1995. "Historias de vida de mujeres líderes: 5 mujeres de base y 5 mujeres desplazadas." Ms., CEPRODEP, Lima.

Arendt, Hannah. 1970. *On Violence.* New York: Harcourt, Brace, Jovanovich.

————. 1973. *The Origins of Totalitarianism.* New York: Harcourt, Brace and World.

Arguedas, José María. 1941. *Yawar Fiesta.* Buenos Aires: Editorial Losada. (Also available in English under the same title. Austin: University of Texas Press, 1985.)

————. 1944. "En defensa del folklore musical andino." *La Prensa* (Lima), 19 November.

————. 1958. *Los ríos profundos.* Buenos Aires: Editorial Losada. (Also available in English as *Deep Rivers.* Austin: University of Texas Press, 1985.)

————. 1964. *Todas las sangres.* Buenos Aires: Editorial Losada.

————. 1976. *Señores e indios. Acerca de la cultura quechua.* Montevideo: Calicanto.

————. 1977. *Formación de una cultura nacional indoamericana.* Mexico: Siglo XXI.

Armaza, Emilio. 1928. "Confesiones de izquierda." *Boletín Titikaka* 2 (Puno) (25).

Atauje, Fortunato. 1995. "Vías de esperanza." Thesis, Universidad Nacional de San Cristóbal de Huamanga.

Balaguer, Alejandro. 1993. *Rostros de la guerra/Faces of War.* Lima: Peru Reporting.

Balbi, Carmen Rosa. 1989. *Identidad clasista en el sindicalismo.* Lima: DESCO.

————. 1992. "Sendero en las fábricas. Encendiendo la mecha." *QueHacer* 77 (Lima): 76–81.

Ballón, Eduardo, et al. 1986. *Movimientos sociales y democracia: La fundación de un nuevo orden.* Lima: DESCO.

————. 1990. *Movimientos sociales: Elementos para una relectura.* Lima: DESCO.

Barrenechea, Carlos, ed. 1983. *El problema regional hoy.* Lima: Ediciones Tarea.

Basadre, Jorge. 1960. *Historia de la República del Perú.* Lima: Ediciones Historia.

Basombrío, Carlos. 1994. "Para la historia de una guerra con nombre: ¡Ayacucho!" *Ideéle* 62 (April): 27–33.

Belaúnde, Fernando. 1993. "El destino reparador." In Roland Forgues, *Perú. Entre el desafío y el sueño de loposible*, 25–35. Lima: Minerva.

Belaúnde, Víctor Andrés. 1933. *Meditaciones peruanas*. Lima: Compañía de Impresiones y Publicidad.

———. 1945. *Peruanidad, elementos esenciales*. Lima: Lumen.

———. 1964. *La realidad nacional*. Lima: no publisher.

Benavides, Margarita. 1992. "Autodefensa asháninka, organizaciones nativas y autonomía indígena." In Carlos Iván Degregori et al., eds., *Tiempos de ira y amor*, 539–59. Lima: DESCO, Centro de Estudios y Promoción del Desarrollo.

Benjamin, Walter. 1968. *Iluminations: Essays and Reflections*. New York: Harcourt, Brace, and World.

Berg, Ronald. 1984. "The Effects of Return Migration on a Highland Peruvian Community," Ph.D. dissertation, University of Michigan, Ann Arbor.

———. 1986. "Sendero Luminoso and the Peasantry of Andahuaylas." *Journal of Interamerican Studies and World Affairs* 28 (4): 165–96.

———. 1992. "Peasant Responses to Shining Path in Andahuaylas." In David Scott Palmer, ed., *The Shining Path of Peru*, 83–104. New York: St. Martin's Press.

Berger, Peter L., and Thomas Luckman. 1966. *The Social Construction of Reality: A Treatise on the Sociology of Knowledge*. New York: Doubleday Press.

Bernales, Enrique. 1972. "Universidad y temas socio-políticos." Ms.

Bernales, Enrique, et al. 1989. "Violencia y pacificación." *Comisión especial del Senado sobre las causas de la violencia y alternativas de pacificación en el Perú*. Lima: DESCO and Comisión Andina de Juristas.

Bertram, Geoffrey. 1991. In Leslie Bethell, ed., *The Cambridge History of Latin America*, vol. 8, 385–449. Cambridge: Cambridge University Press.

Bland, Gary, and Joseph Tulchin, eds. 1994. *Peru in Crisis: Dictatorship or Democracy*. Boulder: Lynne Rienner.

Bloch, Marc. 1961. *Feudal Society*, vol. 1. Translated by L.A. Mannion. Chicago: University of Chicago Press.

Blondet, Cecilia M. 1991. *Las mujeres y el poder: Una historia de Villa El Salvador*. Lima: Instituto de Estudios Peruanos.

Blondet, Cecilia M., and Carmen María Montero. 1994. "La situación de la mujer en el Perú, 1980–1994." Working Paper No. 68, Instituto de Estudios Peruanos, Lima.

———. 1995. *Hoy, menú popular: Comedores en Lima*. Instituto de Estudios Peruanos and UNICEF.

Boggio, Ana María, Fernando Romero, and Juan Ansión. 1991. *El pueblo es así y también asá: Lógicas culturales en el voto popular*. Lima: Instituto Democracia y Socialismo.

Bolton, Ralph, and Enrique Mayer. 1977. *Andean Kinship and Marriage*. Washington, D.C.: American Anthropological Association.

Bonilla, Heraclio, ed. 1987. *Comunidades campesinas: Cambios y permanencias.* Chiclayo, Peru: Centro de Estudios Sociales Solidaridad, and Lima: Consejo Nacional de Ciencia y Tecnología.

Bourque, Susan C., and Kay B. Warren. 1989. "Democracy without Peace: The Cultural Politics of Terror in Peru." *Latin American Research Review* 24 (1): 7–34.

Bourricaud, François. 1989. *Poder y sociedad en el Perú contemporáneo.* Lima: Instituto de Estudios Peruanos and Instituto Francés de Estudios Andinos.

Brading, David. 1988. "Manuel Gamio and Official Indigenismo in Mexico." *Bulletin of Latin American Research* 7 (1): 75–89.

Brown, Michael F., and Eduardo Fernández. 1991. *War of Shadows: The Struggle for Utopia in the Peruvian Amazon.* Berkeley: University of California Press.

Burga, Manuel, and Wilson Reátegui. 1981. *Lanas y capital mercantil en el sur, la Casa Ricketts, 1895–1935.* Lima: Instituto de Estudios Peruanos.

Burneo, José, and Marianne Eyde. 1986. *Rondas campesinas y defensa civil.* Lima: SER.

Burt, Jo-Marie. 1994. "La inquisición pos-senderista." *QueHacer,* 92: 30–55.

——. 1997. "Political Violence and the Grassroots in Lima, Peru." In Douglas Chalmers, et al., eds., *The New Politics of Inequality in Latin America: Rethinking Participation and Representation,* 281–309. London: Oxford University Press.

Burt, Jo-Marie, and César Espejo. 1995. "The Struggles of a Self-Built Community." *NACLA Report on the Americas* 28 (4): 19–25.

Burt, Jo-Marie, and Aldo Panfichi. 1992. *Peru: Caught in the Crossfire.* Jefferson City, MO: Peru Peace Network.

Burt, Jo-Marie, and José López Ricci. 1994. "Peru: Shining Path after Guzmán." *NACLA Report on the Americas* 28 (3): 6–9.

Byrne, Bridget. 1996. "Género, conflicto y desarrollo." Lima: no publisher.

Caballero Martín, Víctor. 1981. *Imperialismo y campesinado en la sierra central.* Huancayo: Instituto de Estudios Andinos.

——. 1984. *La crisis de las empresas asociativas en el agro puneño.* Puno: Servicios Populares/Escuelas Campesinas de la CCP.

——. 1990. "El modelo asociativo en Junín y Puno: Balance y perspectivas del problema de la tierra." In Alberto Fernández and Alberto González, eds., *La Reforma Agraria, 20 años después.* Chiclayo: CONCYTEC.

——. 1991. "La realidad de la reestructuración de las empresas asociativas en Puno." In Víctor Caballero Martín and Dante Zurita, *Puno, Tierra y alternativa comunal (Experiencias y propuestas de politica agraria).* Lima: no publisher.

Caballero Martín, Victor, and Dante Zurita. 1991. *Puno, tierra y alternativa comunal (Experiencias y propuestas de política agraria).* Lima: no publisher.

Cáceres, Andrés. 1973. *La guerra de 1879. Sus campañas (Memorias).* Lima: Editorial Carlos Milla Batres.

Calderón, Mateo Jesús. 1991. "Entre la emergencia y la pacificación. *Ideéle* no. 28 (August): 11–12.

Campredón, Gabriel. 1992. *Luis Dalle: Un hombre libre.* Lima: Tarea.

Carmack, Robert M., ed. 1988. *Harvest of Violence: The Maya Indian and the Guatemalan Crisis.* Norman: University of Oklahoma Press.

Caro, Nelly. 1993. "Democracia interna y las organizaciones de sobrevivencia en Lima." Masters thesis, Pontífica Universidad Católica del Perú, Lima.

Carpentier, Alejo. 1957. *The Lost Steps (Los pasos perdidos).* Translated by Harriet de Onís. New York: Avon. Originally published in 1953.

Carr, Barry, and Steve Ellner, eds. 1993. *The Latin American Left: From the Fall of Allende to Perestroika.* Boulder: Westview Press.

Casanova, Julio, et al. 1971. "Análisis de la economía terrateniente en Ayacucho." *Boletín de Investigaciones Histórico Sociales* (Ayacucho) 2: 14–19.

Castañeda, Jorge G. 1993. *Utopia Unarmed: The Latin American Left after the Cold War.* New York: Vintage.

Castro Caripio, Augusto. 1983. "Gobierno autónomo para Puno." In Carlos Barrenechea, ed. *El problema regional hoy.* Lima: Ediciones Tarea.

Castro Pozo, Hildebrando. 1934. *Renuevo de la peruanidad.* Lima: no publisher.

———. 1979. *Nuestra comunidad indígena,* 2d ed. Lima: no publisher.

Central Committee of the Communist Party of Peru. 1989. "Interview of Chairman Gonzalo." Mimeo.

Centro Bartolomé de las Casas. 1987. *Rimanakuy 86: Hablan los campesinos del Perú.* Cuzco: Centro Bartolomé de las Casas.

———. 1991. *Poder y violencia en los Andes.* Cuzco: Centro de Estudios Rurales Andinos 'Bartolomé de las Casas' and Consejo Latinoamericano de Ciencias Sociales (CLACSO).

Centro Manuela Ramos. 1996. "VI Conferencia mundial sobre la mujer. Acción sobre la igualdad, el desarrollo y la paz." Lima: Centro Manuela Ramos. Separata.

Chalmers, Douglas et al., eds. 1997. *The New Politics of Inequality in Latin America: Rethinking Participation and Representation.* London: Oxford University Press.

Chávez de Paz, Dennis. 1989. *Juventud y terrorismo. Características sociales de los condenados por terrorismo y otros delitos.* Lima: Instituto de Estudios Peruanos.

Chipoco, Carlos. 1988. "Delitos de función y delitos contra los Derechos Humanos cometidos por miembros de las Fuerzas Armadas y Policiales." In CODEPP, *Violencia y Democracia,* 11–48. Lima: CODEPP.

———. 1992. *En defensa de la vida.* Lima: CEP (Centro de Estudios y Publicaciones).

CNDDHH (Coordinadora Nacional de Derechos Humanos). 1990. *Tribunal permanente de los pueblos. Contra la impunidad en América Latina. Sesión peruana. Lima, 5–6–7 de julio–1990.* Lima: Instituto de Defensa Legal.

———. 1996. *Informe sobre la situación de Derechos Humanos en el Perú en 1995.* Lima: CNDDHH.

CODEPP (Comisión de Derechos de la Persona y Construcción de la Paz). 1988. *Violencia y democracia.* Lima: CODEPP.

Cohen, Jean. 1985. "Strategy or Identity: New Theoretical Paradigms and Contemporary Social Movements." *Social Research* 52 (4): 663–716.

Collier, David. 1976. *Squatters and Oligarchs: Authoritarian Rule and Policy Change in Peru*. Baltimore: Johns Hopkins University Press.

Collier, George, and Elizabeth Lowery Quaratiello. 1994. *Basta! Land and the Zapatista Rebellion in Chiapas*. Oakland: Food First.

Comisión Andina de Juristas. 1991. *Análisis de los decretos legislativos por el Gobierno Peruano en materia de pacificación nacional*. Lima: Codice.

Comunidad Campesina de Chapioco. 1987. Oficio No. 012-87. Comunidad Campesina de Chapioco, Distrito de Ocuviri, Provincia de Lampa, 2 March.

Consejo de Desarrollo Alternativo de Puno. 1992. "Situación y perspectivas del proceso político-social y de la guerra interna en Puno. Propuestas y alternativas de pacificación." Puno: Consejo de Desarrollo Alternativo, November.

Contreras, Carlos. 1987. *Mineros y campesinos en los andes. Mercado laboral y economía campesina en la sierra central, siglo XIX*. Lima: Instituto de Estudios Peruanos.

Coral, Isabel. 1990. "La mujer en el contexto de violencia política." Ms.

———. 1993. *Desplazamiento por violencia política en el Perú*. Lima: Instituto de Estudios Peruanos, CEPES; and Miami: North-South Center, University of Miami.

———. 1994. "Desplazamiento por violencia política en el Perú, 1980–1992." Working Paper No. 58. Lima: Instituto de Estudios Peruanos.

———. 1995. "Violencia política en Lima. Estrategia senderista y respuestas." Ms.

Coronel, José. 1996. "Violencia política y respuestas campesinas en Huanta." In Carlos Iván Degregori, ed., *Las rondas campesinas y la derrota de Sendero Luminoso*, 29–116. Lima: Instituto de Estudios Peruanos/Universidad Nacional de San Cristóbal de Huamanga.

———. n.d. "Comités de Defensa: Un proceso social abierto." *Ideéle*, No. 59–60: 113–15.

Coronel, José, and Carlos Loayza. 1992. "Violencia política: formas de respuesta comunera en Ayacucho." In Carlos Iván Degregori et al., eds., *Perú: El problema agrario en debate/SEPIA IV*, 509–37. Lima: SEPIA.

Corpuno, Comision Multisectorial de Sequía. 1984. "Situación y planteamientos por la catástrofe en Puno. *Problemática Sur Andina*, No. 7: 147–68.

Corradi, Juan E., et al. 1992. *Fear at the Edge: State Terror and Resistance in Latin America*. Berkeley: University of California Press.

Cotler, Julio. 1968. "La mecánica de la dominación interna y del cambio social en la sociedad rural." *Perú Problema* (Lima) 1: 153–97.

———. 1978. *Clases, estado y nación en el Perú*. Lima: Instituto de Estudios Peruanos.

———. 1986. "Military Interventions and 'Transfer of Power to Civilians' in Peru." In O'Donnell et al., eds., 148–72.

———. 1987. *Para afirmar la democracia*. Lima: Instituto de Estudios Peruanos.

———. 1989. *Clases populares, crisis y democracia en América Latina*. Lima: Instituto de Estudios Peruanos.

———. 1991. "Peru since 1960." In Leslie Bethell, ed., *The Cambridge History of Latin America*, vol. 8, 451–508. Cambridge: Cambridge University Press.

———. 1993. "Descomposición política y autoritarismo en el Perú." Working Paper No. 51. Lima: Instituto de Estudios Peruanos.

———. 1995. *Perú 1964–1994. Economía, sociedad y política*. Lima: Instituto de Estudios Peruanos.

Crabtree, John. 1992. *Peru Under Garcia: An Opportunity Lost*. Oxford: St. Anthony's College and McMillan.

Crenshaw, Martha, ed. 1995. *Terrorism in Context*. University Park: Pennsylvania State University Press.

CUAVES/CIDIAG. 1984. *Un pueblo, una realidad: Villa El Salvador. Resultados del II Censo organizado por la CUAVES el 8 de abril de 1984*. Lima: CUAVES/CIDIAG.

Cueto, Marcos. 1989. *Excelencia científica en la periferia: Actividades, ciencias, e investigación biomédica en el Perú, 1890–1950*. Lima: GRADE.

Degregori, Carlos Iván. 1983. "Jóvenes y campesinos ante la violencia política, 1980–1983." Separata.

———. 1985a. "Entre dos fuegos." *QueHacer* 37: 53–54.

———. 1985b. "Sendero Luminoso: I. Los hondos y mortales desencuentros" and "Sendero Luminoso: II. Luchas armada y utopía autoritaria." Working papers No. 4 and 6. Lima: Instituto de Estudios Peruanos.

———. 1986. "Del mito de Inkarrí al 'mito' del progreso. Poblaciones andinas, cultura e identidad nacional." *Socialismo y Participación* 36: 49–56.

———. 1989a. "Comentario a la Década de la violencia." *Márgenes* 3, No. 5–6: 186–90.

———. 1989b. *Qué difícil es ser Dios. Ideología y violencia política en Sendero Luminoso*. Lima: El Zorro de Abajo.

———. 1990a. *Ayacucho 1969–1979: El surgimiento de Sendero Luminoso*. Lima: Instituto de Estudios Peruanos.

———. 1990b. "La revolución de los manuales. La expansión del marxismo-leninismo en las ciencias sociales y la génesis de Sendero Luminoso." *Revista Peruana de Ciencias Sociales* 2 (Lima) (no. 3; September–December): 103–124.

———. 1991a. "El aprendiz de brujo y el curandero chino: Etnicidad, modernidad y ciudadanía." In Carlos Iván Degregori and Romeo Grompones, *Elecciones 1990: Demonios y Redentores en el Nuevo Peru. Una tragedia en dos vueltas*, 71–136. Lima: Instituto de Estudios Peruanos.

———. 1991b. "La estrategia urbana de sendero: Al filo de la navaja." *QueHacer*, No. 73: 26–29.

———. 1991c. "Jóvenes andinos y criollos frente a la violencia política." In Henrique Urbano, ed., *Poder y violencia de los Andes*, 395–417. Cuzco: Centro Bartolomé de las Casas.

———. 1992a. "Campesinado andino y violencia: balance de una década de estudios." In Carlos Iván Degregori et al. eds., *Perú: El problema agrario en debate/SEPIA IV*, 413–39. Lima, SEPIA.

———. 1992b. "The Origin and Logic of Shining Path: Two Views." In David Scott Palmer, ed., *The Shining Path of Peru*, 33–44. New York: St. Martin's Press.

———. 1993a. "Después de la caída. El pensamiento de Abimael Guzmán y la violencia de Sendero Luminoso." Ms., Instituto de Estudios Peruanos, Lima.

———. 1993b. "Una tierra de nadie." In Roland Forgues, *Perú: Entre el desafío y el sueño de lo posible*, 69–85. Lima: Minerva.

———. 1994. "Identidad étnica, movimientos sociales y participación política en el Perú." In *Etnicidad, género y política en América Latina*, vol. 2. Lima: Instituto de Estudios Peruanos.

———. 1995a. "Croquis del desarrollo de la izquierda peruana," diagram and personal communication to Florencia Mallon, Madison, Wisconsin.

———. 1995b. "Silencios y puntos ciegos. Buscando una explicación al sorprendente colapso de Sendero Luminoso." Paper presented at the Seminar "Shining and Other Paths: Anatomy of a Peruvian Tragedy, Prospects for a Peruvian Future," University of Wisconsin, Madison.

———. 1996. *La última tentación del Presidente Gonzalo y otros escritos sobre el auge y el colapso de Sendero Luminoso*. Lima: Instituto de Estudios Peruanos.

Degregori, Carlos Iván, Cecilia Blondet, and Nicolás Lynch. 1986. *Conquistadores de un nuevo mundo: De invasores a ciudadanos en San Martín de Porres*. Lima: Instituto de Estudios Peruanos.

Degregori, Carlos Iván, and Romeo Grompone. 1991. *Elecciones 1990: Demonios y Redentores en el Nuevo Perú. Una tragedia en dos vueltas*. Lima: Instituto de Estudios Peruanos.

Degregori, Carlos Iván, and José López Ricci. 1990. "Los hijos de la guerra. Jóvenes andinos y criollos frente a la violencia política." In Carlos Iván Degregori et al., *Tiempos de ira y amor*. Lima: DESCO, Centro de Estudios y Promoción del Desarrollo.

Degregori, Carlos Iván, and Carlos Rivera. 1993. *Perú 1980–1990: Fuerzas Armadas, subversión y democracia. Redefinición del papel militar en un contexto de violencia subversiva y colapso del régimen democrático*. Lima: IEP.

Degregori, Carlos Iván, et al. 1990. *Tiempos de ira y amor*. Lima: DESCO, Centro de Estudios y Promoción del Desarrollo.

Degregori, Carlos Iván, et al., eds. 1992. *Perú: El problema agrario en debate/SEPIA IV*. Lima: SEPIA.

Degregori, Carlos Iván, ed. 1996. *Las rondas campesinas y la derrota de Sendero Luminoso*. Lima: Instituto de Estudios Peruanos/Universidad Nacional de San Cristóbal de Huamanga.

de la Cadena, Marisol. 1991. "Las mujeres son más indias: Etnicidad y género en una comunidad del Cusco." *Revista Andina* 9 (1): 7–29.

———. 1995. "Race, Ethnicity, and the Struggle for Indigenous Self-Representation:

De-Indianization in Cuzco-Peru (1919–1991)." Ph.D. dissertation, University of Wisconsin-Madison.

———. 1996. "The Politics of Representations and Misrepresentations: Mestizas vs. Elite Intellectuals in Cuzco." *Journal of Latin American Anthropology* 2 (1): 112–41.

de la Jara, Francisco. 1994. "Militares opinan sobre derechos humanos." *Ideéle* 61 (March).

Delpino, Nena. 1991. "Las organizaciones femininas por la alimentación: un menú sazonado." In Luis Pásara et al., *La otra cara de la luna: Nuevos actores sociales en el pais*, 154–173. Lima: CEDYS.

Delpino, Nena, and Luis Pásara. 1991. "El otro actor en escena: las ONGDs." In Luis Pásara et al., *La otra cara de la luna: Nuevos actores sociales en el Perú*, 154–73. Lima: CEDYS.

del Pino H., Ponciano. 1992. "Los campesinos en la guerra o como la gente comienza ponerse macho." In Carlos Iván Degregori et al. eds., *Perú: El problema agrario en debate/SEPIA IV*, 487–508. Lima: SEPIA.

———. 1994a. "Comités de Autodefensa Civil. Una nueva estructura de poder en el campo." Paper presented at the seminar "Las secuelas de la guerra: cicatarice-mos nuestras heridas," organized by INIDEN, Lima, 14–15 November 1994.

———. 1994b. "Tiempos de guerra y de dioses. Sendero, ronderos y evangélicos." Ms, Instituto de Estudios Peruanos, Lima.

———. 1996. "Tiempos de guerra y de dioses: Ronderos, evangélicos y senderis-tas en el valle del río Apurímac." In Carlos Iván Degregori et al., *Las rondas campesinas y la derrota de Sendero Luminoso*, 117–88. Lima: Instituto de Estudios Peruanos/Universidad Nacional de San Cristóbal de Huamanga.

DESCO. 1989. *Violencia política en el Perú: 1980–1988*, vol. 1. Lima: DESCO.

de Soto, Hernando. 1986. *El otro sendero: La revolución informal*. Lima: Editorial El Barranco.

———. 1989. *The Other Path: The Invisible Revolution in the Third World*. New York: Harper and Row.

Deustua, José. 1986. *La minería peruana y la iniciación de la República 1820–1840*. Lima: Instituto de Estudios Peruanos.

Deustua, José, and José Luis Rénique. 1984. *Intelectuales, indigenismo y decentralismo en el Perú*. Cuzco: Bartolomé de las Casas.

Deutscher, Isaac. 1960. *Stalin. A Political Biography*. New York: Vintage Books.

El Diario. 1991. "Mejores condiciones para Gran Salto en Equilibrio Estratégico. 1991 inició la Década del Triunfo." *El Diario*, December 2–4.

Díaz Martínez, Antonio. 1969. *Ayacucho: Hambre y esperanza*. Ayacucho: Waman Puma.

———. 1985. *Ayacucho: Hambre y esperanza*, 2d ed. revised. Lima: Mosca Azul.

Dirección Nacional de Lucha Contra el Terrorismo. n.d. Cuaderno de notas, Archivo de la Dirección Nacional de Lucha Contra el Terrorismo, Puno.

Driant, Jean-Claude. 1991. *Las barriadas de Lima: Historia e interpretación.* Lima: IFEA/DESCO.

Ebert, Teresa. 1992. "Luddic Feminism, the Body, Performance, and Labor: Bringing Materialism Back into Feminist Cultural Studies," *Cultural Critique* Winter: 5–50.

Eckstein, Susan, ed. 1989. *Power and Popular Protest: Latin American Social Movements.* Berkeley: University of California Press.

Encinas, José Antonio. 1920. *Contribución a una Ley Tutelar Indígena.* Lima: Editorial Villarán.

———. 1954. "Prólogo." In José G. Guevara, *La Rebelión de los Provincianos.* Lima: Ediciones Folklore.

Escalante, José Angel. 1928. "Cuzqueñismo." *Mundial,* special edition (December).

Escobar, Arturo, and Sonia Alvarez, eds. 1992. *The Making of Social Movements in Latin America: Identity, Strategy, Democracy.* Boulder: Westview.

Escuela Superior de Guerra. 1980a. *Guerra revolucionaria: doctrina.* Chorrillos: Escuela Superior de Guerra.

———. 1980b. *Guerra revolucionaria: subversión.* Chorrillos: Escuela Superior de Guerra.

Espinosa, Oscar. 1995. *Rondas campesinas y nativas en la amazonía peruana.* Lima: CAAAP.

Espinoza, Gustavo. 1993. "Un PC hace lo que puede." *Gaceta Sanmarquina* (Lima) 4 (19): 9.

Espinoza Soriano, Waldemar. 1973. *Enciclopedia departamental de Junín.* Huancayo: Enrique Chipoco Tovar.

Falla, Ricardo. 1992. *Massacres in the Jungle: Ixcan, Guatemala, 1975–1982.* Boulder: Westview Press.

Favre, Henri. 1966. *La evolución de las haciendas en la región de Huancavelica, Perú.* Lima: Instituto de Estudios Peruanos.

———. 1967. *La hacienda en el Perú.* Lima: Instituto de Estudios Peruanos.

———. 1984. "Perú: Sendero Luminoso, horizontes oscuros," *QueHacer* (Lima) 31: 25–34.

FDCP. 1987. "Viva el paro nacional agrario. Viva la liquidación de la SAIS Buenavista." *La República,* 13 November.

FEDEFAM. 1989. "Conclusiones del IX Congreso." Lima.

Feierman, Steven. 1990. *Peasant Intellectuals: Anthropology and History in Tanzania.* Madison: University of Wisconsin Press.

Fernández, Alberto, and Alberto González, eds. 1990. *La reforma agraria, 20 años después.* Chiclayo: CONCYTEC.

Fernández Baca, Jorge, and Jeanice Seinfield. 1993. "Gasto social y políticas sociales en América Latina." *Desarrollo Social* 5.

Fioravanti, Eduardo. 1974. *Latifundio y sindicalismo agrario en el Perú: El caso de los Valles de la Convención y Lares.* Lima: Instituto de Estudios Peruanos.

Fitzgerald, E.V.K. 1979. *The Political Economy of Peru, 1856–1978: Economic Development and the Restructuring of Capital.* Cambridge: University Press.

Flores Galindo, Alberto. 1972. *Los mineros de la Cerro de Pasco 1900–1930.* Lima: Pontífica Universidad Católica del Perú.

———. 1979. "Los intelectuales y el problema nacional." In Emilio Romero et al., *Siete Ensayos: 50 Años de la historia.* Lima: Biblioteca Amauta.

———. 1980. *La agonía de Mariátegui: La polémica con el Komintern.* Lima: DESCO, Centro de Estudios y Promoción de Desarrollo.

———. 1987. *Buscando un inca: Identidad y utopía en los andes.* Lima: Instituto de Apoyo Agrario.

———. 1988a. *Buscando un inca: Identidad y utopía en los Andes,* 3d ed. Lima: Horizonte. Originally published in 1987.

———. 1988b. "La nueva izquierda: sin faros ni mapas." In Alberto Flores Galindo, ed., *Independencia y revolución, 1780–1840,* 136–144. Lima: Instituto Nacional de Cultura.

———. 1988c. *Tiempo de plagas.* Lima: Caballo Rojo.

———. 1989. *La agonía de Mariátegui.* 3d ed. Lima: Instituto de Apoyo Agrario.

———. 1991. *La agonía de Mariátegui.* Madrid: Editorial Revolución.

———. 1993. *Obras Completas.* Lima: Sur.

Flores Galindo, Alberto, ed. 1987. *Independencia y revolución 1780–1840,* 2 vols. Lima: Instituto Nacional de Cultura.

Flores Galindo, Alberto, and José Deustua. 1993. "Los comunistas y el movimiento obrero," in Flores Galindo 1993.

Flores Galindo, Alberto, and Nelson Manrique. 1986. *Violencia y campesinado.* Lima: Instituto de Apoyo Agrario.

FONCODES (Fondo de Compensación y Desarrollo Social). 1994. *El Mapa de la Inversión Social: Pobreza y Actuación de FONCODES a nivel departamental y provincial.* Lima: Instituto Cuanto and UNICEF.

Fontana, Josep. 1992. *La historia después del fin de la historia. Reflexiones acerca de la situación actual de la ciencia histórica.* Barcelona: Crítica.

Forgues, Roland. 1993. *Perú. Entre el desafío y el sueño de lo posible.* Lima: Minerva.

Foucault, Michel. 1971. *The Order of Things: An Archaeology of the Human Sciences.* New York: Pantheon.

Fox, Jonathon, and Luis Hernández. 1989. "Offsetting the Iron Law of Oligarchy." *Grassroots Development* 13 (2): 8–15.

Franco, Carlos. 1991. *Imágenes de la sociedad peruana: La otra modernidad.* Lima: CEDEP.

Fujimori, Alberto. 1995. "Discurso del señor Presidente de la República del Perú ante la Conferencia de la mujer de Beijing, China." Ms in possession of authors.

Galeano, Eduardo. 1992. *We Say No: Chronicles 1963–1991.* New York: Norton.

Gall, Norman. 1971. "Peru: the Master is Dead." *Dissent* 17 (3): 281–320.

Gallegos, Guido. 1991. "Sendero nos ve como sus enemigos políticos." *Ideéle*, no. 32–33 (December).

Gálvez, José. 1921. "La Obra de Sabogal." In *Mundial*, No. 62 (1 July).

Gálvez, Modesto. 1987. "El derecho en el campesinado andino del Perú." In García Sayán, ed. 1987: 233–49.

García Canclini, Nestor. 1990. *Culturas híbridas: Estrategias para entrar y salir de la modernidad.* Mexico City: Horizonte.

García Sayán, Diego. 1982. *Tomas de tierras en el Perú.* Lima: Desco.

———. 1987a. *Derechos humanos y servicios legales en el campo.* Lima: Comisión Andina de Juristas and Comisión Internacional de Juristas.

———. 1987b. "Para asegurar la violencia de los Derechos Humanos." In Julio Cotler, *Para afirmar la democracia,* 127–89. Lima: Instituto de Estudios Peruanos.

Garmendia, Roberto F. 1928. "Lima y Cuzco." *Mundial,* special edition (December).

Gitlitz, John, and Telmo Rojas. 1983. "Peasant Vigilante Committees in Northern Peru," *Journal of Latin American Studies* 15 (1): 163–97.

———. 1985. "Las rondas campesinas en Cajamarca-Perú." *Apuntes* 16: 115–41.

Golte, Jürgen. 1994. "Las contradicciones culturales y la política en el Perú. *Ideéle,* No. 63–64 (May): 40–41.

Golte, Jürgen, and Norma Adams. 1987. *Los caballos de troya de los invasores: Estrategias campesinas en la conquista de la gran Lima.* Lima: Instituto de Estudios Peruanos.

Gonzales de Olarte, Efraín. 1992. *La economía regional de Lima.* Lima: Consorcio de Investigación Económica and Instituto de Estudios Peruanos.

Gonzales, José E. 1992. "Guerrillas and Coca in the Upper Huallaga Valley." In David Scott Palmer, ed., *The Shining Path of Peru,* 105–126. New York: St. Martin's Press.

Gonzales, Raúl. 1982. "Por los caminos de Sendero." *QueHacer* 19: 39–47.

———. 1985. "Sendero: cinco años después de Belaúnde." *QueHacer* 36: 37–40.

———. 1988. "Sendero: los problemas del campo, la ciudad . . . y además el MRTA." *QueHacer* (Lima) 50: 46–63.

———. 1990. "Informe sobre Puno." Ms in possession of authors.

Gonzales Vigil. 1983. *Gonzales Vigil: Libro Jubilar 1933–1983.* Huanta: no publisher.

Gonzales de Olarte, Efraín, and Lilian Samamé. 1991. *El péndulo peruano: Políticas económicas, gobernabilidad y subdesarrollo, 1963–1990.* Lima: Consorcio de Investigación Económica y el Instituto de Estudios Peruanos.

Gorriti Ellenbogen, Gustavo. 1990. *Sendero: Historia de la guerra milenaria en el Perú,* vol. 1. Lima: Editorial Apoyo.

———. 1992. "Shining Path's Stalin and Trotsky." In David Scott Palmer, ed., *The Shining Path in Peru,* 140–70. New York: St. Martin's Press.

Graham, Carol. 1992. *Peru's Apra, Party Politics and the Elusive Quest for Democracy.* Boulder: Lynne Rienner.

Graham, Richard, ed. 1990. *The Idea of Race in Latin America*. Austin: University of Texas Press.

Granados Aponte, Manuel Jesus. 1981. "La conducta política: un caso particular." Thesis, Universidad Nacional de San Cristóbal de Huamanga, Ayacucho.

————. 1987. "El PCP Sendero Luminoso: aproximaciones a su ideología." *Socialismo y participación* (Lima) 37: 15–36.

Granda, Juan. 1989. "Los tiempos del temor: cronología ayacuchana." *QueHacer* (Lima) 60: 84–89.

Grompone, Romeo. 1990. "Perú: La vertiginosa irrupción de Fujimori. Buscando las razones de un sorprendente resultado electoral." *Revista mexicana de sociología* (Mexico) No. 4.

————. 1991. "Fujimori: razones y desconciertos." In Carlos Iván Degregori and Romeo Grompone, *Elecciones 1990: Demonios y Redentores en el Nuevo Perú. Una tragedia en dos vueltas*. Lima: Instituto de Estudios Peruanos.

Guevara, José G. 1929. "La rebelión de los provincianos." *El Sol* (Cuzco), 30 February.

————. 1954. *La rebelión de los provincianos*. Lima: Ediciones Folklore.

Guillermoprieto, Alma. 1994. *The Heart That Bleeds: Latin America Now*. New York: Vintage.

Guzmán, Abimael. 1988. "Entrevista del siglo. Presidente Gonzalo rompe el silencio." *El Diario*, 24 July.

————. 1989. *Por la Nueva Bandera*. In Luis Arce Borja, ed. *Guerra popular en el Perú: El pensamiento Gonzalo*, 139–60. Brussels: No publisher. Original document is dated 1979.

————. 1991. " 'Sobre las dos colinas'. Documento de estudio para el balance de la tercera campaña. La guerra contrasubversiva y sus aliados." Document in possession of author (Basombrío).

Hale, Charles A. 1984. "Political and Social Ideas in Latin America, 1870–1930." In Leslie Bethell, ed., *The Cambridge History of Latin America*, vol. 4, 367–442. Cambridge: Cambridge University Press, 1984.

Hall, Stuart. 1992. "What is this 'Black' in Black Popular Culture?" In Gina Dent, ed., *Black Popular Culture*, 21–33. Seattle: Bay Press.

Handelman, Howard. 1974. *Struggle in the Andes: Peasant Political Mobilization in Peru*. Austin: Institute of Latin American Studies, University of Texas Press.

Harding, Colin. 1988. "Antonio Díaz Martínez and the Ideology of Sendero Luminoso." *Bulletin of Latin American Research* 7 (1): 65–73.

Harnecker, Martha. 1990. *América Latina: Izquierda y crisis actual*. Mexico City: Siglo XXI Editores.

Harvey, David. 1989. *The Condition of Postmodernity*. London: Basil Blackwell.

Haworth, Nigel. 1993. "Radicalization and the Left in Peru, 1976–1991." In Barry Carr and Steve Ellner, eds., *The Latin American Left: From the Fall of Allende to Perestroika*, 41–60. New York: Westview Press.

Haya de la Torre, Víctor Raúl. 1928. "Carta de Haya de la Torre a la Sierra." *La Sierra* 2 (June) No. 18.

———. 1984. *Obras completas*, vol 1. Lima: Editorial J. Mejía Baca.

Hazen, Dan C. 1974. "The Awakening of Puno: Government Policy and the Indian Problem in Southern Peru, 1900–1974," Ph.D. dissertation, Yale University, New Haven.

Hemming, John. 1970. *The Conquest of the Incas*. New York: Harcourt, Brace, Jovanovich.

Hildebrandt, César. 1981. *Cambio de palabra: 26 entrevistas*. Lima: Mosca Azul.

Hinojosa, Iván. 1992. "Entre el poder y la ilusión: Pol Pot, Sendero y las utopías campesinas." *Debate Agrario* (Lima) 15: 69–93.

Hobsbawm, Eric. 1993. *Nations and Nationalism since 1780. Programme, Myth, Reality*. Cambridge: Canto.

Huber, Ludwig. 1995. *Después de Dios y la Virgen está la ronda. Las rondas campesinas de Piura*. Lima: Instituto de Estudios Peruanos/IFEA.

Husson, Patrick. 1992. *De la guerra a la rebelión: Huanta, Siglo XIX*. Lima: Centro de Estudios Regionales "Bartolomé de las Casas."

———. 1993. "Democracia vs. totalitarianismo: El impacto político de la 'masificación' de la sociedad peruana contemporánea." In *Democracia, etnicidad y violencia política en los países andinos*, 245–65. Lima: IFEA-Instituto de Estudios Peruanos.

Huxley, Aldous. 1983. *Un mundo feliz*. Mexico City: Mexicanos Unidos, 1983.

Ideología. 1987. "Testimonios rurales." *Ideología* 10: 31–92.

IDL (Instituto de Defensa Legal). 1990. *Perú 1989. En la espiral de violencia*. Lima: IDL.

———. 1991. *Perú 1990. La oportunidad perdida*. Lima: IDL.

———. 1992. *Perú Hoy. En el oscuro sendero de la guerra*. Lima: IDL.

———. n.d. *El papel de la organización social campesina en la estrategia campesina*. Lima: IDL.

IDS (Instituto de Democracia y Socialismo). 1989. *Perú: La violencia política vista desde el pueblo*. Serie: Estrategia Integral de Paz; Lima: Instituto de Democracia y Socialismo.

IEP (Instituto de Estudios Peruanos). 1985. *¿He vivido en vano? Mesa redonda sobre 'Todas las Sangres.'* Lima: Instituto de Estudios Peruanos.

———. 1986. *Estados y naciones en los Andes. Hacia una historia comparativa: Bolivia-Colombia-Ecuador-Perú*, 2 vols. Lima: Instituto de Estudios Peruanos and Instituto Francés de Estudios Andinos.

IER "José María Arguedas." 1985. *Comunidades campesinas de Ayacucho: Economía, ideología y organización social*. Ayacucho: IER "José María Arguedas" and CCTA.

INE. 1983. *Censos Nacionales VIII de Población. III de Vivienda. 12 de julio de 1981, Departamento de Ayacucho*, vol. 1. Lima: INE.

INEI. 1994. *Censos Nacionales 1993. IX de Población, IV de Vivienda, Departamento de Ayacucho*, vols. 1–4. Lima: INEI.

Instituto Indigenista Peruano. 1948. "Editorial." *Perú Indígena: Organo del Instituto Indigenista Peruano* 1, No. 1.

Isbell, Billie Jean. 1977. "'Those Who Love Me:' An Analysis of Andean Kinship and Reciprocity Within a Ritual Context." In Ralph Bolton and Enrique Mayer, *Andean Kinship and Marriage*, 81–105. Washington, D.C. American Anthropological Association.

———. 1988. *The Emerging Patterns of Peasants' Responses to Sendero Luminoso*. Latin American, Caribbean, and Iberian Occasional Papers No. 7. New York: Columbia University and New York University.

———. 1992. "Shining Path and Peasant Responses in Rural Ayacucho." In David Scott Palmer, ed., *The Shining Path of Peru*, 59–81. New York: St. Martin's Press.

IU (Izquierda Unida). 1985. *Estrategia y táctica. Normas orgánicas*. Lima: Ediciones PCP.

Jacobsen, Nils. 1993. *Mirages of Transition: The Peruvian Altiplano, 1780–1930*. Berkeley: University of California Press.

Jochamowitz, Luis. 1993. *Ciudadano Fujimori: La construcción de un político*. Lima: Peisa.

Judd, Stephen. 1987. "The Emergent Andean Church: Inculturation and Liberation in Southern Peru, 1968–1986." Ph.D. dissertation, Graduate Theological Union, Berkeley.

Kapsoli, Wilfredo. 1977. *Los movimientos campesinos en el Perú 1879–1965*. Lima: Delva.

———. 1984. *Ayllus del Sol: Anarquismo v utopía andina*. Lima: Tarea.

Khosrokhavar, Farhad. 1993. *L'Utopie Sacrifiée. Sociologie de la révolution iranienne*. Paris: Presses de la Fondation Nationale des Sciences Politiques.

Kirk, Robin. 1991. *The Decade of Chaqwa: Peru's Internal Refugees*. Washington, D.C.: U.S. Committee for Refugees.

———. 1993a. *To Build Anew: An Update on Peru's Internally Displaced People*. Washington, D.C.: U.S. Committee for Refugees.

———. 1993b. *Grabado en piedra. Las mujeres de Sendero Luminoso*. Lima: Instituto de Estudios Peruanos.

Klaiber, Jeffrey. 1988. *La Iglesia en el Perú*. Lima: Fondo Editorial de la Universidad Católica del Perú.

Klarén, Peter F. 1973. *Modernization, Dislocation, and Aprismo: Origins of the Peruvian Aprista Party, 1870–1932*. Austin: University of Texas.

———. 1976. *Las haciendas azucareras y el Apra*, 2d. ed. revised. Lima: Instituto de Estudios Peruanos.

———. 1986. "The Origins of Modern Peru, 1880–1930." In Leslie Bethell, ed., *The Cambridge History of Latin America*, vol. 5, 587–640. Cambridge: Cambridge University Press.

Knight, Alan. 1990. "Racism, Revolution, and Indigenismo: Mexico, 1910–1940." In

Richard Graham, ed., *The Idea of Race in Latin America*, 71–113. Austin: University of Texas Press.

Kruijt, Dirk. 1989. *La revolución por decreto: Perú durante el gobierno militar*. Lima: Mosca Azul.

———. 1991. *Entre sendero y los militares*. Lima: Editorial Robles.

Larson, Brooke, Olivia Harris, and Enrique Tandeter, eds. 1995. *Ethnicity, Markets, and Migration in the Andes: At the Crossroads of History and Anthropology*. Durham: Duke University Press.

Lavalle, Bernard. 1988. *El Mercader y el Marqués: las luchas del poder en el Cuzco (1700–1730)*. Lima: Banco Central de Reserva.

Leguía, Augusto B. 1929. "Respuesta a José Angel Escalante." *Mundial*, No. 472.

Lenin, Vladimir I. 1975. *La enfermedad infantil del "izquierdismo" en el comunismo*. Beijing: Ediciones en Lenguas Extranjeras. Originally published in 1920.

Letts, Ricardo. 1981. *La izquierda peruana: Organizaciones y tendencias*. Lima: Mosca Azul.

Llanque, Domingo. 1985. "Pastoral misional en Juli (1957–1967)." *Boletín de Estudios Aymaras*, No. 21 (December): 23–48.

Loayza Camargo, Jorge E. 1988. "El repliegue de la economía comunera en Ayacucho (Pacaycasa, Quinua y Acos Vinchos)." In SEPIA, *Perú: El problema agrario en debate—SEPIA II*, 495–514. Lima: Universidad Nacional de San Cristóbal de Humanga and SEPIA.

Lombardi, Guido. 1994. "Puntos positivos y negativos." *Ideéle* 70 (November).

López, Sinesio. 1989. "¿Militarizar la política o politizar la guerra?" *Temas de debate*. Lima: Instituto Democracia y Socialismo.

———. 1991. *El dios mortal. Estado, sociedad y política en el Perú del siglo XX*. Lima: Instituto Democracia y Socialismo.

López Ricci, José. 1993. "Las organizaciones populares en San Martín de Porres." Informe de Investigación. Ms., Centro Alternativa, Lima.

Lowenthal, Abraham. 1976. *The Peruvian Experiment: Continuity and Change under Military Rule*. Princeton: Princeton University Press.

Lynch, Nicolás. 1990. *Los jóvenes rojos de San Marcos: El radicalismo universitario de los años sesenta*. Lima: El Zorro de Abajo.

———. 1992. *La transición conservadora: Movimiento social y democracia en el Perú, 1975–1978*. Lima: El Zorro de Abajo Ediciones.

McClintock, Cynthia. 1984. "Why Peasants Rebel: The Case of Peru's Sendero Luminoso." *World Politics* 27 (1): 48–84.

———. 1989. "Peru's Sendero Luminoso Rebellion: Origins and Trajectory." In Susan Eckstein, *Power and Popular Protest: Latin American Social Movements*, 61–101. Berkeley: University of California Press.

McCormick, Gordon. 1990. *The Shining Path and the Future of Peru*. Santa Monica: The Rand Corporation.

————. 1992. *From the Sierra to the Cities: The Urban Campaign of the Shining Path.* Santa Monica: The Rand Corporation.

MacGregor, Felipe, and José Luis Rouillon. 1985. *Siete ensayos sobre la violencia política en el Perú.* Lima: Fundación Friedrich Ebert and Asociación Peruana de Estudios e Investigaciones para la Paz-APEP.

Mallon, Florencia E. 1983. *The Defense of Community in Peru's Central Highlands: Peasant Struggle and Capitalist Transition, 1860–1940.* New Jersey: Princeton University Press.

————. 1990. "Coaliciones nacionalistas y antiestatales en la Guerra del Pacífico: Junín y Cajamarca, 1879–1902." In Steve J. Stern, ed., *Resistencia, rebelión y conciencia campesina en los Andes, siglo XVIII al XX.* Lima: Instituto de Estudios Peruanos. (Original English version in Steve J. Stern, ed., 1987, *Resistance, Rebellion, and Consciousness in the Andean Peasant World.* Madison: University of Wisconsin Press.)

————. 1995. *Peasant and Nation: The Making of Postcolonial Mexico and Peru.* Berkeley: University of California Press, 1995.

Manrique, Nelson. 1981. *Campesinado y nación. Las guerrillas indígenas en la guerra con Chile.* Lima: Centro de Investigación y Capacitación.

————. 1986a. "Campesinado, guerra y conciencia nacional." *Revista Andina* 4 (1) (July).

————. 1986b. "Desarrollo del mercado interior y cambios en la demarcación territorial en los Andes centrales del Perú." In Instituto de Estudios Peruanos 1986.

————. 1987a. "Las comunidades campesinas en la sierra central en el siglo XIX." In Heraclio Bonilla, ed., *Comunidades campesinas: Cambios y permanencios.* Chiclayo: Centro de Estudios Sociales Solidaridad, and Lima: Consejo Nacional de Ciencia y Tecnología.

————. 1987b. *Mercado interno y región: La sierra central 1820–1930.* Lima: DESCO (Centro de Estudios y Promoción del Desarrollo).

————. 1988a. "Historia y utopía en los Andes." *Debates en Sociología* (Lima) Nos. 12 and 14.

————. 1988b. *Yawar mayu. Sociedades terratenientes serranas 1870–1910.* Lima: DESCO (Centro de Estudios y Promoción del Desarrollo) and Instituto Francés de Estudios Andinos.

————. 1989a. "La década de la violencia." *Márgenes* 3 (5–6) (Lima): 137–82.

————. 1989b. "Violencia e imaginario social en el Perú contemporáneo." In DESCO, *Violencia política en el Perú: 1980–1988,* vol. 1. Lima: DESCO.

————. 1991. "Gamonalismo, lanas y violencia en los andes." In Centro Bartolomé de las Casas, *Poder y violencia en los Andes,* 211–23. Cuzco: CLACSO.

————. 1995a. "La caída de la cuarta espada y los senderos que se bifurcan." *Márgenes* 13–14: 11–42.

————. 1995b. "Political Violence, Ethnicity, and Racism in Peru in the Time of War," *Journal of Latin American Studies* 4 (1).

————. 1996. "Mestizaje, etnicidad y violencia en el Perú de los ochenta." *Pretextos* (Lima), No. 8 (March).

Manrique, Nelson, ed. 1995. *Amor y fuego. José María Arguedas. 25 años después.* Lima: DESCO.

Manrique, Nelson, Alberto Chirif, and Benjamín Quijandria. 1989. *SEPIA III. Perú: El problema agrario en debate.* Lima: SEPIA.

Manrique Castro, Manuel. n.d. *La Peruvian Corporation en la selva central del Perú.* Lima: Centro de Investigación y Promoción Amazónica.

Mao Zedong. 1971a. "Informe sobre una investigación del movimiento campesino de Junan." In Mao, *Obras escogidas*, vol. 1, 19–59. Peking: Ediciones en Lenguas Extranjeras. Original date is 1927.

————. 1971b. *Obras Escogidas*, 11 vols. Peking (Beijing): Ediciones en Lenguas Extranjeras.

————. 1971c. "Sobre la Guerra Prolongada." In Mao, *Obras escogidas*, vol. 2, 113–200. Peking: Ediciones en Lenguas Extranjeras. Original date is 1939.

Mariátegui, José Carlos. 1928a. "El Cuzco y el indio." *Mundial*, special edition.

————. 1928b. "El indio mestizo." *Mundial*, No. 428.

————. 1929. "Civilización y feudalidad." *Mundial*, No. 467.

————. 1968. *Siete ensayos de interpretación de la realidad peruana.* Lima: Empresa Editora Amauta.

————. 1977. *Ideología y Política.* Lima: Amauta.

Márquez, Gabriel. 1989. "¿Cuál arte alienante?" *El Diario* 24 May: 16.

Martínez, Héctor. 1991. *Reforma agraria peruana: Las empresas asociativas altoandinas.* Lima: Centro de Estudios Para el Desarrollo y la Participación.

Martínez, Héctor, and Jorge P. Osterling. 1983. "Notes for a history of Peruvian Social Anthropology, 1940–1980." *Current Anthropology* 24 (3): 343–80.

Martínez de la Torre, Ricardo. 1928. *El movimiento obrero de 1919.* Lima: Amauta.

————. 1947–1949. *Apuntes para una historia marxista de historia social del Perú.* Lima: Empresa Editora Peruana.

Matos Mar, José. 1984. *Desborde popular y crisis del estado.* Lima: Instituto de Estudios Peruanos.

Mauceri, Philip. 1989. *Militares, insurgencia y democratización en el Perú: 1980–1988.* Lima: Instituto de Estudios Peruanos. (Also available as: *The Military, Insurgency and Democratic Power: Peru, 1980.* New York: Institute of Latin American and Iberian Studies, School of International and Public Affairs, Columbia University, 1989.)

Mayer, Enrique. 1991. "Peru in Deep Trouble: Mario Vargas Llosa's 'Inquest in the Andes' Reexamined." *Cultural Anthropology* 6 (4): 466–504.

Méndez S., José Fernando. 1981. *La derrota de Andahuaylas (1974).* Lima: Talleres Gráficos de Proyecciones Perú S.R.L.

Mendoza-Walker, Zoila. 1993. "Shaping Society Through Dance: Mestizo Ritual Performance in the Southern Peruvian Andes." Ph.D. dissertation, University of Chicago, Chicago.

Migdal, Joel. 1974. *Peasants, Politics, and Revolution. Pressures Toward Political and Social Change in the Third World.* Princeton: Princeton University Press.

Ministerio de Agricultura. 1970. "Chuyama-Chacchuahua y Río Blanco: Historia de una 'reivindicación'." Mimeo, ZAC-Andahuaylas No. 1, Dirección de Comunidades Campesinas, Lima.

———. 1971. "Datos básicos e inventarios del patrimonio cultural de las comunidades de la provincia de Andahuaylas." Mimeo, ZAC-Andahuaylas No. 2, Dirección de Comunidades Campesinas, Lima.

Ministerio de la Presidencia. 1993. "Lineamientos básicos de la política social." Mimeo, Lima.

Ministerio de Trabajo y Asuntos Indígenas. 1983. *Informe del Plan Nacional de la Población Aborigen.* Lima: Ministerio de Trabajo y Asuntos Indígenas.

Montoya, David, and Carlos Reyna. 1992. "Sendero: Informe de Lima," *QueHacer* 76: 34–55.

Montoya, Rodrigo. 1974. *Capitalismo y no-capitalismo en el Perú (Un estudio histórico de su articulación en un eje regional).* Lima: Mosca Azul Editores.

———. 1980. *Capitalismo y no capitalismo en el Perú. Un estudio histórico de su articulación en un eje regional.* Lima: Mosca Azul.

Montoya, Rodrigo, et al. 1974. *La SAIS Cahuide y sus contradicciones.* Lima: Universidad Nacional Mayor de San Marcos.

———. 1987. *La sangre de los cerros. Urqukunapa Yawarnin.* Lima: Cepes, Mosca Azul, and UNMSM.

Moore, Barrington. 1966. *The Social Bases of Democracy and Dictatorship. Lord and Peasant in the Making of the Modern World.* Boston: Beacon Press.

———. 1978. *Injustice. The Social Bases of Obedience and Revolt.* New York: M.E. Sharp.

More, Federico. 1929. "Lo que he visto en el Perú después de 12 años de accidentada ausencia." In *Mundial* 29 November.

Moreiras, Alberto. 1990. "Transculturación y pérdida de sentimiento." *Nuevo Texto Crítico* 6: 15–33.

Moreyra, Manuel. 1987. "Para afirmar las instituciones democráticas." In Julio Cotler, *Para afirmar la democracia,* 59–124. Lima: Instituto de Estudios Peruanos.

Mossbrucker, Harold. 1990. *El concepto de la comunidad: Un enfoque crítico.* Lima: Instituto de Estudios Peruanos.

Murra, John. 1975. *Formaciones económicas y políticas del mundo andino.* Lima: Instituto de Estudios Peruanos.

NACLA (North American Congress on Latin America). 1990–1991. "Fatal Attraction: Peru's Shining Path." Issue theme, *NACLA Report on the Americas* 24 (4) (Dec./Jan.).

————. 1996. "Privilege and Power in Fujimori's Peru." Issue theme, *NACLA Report on the Americas* 30, no. 1 (July/Aug.).

Nash, June. 1978. *We Eat the Mines and the Mines Eat Us.* New York: Columbia University Press.

Neira, Hugo. 1987. "Violencia y anomia: Reflexiones para intentar comprender." *Socialismo y Participación,* No. 37, 1–13.

Nieto, Jorge. 1983. *Izquierda y democracia en el Perú, 1975–1982.* Lima: DESCO.

Nietzsche, Friedrich. 1990. *Beyond Good and Evil.* Translated by Michael Tanner. London: Penguin.

No Basta Tener La Razón. 1975. *No basta tener la razón: Documento para la historia de la universidad peruana.* Ayacucho and Lima: Editorial Pedagógica Asencios.

Noel Moral, Roberto. 1989. *Ayacucho: Testimonio de un soldado.* Lima: Publinor.

Nordstrom, Carol, and Joann Martin, eds. 1992. *Paths to Domination, Resistance and Terror.* Berkeley: University of California Press.

Nun, José. 1989. *La rebelión del coro: Estudios sobre la racionalidad política y el sentido común.* Buenos Aires: Ediciones Nueva Visión.

Obando, Enrique. 1991. "Diez años de estrategia antisubversiva: una pequeña historia." *QueHacer* 72: 46–53.

————. 1993. "El narcotráfico en el Perú: una aproximación histórica." *Análisis Internacional,* No. 2 (Lima).

————. 1994. "The Power of Peru's Armed Forces." In Gary Bland and Joseph Tulchin, eds., *Peru in Crisis: Dictatorship or Democracy.* Boulder: Lynne Rienner.

————. 1995. "Perú: Fuerzas Armadas y Proyecto Nacional." *Revista de Defensa Nacional* (Tegucigalpa).

O'Donnell, Guillermo, Philippe C. Schmitter, and Laurence Whitehead, eds. 1986. *Transitions from Authoritarian Rule: Latin America.* Baltimore: Johns Hopkins University Press.

O'Donnell, Daniel. 1988. *Protección internacional de los derechos humanos.* Lima: Comisión Andina de Juristas.

Olalquiaga, Celeste. 1992. *Megalopolis: Contemporary Cultural Sensibilities.* Minneapolis: University of Minnesota Press.

Oliart, María Patricia. 1994. "Imágenes de género y raza." Ms in possession of author.

Olivera, Luis, and Eduardo Ballón. 1993. "Lima y su organización popular." Paper presented at the Foro de Iberoamérica, Participación Ciudadana y Movimientos Sociales en las Metropolis Latinoamericanas, Salamanca.

Orlove, Benjamin. 1994. "The Dead Policemen Speak: Power, Fear, and Narrative in the 1931 Molloccahua Killings." In Deborah Poole, *Unruly Order: Violence, Power and Cultural Identity in the High Provinces of Southern Peru,* 133–64. Boulder: Westview Press.

ONAMS (Oficina Nacional de Apoyo a la Movilización Social). 1975? "Grupos pro-chinos." Mimeo, ONAMS, Lima.

Orrego, Antenor. 1926. "Prólogo." In Alcides Spelucín, *El Libro de la Nave Dorada: Poemas.* La Libertad: Ediciones El Norte.

Otárola Peñaranda, Alberto. 1994. "El otro desborde popular: Violencia urbana." *PeruPaz* 3 (18).

Paca, Romeo. 1991. "Política de Pacificación en la Región José Carlos Mariátegui." In *Una ruta posible (Propuestas de la I Conferencia por la Paz)*, 81–91. Lima: IDS.

Palmer, David Scott. 1982. "Reformist Military Rule in Peru." In Robert Wesson, ed., *New Military Politics in Latin America*, 117–49. New York: Praeger.

———. 1986. "Rebellion in Rural Perú. The Origins and Evolution of Sendero Luminoso." *Comparative Politics* 18: 127–46.

———. 1995. "The Revolutionary Terrorism of Peru's Shining Path." In Martha Crenshaw, ed., *Terrorism in Context*, 249–308. University Park: Pennsylvania State University Press.

Palmer, David Scott, ed. 1992. *The Shining Path of Peru.* New York: St. Martin's Press.

———. 1994. *The Shining Path of Peru*, 2d. ed. revised. New York: St. Martin's Press.

Panfichi, Aldo, and Felipe Portocarrero, eds. 1995. *Mundos interiores: Lima 1850–1950.* Lima: Universidad del Pacífico.

Paredes, Saturnino. 1970. "El trabajo en el frente campesino." Lima: Trabajo y Lucha.

Pareja, Piedad. 1980. *Aprismo y sindicalismo en el Perú.* Lima: Editorial Rikchay Perú.

Pareja Paz-Soldán, José. 1954. *Las Constituciones del Perú.* Madrid: Ediciones Cultura Básica.

Parodi, Jorge. 1993. "Entre la utopía y la tradición: Izquierda y democracia en los municipios de los pobladores." In Jorge Parodi et al., *Los pobres, la ciudad y la política*, 121–23. Lima: Centro de Estudios de Democracia y Sociedad.

Parodi, Jorge, and Walter Twanama. 1993. "Los pobladores, la ciudad y la política: un estudio de actitudes." In Jorge Parodi et al., *Los pobres, la ciudad y la política*, 19–89. Lima: Centro de Estudios de Democracia y Sociedad.

Parodi, Jorge, et al. 1993. *Los pobres, la ciudad y la política.* Lima: Centro de Estudios de Democracia y Sociedad.

Pásara, Luis. 1978a. "El proyecto de Velasco y la organización campesina." *Apuntes* 8 VI (8): 59–80.

———. 1978b. *Reforma agraria: derecho y conflicto.* Lima: Instituto de Estudios Peruanos.

———. 1986. *Radicalización y conflicto en la iglesia peruana.* Lima: Ediciones el Virrey.

———. 1989. "Rasgos políticos de la demarcación regional." *Debate Agrario* 6 (April–June): 69–80.

———. 1990. "El doble sendero y la izquierda peruana." *Nueva Sociedad* 106: 58–72.

Pásara, Luis, and Alonso Zarzar. 1991. "Ambigüedades, contradicciones e incertidumbres." In Luis Pásara et al., *La otra cara de la luna: Nuevos actores sociales en el Perú*, 174–203. Lima: CEDYS.

Pásara, Luis, et al. 1991. *La otra cara de la luna: Nuevos actores sociales en el Perú.* Lima: CEDYS.

Pastor, Manuel, Jr., and Carol Wise. 1992. "Peruvian Economic Policy in the 1980s: From Orthodoxy to Heterodoxy and Back." *Latin American Research Review* 27 (2): 83–117.

PCP-PR (Partido Comunista del Peru-Patria Roja). 1976. *VII Conferencia Nacional: Sobre el carácter de la sociedad y los problemas de la revolución peruana,* 3d. ed. Lima (?): Ediciones Bandera Roja. Originally published in 1972.

PCP-SL (Partido Comunista del Peru-Sendero Luminoso). 1975. *¡Retomemos a Mariátegui y reconstituyamos su partido!* Ayacucho (?): PCP-SL.

———. 1979. *El desarrollo de las ideas marxistas en el Perú.* Lima: Editorial Pedagógica Asencios.

———. 1982. *¡Desarrollemos la guerra de guerrillas!* Lima (?): Ediciones Bandera Roja.

———. 1984. "Conclusiones del proceso de la lucha armada." Gorriti Archive, Princeton University Library, Princeton.

———. 1986. "Reunión nacional de dirigentes y cuadros." (7 April). Goritti Archive, Princeton University Library, Princeton.

———. 1988a. "Documentos Fundamentales del Primer Congreso del Partido Comunista del Perú. (Congreso marxista, congreso marxista-leninista-maoista, pensamiento Gonzalo." *El Diario,* 7 February.

———. 1988b. "Tercera sesión preparatoria del Primer Congreso," January.

———. 1989. "Desarrollar la guerra popular sirviendo a la revolución mundial." In Luis Arce Borja, ed., *Guerra popular en el Perú: El pensamiento Gonzalo,* 219–304. Brussels: No publisher. Original date is 1986.

———. 1991. "Informe sobre gran culminación del Plan Piloto presentado al Comité Central." *El Diario,* 8 February. Original date is June 1989.

———. 1991a. "¡Que el Equilibrio Estratégio remezca más al país!" November. Mimeo in possession of authors.

———. 1991b. "Sobre dos colinas: La guerra contrasubversiva y sus aliados." Mimeo in possession of authors.

———. 1992. "III Pleno del Comité Central del PCP." Mimeo.

PCR-Co (Partido Comunista Revolucionario-Clase Obrera). 1979. *II Conferencia Nacional: Línea básica de la revolución peruana.* Lima: Editora Peruana.

Pease, Henry. 1979. *Los caminos del poder: Tres años de crisis en la escena política.* Lima: DESCO.

———. 1980. *El ocaso del poder oligárquico: Lucha política en la escena oficial, 1968–1975.* Lima: DESCO.

———. 1983. "Uchuraccay, Lucanamarca y muchos más." *QuéHacer* 22: 48–57.

Pedraglio, Santiago. 1990. *Seguridad democrática integral: Armas para la paz.* Lima: Instituto de Defensa Legal.

Pérez Liu, Rosario. 1988. "Violencia, migración y productividad: cuatro estudios de caso en las comunidades ayacuchanas." In SEPIA, *Perú: El problema agraro en debate–SEPIA II*, 515–36. Lima: Universidad Nacional de San Cristóbal de Huamanga and SEPIA.

Poole, Deborah, ed. 1994. *Unruly Order: Violence, Power and Cultural Identity in the High Provinces of Southern Peru.* Boulder: Westview Press.

Poole, Deborah, and Gerardo Rénique. 1991. "The New Chroniclers of Peru: U.S. Scholars and their 'Shining Path' of Peasant Rebellion." *Bulletin of Latin American Research* 10 (2): 133–91.

———. 1992. *Peru, Time of Fear.* London: Latin American Bureau.

Popkin, Samuel. 1979. *The Rational Peasant: The Political Economy of Rural Society in Vietnam.* Berkeley: University of California Press.

Portocarrero, Gonzalo. 1984. "La dominación total." In *Debates en Sociología* (Lima), No. 10.

———. 1989. "El silencio, la queja y la acción. Respuestas al sufrimiento en la cultura peruana." In DESCO, 1989.

———. 1990. *Violencia estructural en el Perú: Sociología.* Lima: APEP.

———. 1993. "La dominación total." In *Racismo y mestizaje*, 17–31. Lima: SUR.

———. 1995. "El fundamento invisible: Función y lugar de las ideas racistas en la Lima del siglo XIX." In Aldo Panfichi and Felipe Portocarrero, eds., *Mundos interiores: Lima 1850–1950*, 219–59. Lima: Universidad del Pacífico.

Portocarrero, Gonzalo, ed. 1993. *Los nuevos limeños: Sueños, fervores y caminos en el mundo popular.* Lima: SUR and TAFOS.

Portocarrero, Gonzalo, and Patricia Oliart. 1989. *El Perú desde la escuela.* Lima: IAA.

Portocarrero, Gonzalo, et al. 1991. *Sacaojos, crisis social y fantasmas coloniales.* Lima: TAREA.

Pred, Allen, and Michael Watts. 1992. *Reworking Modernity.* New Brunswick: Rutgers University Press.

Protzel, Javier. 1994. "El paradigma del príncipe: El líder, la razón de estado y los medios electrónicos." *Contratexto* 7 (February).

PUM (Partido Unificado Mariateguista). n.d. "Esquema de asentamiento estratégico del Partido," Comisión de Organización Nacional.

———. 1985. "Sobre la táctica: El camino hacia el poder popular." Lima: PUM.

———. 1986. "III Sesión Plena del Comité Central del PUM," January 9–14.

———. 1987. "Estrategia del Poder Popular: Unidad de todas las sangres en el autogobierno del pueblo" (Documento en minoría presentado al VI Pleno del Comité Central), II Congreso Nacional, Lima, December.

———. 1988a. "Informe político: Crear, forjar y conquistar poder popular." Lima: II Congreso Nacional del Partido Unificado Mariateguista.

———. 1988b. "II Congreso Nacional del Partido (Informes y Resoluciones)." *El Mariateguista* No. 17 (August).

———. 1990. "Balance de la situación del partido." VII Comité Central, June.

———. 1991a. "Balance de la exitosa huelga campesina." Cuzco, 26 April.

———. 1991b. "El camino a lo nuevo (Informe y balance de dos años del Plan Piloto

Ande Rojo y de los esfuerzos por llevar a cabo los acuerdos del II Congreso Nacional)," November.

————. 1991c. "Elementos para un balance de la situación política actual," July.

————. 1991d. "Lineamientos de táctica sobre la pacificación," May 24.

————. 1991e. "Resolución sobre la campaña en torno a la pacificación," June 1.

————. 1993. *Documentos aprobados en el III Congreso Nacional*. Lima: PUM.

Quijano, Aníbal. 1980. *Dominación y cultura. Lo cholo y el conflicto cultural en el Perú*. Lima: Mosca Azul Editores.

Quintanilla, Lino. 1981. *Andahuaylas: La lucha por la tierra (Testimonio de un militante)*. Lima: Mosca Azul Editores.

Redfield, Robert. 1941. *The Folk Culture of Yucatan*. Chicago: University of Chicago.

————. 1956. *The Primitive World and its Transformations*. Ithaca: Cornell University Press.

Rénique, Gerardo. 1996. "Crisis, política y cultura: La izquierda peruana en perspectiva histórica." Ms.

Rénique, José Luis. 1991a. "La batalla por Puno: Violencia y democracia en la sierra sur." *Debate Agrario* 10 (Lima): 83–108.

————. 1991b. *Los sueños de la sierra: Cusco en el siglo XX*. Lima: CEPES.

————. 1993. "La Battalla por Puno." Seminario sobre la Violencia Política en el Perú: Análisis y Perspectivas. Organizado por el Centro Peruano de Estudios Sociales (CEPES) y el Instituto de Estudios Peruanos (Instituto de Estudios Peruanos), Lima, 12–14 de julio.

————. 1995. *The 1995 Electoral Process in Peru (A Delegation Report of the Latin American Studies Association.)* Miami: Latin American Studies Association and North-South Center, University of Miami.

Riofrío, Gustavo. 1978. *Se busca terreno para próxima barriada*. Lima: DESCO.

Riva Agüero, José de la. 1965. *Paisajes peruanos*. Lima: Pontífica Universidad Católica del Perú.

Rivera Serna, Raúl. 1958. *Las guerrillas del centro en la emancipación peruana*. Lima: Edición Talleres Gráficos Villanueva.

Robles, Fernando. 1987. *Reestructuración y desarrollo regional de Puno*. Puno: Universidad Nacional del Altiplano.

Rochabrún, Guillermo. 1980. *El ocaso del poder oligárquico: Lucha política en la escena oficial, 1968–1975*. Lima: DESCO.

————. 1989. "Izquierda, democracia y crisis en el Perú." *Márgenes* 3 (Lima): 79–99.

————. 1994. "¿Mirando el campo con ojos urbanos?" In SEPIA, *Perú: El problema agrario en debate-SEPIA V*, 14–31. Lima: Universidad Nacional San Agustin, SEPIA and CAPRODA.

Rodríguez Beruff, Jorge. 1983. *Los militares y el poder: Un ensayo sobre la doctrina militar en el Perú: 1948–1968*. Lima: Mosca Azul.

Rodríguez Vargas, Marisol. 1993. *Desplazados de la selva central: El caso de los asháninka*. Lima: Centro Amazónico de Antropología y Aplicación Práctica.

Rodríquez, Yolanda. 1992. "Los actores sociales y la violencia política en Puno." *Allpanchis* 39: 131–54.

Rojas Samanez, Álvaro. 1985. *Partidos políticos en el Perú: Manual y registro.* Lima: Ediciones F&A.

Romero, Emilio. 1979. "El siglo de Mariátegui." In Emilio Romero et al., *Siete Ensayos: 50 Años de la historia,* 11–18. Lima: Biblioteca Amauta.

Romero, Emilio, et al. 1979. *Siete Ensayos: 50 Años de la historia.* Lima: Biblioteca Amauta.

Rosenberg, Tina. 1991. *Children of Cain: Violence and the Violent in Latin America.* New York: Penguin.

Rospigliosi, Fernando. 1989. "Izquierdas y clases populares: Democracia y subversión en el Perú." In Julio Cotler, *Clases populares, crisis y democracia en América Latina.* Lima: Instituto de Estudios Peruanos, 103–142.

Rubio, Marcial. 1994. "Ley Cantuta o cómo fabricar una sentencia." *QueHacer* (Lima) No. 87.

———. 1995. "Los derechos humanos en la legislación y la práctica jurisdiccional del Estado." In Julio Cotler, *Perú 1964–1994. Economía, sociedad y politica,* 201–14. Lima: Instituto de Estudios Peruanos.

Salcedo, José María. 1986. "Con Sendero en Lurigancho." *QueHacer* 39: 60–67.

———. 1987. "El caso Uchuraccay, cuatro años después." *QueHacer* 45: 14–15.

Sánchez, Luis A. 1929. "La aparición del cholo." *Mundial,* No. 470.

Sánchez E., Rodrigo. 1981. *Toma de tierras y conciencia política campesina: Las lecciones de Andahuaylas.* Lima: Instituto de Estudios Peruanos.

Sase-Instituto Apoyo. 1993. *El desarrollo institucional de las Organizaciones No-Gubernamentales de Desarrollo (ONGDS) en el Perú.* Lima: SASE/Instituto APOYO.

Sauer, Carl O. 1982. *Andean Reflections: Letters from Carl O. Sauer While on a South American Trip Under a Grant from the Rockefeller Foundation, 1942.* Boulder: Westview Press, 1982.

Scott, James. 1985. *Weapons of the Weak: Everyday Forms of Peasant Resistance.* New Haven: Yale University Press.

———. 1990. *Domination and the Arts of Resistance.* New Haven: Yale University Press.

Scurrah, Martin, ed. 1987. *Empresas asociativas y comunidades campesinas, Puno después de la reforma agraria.* Lima: GREDES.

Seligmann, Linda J. 1993. "Between Worlds of Exchange: Ethnicity among Peruvian Market Women." *Cultural Anthropology* 8 (2): 187–213.

———. 1995. *Between Reform and Revolution: Political Struggles in the Peruvian Andes, 1969–1991.* Stanford: Stanford University Press.

SEPAR (Servicios Educativos, Promoción y Apoyo Rural, Huancayo). 1992. *Cifras y cronología de la violencia política en la Región Central del Perú (1980–1991).* Huancayo: SEPAR.

SEPIA (Seminario Permanente de Investigación Agraria). 1988. *Perú: el problema agraro en debate—SEPIA II.* Lima: Universidad Nacional de San Cristóbal de Huamanga and SEPIA.

———. 1994. *Perú: el problema agrario en debate—SEPIA V.* Lima: Universidad Nacional San Agustín, SEPIA and CAPRODA.

Shohat, Ella. 1992. "Notes on the 'Post-Colonial.'" *Social Text* 31–32: 99–113.

Silverblatt, Irene. 1994. "Becoming 'Indian' in the Central Andes of 17th Century Peru." In Gyan Prakash, ed., *After Colonialism: Colonial Histories, Postcolonial Displacements,* 272–94. Princeton: Princeton University Press.

SINAMOS (Sistema Nacional de Apoyo a la Movilización Social). 1975 (?). "Grupos maoístas. Primera parte." Mimeo, Lima.

SIPRI Yearbook. 1982–1987. *World Armaments and Disarmament.* New York: Humanities Press.

Sivirichii, Atilio. 1929. "Con el maestro Ricardo Rojas." *La Sierra,* No. 29.

Skar, Harold O. 1988. *The Warm Valley People: Duality and Land Reform Among the Quechua Indians of Highland Peru,* 2d. ed. Goteborg: Goteborgs Etnografiska Museum.

Smith, Carol. 1990. *Guatemalan Indians and the State: 1540 to 1988.* Austin: University of Texas Press.

Smith, Gavin. 1989. *Livelihood and Resistance: Peasants and the Politics of Land in Peru.* Berkeley: University of California Press.

Smith, Michael L. 1992a. *Entre dos fuegos. ONG, desarrollo rural y violencia política.* Lima: Instituto de Estudios Peruanos.

———. 1992b. "Shining Path's Urban Strategy: Ate-Vitarte." In David Scott Palmer, ed., *The Shining Path of Peru,* 127–48. New York: St. Martin's Press.

Spelucín, Alcides. 1926. *El libro de la nave dorada: Poemas.* La Libertad: Ediciones El Norte.

Starn, Orin. 1991a. "Missing the Revolution: Anthropologists and the War in Peru." *Cultural Anthropology* 6 (Feb.): 63–91.

———. 1991b. *Reflexiones sobre rondas campesinas, protesta rural y nuevos movimientos sociales.* Lima: Instituto de Estudios Peruanos.

———. 1991c. "Sendero, soldados y ronderos en el Mantaro." *QueHacer* 74: 60–68.

———. 1992. "'I dreamed of Foxes and Hawks': Reflections on Peasant Protest, New Social Movements and the Rondas Campesinas of Northern Peru." In Arturo Escobar and Sonia Alvarez, *The Making of Social Movements in Latin America: Identity, Strategy, Democracy,* 89–111. Boulder: Westview.

———. 1993a. "Antropología andina, 'andinismo' y Sendero Luminoso." *Allpanchis* 39: 15–72.

———. 1993b. "La resistencia en Huanta." *QueHacer* 84: 34–41.

Starn, Orin, ed. 1993. *Hablan los ronderos: La búsqueda por la paz en los Andes.* Lima: Instituto de Estudios Peruanos.

Starn, Orin, Carlos Iván Degregori, and Robin Kirk, eds. 1995. *The Peru Reader: History, Culture, Politics.* Durham: Duke University Press.

Stein, Steve. 1980. *Populism in Peru: The Emergence of the Masses and the Politics of Social Control.* Madison: University of Wisconsin Press.

Steinhauf, Andrés. 1991. "Diferenciación étnica y redes de larga distancia entre migrantes andinos: El caso de Sanka y Colcha." *Bulletin del Institut Francais de Etudes Andines* 20 (2): 93–114.

Stepan, Alfred. 1978. *The State and Society: Peru in Comparative Perspective.* Princeton: Princeton University Press.

Stepan, Nancy Leys. 1991. *The Hour of Eugenics: Race, Gender, and Nation in Latin America.* Ithaca: Cornell University Press.

Stern, Peter A. 1995. *Sendero Luminoso: An Annotated Bibliography of the Shining Path Guerrilla Movement.* Albuquerque: SALALM Secretariat.

Stern, Steve J. 1982. *Peru's Indian Peoples and the Challenge of Spanish Conquest: Huamanga to 1640.* Madison: University of Wisconsin Press.

———. 1987. "New Approaches to the Study of Peasant Rebellion and Consciousness: Implications of the Andean Experience." In Steve J. Stern, ed., *Resistance, Rebellion, and Consciousness in the Andean Peasant World,* 3–25. Madison: University of Wisconsin Press.

———. 1990. "Nueva aproximación al estudio de la conciencia y de las rebeliones campesinas: Las implicancias de la experiencia andina." In Steve J. Stern, ed., *Resistencia, rebelión y conciencia campesina en los Andes, siglos XVIII al XX.* Lima: Instituto de Estudios Peruanos.

———. 1995. *The Secret History of Gender: Women, Men, and Power in Late Colonial Mexico.* Chapel Hill: Univ. of North Carolina Press.

Stern, Steve J., ed. 1987. *Resistance, Rebellion, and Consciousness in the Andean Peasant World.* Madison: University of Wisconsin Press.

———. 1990. *Resistencia, rebelión y conciencia campesina en los Andes, siglos XVIII al XX.* Lima: Instituto de Estudios Peruanos.

Stokes, Susan. 1991. "Hegemony, Consciousness and Political Change in Peru." *Politics and Society* 19 (3): 265–90.

Stoll, David. 1993. *Between Two Armies in the Ixil Town of Guatemala.* New York: Columbia University Press.

Strong, Simon. 1992a. *Shining Path: Terror and Revolution in Peru.* New York: Times Books.

———. 1992b. *Shining Path: The World's Deadliest Revolutionary Force.* London: HarperCollins.

Sulmont, Denis. 1975. *El movimiento obrero peruano (1900–1956).* Lima: PUC.

———. 1982. *El movimiento obrero peruano (1890–1980). Reseña histórico,* 3d ed. Lima: TAREA.

Sulmont, Denis, Javier Mújica, Vicente Otta, and Raúl Aramendy. 1989. *Violencia y movimiento sindical.* Lima: Red Peruana de Educación Popular y Sindicalismo.

SUTEP (Sindicato Único de Trabajadores de la Educación). 1977. *Ni botas, ni votos.* Callao: SUTE, Tercer Sector.

Tamayo, Giulia. 1992. "Desplazamiento, género y desarrollo: informe de consultoría UNIFEM-PENUD." Document seen by author.

Tamayo Herrera, José. 1982. *Historia social e indigenismo en el Altiplano*. Lima: Ediciones Treintaitrés.

———. 1989. *Memorias de un historiador: Ensayo de egohistoria*. Lima: CEPER.

Tapia, Carlos. 1995. *Autodefensa armada del campesinado*. Lima: CEDEP.

———. Forthcoming. *Del "Equilibrio Estratégico" a la derrota de Sendero Luminoso*. Lima: Instituto de Estudios Peruanos.

Tello, Julio. 1950. *Páginas escogidas*. Lima: Universidad Nacional Mayor San Marcos.

Thorndike, Guillermo. 1969. *El año de la barbarie: Perú, 1932*. Lima: Mosca Azul.

Thorp, Rosemary, and Geoffrey Bertram. 1985. *Perú: crecimiento económico y políticas en una economía abierta*. Lima: Mosca Azul Editores, Fundación Friedrich Ebert, and Universidad del Pacífico.

Thurner, Mark. 1997. *From Two Republics to One Divided: Contradictions of Postcolonial Nationmaking in Andean Peru*. Durham: Duke University Press.

Tincopa, Nilda, and María Luisa Mollo. 1992. *Nueva legislación antiterrorista: Análisis y comentarios*. Lima: No publisher.

Torres y Torres Lara, Carlos. 1995. *Hito 1424: El pacto de caballeros*. Lima: Informe para la Comisión de Relaciones Exteriores del Congreso de la República.

Tovar, Teresa. 1986. "Barrios, ciudad, democracia y política." In Eduardo Ballón, et al., *Movimientos sociales y democracia: La fundación de un nuevo orden*, 143–84. Lima: DESCO.

Trivelli, C. 1992. "Reconocimiento legal de comunidades campesinas: Una revisión estadística." *Debate Agrario* 14 (June): 23–37.

Tuesta, Fernando. 1989. "Villa El Salvador: Izquierda, gestión municipal y organización popular." Mimeo, CEDYS, Lima.

———. 1994. *Perú político en cifras*. Lima: Fundación Friedrich Ebert.

Tulberg, Rita. 1987. "Deuda relacionada con lo militar en América Latina." In Augusto Varas, *Paz, desarme y desarrollo en América Latina*. Santiago, Chile: Grupo Editor Latinoamericano.

Universidad del Pacifico. 1980. *Guía del elector*. Lima: Centro de Investigaciones de la Universidad del Pacífico.

Urbano, Henrique, ed. 1991. *Poder y violencia en los Andes*. Cusco: Centro Bartolomé de las Casas.

Urriza, Manuel. 1978. *Perú: Cuando los generales se van*. Caracas: Ediciones CIDAL.

Urrutia, Jaime. 1985. "Ayacucho: los frutos de la guerra." *El zorro de abajo* 3: 51–53.

———. 1993. "Ayacucho: Un escenario pos-Gonzalo, ¿Ya?" *Ideéle* 59–60: 8–90.

Valcárcel, Luis E. 1916–1917. "Política nacional. Los problemas actuales." Archivo Departamental del Cuzco, Fondo UNSAAC, libro 11.

———. 1925. *Del ayllu al imperio: La evolución político-social en el antiguo Perú y otros estudios*. Lima: Editorial Garcilaso.

———. 1950. "Introduction." In Pierre Verger, *Indians of Peru*. New York: Pantheon.

———. 1964. "Indigenismo en el Perú." In Luis E. Valcárcel, et al., *Estudios sobre la Cultura Actual de Perú*, 9–15. Lima: Universidad Mayor de San Marcos.

———. 1975. *Tempestad en los andes*. Lima: Universo. Originally published in 1925.

———. 1981. *Memorias*. Lima: Instituto de Estudios Peruanos.

Valcárcel, Luis E., et al. 1964. *Estudios sobre la cultura actual del Perú*. Lima: Universidad Mayor de San Marcos.

Valencia Quintanilla, Felix. 1983. *Crítica de las tesis reaccionarias sobre el movimiento campesino*. Lima: Centro Popular de Estudios Agrarios.

Valentín, Isidro. 1993. "Tsunami Fujimori: una propuesta de interpretación." In Gonzalo Portocarrero, ed., *Los nuevos limeños: Sueños, fervores y caminos en el mundo popular*, 95–114. Lima: SUR and TAFOS.

Varas, Augusto. 1987. *Paz, desarme y desarrollo en América Latina*. Santiago, Chile: Grupo Editor Latinoamericano.

Varese, Stefano. 1973. *La sal de los cerros*. Lima: Retablo de Papel Ediciones.

Vargas Llosa, Mario. 1983. "The Story of a Massacre." *Granta* 9: 62–83.

———. 1984. *Historia de Mayta*. Barcelona: Seix Barral. (Also available in English as *The Real Life of Alejandro Mayta*. Translated by Alfred MacAdam. New York: Farrar, Straus, and Giroux, 1986.)

Vargas Llosa, Mario, et al. 1983. *Informe de la Comisión Investigadora de los sucesos de Uchuraccay*. Lima: Editora Perú.

Vargas, Virginia. 1992. "Women: Tragic Encounters with the Left." *NACLA Report on the Americas* 15 (5) (May): 30–34.

Vega, Ricardo. 1989. "Empresa comunal y vía campesina comunera (Apuntes desde la experiencia de Puno)." *Allpanchis* 33: 125–34.

Vergara, Abilio. 1983. "Subregión de Huanta: apuntes para su comprensión." In Gonzales Vigil, *Gonzales Vigil: Libro Jubilar 1933–1983*, Huanta: 155–77.

Vergara, Abilio, et al. 1985. "Culluchaca: Algunos elementso sobre la ideología comunal." In IER "José María Arguedas," *Comunidades campesinas de Ayacucho: Economía, ideología y organización social*, 107–156. Ayacucho: IER "José María Arguedas" and CCTA.

Vidal, Ana María. 1993. *Los decretos de la guerra*. Lima: IDS.

Villanueva, Víctor. 1997. *Así cayó Leguía*. Lima: Retama Editorial.

Webster, Steven S. 1977. "Kinship and Affinity in a Native Quechua Community." In Ralph Bolton and Enrique Mayer, *Andean Kinship and Marriage*, 28–42. Washington, D.C.: Anthropological Association.

Weiss, Jean. 1996. "Gender and Reconstruction in Ayacucho, Peru." M.A. paper, Latin American and Iberian Studies Program, University of Wisconsin-Madison.

Wesson, Robert, ed. 1982. *New Military Politics in Latin America*. New York: Praeger.

Wiener, Raúl. 1987. *El Antizorro. El debate sobre el "Acuerdo Nacional."* Lima: Ediciones Debate Mariateguista.

Wieviorka, Michel. 1988. *Société et terrorisme*. Paris: Fayard.

———. 1993. *El terrorismo, la violencia política en el mundo.* Lima (?): Plaza Janes and Editorial Cambio 16.

Williams, Raymond. 1985. *Marxism and Literature.* London: Verso.

Wolf, Eric. 1969. *Peasant Wars of the 20th Century.* New York: Harper and Row.

———. 1982. *Europe and the People without History.* Berkeley: University of California Press.

Woy-Hazleton, Sandra, and William A. Hazleton. 1992. "Shining Path and the Marxist Left." In David Scott Palmer, ed., *The Shining Path of Peru,* 207–24. New York: St. Martin's Press.

Xespe, Toribio Mejia. 1950. "Prólogo." In Julio Tello, *Páginas escogidas.* Lima: Universidad Nacional Mayor San Marcos.

Yawar, Evaristo. 1972. "Las tareas actuales del proletariado y la izquierda marxista (A propósito de la aparición del Frente de Apoyo y Solidaridad Obrero-Campesino-Intelectual)." *Crítica Marxista Leninista* (Lima) 4: 5–17.

Yépez Miranda, Alfredo. 1928. "El Cusco que recuerdo." In *Mundial,* special edition.

Yúdice, George. 1992. "Postmodernism on the Periphery." *South Atlantic Quarterly* 92 (3): 543–56.

Gorriti, Gustavo, 115

Grassroots organizations: in Lima, 268, 282, 363–64, 367; in Villa El Salvador, 277, 278, 294; women and, 342–43, 357–60, 367, 371, 372–73

Green Book, 394

Gregorio, 176, 182

Guerrillas, 4–5, 15, 81–82 n.33, 121, 125, 154 n.5, 163; in selva, 212–18

Guerrilla zones, 176

Guillermo, 172

Guzmán Reynoso, Abimael (President Gonzalo), 4, 23, 53, 54, 75, 79 n.12, 80 n.15, 159, 166, 179, 192 n.22, 195, 224, 267, 292, 307, 318, 350, 352–53, 383, 414, 418(fig.), 434, 439, 445–46 n.25; on armed struggle, 155 n.11, 162; capture of, 225, 297, 377, 397, 398; on human rights, 431–32, 436–37, 444 n.12; ideology of, 65, 66; leadership of, 67–68, 74(fig.), 285, 350, 430; on violence, 136, 143, 434–35

Guzmán y Valle University, Enrique ("La Cantuta"), 399, 402

Haciendas, 50–51, 92, 94–95, 222 n.8, 333. *See also* Agrarian reform; Land invasions

Harvey, David, 249

Haya de la Torre, Víctor Raúl, 29–30, 31, 35–36, 38, 40, 57 n.43

Hermoza Ríos, Nicolás, 186, 379, 385, 396, 398–400, 401, 402–3, 404

HIERROPERU, 197

Highlands: culture of, 47, 49–50; peasant mobilizations in, 15, 42, 84–85

Historical Insitute of Cuzco, 36

Holidays, 175–76

Hoyos Rubio, Rafael, 386

Huallaga Front, 400

Huallaga Valley, 145, 215, 409 n.40, 441–42

Huamán Centeno, Adrián, 238, 389

Huamanga, 67, 160, 169, 190 n.5, 353, 359, 467 n.30

Huamanguilla, 164

Huamani, José, 230

Huancahuacho, 92, 103, 108, 109–10, 111, 113

Huancané, 329

Huancas, 105

Huancasancos, 136–37, 152, 239

Huancavelica, 121, 195, 201, 222 n.8, 228, 247; deaths in, 193, 194; military in, 238, 388

Huancayo: attacks on, 196, 197, 198; education in, 199–201

Huanchi, 170

Huanta, 141, 142, 146, 169, 170, 190 n.5, 239, 241, 243, 252, 353, 444–45 n.14; killings in, 448–49; Shining Path in, 160, 162, 163, 164, 166, 236

Huánuco, 164, 388

Huarcaya, Máximo, 290, 291, 296

Huarochirí, 22

Huaycán, 269

Huaychao, 152, 162, 163, 464–65 n.5

Huayhuaco, 169

Huayllao, 168

Huayucachi, 196

Huicho, Marina, 186

Huillca, Hugo, 244

Human rights, 381–83, 402, 417, 443, 461–63, 464 n.2, 468 n.53, 472; activists in, 437–38, 445 nn.20–23, 467 nn.37, 38; Catholic Church and, 450–51; defense of, 447–48; in García administration, 390–91; in Lima, 452–53; Shining Path and, 431–33, 434, 436–37, 438–39, 440–42, 444 nn.12, 13, 468 n.44; United States and, 435–36; violations of, 326, 381–83, 399, 404–5, 425–27, 428–29,

and Shining Path, 320–21; unity of, 321–22

Pasco, 121, 193, 194

Pasos perdidos, Los (Carpentier), 5

Pastor, José, 396

Pataqocha, 172

Patria Nueva, 25, 28, 31–32

Patria Roja. *See* Partido Comunista del Perú-Patria Roja

Patrols. *See Rondas campesinas, ronderos*

PCP. *See* Partido Comunista del Peru

PCP-BR. *See* Partido Comunista del Perú-Bandera Roja

PCP-SL. *See* Partido Comunista del Perú-Sendero Luminoso; Shining Path

PCP-U. *See* Partido Comunista del Perú-Unidad

PCR-CO. *See* Partido Comunista Revolucionario-Clase Obrera

Peace and Development Forum (Peace Forum), 290

Peace Commission, 452

Peasant Federation of Peru. *See* Confederación Campesina del Perú

Peasant Federation of Puno (FDCP), 310, 314, 315, 316, 317

Peasant mobilizations, 15, 307–8; in Andahuaylas, 84–85, 102–16; rondas campesinas as, 235–39

Peasants, 45, 96, 100, 154 n.6, 191 n.9, 219, 221–22 n.6, 230, 240, 311, 460; and Armed Forces, 146–48, 325–26; culture and politics of, 19–20, 51–52, 90–92, 137–38, 151–53, 249–51, 265; family obligations of, 88–90; Indians as, 43, 50–51; land invasions by, 93, 324–25; and Left, 80 n.14, 201–2; opposition by, 138–40; in Puno, 332–34; recruitment of, 172–73, 227–29, 238; resistance by, 125–27, 142–43,

163, 189; resistant adaptation by, 178–80; revolutionary role of, 133–34; and rondas campesinas, 207–8, 231, 232, 234–35, 238–39; and Shining Path, 54, 122–23, 131, 150, 151, 154 n.7, 160–63, 170, 209–11, 267; support of, 145–46

Pease, Henry, 287, 445 n.19

Pentecostal Church, 167, 172, 239

People's Committees. *See* Open People's Committees

People's tribunals, 136–37

People's war, 77, 79 n.11, 81 n.29, 145, 151, 160–61, 307

Pérez de Cuéllar, Javier, 400, 401, 422

Pérez Silva, MacDonald, 400

Permanent Peoples' Tribunals, 468 n.44

Permanent Seminar on Agrarian Research, 459–60

Peru-Cornell agreement, 46

Peruvian Association of Studies and Research for Peace. *See* Asociación Peruana de Estudios e Investigación para la Paz

Peruvian Communist Party (PCP), 43, 97, 98, 117 n.15

Peruvian Indigenista Institute, 45, 46

Peruvian Peasant Federation. *See* Confederación Campesina del Perú

Pichis River, 213, 214

Pichiwillca, 166, 169, 172

Pino, Indalecio, 201

Pioneer Children Movement, 176

Píter, 184, 187

Piura, 40, 135, 235, 313

Plan Piloto Ande Rojo (PPAR), 322–23

PMR. *See* Revolutionary Mariateguista Party

Polay, Víctor, 398

Police forces, 326, 329, 390, 391, 407 n.14

Political parties, 14, 78 n.5, 348, 473; formation of, 39–40; in Lima, 268, 272–73

Politics, 3–5, 55 n.6, 56 n.31, 190 n.2, 250, 302 n.20; of barriadas, 270–74, 275–80; and bossism, 240, 241; civilismo, 24–25; class consciousness and, 43–44; community, 114–15; confrontational, 284–86, 288–96; Fujimori's, 379–81, 411–12, 415–23; leftist, 286–88, 443–44 n.4, 470–71, 472; modernization of, 41–42; of opposition, 13–14; and peasants, 51–52, 90–92, 126–27; and rondas, 241–42, 251–52; scientific, 25, 28; and Sendero Luminoso, 133–35, 158, 263, 472–73; women and, 347–48

Pongos, 43

Poor Peasants Movement, 176

Popkin, Samuel, 273

Popular Action. *See* Acción Popular

Popular Christian Party (PPC), 268, 302 n.24, 445 n.19

Popular Committee of Viscatán, 170

Popular Guerrilla Army, 160

Popular Women's Federation (FEPOMUVES), 277, 278, 279, 286, 289, 292, 298, 299

Populism, 14, 21 n.3, 237, 262, 264

Poverty, 177–78, 300–301 n.13, 303–4 n.39

PPAR. *See* Plan Piloto Ande Rojo

PPC. *See* Partido Popular Cristiano

Prado, Manuel, 58 n.68

Praeli, Cesár Enrico, 390

Primera Escuela Miltar (First Military School), 74(fig.)

Prince of Asturias Award, 279

Principal Regional Committee, 164, 166, 171

Prisons, prisoners, 397; massacres in, 390–91, 466 n.20; Shining Path in, 458–59, 468 n.40

PROCAD. *See* Centro Promoción, Capitación y Desarrollo

Promoción Comunal, 87–88

Promotion, Training, and Development Center (PROCAD), 202–3

Protestants, 123–24, 152

Protzel, Javier, 416

Provincial Federation of Peasants of Andahuaylas. *See* Federación Provincial de Campesinos de Andahuaylas

Provincials, 23, 25, 30; politics of, 27–32, 39–40, 56 n.31

PSR. *See* Revolutionary Socialist Party

Pucayacu, 147

Pueblos jóvenes, 270, 271

Puerto Ocopa, 214, 215

Puitoc, 105

Puka Llacta, 82 n.44

Pulperia, 169

PUM. *See* Partido Unificado Mariáteguista

Puno, 26, 27, 39, 264–65, 268, 300 n.6, 308, 309(fig.), 335 n.18, 337–38 n.78, 467 n.37; counterinsurgency in, 325–28, 331–33; culture and politics in, 308, 310–12; land invasions in, 316–17; political mobilization in, 42, 313–15; and PUM, 321–22; and Shining Path, 317–21

Puno-Tambopata project, 46

Purus, 140

Putina, 329

Qahuasana, 170, 172

Qano, 167

Qaqasmayo, 172

Qarapa, 168

Qawasana, 170, 172

Qisni, 169

Seminario Permanente de Investigación Agraria, 459–60

Sendero Luminoso. *See* Shining Path

Sendero Rojo, 220, 378

Serranos, serranitos, 22, 24, 125, 413

Servicio de Inteligencia Nacional (SIN), 379, 394–95, 398, 403, 408–9 nn.26, 27

Shining Path, 4, 71, 85, 154 n.5, 157 n.32, 223 n.14, 255 n.28, 301 n.14, 384 n.2, 421; and Armed Forces, 141–42, 155–56 n.18, 326–27, 329–30, 386, 390, 391, 397–98; and armed struggle, 76, 77, 79 n.11, 81 n.27, 145–46, 155 n.11; and Ayacucho, 121–22, 128–33, 353–54; community support for, 170–71; confrontational politics of, 284–86, 288–96; elections and, 72, 302 n.23; emergence of, 13, 18, 20, 53, 75, 76, 428, 470; failure of, 126–27, 149–53; families and, 181–82; and human rights, 426, 427, 431–33, 436–37, 438–39, 440–42, 444 nn.12, 13, 445 n.22, 468 n.44; ideology of, 65, 153–54 n.2, 191–92 n.18, 229, 233–34, 305 n.48, 429–30, 471, 475–76 n.1; and Indians, 2–3, 54; internal sanctions in, 184–87; and jungle districts, 124–25, 213–18; in Junín, 196–99; leadership of, 67–68, 79 n.12, 190 n.3, 267–68, 350; and Left, 60–64, 78, 262, 263–64, 303 nn.30–32, 427–28, 472–73; in Lima, 271–72, 273–74, 279–81, 305–6 nn.53, 57, 307, 362–64; makeup of, 79 n.12, 172–74; and military government, 18–19; and mothers' clubs, 359–60; and nuevo poder, 133–35; opposition to, 148, 156 nn.22, 26, 159–60, 163–64, 182–84; organization of, 176–77; and peasants, 151–53, 200–12; and prisons, 458–59, 468 n.40; and Puno, 317–21, 324–25, 331–32; recruitment by, 342, 354–55; and religion, 175–76; repression by, 162–63; resistance to, 123–24, 178–81, 189, 377–78; retreat by, 164, 166; in rural areas, 200–216; support of, 166–67, 170, 171–72; terrorism of, 144, 297; in Villa El Salvador, 269–70, 283–96, 298–99, 305 n.51; violence of, 135–41, 150, 167–69, 171–72, 190 n.5, 192 n.30, 193, 194–95, 218, 262–63, 281–82, 304 n.40, 358, 433–35, 448, 449; war of, 1–2, 76, 81 n.29, 116, 128, 160–61, 261–62; women and, 341–42, 343, 349–53, 354, 361(fig.), 367–68

Shiriari, 168

Sicaya, 196

SIDERPERU, 197

Silva Tuesta, Raúl, 393

Simariva, 171–72

SIN. *See* Servicio de Inteligencia Nacional

SINAMOS. *See* Sistema Nacional de Apoyo a la Movilización Social

Sinchitullo, Juan, 231

Sindicato Unico de Trabajadores de la Educación (SUTEP), 70, 71, 72

Sistema Nacional de Apoyo a la Movilización Social (SINAMOS), 19, 84, 95, 96, 99, 100, 110, 114

Small business owners' federation (APEMIVES), 277, 286, 290–91, 296

Sobrevilla, David Jaime, 400

Social class. *See* Class

Socialism, 39, 58 n.58

Socialist Left (IS), 287

Socialist Party, 40, 41

Socialist Vanguard, 41

Social spending, 300–301 n.13

Sociedades Agrícolas de Interés Social (SAIS), 131, 156 n.22, 198, 201, 202, 209, 219, 310, 311

Universidad Agraria de La Molina, 50
Universidad Comunal del Central, 199
Universidad del Pacifico, 82–83 n.45
Universidad Nacional del Centro, 199–201, 221 n.5
Universidad Nacional de San Cristóbal de Huamanga, 47, 65, 80 n.15, 161, 200, 224, 225
Universities, 47, 414; and leftist groups, 63–64, 80 n.15, 221 n.5; women in, 349, 351
University of Cuzco, 47
University of San Marcos, 29, 30, 40–41, 63, 225, 281
UPP. *See* Unión por el Perú
Urbanization, 46, 51, 270–71, 282–83
Urban sector, 38–39, 42, 50
Urban workers, 45
Urubamba, 214

Valcárcel, Luis E., 17, 28, 33, 45, 54; and indigenismo, 35–36, 38, 45, 46, 47, 49, 59 n.91
Valcárcel, Teodoro, 56–57 n.33
Valderrama, Carlos, 56–57 n.33
Valdivia, José, 398
Valentín, Isidro, 413
Valencia Quintanilla, Félix, 112
Vallejo, César (El Indio), 252
Valle Riestra, Javier, 445 n.19
Vargas Llosaa, Mario, 3, 5, 227, 273, 380, 394, 412, 415, 464–65 n.5
Vanguardia Revolucionaria (VR), 63, 64–65, 70, 73, 80 n.14, 81 n.27, 97, 98, 100, 108, 334 n.6; and peasant mobilizations, 84, 85, 111, 112
Vanguardia Socialista, 41
Vara system, 134–35
Varayocc, 91–92, 116 n.5, 134
Vásquez, Jorge, 306 n.60
Vásquez, Lidia, 230

Velando, Máximo, 212, 213
Velasco Alvarado, Juan, 15–16, 18, 19, 61, 68, 70, 81–82 n.33, 275, 406, 470; agrarian reform under, 44–45, 84, 310
Velasquistas, 387
Vicariates of Solidarity, 326
Víctor Fajardo, 160, 190 n.5, 231, 239
Vilcashuamán, 152, 190 n.5, 239, 353
Villa El Salvador, 262, 302 n.25, 303 n.33, 305 n.52, 306 n.60, 368; confrontational politics in, 284–86, 288–96; Left in, 268–69, 276–80, 286–88; mobilization of, 275–76; Shining Path in, 269–70, 274, 283–84, 298–99, 305 n.51, 363
Villages: corruption and bossism in, 240–41; defense of, 227–28, 231; and Otherness, 233–35; resettlement of, 226–28, 231; and rondas, 245, 247. *See also* Communities
Villa María del Triunfo, 276
Villanueva, Armando, 391
Vinchos, 164, 243
Violence, 155 nn.14, 15, 180, 210, 451, 462–63; among Asháninka, 217, 218; human rights and, 382–83, 425–26; internal, 167, 184–87; levels of, 193–96; and nuevo poder, 135–41; against peasant economy, 459–60; political, 428–29; of rondas, 243–44; by Shining Path, 61, 147, 150, 167–69, 190 n.5, 192 n.30, 262–63, 281–82, 289, 358, 433–35
Viru Viru, 228, 231
Viscatán, 160, 164, 190 n.5
Vista Alegre, 206
Vista Alegre People's Committee, 170
VR. *See* Vanguardia Revolucionaria
Vucetich, Germán, 392, 408 n.18

Wars, 313; and peasants, 219, 247; popu-

Steve J. Stern, a professor of Latin American history at the University of Wisconsin-Madison, has published numerous works on the history of Peru and other Latin American countries.

Marisol de la Cadena, an anthropologist at the University of North Carolina-Chapel Hill, has written on ethnicity and power, and is completing a book on indigenismo and regional culture in Cuzco.

Iván Hinojosa has conducted research on the history of the Left in Peru and is completing a doctoral dissertation on the topic at the University of Chicago.

Florencia E. Mallon teaches Latin American history at the University of Wisconsin-Madison; her recent book, *Peasant and Nation,* won the Bryce Wood Award of the Latin American Studies Association.

Carlos Iván Degregori, a researcher at the Instituto de Estudios Peruanos, has taught at the Universidad Nacional de San Cristóbal de Huamanga and has written numerous works on the origins of Shining Path and Peru's war experience.

Ponciano del Pino H., a historian at the Universidad Nacional de San Cristóbal de Huamanga, has conducted extensive field research with survivors of the war that convulsed the Ayacucho region.

Nelson Manrique, a historian at DESCO and the Universidad Pontífica Católica del Perú, has written numerous books and articles on peasants, war, and politics in the nineteenth and twentieth centuries.

Orin Starn teaches cultural anthropology at Duke University and has published widely on war and community self-defense in rural Peru.

Jo-Marie Burt, an associate editor at NACLA *Report on the Americas,* has conducted extensive field research on politics in metropolitan Lima and is completing a dissertation on the topic at Columbia University.

José Luis Rénique, a historian at Herbert H. Lehman College of the City University of New York, has published widely on politics, intellectuals, and social movements in the Puno region.

Isabel Coral Cordero, as president of CEPRODEP (Centro de Promoción y Desarrollo Poblacional), is a participant-observer of life and struggle among war refugees and subaltern women.

Enrique Obando is a research consultant on the Peruvian military who has participated in various research and publication projects at CEPEI (Centro Peruano de Estudios Internacionales).

Patricia Oliart has written on history, political culture, and ethnicity in Peru and is a member of the Instituto de Estudios Peruanos.

Carlos Basombrío Iglesias, the Associate Director of the Instituto de Defense Legal, has acquired extensive experience in the human rights movement in Peru.

Hortensia Muñoz, a human rights activist in Peru, has served as Executive Secretary of the Comisión de Derechos de la Persona y Construcción de la Paz and coordinates the national network of Peru, Vida y Paz.

LIBRARY OF CONGRESS CATALOGING-IN-PUBLICATION DATA

Shining and other paths : war and society in Peru, 1980–1995 / edited by
Steve J. Stern.

p. cm.

Includes bibliographical references and index.

ISBN 0-8223-2201-3 (cloth : alk. paper). — ISBN 0-8223-2217-x (paper :
alk. paper)

1. Sendero Luminoso (Guerrilla group)   2. Peru—Politics and
government—1968–1980.   3. Peru—Politics and government—1980–
4. Peasantry—Peru—Political activity—History—20th century.
5. Insurgency—Peru—History—20th century.   6. War and society—
Peru—History—20th century.   I. Stern, Steve J., 1951–

F3448.2.S53   1998

322.4'2'0985—dc21   97-43279   CIP